ISBN 978-1-331-15832-5
PIBN 10151942

This book is a reproduction of an important historical work. Forgotten Books uses
state-of-the-art technology to digitally reconstruct the work, preserving the original format
whilst repairing imperfections present in the aged copy. In rare cases, an imperfection in
the original, such as a blemish or missing page, may be replicated in our edition. We do,
however, repair the vast majority of imperfections successfully; any imperfections that
remain are intentionally left to preserve the state of such historical works.

1 MONTH OF
FREE
READING

at
www.ForgottenBooks.com

By purchasing this book you are eligible for one month membership to ForgottenBooks.com, giving you unlimited access to our entire collection of over 700,000 titles via our web site and mobile apps.

To claim your free month visit: www.forgottenbooks.com/free151942

English
Français
Deutsche
Italiano
Español
Português

www.forgottenbooks.com

Mythology Photography **Fiction**
Fishing Christianity **Art** Cooking
Essays Buddhism Freemasonry
Medicine **Biology** Music **Ancient
Egypt** Evolution Carpentry Physics
Dance Geology **Mathematics** Fitness
Shakespeare **Folklore** Yoga Marketing
Confidence Immortality Biographies
Poetry **Psychology** Witchcraft
Electronics Chemistry History **Law**
Accounting **Philosophy** Anthropology
Alchemy Drama Quantum Mechanics
Atheism Sexual Health **Ancient History**
Entrepreneurship Languages Sport
Paleontology Needlework Islam
Metaphysics Investment Archaeology
Parenting Statistics Criminology
Motivational

REPORTS OF CASES

DECIDED IN THE

COURT OF APPEALS

OF THE

9L

STATE OF NEW YORK,

FROM AND INCLUDING THE DECISIONS HANDED DOWN MARCH 20, 1883,
TO AND INCLUDING DECISIONS OF JUNE 5, 1883.

WITH

NOTES, REFERENCES AND INDEX.

By H. E. SICKELS,

STATE REPORTER.

VOL. XLVII.

ALBANY:

WEED, PARSONS & CO., CONTRACTORS.

1883.

JUDGES OF THE COURT OF APPEALS.

TABLE OF CASES

REPORTED IN THIS VOLUME.

TABLE OF CASES REPORTED.

TABLE OF CASES

CITED IN THE OPINIONS IN THIS VOLUME.

Q.

R.

CASES DECIDED

IN THE

COURT OF APPEALS

OF THE

STATE OF NEW YORK,

COMMENCING MARCH 20, 1883.

In the Matter of the Application of THOMAS T. CHURCH for the Appointment of Commissioners, etc.

126
139—

The act (Subd. 9, § 1, chap. 482, Laws of 1875, as amended by chap. 365, Laws of 1880, and by chap. 554, Laws of 1881), giving to the board of supervisors in any county containing an incorporated city of over one hundred thousand inhabitants, where contiguous territory in the county has been mapped out into streets and avenues, power to lay out, open, grade and construct the same, and to provide for the assessment of damages on the property benefited, is not a local law within the meaning of the State Constitution, and so is not violative of the constitutional provision (Art. 3, § 18) prohibiting the passage of a local or private law laying out or opening highways, or of the provision (Art. 3, § 23) requiring the legislature to act by general laws in conferring upon boards of supervisors any power of local legislation.

Where a board of supervisors, acting within the authority so conferred, has created the occasion for and has required the appointment of commissioners to estimate and appraise the damages and benefits, the Supreme Court has jurisdiction to make such appointment.

The board of supervisors may impose the whole cost of the improvement upon the property included in the area which it decides has been benefited to that extent.

By resolution of the board of supervisors of the county of K. which had directed the opening of a street, under said act, in the town of N. U., the town was authorized to issue bonds to pay for the improvement, to be paid out of the general tax, so far as the assessments proved inadequate. *Held*, that adequate and certain provision was thus made for compensation for property taken, sufficient to meet the constitutional prohibition against the taking of property without compensation.

(Argued March 6, 1883 ; decided March 20, 1883.)

APPEAL from order of the General Term of the Supreme Court, in the second judicial department, made December 12, 1882, which affirmed an order of Special Term appointing commissioners for the purpose of opening Ninety-second street, in the town of New Utrecht, Kings county, from Seventh avenue to the Shore road ; also to appraise the damages for lands taken for such improvement, and to assess the amount, together with expenses, upon the property benefited. (Reported below, 28 Hun, 476.)

In 1869 an act of the legislature constituted certain town officers of some of the towns in the county of Kings, contiguous to the city of Brooklyn, commissioners to lay out a plan for streets and roads in those towns, respectively. (Chapter 670, Laws of 1869.) Exclusive power was conferred on these commissioners to lay out streets, roads and avenues in such towns conformable to plan of streets of said city, terminating at the city line, as nearly as might be practicable and judicious.

In performance of the duties imposed on them the commissioners prepared a map, including among others the town of New Utrecht, and laying out the whole area of that town in projected avenues and streets similar to those in Brooklyn city.

In November, 1881, the supervisors, justices of the peace and commissioners of highways of the town of New Utrecht claiming authority, under chapter 554, Laws of 1881, having met in that town, pursuant to public notice, certified to the necessity of opening said Ninety-second street, said certificate being signed by more than two-thirds of said officers, upon which certificate the board of supervisors of Kings county passed resolutions making certain alterations in the map of said street, as filed, and also the following :

" SEC. 3. The County Court or the Supreme Court at Special Term, in Kings county, upon the application of any freeholder of the town, or of the trustees of the school district within which said street is situated, upon five days' notice of such application in one of the daily newspapers of the county, shall appoint three disinterested persons, residents and freeholders of said town, as opening commissioners, for the purpose of opening said street," following which were resolutions as to the mode of proceedings, on the part of the commissioners so appointed, and as to the confirmation of their report.

By further resolutions it was directed that the supervisors of the town borrow on its credit the amount of unpaid assessments, and give the bonds of the town therefor, with directions to apply all sums received in payment of the assessments, and it was provided that "any deficiency, required to meet the principal and interest on said bonds, shall be made a tax on the real and personal estate of the town, and collected in and with the annual taxes."

Thereupon the petitioner above-named made application to the Supreme Court for the appointment of commissioners.

George B. Ely for appellants. The act of 1881 (Chap. 554) was violative of section 18 of article 3 of the Constitution, which prohibits the legislature from providing for "the laying out, opening, altering, working or discontinuing roads, highways or alleys except by general laws." (*State, ex rel. Richards,* v. *Hammer,* 42 N. J. L. 438; *State, ex rel. Anderson,* v. *Trenton,* id. 486; *People, ex rel. Clauson,* v. *Newburgh, etc., P. R. Co.,* 86 N. Y. 1; *People* v. *O'Brien,* 38 id. 194; *People, ex rel. Burroughs,* v. *Brinkerhoff,* 68 id. 265.) The commissioners could be appointed only on the application of owners of the lands through which the road is laid out. (1 Laws of 1872, chap. 315; 1 R. S. [7th ed.].844, § 5.) The act of 1881 (Chap. 554) is void because it authorizes the county board to provide arbitrarily at its discretion for the estimation and award of the damages to be sustained, and for the assessment on property intended to be benefited thereby, and fixing assessment district therefor; the levying, collection and payment of the amount of such damages. (*People, ex rel. Bur-roughs,* v. *Brinkerhoff*, 68 N. Y. 264.)

William Sullivan for respondent. The act of 1881 (Chap. 554) is a general law, for it in terms applies to a specified class of things wherever situated. (*Walker* v. *Potter*, 18 Ohio, 85; *Wheeler* v. *Philadelphia*, 77 Penn. St. 348, 351; *Kilgore* v. *Magee*, 85 id. 401; *Matter of N. Y. El. R. R. Co.*, 70 id. 328; *People* v. *N. & S. P. R. Co.*, 86 id. 1.) The enactment of the board of supervisors is warranted by the act on which it is based, and it does not infringe on the constitutional rights of the parties affected by the opening and construction of the street. (*Mayor* v. *Livingston*, 8 Wend. 85; *Betts* v. *City of Williamsburgh*, 15 Barb. 255; *People* v. *Mayor of Brooklyn*, 4 N. Y. 419; *Matter of Sackett St.*, 74 id. 107; Cooley on Taxation, chap. 20.) The requirement of the enactment that notices shall be given to all parties affected by the acts of the commissioners, and that they shall have an opportunity to be heard, and to protect and enforce their rights, is a sufficient compliance with the constitutional provision that no person shall be deprived of his property without due process of law. (*Stuart* v. *Palmer*, 74 N. Y. 185; *Matter of DePeyster*, 80 id. 504.)

FINCH, J. We are satisfied that the law under which the present application was made is constitutional. It is not a local, as distinguished from a general, act, and so is not prohibited by the fundamental law. (Const., art. 3, §§ 18, 23) It is not easy to define with accuracy the difference between the two forms of legislation, and the difficulty is better solved by adding examples to definitions. Of the latter, the most useful and accurate is that given in *The Matter of the N. Y. Elevated R. R.* (70 N. Y. 328). A law relating to particular persons or things *as a class* was said to be general; while one relating to particular persons or things *of a class* was deemed local and private. The act of 1881 relates to a class, and applies to it as such, and not to the selected or particular elements of which it is composed. The class consists of every county in the State, having within its boundaries a city of one hundred thousand inhabitants, and territory beyond the city limits mapped into streets and avenues. How many such counties there are now, or may be in the future, we do not know, and it is not material that we should. Whether many or few, the law operates upon them all alike, and reaches them, not by a separate selection of one or more, but through the general class of which they are individual elements. The force of the law of 1881 is not localized in Kings county and confined to its territory. By its terms it applies equally to every other county which may prove to be within the constituted class. It is said there is but one such county; and so it was said there was but one elevated railroad. Neither fact at all narrowed the terms of the law. Those terms in each case were broad enough to cover every county in the State if it had the required city and the mapped territory on the one hand, or its own elevated road on the other. The case cited adds example to definition, and, following its doctrine, we must hold the law of 1881 to be general and not local, and so not a violation of the Constitution.

The jurisdiction of the Supreme Court to appoint the commissioners of estimate is assailed upon the ground that its sole authority to act came from the mandate of the county board, which was ineffectual for that purpose. But the Constitution gave to the Supreme Court general jurisdiction in law and equity, and, by the specific provision requiring the damages for property diverted to the public use to be ascertained by a jury or commissioners appointed by a court of record, conferred upon all such courts the necessary jurisdiction. The mode and manner of its exercise was put within the control and regulating power of the legislature, because it was to be exercised "as prescribed by law." In that respect the legislature could not delegate its authority except by the permission of the Constitution. Such permission was given. (Art. 3, § 23.) The legislature was allowed to transfer a power of local legislation, so far as it should deem necessary or prudent, to the county boards. What it could do, over all the State and in every locality, in providing the occasion for and requiring the appointment of commissioners of estimate, it could transfer for a particular county to the board of supervisors of that county, so that the latter became within its prescribed authority a local legislature. This was done in the county of Kings by the act of 1875 as amended in 1881. Thereby the local legislature, acting within the authority conferred, could create the occasion for and call into exercise the power of the Supreme Court to appoint commissioners, and that appointment when made was "as prescribed by law." The county board did not create the jurisdiction. That came from the fundamental law. What it did was to call it into play, to furnish occasion for its exercise, and to require its aid. When it did that the jurisdiction of the court in the particular instance was complete.

There is no force in the objection that after fixing the assessment district the total expense cannot be assessed upon the property included, but only so much as is found to be the actual benefit. That is but another form of saying that the legislature cannot impose the whole cost upon the area which it decides is benefited to that extent. The case of *Stuart* v. *Palmer* (74 N. Y. 185), cited by the appellant, expressly holds that the legislature may cause local improvements to be made and authorize the expense thereof to be assessed upon the land benefited thereby. The resolution of the county board imposes upon each owner his share of the cost in proportion to his benefit accruing.

Nor is the system of awards and the provision for the payment thereof inadequate and uncertain. By force of the resolutions of the county board the public purse of the town is made responsible for any deficiency in the awards resulting from failure of the assessments, and to enable payment to be more readily made, the town is authorized to borrow the necessary amount by the issue of its bonds, and these are to be paid out of the general tax of the whole town so far as the assessments are inadequate. The difficulty and uncertainty of payment commented upon in *Chapman* v. *Gates* (54 N. Y. 145) and *Sage* v. *City of Brooklyn* (89 id. 189) does not here exist.

Other objections taken are founded upon the general system of laying out and opening highways which have no application to the present case.

The order should be affirmed, with costs.

All concur.

Order affirmed.

THE PEOPLE OF THE STATE OF NEW YORK *v.* THE MECHANICS AND TRADERS' SAVINGS INSTITUTION.

W. H. M. SISTARE, Judgment Creditor, Respondent, *v.* WILLIAM J. BEST, Receiver, etc., Appellant.

The primary relation of a depositor in a savings bank to the corporation is that of creditor.

Upon insolvency of the corporation, the depositors stand as other creditors, having no greater, but equal rights to be paid ratably out of the insolvent estate.

Accordingly *held*, where a creditor of a savings bank obtained a judgment against a receiver thereof in an action brought against the bank before the appointment of the receiver, in which action the receiver was substituted as defendant, that the plaintiff was not entitled to a preference over depositors in the payment of his judgment.

People v. *M. and T. S. Institution* (28 Hun, 375), reversed.

(Argued March 6, 1883 ; decided March 20, 1883.)

APPEAL by William J. Best, receiver of The Mechanics and Traders' Savings Institution, from so much of an order of the General Term of the Supreme Court, in the third judicial department, as reversed a portion of order of Special Term, and directed William J. Best, the receiver of said institution, to pay in full certain judgments rendered against him in favor of William H. Sistare. (Reported below, 28 Hun, 375.)

This institution was incorporated as a savings bank by chapter 368, Laws of 1852. Mr. Sistare was a New York broker, and in 1872, the savings institution employed him as such broker to sell certain stock. The result of the transaction was that on the 5th day of April, 1872, the savings institution became liable to him for a large sum. For this Mr. Sistare commenced an action against it in November, 1875. The action was pending on the 26th day of December, 1877, when an order was entered in the matter above entitled, dissolving the corporation and appointing Mr. Best receiver. On the 29th of April, 1878, an order was made substituting Mr. Best as receiver in place of the corporation in the action brought by Mr. Sistare, and judgment was thereafter rendered therein in favor of plaintiff. It was appealed to the Court of Appeals where judgment was affirmed, and judgments for costs were perfected.

Mr. Sistare applied to the court at Special Term that his judgments be paid in preference to the claims of depositors. This motion was granted as to his costs and disbursements, but denied as to his claim. The General Term, on appeal, held that he was entitled to a preference for the full amount of his judgments, with interest, and directed the receiver to pay the same out of the funds in his hands.

A. J. Vanderpoel for appellant. The legislature intended to place the creditors and depositors of savings banks on the same footing. (Laws of 1852, chap. 368, § 13; Laws of 1875, chap. 371, § 476; Laws of 1879, chap. 422, § 473; 2 R. S. [Edm. ed.] 471, 492; 3 R. S. [7th ed.] 2401.) The depositors in a savings bank are simply creditors of the institution. (*Macin* v. *Savings Institution*, 23 Me. 350; *Lund* v. *Seaman's Savings B'k*, 37 Barb. 129; *Van Dyck* v. *McQuade*, 86 N. Y. 39, 52.)

A. D. Pape for respondent. Where a stock corporation is dissolved, its creditors must be paid before its stockholders, because the money paid for the stock constitutes the capital which the stockholders invest and risk in the business, and they, being entitled to the profits, must suffer the loss. (*Huntington* v. *Savings Bank*, 96 U. S. 388.) A savings bank is a corporate trustee, and in the management of its trust, the bank, through its board of directors, is authorized to incur reasonable expenses.

(*Hun* v. *Cary*, 82 N. Y. 65–67; 2 Perry on Trusts [3d ed.], §§ 907, 908; *New* v. *Nicoll*, 73 N.Y. 131; *Stockton* v. *M. and T. Savings Bank*, 32 N. J. Eq. 163; 22 Alb. L. J. 157-8; *Osborn* v *Byrne*, 21 Am. Rep. 641; *Hannon* v. *Williams*, 38 id. 383; *Hyde* v. *Lynde*, 4 N. Y. 391; *Mann* v. *Rentz*, 3 Comst. 423; *M. Savings Bank* v. *Bastin*, Penn. Sup. Ct., March, 1881.) A receiver takes merely the same rights which the corporation had and subject to the same equities. (*Lincoln* v. *Fitch*, 42 Me. 456; *Robinson* v. *Howes*, 20 N. Y. 84; *Smith* v. *Felton*, 43 id. 419.) The defendant is not bound to await the administration of the fund as a general creditor to share with others *pro rata*, but is entitled to an immediate order for the payment of his costs in full. (*Columbia Ins. Co.* v. *Stevens*, 37 N. Y. 536.)

ANDREWS, J. The primary relation of a depositor in a savings bank, to the corporation, is that of creditor and not that of a beneficiary of a trust. The deposit when made becomes the property of the corporation. The depositor is a creditor for the amount of the deposit, which the corporation becomes liable to pay, according to the terms of the contract under which it is made. When payment is made, the claim of the depositor is extinguished; and he has no further claim upon the funds or assets of the bank. Upon insolvency the assets and property of the corporation, as in the case of other corporations, is a trust fund for the payment of creditors, and depositors we think stand as other creditors, having no greater, but equal rights to be paid ratably out of the insolvent estate. The fact that savings banks are public agencies created by law to receive and invest the money deposited in them does not change the status of depositors, upon insolvency of the bank, from that of creditors to that of beneficiaries of a trust, so as to subject the assets of the bank to the payment in the first instance of other creditors. The statutes under which savings banks are organized contain restrictions and provisions intended to secure depositors against loss. These institutions are designed to encourage economy and frugality among persons of small

means.   But the depositors have no voice in the management.
The directors or trustees are designated in the charter or the
certificate of incorporation, and constitute a self-perpetuating
body.   There is nothing like a private trust between the corporation or its trustees, and the depositors, in respect to the
deposits.   The trustees assume the management of the aggregate fund under the special provisions of the statute, and the
depositors can, under the most favorable circumstances, receive but a moderate rate of interest on their deposits.   The
deposits are not made as a business venture, but the supposed
security of the fund is the great motive put forward to induce
deposits.   The other creditors of the corporation have no superior equity to the depositors to payment in case of deficiency
of assets.   They deal with the corporation upon the footing of
general creditors, and the fact that the corporate franchises are
granted primarily for the management of funds of depositors,
does not entitle the former to priority of payment.   The statutes certainly do not contemplate that the rights of depositors
shall be inferior to those of other creditors.   The statutes regulating the distribution of the assets of insolvent corporations
recognize the equitable principle of equality between creditors
and furnish, we think, the proper rule of distribution in this
case. (2 R. S. 464, § 42 ; id. 477, § 79.)

We are therefore of the opinion that the claimant is not en-
titled to the preference claimed, and that the order of the
General Term should be reversed and the order of the Special
Term affirmed, with costs.

All concur.

Judgment accordingly.

GEORGE A. VOGEL, Appellant, *v.* THE MAYOR, ALDERMEN AND
COMMONALTY OF THE CITY OF NEW YORK, Respondent.

One who employs a contractor to do a work, not in its nature a nuisance,
but which becomes so by reason of the manner in which the contractor

has performed it, if he accepts the work in that condition, becomes at once responsible for the nuisance.

In May, 1857, one K. entered into a contract with defendant to regulate, grade, etc., a portion of one of its streets, the work to be completed on or before August 19, 1858. The contract required the work to be done under the supervision of a person appointed by the street commissioner, and to be approved of by that officer or the person so appointed, and if at any time the work should not progress according to the terms of the contract, said officer was authorized to complete the work at the expense of the contractor. K. commenced the work and dug a deep hole or trench in the street near plaintiff's lots, adjoining the street; in 1859 he dug another hole, but did little else toward the performance of the contract, and in 1859 abandoned it. In 1873 the city employed another person who completed the work. In consequence of said excavations, surface water, which before that had been accustomed to flow in a natural channel, was diverted and thrown upon plaintiff's premises, causing damage. This damage was done after the time for the performance of the contract had expired, and ceased when the work was completed. In an action to recover said damage, *held* (MILLER, DANFORTH and FINCH, JJ., dissenting), that defendant was liable, as it permitted these excavations to remain when it had the power and right to take charge of and complete the work, and thus protect plaintiff's property from injury.

Blake v. *Ferris* (5 N. Y. 48), *Pack* v. *The Mayor* (8 id. 222), *Kelly* v. *The Mayor* (11 id. 432), distinguished.

(Argued March 7, 1883; decided March 20, 1883.)

APPEAL from judgment of the General Term of the Supreme Court, in the first judicial department, entered upon an order made May 20, 1881, which affirmed a judgment in favor of defendant, entered upon an order nonsuiting plaintiff on trial, and affirmed an order denying a motion for a new trial.

The nature of the action and the material facts are stated in the opinion.

Samuel Hand for appellant. The title to a street, when acquired by the city, is vested in it in fee. (Val. Laws, 1198.) The power of the city to regulate and grade streets exists only in regard to streets of or belonging to it. (Val. Laws, 1190, 1191.) The power to regulate and grade streets is conferred by statute upon the mayor, etc., of the city of New York, and its exercise in fact is the performance of a public ministerial

duty. (*Barton* v. *City of Syracuse*, 36 N. Y. 54.) A municipal corporation in performing a public duty, ministerial in
its nature and within its powers, is liable for any injury occasioned by the negligence of its agents, whether the latter hold
the relation of immediate employes or apparently independent contractors, unless it arises from a collateral act or omission of an employe, and not his unskillfulness in doing the
very act which was authorized. (*Water Co.* v. *Ware*, 16 Wall.
566 ; *Mersey Dock* v. *Gibbs*, L. R., 1 Eng. & Ir. App. 93,
114, 115; *Ellis* v. *Gas Co.*, 2 E. & B. 167 ; *Butler* v. *Hunter*,
7 H. & N. 826 ; *Storrs* v. *Utica*, 17 N. Y. 104; Dillon on
Mun. Corp., § 753 ; *Hines* v. *City of Lockport*, 50 N. Y. 236 ;
Britton v. *The Mayor, etc.*, 21 How. Pr. 251 ; *King* v. *N. Y.
C. & H. R. R. R. Co.*, 66 N. Y. 185, 186.) Under the circumstances, the defendant is liable, whether the contractor was its servant or independent of it, particularly as the injury was directly
caused by diverting the natural water-course. (*Byrnes* v. *Cohoes*, 67 N. Y. 204 ; *Storrs* v. *City of Utica*, 17 id. 108; *Lynch*
v. *Mayor*, 76 id. 62 ; *Bastable* v. *Syracuse*, 8 Hun, 587.) A
municipal corporation, in using its real estate, is liable in the
same manner and to the same extent as an individual owner
for injury done adjoining or other lands. (*Bailey* v. *Mayor*,
3 Hill, 541 ; *Rochester White L. Co.* v. *City of Rochester*, 3
N. Y. 463.) Defendant having continued the nuisance upon
Fortieth street, which resulted in the injury to the plaintiff, is
liable therefor. (*Vedder* v. *Vedder*, 1 Denio, 257; *Fish* v.
Dodge, 4 id. 317 ; *Brown* v. *C. & S. R. R. Co.*, 12 N. Y. 492 ;
2 Greenl. on Ev., § 472 ; *Todd* v. *City of Troy*, 61 N. Y. 506 ;
2 Greenl. on Ev., § 472.)

D. J. Dean for respondent. The defendant is not liable
for damages occasioned by the unskillfulness or neglect of the
contractor or his servants, or consequent upon a want of care in
the method of prosecuting the work. (*Blake* v. *Ferris*, 5 N.
Y. 48; *Pack* v. *The Mayor*, 8 id. 222 ; *Kelly* v. *The Mayor*,
11 id. 432 ; 4 E. D. Smith, 291.) It is only when the work
which has been directed to be done is intrinsically dangerous,

however skillfully performed, and the plaintiff, without neglect on his part, has suffered injury, that the city becomes liable, if proper and reasonable care has not been used to prevent the accident, and cannot escape the liability by pleading the contractor's neglect. (*Storrs* v. *Utica,* 17 N. Y. 104; *McCafferty* v. *P. M. & S. D. R. R. Co.,* 61 id. 181; *King* v. *Livermore,* 9 Hun, 299; *Gardner* v. *Bennett,* 38 N. Y. Sup. Ct. 198; *Cuff* v. *N. R. R. Co.,* 35 N. Y. 17; 10 Am. Rep. 205; Dillon on Municipal Corporations, §§ 1028–1031 [3d ed.]; *City of Erie* v. *Caulkins,* 85 Penn. St. 247; 27 Am. Rep. 642.) The damage suffered by the plaintiff was the consequence of the method of prosecuting the work adopted by the contractor, who was in this respect beyond the control of the defendant. (*Kelly* v. *Mayor,* 11 N. Y. 432; *Reedie* v. *N. W. R'y,* 4 Exch. 244; Wood on Master and Servant, 619; *Water Co.* v. *Ware,* 16 Wall. 566.) The city had the right to contract for the grading of the street, and to cause the surface of the land to be changed at its pleasure, and without regard to the permanent or temporary effect of such changes upon the flow of surface water. (Dillon on Municipal Corporations, § 1041 [3d ed.]; *Turner* v. *Dartmouth,* 13 Allen, 291; *Greely* v. *R. R. Co.,* 53 Me. 200; *Dickenson* v. *Wooster,* 7 Allen, 19; *Flagg* v. *Wooster,* 13 Gray, 601; *Franklin* v. *Fisk,* 13 Allen, 211; *Barry* v. *Lowell,* 8 id. 127; *Parks* v. *Newburyport,* 10 Gray, 28; *Lynch* v. *The Mayor,* 76 N. Y. 60; *Gould* v. *Booth,* 66 id. 62; *Wilson* v. *The Mayor,* 1 Denio, 595; *Mills* v. *Brooklyn,* 32 N. Y. 489; *Town of Union* v. *Durkes,* 38 N. J. L. 21; *Imler* v. *City of Springfield,* 55 Mo. 119; 17 Am. Rep. 645.) When the contractor failed to complete his contract, and became in default to the corporation, leaving the street in the condition described, it was a matter for the discretion of the defendant to determine when and how the work on the street should be continued. (*Wilson* v. *The Mayor,* 1 Denio, 595; *Mills* v. *Brooklyn,* 32 N. Y. 489; *Rivers* v. *The City Council of Augusta,* 23 Alb. L. J. 17; *Cuff* v. *Newark & N. Y. R. R. Co.,* 35 N. J. 17; 10 Am. Rep. 205; Anson on Contracts, 200.) If the injuries to plaintiff's property were caused by the act or neglect of the contractor, by the method adopted by him in prosecuting the work, he alone is liable, but if they were necessarily incidental to the work, either as a permanent or temporary consequence thereof, defendant is not liable. (*Radcliff* v. *The Mayor*, 4 N. Y. 195; *Hoyt* v. *Hudson*, 9 Am. Rep. 473; Dillon on Municipal Corporations [3d ed.], §§ 989, 991.) It was the duty of the plaintiff in a case of this kind to use all possible means to reduce the amount of his damage as much as possible. (Sedgwick on Measure of Damages, 164 [7th ed.]; *Lawson* v. *Price*, 2 Law & Eq. 427; *Loker* v. *Damon*, 17 Pick. 284.)

Earl, J. This action was brought to recover damages, for injuries to two houses belonging to the plaintiff, and for consequent loss and diminution of rents, by reason of water turned and caused to flow, from time to time, between August, 1858, and December, 1874, into and upon the premises of the plaintiff, situated on the south-east corner of Second avenue and Fortieth street, in the city of New York. The plaintiff was nonsuited upon the trial, and from the judgment entered against him upon the nonsuit, he appealed to the General Term, and from affirmance there, to this court.

In reviewing this nonsuit we must take the facts as the evidence most favorable to the plaintiff tended to establish them, and they are as follows:

The plaintiff, from 1852 to the commencement of this action, owned two lots on the south-east corner of Fortieth street and Second avenue. The land between Thirty-ninth and Forty-second streets and First and Second avenues, was a hill, highest at Forty-second street and First avenue, and lowest at Thirty-ninth street, and it sloped down southerly and westerly from Forty-second street toward Thirty-ninth street. A water-course crossed Fortieth street about one hundred and seventy-five feet east of Second avenue, and seventy-five feet east of the rear line of plaintiff's lots, and the surface water coming down from about twenty acres of the elevated land ran through this water-course, a natual depression in the land, toward Thirty-ninth street, and then down that street to the East river, doing the plaintiff's lots, prior to 1858, no damage.

Prior to May, 1857, Fortieth street between Second and First avenues had not been regulated and graded, although the title to the land in the street belonged to the city; but the city had established the grade of the street so that when the street should be completed it would have a descent toward the First avenue and the East river. On the 19th day of May, 1857, the city made a contract with one Kinsley to furnish all the materials and labor to regulate, grade, curb and gutter Fortieth street between the two avenues named, and he was to complete his contract on or before August 19, 1858. The plaintiff, learning that the grade of the street had been established and that the contract with Kinsley had been made, entered into a contract with a builder to erect two buildings upon his lots, in reference to the grade so established and the contract with Kinsley so made by the city. The buildings were commenced in the latter part of the summer of 1858, and were completed about May 1, 1859.

The contract with Kinsley provided that the work should be "under the supervision of the surveyor, or such person as may be appointed by the street commissioner;" that if at any time the work should not progress according to the terms of the contract, and the street commissioner should be of opinion that the work was delayed, "he shall have the power to place such and so many other persons, by contract or otherwise, to work at and complete the same, as he shall deem advisable," and charge the expense of completing the work to the contractor, and deduct the amount thereof from the compensation to be paid to him under the contract; that the work should conform "to such further directions as shall be given by the street commissioner;" "that a sufficient number of persons shall be at all times employed to execute the work, the whole to be approved of by the street commissioner or such person as shall be appointed to superintend the work;" that "the contractor would commence the work within   days from signing the contract, and progress therein so as to complete the same on or before the 19th day of August, 1858."

The contractor commenced to work under his contract in 1858. If he had commenced his work on the First avenue and worked toward the Second avenue, the topography of the district was such that he could have completed the contract without damaging the plaintiff. But he commenced at the Second avenue, and dug a deep hole or trench in the street, near the plaintiff's lots, and in the year 1859 he dug another hole in the street, making, however, but little progress with the work upon his contract. After 1859, all he did was in each year to draw a little sand from the street, and occasionally some rock, as it is to be inferred, for his own use elsewhere. In that year he practically abandoned the work, and never again resumed it. In 1873, a new man, employed, as it may be inferred, in some way by the city, took hold of the work and completed the contract. During all these years, from 1858 to the completion of the work by the new man in 1873, in consequence of the excavations made in the street, the water which had been accustomed to flow in the natural channel above described, in the times of rain, was diverted and thrown in great volumes upon plaintiff's lots, doing him great damage. The plaintiff endeavored to protect his lots against the floods, but was unable to do so. After the completion of the work, he suffered no further damage.

Upon these facts, if the city had directly through its agents caused the excavations upon its own land in the street, and thus diverted the great volume of water upon plaintiff's lots, there would have been little or no room for contention that it would not have been liable for the damage done. Its liability in such case could be based upon principles laid down and decided in *Byrnes* v. *City of Cohoes* (67 N. Y. 204), and *Noonan* v. *City of Albany* (79 id. 470), and other like cases.

But it is claimed on behalf of the city that it is not liable for these damages, because of the contract it had entered into with Kinsley, by whom the excavations in the street were made. The claim is that the damages were caused by the improper and negligent manner in which he performed his contract; that he was an independent contractor, and that the city had no control over the manner in which he should perform his work, and hence was not responsible for his wrongs or carelessness, he alone being responsible upon principles laid down in *Blake* v. *Ferris* (5 N. Y. 48), *Pack* v. *The Mayor* (8 id. 222), *Kelly* v. *The Mayor* (11 id. 432); and other similar cases. But those cases are not in point. In *Blake* v. *Ferris* the defendants, having a license at their own expense to construct a sewer in one of the streets of the city of New York, entered into contract with another person to construct it at a stipulated price for the whole work, and the plaintiff was injured in consequence of the negligent manner in which the unfinished sewer was left open and unguarded in the night-time. In an action against the defendants to recover damages for the injuries thus sustained, it was held that they were not liable, for the reason that the contractor was not their agent, and that they were not responsible for his negligence. That case was criticised and questioned by Comstock, J., in the case of *Storrs* v. *The City of Utica* (17 N. Y. 104), where he said in substance that the doctrine of *respondeat superior* was correctly expounded in that case, but improperly applied. But to make that case analogous to this, suppose the contractor, after digging the trench in the street, had abandoned his work and left the trench there for weeks and years, could the defendants have escaped liability? Could they permit an excavation which they had caused to be made in the street, to remain there an indefinite time after the work had practically ceased, and claim exemption from liability because they had committed the work to a contractor? Here, if this damage had been done to the plaintiff while Kinsley was in the active and proper performance of his contract, there would be some ground for claiming that the city should not be made liable for the damage resulting from the improper manner in which he performed his work. Suppose A. enters into contract with B. to do some work upon his land, his private property, and in doing this work B. does it so carelessly as to turn a stream of

water upon the land of C. and then B. abandons his contract
and for years omits to proceed with it ; could A. permit the
water to run upon the land of C. for years and escape liability
for the damage which should thus be caused ? Clearly he
would be held responsible for what he had caused to be done,
or suffered to be done, upon his own land, to the injury of his
neighbor, and he could not shield himself behind the claim
that B. was an independent contractor when he did the act
which first diverted the water.

In *Pack* v. *The Mayor*, the city had made a contract with
a person to grade a street, and .the damage complained of was
done by the carelessness of a sub-contractor in blasting rock. It
was held that the person actually guilty of the careless act was.
liable for the damage, and that the city was not liable, as it had
no control over the workmen of the contractor — could not dismiss them or direct the manner in which the blasting should
be done. In reference to a clause in the contract in that case,
which bound the contractor to conform the work to such further directions as might be given by the city or its officers, the
court held, as stated in the head-note, " It gives to the corporation power to direct as to the *results* of the work ; but without control over the contractor or his workmen, as to the
manner of performing it; which control alone furnishes a
ground for holding the master or principal liable for the act of
the servant or agent.'' But the plain inference is that the city
in such a case is liable for the consequences of operations which
are subject to its control.

The case of *Kelly* v. *The Mayor* was similar to the case of
Pack v. *The Mayor*, and was disposed of upon precisely the
same principles. The doctrine was again announced that to
make the city liable it must have the power to direct and control the manner of performing the very work in which the
carelessness occurred.

In the case now under consideration the damage was
occasioned to the plaintiff after the time for the performance
of the contract by Kinsley had expired, at a time when he
could not, as against the city, claim the possession of the street

or the right to do any work therein. The damage was done because the work was improperly delayed and practically abandoned for about fourteen years, during all of which time the city had the right, by the very terms of the contract, to assume control of the work and finish it at the expense of the contractor. The city is liable because it permitted its contractor, in the execution of a contract with it, to make these excavations in the street and to thus turn the water upon plaintiff's lots when it had the power and right, at any time within the fourteen years, to take charge of the work, complete the contract and thus protect the plaintiff's property against injury.

The city owed plaintiff a duty, and the breach of that duty imposes the liability. The city is in the same position as it would have been if it had contracted for making the very excavations, and then had left them to do the injury complained of. This bears some analogy to the case of a continuing nuisance. One must not suffer a nuisance to continue on his premises to the injury of others, although he was not responsible for its creation. (*Osborn* v. *The Union Ferry Company*, 53 Barb. 629; *Burgess* v. *Gray*, 1 C. B. 578.) If one employs a contractor to do a work not in its nature a nuisance, but when completed it is so by reason of the manner in which the contractor has done it, and he accepts the work in that condition, he becomes at once responsible for the creation of the nuisance, upon a principle very similar to that which makes a principal responsible for unauthorized wrongs committed by his agent by ratifying them. (*Boswell* v. *Laird*, 8 Cal. 49.)

This is not like the case supposed of a convulsion of nature causing these chasms and thus turning the water, and the responsibility of the city is not such as it would have been in that case. Here the excavations were made by agencies put in motion by the city, in the execution of a contract for it, upon its land. The excavations were not necessarily damaging to the plaintiff. If the work had been carried to completion in a reasonable time, no serious damage would have been done,

as the plaintiff's houses were not finished until 1859, nearly a
year after Kinsley's contract was to have been completed. But
the damage came because the excavations were needlessly,
negligently and heedlessly suffered to remain in the street for
an unreasonable length of time, and for that responsibility
attached to the city.

We are, therefore, of opinion that upon the facts which
the evidence tended to establish, there is no rule of law which
shields the city from liability to the plaintiff for his damages,
and that the nonsuit was improperly granted.

The judgment should be reversed and a new trial granted,
costs to abide the event.

All concur, except MILLER, DANFORTH and FINCH, JJ., dissenting.

Judgment reversed.

ELISHA MACK, Respondent, *v.* THOMAS PHELAN, Administrator,
etc., Appellant.

The provision of the statute in reference to chattel mortgages (§ 3,
chap. 279, Laws of 1833), providing that, unless such a mortgage is
re-filed, as prescribed, it shall cease to be a lien as against subsequent
purchasers in good faith, after the expiration of a year from the time
of filing, does not relieve a purchaser having actual notice of a mortgage when he purchased, which, at the time it was executed, accurately described the mortgaged property, although the appearance of the
property had, for the purpose of deception, without the fault of the
mortgagee, been changed by the mortgagor.

In November, 1871, C. executed to H. a chattel mortgage on three
machines, which were described by numbers and other descriptive particulars, and were stated to be in the possession of the mortgagor in a
certain mill. In October, 1872, the mortgagee attempted to renew the
mortgage by refiling a copy ; this was held not to be effectual, because
the paper filed was not an exact copy ; it, however, stated accurately the
debt and the mortgaged property, and the statement signed by the
mortgagee stated correctly the amount unpaid. C. sold the machines to
A. H. H. & Co. ; immediately prior to the purchase the agent of that
firm saw and read the original mortgage, and the copy filed as a renewal,

but was informed by the mortgagor that it did not cover the machines in question, and to support this he referred to the fact that the numbers of the machines he was about to sell did not correspond with the numbers as stated in the mortgage; these had in fact been removed, and other numbers appeared upon the machines. The agent, satisfied with this information, concluded the purchase without making further inquiry or going to the mill. In an action for the conversion of the machines, *held*, that the purchasers were chargeable with notice of the mortgage, and of the legal rights of the mortgagee under it; that the paper filed as a copy, although inaccurate, was, with the statement of the mortgagee accompanying it, notice to them that the original mortgage was as between the parties a subsisting security, and the debt secured unpaid; and that it was not essential that they should have had actual knowledge, at the time of the purchase, that the machines were those embraced in the mortgage.

C. received for the machines a sum of money, and three other machines; these latter were stored by him with other machinery covered by the mortgage; he procured insurance on all of the machinery, loss, if any payable to H., as mortgagee. The policies were forwarded to H., who lived in Missouri. A loss having occurred, H. came to this State to collect the insurance. He then learned all the facts of the sale and exchange, of which before he had been ignorant. After acquiring such knowledge H. obtained from C. a power of attorney and assignment of all his interest in the policies. H. then informed A. H. H. & Co. of his claim upon, and demanded the three machines, offering, if they would surrender them, to transfer the claim for insurance; this they refused, and H. thereupon settled with the insurance companies. *Held*, that there was no ratification, either in law or fact, of the acts of C., and no estoppel upon H. from asserting his claim under the mortgage.

After the adjustment of the loss H. sold the old iron, the remnants of the property. *Held,* that this did not amount to a ratification of the acts of C.

It seems that the most A. H. H. & Co. could claim was that H. should account for the portion of the sum received on sales realized from the remnants of machines sold by them.

(Argued March 8, 1883; decided March 27, 1883.)

APPEAL from a judgment of the General Term of the Supreme Court, in the third judicial department, entered upon an order made the first Tuesday of May, 1882, which affirmed a judgment in favor of plaintiff, entered upon the report of a referee.

This action was originally brought by plaintiff against Patrick Butler, as surviving member of the firm of A. H. Hart & Co., to recover damages for the alleged conversion of three machines used in the manufacture of flax. Butler having died during the pendency of the action, his administrator, the present defendant was substituted. Plaintiff claimed, as assignee of one Hayward, who claimed as mortgagee under a chattel mortgage, executed to him by one Crane.

The material facts are stated in the opinion.

E. Countryman for appellant. The referee was right in holding that the chattel mortgage was not properly renewed, as a true copy thereof was not refiled. (*Moredon* v. *Cornell*, 62 N. Y. 215; *Porter* v. *Parmley*, 52 id. 185; *Ely* v. *Carnley*, 19 id. 496; *Patterson* v. *Gillies*, 64 Barb. 563; *Stackhouse* v. *Allard*, 4 T. & C. 279.) Actual notice to be effectual should be equivalent to actual knowledge, and cannot be inferred even from an opportunity of knowledge unless the opportunity be such that the inference of knowledge is conclusive. (*Foster* v. *Gillespie*, 68 Mo. 644; *Hill* v. *Gillman*, 39 N. H. 88; *Stearns* v. *Gage*, 79 N. Y. 103, 107; *Sawyer* v. *Pennell*, 19 Me. 167, 173; *Bacon* v. *Van Schoonhoven*, 87 N. Y. 446, 452; *Farley* v. *Carpenter*, 27 Hun, 359, 361; *Bowman* v. *Roberts*, 58 Miss. 126; *Tootle* v. *Lyster*, 26 Kan. 590.) The referee erred in his legal conclusion that the facts found or proved upon the trial did not constitute a ratification by Hayward of the sale of the property by Crane to said firm, nor an estoppel as against the claim of the plaintiff. (*Bennett* v. *Judson*, 21 N. Y. 239; *Elwell* v. *Chamberlain*, 31 id. 611, 619; *Murray* v. *Binninger*, 3 Abb. Ct. of App. Dec. 336; *Carter* v. *Hamilton*, Selden's Notes, 251; *Leslie* v. *Wiley*, 47 N. Y. 648; *Lowenstein* v. *McIntosh*, 37 Barb. 251; *Palmertier* v. *Huxford*, 4 Denio, 166; *Phillips* v. *McKellor*, 12 Wk'ly Dig. 521; *Crouse* v. *Hunter*, 28 N. Y. 389; *Baker* v. *Union Ins. Co.*, 43 id. 284, 288; *Cobb* v. *Dows*, 10 id. 336, 345; *Bonner* v. *America, etc., Co.*, 81 id. 469; *Scott* v. *Middletown, etc., R. R. Co.*, 86 id. 200; *Krumm* v. *Beach*, 25 Hun, 294; *Bryant* v. *Moore*, 26 Me. 84; *Sortwell* v. *Frost*, 122 Mass. 184; *Cook* v. *Tullis*, 18 Wall. 332; *Commercial*

B'k v. *Warren*, 15 N. Y. 577; *Farmer's, etc., Co.* v. *Walworth*, 1 id. 433; *N. Y. & N. H. R. R. Co.* v. *Schuyler*, 34 id. 87, 88; *Baker* v. *Union, etc., Ins. Co.*, 43 id. 289; *Brewster* v. *Baker*, 16 Barb. 613; *Tilton* v. *Nelson*, 27 id. 595; *Garnor* v. *Bird*, 57 id. 277; *Storrs* v. *Barker*, 6 Johns. Ch. 166; *Sherman* v. *McKeon*, 38 N. Y. 267; *Thompson* v. *Blanchard*, 4 id. 303, 310; *Brainard* v. *Duning*, 30 id. 211.)

Matthew Hale for respondent. The actual notice given to the agent made it immaterial whether the mortgage was properly filed or refiled. (*F. L. & T. Co.* v. *Hendrickson*, 25 Barb. 484; *Hill* v. *Beebe*, 3 Kern. 556; *Lewis* v. *Palmer*, 28 N. Y. 271; *Gildersleeve* v. *Landon*, 73 id. 609; *B'k of U. S.* v. *Davis*, 2 Hill, 451; *Sutton* v. *Dillaye*, 3 Barb. 329; *Ingalls* v. *Morgan*, 6 Seld. 178; *Reed* v. *Gannon*, 50 N. Y. 345; *Goodenough* v. *Spencer*, 15 Abb. [N. S.] 248, 255.) The proof of conversion is ample. (*Fallon* v. *Durant*, 60 How. Pr. 178; *McEnroe* v. *Decker*, 58 id. 250; Code of Civil Proc., § 500; *Holmes* v. *Wood*, 88 N. Y. 650.) Any assumption of right over property in exclusion or defiance of plaintiff's right, is a conversion. (*Bristol* v. *Burt*, 7 Johns. 254; *Murray* v. *Burling*, 10 id. 172; *Reynolds* v. *Shuler*, 5 Cow. 323; *Connah* v. *Hale*, 23 Wend. 462.) A mortgagor cannot, by changing the appearance of the property, or mixing it with other property, by adding to or subtracting from it, impair the title of the mortgagee. (*Dunning* v. *Stearns*, 9 Barb. 630; *Willard* v. *Rice*, 11 Metc. 493; *Southworth* v. *Isham*, 3 Sandf. 448; *Adam* v. *Wilds*, 107 Mass. 123; *Simmons* v. *Jenkins*, 78 Ill. 479.) The assignment being absolute on its face, and conveying to plaintiff legal title to the claim, no inquiry as to its consideration or motive is permissible. (*Sheridan* v. *Mayor*, 68 N. Y. 30, 32; *Stone* v. *Frost*, 61 id. 614; *Allen* v. *Brown*, 44 id. 228.)

ANDREWS, J. The chattel mortgage from Crane to Hayward, included, among other articles, the three machines for the conversion of which this action is brought. They are described in the mortgage by numbers and by other descriptive particulars, and the mortgage stated that the property was then in the possession of the mortgagor, in the upper mill known as the tow mill, in Rotterdam. The mortgagor, when the mortgage was executed, resided in the town of Rotterdam, and the machinery mortgaged was then in his flax mills in that town. The mortgage was dated November 11, 1871, and was filed on the same day in the town clerk's office of the town. It was given to secure the payment by Crane to Hayward of $6,000 with interest in one year from its date, the consideration being a loan of that amount made by Hayward to Crane at the date of the mortgage. The mortgagee, on the 14th of October, 1872, attempted to renew the mortgage by refiling a copy thereof, with a statement indorsed •thereon, exhibiting his interest in the property by virtue of the mortgage; but the copy was not an exact copy of the original mortgage, there being some slight variance between them. It was, however, accurate as to the statement of the debt for which the mortgage was given, and of the property embraced in the mortgage, and the statement, which was signed by the mortgagee, correctly set forth the amount then due upon the mortgage. The referee, however, having found that by reason of the fact that the alleged copy was not an exact transcript of the original mortgage, the refiling did not operate to renew it, this finding must be taken to be the law of the case, and cannot be questioned by the respondent upon this appeal.

The original defendant in the action was one of the firm of A. H. Hart & Co., and claimed title to the machinery in question under a purchase made by that firm from Crane in April, 1873, and one of the questions in the case is whether, at the time of such purchase, the firm of A. H. Hart & Co. had notice of the original mortgage, and that it was then a subsisting lien upon the property. By the third section of chapter 279, Laws of 1833, relating to the filing of chattel mortgages, it is provided that a mortgage filed under the first section of the act, shall cease to be valid as against the creditors of the person making the same, or against subsequent purchasers or mortgagees in good faith, after the expiration of one year from the filing thereof, unless it is refiled as provided in that section. The object of the statute, requiring mortgages of personal property to be filed, is the same as that of the registry acts respecting mortgages of real estate, viz.: to prevent imposition upon subsequent mortgagees and purchasers (DENIO, J., *Meech* v. *Patchin*, 14 N. Y. 71), and if at the time of the purchase by Hart & Co. they had notice of the mortgage to Hayward, such notice stands in the place of filing, and their purchase would be subject to the lien of the mortgage. It appears by the evidence that immediately prior to the purchase of the machines by the firm of Hart & Co. their agent saw and read the original mortgage and the copy filed as a renewal in the town clerk's office of Rotterdam, but was informed by the mortgagor that it did not cover the machines in question, and in support of the statement he referred to the fact that the numbers on the machines which he was about to sell did not correspond with the numbers of the machines stated in the mortgage. The agent being satisfied with this information, without making further inquiry, or going to the mill to ascertain whether the machines covered by the mortgage were still there, concluded the purchase, Crane receiving for the machines $3,000 in cash and three other machines of the same general character as those described in the mortgage. There is no ground to impute any actual bad faith to Hart & Co. in the purchase of the property, nor is there any reason to question that they had no actual knowledge at the time that the machines purchased by them were covered by the mortgage. It appears that when the mortgage was taken by Hayward he examined the property, and there were at that time numbers upon the several machines, upon brass plates attached to them, corresponding with the numbers in the mortgage, but at the time of the purchase by Hart & Co. these numbers had been removed, and the only numbers then upon the machines were numbers which had been cast therein at the time they were made and which did correspond with the numbers mentioned in the bill of sale to the firm. How the numbers came to be changed does not distinctly appear. It

may be inferred, however, that it was done by Crane with the
intention of defrauding the purchasers. But it was not essential to charge the purchasers with notice of the plaintiff's
mortgage that they should have actually known at the time of
the purchase that the machines were those embraced in the
mortgage. They had actual notice of the instrument executed
to Hayward, and the paper filed as a copy of the mortgage
although not accurate in every respect, was, in connection with
the statement accompanying it, notice to them that the original
mortgage between the parties was a subsisting security, and
that the debt which it was given to secure was unpaid.

The statute which declares that unless a mortgage is refiled,
it shall cease to be a lien as against subsequent purchasers in
good faith of the mortgaged property, does not relieve the
purchaser who has actual notice of a mortgage, which at the
time it was executed correctly described the property mortgaged, but the appearance of which, for purposes of deception,
and without the fault of the mortgagee, has been changed by
the mortgagor. The language of the third section of the
statute in this respect is the same as the language of the first
section, requiring the original filing of a chattel mortgage, and
it could not be claimed that if the purchase had been made
before the expiration of the year from the original filing, the
lien of the mortgage was lost as against a purchaser upon whom
such a fraud had been practiced. Hart & Co. were chargeable
in law with notice of the mortgage and with the legal rights
of the mortgagee thereunder, notwithstanding the deception,
and they cannot transfer the loss resulting therefrom from
themselves to the mortgagee, so long as they had actual notice
of the mortgage.

In another view also the objection of want of notice cannot
prevail. The purchasers purchased property of the same
general description, aside from the numbers, as that contained
in the mortgage. Knowing of the mortgage and of the attempt
to renew it, they were put upon inquiry, and this amounts to
actual notice of the mortgage, unless they pursued the inquiry
with diligence, and were unable thereby to ascertain the exist-

ence of the lien. (*Williamson* v. *Brown*, 15 N. Y. 354.) The
purchasers in this case relied alone upon the statements of the
mortgagor in respect to the lien. They did not see the
machines purchased by them until after they had paid the
purchase-money. They made no inquiry of the mortgagee,
nor did they go to the mills where the mortgaged property was
stated in the mortgage to be, to ascertain whether there were
machines there corresponding to those described in the mortgage. Under the circumstances it cannot, we think, be held
as matter of law that they used due diligence in prosecuting
the inquiry to ascertain whether the property purchased was
covered by the mortgage.

It is claimed, however, by the defendant that certain facts
proved and found upon the trial, constitute a ratification by
Hayward, of the sale by Crane, or estop him and his assignee
from claiming title under the mortgage. The referee found
that after the transfer and exchange of machinery between
Crane and the firm of Hart & Co., the machines received by
Crane from the firm, were stored by him with other machinery
covered by the mortgage, and that Crane in March, 1876,
obtained two policies of insurance thereon for $1,750 each,
which were payable "in case of loss, to John T. K. Hayward,
mortgagee, as his interest may appear; balance, if any, to
assured," and that the policies were forwarded to, and received
and held by, Hayward, and that in the fall of 1876, while the
policies remained in force, the insured property was destroyed
by fire. It is further found that in June, 1877, Hayward
came from Missouri, where he resided, to this State, for the
purpose of collecting the insurance, and that he then ascertained all the facts relating to the sale and exchange of the
machinery by Crane to and with the firm of Hart & Co., and
that after acquiring such knowledge, Hayward obtained a
power of attorney and an assignment from Crane, of all his
rights and interest in the policies of insurance, and subsequently compromised the claims, receiving on the compromise,
about the sum of $1,300. It is insisted that this dealing by
Hayward in respect to the policies of insurance, and the com-

promise and collection of the loss, was a ratification of the wrongful act of Crane in selling the mortgaged property. But we are of opinion that this contention is not well founded. The description of the insured property in the policies of insurance, was in general terms, and did not convey any notice to Hayward that it was upon any property other than that which was covered by his mortgage, and when he first ascertained the fraud committed by Crane, the insured property had been destroyed by fire. Hayward had an interest as mortgagee, in the claim against the insurance companies, for the policies embraced not only the machines exchanged by Hart & Co. with Crane, but also the machinery covered by the mortgage other than the three machines in question. Before making the compromise with the insurance companies, Hayward informed Hart & Co. of his claim upon the three machines then in their possession, and demanded them as mortgagee, and he also offered to transfer to Hart & Co. the claim against the insurance companies, in case they would surrender the mortgaged property. Hart & Co. having declined this offer and refused to surrender the machinery, Hayward was justified in adjusting the loss upon the policies, in his character both as mortgagee, and as assignee of Crane. The legal title to the insurance money beyond the portion which belonged to Hayward as mortgagee, was in Crane. Hart & Co. could not claim any portion of it, at least until after a rescission of the contract of exchange between them and Crane. They did not rescind this contract, but on the contrary insisted upon retaining the mortgaged property. The defendant has been allowed in diminution of damages for the conversion, the whole amount received by Hayward on the insurance policies, and under the circumstances we think there was no ratification either in fact or law, of the wrongful acts of Crane arising out of this transaction, and no estoppel upon Hayward from asserting his claim under the mortgage.

It further appears that after adjustment of the loss, Hayward sold the remnants of the property remaining from the fire, consisting of old iron, for the sum of about $70, and this is also claimed to have been a ratification of the acts of Crane. What proportion of the sum received upon this sale, represented the mortgaged property, does not appear. The most that Hart & Co. could claim in respect to it, is that Hayward should account for the proportion of the sum received on the sale, which represents the machines sold by them; and the whole sum so received, was also credited in the action in diminution of damages.

These are the only questions in the case, and we think the judgment should be affirmed.

All concur, except RUGER, Ch., J., not voting.

Judgment affirmed.

THE PEOPLE, Plaintiff in Error, v. GEORGE H. WILLETT, Defendant in Error.

92
154

92
164

The rule allowing the silence of a person to be taken as an implied admission of the truth of allegations spoken or uttered in his presence does not apply to silence at a judicial proceeding or hearing.

Upon the trial of an indictment for murder, evidence was received on the part of the prosecution, under objection and exception, to the effect, that upon the coroner's inquest a witness testified that shortly after the murder a stranger called at her house and asked the way to Sandy Hill and also for a drink of water ; that the prisoner with a number of others was placed around a room and the witness pointed out the prisoner as the one who so called ; also, that a number of persons, including the prisoner, passed behind her, each one repeating the question asked her by the stranger, and that she identified the prisoner by his voice, and that the prisoner on that occasion did not deny that he was such stranger. *Held,* that the examination before the coroner was of a judicial character ; that the experiments so made were part of the proceedings; that the prisoner was not bound to speak, and his silence could not be regarded as an evidence of guilt ; and therefore that the evidence was improperly received.

(Argued March 5, 1883 ; decided March 27, 1883.)

ERROR to the General Term of the Supreme Court in the third judicial department to review judgment entered upon an

order made September 5, 1882, which affirmed a judgment of
the Court of Oyer and Terminer in and for the county of
Warren, entered upon a verdict convicting the defendant in
error of the crime of murder in the first degree. (Reported
below, 27 Hun, 469.)

The facts material to the question discussed are stated in the
opinion.

John L. Hill and *H. A. Howard,* district attorney, for
plaintiff in error.   Evidence of the experiments at the inquest
to prove the identity of the prisoner with the man who was
at Mrs. Wing's house the night of the murder, was competent.
(2 Wharton on Ev. [2d ed.], §§ 1136–1155 ; 1 Taylor on Ev.
680–1, § 812 ; *Watson's Trial,* 32 St. Trials, 347 ; *Gibney* v.
Marchay, 34 N. Y. 305 ; 1 Phil. on Ev., C., H. & Edwards'
Notes [5th ed.], top-paging 357–9,* pp. 436–8, note, 127 ;
People v. *Kelly,* 55 N. Y. 571.) The mere fact that the prisoner
was then under arrest is not important, provided his acts were
voluntary. (*People* v. *Mentz,* 37 N. Y. 303 ; *People* v. *Green-
field,* 23 Hun, 471 ; 85 N. Y. 75 ; *People* v. *Kelley,* 55 id. 571 ;
People v. *Teachout,* 41 id. 7 ; *People* v. *Reinhardt,* 82 id. 607 ;
People v. *Thoms,* 3 Park. C. R. 256 ; *People* v. *Cox,* 80 N. Y.
515 ; *People* v. *Balbo,* id. 499.) It was not a judicial proceeding. (*People* v. *McMahon,* 2 Park. C. R. 670 ; *People* v.
Montgomery, 13 Abb. [N. S.] 251.)

Charles Hughes for defendant in error.   The evidence of
what occurred before the coroner's jury, and the prisoner's
silence when Mrs. Wing stated she thought she recognized the
prisoner as the man she saw at her house on the night of the
murder, was inadmissible. (*Robb* v. *Hackley,* 23 Wend. 50 ;
Dudley v. *Bolles,* 24 id. 464.) The doctrine as to silence
being taken as an implied admission of the truth of allegations
spoken or uttered in the presence of a person, does not apply
to silence at a judicial proceeding or hearing. (1 Wharton's
Cr. L. [7th ed.], § 696 ; *Reg.* v. *Turner,* 1 Moody's Cr. C. 347 ;
Melven v. *Andrews,* Moody & Mal. 336 ; *Reg.* v. *Appleby,* 3

Starkie's N. P. C. 33 ; Wharton's Cr. Ev., § 680 ; 123 Mass.
440 ; *Broyle* v. *DeLong*, 47 Ind. 251 ; *Howard* v. *Howard*,
69 id. 592 ; *Berry* v. *Cooper*, 33 Ga. 155 ; *State* v. *Smith*, 3
La. 457 ; 1 Greenleaf's Ev., § 197, note ; *Child* v. *Grace*, 2 C.
& P. 193 ; 1 Cow. & Hill's Notes to Phillip's ed., note 191, p.
193 ; *Sheridan* v. *Smith*, 2 Hill, 538 ; *Kelly* v. *People*, 55 N.
Y. 571, 572 ; 126 Mass. 519, 522 ; 2 Allen, 34, 35 ; 12 Metc.
235 ; 10 Gray, 72, 75 ; 1 Am. Cr. Rep. 29 note ; *Com.* v.
Walker, 13 Allen, 570 ; 1 Greenleaf's L. of Ev., § 49 ; 1
Wharton's L. of Ev., § 391 ; 1 Greenleaf on Ev. [12th ed.],
§ 160 ; *Com.* v. *Harvey*, 1 Gray [Mass.], 487 ; 44 Ind. 72 ;
Slattery v. *People*, 76 Ill. 217 ; Joy on Confession and Challenges, 323 ; Wharton's Cr. Ev. 644 ; 11 Vt. 152 ; *Fearing* v.
Kimball, 4 Allen [Mass.], 125 ; *Com.* v. *McDermott*, 123 Mass.
441 ; 16 Vt. 113 ; *Gorton* v. *Hadsell*, 9 Cush. 911 ; *Bartlett*
v. *Smith*, 11 M. & W. 483 ; Law Review No. 3, for May, 1845,
pp. 27–44 ; *Vrooman* v. *King*, 36 N. Y. 477, 478, 479 ; *Hector*
v. *State*, 2 Mo. 135 ; *Boyd* v. *State*, 2 Humphrey, 39 ; *Reg.* v.
Gould, 9 C. & P. 364 ; *Whaley* v. *State*, 11 Ga. 125 ; *Fife* v.
Com., 29 Penn. St. 429 ; *Simon* v. *State*, 5 Florida, 285 ;
Brister v. *State*, 26 Ala. 107 ; *Clark* v. *State*, 35 Ga. 75 ;
State v. *Squires*, 48 N. H. 364 ; *Thompson* v. *Com.* 20 Grattan, 724 ; *Com.* v. *Harmon*, 4 Barr. 569 ; 1 Greenleaf on Ev.,
§ 2 ; *Young* v. *Com.*, 8 Bush, 366 ; *Kelley* v. *People*, 55 N.
Y. 565 ; *People* v. *Wentz*, 37 id. 303 ; *People* v. *Teachout*,
41 id. 7.)

MILLER, J.　This case arises upon a writ of error, on behalf
of the people, to review the judgment of the General Term of
the Supreme Court, reversing judgment of conviction of defendant, on an indictment for murder in the first degree.

Upon the examination before the coroner a witness, Mrs.
Wing, was sworn who identified the defendant as the person
whom she had seen at her house, on the night of the murder,
a few miles from the place where the crime was committed, and
with whom she had some conversation. Experiments were
made before the coroner for the purpose of testing the recol-

lection of Mrs. Wing. The defendant and others were placed
around the room, and the witness was asked to pick out the
person she saw at her house that night, and she designated the
defendant. The same persons were made to pass behind her
each repeating the words, as to asking for a drink of water,
which, as she testified, had been used at her house on the night
of the murder, and she was asked to detect by the voice the
one who had used the same language at her house on the night
in question, and she recognized the defendant's voice as belonging to such person. The defendant did not deny, in answer to either test, that he was the person Mrs. Wing saw that
night. These experiments were admitted as evidence upon the
trial on the ground that the silence of the defendant was an
admission of his guilt. The evidence was objected to and the
objection overruled. It is claimed that the ruling of the court,
in this respect, was erroneous. The same question was raised
by the defendant's counsel on motion to strike out the evidence
which was denied, and an exception duly taken. Also by a request to the court to charge the jury to disregard it, which was
refused and an exception taken.

The question whether the defendant was bound to speak, and
understood that he was at liberty to speak, if he chose, was
submitted to the jury by the court in his charge, and an exception taken thereto. The doctrine as to silence being taken
as an implied admission of the truth of allegations spoken or
uttered in the presence of a person, does not apply to silence
at a judicial proceeding or hearing. And if the proceedings
before the coroner were of a judicial character the evidence
was erroneously received. It is very apparent that the examination before the coroner partook of a judicial character, and
what there transpired must be considered as a part of the
proceedings; the coroner was there, a jury had been impaneled,
and witnesses were examined whose testimony was returned
as a portion of the coroner's proceedings. It is difficult to
see upon what ground it can be claimed that the experiments
which were made were not in connection with the proceedings
before the coroner and a part thereof.

The claim that they were informal and outside of the proceedings is not well founded, and it would be extremely difficult to draw the line between the other proceedings and these which are said to have been outside of them. We think the submission of the question to the jury, whether it was a judicial proceeding, was erroneous; the court should have held whether the proceedings before the coroner were judicial or otherwise, thus giving to the defendant's counsel the benefit of an exception, if he chose to take one. The evidence in regard to the coroner's proceedings was before the court, and it should have determined whether the facts referred to constituted a part of these proceedings, and it cannot, we think, be said that it was proper to leave the same to the jury, for the reason that it could have done no harm. It is very evident these experiments were made with a view of sustaining the correctness of Mrs. Wing's testimony, and hence they constituted a part of the proceedings before the coroner. The evidence of Mrs. Wing was for the purpose of showing circumstances tending to prove that the defendant was in the vicinity at the time of the commission of the crime, and his silence might be taken as assenting to that fact. It might well have affected the minds of the jurors that he thus remained silent, and did not deny that he was present at the time stated by Mrs. Wing.

Under the circumstances presented the proceedings before the coroner were clearly of a judicial character and the defendant was not bound to speak. His silence could not be regarded as an evidence of guilt.

There are other questions in the case, but inasmuch as they may not arise upon another trial we do not deem it necessary to consider them.

The judgment of the General Term should be affirmed.

All concur.

Judgment affirmed.

WILLIAM H. PHILIPS et al., Executors, etc., Appellants, *v.*
WILLIAM MACKELLAR, Impleaded, etc., Respondent.

The fact that an agent, without the authority, consent or knowledge of his
principal, upon loaning the money of the latter, exacted a sum in excess
of lawful interest, does not make the loan usurious ; nor does the fact
of the receipt by the principal of the sum so paid, in the absence of
evidence of knowledge on his part that it was paid as a usurious consideration for the loan, establish a ratification of the act of the agent.

To make out the defense of usury, it must be made to appear that the
lender had knowledge of the usurious agreement and assented to the
same.

It seems, however, in such case, the sum so paid should be allowed and
applied as a payment.

(Argued March 8, 1883 ; decided March 27, 1883.)

APPEAL from judgment of the General Term of the Supreme Court, in the first judicial department, entered upon an
order made May 23, 1881, which affirmed a judgment in favor
of defendant, entered upon a decision of the court on trial at
Special Term.

This action was brought to foreclose a mortgage given by
defendant William Mackellar and his wife to the plaintiff's
testator, on the 17th day of October, 1873, to secure the payment of $12,000, the amount of a loan made to Mackellar.

It appeared that the whole amount of the loan was paid to
Mackellar on the 18th day of October, 1873. The loan was made
under an arrangement effected between Abner C. Thomas, who
acted as the lender's attorney and agent in the transaction, and
Thomas Mackellar, son of said William Mackellar. The further material facts are stated in the opinion.

Amasa J. Parker for appellent. In order that the deceased plaintiff may successfully be implicated in a contract to
take usury, it must be shown that he either made the contract
or authorized it to be made in his behalf. (*Farmers' Loan & T.
Co.* v. *Clowes,* 3 N. Y. 470; *Condit* v. *Baldwin,* 21 id. 219;
Bell v. *Day,* 32 id. 165; *Algur* v. *Gardner,* 54 id. 360;

Estevez v. *Purdy*, 66 id. 446; *Guard. Mut. L. Ins. Co.* v. *Kashaw*, id. 544; *S. C.*, 3 Hun, 616; *Lee* v. *Chadsey*, 2 Keyes, 543; *S. C.*, 3 Abb. Ct. App. Dec. 43; *Van Wyck* v. *Watters*, 81 N. Y. 352; *Crane* v. *Hubbel*, 7 Paige, 413.) To constitute usury it is not sufficient to show payment. The vice, if it exists at all, is found in the original contract and in the meeting of the minds of the parties in the undertaking, on the one side to pay and on the other side to receive excessive and unlawful interest. (*L. & T. Co.* v. *Clowes*, 3 N. Y. 470; *Smith* v. *Bird*, 3 Day [Conn.], 268.) In the absence of proof of an agreement made by the defendant, William Mackellar, or in pursuance of his authority and on his behalf to pay usury, this defense cannot be sustained. (*Morton* v. *Thurber*, 85 N. Y. 550; *McArthur* v. *Schenck*, 31 Wis. 673; 11 Am. Rep. 643; *Guggenheimer* v. *Geiszler*, 81 N. Y. 293.) At the worst, the plaintiff should only be required to deduct from the mortgage debt the amount of the alleged bonus. (*Real Estate T. Co.* v. *Keech*, 69 N. Y. 248; *Abrahams* v. *Claussen*, 52 How. Pr. 241; *Langdon* v. *Gray*, id. 387.)

A. J. Vanderpoel for respondent. When the agent of the loaner has exacted a premium in the course of the negotiation of a loan, it is a question of fact whether the agent's demand for the additional sum, and the agreement of the borrower to pay the same were separate and divisible from the contract of loaning, or whether the loaning and the agreement for premium were a single and entire transaction. (*Condit* v. *Baldwin*, 21 N. Y. 219; *Bell* v. *Day*, 32 id. 165; *Algur* v. *Gardner*, 54 id. 360; *Estevez* v. *Purdy*, 66 id. 446; *Van Wyck* v. *Watters*, 81 id. 352; *Wyeth* v. *Braniff*, 84 id. 627, 632.)

MILLER, J. Upon the trial of this action the court found, in substance, that the bond and mortgage in controversy were made and executed under a corrupt and usurious agreement; that the defendant paid and the plaintiff took and received a greater rate of interest than seven per cent, namely, the sum of $1,200 over and above the lawful rate of interest for the use and forbearance of the money loaned, and that this agreement was carried into effect by the parties. The testimony in reference to said alleged agreement was conflicting. It was proved by the defendant's son that a check of the defendant, embracing the $1,200, was made and delivered to the attorney of the plaintiff on the 20th of October, 1873, two days after the money loaned had been paid to the defendant, and that this $1,200 was paid for the loan of $12,000. The plaintiff's attorney on the next day made and delivered his check to the plaintiff for the same amount of the check he received from defendant's son. The plaintiff and his attorney both deny that this $1,200 was received as a usurious consideration for the money loaned. It appeared that the plaintiff held two mortgages, amounting to $10,000, against the defendant upon other real estate, and by an arrangement between him and the defendant these mortgages were taken up and another mortgage taken for the same amount, subsequent to the mortgage in controversy, upon the real estate covered by the same. This last mortgage being a subsequent lien upon the premises was not as safe a security as the one for which it was substituted, and the evidence of the plaintiff's attorney was to the effect that the $1,200 was given in consideration of this change and not as a usurious premium for the loan of $12,000.

The judge upon the trial found in favor of the defendant. It does not, however, necessarily follow that his conclusion, that the loan was usurious, must be upheld. If the loan was made by the attorney or agent of the plaintiff for a usurious consideration, without the authority, consent or knowledge of the plaintiff, and if the plaintiff, when he received the $1,200, supposed and believed that it related to the other transaction to which reference has been had, it is by no means clear that the loan in question was tainted with a usurious and unlawful consideration. In order to establish the defense set up it must be shown that the plaintiff had knowledge of the usury and that it was taken with his consent. There is no evidence in the case which establishes the fact that, prior to the making of the loan, the plaintiff consented to the taking of the unlawful premium as a consideration for the same. He swears directly to the contrary, and there is no proof from which it can be claimed that the plaintiff ever authorized his attorney to make a usurious contract for the loan in question. Neither by declaration nor act does it appear that the plaintiff was apprised, prior to the service of the answer interposed in this case, that the claim was made that a usurious premium had been charged for the loan; his attorney testifies, as we have seen, that the money was paid in connection with an entirely different and another transaction, and the proof does not show the plaintiff had any other knowledge or information on the subject until the trial of the case. There can be no question, it seems to us, in regard to this aspect of the matter. In view of the fact referred to it is difficult to see upon what ground it can be claimed that the plaintiff had knowledge of the alleged usurious contract testified to by the defendant's witness. The authorities fully sustain the position that, where an agent acts without the authority or knowledge of his principal, the latter is not bound by the usurious contract made by the agent. (*Van Wyck* v. *Watters*, 81 N. Y. 352; *Crane* v. *Hubbel*, 7 Paige, 413.) The evidence also shows that the defendant William Mackellar never contracted to pay the usurious consideration; he took no part in negotiating the loan, and, according to the evidence of his son, it was made mainly for that son's benefit, he having contracted for the alleged usurious premium, and he does not swear, nor does the evidence show, that he was authorized by his father to contract on his behalf to pay more than the legal rate. This is corroborated also by the plaintiff's attorney, who testifies that the defendant's son contracted for himself. It is true there is some evidence to establish the fact that the alleged usury was paid by the defendant's son out of the funds of the mortgagor, but this does not prove usury, as such contract rests upon the basis that there was an agreement of the parties by which their minds met, and the one agreed to receive and the other to take an unlawful premium upon the loan made. There being no such proof it is not manifest how the defense in this action can be sustained. It is apparent that the arrangement found to be usurious was between the defendant's son and the attorney of the plaintiff, without the concurrence of the plaintiff, and hence the mortgage in question was not usurious.

While the question is not entirely free from difficulty we are unable to perceive why the plaintiff, as the case stands, is not entitled to claim that he is not bound by the contract, alleged to have been made with his agent, on the ground that it was unauthorized and without his consent.

It is claimed by the counsel for the respondent that the position that the principal received the $1,200 on another and separate transaction is contrary to the findings and is not entitled to consideration. We do not think that the findings can be regarded as going to the extent claimed for them. They merely cover the question whether there was a usurious contract made and carried out between the plaintiff and the defendant and hold that there was, but inasmuch as it is clearly established that such contract was made without the knowledge or consent of the plaintiff and without his authority it is perfectly legitimate to look at the facts for the purpose of determining whether the money received by the plaintiff was not received upon a different contract and in a different transaction. That question was not directly passed upon by any finding of the court below. If the money had not been received by the plaintiff, as the contract was made by his attorney without his knowledge, authority or consent, the defense of usury clearly could not be maintained. The findings relate simply to the question whether more than the legal rate of interest was paid and the conclusion is based evidently upon that ground. If the plaintiff supposed and understood he received this money on account of another transaction, it cannot we think be said that the findings included and covered such transaction. The fact that the $1,200 came into the hands of the plaintiff does not establish the usury so long as there was no knowledge of the plaintiff at the time of the loan that he was to receive it as a usurious consideration for the same, nor under the circumstances did the payment of the $1,200, three days after the transaction, render the loan invalid.

The acceptance of the check by the plaintiff, of itself, cannot be regarded as a ratification of the alleged agreement made by his attorney. The plaintiff denies that there was any usury and there is no testimony that he had any knowledge of it. It is no answer to such denial that the plaintiff did not give evidence on the trial as to the other transaction. If the evidence of the plaintiff's attorney, as to the fact that the $1,200 was received on account of another transaction, be stricken out and disregarded, there is no proof whatever to establish that it was received as usury. The defendant is bound to make out the defense of usury, and the receipt of this money by the plaintiff, standing alone, without knowledge of any corrupt or usurious agreement, does not prove it was taken in pursuance of an unlawful contract.

After a careful consideration of the case we are satisfied that the trial court was wrong in its conclusion that the contract for the loan, for which the bond and mortgage were executed, was usurious.

As to the $1,200 paid to the plaintiff we think it should be allowed as a payment upon the bond and mortgage. If the money was received, as is claimed, to apply under another arrangement it is not to be assumed that the plaintiff received it as a usurious premium on the loan, and upon receiving information that it was such he should have returned the same to defendant or applied it upon the mortgage. It cannot, we think, be said he had knowledge it was usurious until the judgment of the court to that effect. And it is not too late now to apply the $1,200 upon the mortgage.

It follows, that the judgment should be reversed and a new trial granted, costs to abide the event.

All concur, except RAPALLO and ANDREWS, JJ., dissenting.

Judgment reversed.

92   40,
17   27v

GEORGE C. HARRINGTON, Administrator, etc., Respondent, *v.*
EUGENE M. KETELTAS et al., Appellants.

An executor, having notice that there is a debt due the estate, is bound to
active diligence for its collection ; he may not wait for a request from the
distributees.

In case the debt is lost through his negligence he becomes liable as for a
devastavit.

It seems, that if the case is one of such doubt, that an indemnity is proper,
he must at least ask for it ; and at any rate he takes the risk of showing
that the debt was not lost through his negligence.

Where the question was as to whether one person received a certain sum
for another, *held*, that a deposit ticket made out by the former, showing a deposit by him of about the same amount on the day of the alleged
receipt was proper evidence.

The statute of limitations does not begin to run in favor of an executor,
as against a claim for damages occasioned by his negligence in collecting
a debt due the estate from the time of the probate of the will, but at
best only from the time of the loss.

Where, therefore, it was claimed that a debt was lost by reason of the
running of the said statute, and it appeared that the will was admitted
to probate in 1870, that the defense of the statute became available to
the debtor in 1874, and his pecuniary ability up to that time was
unquestioned, that the executor died in 1876, and that an action against
his executors was commenced in 1878. *Held*, that the action was not
barred by the said statute.

As to whether an executor will be permitted to allege his own wrong
so as to have time run in his favor, or whether each day before his
accounting will not be deemed a commencement of the cause of action, or
he be chargeable for the amount he could have collected as for assets in
his hands, *quære*.

(Argued March 8, 1888 ; decided March 27, 1888.)

APPEAL from judgment of the General Term of the Supreme
Court, in the first judicial department, entered upon an order
made April 10, 1882, which affirmed a judgment in favor of
plaintiff, entered upon the report of a referee.

This action was brought by plaintiff, as administrator, with
the will annexed, of Harriet E. Christy, deceased, against defendants, as executors of the will of William M. Keteltas, who was
the executor of the will of said Harriet E. Christy, to recover

the amount of a debt alleged to have been due and owing to
her estate at the time of her death from one Smith, and to
have been lost through the neglect of the said executor to
collect the same. The referee found in substance these facts :
In July, 1868, said Harriet E. Christy sold certain real estate ;
said Smith, who was her attorney and counsel, at her request and
for her use and benefit, received the purchase-money, to-wit,
$29,000, and at the time of her death, which occurred in June,
1870, there remained in his hands of such purchase-money the
sum of $20,000. Said Smith drew the will of Mrs. Christy,
who was in feeble health, and relied entirely upon him in legal
and business matters ; at his instigation she named said
Keteltas, who was a stranger to her, but a client and intimate
friend and relative of Smith's, as her executor ; Smith, acting as
counsel for Keteltas, filed a pretended inventory of the personal
estate of the deceased, omitting therefrom entirely his said indebtedness, which was known to Keteltas, who believed, and had
good reason to believe, that Smith was indebted to the amount of
$20,000 with accrued interest ; Keteltas neglected and refused
to render to the legatees named in the will, or to the surrogate,
any account until November, 1874, when under an order of the
surrogate he filed an account, in which no reference was made
to said indebtedness ; Keteltas wholly neglected to demand of
or to receive from Smith said indebtedness, or to attempt to
collect the same. Keteltas died in January, 1876, and in January, 1878, plaintiff was appointed administrator with the will
annexed ; as such he commenced suit against Smith to recover
said indebtedness, who pleaded the statute of limitations, and
in consequence of the neglect and failure of duty on the part
of Keteltas, the claim against Smith was barred by said statute,
and plaintiff was obliged to discontinue said action. Further
facts appear in the opinion.

Francis Lynde Stetson for appellants. An executor without
funds in his hands, and without any offer to indemnify,
cannot be required to personally make good the amount of a
doubtful and disputed claim, upon the mere ground that he has

neglected to bring suit therefor. (*Griswold* v. *Chandler*, 5 N.
H. 492–494; *Sanborn* v. *Goodhue*, 28 id. 48–58; *Hepburn* v.
Hepburn, 2 Bradf. 74.) The referee erred in finding that the
alleged cause of action against the defendants as representatives
of William A. Keteltas, deceased, had accrued within six years
prior to the commencement of the action. (*Argall* v. *Bryant*,
1 Sandf. 98; *Northrup* v. *Hill*, 57 N. Y. 351; *Moore* v.
Juvenel, Sup. Ct. Penn., Jan. 19, 1880; 8 Weekly Notes of
Cases; *Sanford* v. *Sanford*, 62 N. Y. 553.) If Smith, subsequent to the alleged demand upon him, began to make payments of interest, or partial payments on account, the statute
would not run in his favor until at least six years after
the last of such payments. (Angell on Limitations, §§ 240–247;
First Nat. B'k of Utica v. *Ballou*, 49 N. Y. 155; *Putnam*
v. *Hubbell*, 42 id. 106–113.)

Ira Shafer for respondent. William A. Keteltas, the executor, dying, the plaintiff was properly appointed administrator
with the will annexed. (3 R. S. [6th ed.] 83, § 45.) Plaintiff had a right to bring this action under the circumstances disclosed by the evidence. (*Walton* v. *Walton*, 2 Abb. [N. S.]
428, 451; *McMahon* v. *Allen*, 4 E. D. Smith, 519, 525;
Luers v. *Brunges*, 56 How. Pr. 282, 285; *Petrie* v. *Petrie*,
7 Lans. 90; *Deland* v. *Richardson*, 4 Den. 95.) The defendants are liable, as the representatives of William A. Keteltas,
for the wrongs done by him as executor, and because of his
having "wasted". the estate of Mrs. Harriet E. Christy. (2
R. S. 647, § 1; *Elder* v. *Bogardus*, Hill & Denio's Sup.;
Potter v. *Van Ranken*, 36 N. Y. 619, 625; *Heinmuller* v.
Gray, 13 Abb. [N. S.] 299, 301, 302; *Haight* v. *Hoyt*, 19 N.
Y. 465, 467, 468; *Smith* v. *N. Y. & N. H. R. R. Co.*, 28
Barb. 605, 607, 608; *Dininny* v. *Fay*, 38 id. 18, 20, 21, 22;
Bond v. *Smith*, 4 Hun, 48, 49; *Paine* v. *Elmer*, 7 Mass. 317;
2 R. S. 114, § 6; Bac. Abr., Executors, L.) When the action
was commenced against C. Bainbridge Smith, January 30,
1878, it was barred by the statute of limitations. (*Stafford* v.
Richardson, 15 Wend. 302, 307; *Bommer* v. *Am. Spiral*,

etc., Hinge Co., 81 N. Y. 408; *Stewart v. Smith*, 14 Abb. Pr. 75; *Judd* v. *O'Brien*, 21 N. Y. 186; *Merritt* v. *Seaman*, 6 Barb. 330, 335; *Underhill* v. *Pomeroy*, 2 Hill, 603; *Wenham* v. *Mohawk Ins. Co.*, 13 Wend. 267, 269; *Christopher* v. *Garr*, 2 Seld. 61; *Sandford* v. *Sandford*, 62 N. Y. 553, 555, 556; *Smith* v. *Newby*, 13 Miss. 159.) The statute had not run against Keteltas, or his representatives, when the action was commenced, June 11, 1878. (2 R. S., § 52; id. 90, § 43; Ang. on Lim. 298; *Wenman* v. *Mohawk Ins. Co.*, 13 Wend. 267, 269; *Sandford* v. *Sandford*, 62 N. Y. 553, 555; *Munny* v. *East India Co.*, 5 B. & Ald. 204; *Burklin* v. *Ford*, 5 Barb. 393; *Cary* v. *Stephenson*, 2 Sack. 421; Ang. on Lim. 54–59.) The representatives of Keteltas are liable irrespective of the question of the statute having run against Smith. (*Schultz* v. *Pulver*, 3 Paige, 182; *S. C.*, 11 Wend. 361, 365.) If property is wasted through the carelessness or want of proper attention of an executor or administrator, or debts are not collected within a reasonable time by personal application or suit, the law will hold him personally responsible, whether his motives have been pure or not, and whether or not the delay caused the loss of the debts. (4 Johns. Ch. 284; *Parsons* v. *Mills*, 2 Mass. 80; *Mitchell* v. *Lunt*, 4 id. 653, 658; *Wakeman* v. *Hazleton*, 3 Barb. Ch. 148; *Keller's Appeal*, 18 Barr. 288; *Wilson* v. *Doster*, 7 Ired. Eq. 231; *Williams* v. *Harrell*, 8 id. 123; *Skime* v. *Simmons*, 11 Ga. 401; *Scarborough* v. *Watkins*, 9 B. Monroe; *Nelson* v. *Hull*, 5 Jones' Eq. [N. C.] 32; *Holmes* v. *Bridgman*, 37 Vt. 28; Wms. on Exrs. 1804; Bac. Abr. Exrs. [L] 1; *Tebbs* v. *Carpenter*, 1 Madd. 298, 290; *Lawson* v. *Copeland*, 2 Bro. Ch. Cas. 156; *Moyle* v. *Moyle*, 2 Russ. & M. 710; *Argall* v. *Bryant*, 1 Sandf. 98; *Northrup* v. *Hill*, 57 N. Y. 351; *Moore* v. *Juvenal*, 8 Weekly Notes of Cases, June 17, 1880; 2 Wms. on Exrs. 1064.) The defendant's point that the onus was upon the plaintiff to show that the claim could have been collected by Keteltas, is untenable. (*Walron* v. *Ball*, 9 Barb. 271, 277; *Ingalls* v. *Levy*, 1 Cow. 240, 241.)

DANFORTH, J. The complaint is upon the theory that a cause of action existed in favor of Mrs. Christy, against Smith, for about $20,000, received by him for her use; that it was a valid and subsisting claim when she died, and that when William A. Keteltas (the defendant's testator) undertook the office of executor of her will, he had notice of it. If these things were so it was his plain duty to reduce the debt to his possession, as part of the assets of the estate which he represented. But he took no steps to that end, and allowed time to run in favor of the debtor. He became, therefore, liable as for a *devastavit.* (Williams on Ex'rs, vol. 2, p. 1636 [5th Am. ed.]; *Shultz* v. *Pulver*, 3 Paige, 184; 11 Wend. 366.) And it follows that he having died, his estate should make good the loss. It has been so adjudged. It is now objected, however, by the appellants that the money was for the enjoyment of Mrs. Christy during life only, and that no interest passed by her death to her representatives. It is a sufficient answer that the objection comes too late. (*Peck* v. *Gurney*, 2 Hill, 605; *Judd* v. *O'Brien*, 21 N. Y. 186; *Bommer* v. *Am. Spiral, etc., Butt. Hinge Co.*, 81 id. 468.) It was proven at the trial that the money was part of the proceeds of certain real estate, bought by one Cowdin; that the amount in question was the residue of the share of Mrs. Christy, and was received by Smith "for her," and by stipulation between the parties it was agreed that certain "conveyances" referred to in the case, but not set out, "constituted evidence showing that Harriet E. Christy's share of the purchase-money of the premises described" therein "was $34,000." It may be that other evidence tended to qualify her estate, but if so, it by no means follows that had the objection been urged, still other evidence might not have been produced to answer it. At the trial the objections to the recovery were, "*first*, that the facts proved do not constitute the cause of action stated in the complaint; *second*, do not constitute any cause of action in favor of the plaintiff against the defendant; and, *third*, that there is not sufficient evidence to raise any question of fact for a jury." There was no request to the referee to find upon the point, now presented, nor was it adverted to. To be available to the defendant it should have been specifically stated. (*Bills* v. *N. Y. C. R. R. Co.*, 84 N. Y. 15; *Spears* v. *The Mayor*, 87 id. 359.) A careful examination of the record shows that the trial was conducted throughout upon the theory that such money as Smith received was for Mrs. Christy, and that he was accountable to her for it. The idea that the interest or income only belonged to her, and the principal to remaindermen, was not once suggested. Indeed, the trial proceeded upon the theory enunciated in the complaint that the money was her money — that is altogether hers — and for aught that appears it was assumed by both parties that it was the value of her interest in the land, whatever it might be, the defendant raising no question as to its character. It is also urged by the appellant that Keteltas was not required to proceed against Smith until indemnified by the parties interested. There is no such rule of law. It may be that an executor is not bound to prosecute a doubtful claim merely because those interested think it well founded, but an executor with notice that there is a debt due the estate is bound to active diligence for its collection, and must proceed without waiting for the request even of the distributees. If the case is one of such doubt that indemnity is proper, he must, at least, ask for it, and at any rate takes the risk of showing that the debt is not lost by his own negligence. (*Schultz* v. *Pulver*, 11 Wend. 363; *Stiles* v. *Guy*, 16 Simons, 229.) Here, however, there is evidence not only of neglect, but of willful default, amounting to positive collusion with Smith, in permitting the latter to retain the debt upon his assurance that "the claim would soon be outlawed," and that "if he had to pay any thing on it, he" (Smith) "would make it all right with him" (Keteltas). There is, therefore, no merit in the position that he should have been indemnified also by the other side. It is not even plausible. By accepting the trust he came under an obligation to perform it with diligence, and neither the omission of those interested to proffer indemnity, nor the assurance of the debtor, should excuse him from the consequence of neglect.

It is urged, however, that incompetent evidence was received by the referee upon the question of Smith's indebtedness to Mrs. Christy. The complaint stated that the money was received by him on the 30th of July, 1868, and it must be presumed that in opening the case to the referee, the circumstances surrounding the transaction, and afterward disclosed in evidence, were presented by the plaintiff's counsel. Among them were the source from which the money was derived, its form, its disposition, and the relation which Smith sustained toward it, and toward Mrs. Christy. Her share was part of a large sum received by Smith and others, and it was material to show Smith's individual control of the portion going to her. It was not necessarily to be established by one item of evidence, and the order of its introduction was in the discretion of the referee. When, therefore, at the outset of the case the plaintiff proved by the teller of the Fulton Bank that Smith was a depositor in that bank, and that the witness then had, from the files of the bank, a deposit ticket of July 30, 1868, written by Smith, himself, on that day, it was not irrelevant to the issue. It was Smith's declaration that he deposited in the Fulton National Bank, July 30, 1868, $31,075.30 in bills, and although not sufficient to prove that he did, in fact, make the deposit, its tendency was that way, and, with other circumstances, indicated that he exercised control over a sum of money, shown, by other evidence, to be about equal to the money received by him at an earlier hour, on the same day, and in bills, for Mrs. Christy. The deposit ticket was, therefore, properly admitted.

But rejecting this evidence, the liability of Smith to Mrs. Christy was conclusively established, and the referee justified in finding that Keteltas (her executor) believed such indebtedness to exist when in June, 1871, he filed what purported to be an inventory of her personal estate. It exhibited articles of small value, amounting in the aggregate to less than $200. It was prepared by Smith as the attorney for Keteltas and contained no allusion to the money due from him. Keteltas says Smith told him " he was Mrs. Christy's attorney before her death, and prepared her will and named him as executor." He adds, "he told me there was money in it." "I understood that the estate was quite large; worth about $30,000;" this "was hearsay;" he got that impression "from what Smith had said." He also says, "Mrs. Christy while she was living had been in the hands of Smith; he appointed me in her will as executor, and her estate being in his hands he went on with the business for her estate, she being dead." He never "asked any investigation to ascertain what property Mrs. Christy left," and he went to no one other than Smith to inquire, nor asked any other person about the assets, and although he says he "asked Smith to make out an account," he "never inquired what he had received or paid out."

Mrs. Christy died in June, 1870, and the next winter Miss Wright, one of the beneficiaries under her will, called upon Keteltas, and he says, "he referred her to Smith," and she replied, "she could get no account from him." The testimony of Miss Wright as to this interview is explicit. She asked for money and he said, "he had no money of mine * * * that Smith had some money." She said, "Yes, he must have $30,000 at least." He said, "he supposed it was so, but thought Smith had settled that long ago." She replied, "he had not done any thing about it." Upon cross-examination the witness gives a somewhat fuller account of the interview, and says that Keteltas asked, "Is not that settled yet? and I said no, sir, we have not got any thing from it at all. He then spoke about being executor, and said he would see Mr. Smith. I said there was a great deal of money there and I think it strange we do not get it, and he said, yes, I think there was; and I told him I had an idea it was over $30,000; and he said, I think, I am not positive, he said thirty, I think it was about $30,000; he knew there was money there, and thought it was strange that we had never received any thing."

Q. "Money, where?" A. "In Mr. Smith's hands." Q. "Did he not say, 'I thought Mr. Smith had settled that long ago?'" A. "Yes." Q. "You said nothing?" A. "I said he had not settled, of course." Birdsall, a lawyer, in the latter part of 1870, or winter or spring of 1871, called upon Keteltas at the request of one of the legatees under the will, and says, "he seemed to be annoyed about it, and professed not to know any thing about it, and said that it was altogether in Smith's hands, and that he knew all about it, and that he, Keteltas, did not." "I then said to him that inasmuch as he was the executor, he was the only one the children had to look to, and it was better for him to look into it, as they proposed to have what was their rights." Nothing was accomplished at that interview, but soon after the conversation was renewed, when the witness presented to him a memorandum containing statements of items given to witness by Smith, showing that there was due to Mrs. Christy's estate somewhere between $20,000 and $21,000. Keteltas replied that Smith had given him to understand that there was little or nothing in the estate. "I told him," says Birdsall, "that was not so, and that from the statements he (Keteltas) had made to me, I believed Mr. Smith was deceiving him in the matter. A few days after that I met him in the street and asked if he had seen Smith, and he then said Smith had told him there was nothing left of the estate, and it was all bosh, and he believed Smith and he would be damned if he would bother himself any thing more about it." Q. "Did you tell him what his liability would be?" A. "I told him he would be held liable for the whole amount of that money if he did not get it out of Smith's hands. He said that Smith had been his counsel for many years, that he had married a relative of his, and that he believed his statements."

Upon a further examination of this witness it appeared that in a conversation with Keteltas, he stated to him that he had seen the papers relating to the matter, "and if he would call upon Mr. Cowdin he could see the check indorsed by Mr. Smith for the money that Mr. Smith admitted he had in his possession, and asked Keteltas to go to Mr. Cowdin's office and see the papers; he said he did not care to see them."

There is enough in these statements to warrant the conclusion that Keteltas had information sufficient to excite a belief in the indebtedness of Smith to the estate of Mrs. Christy, and warning enough to put him to the exercise of vigilance in recovering it, but that notwithstanding this he suffered Smith to retain possession of the money. Undoubtedly Keteltas also stated, as the counsel for the appellant claims, that he would have tried to get the money from Smith if he had known that he had any belonging to Mrs. Christy's estate, that he had asked Smith over and over again "what moneys he had received from Mrs. Christy during her life-time, and he said there was not a copper." But in view of the testimony to which I have adverted, it is plain that Keteltas poorly performed the duty of executor; in fact he did not perform it at all, when he relied upon the assurances of Smith in the face of positive information, not only that the debt did exist, but that Smith admitted its existence. We agree, therefore, with the referee and the General Term in the conclusion that with good reason Keteltas believed Smith was indebted to Mrs. Christy in the sum of $20,000; that he failed to demand it from him and suffered him to retain possession of it. Nor was there error on the part of the referee in refusing to find that Smith denied to Keteltas his liability. There are words, as we have seen, which would have justified that finding, but the referee was to look at the whole testimony, and was not bound to credit the statement, nor could he in any just sense have found that upon any serious demand by Keteltas, there had been a denial.

The lapse of time will not aid the defendant: First, the liability of Smith accrued as early as August, 1868, and no point was made upon the trial that by payment or otherwise he had prevented the statute of limitations from running against it. He indeed paid money to Mrs. Christy in small sums from time to time, but there is no finding that the payments related to the debt involved in this claim, nor as to the time of payment, nor was any request to find in these particulars presented to the referee. The complaint alleged that the statute became a bar by reason of the neglect of Keteltas to prosecute Smith, and at the close of the evidence, although the

defendant moved to dismiss the complaint, there was no suggestion that this averment was not proved, and aside from the
general grounds taken on that occasion, and above adverted to,
it was only insisted that the cause of action against Keteltas
accrued more than seven and one-half years before the commencement of the suit, viz., on the 3d of December, 1870 —
that being the time the will went to probate. Second, it is
again claimed by the appellant that the plea of the statute of
limitations to the cause of action against Keteltas was sustained.
This also is unfounded. The statute was available to Smith
in August, 1874. His pecuniary ability up to that time has
not been denied. Then at all events Keteltas became liable to
account to the beneficiaries under the will for the amount uncollected from Smith, to the same extent precisely as if he had
received and actually held the money. There was no period
after that until his death, when he ceased to be liable. He
died on the 16th of July, 1876, and the liability was transferred to his executors. (2 R. S. 114, § 6, title 5, p. 11, chap.
6; *Walton* v. *Walton,* 2 Abb. [N. S.] 428.) This action
was commenced on the 11th of June, 1878, manifestly less
than six years from the time the statute run in Smith's favor.

It is unnecessary, therefore, to consider whether after a greater
lapse of time an executor would be permitted to allege his own
wrong so as to have time run in his favor from the beginning
of his neglect, or whether each day before accounting would
not be deemed the commencement of the cause of action, or he
be chargeable for the money he might have collected, as for
assets in his hands.

The cause was properly disposed of by the referee and General Term, and the judgment appealed from should be affirmed,
with costs.

All concur.

Judgment affirmed.

BEVERLY HAIGHT et al., Respondents, *v.* THE CONTINENTAL INSURANCE COMPANY, Appellant.

132-
13(-
13 7-
92
149

A policy of insurance, issued by defendant upon a dwelling-house, contained a condition, avoiding it, "if the building *become* unoccupied without the consent of the company indorsed" thereon; this was in connection with other conditions relating to the future. It was provided in the policy that nothing but a specific agreement, indorsed thereon, should be construed as a waiver of any of its conditions, and that an agent "has no authority to waive, modify or strike from this policy any of its printed conditions." The insurance was effected, and the policy delivered by an agent of the defendant. The building was then unoccupied, which fact was known to the agent. He had authority to insure unoccupied buildings, and the premium charged was at the rate for such buildings, which was more than double that for those occupied. No indorsement, however, of defendant's consent was made upon the policy. In an action upon the policy *held*, that the condition as to indorsement might have been fairly interpreted by the insured as relating only to the future; but, assuming it to be otherwise, it was to be assumed that the agent accounted for and paid over to defendant the premium received, and as it had not only not repudiated the contract, but recognized its original validity, it must be deemed to have waived the condition essential to such validity; that it would not be permitted to receive and keep the fruits of the contract and yet repudiate its existence.

The premises had been sold on foreclosure, but no deed had been executed or report of sale made. *Held*, that as the sale yet remained inchoate and conditional, there was no breach of a condition of the policy avoiding it in case of a transfer of interest without consent indorsed.

(Argued March 9, 1883; decided March 27, 1883.)

APPEAL from order of the General Term of the Supreme Court, in the second judicial department, entered upon an order made September 11, 1882, which affirmed a judgment in favor of plaintiffs, entered upon a verdict.

This action was brought upon a policy of insurance upon a dwelling-house, issued by the defendant, by its terms insuring Walter L. Thompson, assignee, for the benefit of creditors of Angelina Cooper, "loss, if any, payable to" plaintiffs, "mortgagees as their interest may appear."

The material facts are stated in the opinion.

Frank B. Lown for appellant. The fact that the policy contained a provision that the same should be void if the building " become unoccupied " was notice to plaintiffs, upon their receiving the policy, that the company considered non-occupancy "material to the risk," and they were, therefore, bound, by its terms, to make the fact known to the company. (*Browning* v. *Home Ins. Co.*, 71 N. Y. 508; *Findar* v *Resolute Ins. Co.*, 47 id. 114; *Short* v. *Home Ins. Co.*, 20 Alb. L. J. 54.) Where a policy, on its face, informs the applicant that the agent could waive nothing, no supposition, on his part, can or should avail him. (*Walsh* v. *Hartford Ins. Co.*, 73 N. Y. 5.) The compromise agreement entered into between the plaintiffs and the defendant should not be disturbed. (*Wehrum* v. *Kuhn*, 61 N. Y. 623; *Coon* v. *Knapp*, 8 id. 402; *Brooks* v. *Moore*, 67 Barb. 395; *Ludington* v. *Miller*, 6 J. & S. 478; *Farmers' Bank of Amsterdam* v. *Blaic*, 44 Barb. 652.)

H. H. Hustis for respondents. The knowledge of the defendant's agents that the building was vacant when the policy of insurance was issued was knowledge of the defendant, and that condition of the policy, in reference to vacant buildings, was waived. (*Van Schaick* v. *Niagara Ins. Co.*, 68 N. Y. 434; *Browning* v. *Home Ins. Co.*, 70 id. 508; *Bennett* v. *North British Ins. Co.*, 81 id. 273; *Woodruff* v. *Imperial Ins. Co.*, 83 id. 133.) Where the owner of the property refuses to make proof of loss, the mortgagees have a right to make such proof. (*Graham* v. *Phœnix Ins. Co.*, 17 Hun, 156; *Graham* v. *Fireman's Ins. Co.*, 8 Daly, 421.) There was no change of title. (*Browning* v. *The Home Ins. Co.*, 70 N. Y. 508.)

FINCH, J. Certain provisions of the policy of insurance issued by the defendant company are relied upon as constituting a defense to the plaintiffs' recovery. These are that the contract shall be void " if the building *become* unoccupied without the assent of the company indorsed " on the policy; that "the use of general terms, or any thing less than a distinct, specific agreement, clearly expressed and indorsed on the policy, shall not be construed as a waiver of any printed or written condition contained in it; and that the agent of the company " has no authority to waive, modify or strike from this policy any of its printed conditions; nor is his knowledge of, or assent to insurance in other companies, or to an increase of risk, even if within the limit of his authority herein expressed, binding upon the company, until the same is indorsed in writing on the policy, and the increased premium (if any) paid therefor." As matter of fact the building insured was unoccupied when the policy was issued, as well as when it was burned. We must assume from the verdict that such fact was known to the agent who delivered the policy at the inception of the contract, and who issued it without indorsing upon it the assent of the company. The insurance was obtained by mortgagees, and, although in the name of the assignee of the mortgagor, was for the benefit of the mortgagees, and the loss payable to them. The insurance was temporary, and for a brief period, running only for two months, and the premium charged was at the rate of twenty-five cents per hundred, which the evidence shows was appropriate to a case of unoccupied property, but at least double the rate charged for the same time on an occupied building. The defense rests upon the omission of any indorsement on the policy. The case of *Woodruff* v. *Imperial Fire Ins. Co.* (83 N. Y. 133) is fatal to the defense unless the effort of the appellant to point out a material difference proves successful. It was there held that when a policy is issued upon an unoccupied house, the agent having knowledge of the fact, the defendant cannot be permitted to say it never assumed the risk; and in such case the stipulation requiring an indorsement of the company's consent must be deemed waived by the agent, and through him by the company. But in that case it did not appear that the policy contained the provision present in this, which expressly denied to the agent any power to waive, modify or strike from the policy any of its printed conditions; and it is argued that this limitation of the agent's authority, plainly expressed in the policy, was thus brought to the knowledge of the insured, and the company was not bound and could not be affected by the knowledge and waiver of the agent. But the latter had authority to insure an unoccupied building, and could bind his company by so doing. There was no restraint upon his power to make the precise contract which he did make. Only the manner of his doing it was regulated, and as to that it is not clear that he violated the instructions of his principal, and it is certain that the insured was not fairly chargeable with knowledge that he was so doing. The condition of indorsement as it exists in the language of the policy might have been fairly interpreted by the insured as relating only to the future, and as not affecting the inception of the contract. The language is "if the building *become* unoccupied without the consent of the company indorsed hereon," and the condition is associated with others equally relating to the future. If the building "shall, at any time, be occupied or used so as to increase the risk," if "the risk be increased by the erection or occupation of neighboring buildings;" if the property "be sold or transferred;" if it "be assigned under any insolvent or bankrupt law;" "or if the policy shall be assigned before a loss;" these, and others like them, are the surrounding and accompanying conditions printed in the policy. All of them apparently relate to changes following after an existing and valid contract. The mode of assent to such changes by an indorsement upon the policy indicates the same construction. It assumes a policy already existing, and valid in its inception, upon which a change of its terms is to be noted. So that it will hardly do to say that the insured, upon reading the instrument, was bound to know that an indorsement was essential to its original existence. He might fairly, and naturally, read it as referring only to possible events occurring in the future. But were it otherwise, if not the agent, at least the company, could and did waive the condition. Their agent had authority to insure an unoccupied dwelling; he did so in fact; he charged and received the appropriate premium; we must assume that he accounted for it to the company, which has neither returned nor offered to return the money; the insurer did not repudiate the contract, but has admitted its original validity, recognizing it as a policy of insurance by the letter of its general agent pointing out by whom proofs of loss should have been made, and by its answer when sued. The waiver of conditions at the inception of a policy grows out of the consideration that the company must have intended to make a valid contract, or else to perpetrate a fraud. Their agent had authority to insure the building, although unoccupied, and having done so the company must be held to have waived a condition essential to its validity, and cannot be permitted to receive and keep its fruits, and yet repudiate its existence.

We cannot interfere with the verdict of the jury upon the question whether the compromise between the parties was procured by fraud, and was for that reason invalid. The evidence on the subject shows that Haight was an old man, putting confidence in Thompson, in whose name the policy ran, and influenced by his advice while unconscious that a promise to retain him had been made by the company. The proof is not convincing, but there was enough of it to take the question to the jury, and we cannot review their conclusion.

Nor was the policy avoided by the sale on foreclosure. There was no change of title. No deed was given, and not even a report of sale made and presented to the court for confirmation. Until then the sale and transfer of possession were *inchoate* and conditional, and had not become absolute and complete. (*Browning* v. *Home Ins. Co.*, 71 N. Y. 508; 27 Am. Rep. 86.)

The judgment should be affirmed, with costs.

All concur.

Judgment affirmed.

MARGARETTA CRABB, Appellant and Respondent, *v.* ISAAC H. YOUNG et al., Executors, etc., Appellants and Respondents.

In an action brought by one of the beneficiaries under a will against the executors, who by the will were authorized to sell the real estate, and to invest and hold the proceeds with that of the personalty, as trustees for certain specified trusts, to recover damages for alleged willful delay and neglect in selling the real estate, and for improvident investments of the trust funds and to remove the trustees, it appeared that a former action was brought by plaintiff against defendants and others, wherein the complaint charged willful and fraudulent misconduct in the management of the estate and delay in selling the real estate, and demanded judgment that the executors be directed to sell immediately, also, to pay plaintiff the sums lost by such negligence, and that some other person be appointed to take charge of the portion of the funds in which plaintiff was interested. By the judgment in that action the trustees were directed to sell the real estate at auction within five months, and one of the trustees was suspended until the further order of the court on the ground of his insolvency. It also appeared and the court found that plaintiff upon being paid a consideration by the other *cestuis que trust*, who were satisfied with defendants' management, consented to a delay in the sale ; that certain securities were set aside as and for her portion of the trust fund, and that the lands were sold within the time agreed. *Held*, that the former judgment in effect determined that upon the facts existing at the time it was rendered plaintiff was neither entitled to recover damages for delay, nor for a judgment removing defendants from their trusteeship; and that said judgment was conclusive and estopped plaintiff from any claim for relief based on facts occurring prior to said judgment; also, that no claim could be based upon the subsequent delay in selling the real estate.

The will provided that the executors should not be liable for any loss or damage except such as occurred "from their willful default, misconduct or neglect." The complaint alleged and the court found that defendants imprudently and carelessly invested a portion of the fund set apart for plaintiff in insufficient securities, but such imprudence was not alleged or found to have been "willful." *Held*, that a judgment requiring defendants to restore to the trust fund the amount so invested was not authorized.

A testator has the right to impose the terms and conditions under which his bounty shall be distributed, and the court has no authority to increase the responsibility of, or impose obligations upon, the trustees selected by him from the burden of which he has in his will protected them.

It did not appear that any loss had actually occurred to the income because of such investments, and it seemed probable that no loss would even eventually occur to the fund itself, and the evidence disclosed no ground for imputing bad faith or want of prudence in making said investments. *Held*, that a judgment removing defendants was not justified ; that if they acted in good faith subsequent events which they could not foresee, over which they had no control, could not render them liable.

While trustees will be held to great strictness in their dealings with trust property, the courts will regard them with leniency when it appears they have acted in good faith.

Defendants were required by the will to invest in bonds and mortgages "on unincumbered real estate." At the time of a loan upon bond and mortgage there was an unpaid tax upon the land. *Held*, that this was not a violation of the provision ; that the tax was not an incumbrance within the meaning of the provision.

(Argued March 9, 1883 ; decided March 27, 1883.)

CROSS APPEALS from judgment of the General Term of the City Court of Brooklyn, entered upon an order made February 27, 1882, which affirmed a judgment entered upon a decision of the court at Special Term.

The nature of the action and the material facts are stated in the opinion.

Nathaniel C. Moak for plaintiff. The trustees were creatures of the will, and compelled to follow exactly any explicit directions therein contained. (Perry on Trusts, § 460.) Where an unauthorized investment is made, a trustee is invariably liable ; and his good faith, purity of intention and subsequent diligence in endeavoring to prevent the loss will be no protection to him. (*May* v. *Dreker*, 61 Ala. 53.) The provision of the will that investments should be made on unincumbered real estate was not complied with when the loan of $5,000 was made as there were unpaid taxes on the land, and the executors were not relieved from liability by the provision of the will that they should not be liable for any loss or damage except what occurred " from their willful default, misconduct or neglect." (*Dosier* v. *Brereton*, 15 Beav. 221 ; *Adair* v. *Brimmer*, 74 N. Y. 552; *Kimball* v. *Beding*, 31 N. H. 352; *Baker* v. *Disbrow*, 18 Hun, 29 ; *Quackenbush* v. *Southwick*, 41 N. Y.

117, 122; *Matter of Morgan* 63 Barb. 621; Perry on Trusts, §§ 279, 427, 539–549.) The prior suit was no bar to the relief allowed by the present judgment. (*Dawley* v. *Brown*, 79 N. Y. 390, 397–400; *Van Boskirck* v. *Herrick*, 65 Barb. 250; *Brown* v. *Gallaudet*, 80 N. Y. 413; *Kirby* v. *Daly*, 63 id. 659; *Kerr* v. *Hayes*, 35 id. 331; *White* v. *Madison*, 26 id. 117; *Lawrence* v. *Cabot*, 41 N. Y. Sup. Ct. 123; *Jones* v. *Underwood*, 13 Abb. Pr. 393; *Tyler* v. *Willis*, 35 Barb. 213; *McDonald* v. *Christie*, 42 id. 37; *Smith* v. *Weeks*, 26 id. 464; *East N. Y. & J. R. R. Co.* v. *Elmore*, 53 id. 624; Greenl. on Ev., § 532 [13th ed.]; Wharton on Ev., § 988; *Dawley* v. *Brown*, 79 N. Y. 390, 397–400; *Kirby* v. *Daly*, 63 id. 659; *Smith* v. *Weeks*, 26 Barb. 464; *Stowell* v. *Chamberlain*, 60 N. Y. 273.) The claim for loss on the real estate was not barred by the former action, because it was not asserted in the complaint or on the trial of that action. (Perry on Trusts, §§ 439, 462; *Cromwell* v. *County of Sac*, 94 U. S. 351; *Stowell* v. *Chamberlain*, 60 N. Y. 273 · *Marcellus* v. *Countryman*, 65 Barb. 201.)

Matthew Hale for defendants. Plaintiff has already had her day in court to obtain the relief which she now asks for. If the judgment then awarded her was not as full as she was entitled to, her remedy was by appeal, and not by a new action. (*Cook* v. *Grant's Adm.*, 1 Paige, 407; *Lockwood* v. *Fawcett*, 24 S. C. 146; *Inslee* v. *Hampton*, 11 Hun, 156; *Hoff* v. *Myers*, 42 Barb. 270; *Gates* v. *Preston*, 41 N. Y. 113; *Brown* v. *Mayor*, 66 id. 385, 390; *Blair* v. *Bartlett*, 75 id. 150; *Jordan* v. *Van Epps*, 85 id. 427–432; *Church* v. *Kidd*, 88 id. 652.) The only cases in which it is allowable to inquire into the evidence produced on the trial of the former action are cases where, from the absence of formal pleadings in the first suit, or their obscurity, the record fails to show what were the actual issues between the parties. (*Young* v. *Rummell*, 2 Hill, 478; *Campbell* v. *Butts*, 3 N. Y. 173; *Doty* v. *Brown*, 4 id. 71; *Brown* v. *Gallaudet*, 80 id. 413; *Wood* v. *Genet*, 8 Wend. 9; *Ehle* v. *Bingham*, 7 Barb. 494; *Gardner* v. *Buck-*

bee, 3 Cow. 120.) The fact that the plaintiff, whether intentionally or unintentionally, failed to produce any evidence or sufficient evidence in support of any of the issues presented by the pleadings, does not entitle her to bring another suit upon those issues. (*Ogsbury* v. *La Farge,* 2 N. Y. 113.) The question of negligence was a question of law, and had the case been tried by a jury upon the evidence it would have been the duty of the court to direct a verdict for the defendants. (*Mitchell* v. *N. Y. C. & H. R. R. R. Co.,* 64 N. Y. 655.) The taxes, which were unpaid on the property on which $5,000 was loaned by the executors, were not such an incumbrance as was contemplated by the testator when he directed the investments to be made upon unincumbered real estate. (*Craft* v. *Williams,* 88 N. Y. 384, 391; *Chesterman* v. *Eyland,* 81 id. 398; *Wiggins* v. *Howard,* 83 id. 613; *Ormiston* v. *Olcott,* 84 id. 339; *Lansing* v. *Olcott,* 1 Abb. Pr. [N. S.] 280, 288-9; *Sidenberg* v. *Ely,* N. Y. Daily Reg., Nov. 13, 1882.) The care required of trustees is such as prudent and intelligent men use in their own affairs. (*Roosevelt* v. *Roosevelt,* 6 Abb. N. C. 447; *Knight* v. *Earl of Plymouth,* 3 Atk. 480; Dickens, 120; *Thompson* v. *Brown,* 4 Johns. Ch. 619; *Higgins* v. *Whitson,* 20 Barb. 141; Lewin on Trustees, 152; Story's Eq. Jur., § 1273; *Ormiston* v. *Olcott,* 84 N. Y. 339-347; *Litchfield* v. *White,* 7 id. 438.) The objection to the admission of Mr. New's evidence, as to what occurred on the former trial, was well taken, and is fatal to the judgment. (*Tabor* v. *Van Tassell,* 86 N. Y. 642-643; *Foot* v. *Beecher,* 78 id. 155; *New York Guaranty Co.* v. *Gleason,* id. 503-517; *Capron* v. *Thompson,* 86 id. 418-421; *Pinney* v. *Orth,* 88 id. 447.) Trustees are to be allowed six months to find an investment. (*Dunscomb* v. *Dunscomb,* 1 Johns. Ch. 508; *Gilman* v. *Gilman,* 2 Lans. 1; *DePeyster* v. *Clarkson,* 2 Wend. 77.) The court had no jurisdiction to appoint a new trustee in this action. The necessary parties were not before it. (*Powers* v. *Bergen,* 6 N. Y. 358; *In re Empire City B'k,* 18 id. 199; *Rockwell* v. *Nearing,* 35 id. 302; *Shaver* v. *Brainard,* 29 Barb. 25; *Stuart* v. *Palmer,* 74 N. Y. 183.)

RUGER, Ch. J.   This case comes here on cross appeals from the judgment of the General Term, affirming a final judgment rendered in the City Court of Brooklyn. Each party by appropriate provisions contained in their respective notices of appeal seeks also to review an interlocutory judgment previously rendered in the action.

The circumstances out of which this action arose are as follows : Isaac Young died before July, 1868, having previously made his will, and leaving a considerable estate to his five children, Isaac H., Robert B., John L., William A. and Margaretta Young, the plaintiff, the defendants Isaac H. and Robert L. Young were made executors. The estate consisted of four pieces of real property, some of which were unproductive, and personal property of the value of about $80,000.

The will and codicils made provisions which may be stated concisely as follows : To each of the defendants was devised one-fifth of all of his property absolutely.   The shares of the other three children, each consisting of one-fifth of the estate, were devised to the defendants in trust to invest and pay over the income arising therefrom to the respective devisees during their natural lives, and the share to the income of which the plaintiff was entitled, was upon her death to go to her heirs and next of kin.

The executors were empowered to sell, lease and dispose of, or to partition the real estate, and they were directed to invest the moneys accruing from plaintiff's share of the proceeds in bonds, secured by mortgages upon unincumbered real estate, situated in the State of New York, and to keep said trust funds at all times distinct from the other trust estates created by said will. It was further provided that said executors should not be answerable for any loss or damage happening to the estate, except such as occurred from their willful default, misconduct or neglect, and that each of said executors should be liable to account only for the moneys which come into his individual hands.   The plaintiff had no parents or children living, and in the event of her decease, her brothers would apparently become her heirs at law.

This action was commenced in March, 1879, against the

executors, and sought substantially these measures of relief: *First.* To recover of the defendants the sum of $10,000 for loss of income, to which the plaintiff claimed she was entitled, by reason of an alleged willful and fraudulent delay of said executors and trustees in selling the real estate left by the testator, and adding one-fifth thereof to the plaintiff's trust fund. *Second.* To cause the defendants to reimburse to the plaintiff's trust fund the sum of $8,000, alleged to have been imprudently loaned by them in two several mortgages of the respective amounts of $5,000 and $3,000, and which are claimed to have resulted in an apparent loss to the trust fund. *Third.* To obtain the removal of the defendants as trustees of said estate. The grounds for this claim of relief do not appear in said complaint, except inferentially they may be presumed to be founded upon the allegations of misconduct thereinbefore described.

The answer consists: *First.* Of what may be briefly termed a general denial. *Second.* A former adjudication of all matters of difference between the parties by the surrogate of the proper county in October, 1874. *Third.* A former adjudication of all of the alleged causes of action arising out of the delay of the executors in selling said real estate, in an action in the City Court of Brooklyn, in which final judgment was rendered in June, 1876. *Fourth.* The statute of limitations. Under this state of the pleadings, a trial was had at Special Term which resulted in a judgment for $1,826.69 and interest in favor of plaintiff for defendants' delay in selling real estate, also removing them as trustees of plaintiff's share in said estate, and appointing another trustee, and requiring Isaac H. Young to restore to said trust fund $8,000 and interest thereon, on account of the said alleged improvident investment, and gave the plaintiff's attorney an allowance of $1,500 with costs, to be collected personally out of the defendants.

Upon appeal to the General Term of the City Court, taken by defendants, that court reversed so much of the judgment of the Special Term as awarded $1,826.69 and interest to the plaintiff, and affirmed the remainder thereof, and remitted the parties to the Special Term to carry out certain special provisions contained in the judgment. After an appearance by the parties before the Special Term, and their compliance with the special direction required by what was termed the interlocutory judgment, final judgment was rendered at said Special Term to the effect above described, which was on appeal affirmed at the General Term. From this judgment both parties appeal to this Court, the plaintiff from so much of said interlocutory judgment as reversed the award to her by the Special Term of $1,826.69 and interest, as damages for defendants' delay in selling real estate, and the defendants from the rest of said judgment.

Appropriate exceptions have been taken to raise each of these questions, and their consideration requires us to examine the findings of the court below and such evidence as bears legitimately upon them.

On the trial the plaintiff put in evidence a judgment of the City Court of Brooklyn in an action wherein she was plaintiff and Isaac H. Young, Robert B. Young, John L. Young, William A. Young and others were defendants. The complaint in the action, among other allegations, charged Isaac H. and Robert B. Young with willful and fraudulent misconduct in the management of the estate of Isaac Young, deceased, and delay in selling the real estate, whereby she claimed that she had suffered great damages in the loss of income therefrom, and demanded judgment that the executors be directed immediately to sell said real estate and invest her share thereof, and that they pay over to her the income which they had and also that which they might with due diligence have received from the one-fifth part of said estate, and that some suitable person be appointed to take charge of that part of the funds in which she was interested, or that the trustees give security for the performance of their duties as trustees. The defendants Isaac H., Robert B., John L. and William A. Young, each answered said complaint substantially denying the allegations of improper conduct therein charged against Isaac H. and Robert B. Young, and alleged that there had been no intentional delay in selling said real estate, that constant efforts had been made to effect a sale thereof, but the same had been ineffectual for the reason that the market for the sale of real estate had been so depressed that it could only be made at any time previous thereto except at inadequate prices with great loss to all of the parties interested.

Upon the issues thus formed a trial was had between these parties and judgment rendered therein in June, 1876, whereby the trustees were directed to sell said real estate at public auction within five months from the entry of said judgment, and proceed to divide said estate into five equal parts, keeping the trust funds separate and distinct from each other, and pay over the income of one of said shares, after deducting all proper and necessary charges thereon, to said plaintiff. Extra allowances were ordered of $2,000 to the plaintiff and $1,250 to the defendants Isaac H., Robert B. and John L. Young, to be paid out of the estate. The judgment also suspended Robert B. Young on the ground of his insolvency from acting as trustee until the further order of the court. The court below on the trial of the present action found the further fact that all of said lands were sold by the executors in the year 1878 for the aggregate sum of $15,950, and that the delay in the sale thereof after the said judgment in June, 1876, was consented to by plaintiff upon the request of defendants. It appeared in evidence that she received a pecuniary consideration from defendants for such consent. Immediately on the heel of this former judgment and apparently with a view of complying with its provisions, the defendants set apart securities of the appraised value of $21,673.97, and executed a written declaration stating that they held such securities in trust for the plaintiff under the provisions of the will of Isaac Young, deceased. This selection of securities was approved as to character and amount by the plaintiff's attorney in that and also the present action.

Upon these facts we are of the opinion that there was no evidence in the case which authorized the court below to charge the defendants with damages occasioned to the plaintiff on account of the delay in selling the real estate in question and investing its proceeds, neither do we think that any evidence in relation to such delay was competent or material as the basis of a charge against these defendants of improvidency or willful or fraudulent misconduct in the management of such trust estate. So far as the charge of misconduct related to the period subsequent to the former judgment the court find that the delay was expressly authorized and approved by the plaintiff, and there is nothing in the case to show that it was not a wise and prudent measure. In fact the other four joint-owners, two of whom were *cestuis que trust*, with interests identical with those of plaintiff, approved the management of the trustees and voluntarily paid the plaintiff a considerable sum to induce her to consent to such delay.

The determination of the former action by the judgment of the City Court was an adjudication as to all of the questions litigated therein and was conclusive upon the parties to this action until reversed. It is, therefore, seen that that action adjudicated the question that upon the facts existing at the time of such judgment the plaintiff was neither entitled to recover damages for delay in selling said real estate, or to a judgment removing the defendants from their trusteeship under the will. That judgment shows that the court passed not only upon the question of the amount of the fund to the income from which plaintiff was then entitled, as was held by the General Term, but also upon the question of the removal of the defendants. In fact they did suspend one of said trustees upon the ground of his insolvency, and as to the other trustee they directed him to proceed and execute the duties of his trust, thus impliedly refusing to remove him from his position as trustee.

These questions were all legitimately raised by the pleading in that action, and were either actually decided or necessarily determined in arriving at the conclusion embodied in the judgment. We, therefore, affirm the decision of the General Term, holding that the plaintiff was estopped by that judgment from claiming or recovering damages on account of the delay exercised by the executors in disposing of the testator's real estate.

The only finding of fact in the court below charging the defendants with willful misconduct in the management of said estate related solely to their action in delaying the sale of said real estate, and we must assume that the judgment of removal was based largely if not wholly upon this finding. We see no reason why the former adjudication was not as conclusive of the question of defendants' misconduct as it was upon the question of delay in selling the real estate, and we are, therefore, of the opinion that the court below erred in directing the removal of the defendants from their trusteeship unless some other sufficient ground therefor arising subsequent to June, 1876, appears in the evidence.

It is claimed that the defendants were also guilty of misconduct in the year 1876 in relation to the investment of trust funds in bonds and mortgages upon real estate in the city of Brooklyn. The complaint does not allege the carelessness or imprudence of the defendants in respect to such investment to have been "willful," neither do the findings of the court below thus characterize the action of these trustees. It is quite clear that they cannot be held liable to replace the moneys lost through even an improvident or careless investment, unless they have acted willfully and have intentionally disregarded the rules which control and regulate the action of prudent and careful men in conducting their own business affairs.

The will of the testator expressly exempts them from liability " for any loss or damage that may happen to my estate except the same shall occur or take place from their own willful default, misconduct or neglect." The testator had an absolute right to select the agencies by which his bounty should be distributed and to impose the terms and conditions under which it should be done. He well knew the character and qualification of those whom he selected as his trustees, for they were his own children, and while they were engaged in the performance of a lawful duty which he intrusted to them, the court has not the right to increase the measure of their responsibility or impose obligations from the burden of which he has in his will so carefully protected them. We think, therefore, in the absence of any finding to the effect that the conduct of the defendant Isaac H. in making such investments was willful or fraudulent, that the court below erred in holding that he was liable to replace the amount of such investment in the trust fund.

There still remains to be considered the question as to whether the conduct of these defendants in dealing with this estate since June, 1876, has been so negligent, careless and improvident as to justify the claim that it was willful and authorized their removal from the trusteeship and the appointment of another in their place.

Trusts of property are generally created for the benefit and support of the young, helpless and inexperienced, and depend largely for their proper administration upon the honesty and capacity of those to whom they are confided. From the fact that those who are most immediately interested are usually incapable of properly guarding their own interests, and must necessarily depend so much upon the good faith of others, the court will guard their rights with jealous care and scrutinize closely the conduct of trustees with the view of holding them to a high degree of responsibility in the management and control of trust estates. But while trustees are thus held to great strictness in their dealings with the interests of their beneficiaries, the court will regard them leniently when it appears they have acted in good faith, and if no improper motive can be attributed to them, the court have even excused an apparent breach of trust, unless the negligence is very gross. (Perry on Trusts; *Lansing* v. *Lansing,* 1 Abb. Pr. [N. S.] 288.) We would not in the least degree impair the force of the well-settled rules on that subject or encourage laxity in the conduct of trustees in the management of trust estates, but in this case and with reference to these defendants, we think the court below have gone beyond any established rule and have held them to a stricter degree of responsibility than ought generally to be required from executors and trustees. It does not appear from

the evidence given on the trial that any loss has actually occurred to the income from the trust fund in consequence of
these investments; indeed it seems quite probable that no loss
will even eventually occur to the fund itself.

Although the defendants in the exercise of a permissible discretion (*Chesterman* v. *Eyland*, 81 N. Y. 398; *Ormiston* v.
Olcott, 84 id. 339), and in order to avoid eventual loss, have
felt obliged to foreclose the mortgages and take the title to the
real estate upon which they were liens, there has nothing yet
transpired to show that this proceeding will result in any loss.
In fact it was shown upon the trial that upon this investment
of $8,000, the trustees are now in the receipt of rents amounting
to about $800 annually, and with a reasonable probability that
the property may be sold for enough to cover the entire amount
of both of the loans complained of.   The presumptions against
careless or imprudent conduct on the part of these defendants
in the investment and management of this fund are natural and
almost irresistible.   They are apparently the natural heirs of
the plaintiff and presumptively will be entitled to the trust
fund after the termination of her life estate.   They, therefore,
have every interest in preserving instead of wasting it.   They
are required by the will to invest the funds in a limited way,
viz., on bond and mortgage upon unincumbered real estate
situated in the State.   They invested these moneys in strict
accordance with their authority, and at a time when from the
abundance in the money market such securities were scarce
and difficult to obtain.

The evidence produced by the plaintiff on the trial in support of the charges of misconduct on the part of the trustees
in making the investments in question seems entirely insufficient to sustain the findings.   Except the strong apparent desire of the plaintiff to direct and control the management of
the trust estate, and the refusal of one of the defendants when
giving evidence in this case to say that he would take the two
lots in question and replace their cost in the trust fund, there
is but little proved or alleged against the defendants

The only witness produced by the plaintiff upon the value

of this property testifies that the McComb street lot and building upon which the $5,000 loan was made was worth in 1876 from $5,100 to $5,400, and that the lot and building on Ninth street would have cost about $4,000 in 1876. It further appeared that the loan on the McComb street house was made by the purchase of an existing mortgage thereon, which was at the time of the loan paid down from $7,500 to $5,000 to meet the amount which the defendants desired to invest. In opposition to this evidence, the defendants proved by a number of capable and apparently experienced witnesses that the McComb street house was worth from $9,000 to $10,000 in 1876, and that the officers of a banking institution in Brooklyn at the same time, with the loan in question, loaned $5,000 on a mortgage upon a similar house in the same block.

The Ninth street house was by the same witnesses shown to be worth in 1876 from $4,600 to $6,000 and rented for $350 per annum. Upon this evidence we cannot see any ground for imputing a want of prudence to the defendants in making the loan in question, much less bad faith in the management of this estate. If the defendants acted in good faith in making these loans, subsequent events which they could not foresee and over which they had no control, operating to depreciate the value of these securities, would not render them liable to make good such loss to the estate. Such a rule would require a trustee to forecast the future with infallible accuracy, and in case of failure to do so, make him responsible for the consequences, even though he exercised the greatest caution and prudence in making investments. Under such a rule no prudent man would or could safely undertake the management of a trust estate, and it would be difficult to obtain honest and reliable men to accept what is a very necessary but is often a thankless and troublesome duty.

We apprehend the court below mistook the actual position of these parties and did not sufficiently realize that the defendants were by the testator exclusively intrusted with the duty of managing and controlling this fund. The testator deliberately excluded the plaintiff from the performance of this duty, and conferred it upon the defendants, and when she seeks to over-see and supervise the management of the trust fund, she exceeds the power which the will confers upon her. While it would not be improper that these trustees should consult the plaintiff with reference to the investment and management of such fund, yet they were under no legal obligation to do this, and their neglect to do so is not misconduct or conclusive evidence of carelessness or bad faith. It was suggested on the argument as a reason why the defendants should be removed from their trusteeship that their interests were hostile to those of the plaintiff. We think this is not necessarily so, but even if it was, the testator, who knew the relations of the parties and their opposing interests, if any such there were, chose to impose this trust as the condition upon which he gave the plaintiff an interest in his estate, and she can acquire that interest only through an acquiescence in the terms which accompany the gift. It is also claimed that the existence of an unpaid tax of about $160 upon one of these lots at the time of the loan in question was a violation of that provision of the will which required investments to be made in mortgages upon unincumbered real estate. Although an unpaid tax is doubtless an incumbrance on the land upon which it is laid, yet we think it was not such an incumbrance as was in the contemplation of the testator when he inserted this provision in his will. Not only was its amount trivial in comparison with the value of the lot, but there is comparatively but a short time in the course of a year when a tax upon real estate is not either levied or impending over it, and to call a tax an incumbrance within the meaning of this provision would give it an unreasonable and impracticable construction. (*Croft* v. *Williams*, 88 N. Y. 384; *Chesterman* v. *Eyland*, 81 id. 398.)

The views which we have expressed in regard to this case render it unnecessary to discuss the effect of the adjudication before the surrogate in 1874, or as to whether all of the parties interested in the trust fund and entitled to be heard on the question of a change of trustees are now before the court.

The interlocutory judgment of the General Term reversing

the judgment of Special Term awarding $1,826.69 and interest to the plaintiff should be affirmed.   And the judgments of General and Special Terms removing the defendants as trustees, and appointing another in their place, and requiring the defendant Isaac H. Young to restore the sum of $8,000 and interest to the trust fund, should be reversed and a new trial ordered, costs to abide the event.

All concur.

Judgment accordingly.

CATHARINE MARTIN, as Administratrix, etc., Respondent, v. THE DRY DOCK, EAST BROADWAY AND BATTERY RAILROAD COMPANY, Appellant.

A surrogate, in issuing letters of administration, has authority, and it is within his discretion, to limit the powers conferred upon the administrator.

Where, therefore, such letters contain this clause, " these letters are issued with limited authority to prosecute only, and not with power to collect or compromise," *held*, that the surrogate had power to insert the limitation.

It seems, that if such a limitation was in excess of the powers of the surrogate, it did not invalidate the letters, but was at most only an irregularity.

It seems also (MILLER, J., DANFORTH and FINCH, JJ., concurring), that the objection is one that may not be raised collaterally, in a suit brought by the administrator.

(Argued March 12, 1883 ; decided March 27, 1883.)

APPEAL from judgment of the General Term of the Supreme Court, in the first judicial department, entered upon an order made April 10, 1882, which affirmed a judgment in favor of plaintiff, entered upon a verdict.

This action was brought to recover damages for alleged negligence causing the death of Nicholas Martin, plaintiff's intestate.

The letters of administration issued to plaintiff were offered in evidence; in the body thereof in the clause granting power was inserted the following, "with the limited power expressed in the margin." Upon the margin was written the following : " These letters are issued with limited authority to prosecute only, and not with power to collect or compromise."

Defendant's counsel objected to the letters as evidence, upon the ground that they were invalid upon their face, and did not authorize plaintiff to bring the action. The objection was overruled, and said counsel duly excepted.

John M. Scribner for appellant. The Surrogate's Court being a creature of the statute, its proceedings in the manner authorized by the statute, or they are absolutely void. (Redfield's Law and Practice of Surrogates' Courts, 43 ; *Converse* v. *Barber*, 1 Redf. 330; *Riegelman* v. *Riegelman*, 4 id. 492– 495; *Corwin* v. *Merritt*, 3 Barb. 343; *People* v. *Corlies*, 1 Sandf. 247; 14 Am. Law Review, 347; *People* v. *Barnes*, 12 Wend. 492–494; *Roderigas* v. *East River B'k*, 76 N. Y. 316; R. S., chap. 2 of Part 3, title 1; 2 R. S. [Edm. ed.] 230; *Bevan* v. *Cooper*, 72 N. Y. 327; *Matter of Parker*, 1 Barb. Ch. 154.) Limited administrations seldom or never obtain in the American practice. (Williams on Executors and Administrators [6th Am. ed.], 520, 580; 3 Redf. on the Law of Wills, 112.) The limited administration attempted to be conferred by the surrogate in the present case does not fall within either of the kinds of special administrations authorized. (Code, §§ 2660, 2667; 2 R. S. 73, § 23 ; id. 82, § 6 ; id. 114, § 3 ; Laws of 1847, chap. 450 ; 4 Edm. Stat. 526–527; Code, § 1902.) Prior to the passage of the act of 1881 (Chap. 535) the surrogate did not have power to grant the limited administration in question. (*Bevan* v. *Cooper*, 72 N. Y. 329; *Smith* v. *The State*, 27 Ind. 375; *Pike* v. *Megoun*, 44 Mo. 499 ; Sedgwick on Construction of Statutory Law [Pomeroy's ed.], 214, 215; Hardcastle's Statutory Law, 67.) If the surrogate had no power to grant the limited administration in question, the plaintiff's right to maintain the action necessarily falls, and the motion to dismiss the complaint should have been granted. (Williams on Executors and Administrators

[6th Am. ed.], 468, 469 [404]; *Griffith* v. *Frazier*, 8 Cranch, 28.; *Slade* v. *Washburn*, 3 Ired. L. 557, 562; Leake's Digest of the Law of Contracts, 780; Coke on Littleton, 258; *Farmers' B'k* v. *Harrison*, 57 Mo. 503; *Bonesteel* v. *The Mayor*, 22 N. Y. 162; *National B'k of Chemung* v. *Elmira*, 39 How. Pr. 373; 53 N. Y. 49; *Brady* v. *The Mayor*, 20 id. 312; *Roderigas* v. *East River B'k*, 76 id. 316.) The appointment being the judicial action of the surrogate could only be proved by the letters of administration themselves, or by the record or a certified copy of the proceedings, or of the appointment, as the action of the courts is proved in other cases. (*Albright* v. *Cobb*, 30 Mich. 355.) The plaintiff was bound to establish at the trial the regularity of her appointment as administratrix. (*Green* v. *H. R. R. R. Co.*, 2 Abb. Ct. of App. Dec. 277.)

Samuel Greenbaum for respondent. The letters of administration not being incompetent on their face were properly admitted in evidence. (2 R. S. 80, § 55; id. 73, § 23; id. 81, § 56; *Roderigas* v. *East River B'k*, 63 N. Y. 453; Redfield's Surrogates' Pr. [ed. of 1881] 316; *Belden* v. *Meeker*, 47 N. Y. 307; *Parham* v. *Moran*, 4 Hun, 717.) They cannot be attacked or reviewed collaterally. (*Wetmore* v. *Parker*, 52 N. Y. 450; *Roderigas* v. *East River S'vgs B'k*, 76 id. 316; *Bearns* v. *Gould*, 77 id. 455; *Harrison* v. *Clark*, 87 id. 572; *Kelly* v. *West*, 80 id. 139; Redfield's Surrogates [ed. 1881], 52; Code of Civ. Proc., § 2474; Re-enacting Laws of 1870, chap. 359, § 1; *Maloney* v. *Woodin*, 11 Hun, 202; *Potter* v. *Purdy*, 29 N. Y. 196; *Bumstead* v. *Read*, 31 Barb. 661; *Bolton* v. *Brewster*, 32 id. 389; *Doty* v. *Brown*, 4 How. Pr. 428.) The validity of a surrogate's appointment of an administrator, on the ground that he had failed to comply with the directory provisions of the law prescribing his duty in cases where he has become possessed of the jurisdiction to make such appointment, cannot be attacked collaterally. (*Lawrence* v. *Parsons*, 27 How. Pr. 26; *Price* v. *Peters*, 15 Abb. Pr. 197; *Matter of Harvey*, 3 Redf. 214; *Atkins* v. *Kennon*, 20 Wend. 241; *Morrell* v. *Dennison*, 8 Abb. Pr.

401; *Monell* v. *Dennison*, 17 How. Pr. 422; *Wetmore* v. *Parker*, 52 N. Y. 450; 1 Banning and Alden's Patent Cases, 182; *Jackson* v. *Robinson*, 4 Wend. 436; *Van Deusen* v. *Sweet*, 51 N. Y. 378; Redfield's Surrogates [ed. 1881], 51, 314; 3 Phillips' Evidence [3d Am. ed.], 363.) The surrogate had full power to issue the letters of administration. (2 R. S. 220, § 1; Redfield's "Law and Practice of Surrogates' Courts" [ed. 1881], 43; *Kohler* v. *Knapp*, 1 Bradf. 241; *Campbell* v. *Logan*, 2 id. 90; 3 Redfield on Wills [ed. 1877], 113; *Campbell* v. *Logan*, 2 Bradf. 90; *Dubois* v. *Sands*, 43 Barb. 412; *Harnett* v. *Wandell*, 60 N. Y. 353.) Even if the surrogate improperly limited the authority of the administratrix, still the letters cannot be held void. (*Hutchinson* v. *Brand*, 9 N. Y. 209; *Bingham* v. *Disbrow*, 14 Abb. Pr. 251; *Viburt* v. *Frost*, 3 id. 121; *Bucklin* v. *Chapin*, 53 Barb. 488; *Sheldon* v. *Wright*, 5 N. Y. 497; *Bumstead* v. *Read*, 31 Barb. 661; *Lawrence* v. *Parsons*, 27 How. Pr. 26; *Everts* v. *Everts*, 62 Barb. 577; *D'Ivernois* v. *Leavitt*, 8 Abb. Pr. 59, 62; *Roderigas* v. *East River S'vgs B'k*, 63 N. Y. 474; 76 id. 321.)

Per Curiam. The letters of administration issued to the plaintiff in this case contained a limitation, which was written on the margin, limiting the power of the administratrix to prosecute only and not giving her power to collect or compromise.

The limitation referred to was not, at the time of granting the letters, expressly authorized by any statute of this State, but, with this exception, the letters were in the usual form of those issued to an administrator and conferred the usual powers granted to such officer for the purpose of enabling him to discharge the duties thereby imposed. There can be no question that, without such limitation, the letters issued were fully authorized and within the power of the surrogate to grant. That officer had jurisdiction over the person and the subject-matter, and unless he exceeded his authority there is no ground for insisting that the letters were unauthorized. They certainly contained sufficient to confer general authority and power over

the assets of the deceased, and it is not clear upon what ground
it can be claimed that the right to administer, which was thus
conferred, can be disregarded and set at naught for the reason
that the letters contained matter which was not within the
scope of the surrogate's power.   Such matter, we think, being
unnecessary, may be regarded as surplusage, and the letters may
be considered as if it had not constituted a part of or been incorporated in the same.   If the matter objected to be stricken
out then the letters are perfect and complete.   Within well-
settled rules we think they may be considered as if they contained no such limitation, and the objection taken to their validity cannot be upheld.

We are also of the opinion that the surrogate had full power
and authority to issue the letters in question in the form in
which they were made out and that they were properly issued
by him.

By 2 R. S. 220 the surrogate is vested with authority " to
grant letters testamentary and of administration " and " to direct and control " and settle the accounts of executors and administrators.   Although the Surrogate's Court is limited in its
jurisdiction it by no means follows that the surrogate had no
power to issue the letters in question ; he acted strictly within
his jurisdiction and in granting the letters he did that which
was directly within the scope of his powers and the line of his
duties ; the law does not direct what language shall be employed in letters issued by him or what precise powers or duties
shall be laid down in the same ; it does not prohibit letters in
the form used in the case considered.   The power being general
for such a purpose the surrogate must be governed by established rules not inconsistent with the statutes relating to the
organization of the Surrogate's Court.   In all matters relating
to estates the court proceeds in accordance with established
usage as modified by statutory enactment.   (Redf. Law and
Practice, 43.)

In the English practice letters of administration are granted,
limited to certain effects of the deceased, while the general
administration is committed to another.   Also administration

is sometimes granted in reference to a particular fund and to defend proceedings in chancery. (3 Redfield on Wills, 113.) There would seem to be no objection to intrusting to the surrogate the necessary powers in regard to the administration of estates, subject to such restrictions as may be imposed by statutory enactment. The statutes contain no restriction in regard to the right of the surrogate to issue letters in the form of those which were proven on the trial of this action; they empower the surrogate " to control and direct " administrators, and no sound reason exists why the surrogate, in the exercise of his authority, should not limit the application of the letters issued by him. We think it rests with him to say, in the exercise of his discretion, what powers should be conferred upon an administrator, and so long as he does not exceed the authority vested in him by law there is no valid ground for assuming that the letters issued by him are unauthorized; he has kept himself within the letter and the spirit of the statute, already cited, which authorizes him "to direct and control." In this case he merely allowed the administratrix to institute the first step to be taken for the collection of a claim which existed against the defendant. The law does not prevent or forbid him from issuing letters in the form which he followed; he therein limited the power of the administratrix instead of extending it. The extent of the surrogate's authority has been the subject of consideration in the Supreme Court of this State. In *Dubois* v. *Sands* (43 Barb. 412) it was laid down that the Surrogate's Court can only exercise such power as the statute confers, yet the authority to do certain acts or to exert a certain degree of power need not be given in express words, but may fairly be inferred from the general language of the statute, or, if necessary to accomplish its object and to the just and useful exercise of the powers which are expressly given, it may be taken for granted. And in *Hartnett* v. *Wandell* (60 N. Y. 353; 19 Am. Rep. 194) it is held that the statutes regulating the mode of procedure in the Surrogate's Court, like all rules of justice, should be liberally construed in furtherance of justice.

The authorities cited and the principle applicable to the right of this officer to exercise his power fully justified the issuing of the letters in question in the form granted and we think it was warranted by law. Even if it be conceded that the surrogate improperly limited the power of the administratrix, in the letters issued, the objection is one that cannot be raised collaterally in a suit by the administratrix and the letters cannot be held void. At most it was an irregularity which can only be made available by the parties in interest upon appeal from the surrogate's decision, and the defendant was not in a position to take advantage of the irregularity, by objecting upon the trial to the right of the administratrix to maintain the action and by a motion to dismiss the complaint on that ground.

As we have arrived at the conclusion that the letters of administration were valid, it is not necessary to consider the other questions relating to the same which have been urged by the appellant's counsel. No other point is made which demands examination, and the judgment should be affirmed.

DANFORTH and FINCH, JJ., concur.

RUGER, Ch. J., ANDREWS and RAPALLO, JJ., concur on the ground that the surrogate had power to place the limitation in the letters.

EARL, J., concurs on the ground that the limitation was at most an irregularity and did not render the letters void.

Judgment affirmed.

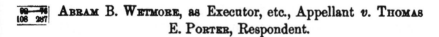

ABRAM B. WETMORE, as Executor, etc., Appellant *v.* THOMAS E. PORTER, Respondent.

It is no defense to an action brought by an executor as such, to recover assets of the estate in the hands of defendant, or for the conversion thereof, that plaintiff in his individual capacity acted in collusion with the defendant in despoiling the estate.

Whoever receives property knowing that it is the subject of a trust, and has been transferred by the trustee in violation of his duty or power, takes it subject to the right, not only of the *cestui que trust*, but also of the trustee, to reclaim possession or to recover for its conversion.

The complaint in an action brought by an executor to recover the value or possession of certain railroad bonds, after alleging the issuing of letters testamentary to plaintiff and his qualification, and that the bonds in question belonged to the estate, alleged in substance that plaintiff, at the request of defendant, who was his partner in business, and who knew that the bonds were trust funds, pledged the same as security for loans made to the firm ; that the firm had funds sufficient to pay the debt, and defendant was largely indebted to plaintiff, yet that defendant, without the knowledge or consent of plaintiff, procured the pledgee to sell the bonds, and the proceeds were applied to the payment of the firm debt ; that the bonds came into the custody and control of defendant, who refused to return them or pay their value. Upon demurrer to the complaint, *held*, that it set forth a good cause of action ; and that it was not necessary that plaintiff should have been made individually a party defendant.

Dillaye v. *Greenough* (45 N. Y. 488), distinguished.

A complaint which states facts constituting a good cause of action is not demurrable, simply because the facts are inartificially stated or because several different causes of action are joined in one count.

Nor is a complaint demurrable where the facts stated show that plaintiff is entitled to some relief because the relief demanded is not precisely that to which plaintiff is entitled.

(Argued March 13, 1883 ; decided March 27, 1883.)

APPEAL from judgment of the General Term of the Superior Court of the city of New York, entered upon an order made April 3, 1882, which affirmed a judgment in favor of defendant, entered upon an order sustaining a demurrer to plaintiff's complaint herein.

The substance of the complaint and of the demurrer is stated in the opinion.

E. Terry for appellant. It is competent for partners to make contracts between themselves in reference to partnership matters. (*Glover* v. *Tuck*, 24 Wend. 153 ; *Casey* v. *Brush*, 2 Cin. 293 ; *Clough* v. *Hoffman*, 5 Wend. 499 ; *Musier* v. *Trumpbour*, id. 274 ; *Paine* v. *Thatcher*, 25 id. 450.) The action is properly brought by Wetmore as the executor or trustee of an express trust, and as the representative of all parties interested in the estate. (Code, § 449.) The complaint states a good cause of action. (2 Kent's Com. 449; Comyn on Contracts, 2; *Pierson, Rec'r,* v. *McCurdy,* 61 How. Pr. 134; *Holsapple* v. *R. W. & O. R. R.,* 86 N. Y. 275; *Trust and Deposit Co.* v. *Price,* 87 id. 542, 549; Laws of 1858, chap. 314; 4 Edm. 483; Code, §§ 452, 1317.) The maxim "*ex turpi causa, non oritur actio,*" does not apply to transactions of this kind. It only applies to unlawful bargains or illegal contracts. (*Shiffner* v. *Gordon,* 12 East, 304; *Belding* v. *Pitkin,* 2 Caines, 149; *Springfield B'k* v. *Merrick,* 14 Mass. 322; *Russell* v. *De-Grand,* 15 id. 39; *Allen* v. *Rescons,* 2 Lev. 174; *Fletcher* v. *Harcot,* Hutton, 56; *Holman* v. *Johnson,* Cowp. 343; *Gas-light Co.* v. *Turner,* 7 Scott, 779; *Wetherell* v. *Jones,* 3 B. & Ald. 221; *Fivaz* v. *Nichols,* 2 C. B. 501; *Simpson* v. *Bloss,* 7 Taunt. 246; *Wheeler* v. *Russel,* 17 Mass. 281.) If all the statements of facts in the complaint were denied by an answer and proved, there would be sufficient to allow the plaintiff to go to the jury. (*Powers* v. *Benedict,* 14 Weekly Dig. 249, Ct. of App., Aug. 11, 1882.) When all the parties in interest are before the court, the court may determine the controversy (Code, § 3452); and may determine the ultimate rights of the parties on the same side, as between themselves. (Code, § 31204.)

Edward Fitch for respondent. Even if all wrong were eliminated from the matters stated in the complaint the plaintiff would be claiming a recovery against defendant alone on a demand jointly obligatory upon plaintiff and defendant, which is not permissible. (*De Puy* v. *Strong,* 13 N. Y. 372; 4 Abb. [N. S.] 340; *Dennison* v. *Dennison,* 9 How. 247; *Osgood* v. *Whittlesey,* 10 Abb. 134; *Zabriskie* v. *Smith,* 13 N. Y. 322.) The complaint does not state facts sufficient to constitute a cause of action in favor of the plaintiff against the defendant. (Code, §§ 487, 488.)

RUGER, Ch. J. The defendant demurred to the complaint upon the grounds:

1st. That there was a defect in the parties defendant, in that the plaintiff should also have been made a defendant.

2d. That the complaint did not state facts sufficient to constitute a cause of action.

The action was brought to recover the value or the possession of certain railroad bonds. The complaint states facts sufficient to justify either form of relief, and if there is any other objection to such a form of complaint it is not raised by this demurrer.

The complaint sets forth among other things that one Alpheus Fobes died at New York city about the 1st day of July, 1872, having executed a last will and testament, which was admitted to probate by the surrogate of the county of New York, and letters testamentary were duly issued thereon to Abram B. Wetmore as sole executor, who thereafter took the oath of office and duly qualified; that nine $1,000 railroad bonds were of the assets belonging to said estate and were of the value of $12,000; that by an order of the surrogate made on or about the 26th day of May, 1874, the plaintiff was directed to keep the property of the estate, including said bonds, then remaining in his hands invested, and to continue in the discharge of his trust according to the terms of the will; that said bonds came into the custody of the defendant by an arrangement between the plaintiff and defendant (who then knew that the same were trust funds) whereby they were to be used as collateral security at a bank in New York for the firm notes of Porter & Wetmore. That firm consisted of the plaintiff and defendant, who were engaged in carrying on a general commission business for their joint individual benefit. The complaint further alleges that the bonds did not belong to the plaintiff individually, but were owned by the estate, and that plaintiff had long tried to re-obtain possession of them for the purpose of holding them to accomplish the objects of the trust, but that his efforts had been defeated by defendant; that on the 11th day of April, 1881, the bonds were procured to be sold by the defendant, and on the 12th day of April, 1881, and on several occasions previous thereto, the plaintiff demanded the return of the bonds or the payment of the value thereof from the defendant, but that the defendant, admitting that they were in his custody or control, refused to return them or pay their value to the plaintiff. The complaint closed by demanding judgment for the sum of $15,000, with costs.

While the complaint contains the facts substantially as above set forth, it also contains much more, and perhaps the only question in the case is, whether the pleader in relating many unnecessary facts has stated, not only a cause of action, but also a defense. The facts above set forth contain all that is required in an action of trover, and are sufficient to sustain not only a judgment for the value of the bonds as for an unlawful conversion thereof by the defendant, but also a decree requiring them to be re-delivered into the possession of the trustee.

Under the liberal rule prevailing under the Code of Procedure for the construction of pleadings it would be contrary to its spirit to turn a party out of court who appears to have a good cause of action, simply because the pleader has stated those facts in an artificial manner, or has joined several different causes of action in one count, unless the objection thereto is specifically raised. Even under the former practice this complaint would have been held good in an action of trover, and the non-joinder as a defendant of a joint wrong-doer would not have been a defense to such an action.

It has been repeatedly held under the Code, that if the facts stated in a complaint show that the plaintiff is entitled to any relief, either legal or equitable, it is not demurrable upon the ground that the party has not demanded the precise relief to which he appears to be entitled. (*Wright* v. *Wright*, 54 N. Y. 437; *Emery* v. *Pease*, 20 id. 62; *Williams* v. *Slote*, 70 id. 601.) But perhaps it is unnecessary to pursue this subject further, as the General Term, by a memorandum indorsed upon the papers, and which contains the only information we have of the reasons for their decision, seem to have placed it upon the ground that the complaint showed upon its face that there was a defect of parties defendant. In other words, that the plaintiff should have been made a party defendant with Thomas E. Porter in any action to recover the value or possession of the bonds in question. It, therefore, becomes necessary to refer briefly to the additional allegations contained in the complaint.

It substantially alleges in addition to what has been recited, that the plaintiff, at the request of the defendant, removed the bonds from the Safe Deposit Company, where the securities of the estate were deposited for safe-keeping, and also at defendant's request left them at the Shoe and Leather Bank in New York as security for loans made, and to be made of said bank, by the firm of Porter & Wetmore, to carry on the partnership business, and that the bonds were ordered by defendant on or about the 11th day of April, 1881, to be sold by the Shoe and Leather Bank, and the proceeds applied to pay a firm note of the amount of $10,000, then held by the bank. It was also alleged that Porter was then owing the plaintiff a large sum of money in respect to the firm business, and had sufficient money belonging to the firm to more than pay the amount of the note, at the time of the sale of the bonds.

Upon this state of facts the court below has held upon the strength of the maxim " *Ex turpi causa non oritur actio*," that inasmuch as Abram B. Wetmore in his individual capacity was in collusion with the defendant in despoiling this estate, that he could not in his representative capacity re-claim these bonds from one who had wrongfully come into their possession, and restore them to the trust estate. The court further said that " the remedy of the *cestui que trust* is to have another trustee appointed who shall bring the proper action." In this, we think, it proceeded upon a mistaken view of the rights and duties of the parties. The legal title to these bonds, and the right to their custody, was and remains in the trustee, at least until they reach the possession of some person who has paid full value, and is ignorant of their trust character. Whoever receives property knowing that it is the subject of a trust, and has been transferred in violation of the duty or power of the trustee, takes it subject to the right, not only of the *cestui que trust*, but also of the trustee to reclaim possession of the specific property, or to recover damages for its conversion in case it has been converted. (*Briggs* v. *Davis*, 20 N. Y. 15.)

In the case of the *Western R. R. Co.* v. *Nolan* (48 N. Y. 517), this court say : " The trustees are the parties in whom the fund is vested, and whose duty it is to maintain and defend it against wrongful attacks or injury tending to impair its safety or amount. The title to the fund being in them, neither the *cestui que trust*, nor the beneficiaries can maintain an action in relation to it as against third parties, except in case the trustees refuse to perform their duty in that respect, and then the trustees should be brought before the court as parties defendant."

It is an alarming proposition to urge against the legal title which a trustee has to trust funds that his recovery of their possession may be defeated by a wrong-doer, upon the allegation that the lawful guardian of the funds colluded with him in obtaining their possession. This action is sought to be maintained by the plaintiff solely in his representative capacity as executor or trustee under the will of Alpheus Fobes.

The contracts and engagements entered into by him in his individual capacity are extraneous to the power conferred upon him by the will of Alpheus Fobes, and cannot be made the foundation of a defense to such an action. The dual character maintained by an individual who is also engaged in the administration of a trust involving the control and custody of another's property is not only recognized by numerous decisions in the courts, but has also been the subject of frequent statutory enactments.

Thus it has been held that a contract made by executors in form as such, even when made for the benefit of the estate which they represent, does not bind such estate or create a charge upon the assets in the hands of the executors. (*Austin* v. *Munro*, 47 N. Y. 360 ; *Ferrin* v. *Myrick*, 41 id. 315.) Neither can they be charged in the same action upon liabilities existing against the testator during his life-time and those arising against the executors with respect to the estate after the testator's death. (*Reynolds* v. *Reynolds*, 3 Wend. 244; *Demott* v. *Field*, 7 Cow. 58.)

A complaint in an action by an administrator as such which does not show a cause of action existing in favor of his intestate against the defendant is bad. (*Christopher* v. *Stockholm*, 5 Wend. 36.) Where a plaintiff sued upon a note given to himself as executor of the estate of John Sampson, it was held that the defendants could not set off a cross demand accruing to them against the testator. (*Merritt* v. *Seaman*, 6 N. Y. 168.)

The distinction between the rights which belong to individuals as such and those accruing to or against them in their representative capacity are recognized and regulated by the Code of Civil Procedure, sections 449, 502, 505, 506.

Section 1814 provides that "actions or special proceedings hereafter commenced by an executor or administrator upon a cause of action belonging to him in his representative capacity, or an action or special proceeding hereafter commenced against him, except when it is brought to charge him personally, must be brought by or against him in his representative capacity." Any conveyance by a trustee of real estate in violation of the terms of the trust expressed in the instrument creating it is declared by statute to be absolutely void. (3 R. S. [7th ed.], § 665, p. 2183.)

An executor or administrator being powerless to bind or charge the estate which he represents by his express contract, it is difficult to see how any right as against such estate can grow out of what is known to be an unauthorized exercise of power by such representative in favor of a wrong-doer.

Upon the facts shown in this case the bonds in question are subject to the conditions imposed by the creator of the trust, and the trustee is still the legal owner of the trust fund and responsible for the due execution of such trust.

Lewin on Trusts, page 279, lays down the rule as follows: "It is a universal rule as trusts are now regulated that all persons who take through or under the trustee shall be liable to the execution of the trust," "so all assigns of the trustee by

The authorities cited and the principle applicable to the right of this officer to exercise his power fully justified the issuing of the letters in question in the form granted and we think it was warranted by law. Even if it be conceded that the surrogate improperly limited the power of the administratrix, in the letters issued, the objection is one that cannot be raised collaterally in a suit by the administratrix and the letters cannot be held void. At most it was an irregularity which can only be made available by the parties in interest upon appeal from the surrogate's decision, and the defendant was not in a position to take advantage of the irregularity, by objecting upon the trial to the right of the administratrix to maintain the action and by a motion to dismiss the complaint on that ground.

As we have arrived at the conclusion that the letters of administration were valid, it is not necessary to consider the other questions relating to the same which have been urged by the appellant's counsel. No other point is made which demands examination, and the judgment should be affirmed.

DANFORTH and FINCH, JJ., concur.

RUGER, Ch. J., ANDREWS and RAPALLO, JJ., concur on the ground that the surrogate had power to place the limitation in the letters.

EARL, J., concurs on the ground that the limitation was at most an irregularity and did not render the letters void.

Judgment affirmed.

———

ABRAM B. WETMORE, as Executor, etc., Appellant v. THOMAS E. PORTER, Respondent.

It is no defense to an action brought by an executor as such, to recover assets of the estate in the hands of defendant, or for the conversion thereof, that plaintiff in his individual capacity acted in collusion with the defendant in despoiling the estate.

Whoever receives property knowing that it is the subject of a trust, and has been transferred by the trustee in violation of his duty or power, takes it subject to the right, not only of the *cestui que trust*, but also of the trustee, to reclaim possession or to recover for its conversion.

The complaint in an action brought by an executor to recover the value or possession of certain railroad bonds, after alleging the issuing of letters testamentary to plaintiff and his qualification, and that the bonds in question belonged to the estate, alleged in substance that plaintiff, at the request of defendant, who was his partner in business, and who knew that the bonds were trust funds, pledged the same as security for loans made to the firm ; that the firm had funds sufficient to pay the debt, and defendant was largely indebted to plaintiff, yet that defendant, without the knowledge or consent of plaintiff, procured the pledgee to sell the bonds, and the proceeds were applied to the payment of the firm debt; that the bonds came into the custody and control of defendant, who refused to return them or pay their value. Upon demurrer to the complaint, *held*, that it set forth a good cause of action ; and that it was not necessary that plaintiff should have been made individually a party defendant.

Dillaye v. *Greenough* (45 N. Y. 488), distinguished.

A complaint which states facts constituting a good cause of action is not demurrable, simply because the facts are inartificially stated or because several different causes of action are joined in one count.

Nor is a complaint demurrable where the facts stated show that plaintiff is entitled to some relief because the relief demanded is not precisely that to which plaintiff is entitled.

(Argued March 13, 1883 ; decided March 27, 1883.)

APPEAL from judgment of the General Term of the Superior Court of the city of New York, entered upon an order made April 3, 1882, which affirmed a judgment in favor of defendant, entered upon an order sustaining a demurrer to plaintiff's complaint herein.

The substance of the complaint and of the demurrer is stated in the opinion.

E. Terry for appellant. It is competent for partners to make contracts between themselves in reference to partnership matters. (*Glover* v. *Tuck*, 24 Wend. 153 ; *Casey* v. *Brush*, 2 Cin. 293 ; *Clough* v. *Hoffman*, 5 Wend. 499 ; *Musier* v. *Trumpbour*, id. 274 ; *Paine* v. *Thatcher*, 25 id. 450.) The action is properly brought by Wetmore as the executor or trustee of an express trust, and as the repre-

innocence of the prisoner, but that such opinion would not, as he believed, influence his verdict, and that he could render an impartial verdict. *Held*, that the challenge was properly overruled. (Code of Criminal Procedure, § 376.)

It appeared that the prisoner and C., the deceased, were at the time of the homicide convicts confined in a State prison. On the morning of the homicide another convict, after sharpening a case-knife, laid it down and went to another part of the room ; on his return he found the knife had been taken away. The, prisoner was near where the knife was left and in a position where he could have seen it. A few moments thereafter the prisoner approached C. and stabbed him with a knife, which was identified as the one so sharpened. C. died in a few minutes. The witnesses for the prosecution testified that no words passed between C. and the prisoner, and there was no assault or provocation by the former. *Held*, that the prisoner was properly convicted of murder in the first degree.

(Argued March 13, 1883 ; decided March 27, 1883.)

APPEAL from judgment of the General Term of the Supreme Court, in the second judicial department, entered upon an order made December 12, 1882, which affirmed a judgment of the Court of Oyer and Terminer in and for the county of Westchester, entered upon a verdict convicting the defendant of the crime of murder in the first degree.

The material facts are stated in the opinion.

E. T. Lovatt for appellant.

Nelson H. Baker, district attorney, for respondent. The prisoner was properly convicted of murder in the first degree. (*People* v. *Williams*, 43 Cal. 344 ; 1 Green's Cr. Law, § 412; *People* v. *Leighton*, 88 N. Y. 117.)

ANDREWS, J. The defendant was convicted at the Court of Oyer and Terminer of Westchester county, held in June, 1882, of the crime of murder in the first degree, in killing one Daniel Cash, by stabbing, in the mess-room of the State prison at Sing Sing on the 31st day of December, 1881. The prisoner and Cash were convicts in the prison at the time of the homicide, and were assigned to duty in the mess-room. The evidence shows that on the morning of the day of the homicide, another prisoner, after sharpening a case knife used by him, laid it down and went to another part of the room. The prisoner was within a few feet of the place where the knife was left, and in a position where he could have seen it. The convict who sharpened and left the knife, returned after a short absence to the place where he had left it and found that it had been taken away. In a few moments the prisoner was seen to approach the deceased, and when he came near him struck him twice in the neck with a knife. The deceased immediately cried out that he was cut, and started to leave the room. He was taken to the hospital and died in about twenty minutes. It was found that the knife had severed the internal jugular vein. The knife with which the blow was struck, was taken from the hands of the prisoner. It was identified as the one which had been sharpened and laid down by the convict, before referred to. Two witnesses of the transaction testified that no words passed between the prisoner and deceased before the homicide, and that there was no assault or provocation by the latter. The evidence on the part of the people does not disclose any motive for the homicide. It appears that the prisoner and the deceased had been witnesses on the trial of another convict by the name of Mangano, on opposite sides, but whether any ill feeling between them grew out of this circumstance does not appear. The prisoner was examined on his own behalf and testified that the deceased before the day of the homicide called him bad names, and threatened to kill him, and that just before the homicide had struck him and drew a knife upon him. The question whether the killing was in self-defense or under an apprehension on the part of the prisoner of personal injury was submitted to the jury. The case as presented upon the record, leaves no doubt in our minds that it was one of deliberate and premeditated murder, and no other reasonable conclusion could have been reached by the jury.

Two exceptions were taken by the prisoner's counsel on impaneling the jury. The juror Onderdonk, was challenged by the prisoner's counsel for principal cause, and testified on his examination in chief, that he had read and talked about the case, and had formed an opinion as to the guilt or innocence of the accused, but he subsequently declared in substance that such opinion would not, as he believed, influence his verdict, and that he could render an impartial verdict according to the evidence. The court, therefore, overruled the challenge, and the juror was sworn. The exception taken to this ruling is answered by section 376 of the Code of Criminal Procedure, which is a re-enactment of chapter 475 of the Laws of 1875, which was considered in *Balbo* v. *People* (80 N. Y. 484). In the case of the juror Harris, the same ruling was made under similar circumstances, but this juror was peremptorily challenged by the prisoner's counsel and did not sit in the case.

It is claimed that the Court of Oyer and Terminer by which the prisoner was tried, was not legally constituted, the allegation being that the justices of the Sessions, who in part composed it, were not legally designated or elected. This point is taken here for the first time. It was not raised at the trial, and there is no evidence and no exception bearing upon it. It must be assumed, therefore, that the court was properly constituted, and that the justices of the Sessions who acted, were duly designated according to law. There are no other points presented as ground of reversal, and no other exceptions of any moment beside those considered.

There is no error in the judgment, and it should therefore be affirmed.

All concur.

Judgment affirmed.

SARAH F. HAND as Executrix, etc., Respondent, *v.* JOHN NEWTON, Appellant.

88|
6|
10.
4 88
1 639
88|
262|
264|

The town of B., which claimed title under certain letters patent executed in 1666 and 1686 by the Colonial governors of the Province of New York, executed to plaintiff a lease of certain lands under water in a bay included in the boundaries of the said grants. In an action for alleged trespass in entering upon said lands and removing oysters therefrom, it appeared that the town, by various acts continuing from the time of said grants, assumed the rights of rental and exercised control of the lands under water in the bay. *Held*, that the title was in the town and the lease conferred upon plaintiff the exclusive right to take oysters from the lands covered by the lease ; and that it was immaterial whether or not there was a natural oyster-bed on the land.

The board of trustees of the town in 1871 passed a resolution declaring it not to be the intention of the trustees "to lease oyster lots on ground where oysters are naturally growing." In 1880 and before the granting of the lease in question, said resolution was, by another resolution passed by said board, repealed or modified so as to allow such leasing. *Held*, that the first resolution did not affect the validity of the lease ; but that in any event the trustees had the right to repeal or modify it, and having so done, their right to lease without regard to the fact of the existence of a natural oyster-bed was restored.

(Argued March 13, 1883 ; decided March 27, 1883.)

APPEAL from judgment of the General Term of the Supreme Court, in the second judicial department, entered upon an order made February 13, 1882, which affirmed a judgment in favor of plaintiff, entered upon a verdict.

This action was brought originally by Robert N. Hand, the present plaintiff's testator, to recover damages for entering upon lands under water in Port Jefferson bay or harbor and removing oysters therefrom.

The material facts are stated in the opinion.

Clifford A. H. Bartlett for appellant. The town of Brookhaven can only claim an exclusive fishery in the waters of Port Jefferson bay by virtue of its ownership of the soil under water. The charters do not convey any land, nor is there any evidence that the town ever acquired the land covered by plaintiff's lease. (*Palmer* v. *Hicks*, 6 Johns. 135 ; *Jackson* v. *Hudson*, 3 id. 384 ; *La Plaisance Bay Harbor Co.* v. *City of Monroe*, Walker's Ch. [Mich.] 169 ; *Duke of Somerset* v. *Fogwell*, 5 B. & C. 885 ; *Duke of Beaufort* v. *Mayor of Swansea*, 3 Exch. 414, 424 ; *Atty.-Gen.* v. *Parsons*, 2 C. & J. 279 ; *Feather* v. *The Queen*, 6 B. & S. 283 ; *Bristow* v. *Cormican*, 3 Eng. L. R. [App. Cas.] 652, 653, 655 ; *Murphy* v. *Ryan*, 2 Irish R. 149 ; *Mayor of Carlisle* v. *Graham*, L. R.,

4 Exch. 368; *Bristow* v. *Cormican,* 10 Irish C. L. 407; 60
N. Y 71.) The defendant had a common right and liberty in
fishing and taking oysters in the *locus in quo* acquired by the
inhabitants of the town of Brookhaven, by long user, or by
adverse enjoyment on their part, or by the intentional abandonment or non-user on the part of the trustees. In any event
this question should have been submitted to the jury. (Angell
on Water-courses, §§ 201, 221; Hall on Sea Shore, 25;
Ricard v. *Williams,* 7 Wheat. 109, 110; *Hazard* v. *Robinson,* 3 Mason, 275, 276; *Adams* v. *Van Alstyne,* 25 N. Y.
237; *Parker* v. *Foote,* 19 Wend. 311; *Friend* v. *Braintree
Man. Co.,* 23 Pick. 221, 222; *Hodges* v. *Hodges,* 46 Mass.
212; *'Hatch* v. *Wright,* 17 id. 297; *Fuller* v. *French,* 10
Metc. 363; *Jennison* v. *Walker,* 11 Gray, 425; *Farrar* v.
Cooper, 34 Me. 400, 401; 2 Irish L. R. 118; 3 Eng. L. R.
[App. Cas.] 652; *Reece* v. *Miller,* 8 Eng. L. R. [Q. B.] 626.)
The attempted leasing of any natural oyster bed in the town by
the trustees thereof is invalid and inoperative, because it is in
violation of an existing law of the town. (*Brick Church* v. *New
York,* 5 Cow. 540, 541; *McDermott* v. *Bd. Police,* 5 Abb.
434; *Kent* v. *Quicksilver Mining Co.,* 78 N. Y. 179.)
Wherever oysters have previously existed in their native state
no one can deprive other persons of the right to take them by
depositing oysters in the same place. (*McCarty* v. *Holman,*
22 Hun, 53; *Decker* v. *Fisher,* 4 Barb. 595; *Brinkerhoff* v.
Starkins, 11 id. 250; *Lowndes* v. *Dickinson,* 34 id. 589;
Fleet v. *Hegeman,* 14 Wend. 42; *Gulf Pond Oyster Co.* v.
Baldwin, 42 Conn. 258; *State* v. *Taylor,* 27 N. J. 122, 123;
Paul v. *Hazleton,* 37 id. 106.)

Thos. S. Strong for respondent. The town patents, granted
by the English Crown in 1666 and 1686, expressly conveyed
to the patentees the land under the water of the bays and harbors included within the bounds of the grant, as well as the
exclusive right to the oyster fisheries therein. (*Trustees of
Brookhaven* v. *Strong,* 60 N. Y. 56.) It can make no difference whether the lands covered by respondent's lease were

natural oyster lands or not. (*Robbins* v. *Ackerly*, 24 Hun, 499.)

MILLER, J. The plaintiff's title rests upon two ancient patents granted to the inhabitants and freeholders of the town of Brookhaven. These patents, one dated 1666 and the other 1686, granted to the inhabitants and freeholders of the town of Brookhaven the lands under the water in the bays and harbors, included within the bounds of the patents, and the exclusive right to the oyster fisheries therein. The land upon which the alleged trespass was committed is included within the boundaries of these charters. In the case of *Trustees of Brookhaven* v. *Strong* (60 N. Y. 56), it was held, "That by the common law the king had the right to grant the soil under water and with it the exclusive right of fishery, and that a grant by the Colonial Government, confirmed by subsequent legislation, conveyed an exclusive right to the oyster fishery," and the right of the plaintiff to sue for taking oysters, within the limits of the patent, was sustained. The trustees have exercised the power conferred upon them, by the grants in question, by various acts from the time of said grants and in later years by leasing the bottom of the bay for raising oysters. It must, therefore, be assumed that the title to the land was in the town and we are unable to perceive upon what ground it can be maintained that the trustees were not entitled to lease the oyster beds, lying on the land under water, for the purpose of raising oysters under the power conferred by the grants in question.

That the land in question in this action was a part of a natural oyster bed cannot, we think, make any difference. The town had a right to lease the land whether natural oysters were growing thereon or otherwise under the decision cited.

This principle is also fully upheld in the case of *Robins* v. *Ackerly* recently decided in this court.* In view of these decisions the question as to the right of the town to lease the land under water for oyster beds and to control and dispose of

*91 N. Y. 98.

the same must be regarded as *res adjudicata,* and under the
decisions it is very manifest that the right to the plaintiff must
be upheld unless a case is made out which is excepted from
the operation and effect of the principle established by the
cases cited.   There is nothing in this case that vests a common
right in the defendant, by user or otherwise, or by non-user or
abandonment on the part of the board of trustees to take oysters, nor was there any question of fact for the jury to pass
upon in this respect.   The appellant claims that the lease by
the trustees to the plaintiff does not include the natural oyster
bed in controversy because it was not the intention of the
trustees to lease such oyster lots.   This claim is based upon the
resolution of the trustees passed in 1871 by which it was declared " it is not and has not been the intention of the trustees
to lease oyster lots on ground where oysters are naturally
growing," etc., and that for this reason the lease in question
was invalid.   This position is not maintainable.   Although
the resolution referred to had been adopted no reason existed
why the trustees had not the right and the power to change
their action and to execute a lease for the land under water
where oysters naturally grew.   The resolution merely declared
that it had not been and was not the intention of the trustees
to lease lands where oysters naturally grew, and that in future
applications the lots should be examined before letting at the
expense of the applicant.   The resolution was not, therefore,
absolute in its terms, and it appears the examination was had
pursuant to the resolution of the board of trustees before the
granting of the lease to the plaintiff in this action.   But a
complete answer to the point is that on the 11th of September,
1880, and before the granting of the lease in question to the
plaintiff, a resolution was passed by the board of trustees, by
which the resolution of 1871 was repealed or modified, and
under this resolution a lease was granted to the plaintiff of the
lands under water, which are now in dispute, for the purpose
of raising oysters.   We think there was no legal objection to the
last-named resolution, and that the trustees, in the exercise of
their right to the land under water, were justified in changing

the policy, which had been indicated by the previous resolution. There is no law which prohibited such action, and the last resolution must be considered as superseding the former one and as conferring a perfect right and title to the plaintiff in this action to the oyster beds in question.

The case of *Averill* v. *Hull*, decided in Connecticut in 1870, cited by the appellant's counsel, we think has no application and is not in point. We have considered all the points and suggestions made by the appellant, and we do not find in any of them sufficient ground for a reversal of the judgment, which should be affirmed, with costs.

All concur.

Judgment affirmed.

In the Matter of the Distribution of the Proceeds, etc., of the Estate of PETER G. Fox, deceased.

During the pendency of an action against an executor for misappropriation of moneys belonging to the estate, he died and his executor was substituted as party defendant. Judgment was recovered, which the defendant was directed to pay out of the estate; costs were also given, which were directed to be paid in like manner. The real estate of the deceased executor was sold by order of the surrogate. *Held*, that in the distribution of the proceeds said judgment creditor was not entitled to a preference for the damages recovered over the other creditors of the decedent, but was entitled to share *pro rata ;* and that the surrogate properly disallowed the costs, as a claim, payable out of such proceeds. (Code of Civil Procedure, §§ 2756, 2757.)

(Argued March 16, 1883 ; decided March 27, 1883.)

APPEAL from order of the General Term of the Supreme Court, in the third judicial department, made May 2, 1882, which affirmed a decree of the surrogate of Montgomery county, directing as to the distribution of the proceeds of sale of the real estate of the decedent above named.

The facts, so far as material, are stated in the opinion.

D. C. Calvin for appellant. The court had power to restore to plaintiff, from the estate of the testator of the present defendant, the amount of which he had been defrauded. (*French's Case*, 4 Co. 31; Gr. & Rud. 405; Story's Eq. Jur., § 266, note 2; Paulus Dig. L. 17, fr. 141; Ulpian Dig. id. 134, § 1; Gothofred, the Div. Reg. Jur. c. xxxiv, § 1; Paulus Dig. 17, fr. 15; v. Gothofred, the Div. Reg. Jur. xv; Paulus Dig. vi, 1, fr. 27, § 3; 7 Co. 19; Bracton, lib. iii, c. 3, § 5, fol. 102 *a*; 1 Story's Eq. Jur., § 553, note 2.) The surrogate's decree was erroneous in disallowing to be paid to the plaintiff from the same fund, "any part of his costs recovered in his judgment against the executor.", (Code of Civil Procedure, §§ 2756, 2757.)

L. M. Weller for respondent. Where a judgment has been rendered against an executor for a debt due from the decedent, the debt for which the judgment was rendered cannot be allowed, as against the real estate of the decedent, in proceedings before the surrogate to sell the same for the payment of debts at any greater sum than the amount recovered exclusive of costs. (Code of Civil Procedure, §§ 2756, 2757; 4 R. S. [Edm. ed.] 499, § 72; *Burnham* v. *Harrison*, 3 Redf. 345; *Sanford* v. *Granger*, 12 Barb. 392–403; *Colson* v. *Brainard*, 1 Redf. 328; *Ferguson* v. *Broome*, 1 Bradf. 10; *Wood* v. *Byington*, 2 Barb. Ch. 57; Dayton on Surrogates [2d ed.], 559, 560) Peter G. Fox being executor of an estate, by paying to another, as such executor, moneys which he should have paid to the appellant, became personally responsible to him. Still as respects the said Fox and his individual estate, it is only a simple contract debt, and the appellant can only take equally with the simple contract creditors of the said Fox. (*Carow* v. *Mowatt*, 2 Edw. Ch. 57; *Charlton* v. *Low*, 3 P. Wms. 330–331; *People, ex rel. Adams*, v. *Westbrook*, 61 How. Pr. 140.) The heirs and creditors of the decedent should have been made parties respondent to the appeal from the surrogate's decree. (Code of Civil Procedure, § 2573; *Patterson* v. *Hamilton*, 26 Hun, 665; *Brown* v. *Evans*, 34 Barb. 594; *People* v. *Com.*

Council of Troy, 82 N. Y. 575–6; *People* v. *Clark*, 70 id. 520; *Kilmer* v. *Bradley*, 80 id. 630.)

MILLER, J. The appellant brought an action against Peter G. Fox, executor, for the misappropriation of moneys received by him as such executor and obtained a judgment. Fox having died before judgment was entered Jacob C. Nellis was substituted, as his executor, in his place as defendant, and the judgment declared that the estate of the said Peter G. Fox was liable therefor and his executor was directed to pay the same out of his estate by due course of administration, and also it was directed that the appellant recover against Nellis, the executor, costs and disbursements to be paid in like manner. Proceedings were instituted in the Surrogate's Court for the sale of the real estate, and an order was made directing such sale, which was had and the money realized therefor. The surrogate also made an order for the distribution of such proceeds, and upon the hearing before him allowed the appellant the amount of the judgment obtained by him against the executor of Fox, together with the interest, and disallowed the costs and refused to allow a preference to the appellant over the other creditors.

Upon the facts stated two questions arise. First, whether the surrogate erred in not preferring the appellant as a creditor before the other creditors; and, second, whether the appellant was entitled to the costs incurred in obtaining the judgment against the executor.

In reference to the first question we think there is no ground upon which the recovery in question against the estate of Peter G. Fox was entitled to a preference over the other creditors of the deceased, and we think the judgment was not entitled to a preference over the creditors of the estate in the distribution of the funds realized from the sale of the real estate. The plaintiff no doubt had a perfect right, if he had obtained judgment before the death of Peter G. Fox, to enforce the judgment, even against his person, but that fact does not confer a preference in favor of a judgment entered after the death of said

Fox against his executor.   The statute provides for no preference in such a case, and therefore the appellant stands, in the
proceedings before the surrogate, in the same position occupied
by other creditors.   The judgment, not having been docketed
prior to the death of Peter G. Fox, did not become a lien upon
his real estate, and therefore it is not apparent how the land of
the deceased, which had been sold under the surrogate's order
for the purpose of paying his debts, could be charged with the
character of a trust-fund which gave such judgment the preference and priority over all other demands which were proved
against said Fox's estate.

Even if it may be conceded that the estate or funds which
Fox held in his hands as executor were impressed with the
character of a trust-fund, that character would not follow the
property which belonged to Fox at the time of his death.
We think that this is not a case in which trust-funds which
can be identified may be followed and appropriated to the payment of the demand of the *cestui que trust.*

The appellant's counsel claims that applying equitable rules
and principles to the case considered, the court, under the authorities, has the power to appropriate the estate of the defendant to restore the rights of which the appellant has been
deprived; that the action brought against the executor being
a mixed action *in rem* to recover the trust-fund, and *in per-
sonam* to recover a penalty for the unjust detention of such
fund, a court of equity will enforce the claim of the appellant
as an existing lien upon the property.   We are unable to
discover in what way the rule insisted upon can be applied to
the facts presented.   The assets belonging to the estate of
Peter G. Fox were not shown to be a part or parcel of the
estate against which the appellant's claim existed, and it is
very obvious that they cannot be regarded as constituting, in
any sense, the thing itself so as to render them specific property intrusted into Fox's hands which may be appropriated to
the payment of appellant's demand.   The creditors of Peter
G. Fox have rights which entitle them to the appropriation
of his property to the payment of his debts equally and alike,

and upon no principle, in law or equity, can it be maintained that the property, belonging to creditors generally, and not shown to have constituted a portion of the estate of which Fox was the executor, can be applied to the payment of the appellant's demand in preference to other creditors. We do not see how the principle of subrogation of the property of the defendant in place of that which he held as executor can be applied to the case considered, under the authorities to which we have been referred, and there are no cases cited which hold any such doctrine, and it has not been held that under such circumstances property could be regarded to be for the benefit of the creditor as if it was the thing *in rem* which had been misappropriated and fraudulently disposed of. We do not think the surrogate in his decree sought to readjudicate the plaintiff's equities and lien, he merely disposed of and distributed the funds on hand which belonged to the estate of Fox in accordance with the provisions of law, and his decree was not in contravention of the judgment, but in accordance with the statutes under which he acted.

We think, after a careful consideration, there is no valid ground upon which the estate of Peter G. Fox could be held primarily liable for the appellant's demand in preference to other creditors, and the judgment in this respect was not erroneous.

As to the costs they were not a claim against Peter G. Fox prior to his decease, and the judgment being entered afterward, it is difficult to understand upon what ground they can be made such against his estate. It was not determined, prior to the judgment, that the costs were a claim against Fox, as it was uncertain which party would succeed or which would be liable for the payment of the costs. Under the Code of Civil Procedure no such costs can be allowed against an executor in a case like the one considered. (Code of Civil Procedure, §§ 2756, 2757.)

The order appealed from should be affirmed.

All concur.

Order affirmed.

THE PEOPLE OF THE STATE OF NEW YORK *v.* THE OPEN BOARD
OF STOCK BROKERS BUILDING COMPANY OF THE CITY OF NEW
YORK. RASTUS S. RANSOM, Receiver, etc., Respondent;
SAMUEL McMILLAN, Purchaser, Appellant.

In proceedings to compel a purchaser of real estate, at a receiver's sale, to
complete the purchase, the receiver claimed title under two deeds; one
dated March 21, 1863, from an executor, having power under the will to
sell the real estate, to a third person, having the same family name as
the executor; the other dated March 25, 1863, by said grantee, conveying
the premises back to the executor, individually. The deeds were both
recorded April 1, 1863, with an interval of but five minutes between.
The receiver's sale was made January 11, 1882. No accounting or settlement of the estate by the executor had been had; no explanation was
made by the receiver, and no ratification of the transfer by those interested, under the will, was proved. *Held,* that the title was defective as
it appeared that the conveyances were but one transaction, the executor
acting in the double capacity of seller and purchaser; and, therefore, the
title was voidable at the election of the beneficiaries named in the will;
also that the lapse of time, it being less than twenty years, was not conclusive upon them.

The court below directed the purchaser to take the premises if the seller
should produce sufficient evidence showing a confirmation of the executor's purchase by the proper parties. Such evidence to be taken in a
proceeding instituted within sixty days. *Held* error; that the purchaser
should have been relieved wholly from his contract.

People v. *O. B. S. B. B. Co.* (28 Hun, 274), reversed in part.

(Argued March 20, 1883; decided March 30, 1883.)

CROSS APPEALS by Rastus S. Ransom, receiver of the defendant, above-named, and by Samuel McMillen, purchaser, from
portions of an order of the General Term of the Supreme
Court, in the first judicial department, made October 13, 1882,
which reversed two orders of Special Term, one of which
directed said McMillen, the purchaser of certain premises at a
sale made by said receiver, to complete his purchase; the other
denied a motion by said McMillan to be relieved from said
purchase. (Reported below, 28 Hun, 274.)

The order of the General Term contained this clause:

" Said receiver, notwithstanding the reversals of said two orders, may still enforce the contract to purchase said premises, which said McMillan, as the purchaser thereof as aforesaid, entered into, under said terms of sale, provided said receiver can produce evidence which shall be approved as sufficient by a justice of this court sitting at Special Term or Chambers, and to be taken in a proceeding which shall be instituted herein by action or by motion at any time within sixty days from the entry of this order, and of which motion (if that course be adopted), said McMillan is to have due notice, showing acquiescence in, or confirmation of, a purchase of said premises, on or about the 1st April, 1863, by one Albert Smith, from himself as sole surviving executor of the will of one Casper Meier, deceased, through one William H. Smith, by all the heirs at law of said Casper Meier, deceased, who died seized of said premises in February, 1837, and by all the *cestuis que trust* under the will of said Casper Meier, and by all parties to whom the rights and interests of said heirs and *cestuis que trust*, or of any of them, may have passed or may belong.

" Upon the decision of such motion in favor of the receiver (but always provided that said proceeding in which such evidence is to be taken shall have been commenced within sixty days from the time of the entry of this order), said McMillan, notwithstanding the said other preliminary objection which he has raised and presented to the court as aforesaid as to the title to said premises and which is designated as second in said Lindley's affidavit, and within twenty days after the entry of the order upon such motion, is hereby directed to complete his purchase of said premises."

The purchaser appealed from said clause of the order, the receiver from that portion of the order reversing the orders of Special Term.

By the judgment in this action, which was brought to dissolve the defendant, a joint-stock association, said Ransom was appointed receiver of its property and effects on January 11, 1882; he sold the real estate in question at auction and McMillan became the purchaser and paid down ten per cent of the purchase-money, but refused to complete the sale on the ground of alleged defects in title. The premises formerly belonged to one Meier, who died seized of them in 1837. By his will, Albert Smith and Laurenz Von Post were appointed as executors, and power was given them to sell the real estate; said executors qualified, and Von Post thereafter died. The receiver claimed title under two deeds, executed after the death of Von Post, one dated March 21, 1863, from said Albert Smith, as sole surviving executor, to William H. Smith, for the expressed consideration of $35,250, recorded April 1, 1863, at 3 : 05 P. M. ; the other dated March 25, 1863, from said William H. Smith to said Albert Smith, individually, for the expressed consideration of $35,320, which was recorded April 1, 1863, at 3 : 10 P. M.

Further facts appear in the opinion.

George Waddington for purchaser, appellant. The description conveyed to and by McLean as a trustee. (*Christopher* v. *Stockholm*, 5 Wend. 36 ; *Thomas* v. *Dakin*, 22 id. 9 ; *Delafield* v. *Kearney*, 24 id. 345 ; *Hunt* v. *Van Alstyne*, 25 id. 605 ; *Ogdensburgh B'k* v. *Van Rensselaer*, 6 Hill, 240 ; *Merritt* v. *Seaman*, 6 N. Y. 168 ; *Peck* v. *Mallams*, 10 id. 509 ; *Mott* v. *Richtmyer*, 57 id. 63 ; *Towar* v. *Hale*, 46 Barb. 361 ; *Renaud* v. *Conselyea*, 4 Abb. Pr. 280 ; 5 id. 346.) The character or capacity of the grantee, or party to be sued, although differently described in the preamble, will be established by the form of the operative parts of the deed or declaration. (*Sutherland* v. *Carr*, 85 N. Y. 105, 110 ; *People* v. *Keyser*, 28 id. 226.) The misnomer was immaterial, for, both as to persons and corporations, distinguishing and not true names will clothe them with the character of grantor or grantee. (3 Washb. on Real Prop. 565 ; 3 Greenl. Crim. Real Est. 620, 621 ; 3 Greenl. Crim. 586 ; *Jackson* v. *Dunsbagh*, 1 Johns. Cas. 91 ; *Woodgate* v. *Fleet*, 64 N. Y. 566, 570.) The extrinsic circumstances show that there was an attempt to create a trust in McLean. (*Selden* v. *Vermilyea*, 3 N. Y. 525.) Such a trust as this could not exist under the rule of common law. (*Nicoll* v. *Walworth*, 4 Denio, 388 ;

Bennett v. *Garlock*, 79 N. Y. 302, 323.) The Revised Statutes have thoroughly accepted and perpetuated, to the furthest limit of its application, this doctrine of the common law, that the estate of a trustee can only co-exist with the activity of the trust. (1. R. S. 727, §§ 45, 47, 48, 49; 4 Kent's Com. [12th ed.] 308, 310; *Verdin* v. *Slocum*, 71 N. Y. 345, 347; *Rawson* v. *Lampman*, 5 id. 456; *Wright* v. *Douglass*, 7 id. 564.) The trust which the deed to McLean attempted to create cannot be sustained as a power to him to convey the premises to the defendants. (1 R. S. 729, §§ 56, 58; id. 732, §§ 73, 74; *Selden* v. *Vermilyea*, 3 N. Y. 525, 536.) The only force of the deed to McLean could have been to pass the title of the premises it conveyed to the *cestui que trust* named in the deed. (*Jackson* v. *Cory*, 8 Johns. 385; *Hornbeck* v. *Westbrook*, 9 id. 73; 1 Sharswood's Black. Com. 467; *Russell* v. *Topping*, 5 McLean, 194.) The deeds not being between the same parties cannot be construed as parts of one contract. (*Mott* v. *Richtmyer*, 57 N. Y. 49, 65; *Cornell* v. *Todd*, 2 Denio, 133; *Selden* v. *Vermilyea*, 3 N. Y. 535.) As a construction of the deed in this present appeal cannot bind or estop members of the association from claiming that the deed vested them with title, the purchaser is entitled to be relieved from his purchase. (*Jordan* v. *Poillon*, 77 N. Y. 519; *Argale* v. *Raynor*, 20 Hun, 267.) One who stands in a fiduciary capacity cannot, under any circumstances whatsoever, purchase or deal with the property he holds in trust. (Lewin on Trusts and Trustees [2d Am. ed.], 394–398, 402; *Davoue* v. *Fanning*, 2 Johns. Ch. 252, 259; *Monro* v. *Allaire*, 2 Caines' Cas. 182; *Michoud* v. *Girod*, 4 How. 503; *Dobson* v. *Racey*, 3 Sandf. Ch. 60; *Ames* v. *Downing*, 1 Bradf. 321, 324; *Gardner* v. *Ogden*, 22 N. Y. 327; *Forbes* v. *Halsey*, 27 id. 53, 65; *Van Epps* v. *Van Epps*, 9 Paige, 237; *Iddings* v. *Bruen*, 4 Sandf. Ch. 263; *Jewett* v. *Miller*, 10 N. Y. 402; 1 Perry on Trusts, 241.) The heirs of Caspar Meier still retain all their rights to attack the purchase of Albert Smith. (*Hawley* v. *Cramer*, 4 Cow. 717, 743; *Hatch* v. *Hatch*, 9 Ves. 291; *Dobson* v. *Racey*, 3 Sandf. Ch. 66; *Johnson* v. *Bennett*, 39 Barb. 237; Lewin on Trusts and Trustees [2d Am. ed.], 402; *Watson* v. *Town*, 2 Mod. 153; *Jordan* v. *Poillon*, 77 N. Y. 519; *Argale* v. *Raynor*, 20 Hun, 567.) The General Term were correct in including the amount of the mortgage mentioned in the seventh subdivision of the terms of sale in the amount of the bid. (*Williams* v. *Millington*, 1 H. Bl. 81, 85.)

J. Sanford Potter for receiver, respondent. The title was in the deeds of McLean, as trustee for the association of the Open Board of Brokers of the city of New York, must be regarded as nothing more than a *descriptio personae;* the legal title vested in him individually, and he conveyed it to the defendant by the same form of description. (*David* v. *Williamsburgh F. Ins. Co.,* 83 N. Y. 265; *Tower* v. *Hale*, 46 Barb. 361; *Renaud* v. *Consslyea*, 5 Abb. Pr. 346; *Ogdensburgh Bk.* v. *Van Rensselaer*, 6 Hill, 240; *Merritt* v. *Seaman*, 2 Seld. 168; *Nat. Bk.* v. *Vanderwerker*, 74 N. Y. 243; 1 Laws of 1867, chap. 289, p. 576; Const., art. 17, § 7; id., art. 24.) Crocker is estopped to deny that title passed from him to "McLean, as trustee," by his deed. (*Tilton* v. *Nelson*, 27 Barb. 595; *Wood* v. *Seely*, 32 N. Y. 105; *Holbrook* v. *Chamberlin*, 115 Mass. 155; *Johnson* v. *Bennett*, 39 Barb. 237; *Jackson* v. *Stevens*, 16 Johns. 110.) The provisions of the Revised Statutes as to conveyances in trust do not impair this title. (1 R. S. 772, § 64; *Jackson* v. *Schoonmaker*, 2 Johns. 230; *Matter of Mason*, 4 Edw. 418; *Farmers', etc., Co.* v. *Curtis*, 7 N. Y. 466; *Chautauqua Co. Bk.* v. *Risley*, 19 id. 369; *Nelson* v. *Eaton*, 26 id. 410; *Sistare* v. *Best*, 88 id. 527, 537; 1 R. S. 728, § 51; *Hurst* v. *Harper*, 14 Hun, 280; *Everett* v. *Everett*, 48 N. Y. 218; *Hubbard* v. *Gilbert*, 13 W. D. 494.) If the association of the Open Board of Stock Brokers could have taken title, that title would be subject to that of the Building Company, as it was created for the purpose of being transferred to that corporation. (*Ransom* v. *Lampman*, 5 N. Y. 455.) If this deed to McLean was in fact upon some trust, it was not necessary that the trust be declared or evidenced by the deed. (*Wright* v. *Douglass*, 7 N. Y. 564; *Bennett* v.

Garlock, 79 id. 302.) . If the defect can be cured, the purchaser may be compelled to complete his purchase. (*Dutch
Church* v. *Mott,* 7 Paige, 85 ; *Grady* v. *Ward,* 20 Barb. 543.)

FINCH, J. An examination of the title questioned by the purchaser discloses two deeds, which constitute links in the chain,
from an executor to a third person, and from the latter back to
the executor under whom, as an individual, the present vendor
claims. The deeds are dated within four days of each other,
and were recorded upon the same day with an interval of but
five minutes between. The person through whom the title thus
passed to the executor bore the same family name, and a search
in the surrogate's office shows that no accounting or settlement
of the estate has been had before that officer. The deeds in
question were made in 1863. The receiver gives no explanation of these facts, proves no ratification by those interested
under the will of Meier, and relies wholly upon their presumed
acquiescence evidenced by the lapse of time.

It is impossible to avoid the inference that the conveyance
by the executor and the deed back to him were one transaction,
and that the trustee acted in the double capacity of seller and
purchaser of the trust property. His title, therefore, was voidable by those whom he was bound to protect, but whose interests were endangered by the collision with his own. (*Davoue*
v. *Fanning,* 2 Johns. Ch. 252 ; *Gardner* v. *Ogden,* 22 N. Y.
327 ; *Forbes* v. *Halsey,* 26 id. 53 ; *Van Epps* v. *Van Epps,* 9
Paige, 237 ; *Duncomb* v. *N. H. & N. Y. R. R.,* 84 N. Y.
199.) The purchaser here is not protected as one buying in
good faith and without knowledge of the breach of trust, for
he has ascertained the facts, so far as they are known, before
any acceptance of the deed or payment of the purchase-money.
(*Wormley* v. *Wormley,* 8 Wheat. 449.) Nor is the lapse of
time conclusive upon the beneficiaries under the will of Meier.
Twenty years had not elapsed when this attempted sale was
made. In *Hawley* v. *Cramer* (4 Cow. 735), it was said that
an application to set aside the sale must be made within a
reasonable time, of which the court must judge under all the

circumstances, and twenty years was named as the shortest period which a court of equity would be bound to consider an absolute bar. If a resale was refused after eighteen years (*Gregory* v. *Gregory*, Coop. Ch. Cas. 201), and after sixteen years (*Bergen* v. *Bennett*, 1 Caine's Cas. in Error, 1), on the other hand in *Hatch* v. *Hatch* (9 Ves. 292), the sale was set aside after the lapse of twenty years; in *Dobson* v. *Racey* (3 Sandf. Ch. 66), after twenty-seven years ; in *Purcell* v. *McNamara* (14 Ves. 91), after seventeen years. Of course in all these cases diverse and varied circumstances operated to affect the judgment of the court and produced very different results, but they show that such time as has elapsed in the present case is not necessarily conclusive, and that the purchaser taking the receiver's deed, and in total ignorance of the occasion or circumstances of the delay, would run the risk of an adverse decision and hold at the best only a doubtful title. Infancy, ignorance, concealment, or misrepresentation might come to explain and excuse the delay, and prevent it from amounting to acquiescence.

We think the General Term were, therefore, right in holding the proffered title defective, but should have relieved the purchaser wholly from his contract. Admitting the title to be bad, but assuming that it might thereafter be made good, the court directed that the purchaser should take the premises if the seller should produce sufficient evidence to be taken in a proceeding which should be instituted by action or motion within sixty days, showing a confirmation of the executor's purchase by the proper parties. The effect of this order was to change utterly the purchaser's contract, and bind him to an agreement which he never made. It left the period of performance entirely uncertain and indefinite. The seller could begin his proceeding within sixty days, and after that was free to pursue the litigation at his pleasure, while the purchaser remained bound for an unknown period, with no guaranty of getting a title in the end. We can find no authority for such an order. In actions for specific performance, the courts have sometimes decreed that the purchaser should take title when its defects were cured before the final hearing, although existing at the commencement of the action (*Dutch Church* v. *Mott*, 7 Paige, 85 ; *Grady* v. *Ward*, 20 Barb. 543), but have never gone so far as to hold the action open and undetermined to enable the seller to bring a suit against other parties, and try the experiment of an effort to secure a good title at some uncertain date in the future. In this respect the order of the General Term was wrong and should be reversed, McMillan be relieved from his purchase and repaid his deposit and auctioneer's fees with interest thereon, together with the reasonable expenses of investigating the title, and costs of the appeal to the General Term and to this court.

All concur.

Ordered accordingly.

THE PEOPLE OF THE STATE OF NEW YORK *v.* THE EMPIRE MUTUAL LIFE INSURANCE COMPANY, JOHN P. O'NEILL, Receiver, etc., Appellant.

One holding a policy of life insurance does not forfeit his policy by omitting to pay annual premiums thereon after the company issuing the policy has ceased to do business, transferred all of its assets and become insolvent.

The fact that a life insurance company is authorized to reinsure its risks, or that it is by statute permitted to discontinue its business and wind up its affairs, does not release it from any of its existing obligations ; such a company has no power to turn its policy-holders against their consent over to another company, and the policy-holders are under no obligations, in order to protect their legal rights, to protest against an effort so to do.

The implied contract of the company with its policy-holders is, that it will continue its business, keep on hand the fund required by law for their security, and remain in a condition, so long as its contracts continue, to perform its obligations.

The E. M. L. Ins. Co. entered into a contract with the C. L. Ins. Co., by which the latter agreed to insure the outstanding risks of the former for a sum specified, it agreeing to cease business and to wind up its affairs ; it transferred all of its assets to the C. L. Ins. Co., and still owed that company a balance which it had no means of paying and has not paid. The E. M. L.

Ins. Co. thereupon surrendered its offices, notified the comptroller of that fact, and seven years thereafter, at the suit of the attorney-general, it was dissolved and a receiver appointed. Certain of its policy-holders refused or neglected to accept new policies from the C. L. Ins. Co., and omitted to pay premiums after such transfer. *Held,* that the E. M. L. Ins. Co., having voluntarily disabled itself from the performance of its contract, said policy-holders were excused from further performance or offer to perform on their part, and were entitled to recover as damages for the breach on the part of the company, the value of their policies at the time of such breach; that by virtue of their position they were beneficiaries of the fund held by the State as security for policy-holders, and their claims followed that fund into the hands of the receiver and were first entitled to be paid therefrom.

(Argued March 20, 1883; decided March 30, 1883.)

APPEAL by John P. O'Neill, receiver of the defendant, from an order of the General Term of the Supreme Court, in the third judicial department, made December 19, 1882, which reversed an order of Special Term: " In so far as said order rejects and disallows the claims of certain policy-holders in said order named and sustains the exceptions to that portion of the referee's report as holds said claims to be invalid." (Reported below, 28 Hun, 358.)

The material facts are stated in the opinion.

Geo. W. Wingate for John P. O'Neill, receiver, appellant. The contract of reinsurance of the Empire with the Continental was not illegal. (Laws of 1853, pp. 805, 896; Laws of 1853, chap. 643, § 1; Laws of 1865, chap. 328, § 1.) Beyond the deposit with the insurance department, the company was free to deposit its assets where it saw fit. (Laws of 1853, chap. 463, § 17.) A contract of reinsurance of this description is not void, but may be enforced. (*Glen* v. *Hope Mut. L. Ins. Co.*, 56 N. Y. 379; *Fischer* v. *Hope Mut. L. Ins. Co.*, 69 id. 161, 165.) It is too late for parties who have themselves violated their contracts, by failing to pay their premiums, and thereby forfeited them, to claim now the value of those policies. (*Taylor* v. *Charter Oak*, 59 How. 468; *Meade* v. *St. Louis Mut. L. Ins. Co.*, 51 id. 5; *Universal Life* v. *White* head, 10 Ins. L. J. 337, 340; *King's Accum. L. Fund Ann. Co.*, 3 C. B. [N. S.] 151.) Courts of equity have no power to excuse against forfeiture caused by the failure of the assured to comply with their contract to pay premiums as stated in their policy. (*Douglass* v. *Knick. L. Ins. Co.*, 83 N. Y. 499.)

Lucius McAdam for policy-holders, appellants. There was in fact no breach of contract by the company, the reinsurance agreement being valid and within the powers of the companies to make. (*Fischer* v. *Hope L. Ins. Co.*, 69 N. Y. 161.) The breach of contract was by the policy-holders who stopped payment, and thereby lapsed their policies. (*Carpenter* v. *Catlin*, 44 Barb. 75.) If the reinsurance agreement is alleged as an excuse for non-payment of premiums, its effect would be merely that the policy-holder need not have paid his premium actually, and may be allowed to offset the unpaid premiums against the value of the policy. (*Attorney-Gen'l* v. *Guardian L. Ins. Co.*, 82 N. Y. 336.) The valuation should be taken as of the date of the appointment of the receiver, January 14, 1879, and the unpaid premiums deducted, as was done in the former proceeding. (*People* v. *Security L. Ins. Co.*, 78 N. Y. 114; *Attorney-Gen'l* v. *North Am. L. Ins. Co.*, 82 id. 172.) The true nature of these claims is for a rescission of the contracts. (*Mead* v. *St. Louis L. Ins. Co.*, 51 How. Pr. 1.) A rescission must be made promptly, so as to properly protect the rights of all parties. It is too late to rescind ten years after the breach complained of, and after the contract of reinsurance assigned as the breach has been faithfully performed during that period, and after the company has gone into the hands of a receiver. (*Lawrence* v. *Dale*, 3 Johns. Ch. 23; *McNever* v. *Livingston*, 17 Johns. 437; *People* v. *W. O. B. L. Ins. Co.*, 15 Hun, 8.)

Raphael J. Moses, Jr., for respondent. The cessation of business on June 7, 1872, and notice to the superintendent caused the trust in the $100,000 deposited with him to become operative. (Laws of 1853, chap. 463, § 19; *Mead* v. *St. Louis*

L. Ins. Co., 51 How. Pr. 1 ; *Fischer* v. *Hope L. Ins. Co.*, 69
N. Y. 161.) The company, by ceasing to do business and publishing notice thereof in manner required by law, released the
assured from the obligation to tender premiums. (*Attorney-
Gen'l* v. *Guardian Mut. L. Ins. Co.*, 82 N. Y. 336.) The
assured has not waived the breach of contract on the part of
the company. (Code of Civil Pro., §§ 381, 388 ; Story's Eq.
Jur., § 1520 ; *Lyon* v. *Hay*, 51 Barb. 13 ; *Kingsland* v.
Robers, 3 Paige, 193.)

John C. Keeler for attorney-general.

Ruger, Ch. J. The sole question raised upon this appeal is
whether a person insured forfeits his policy by omitting to pay
annual premiums thereon when the company issuing such
policy has ceased its business, transferred all of its assets and
become insolvent.

It would seem to be an inequitable rule that would require
a policy-holder to continue for years in the payment of annual
premiums upon a life insurance policy to a corporation utterly
unable to perform its obligation, and which, by its situation, is
precluded from even possibly improving its condition in the
future, or forfeit all that he has previously paid in performance
of his contract.

In June, 1872, the Empire Mutual Life Insurance Company,
having been in business about three years, entered into a contract with the Continental Life Insurance Company, whereby
the latter agreed to reinsure the outstanding risks of the former
at a specified price, which amounted in the aggregate to about
$656,754, and the Empire company contracted to immediately
relinquish the business of life insurance, and do whatever
might be necessary to wind up its affairs. The Empire Mutual
Life Insurance Company, after transferring all of its assets, including its interest in a deposit of $100,000 in the State insur-
ance department, to the Continental Insurance Company, still
owed that company, on such contract, over $200,000, which it
had no means of paying and never has paid.

Upon the heels of this agreement the Empire company surrendered its offices, went out of the life insurance business, notified the comptroller of that fact, and seven years thereafter was dissolved and had a receiver of its assets appointed at the suit of the attorney-general.   The Continental company continued its existence until the year 1876, when it also became insolvent and was dissolved and a receiver appointed of its effects.   During the period of its existence the Continental company received such of the policy-holders of the Empire as consented to come in and accept policies from it, but the respondents, on this appeal, refused or neglected to accept new policies from the Continental, and omitted to pay their annual premiums to the officers of either the Continental or the Empire companies after June, 1872.

It will be seen that policy-holders in the Empire company, after its sale to the Continental, had the option of three alternatives, either to continue paying premiums to the nominal officers of an insolvent corporation, with the certainty of making an ultimate loss, or to accept an enforced change of policies in a company not of their own selection, and concerning whose responsibility they knew nothing, or to rest on their claim for damages against the company with whom alone they had contracted, and who had voluntarily disabled itself from performing such contract.   They selected the latter alternative, omitted to pay any further premiums, and now claim damages for a breach of contract by the Empire company in June, 1872, asserting the measure of damages to be the value of their policies at the time of the breach.

If the insurer has violated its contract, and voluntarily disabled itself from performance, the insured is doubtless excused from further performance or offer to perform, on his part, and may recover such damage as he can show he has suffered.

The circumstance that an insurance company is authorized by statute to effect an insurance upon its outstanding risks, or is permitted to discontinue its business, and wind up its affairs, does not release it from any of its existing obligations. There is no principle of law which permits an insurance company any more than a private individual by its own act to avoid the performance of its contracts, and the provisions of the statute in question were intended simply to empower an insurance company to protect itself by voluntary engagements with others from eventual or continued loss, and do not at all concern the persons with whom it has previously contracted.

An insurance company has no power to turn its policy-holders against their consent over to another company, and such policy-holders are under no obligation, in order to protect their legal rights, to protest against an effort to do so.

The implied contract of an insurance company with its policy-holders is that it will continue its business, keep on hand the funds required by law for the security of its patrons, and remain in a condition, so long as its contracts continue, to perform its obligations, and when it fails to do this it has broken its engagements. (*People* v. *Security Life Ins. & Ann. Co.*, 78 N. Y. 125; 34 Am. Rep. 522.) It was held in the case of *Shaw* v. *The Republic Life Ins. Co.* (69 N. Y. 286) that when an insurance company announces that it will not perform its contract, and does not withdraw such announcement before the period for paying premiums arrives, the assured is excused from paying or tendering payment of premiums. And in *Att'y-Gen'l* v. *Guardian Mutual Life Ins. Co.* (82 N. Y. 339) it was held that when the further payment of premiums is excused by the insolvency of the company for the purpose of enforcement, the policies are just as effectual as if the premiums had been paid. The rules relating to the rescission of contracts have no application in this case; the claim of the respondents is based upon the validity of the contract and relates to its enforcement. By virtue of their position they are beneficiaries of the funds held by the State as security for policy-holders, and their claims follow that trust fund into the hands of the receiver, and are first entitled to be paid therefrom.

The order of the General Term should be affirmed, with costs to be paid from the fund.

All concur.

Order affirmed.

In the Matter of the Petition of WILLIAM A. RIGHTER to
Vacate an Assessment.

The petition upon which proceedings were instituted to vacate an assessment for regulating and grading a street in the city of New York, authorized by the act of 1871 (Chap. 226, Laws of 1871), charged in substance
that the commissioner of public works fraudulently combined and colluded with the contractors to let the contract at an extravagant price. The
contract in question was not let at a public letting, but was what is known
as "a special contract," the commissioner having invited four persons
to bid for the work. The persons so invited put in bids for
"filling," which was the main item, ranging from $1.43 to $1.60
per cubic yard. The contract was awarded for $1.47. The petitioner
upon the hearing offered in evidence the "bid-book" of the department
of public works, containing a record of bids received for public lettings
prior and subsequent to the contract in question, relating to streets in
the same vicinity, by which it appeared that filling was contracted for
at prices not exceeding eighty cents per cubic yard. This evidence was
rejected. *Held* error; that the commissioner, in the absence of evidence
to the contrary, must be presumed to have known the usual prices paid
for the work, and the evidence was competent on the issue of fraud.
Also *held*, that it was competent as bearing upon the alleged combination
and collusion to prove the bids by the selected bidders for the other
special contract work and the contracts awarded therefor.

(Argued March 20, 1883; decided March 30, 1883.)

APPEAL from order of the General Term of the Supreme
Court, in the first judicial department, made at the February
term, 1883, which affirmed an order of Special Term which
denied the application of the petitioner above named to vacate
an assessment for regulating and grading Eighty-fourth street
in the city of New York.

The material facts are stated in the opinion.

Samuel Hand for appellant. It was error to reject the evidence offered of the bids for filling on previous and subsequent
contracts in the same vicinity. (23 Hun, 355; 85 N. Y. 646;
Harrison v. *Glover*, 72 id. 451, 454; *Cliquot's Champagne*, 3
Wall. 143; *Lusk* v. *Druse*, 4 Wend. 313.) The requirements of the ordinances of the common council were, by force

of the several statutes authorizing them, as obligatory and mandatory as to the manner of contracting for public works as if the same were part of the statutes themselves. (*Smith* v. *Mayor, etc.*, 10 N. Y. 508; *Russ* v. *Mayor, etc.*, 10 N. Y. Leg. Obs.; *People, ex rel. Dunsmore,* v. *Croton Bd.*, 6 Abb. Pr. 58; *People, ex rel. Cummings,* v. *Croton Aq. Bd.*, 26 Barb. 240; *In re Merriam*, 84 N. Y. 601; *Smith* v. *Mayor, etc.*, 10 id. 508.) The expression in the act of 1871 (Chap. 226) "in such manner as by him shall be deemed necessary and proper," did not relieve the superintendent from the necessity of advertising and letting to the lowest bidder. (*In re Weil,* 83 N. Y. 543; *In re Robbins,* 82 id. 131.) It is not open to question that the price at which a contract is let by a public officer, when he lets it at private letting instead of public letting, may be evidence of fraud. (*Matter of Mead,* 74 N. Y. 216; *Matter of Raymond,* BARRETT, J.; *Lawrence* v. *Mayor,* opinion of WHEELER, J.)

D. J. Dean for respondent. The failure of the commissioner of public works to advertise for bids and proposals for the work is no sufficient ground for invalidating the assessment. (Laws of 1861, chap. 308; Laws of 1870, chap. 137, § 104; *Greene* v. *Mayor,* 60 N. Y. 303; *People, ex rel. Ross,* v. *Brooklyn,* 69 id. 605; *Kingsley* v. *Brooklyn,* 7 Abb. N. C. 42; affirmed, 78 N. Y. 200; *Goodrich* v. *Russell,* 42 id. 177–184.) Chapter 226, Laws of 1871, section 5, confers authority to impose the assessment for the expenditure actually made by the city in performing the work, whether incurred legally or otherwise. (*Brown* v. *The Mayor,* 63 N. Y. 240; *In re Van Antwerp,* 56 id. 261; Dillon on Mun. Corp., § 46; *Hoyt* v. *Thompson,* 19 N. Y. 218; *Hasbrouck* v. *Milwaukee,* 21 Wis. 217; *Guilford* v. *Sup'rs of Chenango,* 3 Kern. 143; *Brewster* v. *Syracuse,* 19 N. Y. 116; *Howell* v. *Buffalo,* 37 id. 267; 50 id. 502.) The evidence in relation to bids to regulate and grade other streets during the years 1872 and 1873 was properly excluded. (*Gouge* v. *Roberts,* 53 N. Y. 619; *Jaeger* v. *Kelly,* 52 id. 274; Story on Eq. Jur., §§ 244,

245; *Davidson* v. *Little,* 22 Penn. St. 245–251; *Matter of Eightieth St.,* 31 How. 199; *Kingsley* v. *Brooklyn,* 7 Abb. N. C. 28–44.) The allegation of fraud to be sufficient should be clear and explicit. (Moak's Van Santvoord's Plead. 356; *McMurray* v. *Thomas,* 5 How. Pr. 14; *Barber* v. *Morgan,* 51 Barb. 116.) Mere inadequacy of price is not sufficient to prove fraud. (*Jaeger* v. *Kelly,* 52 N. Y. 274; Story on Eq. Jur., §§ 244, 245; *Davidson* v. *Little,* 22 Penn. St. 245–251; *Matter of Eightieth St.,* 31 How. 199; *Kingsley* v. *Brooklyn,* 7 Abb. N. C. 42.) If the court finds that there was any such excess in the cost, or extravagance or carelessness in the matter of contracting, as to create a reasonable suspicion of bad faith, the only remedy to which the petitioners would be entitled would be a reduction in proportion to the amount to which the expense had been thus unlawfully or negligently increased. (Laws of 1870, chap. 383, § 27; *In re Merriam,* 84 N. Y. 596; *In re Met. Gas-light Co.,* 85 id. 526; *In re Pelton,* id. 651.) The power to reduce and modify the amount according to the merits, as shown by the proof, is inherent in the court without the aid of the statute of 1870. (*In re St. Joseph's Asylum,* 69 N. Y. 353; *In re Merriam,* 84 id. 651.)

Per Curiam. The assessment in question was for the regulating and grading Eighty-fourth street, authorized by chapter 226, Laws of 1871. The petition alleged that the work was let at grossly extravagant prices, greatly in excess of the usual, ordinary and market prices for such work, and much greater than the prices for similar work in the same and other portions of the city, paid to contractors under contracts let at public lettings by the commissioner of public works, and his predecessor in office, and "that the officer by whom the contract (in question) was made, well knowing these facts, and in violation of his duty in the premises, and in pursuance of a corrupt conspiracy and combination, let the contract for this and similar work to a ring of contractors at the aforesaid extravagant prices."

These allegations, fairly construed, charge that the commissioner combined and colluded with the contractors in committing a fraud upon the public and property owners in the letting of the contract in question at an extravagant price, and any proof tending to support the charge was admissible. The contract in question was known as a special contract. ' It was not let at a public letting. The commissioner of public works in the fall of 1872 invited four persons, among whom was the contractor in this case, to bid for work authorized by the act referred to, on a large number of streets, including Eighty-fourth street. The persons so invited put in bids for the several pieces of work, and for *filling*, which was the main item, the bids ranged from $1.43 to $1.60 per cubic yard. The contract for the work on Eighty-fourth street was awarded November 19, 1872, at the price for filling, of $1.47 per cubic yard. Several witnesses called by the petitioner, acquainted with the value of such work, testified that a fair price for filling was from sixty to seventy cents per cubic yard.

No work under any of the contracts was commenced until October, 1873, nearly a year after the contract in question was let. The petitioner offered in evidence the bid book of the department of public works, which contained a record of all bids received in pursuance of public advertisement, for regulating and grading streets and avenues during the years 1872 and 1873, both prior and subsequent to the letting of the contract in question (where filling was required and bid for), and relating to streets in the vicinity of Eighty-fourth street, and in the upper parts of the city, and of the contracts upon such proposals. By these contracts it appeared that the filling was contracted for at a price not exceeding eighty cents per cubic yard.

The petitioner also offered in evidence the bid book of special contracts containing the bids by the four selected contractors, for the grading and regulating of the streets regulated and graded under the act of 1872, as to which bids were specially invited, as before stated, and he also offered in evidence the awards made thereon. This evidence last referred to (the particulars of which are disclosed by the record) would justify an inference of a prior arrangement between the several bidders in respect to their bids.   Five of the contracts were awarded to one of the bidders, four to each of two others, and one to another.

The court at Special Term rejected both classes of evidence. We think the evidence offered was admissible upon the issue of fraud.   The commissioner of public works, in the absence of evidence to the contrary, must be presumed to have known of the usual prices paid for filling at or about the time the special contracts were made under contracts let at public lettings, and the bids made for such work were some evidence of the fair value of this work.   If he knew that the prices in the special contracts were grossly extravagant, it would be a fact bearing upon the alleged fraud.   So also it was competent, as bearing upon the alleged combination and confederacy, to prove the other bids by the selected bidders for the special contract work, and the contracts awarded therefor. If an inspection of those bids would suggest an arrangement between the several bidders, and it should be found that the commissioner of public works was put upon inquiry, the petitioner was entitled to the benefit of this evidence.

We express no opinion as to the force of the evidence offered, but we think the judge erred in rejecting it as he did on the ground that it was irrelevant and incompetent.   This evidence is subject to explanation, and it is not impossible that it may be shown that it is entirely consistent with good faith on the part of the commissioner of public works in letting the contract in question, but this can only be determined when all the competent evidence offered has been received and considered.

Without, therefore, considering the other questions, we are of opinion that upon the ground that competent evidence was rejected the orders of the Special and General Terms should be reversed, and that the case should go back for rehearing.

Orders of Special and General Terms reversed, and a rehearing ordered.

All concur.

Orders reversed.

In the Matter of the Petition of the Trustees of the LEAKE
AND WATTS ORPHAN HOME IN THE CITY OF NEW YORK, to
Vacate an Assessment.

The provision of the act of 1873, entitled " An act to provide for the Eastern
boulevard in the city of New York, and in relation to certain alterations
of the map or plan of said city, and certain local improvements" (§ 4, chap.
528, Laws of 1873), authorizing the department of public parks to do
the work " of regulating, grading or otherwise improving Tenth
avenue," authorized the construction of a sewer in said avenue.
Under said provision the department was authorized to do the work of constructing such a sewer, or any part thereof, by day's work.
In proceedings to vacate an assessment for the construction of such a sewer,
held, that in the absence of evidence that there was no connection or relation between the portion of Tenth avenue specified in the act and the
Eastern boulevard, for the purpose of sustaining the constitutionality of
the act, the connection was to be assumed ; and, therefore, that said
act was not violative of the provision of the State Constitution (Art. 3,
§ 16), declaring that no local or private act shall contain more than one
subject, and requiring that to be expressed in the title.
The greater portion of the work was done by day's work. It appeared that
rock excavation cost over $14 per cubic yard, pipe culvert $7.05 per
lineal foot, and brick sewer $25 per lineal foot, while the fair value was
rock excavation $4 per cubic yard, pipe culvert $1.50 per lineal foot and
brick sewer $4.55 per lineal foot. *Held*, that the evidence disclosed not
merely a case of improvidence and extravagance, but sufficiently established fraud or irregularity.
But *held*, that the petitioner was not entitled to have the assessment wholly
vacated ; and that an order reducing it, by striking out the amount
added by reason of such fraud or irregularity, was proper.
Also *held*, that an objection that the petition contained no averments of
fraud affecting the assessment, not having been taken at Special Term,
would not be heard here.

(Argued March 20, 1883 ; decided March 30, 1883.)

APPEAL from order of the General Term of the Supreme
Court, in the first judicial department, made February 2, 1882,
which affirmed an order of Special Term which reduced an
assessment upon certain lots of the petitioner in the city of
New York for constructing a sewer in Tenth avenue in said

city between One Hundred and Tenth and One Hundred and Fourteenth streets.

The material facts are stated in the opinion.

John C. Shaw for appellant. The work done in the year 1875 by day's work was illegal and unauthorized, being in violation of the ninety-third section of the charter of 1873, and cannot be the foundation of a valid assessment. (*In re Emigrant Sav. B'k*, 75 N. Y. 388; *In re Robbins*, 82 id. 131; *In re Weil*, 83 id. 543; *In re Stephens*, 26 Hun, 22; *In re Holly*, 25 id. 119; *In re Lange*, 85 N. Y. 307.) Chapter 528 of Laws of 1873, is unconstitutional so far as regards the last provision relating to Tenth avenue, being in violation of article 3, section 16 of the Constitution. (*People* v. *Hills*, 35 N. Y. 449; *People* v. *Comm'rs of Highways*, 53 Barb. 70; *People* v. *Com. Council of Brooklyn*, 13 Abb. [N. S.] 121; *People* v. *Briggs*, 50 N. Y. 553; *Matter of Sackett St.*, 74 id. 95; *Matter of Roberts*, 89 id. 618; *In re Eager*, 46 id. 100; *Coffin* v. *McLean*, 80 id. 564; *In re Emigrant Sav. B'k*, 75 id. 388.) The case presents a clear and unmistakable case of fraud. (*In re Mead*, 74 N. Y. 220.) The petitioner is not liable to be assessed even for the fair value of the work as claimed by the city, the same having been done in violation of law or under such circumstances as to amount to a fraud. (*In re Raymond*, 21 Hun, 229; *In re Robbins*, 82 N. Y. 131; *In re Stephens*, 26 Hun, 22.)

D. J. Dean for respondent. The commissioner of public works was clothed with full power to build the sewer in question by day's work. (Laws of 1873, chap. 528, §4.) The objection of fraud in incurring the expense is not available to the petitioner here. (Moak's Van Santvoord's Pleading, 316; *Mc-Murray* v. *Thomas*, 5 How. Pr. 14; *Barber* v. *Morgan*, 51 Barb. 116.) Mere excess of cost will not show fraud, and collusion must be proved. (*Jaeger* v. *Kelly*, 52 N. Y. 274; Story's Eq. Jur., §§ 244, 245; *Davidson* v. *Little*, 22 Penn. St. 245, 251; *In re Eightieth St.*, 31 How. 99; *Kingsley* v. *Brooklyn*,

7 Abb. N. C. 42.) The objection to the constitutionality of the act is not available to the petitioner, not being stated in the petition. (*Rich's Case*, 12 Abb. 118; *Miller's Case*, id. 121; *Horne's Case*, id. 124; *In re Eager*, 46 N. Y. 109.) The title is quite sufficient to fulfill the constitutional requirement. (*Matter of Dep't Pub. Parks*, 86 N. Y. 440; *Matter of Sackett St.*, 74 id. 95; *Harris* v. *People*, 59 id. 596; *Matter of Mayer*, 50 id. 506; *People* v. *Briggs*, id. 553.) If the commissioner of public works was authorized to do the work by day's work, the utmost extent of the petitioner's grievance is the increase in cost of the work done under that system, above the fair and reasonable value thereof. (*In re Merriam*, 84 N. Y. 596; *In re Mut. L. Ins. Co.*, 89 id. 530.)

EARL, J. The cost of the work for which the assessment in question was made was $35,214.25. Of this sum $16,292.60 was assessed upon the property owners, and $18,921.65 upon the city. The sum of $33,804.78 was the expense of work done by day's work, and $1,318.47 was the expense of work done by contract. The cost of work done by day's work was as follows:

1350 cubic yards of rock excavation at $14, 087,	$19, 018 86
1 receiving basin.............................	363 22
23.93 lineal feet 12-inch pipe at $7.05..........	168 79
562.17 lineal feet brick sewer at $25.35	14, 253 91
Total..................................	$33, 804 78

The work done by contract let at a public bidding was:

2 receiving basins at $95 each	$190 00
10 lineal feet 12-inch pipe at 70c	7 00
433 lineal feet of brick sewer at $2.59	1, 121 47
Total	$1, 318 47

All the evidence upon both sides showed that the expense of the work done by day's work was very extravagant, largely, several times in excess of what the work ought to have cost. It was found by the judge at the Special Term, that the fair value for the rock excavation per yard was $4 ; the brick sewer $4.55 per lineal foot, the pipe culvert $1.50 per lineal foot, and the receiving basins $125 each; and he ordered a reduction of the assessment based upon those figures. Both parties have appealed, the petitioner claiming that the assessment should have been entirely vacated, and the city that no reduction whatever should have been made.

We are of opinion that the department of public works was authorized to construct this sewer by virtue of section 4, chapter 528 of the Laws of 1873, which contains the following provision : " The department of public works is hereby authorized to contract for and let to the lowest bidder the work of regulating, grading and otherwise improving Tenth avenue between the said One Hundred and Tenth street and Manhattan avenue, so as to connect both of said boulevards, requiring in such contract adequate security in addition to that now required by law for the proper protection of and against danger to the Croton aqueduct. Should, however, the commissioner of the said department deem it more advisable for the interest of the public and for the better protection of the Croton aqueduct, to do the said work, or any part thereof, by day's work, then he is so authorized to do, and in such manner as may be approved by the chief engineer of the Croton aqueduct department."

It is true that there are no express words in the section authorizing the construction of the sewer; but we may take notice of the fact that sewers in the city of New York are incidents of the streets constructed, in part at least, for the purpose of draining the streets and protecting them against water. They are generally to be found in all the principal streets of the city. They are laid below the pavements of the streets, and unless they are constructed before the streets are regulated, graded and paved, the streets would have to be torn up and the pavement removed in order to construct them. And hence we think that the words, "regulating, grading and otherwise improving Tenth avenue," are sufficiently broad to authorize the construction of a sewer in the avenue.

The claim on the part of the petitioner, that the department of public works was not authorized to do any of the work by the day is not well founded. It is too clear for dispute, that express authority, in plain language, was given to do the work by day's work if the department of public works should deem that method more advantageous for the interest of the public, and the better protection of the Croton aqueduct.

We are of opinion that chapter 528 was not in violation of section 16 of article 3 of the Constitution. The title of the act is as follows: ". An act to provide for the Eastern boulevard in the city of New York, and in relation to certain alterations of the map or plan of said city, and certain local improvements in connection therewith to amend chapter 626 of the Laws of 1870." The subject of this act, as expressed in its title, is the Eastern boulevard and the alteration of the map or plan of the city, and certain local improvements so far as they are connected with the boulevard. All the work authorized by the act was part of one improvement, one system. By referring to chapter 626 of the Laws of 1870, and to section 4 of chapter 528 it appears that Tenth avenue above One Hundred and Tenth street was in some way connected with the Eastern boulevard and was expected to be used therewith. It was to be improved so as to connect the two portions of the boulevard. How intimate or important its connection was does not precisely appear. There is no proof, however, showing that it had no connection with, or relation to, the boulevard, and for the purpose of sustaining the constitutionality of the act we must assume that it had. Hence there was but one subject and the title was sufficient within the following authorities. (*Matter of Mayer*, 50 N. Y. 504; *People, ex rel. City of Rochester*, v. *Briggs*, id. 553; *Harris* v. *People*, 59 id. 599; *Matter of Sackett Street*, 74 id. 95; *Matter of the Department of Public Parks*, 86 id. 440.) Assuming, therefore, that the petitioner has the right under his petition to raise this constitutional objection, we are of the opinion that it is not well founded.

We think fraud or irregularity was sufficiently established. An expenditure of $14 per cubic yard for rock excavation which should have cost but $4 ; of $7 per foot for pipe which should have cost but $1.50 ; of $25.35 per lineal foot for brick sewer which should have cost but $4.55, shows not merely a case of improvidence and extravagance, but very satisfactorily that there was either gross fraud, imposition, mistake or irregularity, and fully justifies the finding of the court at Special Term. If the difference in the prices had been such only as could fairly be accounted for upon the theory that the work had been merely improvidently, or perhaps extravagantly done, a case would not have been made for the interference of the court. But here there was more, and the facts lead irresistibly to the conclusion that there was either fraud or some unexplained irregularity.

The claim of the petitioner that the assessment should have been entirely vacated is not well founded. All it can ask under the statutes is, that the amount which has been added to his assessment, otherwise valid, by fraud or irregularity, should be eliminated therefrom, and this relief the Special Term granted.

It is claimed on the part of the city that there is no allegation in the petition of any fraud affecting the assessment. The allegation in the petition is quite imperfect, but no objection to its sufficiency appears in the record to have been taken at the Special Term, and hence the objection should not be listened to here.

We do not understand the city to complain of the amount of the reduction of the assessment, in case any reduction is proper.

We are, therefore, of the opinion that the order appealed from should be affirmed, without costs to either party in this court.

All concur.

Order affirmed.

2 122
3 399

WILLIAM D. MEAD, Respondent, v. PATRICK F. SHEA, as Executor, etc., Appellant.

A request to the court on trial to rule as to the order in which counsel
shall address the jury can only properly be made after the whole evidence has been presented.

Plaintiff's complaint stated two causes of action, one upon two promissory
notes indorsed by S., defendant's testator, the other for goods sold. To
the first defendant pleaded payment, to the second a general denial.
Plaintiff opened the case and gave evidence as to both causes of action.
After the evidence had been substantially closed defendant's counsel
moved for judgment on the last cause of action. To this the court replied, "my impression is there is not evidence to warrant a recovery. I
think I shall so direct the jury." No further request as to that cause of
action was made, and no exception was taken to the omission of the
court to rule on the request. Said counsel then stated to the court "we
have established the affirmative of the issue." The court replied, "I
think not, I think the pleadings control that." To which said counsel
excepted. Some further evidence was given by defendant, and the court,
in submitting the case to the jury, withdrew from their consideration the
claim for goods sold. *Held*, that the colloquy between court and counsel
did not amount to a claim or denial of the right of the latter to the closing address to the jury ; but conceding this, the court properly declined to
allow the right, as at the time nothing had occurred which prevented
the final submission to the jury of the issue as to the second cause of
action, and there was, therefore, at the time the request was made an
issue undisposed of as to which plaintiff had the affirmative and the
right to close.

It appeared that H., in the spring of 1876, doing business in the name of
his wife, purchased stone of plaintiff to the amount of $800, giving in
payment her notes indorsed by S., which were renewed from time to
time until April 7, 1877, when the notes in suit were given. In October,
1876, the H.'s purchased another lot of stone of plaintiff, and on the 27th
of the month Mrs. H. delivered to him an order on R. for $800, which
was accepted and paid in the spring and summer of 1877. The
H.'s both testified that this order was given in payment of the notes indorsed by S. Plaintiff testified in his own behalf that the order was
given to apply on the October purchase. Plaintiff was permitted to prove,
as bearing upon the credibility of the H.'s, their letters and declarations as to the purchases and the manner of payment written and made
both before and after the giving of the order. *Held*, that the evidence
was properly received. Also that the objection that as the evidence
tended to contradict the testimony of the H.'s their attention should have

first been called to, and they interrogated in regard thereto could not be presented here, it not having been raised on the trial.

(Argued March 22, 1883; decided March 30, 1883.)

APPEAL from judgment of the General Term of the Supreme Court, in the third judicial department, made September 6, 1882, which affirmed a judgment in favor of plaintiff, entered upon a verdict.

The nature of the action and the material facts are stated in the opinion.

Jesse Johnson for appellant.   The transactions between Mead and Henright, subsequent to October 25, 1876, were clearly irrelevant and improper as evidence against Shea. (1 Wharton on Evidence, §§ 551, 566; 1 Greenleaf on Evidence, § 462; *Bullis* v. *Montgomery*, 50 N. Y. 352, 358, 359; *Anderson* v. *R. & W. R. R. Co.*, 54 id. 340–343; *Gandolfo* v. *Appleton*, 40 id. 533, 539; *Worrill* v. *Parmerlee*, 1 id. 519, 521; *Wilson* v. *Wilson*, 4 Abb. Ct. App. Dec. 621; *Happy* v. *Mosher*, 48 N. Y. 313, 320.)   The defendant, at the close of the testimony, was entitled to the affirmative in the summing up to the jury. (*Houghton* v. *Townsend*, 8 How. 441; *McKyring* v. *Bull*, 16 N. Y. 297; *Millerd* v. *Thorn*, 56 id. 402; *Elwell* v. *Chamberlain*, 31 id. 611; *DeGraff* v. *Carmichael*, 13 Hun, 129.)

Joseph M. Lawson for respondent.   Plaintiff was properly allowed to close the case. (*Huntington* v. *Conkey*, 33 Barb. 218, 227, 228; *Fry* v. *Bennett*, 28 N. Y. 324, 329; *Elwell* v. *Chamberlain*, 31 id. 611, 620; *DeGraff* v. *Carmichael*, 13 Hun, 129; *Millerd* v. *Thorn*, 56 N. Y. 402; *Murray* v. *N. Y. L. Ins. Co.*, 85 id. 236.)

RUGER, Ch. J.   The defendant seeks to reverse the judgment in this action, because he was not permitted to make the closing argument to the jury.   The question was claimed to have been raised by the following colloquy towards the close of the evidence. Defendant's counsel, "I desire further that we have established that we have the affirmative of the issue." The court, "I think not. I think the pleadings control that."

"Exception by defendant's counsel."

We think that it might very well be said that this language neither constitutes a claim nor a denial of the right of either party to address the jury. The right to deliver the closing address might be one of the consequences of the proposition suggested to the court, but it is not embraced in the language used by the counsel. Even after this ruling by the court further evidence was given in the case by the defendant, and a request that the court should rule on the order in which counsel should address the jury, could only properly be made after the whole evidence had been presented. But we think there was another ground upon which the court might have properly declined to allow the defendant the right of making the closing address. Issues were formed by the pleadings upon two causes of action, and they were both tried together. The first was upon two promissory notes, to which the defendant pleaded payment. The second was upon a sale of merchandise; to this the defendant pleaded a general denial.

The plaintiff opened the case to the jury and gave evidence tending to establish both causes of action. The defendant gave evidence tending to establish a defense to both claims. After the evidence had been substantially closed, the defendant moved for judgment on the last cause of action. To this motion the court replied : " My impression is there is not evidence to warrant a recovery. I think I shall so direct the jury, not sufficient evidence to warrant a recovery for the bill of $58.81." No further request relating to that cause of action was made by the defendant's counsel, neither did he except to the omission of the court to rule upon his request, although the court finally excluded this claim from the consideration of the jury. At this time nothing had occurred which precluded the court from finally submitting it to the jury. It was obviously improper for the court to rule finally upon that question until it had heard the plaintiff's counsel in relation thereto.

It thus appears that at the time when the defendant presented his request to the court to have the final address to the jury, there was an issue in the case undisposed of upon which the plaintiff held the affirmative, and therefore had the right to close. We think the question was properly disposed of by the court below.

It is claimed by the defendant that the court erred in admitting certain evidence offered by the plaintiff under the plea of payment. It appeared in evidence that one Henry Henright, doing business at Brooklyn, in the name of his wife, Bridget Henright, purchased of the plaintiff, in the spring of 1876, a quantity of stone of the value of about $800, that he gave in payment for this stone Bridget Henright's notes indorsed by the defendant Shea, that these notes ran along and were renewed from time to time until April 7, 1877, when the two notes in suit, and a third note for about $279, was given by Shea to take up the prior notes.

It also appeared that in October, 1876, the plaintiff sold another lot of stone to the Henrights, amounting to about $1,035, and that on the 25th day of October, 1876, Bridget Henright delivered to the plaintiff an order on one Russell, which the latter afterward accepted for $800, and which was paid in the spring and summer of 1877.

Upon the trial Henry and Bridget Henright were called as witnesses for the defendant, and both testified, among other things, that the $800 order, upon Russell, was given to the plaintiff in payment of the Shea notes, and that at the time they expressed their gratification at being able to discharge Shea from his obligation, because he had done so much for them. It did not appear that they ever asked Mead to return the Shea notes, but it did appear that six months after this alleged payment, Shea gave the two notes in suit and also another note for about $279, which he paid in October, 1877. It also appeared that the Henrights did not inform Shea, although living in the same city with him, of the alleged payment until after the commencement of this action in January, 1879.

The plaintiff testified, in his own behalf, that the $800 order was given to apply upon the purchase of stone made in October, 1876, and that nothing was said about applying it upon the Shea notes.

The only question left to the jury was which of these two versions was true. It is obvious that any evidence legitimately tending to affect or impair the credibility of either of the witnesses would not only be important but also competent and relevant to the issue.

The evidence objected to was offered by the plaintiff and related to letters written by and acts and declarations of the Henrights both before and after the time of the alleged payment.

The letters and negotiations between the Henrights and plaintiff, relating to the purchases of stone and the manner of its payment, occurring before the date of the alleged payment, were objected to by the defendant upon the ground of their immateriality alone. The court admitted the testimony only as affecting the credibility of the witnesses; — we think it was competent, not only upon that ground, but also as part of the *res gestæ*, and that, therefore, the objection was properly overruled.

While the subsequent acts and declarations of the same witnesses, inconsistent with the testimony given by them on the trial, could not be shown as evidence in chief or as establishing the truth of what was then said or done by them, yet the proof was competent as bearing upon the credibility of the witnesses and the probabilities of the transaction relating to the alleged payment as testified to by them. If the delivery of the order to Mead operated as a payment upon the Shea notes at the time it was made, the subsequent conduct or acts of the Henrights could not change the legal effect of such delivery.

The evidence in question was not received for that purpose, but was limited by the court when offered as bearing solely upon the credibility of the witnesses. Very much of the evidence as to the subsequent correspondence and negotiations between the Henrights and plaintiff had been given before any objection was interposed thereto by the defendant.

The fact that plaintiff received the $800 order from Henright and that it was paid in the spring of 1877 was proved by the defendant upon the plaintiff's cross-examination.

A note for $121.79 given by Henright to plaintiff, dated September 16, 1879, had been received in evidence, and the fact that Henright gave such a note and another order some eighteen months thereafter upon Russell for $134.87 to apply upon the second purchase of stone, and which note and order together amounted to precisely the balance due upon such purchase after applying thereon the $800 order, had also appeared in evidence.

After this evidence had been admitted without exception, the plaintiff again offered to read the note for $121.79 and also a memorandum of the second purchase made by himself at the time of the giving of the second order, and which he claimed to have read to Henright at the time, showing the amount thereof and the application thereon of the two orders and note.

This was objected to as immaterial and incompetent.

We think that this was not only material, but also competent. It was certainly material upon the question of the credit to be given to the testimony of the Henrights and to the application of the $800 order. It tended directly to contradict the evidence which both of the Henrights had given upon the vital issue in the case. We have already seen that the acts and declarations of a witness, which are inconsistent with his testimony, may be given in evidence against him ; this evidence was, therefore, competent and the defendant was not entitled to have it excluded upon the grounds stated by him.

The rule, that a party seeking to avail himself of an exception to the admission of improper evidence on a trial must point out the particular ground of his objection, is a salutary one, and its application here is proper and just. If the objection had been taken that Henright had not been previously interrogated in regard to this transaction, it could easily have been obviated by calling him upon the stand and thus laying the foundation for his contradiction. A party ought not to be allowed to remain silent and conceal the real objections which hê may have to the admissibility of evidence, and then, after misleading his adversary by frivolous objections, for the first time reveal his real complaint in the appellate court.

Under the particular circumstances of this case, it appearing that the evidence objected to directly conflicted with the whole character of the transaction as previously sworn to by the Henrights, no useful object could have been served by calling their attention to the details of the interview occurring at the time the memorandum was presented.

The objections, therefore, were purely technical in their character and the defendant should be held to the application of strict rules in their consideration here.

The exceptions taken to the charge of the court after the jury retired were too general and vague to present any question for review.

It follows from the views expressed that the judgment should be affirmed.

All concur.

Judgment affirmed.

THE PEOPLE OF THE STATE OF NEW YORK, Respondent, *v.* JOHN PETREA, Appellant.

2 128|
1 218|
2 128|
7 585|

The act of 1881 (Chap. 532, Laws of 1881) purporting to amend the provision of the Code of Civil Procedure (§ 1041), in regard to the selection and drawings of jurors in the city and county of Albany, so far as it relates to grand jurors, is a local act and is within the prohibition of the provision of the State Constitution (Art. 3, § 18), forbidding the passage of a local or private bill for " selecting, drawing, summoning or impaneling grand or petit jurors."

Assuming therefore the said act not to have been reported by the commissioners appointed by law to revise the statutes, and so not within the exception (Art. 3, § 25) exempting from the operation of said provision, bills so reported, the said act is as to grand jurors unconstitutional and void.

In the absence of proof to the contrary it will be presumed in support of the constitutionality of the act that it originated in a bill so reported.

It is proper, however, to establish by proof *aliunde* that it did not so originate.

So far as said act relates to the selection of petit jurors, as it is simply an amendment of an existing local law, it is not within the prohibitory provision of the Constitution and is valid.

The amendment of an existing local act in mere matters of detail is not within the mischief aimed at by said provision, and is not violative thereof.

Where an indictment was found by a grand jury drawn from the petit jury list as provided for in said act, *held*, upon the trial thereof, that as the grand jurors were drawn by the proper officer, were regularly summoned and returned, were recognized, impaneled and sworn by the court, were qualified to sit as grand jurors, and as such found the indictment, the arraignment and trial of the accused under it was not a violation of the constitutional guaranty that no person shall be held to answer for a capital or otherwise infamous crime, save as excepted, "unless on presentment or indictment of a grand jury" (Art. 1, § 6); that the indictment was by a grand jury within the meaning of said guaranty.

Also *held*, that under the Code of Criminal Procedure (§§ 312, 313, 321, 328, 329), the accused was not entitled to avail himself by plea or objection in other form of the defect in the proceedings in drawing the grand jury.

(Argued March 30, 1883 ; decided April 17, 1883.)

APPEAL from judgment of the General Term of the Supreme Court, in the third judicial department, entered upon an order made the third Tuesday of November, 1882, which affirmed a judgment of the Court of Sessions of the county of Albany, entered upon a verdict convicting defendant of the crime of grand larceny.

The material facts appear in the opinion.

N. P. Hinman for appellant.   It was unnecessary to prove the facts alleged in the special plea, as the court was bound to take judicial notice of the official acts of public officers like the commissioners to revise the statutes, their powers and duties and the expiration of their term of office, as well as of all legislative proceedings in reference to such officers or to any bill or law in the course of its passage through either house.   (1 Wharton on Evidence, §§ 290, 295, 337 ; *People* v. *Comm'rs of High-*

ways, 54 N. Y. 276; Cooley's Const. Lim. [4th ed.] 164; *Purdy* v. *People*, 4 Hill, 384; *Gardiner* v. *The Collector*, 6 Wall. 499, 511; *Opinions of the Justices*, 52 N. H. 622; *Berry* v. *Balt.*, etc., *R. Co.*, 41 Md. 446, 462; *Town of Ottawa* v. *Perkins*, 94 U. S. 260, 268; *Post* v. *Supervisors*, 105 id. 667; 1 Greenleaf on Evidence, § 6; Laws of 1873, p. 1007; *Clark* v. *Rochester*, 24 Barb. 446, 466.) Chapter 532 of the Laws of 1881, under which the persons composing the grand jury which found the indictment and the petit jury which tried the case, were selected and drawn, is a plain and palpable violation of the Constitution. (2 R. S. [6th ed.] 1015, § 1; 3 R. S. [7th ed.] 2258–2260, §§ 5, 6, 10, 12; Code of Civil Pro., §§ 1035, 1036, 1037, 1038, 1042, 1048.) Chapter 532 of the Laws of 1881 was clearly a "local bill," while in the course of its passage through the legislature. (*People* v. *Sup'rs of Chautauqua*, 43 N. Y. 11, 14 *et seq.*; *People* v. *Hills*, 35 id. 449, 451; *People* v. *O'Brien*, 38 id. 193, 194; *Wanzler* v. *People*, 58 id. 516, 525; *Goskin* v. *Meek*, 42 id. 186; *Huber* v. *People*, 49 id. 132, 135; *Herrigan* v. *Force*, 68 id. 381, 383; *Rogers* v. *Stephens*, 86 id. 623; *In re Met. G. L. Co.*, 85 id. 526.) It is not material that chapter 532 of the Laws of 1881 is in form an amendment of a general statute. (*People* v. *Sup'rs of Chautauqua*, 43 N. Y. 10; *People* v. *O'Brien*, 38 id. 193; *People* v. *Hills*, 35 id. 449; *Earle* v. *Bd. of Education*, 55 Cal. 439, 492; *Matter of Elevated R. R. Co.*, 70 N. Y. 327, 349.) The prohibition contained in section 18 extends to any and all cases of proposed laws, private or local, for any of the purposes specified. (*People* v. *Hills*, 35 N. Y. 449; *People* v. *O'Brien*, 38 id. 193.) The principles of interpretation are the same in reference to contracts, statutes and constitutions. (*Minnis* v. *U. S.*, 15 Peters, 423, 445; *U. S.* v. *Dickson*, id. 141, 165; *People* v. *Albertson*, 55 N. Y. 50.) The accusatory paper on which the defendant was arraigned, tried and convicted of the crime of grand larceny, was not an indictment, and was not found or presented by a grand jury. (*Doyle* v. *State*, 17 Ohio, 222, 224–5; *Wynehamer* v. *People*, 13 N. Y. 427, 457–9, 484; *Cancemi* v. *People*, 18 id. 129, 135; *Mc-*

Guillen v. State, 16 Miss. 587, 597; *State v. McClear*, 11 Nev. 39; *Young v. State*, 6 Ohio, 436; *Dawson v. People*, 25 N. Y. 404; *People v. McKay*, 18 Johns. 212; *McCloskey v. People*, 5 Park. Cr. 306; *Clare v. State*, 30 Md. 164; *State v. Symonds*, 36 Me. 128; *Brown v. Comm.*, 73 Penn. St. 321; *Chase v. State*, 20 N. J. L. 208; *Whitehead v. Comm.*, 19 Gratt. [Va.] 640; *Rawls v. State*, 16 Miss. 599; *Stokes v. State*, 24 id. 621; *Barney v. State*, 20 id. 68; *Miller v. State*, 33 id. 356; *State v. Williams*, 5 Port. [Ala.] 130; *Finley v. State*, 61 Ala. 201; *Scott v. State*, 63 id. 59; *Berry v. State*, id. 126; *Couch v. State*, id. 163; *State v. Connor*, 5 Blackf. [Ind.] 325; *Dutel v. State*, 4 Greene [Iowa], 125; *State v. Jennings*, 15 Rich. [S. C.] 47; *State v. Bryce*, 11 S. C. 242; *Wilbur v. State*, 21 Ark. 198; *State v. Morgan*, 20 La. Ann. 442; *State v. Jacobs*, 6 Texas, 99; *Friery v. People*, 2 Abb. Ct. App. Dec. 216; *Fitzgerald v. State*, 4 Wis. 395; *Low's Case*, 4 Me. 439; *People v. Kings*, 2 Caines, 98; *People v. Thurston*, 5 Cal. 69; *Comm v. Cherry*, 2 Va. Cas. 20; *Comm. v. St. Clair*, 1 Gratt. [Va.] 556; *State v. Griffice*, 74 N. C. 316; *U. S. v. Hammond*, 2 Wood's C. C. 197; *Barney v. State*, 20 Miss. 69; *State v. Rockafellow*, 6 N. J. L. 405; *Reich v. State*, 53 Ga. 73; *State v. Foster*, 9 Texas, 65; *Jackson v. State*, 11 id. 261; 1 Chitty's Crim. Law, 307; 2 Hawkins' P. C. 307; 2 Hale's P. C. 155; *Kill v. Brillinger*, 84 Penn. St. 276; *Williams v. Comm.*, 91 id. 493; *Patterson Gas Co. v. Brady*, 27 N. J. L. 246; *Guykowski v. State*, 2 Ill. 476; *Wilson v. State*, 42 Ind. 224; *Rogers v. State*, 33 id. 543; *Moses v. State*, 60 Ga. 138; *Hamlin v. Fletcher*, 64 id. 549; *Brazier v. State*, 44 Ala. 387; *State v. Stephens*, 11 S. C. 319; *Clark v. Saline Co.*, 9 Neb. 516; *State v. Da Rocha*, 20 La. Ann. 356; *State v. Newhouse*, 29 id. 824; Cooley's Const. Lim. [4th ed.] 227; *Taylor v. Porter*, 4 Hill, 140.) The mere claim to be a public officer, and the performance of a single or even a number of acts in that character would not constitute an individual an officer *de facto*. (*Wilcox v. Smith*, 5 Wend. 231, 234; *Lambert v. People*, 76 N. Y. 221, 237, 238; *Boardman v. Halliday*, 10 Paige, 224, 232; *Dolan v. Mayor*,

68 N. Y. 274, 281-2; *Rex* v. *Verelst*, 3 Camp. 432; *Reg.* v. *Roberts*, 38 L T. [N. S.] 690.) Grand or petit jurors are not public officers. (1 Abbott's Law Dict., 672; *Wynehamer* v. *People*, 13 N. Y. 378; *Williams* v. *Garrett*, 12 How. 456; *Kelly* v. *Bemis*, 4 Gray, 83; *People* v. *Blake*, 49 Barb. 9; *People* v. *Carter*, 29 id. 208; *Gross* v. *Rice*, 71 Me. 241. 252.) There has not been any waiver by the defendant of his legal or constitutional rights. (*McGillen* v. *State*, 16 Miss. 587, 597; *Doyle* v. *State*, 17 Ohio, 222, 225; *Cancemi* v. *People*, 18 N. Y. 129, 135, 136, 137.) The absolute rights of prisoners, especially the constitutional ones, in respect of their defense, cannot be taken away. (1 Bishop's Crim. Proc. [3d ed], §§ 113, 115, 872; Cooley's Const. Lim. [4th ed.] 331; Potter's Dwarris on Stats. 474; *McGuire* v. *People*, 2 Park. Cr. 148, 161, 162.) An objection could be taken to the grand jury on behalf of the defendant by plea in abatement or motion to quash the indictment before pleading to the merits. (*People* v. *McKay*, 18 Johns. 212; *People* v. *Allen*, 43 N. Y. 28; *Clare* v. *State*, 30 Md. 165, 176; *Low's Case*, 4 Me. 439; *State* v. *Symonds*, 36 id. 128; *State* v. *Rockafellow*, 6 N. J. L. 405; *Chase* v. *State*, 20 id. 218; *Brown* v. *Commissioners*, 73 Penn. St. 321; *Doyle* v. *State*, 17 Ohio, 222; *State* v. *Connor*, 5 Blackf. [Ind.] 325; *McGillen* v. *State*, 16 Miss. 587; *Miller* v. *State*, 33 id. 356; *State* v. *Williams*, 5 Port. [Ala.] 130; *Finley* v. *State*, 61 Ala. 201; *Scott* v. *State*, 63 id. 59; *Berry* v. *State*, id. 126; *Whitehead* v. *Commissioners*, 19 Gratt. [Va.] 640; *Commissioners* v. *Cherry*, 2 Va. Cas. 20; *Dutch* v. *State*, 4 Greene [Iowa], 125; *Reich* v. *State*, 53 Ga. 73; *State* v. *Smith*, 80 N. C. 410; *State* v. *Watson*, 86 id. 624; *State* v. *Jennings*, 15 Rich. [S. C.] 42; *State* v. *Pratt*, id. 47; *State* v. *Bryce*, 11 S. C. 342; *State* v. *Morgan*, 20 La. Ann. 442; *Wilburn* v. *State*, 21 Ark. 198; *State* v. *Jacobs*, 6 Texas, 99; *State* v. *Foster*, 9 id. 65; *Jackson* v. *State*, 11 id. 261; *U. S.* v. *Hammond*, 2 Wood's Cr. 197.) The same methods of ascertaining facts are open to the court on a motion to quash or set aside an indictment as in any other legal proceeding. (*U. S.* v. *Shepard*, 1 Abb. [U. S.] 431; *State* v. *Nutting*, 39 Me.

359 ; *State* v. *Horton*, 63 N. C. 595 ; *Gott* v. *Brigham*, 45
Mich. 428.) The appeal brings up the ·judgment-roll which
includes the bill of exceptions. (Code of Crim. Proc., §§ 485,
517, 519.)

D. Cady Herrick, district attorney, for respondent. Unless
some plain rule of law was violated, the decision refusing to
quash the indictment should be sustained, because it is a general
rule that an indictment charging the higher crimes, or which
affect the public at large, will not be summarily set aside on a
motion to quash. (*People* v. *Walters*, 5 Park. 661.) A court
will not listen to an objection made to the constitutionality of
an act by a party whose rights it does not affect, and who, therefore, has no interest in defeating it. (Cooley's Const. Lim.
163, 164; *Wellington's Petition*, 16 Pick. 87.) The manner
in which the jurors were selected is something to which the
defendant cannot take exception. (*Friery* v. *People*, 2 Keyes,
425; 2 Abb. Ct. App. Dec. 229; *Cox* v. *People*, 19 Hun, 430 ;
People v. *Harriott* 3 Park. 112 ; *Carpenter* v. *People*, 64 N.
Y. 483.) It is sufficient to maintain the authority of the
grand jury to investigate criminal charges, and find indictments
valid in their nature, that the body acted under color of lawful
authority. (*People* v. *Dolan*, 6 Hun, 232; *Dolan* v. *People*,
id. 493; 64 N. Y. 485, 492 ; *Carpenter* v. *People*, id. 483;
Thompson v. *People*, 6 Hun, 135 ; *People* v. *Jewett*, 3 Wend.
314; *Cox* v. *People*, 80 N. Y. 500–511 ; *Friery* v. *People*, 2
Keyes, 450; *Ferris* v. *People*, 31 How. 145.) The grand
jurors are public officers. (Jacob's Law Dictionary ; Tomlyn's
Law Dictionary ; 7 Bacon's Abr., Office and Officers.) The
objections to the grand jury come too late. They should have
been taken before indictment found. (*People* v. *Jewett*, 3
Wend. 314; affirmed, 6 id. 386 ; *State* v. *Hamlin*, 36 Am.
Rep. 54.) A law regulating the manner of trial is not *ex post
facto*. (*Stokes' Case*, 53 N. Y. 164.) The Code of Criminal
Procedure expressly prohibits challenge to the array. (Code of
Crim. Proc., § 238.) The objections filed to the indictment
are insufficient, because they show the organization of a grand

jury drawn from the citizens of the county. They show a
proper grand jury as defined by the Code. (Code of Crim. Proc.,
§ 223.) The papers filed in answer to the indictment should
not be considered, because this is not. a motion to set the indictment aside but a demurrer or plea to the indictment, within
the Code of Criminal Procedure. (Code of Criminal Procedure, §§ 273, 312, 321, 342.) The Code of Criminal
Procedure intended to establish a complete system, provided for proceedings on the part of the defendants, to
be taken both before and after indictment; what objections
he may take to grand and petit juries; what objections,
motions and pleas he may take and make to indictment. (*Hick-
mann* v. *Pinkney*, 81 N. Y. 211–215; *People, ex rel. Ross*, v.
City of Brooklyn, 69 id. 605.) The challenge to the petit jury
was properly overruled, both under the Code of Criminal Procedure, and also under the law as it existed prior to the Code.
(Wharton's Pleadings and Practice, § 607; Proffat on Jury
Trial, § 149; *Pringle* v. *Huse*, 1 Cow. 436, note; *Gardner* v.
Turner, 9 Johns. 261; Code of Crim. Proc., §§ 362, 375, '6, '7,
'8, '80; *People* v. *Harriott*, 3 Park. 112.) The fact that a local
law prescribes a different procedure from that in other parts of
the State does not render that law unconstitutional as violating the prisoner's constitutional right of trial by jury. (*Gardner* v. *People*, 6 Park. 155, 193; *Walter* v. *People*, 32 N. Y.
247; *Stokes* v. *People*, 53 id. 164.) The law enacted by a
legislature that cannot be amended or repealed is one that
embodies a contract. (5 McLean, 161; 28 Ind. 364; 23 id.
150; 14 Wis. 623; *Matter of Gilbert El. R. R. Co.*, 70 N.
Y. 371; *Tifft* v. *City of Buffalo*, 84 id. 204–212; *In re
Village of Middletown*, 82 id. 196–9.) Nothing but a clear
violation of the Constitution will justify the court in overriding
the legislative will. (*C. C. R. Co.* v. *Twenty-third St. R. R.
Co.*, 54 How. 180; *Matter of N. Y. El. R. R. Co.*, 3 Abb.
N. C. 413; *Ogden* v. *Saunders*, 12 Whart. 270; *Matter of
N. Y. El. R. R. Co.*, 70 N. Y. 356.) Every intendment and
presumption is in favor of the constitutionality of legislative
enactments. (*Kerrigan* v. *Force*, 9 Hun, 190; *C. C. R. Co.*

v. *Twenty-third St. R. R. Co.*, 54 How. 180 ; *Leavitt* v. *Blatch-ford*, 17 N. Y. 549 ; *Matter of N. Y. El. R. R. Co.*, 3 Abb. N. C. 413 ; *S. C.*, 70 N. Y. 342, 343.) Proof cannot be given to show that the act or amendment in question was not reported by the commissioners. (*People* v. *Devlin*, 33 N. Y. 279, 283 ; *Matter of N. Y. El. R. R. Co.*, 70 id. 351.)

ANDREWS, J. The defendant was indicted at the September term of the Albany County Sessions, 1881, for the crime of grand larceny, committed on the 2d day of August, 1881. He was arraigned at the March term, 1882, and on his arraignment filed a special plea, setting forth in substance, that the grand jury which found the indictment, was not a legal grand jury, for the reason that it was not drawn from any list of grand jurors selected by the supervisors of Albany county, but from a list of petit jurors, pursuant to chapter 532 of the Laws of 1881, which act is alleged in the plea to be unconstitutional, in that it is a local act for selecting and drawing grand juries in the city and county of Albany, and was not reported to the legislature by commissioners appointed to revise the statutes, and was passed in contravention of article 3, section 18, of the Constitution adopted in 1874, which forbids the passing by the legislature of a private or local bill in certain enumerated cases, and among others for " selecting, drawing, summoning or impaneling grand or petit jurors." The defendant accompanied his plea with an offer to prove the facts stated in the plea, and especially to prove by the clerk of the senate, by the commissioners appointed to revise the statutes, by the journal of the legislature of 1881, and by the original act itself, that the act was not reported to the legislature by any commissioner or commissioners appointed to revise the statutes. The court overruled the plea and offer of proof, and the defendant's counsel thereupon moved the court to set aside the indictment upon the grounds set forth in the special plea, and offered to prove the facts as before, which motion was denied, and this was followed by a motion to quash the indictment upon the same grounds, and upon the offer of the same proof, which motion was also denied. The defendant thereupon interposed the plea of not guilty, and a jury was ordered to be impaneled to try the issue. The defendant's counsel thereupon objected to the panel of petit jurors on the ground of the unconstitutionality of the act of 1881, under which the list of petit jurors was selected, and offered to substantiate the facts, hereinbefore stated, by proof. The court overruled the objection, and a jury was impaneled and the trial proceeded, and resulted in the conviction of the defendant of the crime charged in the indictment.

It will contribute to a clear understanding of the question raised in respect to the constitutionality of the act of 1881, to have in view the laws in force at the time of the passage of that act, regulating the selection of grand and petit jurors in the county of Albany. Prior to the act of 1881, grand jurors, in the county of Albany, were selected under the general provisions of the Revised Statutes. The list was prepared by the supervisors of the county (2 R. S. 720, § 1 *et seq.*), and was returned by them to the county clerk, who placed the names in a box, from which from time to time, prior to the terms of the courts, the names of twenty-four persons were drawn to serve as grand jurors. The petit jury list was also made up in accordance with the system prescribed by the general statutes for the selection of petit jurors in the counties of the State, with a single exception, viz.: the selection of persons in the city of Albany to serve as petit jurors, instead of being made by the supervisors, assessors and town clerk, as provided in the case of towns, was made by the supervisor and assessors of the respective wards each ward being for that purpose considered as a town. This method of selecting petit jurors in the city of Albany was first prescribed by the Revised Statutes (2 R. S. 413, § 23), and the provisions of the Revised Statutes upon that subject, as to the city of Albany, were incorporated into the Code of Civil Procedure passed in 1876, in the article relating to the mode of selecting, etc., trial jurors, as section 1041. The next legislation on the subject of grand and petit jurors in Albany county, was chapter 532, Laws of 1881, which is the act now in question. That act purported to amend section

1041 of the Code of Civil Procedure, by inserting therein the following provisions : " In the city of Albany, the recorder of said city shall perform the duties imposed by this title upon the supervisor, town clerk and assessors of towns.   In Albany county, grand jurors shall hereafter be drawn from the box containing the names of petit jurors selected for said county, in the same manner as petit jurors, and hereafter no separate list of grand jurors shall be prepared for said county."

This act, if valid, effected an entire change in the system of selecting grand jurors in Albany county.   It abrogated the provisions of the Revised Statutes, imposing upon the supervisors of the county the duty of preparing a list of grand jurors, and made the petit jury list *pro hac vice*, the grand jury list also. Thereafter there was to be neither a separate grand jury list, nor a separate box containing the names of persons selected as grand jurors.   The change, in respect to the selection of petit jurors, made by the act of 1881, was much less radical, and consisted, simply, in the substitution of the recorder of the city of Albany in place of the supervisors and assessors of the wards, to discharge the duty of preparing the jury lists in that city.

The act of 1881, so far as it relates to the selection and drawing of grand jurors for the city and county of Albany, is a local act upon that subject, and is within the prohibition of article 3, section 18 of the Constitution, unless excepted therefrom by force of section 25 of the same article.   That section is as follows : " Section 25.   Sections 17 and 18 of this article shall not apply to any bill, or the amendments of any bill which shall be reported to the legislature by commissioners appointed pursuant to law to revise the statutes."   It is a part of the legislative history of the State, that prior to the adoption of the constitutional amendments of 1874, commissioners to revise the statutes had been appointed by the legislature, who had from time to time made reports of their proceedings to that body, and when the constitutional amendments were adopted, they had not completed their labors, but were still engaged in the work of the revision.   The plain object of section 25, article 3, which was one of the amendments adopted in

1874, was to exempt from the operation of section 18, private or local bills which had been, or should be reported by the commissioners. But with the exception of bills originating with the commissioners, and reported by them to the legislature, the prohibition of section 18 is absolute. The language of the section needs no interpretation. Construed in connection with section 25, it forbids the enactment of any private or local law by the legislature in the cases enumerated therein, and not falling within the exception in section 25. The legislative power vested in the senate and assembly, is subject to the limitations of the Constitution, and it needs no citation of authorities to show that the legislature, like every other department of the government, is subject to the supreme will of the people, as expressed in the organic law. If the proof offered by the defendant in support of his plea, was admissible, and the facts offered to be proved, were established, there can be no doubt that the part of the act of 1881, relating to the selection and drawing of grand jurors in Albany county, is unconstitutional. The intention of the act was to take Albany county out of the operation of the general statutes of the State, relating to the selection and drawing of grand jurors, and to substitute for that county a special system, applicable to that county alone. But it is insisted by the counsel for the people that the unconstitutionality of the act, cannot be established by proof *aliunde* that the act was not reported to the legislature by commissioners. We have no doubt that the presumption in favor of the constitutionality of statutes, applies in this case, and that in the absence of proof to the contrary, it will be presumed in support of the constitutionality of the act of 1881, that it originated in a bill reported by commissioners. But the question whether a statute is constitutional, is in its nature a judicial one. The question most frequently arises upon the face of the statute itself, and the question of constitutionality is determined by comparing the statute with the Constitution. But it often depends upon extrinsic facts, not appearing upon the statute book. In cases involving the constitutionality of what are known as two-third bills, it has been held that the court may go behind the statute book, and look at the original bill, to ascertain whether it was passed by the constitutional majority. (*People* v. *Purdy*, 2 Hill, 31; *S. C.*, 4 id. 384). The case here is of the same nature, but arises upon a different limitation of legislative power. The proof offered did not contradict any fact asserted on the face of the statute, nor so far as appears in any legislative record. On the contrary, the offer was to show by the journal of the legislature and by the original act, the facts averred in the plea. The Constitution would afford very slight protection against legislative usurpation, and the object sought to be accomplished by the amendment in question, could be easily frustrated, if the mere fact that the legislature had passed a local or private bill in one of the enumerated cases, created a conclusive presumption that the bill was originally reported by commissioners, and was within the exception of section 25. The tendency of judicial authority, supports the proposition that whenever a question arises as to the constitutionality of a statute, the court may resort to any source of information which in its nature is original evidence of any fact relevant to the inquiry. (*Purdy* v. *The People*, 4 Hill, 384; *Gardner* v. *The Collector*, 6 Wall. 499; *Post* v. *Supervisors*, 105 U. S. 667; *Berry* v. *Baltimore, etc., R. Co.*, 41 Md. 446; 20 Am. Rep. 69; *Opinion of Justices*, 52 N. H. 622.) This rule excludes all inquiry as to the motives of the legislature in passing the particular statute. Such an inquiry is wholly irrelevant, the only inquiry permitted being whether the enactment, the constitutionality of which is assailed, is forbidden by the Constitution. We think the offer to prove by the journal of the legislature and by the original act, that the act of 1881 was not reported by commissioners, was improperly overruled, and as the fact alleged must be deemed on this appeal to have been proved, the conclusion that the act so far as it relates to the selection and drawing of grand jurors, is unconstitutional, cannot be avoided.

The question of the constitutionality of the act of 1881, so far as it relates to the selection of petit jurors, depends upon different considerations. When the act of 1881 was passed,

there was a local act then in existence, regulating the selection
of petit jurors in Albany county.   By the existing law, which
was enacted first by the Revised Statutes, and re-enacted by
the Code of Civil Procedure in 1876, the selection of petit
jurors in the city of Albany, was committed to the supervisors
and assessors of the respective wards of the city.   The only
change made by the act of 1881, as has been said, was to make
the recorder the selecting officer, in place of the supervisors
and assessors.   There can be no doubt that the act of 1881, by
which this change was wrought, was a local law.   The point to
be determined is whether it was a local law for the selection of
petit jurors, within the sense and meaning of article 3, section 18,
of the Constitution.   It seems quite plain that the amendment
of an existing local law regulating the selection of petit jurors,
which simply transferred the power to select the petit jurors
within the city, from one local officer or set of officers to another local officer, is not within the mischief at which the constitutional amendment was aimed.   By the existing local
law the city of Albany was taken out of the general plan.
The legislature by the act of 1881, left this law in force,
changing it only in the respect mentioned.   The qualifications
of petit jurors were prescribed by the Revised Statutes, and
the provisions of the Revised Statutes upon the subject, were
substantially re-enacted in the Code in 1876 (2 Rev. Stat. 411,
§ 13; Code Civ. Pro., § 1027).   It was made the duty of the selecting officers to select from the last assessment-roll of the
town (or city) and to make a list of the names of all persons
whom they believed to possess the qualifications prescribed by
the general statute. (Code Civil Pro., § 1036.)   This duty was
in the main ministerial, and in the city of Albany, prior to the
act of 1881, was devolved upon the supervisors and assessors of
the ward, and by that act, on the recorder.   We think it would be
too strict a construction of the constitutional provision, to hold
that no existing local law upon one of the subjects mentioned in
article 3, section 18, of the Constitution, can be amended in any
detail, without violating the Constitution.   This question was
considered to some extent by this court in the *Matter of N. Y.*

El. R. R. Co. (70 N. Y. 327) : *Matter of Gilbert El. Ry. Co.* (id. 361). In the case first referred to, EARL, J., referring to the section of the Constitution now in question, said : " These constitutional provisions do not prohibit a private or local bill to amend the charter of private corporations, by regulating powers, rights, privileges, and franchises which it previously possessed." And in the case last cited, CHURCH, Ch. J., referring to the same provisions, said : " They must be sustained and applied by a rational and practical construction, so as to subserve the purposes intended, and prevent the evils designed to be remedied, but not by an artificial and technical construction, to extend their application to cases never contemplated." It is a plain proposition, recognized in the cases referred to, and in the subsequent case, *In re Brooklyn, etc., R. R. Co.* (75 N. Y. 335), that the legislature cannot, under the guise of an amendment of a private and local bill, make a new and original enactment in evasion of the constitutional prohibition. The act of 1881 in reference to petit jurors, is not, we think, within this principle. It did not inaugurate a local system for the selection of petit jurors in the city of Albany, but, as we have said, continued an existing one, changing it in one of its details. Special laws have been passed, and are now in force, regulating the selection of jurors in the counties of New York and Kings. These laws extend to great detail, and contain many special provisions. It would be a dangerous construction of the constitutional provision which would prohibit any alteration in those and like statutes, and place it beyond the power of the legislature to amend any of their provisions. The question before us is not free from difficulty, but our conclusion is that a reasonable and practical construction of the Constitution upholds the act of 1881 in respect to the substitution of the recorder in place of the supervisors and assessors, to discharge the duty of preparing the petit jury lists, and that this conclusion fairly rests on the ground that the act is not in a proper sense an act for the selection of petit jurors, but an amendment of an existing local law on the subject, not within the purview of the constitutional prohibition.

The next question which arises is whether the arraignment and trial of the defendant upon the indictment in question, was a violation of the constitutional guaranty that no person shall be held to answer for a capital, or otherwise infamous crime (except in certain cases mentioned, not material to the present inquiry), "unless on presentment or indictment of a grand jury." (Const., art 1, § 6.) It is insisted on the part of the defendant that the body of men which found the indictment in question, was not a grand jury, that the paper filed as an indictment was not an indictment, and that the defendant could not be held to answer thereto, or be put upon his trial thereon. In considering this question, it will be convenient in the first place, to recall the actual facts. The objection to the constitution of the grand jury which found the indictment, lies solely in the fact that they were drawn, under the provisions of a void statute, from the petit jury list, whereas they should have been drawn from a list of grand jurors, specially selected to serve as such by the supervisors of Albany county. In all other respects the proceedings were regular. The jurors were drawn by the proper officer, they were regularly summoned and retained by the sheriff, they were recognized, impaneled and sworn as grand jurors by the court, and as grand jurors they found the indictment; and moreover they were good and lawful men, duly qualified to sit as grand jurors. None of these facts are negatived by the plea, and they must be assumed in determining the question before us.

The principle that no person shall be put upon trial for an infamous crime unless on presentment or indictment of a grand jury, has been regarded as one of the securities of civil liberty, and is embodied among the fundamental provisions of the Federal and State Constitutions. The institution of the grand jury has been said by high authority to be one of the barriers between the liberties of the people and the prerogatives of the crown. (4 Bl. Com. 349.) The interposition of a body of competent citizens charged to inquire of offenses between the individual and the State, and the finding of a formal accusation upon such inquiry, before he can be put upon his trial for an infamous crime, forms the substance of the right guaranteed by the law of England and by the Constitution of the State. But the Constitution does not define what shall constitute a grand jury. It refers to the grand jury as an existing institution, and its essential character must be found by reference to the common law, from which it has been derived. By the common law a grand jury must consist of not less than twelve, or more than twenty-three, and twelve must concur in finding an indictment; and they must be good and lawful men of the county. (Hawk. P. C., vol. 2, chap. 25, § 16; Chitty's Crim. Law, vol. 1, p. 307.) The Constitution does not define the mode of selection, and it has never been supposed that the States in adopting the common-law institution of the grand jury, adopted the mode of selection which prevailed in England. In England grand jurors were formerly selected by the sheriffs (2 Hawk. P. C., chap. 25, § 16), but in this State the sheriff is the summoning and returning officer, and has no part in the selection or preparation of the jury lists; and it is doubtless competent for the legislature to enact such regulations and make such changes respecting the mode of selecting and procuring grand jurors, as it may deem expedient, not trenching, however, upon the essential feature of the system. (*Stokes* v. *People*, 53 N. Y. 164; 13 Am. Rep. 492.)

We are of opinion that no constitutional right of the defendant was invaded by holding him to answer to the indictment. The grand jury, although not selected in pursuance of a valid law, were selected under color of law and semblance of legal authority. The defendant, in fact, enjoyed all the protection which he would have had if the jurors had been selected and drawn pursuant to the general statutes. Nothing could well be more unsubstantial than the alleged right asserted by the defendant under the circumstances of the case. He was entitled to have an indictment found by a grand jury before being put upon his trial. An indictment was found by a body, drawn, summoned and sworn as a grand jury, before a competent court and composed of good and lawful men. This we think fulfilled the constitutional guaranty. The jury which

found the indictment was a *de facto* jury selected and organized
under the forms of law. The defect in its constitution, owing
to the invalidity of the law of 1881, affected no substantial
right of the defendant. We confine our decision upon this
point to the case presented by this record, and hold that an indictment found by a jury of good and lawful men selected and
drawn as a grand jury under color of law, and recognized by
the court and sworn as a grand jury, is a good indictment by a
grand jury within the sense of the Constitution, although the
law under which the selection was made, is void. It will be
time to consider the extreme cases suggested by counsel when
occasion shall arise.

The remaining question relates to the right of the defendant to
avail himself by plea, or objection in other form, of the defect
in the proceedings in selecting or drawing the grand jury which
found the indictment. If the defect in the constitution of the
tribunal, deprived it of the character of a grand jury in a constitutional sense, there can be no doubt that the court would
have been bound to take notice of it, although no statute authorized it, or even if the statute assumed to preclude the raising of the objection. But when the defect is not of that
character and the defendant may be held to answer the indictment without invading any constitutional right, then the question is one of procedure merely, and the right of the defendant
to avail himself of the objection is subject to the regulation
and control of the legislature. In times past, courts have been
inclined to go very far in sustaining technical objections in
criminal cases, but there is much less reason for this now than
formerly, when comparatively trivial offenses were punished
with the greatest severity. The indictment in question was
found after the Code of Criminal Procedure was enacted and
took effect, and the proceedings are governed by its provisions.
We are of opinion that under the provisions of the Code the
court was justified in refusing to entertain the objections made.
Section 328 prohibits any challenge to the panel or array of
grand jurors, but the court is authorized in its discretion, for
certain causes stated, to discharge the panel and order another

to be summoned. Section 329 provides for challenges to individual jurors. Both of these sections relate to proceedings to be taken before indictment and are irrelevant to the present inquiry. Section 312 provides that in answer to an indictment the defendant may either move the court to set the same aside or may demur or plead thereto. The causes for which the defendant may move to have the indictment set aside are defined in section 313. Section 321 declares that the only pleading on the part of the defendant is a demurrer or plea; and section 332 declares that pleas are of three kinds: (1) guilty; (2) not guilty; (3) a former judgment of conviction or acquittal.

The paper filed by the defendant was not a plea authorized by the section last mentioned and the motion to quash or set aside the indictment is not for any cause embraced in section 313. The Code by defining the causes for which the indictment may be set aside, must by the general rule of construction, be held to exclude the entertaining of the motion for other causes than those specified. The intention of the Code was to discourage technical defenses to indictments not affecting the merits as is apparent from the sections cited as well as the provisions relating to amendments and the proceedings on the trial. (Code of Crim. Pro., §§ 293, 362.) This general purpose is more directly indicated by section 285, which declares "that no indictment is insufficient, nor can the trial, judgment or other proceedings be affected by reason of an imperfection, in matter of form, which does not tend to the prejudice of the substantial rights of the defendant upon the merits."

We think the objection to the grand jury was not one which, by the new procedure, the defendant could take after indictment, and, as it involved no constitutional right, that it was properly overruled.

These reasons lead to an affirmance of the judgment.

All concur.

Judgment affirmed.

THE PEOPLE OF THE STATE OF NEW YORK, Appellant, *v.*
CONSTANTINE FABER, Respondent.

For the purpose of enforcing the statutory provision (2 R. S. 146, § 49) prohibiting one who has been divorced, on account of his or her adultery,
from marrying again "until the death of the complainant," and under
the provision of the statute in reference to bigamy (2 R. S. 687, § 8),
which declares that "every person having a husband or wife living"
who shall marry again shall, except in the cases specified, be adjudged
guilty of bigamy, a person against whom a divorce has been obtained
because of adultery is regarded as having a husband or wife living, so long
as the party obtaining the divorce lives.
A person, therefore, so divorced who marries again, in this State, in violation of said prohibitory provision, is guilty of the crime of bigamy.
People v. *Hovey* (5 Barb. 117), overruled.
People v. *Faber* (Mem. 29 Hun, 320), reversed.

(Submitted March 5, 1883; decided April 17, 1883.)

APPEAL from judgment of the General Term of the Supreme
Court, in the first judicial department, made February 2, 1883,
which reversed a judgment of the Court of General Sessions
in and for the city and county of New York, entered upon a
verdict convicting the defendant of the crime of bigamy.
(Mem. of decision below, 29 Hun, 320.)

It appeared that defendant was married in 1878. In 1881,
in an action of divorce brought by his wife, a judgment was
rendered dissolving the marriage on the ground of his adultery,
and afterward, during the life of the plaintiff in that action,
he married another woman in this State.

John McKeon, district attorney, for appellant. The defendant, under the law and upon the facts, was guilty of the crime
of bigamy. (Wharton's Law Dictionary, 93; R. S., art. 1,
tit. 1, chap. 8, part 2, § 5; id., art. 2, tit. 5, chap. 1, part 4,
§§ 8, 9; *Fleming* v. *People*, 27 N. Y. 335; *Baker* v. *People*,
2 Hill, 325; *Van Voorhis* v. *Brintnall*, 86 N. Y. 29; *Wait*
v. *Wait*, 4 id. 95.)

William F. Kintzing and *George L. Simonson* for respondent. The conceded facts in the case did not justify a conviction of the appellant of the crime of bigamy. (Shelford on Marriage and Divorce, 1; 2 Edm. R. S. [2d ed.], § 1, p. 144; § 8, p. 709; *People* v. *Hovey*, 5 Barb. 118; *Comm.* v. *Putnam*, 1 Pick. 136; *Porford* v. *Johnson*, 2 Blatchf. 59; *Dickson* v. *Dickson*, 1 Yerg. 110; 1 Revised Laws, 113; 1 Hale's P. C. 691; *King* v. *Burrell*, 12 A. & E. 468; *Lammont* v. *Eiffe*, 3 Q. B. 910; *Everett* and *Wales Case*, 2 Scott N. C. 531; *Rex* v. *Skone*, 6 East, 518; *Mora* v. *Newman*, 6 Bing. 567.)

RAPALLO, J. The question in this case is whether contract- ing a marriage in this State, in violation of section 49 of the act concerning divorces (2 R. S. 146), constitutes the crime of bigamy, as defined in 2 Revised Statutes, 687, sections 8 and 9, or is punishable only as a misdemeanor.

The provisions of the Revised Statutes bearing upon the question are as follows :

Article 1 of title 1, chapter 8, part 2, relating to marriages, provides, section 5 : " No second or other subsequent marriage shall be contracted by any person during the life-time of any former husband or wife of such person, unless (1) the marriage with such former husband or wife shall have been annulled or dissolved for some cause other than the adultery of the accused." (2 R. S. 139.)

Article 3 of the same title, concerning divorces (2 R. S. 144) provides (§ 38): " Divorces may be decreed and marriages may be dissolved by the Court of Chancery whenever adultery has been committed by any husband or wife." Section 49: " Whenever a marriage shall be dissolved pursuant to the pro- visions of this article the complainant may marry again during the life-time of the defendant, but no defendant, convicted of adultery, shall marry again until the death of the complain- ant."

Article 2 of title 5, chapter 1 of part 4 of the Revised Stat- utes, entitled " Of unlawful marriages and of incest " (2 R. S. 687), provides (§ 8): " Every person having a husband or

wife living, who shall marry any other person, whether married or single, shall, except in the cases specified in the next
section, be adjudged guilty of bigamy; and upon conviction
shall be punished by imprisonment in the State prison for a
term not exceeding five years."

Section 9: " The last section shall not extend to the following persons or cases:"

Then follow six subdivisions, the third of which is: " 3. To
any person by reason of any former marriage which shall have
been dissolved by the decree of a competent court for some
cause other than the adultery of such person."

Reading all these provisions together, the conclusion seems
irresistible that the intent of the statute was that section 8
should extend to a divorced person who did not come within
the exception. The language clearly implies that, notwithstanding the divorce, such a person is placed in the situation
of having a husband or wife living for the purposes of the
eighth section.

The third subdivision imports into the statute for the punishment of bigamy almost the identical language which is employed in 2 Revised Statutes, 139, § 5, subd. 1, which prohibits and declares unlawful certain marriages, the only difference
being that in 2 Revised Statutes, 139, a husband or wife of
the first marriage, who has obtained a divorce, is spoken of as
the former husband or wife, and in subdivision 3 of section 8
the prior marriage is spoken of as the former marriage, but the
intent is clear that the prohibition contained in the statutes
concerning marriages and divorces shall be incorporated into
the statutes punishing bigamy. The language of the latter act,
where the sections are connected, is that every person having
a husband or wife living, who shall marry, etc., shall be guilty
of bigamy, except where the former marriage has been dissolved for some cause other than the adultery of the person
contracting the subsequent marriage. There could scarcely be
a plainer implication that for the purpose of enforcing the
statutory prohibition, a person against whom a divorce has
been obtained for that cause is regarded, by the statute, as

having a husband or wife living so long as the party obtaining the divorce lives.

The judgment of the General Term in this case was based upon the case of *People* v. *Hovey* (5 Barb. 117), which was decided in 1849 by the General Term of the Supreme Court in the seventh district. In that case it was held that a violation of the prohibition against marriage of the guilty party, contained in the Divorce Act, did not constitute bigamy, and the reasons assigned for that conclusion were, that the divorce dissolved the former marriage, and after such dissolution neither party could have a husband or wife living. That consequently such a case was not included in the eighth section, and the provisions of that section could not be enlarged by the exception contained in the third subdivision of the ninth section.

This criticism on the language of the section cannot, in our judgment, overcome the clear and unmistakable intent apparent on the face of the provisions when read together. The declaration that the eighth section shall not extend to a person by reason of a former marriage which has been dissolved by the decree of a competent court for some cause other than the adultery of such person, clearly assumes that it does extend to a person whose former marriage has been dissolved for his or her adultery. If not, the third subdivision of section 9 is wholly without meaning or operation.

The same argument which was used in *People* v. *Hovey* was subsequently sought to be employed in the case of *Wait* v. *Wait* (4 N. Y. 95). In that case the plaintiff claimed dower in lands left by a husband from whom she had obtained a divorce *a vinculo* on the ground of his adultery. There is no express provision of the statute, declaring a widow entitled to dower under such circumstances, but the right of dower is not taken away, and its continuance is impliedly recognized in section 48 of the Divorce Act (2 R. S. 146), which provides that a wife convicted of adultery in a suit for a divorce brought by her husband shall not be entitled to dower in her husband's real estate. In the case cited it was argued by Mr. Hill that the right to dower could only be acquired by the death of the husband; that only a widow had a dowable capacity and that she must have such capacity at the time of his death; that she could be endowed of lands of her deceased husband only; that she must survive her husband, and that she must be a wife at the time of his decease or she cannot be his widow; that the marriage being dissolved she ceased to be his wife and could not be his widow. But this criticism on language was not suffered to prevail, and it was held that although the term "widow" might not be the most appropriate term to employ under these circumstances, yet it was sufficient to designate the person entitled to dower, and the conclusion was that the divorced wife was entitled to the benefit of the statute which awards dower to the widow. A reference to section 48 of the Divorce Act (2 R. S. 146) is also instructive as showing that for some purposes the legislature apply the terms "husband" and "wife" to parties between whom a decree of divorce *a vinculo* has been pronounced. The language of section 48 is, "a wife," being a defendant in a suit for a divorce brought by her husband, and "convicted" of adultery, shall not be entitled to dower in "her husband's" real estate. The terms "husband" and "wife" are thus applied to the parties after the judgment of divorce has been rendered, without the addition of the term "former," or any other term indicating that the parties had ceased to answer the description of husband and wife.

A reference to the history of our statute against bigamy shows very conclusively that its framers intended it to apply to a case like the present one. The first act on the subject was passed February 7, 1788, and was re-enacted in 1 Revised Laws, 113, as follows:

"That if any person or persons being married, or who hereafter shall marry, do at any time marry any person or persons, the former husband or wife being alive, then any such person shall be guilty of a felony. * * * But neither this act, nor any thing therein contained, shall extend to any person or persons. * * * " Then follow five specifications, the third of which is: "Nor to any person or persons who are, or shall be at the time of such marriage, divorced by the sentence or decree of any court having cognizance thereof."

In framing the provisions of the Revised Statutes it is stated by the revisers in their original note to section 8 (the statute against bigamy), that it was the same as 1 Revised Laws, 113, varied by inserting "whether married or single," to reach cases not supposed to be within the act, and the note to section 9 states that the first five subdivisions are founded upon 1 Revised Laws, 113, the third being qualified according to 2 Revised Laws, 198, section 4. Section 4 here referred to is contained in the divorce law of 1813, and is the provision that it shall not be lawful for the defendant, who may be convicted of adultery, to marry again until the complainant shall be actually dead. It cannot be doubted that the intention of the revisers was to bring a violation of this prohibition within the statute against bigamy.

The new Penal Code, adopted in 1881, re-enacts the statute in the same language as in the Revised Statutes, except that it has added to the third subdivision of section 9 a further exception in favor of a divorced party who has obtained permission from the court to marry again, pursuant to the act authorizing such permission to be given.

Upon the theory of the respondent all these elaborate provisions are senseless and without any effect whatever.

The utility of the prohibition of such marriages it is not for us to discuss here. So long as it stands upon the statute book we are bound to give it force in the manner prescribed by the legislature, when the violation of it is committed within this State.

The judgment appealed from should be reversed, and that of the Court of General Sessions affirmed and the proceedings remitted.

All concur, except ANDREWS, J., who dissents on the ground that the construction of the statute on bigamy by the General Term in *People* v. *Hovey* (5 Barb. 117) has never been reversed or questioned in any judicial decision until now, and EARL, J., who dissents generally.

Judgment reversed.

09 445

119 516

129 390

ELLEN BERTLES, Respondent, *v.* JAMES NUNAN, Appellant.

-354.

266.

21.

311.

4

152

310

52

38

Under a conveyance to a husband and wife jointly, they take, not as tenants in common or as joint tenants, but as tenants by the entirety, and upon the death of either, the survivor takes the whole estate.

This common-law doctrine has not been abrogated by the statutory provisions (§ 3, chap. 200, Laws of 1848, amended by chap. 375, Laws of 1849; §§ 1, 2, chap. 90, Laws of 1860, amended by chap. 172, Laws of 1862), enabling a wife to acquire and hold a separate estate and to sell and convey the same. (DANFORTH and FINCH, JJ., dissenting.)

As to whether those provisions apply to lands so conveyed, *quære.*

So also as to whether the husband still retains the common-law right of control and use of lands so conveyed, during the joint lives.

Feely v. *Buckley* (28 Hun, 451), overruled.

(Argued March 8, 1883; decided April 17, 1883.)

APPEAL from judgment of the General Term of the Supreme Court, in the fourth judicial department, in favor of plaintiff, entered upon an order directing such judgment, made March 22, 1882, upon a case submitted under section 1279 of the Code of Civil Procedure.

The facts stated were substantially these: In 1868, Nelson K. Hopkins executed a deed to "Cornelius Day and Hannah Day, his wife * * * their heirs and assigns," of certain premises situate in the city of Buffalo. In August, 1877, Cornelius Day died leaving his wife surviving him, and after his death, up to her own death, she had the possession of the whole of said premises. She died intestate in April, 1879, and in proceedings instituted by plaintiff, her administratrix, and who was her sole heir at law, an order was made by the surrogate directing the sale of the premises. Upon such sale defendant became the purchaser, but he refused to complete the purchase on the ground that said Hannah Day was never seized of more than an undivided half interest, and, therefore, that plaintiff could not convey a good title. The question submitted was as to whether this objection was tenable.

Spencer Clinton for appellant. A deed of land to husband

and wife conveys it to them as tenants in common. (Laws of 1849, chap. 375; Laws of 1860, chap. 90, amended by Laws of 1862, chap. 172; 3 R. S., part 1, chap. 1, title 2, art. 2, § 74 [7th ed.], p. 2179; *F. & M. B'k* v. *Gregory*, 49 Barb. 155; *Barber* v. *Harris*, 15 Wend. 615.) There is no inherent disability in a wife to hold land in common with her husband. (*Moore* v. *Moore*, 47 N. Y. 467.) The husband, by the marriage contract, acquires no vested rights in the future acquisitions of the wife, and the legislature can change them at will. (*Sleight* v. *Reed*, 18 Barb. 159–164; *Blood* v. *Humphrey*, 17 id. 660.)

Tracy C. Becker for respondent.   At common law, husband and wife were considered as one person, and when land was conveyed to them as such, they held not as joint tenants but each being seized of the whole *per tout et non per my*, so that the survivor takes the whole, not by survivorship but by virtue of the original estate. (*Stuckey* v. *Keefe's Ex'rs*, 26 Penn. St. 397–9; 1 Dana, 244; 7 Yerger, 319; 4 Kent's Com. 362; 2 Blackst. Com. 182; *Jackson* v. *Stevens*, 16 Johns. 110, 115; *Rogers* v. *Benson*, 3 Johns. Ch. 431, 437; *Barber* v. *Harris*, 15 Wend. 615–617; *Jackson* v. *McConnell*, 19 id. 175, 177; *Burn & Dias* v. *Glover*, 1 Hoff. Ch. 76–77; *Doe* v. *Howland*, 8 Cow. 283; *Torry* v. *Torry*, 14 N. Y. 430; *Den* v. *Hardenburgh*, 5 Halst. [N. J.] 42; *Shaw* v. *Hearsay*, 5 Mass. 521; *Whales* v. *Coffin*, 23 id. 215; *Thornton* v. *Thornton*, 3 Rand. [Va.] 179; *Ames* v. *Norman*, 4 Sneed [Tenn.], 683; *Rogers* v. *Grider*, 1 Dana [Ky.], 94; *Cochran* v. *Kerney*, 9 Bush [Ky.], 199; *Gibson* v. *Zimmerman*, 12 Mo. 385; *Fairchild* v. *Chastellux*, 1 Barr. [Penn.] 176; *Johnson* v. *Hart*, 6 W. & S. [Penn.] 319; *Ketchum* v. *Wadsworth*, 5 Wis. 102; *Brownson* v. *Hall*, 16 Vt. 309; *Fisher* v. *Provin*, 25 Mich. 347–351; *Davis* v. *Clark*, 26 Ind. 428; *McDuff* v. *Beauchamp*, 50 Miss. 531; *Greenlaw* v. *Greenlaw*, 13 Me. 182–186; 1 Washburn on Real Property, 278.) By virtue of her relation as wife, in case of a conveyance to a wife and husband, naming them as such, the wife gained a greater right in the property thus conveyed than if conveyed to her alone during coverture, for by the common law a wife's property was liable for her husband's debts. (Schouler's Dom. Rel. 134; 2 Kent's Com. 134; *Miller* v. *Williams*, 1 P. Wms. 258; *Carterer* v. *Paschal*, 3 id. 351, *a ; Roberts* v. *Palgrean*, 1 H. Bl. 535; 1 Bright on Husband and Wife, 98; *Grute* v. *Lowcroft*, Cro. Eliz. 287; *Jackson* v. *McConnell*, 19 Wend. 175; Co. Inst. 351 *a ;* 4 Blackst. Com. 387; *Steed* v. *Cragh*, 9 Mod. 43; 2 Blackst. Com. 421; Co. Litt. 351; 2 Kent's Com. 133; *Jacques* v. *Meth. Ep. Ch.*, 1 Johns. Ch. 450; *S. C. on appeal*, 17 Johns. 548; Roper on Husband and Wife, 182; 2 Story's Eq., § 1392; *Yale* v. *Dederer*, 18 N. Y. 265, 270.) When land was conveyed to husband and wife together, neither could bind the other, and if the wife survived, she took the whole whether any children were born of the marriage, and irrespective of any deed or will or other alienation made by the husband during his lifetime. (*Stuckey* v. *Keefe's Ex'rs*, 26 Penn. St. 401; *Rogers* v. *Benson*, 3 Johns. Ch. 437; *Jackson* v. *Stevens*, 16 Johns. 15; *Den* v. *Hardenburgh*, 5 Halst. 42; *Shaw* v. *Hearsay*, 5 Mass. 521.) As the act of 1848 (Chap. 200), as amended, gave married women only such rights as they would have if unmarried, and an unmarried woman could not convey to her husband or take lands with him, she having no husband, a married woman could not convey to her husband nor hold lands as tenant in common with him. (*White* v. *Wager*, 25 N. Y. 333; *Winans* v. *Peebles*, 32 id. 423; *Goelet* v. *Gori*, 31 Barb. 314; *Meeker* v. *Wright*, 76 N. Y. 267, 271; *Power* v. *Lester*, 17 How. Pr. 413; *S. C. on appeal*, 23 N. Y. 529; *F. & M. B'k* v. *Gregory*, 49 Barb. 162; *Miller* v. *Miller*, 9 Abb. Pr. [N. S.] 444; *Beach* v. *Hollister*, 3 Hun, 519; *Freeman* v. *Barber*, 3 T. & C. 574; *Bates* v. *Seely*, 46 Penn. St. 248; *French* v. *Mehan*, 56 id. 289; *Diver* v. *Diver*, id. 106; *Fisher* v. *Provin*, 25 Mich. 350; *Davis* v. *Clark*, 26 Ind. 428; *McDuff* v. *Beauchamp*, 50 Miss. 531; *Washburn* v. *Burns*, 34 N. J. 18; *Chandler* v. *Cheney*, 37 Ind. 401; *Hulet* v. *Inlow*, 57 id. 412–414; *Marburgh* v. *Cole*, 49 Md. 402.) Conceding that the act of 1862, or even the act of 1848, as amended in 1849, was broad enough to destroy the common-law doctrine of estates conveyed to husbands and wives, those acts cannot affect marriages contracted before their passage. They are not retroactive. (*Hatfield* v. *Snedon*, 54 N. Y. 280, 287; *Burke* v. *Valentine*, 52 Barb. 412; *S. C.*, 4 Abb. Pr. [N. S.] 164; affirmed by Court of Appeals, 6 Alb. L. J. 167; *Hurd* v. *Cass*, 9 Barb. 366; *Clark* v. *Clark*, 24 id. 581; *Lansing* v. *Gulick*, 26 How. Pr. 250; *Jaycox* v. *Collins*, id. 496; *Ex parte Winne*, 2 Lans. 21; reversing *S. C.*, 1 id. 508, and overruling *Billings* v. *Baker*, 28 Barb. 343; *Beamish* v. *Hoyt*, 2 Robt. 307; *Ransom* v. *Nichols*, 22 N. Y. 110; *Barnes* v. *Underwood*, 47 id. 351; *Westervelt* v. *Gregg*, 12 id. 302; *Snyder* v. *Snyder*, 3 Barb. 621; *Holmes* v. *Holmes*, 4 id. 295; *White* v. *White*, id. 474; *Quackenbush* v. *Danks*, 1 Denio, 128; 1 Comst. 129; *Bronson* v. *Kinzie*, 1 How. [U. S.] 311; *McCracken* v. *Hayward*, 2 id. 608; *Morse* v. *Gould*, 11 N. Y. 281; *Edwards* v. *Kearzey*, 96 U. S. 595.) The rule of law should be applied in cases of this character which obtains in England in the matter of personal property, viz.: that where property is purchased by the husband in the joint names of himself and wife, it is presumed to have been a gift and advancement to her, unless evidence of a different intention be adduced. And that the wife, on surviving, will be entitled to such property unless he in his life-time aliens it. (*Kingdon* v. *Bridges*, 2 Vern. 67; *Glaister* v. *Hewer*, 8 id. 99; *Christ's Hospital* v. *Budgin*, 2 id. 683; *Watts* v. *Thomas*, 2 P. Wms. 364; *Coates* v. *Stevens*, 1 Y. & C. Eq. Ex. 66; *George* v. *Bank of England*, 7 Price, 647; *Ridder* v. *Kidder*, 10 Ves. 360; *Lucas* v. *Lucas*, 1 Atk. 270; *Dummer* v. *Pitcher*, 5 Sin. 35; *S. C.*, 2 M. & K. 262, 273; *Low* v. *Carter*, 1 Beav. 426; *Gibson* v. *Todd*, 1 Rawle, 455.) Courts strongly oppose any innovation upon the common-law doctrine of tenancy of the entirety. (*Wright* v. *Sadler*, 20 N. Y. 320; 17 Alb. L. J. 393; 11 id. 375, 402; 20 id. 203; 27 id. 162; 26 Am. Rep. 64; 23 id. 269; Girard's Real Estate Titles [2d ed.], 72, 84; Williams on Real Estate [5th ed.], 225, *n*; *Whiton* v. *Snyder*, 88 N. Y. 297; *Baker* v. *Lamb*, 11 Hun, 519; *Pollock* v. *Webster*, 16 id. 104; *Matteson* v. *N. Y. C. R. R. Co.*, 62

Barb. 373 ; *Wright* v. *Wright*, 54 N. Y. 437 ; Laws of 1880, chap. 472 ; *Taylor* v. *Young*, 71 Penn. St. 81.)

EARL, J. On the 1st day of August, 1868, certain land, which is the subject of this controversy, was conveyed by deed to Cornelius Day and Hannah Day, his wife, and to their heirs and assigns ; and the sole question for our determination is whether the grantees took the land as tenants in common or whether each took and became seized of the entirety.

By the common law, when land was conveyed to husband and wife they did not take as tenants in common, or as joint tenants, but each became seized of the entirety, *per tout, et non per my*, and upon the death of either the whole survived to the other. The survivor took the estate, not by right of survivorship simply, but by virtue of the grant which vested the entire estate in each grantee. During the joint lives the husband could, for his own benefit, use, possess and control the land, and take all the profits thereof, and he could mortgage and convey an estate to continue during the joint lives, but he could not make any disposition of the land that would prejudice the right of his wife in case she survived him.

This rule is based upon the unity of husband and wife, and is very ancient. It must have had its origin in the archaic period of our race, and it colored all the relations of husband and wife to each other, to the law and to society. In 1 Blackst. Com. 442, the learned author says : " Upon this principle, of an union of person in husband and wife, depend almost all the legal rights, duties and disabilities that either of them acquired by the marriage. I speak not, at present, of the rights of property, but of such as are merely personal. For this reason a man cannot grant any thing to his wife or enter into covenant with her ; for the grant would be to suppose her separate existence, and to covenant with her would be only to covenant with himself." They were not allowed to give evidence against each other, mainly because of the union of person, for if they were admitted to be witnesses for each other they would contradict one maxim of the common law, *nemo in propria causa testis esse debet ;* and if against each other they would contradict another maxim, *nemo tenetur se ipsum accusare.*

As one of the consequences of the same rule, the husband was made responsible to society for his wife. He was liable for her torts and frauds, and, in some cases, for her crimes.

This, and the other rules regulating the effect of marriage at common law, were not designed to degrade and oppress the wife. Blackstone (2 Com. 445) says : " Even the disabilities which the wife lies under are, for the most part, intended for her protection and benefit; so great a favorite is the female sex of the laws of England."

The common-law rule as to the effect of a conveyance to husband and wife continued in force, notwithstanding the Revised Statutes, which provided that " every estate granted or devised to two or more persons in their own right shall be a tenancy in common unless expressly declared to be in joint tenancy." (3 R. S. 2179 [7th ed.]; *Dios* v. *Glover,* 1 Hoff. Ch. 71; *Torrey* v. *Torrey,* 14 N. Y. 430 ; *Wright* v. *Saddler,* 20 id. 320.) In the latter case COMSTOCK, J., said : " It appears to be well settled that this statute does not apply to the conveyance of an estate to husband and wife. They are regarded in law as one person."

But the claim is made that the legislation in this State, in the years 1848, 1849, 1860 and 1862, in reference to the rights and property of married women, has changed the common-law rule so that now when land is conveyed to husband and wife they take as tenants in common, as if unmarried. In construing these statutes the rule must be observed, and usually has been observed, that statutes changing the common law must be strictly construed and that the common law must be held no further abrogated than the clear import of the language used in the statutes absolutely requires.

. Section 3 of chapter 200 of the Laws of 1848, as amended by chapter 375 of the Laws of 1849, provides that " any married female may take by inheritance or by gift, grant, devise or bequest, from any person other than her husband, and hold

to her sole and separate use, and convey and devise, real and
personal property, or any interest or estate therein, and the
rents, issues and profits thereof in the same manner and with
like effect as if she were unmarried, and the same shall not be
subject to the disposal of her husband or be liable for his
debts." It is not the effect of this section, and plainly was not
its purpose to change the force and operation of a conveyance
to a wife. It does not enlarge the estate which a wife would
otherwise take in land conveyed to her, and whatever the effect of a conveyance to a husband and wife was prior to that
statute, so it remains. If the operation of such a conveyance
was to convey the entire estate to each of the grantees, so that
each became seized of the entirety, there is nothing in the
force or effect of the language used to change the operation of
such a deed so as to make the grantees tenants in common.
The section gives the wife no greater right to receive conveyances than she had at common law, but its sole purpose was to
secure to her during coverture, what she did not have at common law, the use, benefit and control of her own real estate,
and the right to convey and devise it as if she were unmarried.

By section 1 of the act (Chapter 90 of the Laws of 1860)
it is provided that "the property, both real and personal,
which any married woman now owns as a sole and separate
property; that which comes to her by descent, devise, bequest,
gift or grant; that which she acquires by her trade, business,
labor or services, carried on or performed on her sole and separate account; that which a woman married in this State
owns at the time of her marriage, and the rents, issues and
profits of all such property, shall, notwithstanding her marriage, be and remain her sole and separate property, and may
be used, collected and invested by her in her own name, and
shall not be subject to the interference or control of her husband, or liable for his debts;" and in section 3 of the act of
1860, as amended by the act chapter 172 of the Laws of
1862, it is provided that "any married woman possessed of
real estate as her separate property may bargain, sell and con-

vey such property, and enter into any contract in reference to
the same, with the like effect, in all respects, as if she were
unmarried." There is great plausibility in the claim that
these provisions in the acts of 1860 and 1862 have reference
only to the separate property of a wife, which she owns separate from her husband, and that they have no reference whatever to land conveyed to husband and wife, in which, by the
common law, each became seized of the entirety. The language
is not so strong and direct as that of the Revised Statutes,
which provided that a grant to two or more persons shall create a tenancy in common, and which was yet held not to make
husband and wife tenants in common. But it is not necessary
now to determine that these provisions of law do not apply
to lands conveyed to husband and wife, and we pass that question. It is sufficient now to hold that they do not limit or define what estate the husband and wife shall take in lands conveyed to them jointly. Their utmost effect is to enable the
wife to control and convey whatever estate she gets by any
conveyance made to her solely or to her and others jointly.

The claim is made that the legislation referred to has destroyed the common-law unity of husband and wife, and made
them substantially separate persons for all purposes. We are
of the opinion that the statutes have not gone so far. The
legislature did not intend to sweep away all the disabilities of
married women depending upon the common-law fiction of a
unity of persons, as a brief reference to the statutes will show.
The act of 1848 gave no express authority to a married woman
to grant or dispose of her property; such authority came by
the act of 1849. The legislature clearly understood that the
common-law unity of husband and wife, and the disabilities
dependent thereon still remained, notwithstanding those acts,
because in 1860, by the act of that year, it empowered a married woman to perform labor and to carry on business on her
separate account; to enter into contracts in reference to her
separate real estate ; to sue and be sued in all matters having
relation to her property, and to maintain actions for injuries to
her person. Until 1867 (Chap. 782) husbands retained their

common-law right of survivorship to the personal property of their wives. It was not until chapter 887 of the laws of the same year, that husband and wife could, in civil actions, be compelled to give evidence for or against each other; and in 1876 (Chap. 182), for the first time, they could be examined in criminal proceedings as witnesses for each other; and provision was first made in the Penal Code (§ 715) that they could, in criminal proceedings, be witnesses for and against each other.

From this course of legislation it is quite clear that the legislature did not understand that the common-law rule as to the unity of husband and wife had been abrogated by the acts of 1848, 1849 and 1860, and that whenever it intended an invasion of that rule, it made it by express enactment. Still more significant is the act chapter 472 of the Laws of 1880, which provides that " whenever husband and wife shall hold any lands or tenements as tenants in common, joint tenants or as tenants by entireties, they may make partition or division of the same between themselves," by deeds duly executed under their hands and seals. Here the disability of husband and wife, growing out of their unity of person, to convey to each other is recognized, as is also the estate by entireties created by a deed to them jointly.

So the common-law incidents of marriage are swept away only by express enactments. The ability of the wife to make contracts is limited. Her general engagements are absolutely void, and she can bind herself by contract only as she is expressly authorized to do so by statute. A husband still has his common-law right of tenancy by the curtesy. Although section 7 of the act of 1860 authorizes a married woman to maintain an action against any person for an injury to her person or character, yet we have held that she cannot maintain an action against her husband for such an injury; and so it was held, notwithstanding the acts of 1848, 1849 and 1860, that the common-law disability of husband and wife growing out of their unity of person to convey to each other still existed. (*White* v. *Wager*, 25 N. Y. 333; *Winans et al.* v. *Peebles et al.*, 32 id. 423 ; *Meeker* v. *Wright*, 76 id. 262, 270.) It is believed, also, that the common-law rule as to the liability of the husband for the torts and crimes of his wife are still substantially in force.

We fail, therefore, to find any reason for holding that the common-law rule as to the effect of a conveyance to husband and wife has been abrogated, and this conclusion is sustained by considerable authority. In *Goelet* v. *Gori* (31 Barb. 314), SUTHERLAND, J., at Special Term, held that a lease for a term of years, executed to husband and wife, was unaffected by the acts of 1848 and 1849, and that husband and wife by conveyances to them still took as tenants by the entirety. In *Farmers and Mechanics' National Bank of Rochester* v. *Gregory* (49 Barb. 155) it was held at General Term that the statutes referred to had no relation to or effect upon real estate conveyed to husband and wife jointly, and that in the case of such a conveyance, notwithstanding those statutes, they take as tenants by the entirety. JOHNSON, J., commenced his opinion by saying : " To my mind it is a very clear proposition that our recent statutes for the better protection of the separate property of married women have no relation to or effect upon real estate conveyed to husband and wife jointly." That decision was rendered in 1867, and the conveyance which was there the subject of consideration was executed in 1864. In *Miller* v. *Miller* (9 Abb. Pr. [N. S.] 444) MURRAY, J., at Special Term, in 1871, feeling bound by the decision last referred to, held, that the common-law rule was applicable to a conveyance made to husband and wife in 1867. In *Freeman* v. *Barber* (3 N. Y. Sup. Ct. [T. & C.] 574) the same rule was applied in 1874 by the Supreme Court in the third department. The opinion of the court was written by MILLER, P. J., in which he stated that he regarded the law as settled in this State that, in the case of a conveyance to husband and wife, they take, not as joint tenants or as tenants in common, but as tenants by entireties, notwithstanding the acts referred to. In *Beach* v. *Hollister* (3 Hun, 519), decided in 1875, a similar decision was made. GILBERT, J., writing the opinion of the court, said : "These statutes operate only upon property which is. exclusively the wife's, and were not intended to destroy the legal unity of husband and wife, or to change the rule of the common law governing the effect of conveyances to them jointly." In *Ward* v. *Crum* (54 How. Pr. 95), decided in 1876, VAN VORST, J., at Special Term, held that under a deed executed to husband and wife in 1872, both became seized of the entirety, although the wife paid the entire consideration of the conveyance.

It is true that these decisions are not absolutely binding upon this court, but they settled the law in the Supreme Court. For twenty years after 1849 there was no decision or published opinion in this State in conflict with them, and they are, under the circumstances, entitled to great weight here. They undoubtedly lay down a rule which has been followed and observed by conveyancers, and we have no doubt that property to the value of millions is now held under conveyances made in reliance upon the common-law rule as thus expounded. These decisions were never questioned in this State by any court until the decision in the case of *Meeker* v. *Wright*, which was rendered in this court in 1879 (76 N. Y. 262). In that case the learned judge writing the opinion reached the conclusion that the common-law rule governing conveyances to husband and wife had been abrogated by the modern legislation in this State. But that portion of the opinion was not concurred in by a majority of the judges. The views of that judge were very forcibly and ably expressed, and they have been carefully reconsidered. They do not convince us that the conclusions he reached should be adopted by this court. That case is supposed to have unsettled the law somewhat in this State. In *Feely* v. *Buckley* (28 Hun, 451) it was held upon its authority, by a divided court, that tenancy by the entirety is abrogated by the Married Women's Acts ; and upon the same authority it is said a similar holding was made in *Zorntlein* v. *Brown*, decided in the Superior Court of New York, in January of this year, by a divided court. It is also said that in *Forsyth* v. *McCall*, in the fourth department in June, 1880, and in *Meeker* v. *Wright*, after a new trial, in the third department, in April, 1882, it was decided that the common-law rule was not abrogated. (27 Albany Law Journal, 199.) And these decisions, together with the one which is now under review, are all the decisions made in this State since the case of *Meeker* v. *Wright* was in this court, which have come to our attention.

Legislation similar to that which exists in this State, as to the rights and property of married women, exists in many of the States of the Union, and the decisions are nearly uniform in all the other States where the question has arisen, that a conveyance to husband and wife has the common-law effect, notwithstanding such legislation. Without citing all we call attention to the following cases and authorities: *Bates* v. *Seeley* (46 Penn. St. 248), *French* v. *Mahan* (56 id. 289), *Diver* v. *Diver* (id. 106), *Fisher* v. *Peovin* (25 Mich. 350), *McDuff* v. *Beauchamy* (50 Miss. 531), *Washburn* v. *Burns* (34 N. J. 18), *Chandler* v. *Cheney* (37 Ind. 391), *Morburgh* v. *Cole* (49 Md. 402; 33 Am. Rep. 266), *Bennett* v. *Child* (19 Wis. 362), *Robinson* v. *Eagle* (29 Ark. 202; 1 Washb. on Real Prop. [3d ed.] 577; Schouler on Husband and Wife, §§ 397, 398; 1 Bishop on the Laws of Married Women, 438, §§ 613, etc.; 2 id. 284, § 284). In the last section the learned author says: "Under the late married women's statutes, the effect of which is to prevent any part of the wife's interest in her lands passing to her husband, the rule of the common law, by force of which the two became tenants by the entirety of lands conveyed to both, is not changed," and he says: "The reason for the doctrine, looking at the question in the light of legal principle, is, that the statutes which preserve to married women their separate rights of property do not have, or profess to have, any effect upon the capacity of the wife to take property, or the manner of her taking it, but when she does take it they simply preserve the right in her, to her separate use, forbidding it to pass in part or in full to her husband under the rules of the unwritten law. If, then, land is conveyed to a husband and his wife, they take precisely as at the com-

mon law — that is, as tenants by the entirety." In *Diver* v.
Diver, STRONG, J., said: "But it is said the act of 1848, by
destroying the legal unity of the husband and wife, has converted such an estate into a tenancy in common; that is,
that such a deed conveys a different estate from that which
the same deed would have created if made prior to the
passage of the act. To this we cannot assent. It mistakes
alike the letter and the spirit of the statute, imputing to it a
purpose never intended. The design of the legislature was
single. It was not to destroy the oneness of husband and wife,
but to protect the wife's property, by removing it from under
the dominion of the husband. To effect this object she was
enabled to own, use and enjoy her property, if hers before
marriage, as fully after marriage as before, and the act declared that if her property accrued to her after marriage, it
should be owned, used and enjoyed by her as her own separate
property, exempt from liability for the debts and engagements
of her husband. All this had in view the enjoyment of that
which is hers, not the force and effect of the instrument by
which an estate may be granted to her. It has nothing to do
with the nature of the estate. The act does not operate upon
rights accruing to her until after they have accrued. It takes
such rights of property as it finds them, and regulates the enjoyment, that is the enjoyment of the estate after it has vested
in the wife."

At common law where the estate was conveyed to husband
and wife, as above stated, the husband had the control and use
of the property during the joint lives. It is unnecessary now
to determine whether, under the Married Women's Acts in this
State, the husband still has such a right in real estate conveyed
to him and his wife jointly. It was said in some of the authorities cited that the statutes had changed that common-law
rule, and that while husband and wife, in conveyances to them
jointly, each took the entirety, yet that the land could not be
sold for the husband's debts, or the use and profits thereof during their joint lives be entirely appropriated by him. It is
not important in this case to determine what the relation of

the wife to the land, in such a case, now is, during the life of her husband.

It is said that the reason upon which the common-law rule under consideration was based has ceased to exist, and hence that the rule should be held to disappear. It is impossible, now, to determine how the rule, in the remote past, obtained a foot-ing, or upon what reason it was based, and hence it is impossi-ble now to say that the reason, whatever it was, has entirely ceased to exist. There are many rules appertaining to the ownership of real property originating in the feudal ages, for the existence of which the reason does not now exist, or is not discernible, and yet, on that account, courts are not authorized to disregard them. They must remain until the legislature abrogates or changes them, like statutes founded upon no reason, or upon reasons that have ceased to operate.

It was never, we believe, regarded as a mischief, that under a conveyance to husband and wife they should take as tenants by the entirety, and we have no reason to believe that it was within the contemplation of the legislature to change that rule. Neither do we think that there is any public policy, which re-quires that the statute should be so construed as to change the common-law rule. It was never considered that that rule abridged the rights of married women, but rather that it en-larged their rights, and improved their condition. It would be against the spirit of the statutes to cut down an estate of the wife by the entirety to an estate as tenant in common with her husband. If the rule is to be changed it should be changed by a plain act of the legislature, applicable to future conveyances ; otherwise incalculable mischief may follow by unsettling and disturbing dispositions of property made upon the faith of the common-law rule. The courts certainly ought not to go faster than the legislature in obliterating rules of law under which many generations have lived and flourished and the best civili-zation of any age or country has grown up.

We are, therefore, of opinion that the judgment should be affirmed, with costs.

All concur, except DANFORTH and FINCH, JJ., who dissent

upon the ground that the common-law doctrine was abrogated by the statutes which enable a wife to hold a separate estate, and for the reasons stated by the former in *Meeker* v. *Wright,** and his dissenting opinion in *Schultz* v. *Schultz.†*

Judgment affirmed.

Stephen Cutter et al., as Executors, etc., Appellants, *v.* The Mayor, Aldermen and Commonalty of the City of New York, Respondent.

Where one, entitled to an award for damages by reason of the widening of Broadway in the city of New York, made in proceedings under the act of 1869 (Chap. 890, Laws of 1869), accepted the sum awarded, and gave a receipt acknowledging payment in full of its amount, *held,* that the right to interest was thereby waived, and an action to recover the same could not thereafter be maintained against the city ; and this, although the claimant demanded payment of interest at the time and protested against the refusal of the comptroller to pay the same.

Interest in such case is given as damages for non-payment or detention of the money awarded (§ 183, chap. 86, Laws of 1813), and is only to be recovered with the principal by action; it does not constitute a debt capable of a distinct claim. Acceptance, therefore, without action of the sum awarded, in full payment of the principal, bars an action for such damages.

(Argued March 14, 1883 ; decided April 17, 1883.)

Appeal from judgment of the General Term of the Supreme Court, in the first judicial department, entered upon an order made April 10, 1882, which affirmed a judgment in favor of defendant, entered upon an order dismissing plaintiffs' complaint on trial.

This action was brought to recover interest alleged to be due and unpaid upon an award to Louisiana St. John, plaintiffs' testatrix, for damages to her land because of the widening of Broadway, which damages were awarded to her in proceedings instituted under the act (Chap. 890, Laws of 1869) authorizing that improvement.

* 76 N. Y. 262.   † 89 N. Y. (Mem) 644.

The award was made July 5, 1872. The testatrix made a demand upon the comptroller for the same in December, 1872. In June, 1875, the comptroller paid the sum awarded, which was accepted by testatrix, who at the time gave a receipt at the foot of an account showing the amount awarded "as in full payment of the above account." She at the time served upon the comptroller a paper stating that she demanded interest from January 4, 1873, and protested against his refusal to pay such interest, and accepted said award under protest, "saving to herself all her rights in the premises."

Further facts appear in the opinion.

Cecil Campbell Higgins for appellants. Interest ran on the award from the time of demand of payment thereof by the testatrix. (*Spears* v. *Mayor, etc.*, 87 N. Y. 371.) Payment and acceptance of the award does not preclude plaintiffs' right to recover the interest then due thereon, the interest being demanded at the time, and payment of the principal without interest being accepted under protest. (*Jacot* v. *Emmet*, 11 Paige, 142; *Gillespie* v. *Mayor, etc.*, 3 Edw. Ch. 512; *Tillotson* v. *Preston*, 3 Johns. 229; *Johnson* v. *Brannan*, 5 id. 268; *Williams* v. *Houghtaling*, 3 Cow. 86; *Consequa* v. *Fanning*, 3 Johns. Ch. 587; *So. Cent. R. R. Co.* v. *Town of Moravia*, 61 Barb. 180–188; *People* v. *County of New York*, 5 Cow. 331; *Fake* v. *Eddy's Ex'rs*, 15 Wend. 76; *Luddington* v. *Miller*, 38 N. Y. Super. [6 J. & S.] 478; *Bender* v. *Bender*, 7 Barb. 561; *Craft* v. *Morrill*, 14 N. Y. 463; *Tenth Nat. B'k* v. *Mayor, etc.*, 4 Hun, 429; *S. C.*, 80 N. Y. 660.) The plaintiffs' legal right to recover in this action being established, they are not estopped from recovery by the receipt given by the testatrix. (*Geary* v. *Page*, 9 Bosw. 290; *Allen* v. *Roosevelt*, 14 Wend. 100; *Hawley* v. *Foote*, 19 id. 516; *Brooklyn B'k* v. *DeGraw*, 23 id. 342; *Tilton* v. *Alcott*, 16 Barb. 598; *Day* v. *Roth*, 18 N. Y. 448; *Hammond* v. *Christie*, 5 Rob. 166; *Ryan* v. *Ward*, 48 N. Y. 204; *Keeler* v. *Salisbury*, 33 id. 153; 46 id. 310; *People, ex rel. Kinney*, v. *Supervisors*, 58 Barb 139; *Bunge* v. *Koop*, 48 N. Y. 225.) Where there are more instruments than one in existence between the same parties, cotemporaneous and relating to the same subject-matter, they must be construed together, treated as one writing, and the rights of the parties then determined upon the proper construction thereof. (Greenleaf on Evidence, § 283; *Kittle & Chandler* v. *Massasoit Ins. Co.*, 56 Barb. 177; *Meriden Britt. Co.* v. *Zingson*, 48 N. Y. 251; *Jackson, ex dem. Watson,* v. *McKinney*, 3 Wend. 233; *Shaw* v. *Leavitt*, 3 Sandf. Ch. 178; *Mott* v. *Richtmyer*, 57 N. Y. 49, 65; *Connell* v. *Todd*, 2 Denio, 133; *Marsh* v. *Dodge*, 66 N. Y. 533; *Reynolds* v. *Commerce Ins. Co.*, 47 id. 605; *N. Y. D. D. Co.* v. *Stillman*, 30 id. 176; *Ford* v. *Belmont*, 7 Rob. 97, 508.)

D. J. Dean for respondent. The payment of the principal sum awarded to the plaintiffs' testatrix as principal has satisfied her entire cause of action growing out of the award, and is a bar to recovery of interest thereon. (*Gillespie* v. *Mayor*, 3 Edw. Ch. 512; *Jacob* v. *Emmett*, 11 Paige, 142; *Johnston* v. *Brannan*, 5 Johns. 267; *Tillotson* v. *Preston*, 3 id. 299; *Consequa* v. *Fanning*, 3 Johns. Ch. 587; *Fake* v. *Eddy*, 15 Wend. 76; *Tenth Nat. B'k* v. *Mayor*, 4 Hun, 429; *S. C.*, 80 N. Y. 660; *People* v. *County of New York*, 5 Cow. 331; 1 Abbott's Dig. title "Application of Payments," 220; *Fleetwood* v. *Mayor*, 2 Sandf. 481.) Under any circumstances the city could become liable to pay interest upon the award only as damages for the wrongful detention of the sum awarded to the plaintiffs and for negligent default in the duty of payment. (*Ex parte Marlar*, 1 Atk. 151; *Watkins* v. *Morgan*, 6 C. & P. 661; *Cameron* v. *Smith*, 2 B. & Ald. 305; *Cook* v. *Fowler*, E. L. R., 7 H. L. Cas. 27; *Brewster* v. *Wakefield*, 22 How. 118–127; *Young* v. *Goodby*, 15 Wall. 562–565; *Burnhisel* v. *Firman*, 22 id. 170–176; *Nat. B'k Comm.* v. *Mech's' Nat. B'k*, 4 Otto, 437; *U. S.* v. *Sherman*, 8 id. 565, 567; *Van Rensselaer* v. *Jewett*, 2 Comst. 135–140; *Brainard* v. *Jones*, 18 N. Y. 35–37; *Hamilton* v. *Van Rensselaer*, 43 id. 244–246, 7; *Melick* v. *Knox*, 44 id. 676–680; *Eaton* v. *Poissonault*, 67 Me. 540; *Pearce* v. *Hennessy*, 10 R. I. 223; *Suffield Educ.*

Soc'y v. *Loomis*, 42 Conn. 570; *Ludwick* v. *Huntzinger*, 5 Watts & S. 51–59; *McLane* v. *Abrams*, 2 Nev. 99; *Hubbard* v. *Charlestown Branch R. R. Co.*, 11 Metc. 124–128.) It was a necessary part of the plaintiffs' case to prove that payment had been unjustly refused and the money unjustly detained, in order to establish a right to interest. (*U. S.* v. *Sherman*, 8 Otto, 565; *People* v. *Canal Comm'rs*, 5 Denio, 405; 67 N. Y. 94; *Spears* v. *Mayor*, 87 id. 359; *Astor* v. *Miller*, 2 Paige, 68; *Astor* v. *Hoyt*, 5 Wend. 602; *Coutant* v. *Catlin*, 2 Sandf. Ch. 485.)

Danforth, J. The report of commissioners appointed to estimate damages incurred by reason of the widening of Broadway was duly confirmed on the 5th of July, 1872, and included an award to plaintiff's testatrix of $23,041, by way of damages to her land, but it also stated that the premises were incumbered by mortgage in the sum of $10,000, and it is now conceded that the amount of the mortgage debt was in fact $8,000. It does not appear when the exact sum was ascertained, or the property taken for the improvement relieved from the lien of the mortgage, or the release delivered to the defendants, but the account for which the testatrix acknowledged payment contains a certificate signed by the auditor of accounts, dated May 13, 1875, and this recites a release dated September 9, 1874. There is no evidence that the defendant refused payment after that time, and without demand it could not be put in default or subjected to the payment of interest. The demand relied upon by the plaintiffs was made on the 31st of December, 1872, and was for the full sum of $23,041. No answer appears to have been made to that demand; at all events it was not complied with.

Where, however, a demand is necessary as a foundation for a claim of interest, it must be a distinct demand for the sum of money to which the party is then entitled. It is not enough that by some change in circumstance, brought about by his own act or the act of others, he may become entitled to it. Here the demand included more than the plaintiffs could

justly claim, for until discharged of record the amount of the
mortgage debt was to be withheld.   Nor have the plaintiffs
brought their case within the statute (Laws of 1869, chap.
890) regulating the proceedings under which the award was
made.   By this act (§ 1) all provisions of law then in
force relative to opening, regulating and widening streets
and avenues in New York city were made applicable to
the improvement in question, and among others section 183,
chapter 86 of the Laws of 1813.   By the terms of this section
damages awarded are directed to be paid by the corporation
within four months after confirmation of the report of the
commissioners, "and in case of neglect or default" in so
doing, leave is given to the party entitled thereto "to sue for
and recover the same with lawful interest from and after the
said application therefor, and the costs of the suit."   No
other provision is made for the accruing or running of interest, and it was in no sense incident to or part of the original
award.   It is given as damages for non-payment or detention
of the money awarded, and does not constitute a debt capable
of a distinct claim.   (*Dixon* v. *Parkes*, 1 Esp. 110; *Churcher*
v. *Stinger*, 2 B. & Ad. 777.)   It could only be recovered
with the principal by action.   Acceptance, therefore, of
the sum awarded in full payment of the principal prevents
an action for those damages.   If the plaintiff meant to have
demanded the interest, she ought not to have received the
principal.   In the face of that fact, protest against the refusal
of the defendant to pay interest is of no importance.   (*Fleetwood* v. *The City of New York*, 2 Sandf. 481; *Forrest* v. *The
City of New York*, 13 Abb. Pr. 350.)   In the cases cited,
the plaintiffs sought to recover back money paid under an assessment for city improvements.   The payment was made
under protest, the plaintiffs alleging that the assessment was
illegal, but the court held that the plaintiffs could not recover, saying, "where there is no legal compulsion, a
party yielding to the assertion of an adverse claim cannot detract from the force of his concession by saying
I object or I protest.   The payment nullifies the protest

as effectually as it obviates the previous denial and contestation of the claim." So in the case before us. Here the demand by the plaintiff of interest in addition to the amount of the award from January 4, 1873, and protest against the refusal of the defendant's comptroller to pay such interest with the award can amount to nothing in view of the fact that she knowingly accepted the award without interest, at the same time acknowledging payment in full of its amount. She might have refused to accept the award without interest; so the defendant could refuse to pay interest even for the purpose of effecting a settlement, but the concession indicated by an actual payment and an actual receipt of payment of principal without interest must be conclusive. The principle relied on by the plaintiffs that payment of part of a just debt furnishes no consideration for the discharge of the whole is inapplicable in the present case. There was no contract liability of the defendant for interest when the settlement was made. It could not become a debt against the defendant until judgment, and would then become due because allowed as damages.

The cases of *Tillotson* v. *Preston* (3 Johns. 229), *Johnston* v. *Brannan* (5 id. 268), *People* v. *County of New York* (5 Cow. 331), were cases in which there was no contract for the payment of interest, and it was held that it could only be recovered as damages for the non-payment of the principal debt when it became due, and that in such a case, if the party to whom the money was payable accepted the amount agreed to be paid in full satisfaction of the principal debt, he could not afterward maintain an action for the mere incidental damages which he had sustained by reason of the debt not having been paid at the time it became due. In *Tillotson* v. *Preston* (*supra*), the court say, "if the plaintiff accepted the principal he cannot afterward bring an action for the interest." In *Hamilton* v. *Van Rensselaer* (43 N. Y. 244), it is said that when interest is only recoverable as damages after default in the payment of the principal, the receipt of the principal debt is a bar to the claim for such interest.

If, by reason of the refusal of the defendant to pay interest,

and persistence of the plaintiffs' testator in demanding it, a
suit had been brought, interest could undoubtedly have been
recovered from the time a proper demand of payment had
been made. But having settled without action, and actually
accepted the money in full payment of the principal, the interest cannot, by any disclaimer or protest on the part of the
plaintiffs' testator be made the subject of a distinct claim;
nor could she, by any avowed reservation, create a right which
had no existence. The complaint, therefore, was properly
dismissed, and the judgment appealed from should be affirmed.

All concur, except RAPALLO and EARL, JJ., dissenting.

Judgment affirmed.

CHARLES FINKELMEIER et al., Executors, etc., Respondents, *v.*
HESTER BATES et al., Appellants.

By a lease for a term of twenty-one years the lessee covenanted to pay
an annual rental, and all taxes and assessment, also to build a "first-class
commercial building," of a size and material specified, to cost not less
than $30,000. A right of re-entry in case of non-payment of the rent
was reserved, and it was covenanted that "at the expiration of the aforesaid term" the value of the building should be appraised, and upon payment of one-half of the appraised value the building should belong to
the lessor, and "on the last day of said term or other sooner determination
of the estate" granted, the lessee would peaceably surrender possession.
The lessor was given the option of giving a renewal lease for a further
term of twenty-one years instead of paying half the value of the building,
and at the expiration of that term it was declared that the building should
belong to him. The lessee erected the building, and at the expiration
of about five years his assignees were dispossessed for non-payment of
rent. In an action to recover the rent due defendants set up as a counter-
claim the half value of the building, claiming that the words "expiration
of the term" when the lessor was to pay the half value in case he determined not to re-lease related not to time, but to the estate of the lessee,
and that upon termination of the estate the liability of the lessor arose.
Held untenable; that assuming the covenant to pay such half value to be
an independent one, not conditioned upon the prior payment of rent,
the word "term" was used in the sense of time, and such liability did not
arise until the end of the twenty-one years.

The lessor, as part of the original construction, put into the building an
elevator, an engine to run the same; a boiler was also placed in a vault
under the sidewalk to furnish steam for the engine, and for heating the
building.   The boiler was set in brick work, and could only be removed
by taking up the sidewalk.   Defendants sought to counter-claim the
value of the elevator and boiler ; *held* untenable; that in the absence of
evidence to the contrary, it was to be assumed the price of these articles
went to make up the stipulated expenditure of $30,000, and under the
lease, as between the parties, they were to be considered as part of the
building.

(Argued March 30, 1883 ; decided April 17, 1883.)

APPEAL from judgment of the General Term of the Superior
Court of the city of New York, entered upon an order made
December 4, 1882, which modified, and affirmed as modified, a
judgment in favor of plaintiffs, entered upon a decision of the
court on trial without a jury.

This action was originally brought by Selena H. Jewell, the
devisee of the lessor, to recover rent alleged to be due from
defendants, as assignees of the lessee under a lease of certain
lots in the city of New York, executed in 1866 by Charles J.
Jewell to David C. Sturges ; said devisee having died during
the pendency of the action, her executors, the present plaintiffs,
were substituted.

The lease was for a term of twenty-one years from May 1,
1867; the lessee covenanted to pay an annual rent of $3,000,
and to pay all taxes and assessments upon the lots during the
term.   A right of re-entry by the lessor was reserved in case
of non-payment of rent for ten days after any payment became due.   The lease contained these clauses :

"And the said party of the second part further covenants
and agrees to erect and build upon said premises a first-class
commercial building to cover the entire premises, except such
part thereof as it is usual to reserve for light and air in the
rear.   Said building shall not be less than five stories in height
and with a front of white marble, yellow stone or of iron, and
to cost not less than thirty thousand dollars ($30,000); said build-
ing shall be completed on or before the 1st day of May, 1868,
unless the same shall be injured or destroyed by fire, without

the fault or negligence of the party of the second part while in process of erection and completion, in which event a reasonable time hereinafter shall be allowed him to re-erect or repair the same."

" The said party of the second part further covenants and agrees to keep the building so to be erected at all times fully insured in the joint names of the parties hereto in as large an amount as any first-class insurance company in the city of New York will accept; and in the event of neglect so to do, the party of the first part shall be at liberty to insure the same, the said party of the second part agreeing to refund and pay the amount of premium therefor; any and all moneys received from such insurance for loss or damages shall be payable to the party of the second part upon his giving satisfactory security to the party of the first part that the whole of the money so received shall be expended in restoring the building to the like condition in which it was before such loss or damage."

" It is mutually covenanted and agreed by the parties hereto that at the expiration of the aforesaid term the building upon said premises shall be appraised by appraisers to be chosen one by each party hereto, and in case of their disagreement those two shall choose a third, and the decision of said three appraisers, or a majority of them, shall be final and conclusive upon both parties hereto, and upon payment of one-half of such appraised value of said building to the party of the second part, by the party of the first part, the same building shall belong wholly to said party of the first part hereto. And that on the last day of the said term or other sooner determination of the estate hereby granted, the said party of the second part, his executors, administrators or assigns, shall and will peaceably and quietly leave, surrender and yield up unto the said party of the first part, his heirs or assigns, all and singular the said demised premises in good order and condition. It is, however, expressly stipulated and agreed between the parties hereto that the party of the first part, upon giving notice of at least three months to the party of the second part of his election so to do, in lieu of paying one-half of the aforesaid appraised value, may execute and deliver to the party of the second part, who shall accept the same, a lease for the further term of twenty-one years of the premises aforesaid, at a rent to be fixed by appraisers to be appointed as aforesaid, in case the parties hereto cannot agree, such lease to contain similar covenants and stipulations other than as to the amount of rent, erection of building and renewal as are herein contained, and at the expiration of said last term mentioned, or other sooner determination of the estate thereby granted, the said building shall belong wholly to the party hereto of the first part, and to be surrendered to him in like good order and condition."

The building was erected by the lessee in pursuance of the contract in December, 1879; plaintiffs' testator took possession by virtue of a warrant in summary proceedings, because of default in payment of rent. Defendants set up as a counter-claim, half the value of the building, and as a separate counter-claim, the value of an elevator, engine and boiler put into the building by the lessee. The material facts in reference thereto are stated in the opinion.

Edward Van Ness for appellants. The performance of the covenant upon the part of the lessor to pay one-half of the value of the building at the expiration of the term is charged upon his grantee by the statute. (1 R. S. 747, § 24; Smith's Lead. Cas. 22 and notes; *Norman* v. *Wells*, 17 Wend. 146; 1 R. S. 748, § 2; Littleton, 111, chap. 10, par. 585, edition by Thornton, p. 505.) The covenant to pay one-half of the value of the building was not collateral in any possible sense. (*Norman* v. *Wells*, 17 Wend. 146; Taylor's L. & T., § 260, 1 and 2 and note; 1 Washb. on Real Prop. [3d ed.] 327 [5a.], 330 [11], and [12]; 2 id. 16, 17; Taylor's L. & T., § 330; *Ganson* v. *Tift*, 71 N. Y., see opinion, p. 53; Littleton's Tenures, chap. 10; Taylor's L. & T., § 439.) The claim that the defendants cannot enforce the covenant to pay one-half of the value of the building at this time, because the words "at the expiration of the aforesaid term" refer only to a termination of the lease by lapse of time, is untenable. (Washb. on Real

Prop. 292; Taylor's L. & T., § 16; 2 Blackst. 144; *Beach* v. *Nixon,* 9 N. Y. 35; McAdam's L. & T. 644 [new ed.]; *Johnson* v. *Oppenheimer,* 55 N. Y. 293 and 4; *Roe* v. *Conway,* 74 id. 201; McAdam's L. & T., p. 660; Angell on Limitations, 390.) The claim by plaintiffs that the payment of rent and taxes is a condition precedent to any claim for the value of the building is untenable. (Taylor's L. & T., § 278; *Tracy* v. *Albany Ex. Co.,* 7 N. Y. 472.) The plaintiff, as devisee of the reversion in part of the demise, cannot enforce any conditions. The rule is that covenants may be apportioned, but conditions cannot. (Smith's L & T. 292; *Twynain* v. *Pickard,* 2 B. & A. 109.) That a ground of forfeiture exists is of no importance, there must be an actual entry for conditions broken. (*Twynain* v. *Pickard,* 2 B. & A. 109; *Beach* v. *Nixon,* 9 N. Y. 35; *Tallman* v. *Coffin,* 4 id. 138.) The boiler, engine, hoist-way, etc., were chattels for the temporary convenience of tenants, and as such belong to the lessee and his assigns, and passed to defendants under their mortgage. (*Voorhees* v. *McGinnis,* 48 N. Y. 278; Ewell on Fixtures, 275 and note; Taylor's L. & T., §§ 544-545.)

Richard L. Sweezy for respondents. The lessees have failed to perform the covenants of the lease by omitting to pay the taxes and ground rent, and they could not demand payment for the building even if the time for payment had arrived. (*People's B'k* v. *Mitchell,* 73 N. Y. 406; *Pike* v. *Butler,* 4 id. 360.) When there are mutual agreements and an act by one party is to be in point of time previous to an act by the other, the doing of the first act is a condition precedent to the compelling performance of the second, whether so stated in the contract or not. (*People's B'k* v. *Mitchell, supra,* at p. 411; *Grant* v. *Johnson,* 5 N. Y. 247; *Paine* v. *Brown,* 37 id. 228.) The covenant concerning the payment for the building is on the part of the parties only and not of their assigns, and is personal only and does not run with the land, and cannot be enforced against the devisee of the lessor. (1 Washb. on Real Prop. 330, 331; Taylor's Land & Ten. 127, 128, 157; *Coffin* v. *Tallman*, 8 N. Y. 467; *Cole* v. *Hughes*, 54 id. 444.) The counter-claim for the value of the alleged personal property was properly dismissed, it is not a cause of action on contract, but on a tort, and cannot be set up in this action. (Code, § 501; *Peiser* v. *Stearns*, 1 Hilt. 86; *Chambers* v. *Lewis*, 11 Abb. Pr. 212; *Smith* v. *Hall*, 67 N. Y. 48; *Clapp* v. *Wright*, 21 Hun, 240; *Jones* v. *Hoare*, 5 Pick. 285; *Willett* v. *Willett*, 3 Watts, 277; *Coit* v. *Stewart*, 12 Abb. Pr. [N. S.] 216.) The elevator, boiler and heating apparatus are part of the realty, and could not be removed by defendants. (*McRae* v. *Central B'k*, 66 N. Y. 489.) A defendant cannot counter-claim a joint cause of action against the plaintiff and other persons not parties to the action. (Code, § 501.)

FINCH, J. Assuming the position of the appellants, that the covenant of the lessor to pay the value of one-half of the building erected on the leased premises is an independent covenant, and not conditioned upon the prior payment of rent and taxes during the twenty-one years, there yet remain difficulties which bar a recovery. The payment for the building by the lessor was to be made at the "expiration of the term." The meaning of that phrase as used in the contract involves a construction of the agreement to be gathered from its several provisions. The lease, as printed for our use, is divided into separate and numbered paragraphs. That was done for convenience merely, the original instrument having no such subdivisions. By its terms the premises were granted to the lessee for a period of twenty-one years at an agreed rent of $3,000, which the lessee covenanted to pay quarterly in each year, together with the taxes, and if the rent should remain in arrears for ten days, or default be made in any of the lessee's covenants, a right of re-entry was reserved to the lessor. It was further provided that within two years a building should be erected upon the premises by the lessee. Its general purpose and character was described. It was to be a first-class commercial building, not less than five stories in height, with a front of white marble, yellow stone or iron, and to cost not less than $30,000. It was to be kept insured in the joint names of the parties, and in case of fire was to be restored or repaired out of the insurance money received. At the "expiration of the term" the building was to be valued by chosen appraisers, and the lessor was to pay to the lessee one-half of that appraised value, and upon such payment the building "should belong wholly" to the lessor, provided, however, that the latter, at his option, instead of the payment in cash, might make it by giving a new lease for twenty-one years more, at a rental to be agreed upon, or, in case of disagreement, to be fixed by selected appraisers. It is thus apparent in the contract of the parties that the construction of this building was intended to be practically a payment of rent in advance. The rents to be paid quarterly in cash were fixed at such a sum as, with one-half the value of the building at the close of the term, would amount to an adequate rent for the whole term ; and the same process repeated during a renewal of the lease for another twenty-one years was to exhaust in the same way the remaining half of the building. It is also apparent that the lessor was never bound absolutely to pay for one-half of the value of the building in cash. He could do so if he pleased, but was not bound to do so. He was at liberty in lieu thereof to give a new lease for a further term at a rent agreed upon or appraised. This payment was to be made, or the new lease given at "the expiration of the term." The appellants construe the word "term" as relating not to time, but to the estate of the lessee. It is capable of use in both senses. (1 Washburn on Real Prop. 385, *292.) And whether the one sense or the other is to be attached to the form of expression depends upon the construction of the instrument containing it. Here the estate of the lessee had been terminated by his failure to pay rent and taxes, and his dispossession by the landlord under appropriate legal proceedings. The appellants insist that upon such termination of the estate the liability of the lessor arose, and the respondents that it did not come into existence until the end of the twenty-one years. We think the latter is the true construction. The seventh subdivision of the lease, after providing " that at the expiration of the aforesaid term " the building should be appraised, further undertakes to stipulate for the ultimate surrender of the premises by the lessee in good order and condition, and in fixing the date of such surrender uses the expression, " on the last *day* of the said *term*, or other sooner determination of the *estate* hereby granted." The phraseology indicates that the word " term " was used in the sense of time as distinguished from the estate granted. The character of the agreement tends to the same result. The lease provided, at the option of the lessor, for paying the value of the building by the tenant's occupation at a reduced or graded rent for forty-two years; and the lessor reserved a choice at the end of the first twenty-one to pay one-half of the then value of the building. That value at the end of twenty-one years might be very different from the value at the end of five ; and the lessor, after twenty-one years receipt of rents, might easily have saved and accumulated from them the means with which to pay, when at the end of five years such payment might be impossible. The contention of the appellants, if sustained, would enable a lessee to change materially, and to the injury of the lessor, the stipulations of a lease by the mere process of repudiating its conditions. He makes default in the payment of rent and taxes, and so obliges the landlord to remove him, and rests upon that fact as the ground for depriving the lessor of a credit or delay of nearly twenty years, and matures the debt by means of his own wrong. We think the counter-claim was properly rejected for that reason. The demand was not due, and the lessor's option not destroyed. Whether any, and, if so, what right may remain to the lessee in the future, we need not now determine.

But another form of the difficulty growing out of the dispossession of those claiming under the lessee remains to be considered. A separate and distinct counter-claim for the value of the elevator, engine and boiler was asserted and also rejected. The engine was supplied to run the elevator, and the boiler was needed to furnish steam for the engine, and for the heating of the building. The boiler was placed in a vault under the sidewalk, upon a brick foundation prepared for the purpose, and protected on each side by a substantial brick wall. It could only be removed by taking up the sidewalk. The engine was bolted to a bed-plate which rested upon a stone foundation built to receive it. The elevator extended to the top of the building, running upon guide-posts attached to the frame. The elevator and steam-heating apparatus are the common conveniences of a first-class commercial building. They were introduced as part of the original construction under the lessee's contract, and we must assume, in the absence of evidence to the contrary, went to make, up the expenditure of $30,000, which the lessee was bound to incur. There is no evidence and no finding that their cost was in excess of the $30,000. On this state of facts, we think that as between lessor and lessee, under the peculiar contract to which they were parties, the elevator, engine and boiler were a part of the building and of the real estate. They were supplied for its use; were fairly included in the description of a first-class commercial building; could not be removed without substantial injury to the structure; were within the reasonable contemplation of the contract; and were a part of the very expenditure which the lessee was bound to make, and the lessor was entitled to receive. If there be doubt whether as between vendor and vendee of a first-class commercial building an elevator and the machinery necessary to operate it are to be treated as part of the realty, it is dissipated in the present case by the peculiar character of the contract, and the nature of its conditions. If the proof had shown that these appurtenances had been supplied by the tenant in excess of the $30,-000 he was bound to expend, and so for his own convenience, and not in part performance of his contract obligation, the question would have been purely one of fixtures. Upon the evidence as it stands, we do not doubt that the articles in question must be deemed a part and parcel of the building, and so cannot serve as the basis of a separate counter-claim.

These views of the case render unnecessary any consideration of the assignments and transfers of title on both sides. The defendants claiming under and through the original lessee can have no other or greater rights than his.

The·judgment should be affirmed, with costs.

All concur.

Judgment affirmed.

WILLIAM B. MILLS, as Administrator, etc., Appellant, · *v.* FRANCIS R. HOFFMAN, Respondent.

In proceedings before a surrogate to compel an accounting, by an executor, instituted prior to September 1, 1880, a hearing was had and a decree rendered, after that time, which was appealed from. The appellant, at the close of the evidence, requested the surrogate to find upon certain questions of fact, as provided by the Code of Civil Procedure (§ 2545), which he refused. *Held*, that an exception to the refusal was not well taken ; as, by the said Code (§ 3347, subd. 11), all proceedings pending in Surrogate's Court on that date are exempted from the operation of any of the provisions of the chapter (18) containing said provision.

In an action brought by a legatee against the other beneficiaries, and the heirs at law and next of kin of the testator, and against an administrator, with the will annexed, for the purpose of determining, among other things, the rights of the parties in the estate, and for an accounting by the administrator, and payment by him, to the parties entitled, of the amount found in his hands; judgment was rendered determining those questions and adjudging that upon compliance with the provisions of the judgment by the administrator he should be discharged from all claims and demands. A guardian *ad litem* was appointed in said action for an infant who, with her general guardian, was made a party defendant, and by the judgment she was adjudged to be entitled to a certain sum out of the funds in the hands of the administrator. The latter fully performed all the requirements of said judgment, paying over the share of said infant to her general guardian, and was thereupon discharged from such administration. After said infant became of age, with full knowledge of the terms of the judgment, she received from her general guardian the moneys so paid to him, and also other moneys which the judgment required other defendants to pay to her, and which they had previously paid in compliance therewith to said guardian. She also commenced proceedings to vacate said judgment upon the ground that the appointment of the guardian *ad litem* was irregular, and an order was granted vacating the same, so far as she was concerned. Four years after the payment so made to her she commenced proceedings before the surrogate to compel said administrator to account. *Held,* that the proceedings were not maintainable ; that assuming the judgment has, so far as the petitioner is concerned, been deprived of any force as an adjudication of the question involved, she could and did, by acceptance of the moneys paid, ratify the acts of the general guardian and estopped herself from controverting either the judgment or the settlement made thereunder. A party may not enjoy the rights awarded to him by a judgment and deny its force as an adjudication

Mills v. *Hoffman* (26 Hun, 594), reversed.

(Argued March 14, 1883 ; decided April 17, 1888.)

Appéal from judgment of the General Term of the Supreme Court, in the fourth judicial department, entered upon an order made April 8, 1882, which affirmed a decree of the surrogate of the county of Cayuga, in proceedings to compel an accounting by William B. Mills, as administrator, with the will annexed, of David N. Follett, deceased. (Reported below, 26 Hun, 594.)

The material facts are stated in the opinion.

H. V. Howland for appellant. The respondent, by acceptance of the moneys paid, ratified the acts of her general guardian and estopped herself from controverting either the judgment or the settlement made thereunder. (Bigelow on Estoppel, 16 ; *City B'k* v. *Hopkins,* 2 Dana [Ky.], 395 ; *Borrowseale* v. *Tuttle,* 5 Allen, 377 ; *Foote* v. *Essex Co.,* 7 Wall. 107 ; *Talbot* v. *Todd,* 5 Dana [Ky.], 193 ; *Le Guen* v. *Gouverneur,* 1 Johns. Cas. 492, note ; *Danber* v. *Prentice,* 22 Wis. 311 ; *Parkhurst* v. *Sumner,* 23 Vt. 588 ; *Chesapeake Co.* v. *Gittings,* 36 Md. 276 ; *Philon* v. *Gardner,* 43 Cal. 306 ; *Maloney* v. *Horan,* 49 N. Y. 111 ; *Petersire* v. *Thomas,* 28 Ohio St. 596 ; *Whitcomb* v. *Williams,* 4 Pick. 228 ; *King* v. *Chase,* 15 N. H. 13 ; *Blockinton* v. *Blockinton,* 113 Mass. 231 ; *Matter of Place,* 1 Redf. Surr. 276 ; 3 Pick. 365 ; 10 id. 77 ; Bigelow on

Estoppel, 511; *Deford* v. *Mercer*, 24 Iowa, 118; *Pursley*
v. *Hays*, 17 id. 310; Bigelow on Estoppel, 514; *Duff* v. *Wyn-*
coop, 74 Penn. St. 300; Bigelow on Estoppel, 511; *Sherman*
v. *McKeon*, 38 N. Y. 266; *Wood* v. *Seely*, 32 id. 105; *O'Conor*
v. *Varney*, 10 Gray, 231; Bigelow on Estoppel, 516; *Lewis*
v. *Maloney*, 12 Hun, 207; Freeman on Judgments, § 104;
Rogers v. *King* 8 Paige's Ch. 209.) Respondent must
be bound by the acts of her guardian in this matter,
and she is now estopped from requiring Mills to stand
the loss sustained by a failure of an investment which she
through her guardian requested and advised him to hold.
(*Dakin* v. *Dunning*, 6 Paige, 95.) At any rate Mills must be
considered as acting reasonably, and that he was justifiable in
holding stock which he and people generally considered good,
when he was advised and requested so to do by the parties in
interest. (*Higgins* v. *Whitson*, 20 Barb. 141; *Litchfield* v.
White, 7 N. Y. 438; *McRae* v. *McRae*, 3 Bradf. Surr. 199;
Thompson et al. v. *Brown*, 4 Johns. Ch. 619; *Loud* v. *Minot*,
20 Pick. 116; *Rowth* v. *Howell*, 4 Johns. Ch. 629; *Knight*
v. *Earl of Plymouth*, 3 Atk. 480.) There has been no
gross negligence, collusion, fraud or unreasonable delay in
collecting shown. (*Ruggles* v. *Sherman*, 14 Johns. 466;
Marvin v. *Stone*, 2 Cowen, 781; *Moore's Estate*, 1 Tuck.
41.)

Charles M. Baker and *Amasa J. Parker* for respondent.
The surrogate had jurisdiction of the subject-matter, and Mills'
appearance without any objection waived all objections to
irregularities, and to jurisdiction over his person. (1 Abb.
Dig. [new ed.] 219, § 64; *McCormick* v. *Penn. Central R.*
R. Co., 49 N. Y. 308–9; *Burt* v. *Trustees of Lockport*, 3
id. 200.) The judgment which has been (as to the respondent)
set aside on motion in the Supreme Court on the ground that
no guardian *ad litem* was properly appointed for her therein,
cannot be used as a shield to protect Mills from rendering an
account of his proceedings to respondent. (*Wells* v. *Thornton*,
45 Barb. 391; *Simpson* v. *Hornbeck*, 3 Lans. 53, 55.) The

orders setting aside the judgments settled the rights of the parties (Mills and respondent) as to the effect of the judgment and were conclusive between them. (*Dwight* v. *St. John*, 25 N. Y. 203, 205–7; *Demarest* v. *Darg*, 32 id. 281, 287–290; *Embury* v. *Conner*, 3 id. 522; *White* v. *Coatsworth*, 6 id. 143.) The judgment having been set aside, it could not protect Mills from an accounting, nor act as an estoppel against the respondent. (*Wells* v. *Thornton*, 45 Barb. 391, 394; *Simpson* v. *Hornbeck*, 3 Lans. 53, 55; *Smith* v. *Frankfield*, 77 N. Y. 415; *Wood* v. *Jackson*, 8 Wend. 36; *Hall* v. *Andrews*, 65 N. Y. 572.) It appearing upon the face of the record that the judgment was irregular as to Frances and obtained by false affidavits, the court never obtained jurisdiction of Frances, and the judgment was void as to her. (Freeman on Judgments, § 116, p. 87; id., § 117; *Wells* v. *Thornton*, 45 Barb. 391, 394; *Simpson* v. *Hornbeck*, 3 Lans. 53, 55; *Smith* v. *Frankfield*, 77 N. Y. 414, 419; *Wood* v. *Jackson*, 8 Wend. 10, 36; *Hall* v. *Andrews*, 65 N. Y. 572; *Dwight* v. *St. John*, 25 id. 203, 205–7; *Demarest* v. *Darg*, 32 id. 281, 287–290.) Surrogates' Courts have concurrent jurisdiction with the Court of Chancery to call executors to an account, and the pendency of an action for an accounting between some of the legatees or heirs against the administrator is no bar to prevent another heir or legatee from calling him to an account before the surrogate until the first suit has proceeded to a judgment or decree. (*Rogers* v. *King*, 8 Paige, 210, 212; *In re Hood Estate*, 15 N. Y. W. Dig. 333, 334; *Grochen* v. *Lyon*, 16 Barb. 461, 466–8; *Geery* v. *Webster*, 11 Hun, 428, 430.) As Mills has never paid to any one the amount which he should have received from the notes and bank stock, he stands as to that as though he had never accounted to any one, and he is not asked to pay any more than he would have been held to pay if there had been no settlement with Follett, Colvin and Beach. (*Maloney* v. *Horan*, 49 N. Y. 111, 115–117.) Mills should have disposed of the stock, and his holding of it was negligence. (*Baskin* v. *Baskin*, 4 Lans. 94; *Schultz* v. *Pulver*, 11 Wend. 361; *Hasler* v. *Hasler*, 1 Brad. 251; *Mat-*

ter of Gray, 27 Hun, 458; 4 Lans. 94; *Ormiston* v. *Olcott*, 24 Hun, 270, 272-3; *S. C.*, 84 N. Y. 339; *Ackerman* v. *Emott*, 4 Barb. 626; 2 Kent's Com. 416 [note *b*]; McLellan's Probate Practice, 213; *Bullock* v. *Wheatty*, 1 Collyer [130 Eng. Rep.]; *King* v. *Talbot*, 40 N. Y. 76; *Adair* v. *Brimmer*, 74 id. 550-1; *Ormiston* v. *Olcott*, 84 id. 343, 345; Dayton on Surrogates [2d ed.], 481-4; [3d ed.], 519; Wms. on Exrs. 1815-1816; *Lacey* v. *Davis*, 4 Redf. Surr. 406; *Schultz* v. *Pulver*, 11 Wend. 361; *Lawson* v. *Copeland*, 2 Brown's C. C. R. 156 [Eng. Rep.]; *Caffrey* v. *Darby*, 6 Ves. 487, 494-6; *Brazer* v. *Clark*, 5 Pick. 96-97; *Baskin* v. *Baskin*, 4 Lans. 94; *King* v. *Tabor*, 40 N. Y. 76; 2 Bouvier's Inst. 477; *Lacey* v. *Davis*, 5 Redf. Surr. 311; McClellan's Surr. [2d ed.] 433; *Gillespie* v. *Brooks*, 2 Redf. Surr. 349; Wms. on Exrs. [3d Am. ed.] 1535-6-7-8, 1542-1547; *Powell* v. *Evans*, 5 Vesey, 843-844; *Phillips* v. *Phillips*, 2 Freeman [Eng. Rep.], 11; *Tebbs* v. *Carpenter*, 1 Maddock's Ch. 166; *Eagleston & Coventry* v. *Kingston*, 8 Vesey, 466, 467; *Schultz* v. *Pulver*, 11 Wend. 361-5; *Leggett* v. *Leggett*, 24 Hun, 334-5; Story's Eq. Jur., §§ 1274-5.) Such acts of negligence or careless administration as defeat the rights of the parties entitled to distribution amount to a *devastavit*, for if persons accept the trust of executor they must perform it. They must use due diligence and not suffer the estate to be injured by their neglect. (*Hollister* v. *Burnett*, 14 Hun, 293; Dayton on Surrogates [3d ed.], 519; 2 Wms. on Exrs. 1543; *Brown's Accounting*, 16 Abb. Pr. [N. S.] 466; 5 Pick. 96; Dayton on Surrogates [1st ed.], 218; *Piety* v. *Stacy*, 4 Vesey, 622; *King* v. *Talbot*, 40 N. Y. 76; Dayton on Surrogates [2d ed.], 488; Wms. on Exrs. 1567; Redfield's Law and Practice, 501; 4 Lans. 94; 11 Wend. 361-5; *Matter of Gray*, 27 Hun, 458.) Administrators are held liable for loss arising from insolvency or otherwise where they negligently permit assets to remain on personal security longer than absolutely necessary, even if taken during the life of the testator. (*Smith* v. *Smith*, 4 Johns. Ch. 285; 2 Wms. on Exrs. 1536; *Hollister* v. *Burritt*, 14 Hun, 211, 292-

293; *Matter of Foster*, 15 id. 392; *Schultz* v. *Pulver*, 11 Wend. 361; *Powell* v. *Evans*, 5 Vesey, 844.) Mills was not a trustee in the strict legal sense. He was not authorized to retain the stock for any purpose. He should have immediately proceeded to collect the debts and turn the stock into cash and distribute it among the distributees. (84 N. Y. 345.) The investment by Oglesbie was not authorized, and Mills by taking the notes made the investment his own, and if loss followed he should be held liable. (22 Hun, 270, 272–3; 4 Lans. 93–4; *Moore's Estate*, 1 Tuck. 41; 11 Wend. 361–5; *Hollister* v. *Burritt*, 14 Hun, 293; McClellan's Probate Practice, 213.) Good faith and honest intentions will not protect an executor when he departs from prudential rules. (*Bogart* v. *Van Velsor*, 4 Edw. Ch. 718–19; *In the Matter of Ross*, 87 N. Y. 514; *Davis* v. *Clark*, id. 623.)

RUGER, Ch. J. This case comes here upon an appeal from the judgment of the General Term, affirming a decision of the surrogate of Cayuga county in favor of the petitioner, Frances Hoffman.

The proceeding was commenced before the surrogate by petition filed in May, 1880, by one of the next of kin, to compel an accounting by an administrator, and was heard from time to time until the 31st day of May, 1881, when he rendered the decree appealed from.

The case shows that the appellant, at the close of the evidence, requested the surrogate to find upon certain questions of fact in accordance with the provisions of section 2545 of the Code of Civil Procedure, and he having refused to so find except as such facts were embodied in his decree, the appellant excepted to such refusal. We think this exception was not well taken.

By subdivision 11 of section 3347 of the Code of Civil Procedure all proceedings pending in Surrogates' Courts upon the 1st day of September, 1880, were especially excepted from the operation of any of the provisions contained in chapters 14, 15, 16, 17, 18, 19 and 20 of such Code. Section 2545, being a part of chapter 18 and thus excepted, did not, therefore, apply to this proceeding.

But we are further asked to review the conclusions reached by the surrogate upon the uncontradicted evidence in the case upon exceptions taken thereto by the petitioner.

In order to present these questions clearly a statement of the circumstances out of which this controversy arises is necessary. The petitioner claims as one of the heirs at law and next of kin to David N. Follett, deceased. Follett died on the 13th day of May, 1854, leaving a large estate, consisting of both real and personal property. In 1851, he made his will, by which he devised and bequeathed the whole of his property to his wife, Mary A. Follett, and his eight children, Charles P., David, James A., Triphena, Amelia, Mary, Fidelia M. and Fanny Jane Follett, who were born prior to the execution of the will. Preston Thompson, Jesse H. Foreman and Lee Oglesbie were named as his executors. The petitioner, whose maiden name was Frances R. Follett, was born in October, 1853, after the execution of the will, and so far as her rights were concerned, her father died intestate. After the testator's death his will was duly proved, and Lee Oglesbie and Jesse H. Foreman alone qualified and acted as executors under it. A large amount of property came into the hands of these executors, and they continued in the administration of the estate until 1863, when they died. Neither of them rendered an account of their administration of the estate. After their respective deaths, on November 19, 1863, the appellant, William B. Mills, was appointed administrator, with the will annexed, of the testator, and received into his hands such portion of the estate as he could recover, and continued in the administration thereof until 1869, when, under a judgment of the Supreme Court, purporting to determine the rights of all of the parties interested in the estate, he settled with and paid off each of the heirs and legatees of the testator, and was discharged from its further administration. In July, 1854, one Levi Colvin was appointed by the surrogate as the general guardian of the infant children of D. N.

Follett, including Frances R. Follett, the petitioner, and continued to act as such guardian until July, 1869, when the petitioner, having arrived at the age of fourteen years, selected
and the surrogate appointed one Harvey C. Beach as her
guardian. Beach continued to act as such guardian until October, 1874, when the petitioner arrived at majority. The
affairs of the estate having become greatly complicated,
owing to the infancy of many of the persons interested therein,
the birth of issue subsequent to the execution of the will, the
decease of the executors before they had rendered an account,
the necessity for the support of the infants during minority
by their mother, Mary Ann Follett, and the existence of her
dower rights, the action referred to was commenced in November, 1867, in the Supreme Court by James A. Follett, one
of the legatees under the will, against Mary Ann Follett; the
administrator, William B. Mills ; Frances R. Follett, the petitioner, and Levi Colvin, her general guardian, and all other
heirs at law and devisees of David N. Follett, deceased, with a
view of determining their respective rights in the estate, the
amount thereof still remaining subject to division and distribution, the persons who were liable therefor, and the respective amounts for which they were so liable, and for an accounting by the administrator, and the payment by him to the
parties entitled thereto of the amount which should be found
in his hands. Calvin R. Aldrich, an attorney of the Supreme
Court, was appointed guardian *ad litem* for the petitioner in
the action. Each of the other defendants also appeared, and
the action resulted in a decree rendered July 12, 1869, whereby
among other things it was adjudged that the appellant, William B. Mills, had certain moneys in his hands belonging to
the petitioner, and requiring him to pay the same to her, and
that upon the payment thereof and complying with the other
provisions of such judgment he should be released and discharged from all claims and demands against him as administrator of the estate. The record shows that after the rendition of said judgment the appellant fully performed all of

the obligations therein enjoined upon him and paid over
to Harvey C. Beach, the general guardian of the petitioner,
the moneys thereby directed to be paid to her. Other defendants who were also adjudged to pay moneys arising out of
the estate to the petitioner, paid them to her general guardian
in July, 1869. The provisions of the judgment seem to have
been complied with by each of the parties who were required to
perform any act necessary to a complete final settlement of the
estate and of the rights of the respective parties interested therein.
After the petitioner had arrived at majority, in July, 1875,
she commenced proceedings in the Supreme Court to vacate
this judgment upon the ground that the appointment of a
guardian *ad litem* for her in the action was irregular, and that
the court did not thereby acquire jurisdiction to render judgment against her therein. This proceeding resulted in an order,
on October 26, 1875, vacating the judgment so far as it affected
the petitioner.

It is claimed by the petitioner, notwithstanding the receipt
by her general guardian of the sums awarded to her
by the judgment, that by reason of this order she was
entitled to require the appellant to account before the
surrogate as to his entire administration of the estate.
Assuming that she is correct in this contention, and that
such judgment has been deprived, so far as she is concerned, of
any force as an adjudication of the questions involved in this
controversy, she could, nevertheless, upon arriving at majority,
ratify the acts of her general guardian and estop herself from
controverting either the validity of the judgment of which
she had received the benefits or the settlements made thereunder. The judgment operated after its rendition as a contract between all of the parties to the action, and whether the
same was void or voidable, the several parties thereto still had
the power to give it validity by assenting to its terms or accepting the benefits which it conferred.

A principal cannot accept the benefits of an unauthorized
contract made by an agent and repudiate its obligations.
Neither can a party enjoy the rights awarded to him by a

judgment and deny its force as an adjudication. (*Wood* v. *Seely*, 32 N. Y. 105; *Sherman* v. *McKeon*, 38 id. 266; *Paine* v. *Hubbard*, 6 Wis. 175; 1 Redf. Surr. Rep. 276.)

The undisputed facts in the case show that the petitioner, with full knowledge of the terms of the judgment, received from her guardian, Harvey C. Beach, after arriving at her majority, the moneys which had previously been paid to him by the appellant in satisfaction of the amount thereby awarded to her. It also appeared that in 1876 she received other moneys from her guardian, which the same judgment required other defendants to pay to her, and which they had previously paid in compliance with such requirements. And, finally, after all these settlements had been made, and nearly four years after the judgment had been vacated as to her, this proceeding was commenced by the respondent before the surrogate to compel the appellant to account.

In view of all the circumstances of this case, we think that the court below erred in holding that the appellant could again be called upon to account for his administration. It is quite certain that he could not recover back the moneys which he had paid in obedience to the judgment, for the purpose of settling the estate, to any of the parties to the action. Not only had six years elapsed after such payments were made before the judgment was vacated, but the moneys which the appellant had paid the petitioner's representative had been paid over to her before this proceeding was instituted. Neither was the judgment vacated as to any of the parties except the petitioner, and as to them it still remains in force. Moneys paid to them were certainly not recoverable by him as a consequence of the order obtained by the petitioner.

It appears, therefore, that the petitioner has now moneys in her hands which she has received from the appellant solely by force of the judgment in question, and claims to repudiate the obligations of the same judgment under which he paid those moneys.

1883.] PEOPLE, ex rel. GERE et al., v. WHITLOCK et al. **191**

Statement of case.

This we think she cannot do. The receipt by her of such moneys was an unequivocal act of ratification, made with full knowledge of the circumstances, and at a time when she was capable of binding herself, and she cannot now be permitted to deny the validity of an act which she has thus ratified and confirmed.

For these reasons we think the judgment of the surrogate and of the General Term should be reversed, and judgment for a dismissal of her petition, with costs, rendered against the petitioner.

All concur.

Judgment accordingly.

THE PEOPLE, ex rel. DANIEL GERE et al., Appellants, *v.* JOHN R. WHITLOCK et al., Respondents.

1
92
152

The act entitled " An act to amend an act to provide for the election of police commissioners in the city of Syracuse, and to establish a police force therein, and to repeal certain sections thereof " (Chap. 559, Laws of 1881), is not violative of the provision of the State Constitution (Art. 3, § 16) declaring that no local or private bill shall contain more than one subject and that shall be embraced in the title.

Under the provision of said amendatory act (§ 2) giving to the mayor power to remove any police commissioner, the mayor was authorized to remove a commissioner in office when the act took effect.

Under said provision the mayor has power to remove without giving the commissioner notice or opportunity to be heard.

The legislature may abridge the term of an office created by it, by express words, or may specify an event upon the happening of which it shall end.

It is also within the power of the legislature, where it has given the authority to appoint to an office created by it, to authorize the removal of the incumbent without notice or a hearing.

People, ex rel. the Mayor, v. *Nichols* (79 N. Y. 582), distinguished.

(Argued March 16, 1883; decided April 17, 1883.)

APPEAL from judgment of the General Term of the Supreme Court, in the fourth judicial department, entered upon an order made October 20, 1882, which affirmed a judgment in favor of defendants, entered upon a decision of the court on trial at Special Term.

This action was in the nature of a *quo warranto* to try the title of defendants to the office of police commissioners of the city of Syracuse.

On the 29th day of August, 1881, the mayor of Syracuse addressed to each of the relators a written notice that he had removed him from the office of police commissioner, of which he was then an incumbent, by virtue of the act chapter 559, Laws of 1881, and on the same evening he submitted to the common council a statement of his reasons for such removal, together with a message appointing the defendants to fill the vacancies thereby created. No notice of the mayor's intention had been given to the relators, or to either of them, no charges were presented, and no hearing, or opportunity of hearing, or explanation was afforded to them.

The defendants immediately afterward qualified as such police commissioners, and took possession of the books and papers of the board, and have ever since exercised the duties of the office to the exclusion of the relators.

Louis Marshall for appellants. Chapter 559 of the Laws of 1881 is a local act, and is void because it does not comply with the requirements of the Constitution (Art. 3, § 16) as to its title. (*People* v. *The Board of Supervisors of Chautauqua,* 43 N. Y. 10; *The People* v. *Hill,* 35 id. 449; *Stewart* v. *The Father Matthew Society,* 41 Mich. 67; *Dorsey's Appeal,* 72 Penn. St. 192; *Town of Fishkill* v. *Fishkill, etc., Plankroad Co.,* 22 Barb. 634; *People* v. *Commissioners of Highways of Palatine,* 53 id. 70; *People* v. *Allen,* 42 N. Y. 404; *People* v. *O'Brien,* 38 id. 193; *Huber* v. *The People,* 49 id. 132; *Meek* v. *Gaskin,* 42 id. 186; *The Matter of the Town of Flatbush,* 60 id. 398; *City of Watertown* v. *Fairbanks,* 65 id. 588; *The Matter of Sackett Street,* 74 id. 95; *People* v. *Common Council of Brooklyn,* 13 Abb. Pr. [N. S.] 121; *Murray* v. *The Mayor of New York, etc.,* 11 J. & S. 164; *Mat-*

ter of Blodgett, 15 N. Y. W'kly Dig. 21, Court of Appeals, tried 1882; *State* v. *Clinton*, 27 La. Ann. 40; *Moses* v. *The Mayor, etc.*, 52 Ala. 212; *People* v. *The Institution of Deaconesses*, 71 Ill. 229; *Town of Union* v. *Rader*, 39 N. J. Law. 509; *The People, ex rel. Ryan*, v. *Green*, 58 N. Y. 295.) This statute should be construed prospectively. (*Dash* v. *Van Kleek*, 7 Johns. 477; *Hackley* v. *Sprague*, 10 Wend. 133; *Sayre* v. *Wisner*, 8 id. 661; *Jarvis* v. *Jarvis*, 3 Edw. Ch. 462; *Johnson* v. *Burrell*, 2 Hill, 238; *Palmer* v. *Connelly*, 4 Denio, 374; *Sanford* v. *Bennett*, 24 N. Y. 20; *Ely* v. *Holton*, 15 id. 595; *Jackson* v. *Van Zandt*, 12 Johns. 159; *Benton* v. *Wickwire*, 54 N. Y. 226; *Carpenter* v. *Shimer*, 24 Hun, 464; *Williams* v. *City of Oswego*, 25 id. 36; *New York & Oswego Midland R. R. Co.* v. *Van Horn*, 57 N. Y. 473.) If it had been intended that the mayor had a right to remove police commissioners who were in office at the time of the passage of the act, the right of appointing their successors would not have been limited to a time subsequent to the expiration of their terms of office. (*Curtis* v. *Leavitt*, 15 N. Y. 59; *Moulton* v. *Hunt*, 23 id.; *Wait* v. *Wait*, 4 Comst. 95; *People* v. *Tiernan*, 35 Barb. 198; *Frask* v. *Payne*, 43 id. 569; *Childs* v. *Smith*, 55 id. 45.) The removal of the relators without a hearing or an opportunity for an explanation, and upon the grounds specified by the mayor, was not authorized by the statute. (*Bagg's Case*, 11 Coke, 99; Term Reports, 209; *People, ex rel. Gray*, v. *The Medical Society*, 24 Barb. 578; *People, ex rel. Bartlett*, v. *The Medical Society*, 32 N. Y. 181; *People, ex rel. Schmitt*, v. *St. Franciscus Society*, 24 How. Pr. 216; *Queen* v. *Sadlers Co.*, 10 House of Lords Cases, 404; *Black and White Smiths Society* v. *Van Dyke*, 2 Whart. 309; *Washington Society* v. *Bach*, 20 Penn. St. 425; *Sleeper* v. *Franklin Lyceum*, 7 R. I. 523; *People, ex rel. Doyle*, v. *Ben. Society*, 3 Hun, 361; *Wachel* v. *Noah Ben. Society*, 84 N. Y. 28; *People* v. *Sailors' Snug Harbor*, 54 Barb. 532; *Innes* v. *Willey*, 1 C. & K. 257; *Fritz* v. *Muck, Pres't of St. Stephen's Society*, 62 How. Pr.; *People, ex rel. Munday*, v. *Fire Commissioners*, 72 N. Y.

445 ; *Matter of Nichols*, 57 How. 395 ; *People, ex rel. Mayor, etc.*, v. *Nichols*, 79 N. Y. 582 ; 72 id. 445 ; *Murdoch* v. *The Trustees of Phillips Academy*, 12 Pick. 244 ; *Paige* v. *Hardin*, 8 B. Monr. 673 ; *Field* v. *The Commonwealth*, 32 Penn. St. 476 ; *Barnshay's Case*, 18 Q. B. 173 ; *Commonwealth* v. *Stifer*, 25 Penn. St. 23.)

M. A. Knapp for respondents. The title of the act of 1881 (Chap. 559) fully discloses the purpose and intent of its provisions and meets the requirements of the Constitution. (Sedgwick on Construction of Statutory and Constitutional Law, 530, 531, 532, and notes; Const. Tenn., Art. 2, § 17 ; Stat. Tenn [Thompson & Sager], vol. 1, p. 93 ; *People, ex rel. City of Rochester*, v. *Briggs et al.*, 50 N. Y. 554 ; *Harris* v. *The People*, 59 id. 600 ; Bouvier's Law Dictionary, 118 ; *The Cases of Stewart* v. *The Father Matthew Society*, 41 Mich. 67 ; *The Matter of Sackett Street*, 74 N. Y. 95 ; *Murry* v. *The Mayor, etc.*, 11 J. & S. Super. Ct. ; *Huber* v. *People*, 49 N. Y. 132 ; *People, ex rel. City of Rochester*, v. *Briggs*, 50 id. 554 ; *People, ex rel. Davies*, v. *Com. of Taxes of N. Y.*, 47 id. 501 ; *Morford* v. *Nugen*, 8 Iowa, 83 ; *Phillips* v. *Covington & Cincinnati Bridge Co.*, 2 Metc. [Ky.] 219 ; *Leuhrman* v. *Taxing District*, 2 Lea [Tenn.], 426 ; *State* v. *Fox*, 51 Md. 412 ; *Matter of Mayer*, 50 N. Y. 504 ; *People, ex rel. Hayden*, v. *City of Rochester*, id. 525 ; *Matter of Van Antwerp*, 56 id. 264 ; *Neuendorff* v. *Duryea*, 69 id. 557 ; *Kerrigan* v. *Force*, 68 id. 381 ; *Connor* v. *Mayor*, 5 id. 285 ; *Sun Mut. Ins. Co.* v. *Mayor*, 8 id. 241 ; *Brewster* v. *City of Syracuse*, 19 id. 116 ; *People, ex rel. Crowell*, v. *Lawrence*, 41 id. 139 ; *Franklin* v. *Trustees Vis Dansville*, 1 Hun, 593 ; *People, ex rel. H. R. Co.*, v. *Havemeyer, Mayor, etc.*, 3 id. 106 ; *Alexander* v. *Bennett*, 38 N. Y. Super. Ct. 498 ; *People* v. *Bennett*, 54 Barb. 486 ; *Mosier* v. *Hilton*, 15 id. 660 ; *Matter of Wakker*, 9 id. 163 ; *White* v. *Syracuse & Utica R. Co.*, 14 id. 563 ; *Devlin* v. *Mayor*, 50 How. Pr. 12 ; *Cen. C. R. R. Co.* v. *23rd St. R. R. Co.*, 54 id. 168 ; *Outwater* v. *Mayor*, 18 id. 572 ; *In re Petition of Wm. T. Blodgett*,

14 W'kly Dig. 326; *McReynolds* v. *Smallhouse*, 8 Ky. [Bush] 453; *Louisville & O. T. R. Co.* v. *Bullard*, 2 Metc. [Ky.] 166; *Mayor, etc.*, v. *Reitz*, 50 Md. 574; *Mayor of Annapolis* v. *State of Maryland*, 30 id. 118; *Hammond* v. *Lesseps*, 31 La. Ann. 336; *City of Hannibal* v. *County of Marian*, 69 Mo. 571; *People, ex rel. Davies*, v. *Commissioners of Taxes*, 47 N. Y. 501; Cooley's Const. Lim. 148; *Yellow River Improvement Co.* v. *Arnold*, 46 Wis. 224. See *Brandon* v. *State*, 16 Ind. 197; *Harris* v. *People*, 59 N. Y. 600; *City of Eureka* v. *Davis*, 21 Kans. 578.) The provisions of chapter 559 of the Session Laws of 1881 are applicable to the relators. (*Moore* v. *Mausert*, 49 N. Y. 333; *People, ex rel. Sears*, v. *Board of Assessors of Brooklyn*, 84 id. 610; *Matter of Executive Communication*, 15 Fla. 735; *State* v. *Andrews*, 20 Texas, 230; *Long* v. *Mayor*, 81 N. Y. 425; *Holley* v. *Mayor*, 59 id. 166; *D. & L. Plankroad Co.* v. *Allen*, 16 Barb. 15; *Phillips* v. *Mayor*, 1 Hilt. 483.) As the office of police commissioner of the city of Syracuse was first created by chapter 17 of the Session Laws of 1869, it has, therefore, none of the elements or incidents of a common-law office, and the relators can claim no such rights or privileges as custom or ancient usage may have secured to common-law officers. (*Ex parte Hannen*, 13 Peters, 260; *Smyth* v. *Latham*, 9 Bing. 692.) The legislature had ample power, therefore, to provide by law that said police commissioners should be appointed instead of elected by the people, and it is not even necessary that the appointment be made by local authority. (*People* v. *Draper*, 15 N. Y. 532; *People* v. *Palmer*, 52 id. 83; State Const., art. 10, § 3; Session Laws 1881, chap. 559, § 2.) When a person accepts a public office in this State, of the nature of that held by the relators, he accepts it subject to whatever changes and regulations the legislature may thereafter see fit to make concerning it. (*Connor* v. *Mayor*, 5 N. Y. 285; *Smith* v. *Mayor*, 37 id. 518; *Long* v. *Mayor*, 81 id. 425; *Holley* v. *Mayor*, 59 id. 166; *Gillespie* v. *Mayor*, 6 Daly, 286; *City of Wyandotte* v. *Drennen*, 24 Alb. L. J. 401; *Phillips* v. *Mayor*, 1 Hilt. 483; *People* v. *Morris*, 13 Wend.

331–337.) The action of the mayor is fully sustained by authorities in this State and elsewhere. (*People, ex rel. Munday,* v. *Fire Commissioners,* 72 N. Y. 445; *People, ex rel.
Sims,* v. *Fire Commissioners,* 73 id. 437.) The present case
belongs to that class where the proceedings to remove are not
intended to be judicial, but executive or ministerial in their
nature. (*People, ex rel. Westray,* v. *Mayor,* 16 Hun, 309;
Matter of Bartlett, 9 How. Pr. 417; *Queen* v. *Governors
Darlington Free Grammar School,* 6 Ad. & El. 714; *People*
v. *Stout,* 19 How. Pr. 168; *Attorney-General, ex rel. Taylor,*
v. *Brown,* 1 Wis. 513; *State* v. *McGarry,* 21 id. 496;
Keenan v. *Perry,* 24 Texas, 259; *State* v. *Dohert,* 25 La.
Ann. 119; *People* v. *Bearfield,* 35 Barb. 254; *People* v. *Dep't
Police, etc.,* 5 Hun, 457; 1 Dill. Mun. Corp., § 13 [3d ed.].)

DANFORTH, J. The thing in dispute is the office of police
commissioner of the city of Syracuse. The relators claim it
under a statute of 1869, entitled "An act to provide for the
election of police commissioners in the city of Syracuse, and
to establish a police force therein" (Chap. 17, Laws of 1869).
The defendants claim it under chapter 559 of the Laws of 1881,
entitled "An act to amend an act to provide for the election
of police commissioners in the city of Syracuse, and to establish a police force therein, and to repeal certain sections thereof."
The relators argue that the act of 1881 is a local act; that its
subject is not expressed in the title, and that it is, therefore,
void under the prohibition of the Constitution (§ 16, art. 3).
    It is plain that the act is local, for it has no force beyond
the city named in it, and does not affect the people of the
State; but its title expresses an intention of the legislature,
and a single object — to amend a previous and specified statute. Nor do the provisions in the body of the act go beyond
it. The act of 1869 provides for the choice by ballot, by the
electors of the city, of police commissioners, their term of office,
their organization as a board, and their powers. The act of
1881 repeals those provisions of the act of 1869, relating to the
election of the commissioners, and by amendment confers au-

1883.] PEOPLE, ex rel. GERE et al., v. WHITLOCK et al. 197

Opinion of the Court, per DANFORTH, J.

thority upon the mayor, "upon the expiration of the term of office of any of the present commissioners," to appoint his successor, and in like manner fill any vacancy that might otherwise occur, authorizes him to remove from office any commissioner "for any cause deemed sufficient to himself," and prescribes the powers and duties of the commissioners. All these things are properly incident to the subject of the original act, and it is difficult to see how the members of the legislature or the public could in any way be misled by the actual title of the act, or by what other words their vigilance as to the real topic of legislation could be better excited. The selection of the commissioners is dealt with in both statutes, and the amendment consists in the substitution of one mode of selection for another; an important alteration doubtless, but in no respect foreign to the main purpose or subject of the act, which was the establishment of a police force, nor outside the office of an amendment, of which notice was sufficiently given by a title indicating the act to be amended, and its subject-matter. The statute of 1881, therefore, is not broader than its title, and does not contravene the constitutional provision upon which the appellant relies. The object of that provision is fairly answered by a title giving notice to whomsoever reads, that legislation is impending, which, by amending the act referred to, might touch upon the subject-matter of any of its provisions.

By the sixth section of the act of 1869, it was provided that "the commissioners may be removed for cause, in the same manner as sheriffs are removed," and the relators contend that the amendment of 1881, by which this provision was omitted, and power of removal given to the mayor, has no application to them, because they were in office when the last act took effect. This construction is untenable. The authority given to the mayor is general to remove from office any commissioner for any cause sufficient to himself, and we find nothing in the act to restrain in any degree the intent of the legislature as expressed by those words. They merely substitute one tribunal for another, and vest it with power over the commissioner. He was not less subject to removal under the act of

1869 than under the act of 1881, but by the last a new mode of procedure was adopted, and to that each commissioner is made subject. He can no more complain that he is proceeded against by the altered mode than a suitor in our courts could claim to maintain or resist a cause of action by the procedure in force when it accrued. As to that he has no vested right, and, therefore, the cases, *Dash* v. *Van Kleeck* (7 Johns. 477), *People, ex rel. Ryan,* v. *Green* (58 N. Y. 295), and others of like character cited by the appellants, have no application. The office was created by the legislature, and they might abridge its term by express words, or specify an event, upon the happening of which it should end. (*Conner* v. *Mayor, etc.,* 5 N. Y. 285; *Long* v. *Mayor, etc.,* 81 id. 425.) In this case the event specified by the legislature is removal by the mayor.

The next position of the relators raises a more interesting general question : whether they were entitled to have notice or be heard before the final action of the mayor. At common law there could be no doubt as to this. *Bagg's Case* (11 Coke, 99), *King* v. *Gaskin* (8 Term Rep. 209), and many others cited by the learned counsel for the appellant, stand upon the principle that no one shall be condemned unheard, but this, too, when applied to· the term of office, is within the control of the legislature, and as it gave the power to appoint, may also give the power to remove. (Const., art. 10, § 3 ; *People, ex rel. Sims,* v. *Board of Fire Commissioners of the City of New York,* 73 N. Y. 437.) In the act before us (Laws of 1881, § 1, chap. 559) the power of removal has been expressly conferred upon the mayor, to be exercised as to him shall seem meet. In *People, ex rel. The Mayor,* v. *Nichols* (79 N. Y. 582), cited by the appellant, the statute requires not only that cause for removal should exist, but also that the officer should have an opportunity to be heard. The statute before us lacks both conditions. No opportunity to be heard is given, and it is enough if the mayor thinks there is sufficient cause. It may or may not exist, except in his imagination, but his conclusion is final. The diligence of appellants' counsel has found no case like it, and those cited by him do not apply. They require either the actual existence of "cause," or "sufficient cause" for removal, and so by implication impose investigation before action, or by express language give a hearing to the accused member or official. Here the removal is to be determined summarily, and is intrusted to the unrestrained discretion of the mayor. Nor is this without a precedent. Among other cases, like power is given to the governor over the superintendent of public works, and to the latter over his assistant superintendents (Const. of N. Y., art. 5, § 3), and to the board of commissioners of the fire department of New York, over certain subordinates (Laws of 1873, chap. 335, § 28). Under that statute it was held that the power of removal was to be exercised at pleasure, except in cases where there was an express limitation to a removal after notice and a hearing, and for cause. (*People, ex rel. Sims,* v. *Board of Fire Comm'rs, supra.*)

We are, therefore, of opinion that no reason for a reversal of the judgment appealed from is shown, and it should be affirmed.

All concur. RAPALLO and EARL, JJ., on the ground that the title of the amendatory act was sufficient to cover the subject of removal, without passing upon the question, whether it was sufficient to substitute appointment in place of election of commissioners.

Judgment affirmed.

LEWIS J. PHILLIPS et al., Executors, etc., Respondents, *v.* MARIA DAVIES et al., Appellants.

Where, upon examination of a will, taken as a whole, the intention of the testator appears clear, but its plain and definite purposes are endangered by inapt or inaccurate modes of expression, the court may, and it is its duty to, subordinate the language to the intention; it may reject words and limitations, supply or transpose them to get at the correct meaning.

M., at the time of making her will, and of her death, owned a large amount of real estate but only a small amount of personal property. By her will, after providing for the payment of debts, she first gave her estate, real and personal, to her executors in trust, to rent, etc., and apply the rents, income, etc., to the use of her husband during his life. Then followed ten clauses purporting to create separate and independent trusts; also numerous legacies, all of which would substantially fail in the absence of a trust estate, or power in trust vested in the executors, by force of which the real estate could be sold and converted into money. Certain real estate was also specifically devised, and the executors were directed to pay off incumbrances thereon, which, in the absence of such power, could not be done. The clause appointing executors contained the following: "and during the life-time of my said husband my said executors, and such and whichever of them as shall act, are authorized and empowered, by and with the consent of my said husband, to sell and dispose of any part of my estate, real and personal, not specifically bequeathed." In an action for a construction of the will, *held*, that said clause was to be construed as conferring upon her executors a power of sale, which during the life of her husband, was to be exercised only with his consent, but thereafter continuing to exist; and that, therefore, the executors had power to sell after the death of the husband, and convert into money so much of the real estate as was not specifically devised.

(Argued March 16, 1888; decided April 17, 1888.)

APPEAL from judgment of the General Term of the Supreme Court, in the first judicial department, entered upon an order made December 14, 1882, which affirmed a judgment entered upon a decision of the court on trial at Special Term.

This action was brought to obtain a construction of the will of Matilda Phillips, deceased.

The substance of the will and the material facts appear in the opinion.

William Allen Butler for appellants. The due execution of a power requires a substantial compliance with every condition which precedes or accompanies its exercise. After the death of her husband the power of sale given by the testatrix could not by any possibility be exercised. (*Matter of Vanderbilt*, 20 Hun, 122; 1 R. S. 737, §§ 121, 122; Hill. on Trustees, 478; *Allen* v. *De Witt*, 3 N. Y. 276 at 278; *Barber* v. *Cary*, 11 id. 397; *Hetzel* v. *Barber*, 69 id. 1; *Richardson* v. *Sharpe*,

29 Barb. 222.) The sole devise in trust of the real estate having been for the life of John D. Phillips, and the sole power
of sale having been conditioned on its exercise during his life
and with his consent, and neither the devise nor the power having ever taken effect, owing to the failure of the executors to
qualify during his life, the plaintiffs had no right to commence
this action for the construction of the will. (*Dill* v. *Wisner*,
88 N. Y. 153 at 160; *Bailey* v. *Briggs*, 56 id. 407 at 413;
Post v. *Hover*, 33 id. 593; *Bowen* v. *Smith*, 10 Paige, 193;
Chipman v. *Montgomery*, 63 N. Y. 221; *Monarque* v. *Monarque*, 80 id. 320; *Onderdonk* v. *Mott*, 34 Barb. 106; *Bailey*
v. *Briggs*, 56 N. Y. 407, 413; *Mead* v. *Mitchell*, 17 id. 210;
Brevoort v. *Brevoort*, 70 id. 136.) If this action can be sustained and the question of the intent of the testator as to the
powers of the executors is to be inquired into, the title of the
heirs at law will not be disturbed unless it is made plainly to
appear that the testatrix intended that her real estate, if unsold
at her husband's death, should not descend to them, but should
vest in the executors surviving her husband for the purposes
of the will. (2 Jarman on Wills, 744; 1 id. 465; *Lynes* v.
Townsend, 33 N. Y. 558; *Roe* v. *Blackett*, Cowp. 235; 1
Bro. C. C. 441; *Moore* v. *Heaseman*, Willes, 141; *Hay* v.
The Earl of Coventry, 3 T. R. 83; *Wheaton* v. *Andress*, 23
Wend. 462; *Post* v. *Hover*, 33 N. Y. 593 at 599; *Rathbone*
v. *Dyckman*, 3 Paige, 9; Redfield on Wills, 425, n. 5, p. 434,
§ 18; *Allen's Ex.* v. *Allen*, 18 How. [U. S.] 385; *Lynes* v.
Townsend, 33 N. Y. 570; *Roberts* v. *Corning*, 23 Hun, 303;
Harvey v. *Olmstead*, 1 N. Y. 493; *Vanderzee* v. *Vanderzee*,
30 Barb. 331; affirmed, 36 N. Y. 281; *Vanderwerker* v. *Vanderwerker*, 7 Barb. 221; *Van Kleck* v. *The Reformed Dutch
Church*, 6 Paige, 600–612; *Schauber* v. *Jackson*, 2 Wend. 26;
Delafield v. *Parish*, 25 N. Y. 9; *Crowningshield* v. *Crowningshield*, 2 Gray, 526) The court below erred in construing
the will to intend that the trust estate or the power of sale as
to the real estate should extend beyond the life of John D.
Phillips, the husband of the testatrix. (*Richardson* v. *Sharpe*,
29 Barb. 222; *Dunsdee* v. *Goldbacker*, 8 Abb. [N. S.] 439.)

It was error in the court below to assume that the testatrix, when she made her will, had in view a personal estate of only $16,000, and that, therefore, she must have intended to give a power of sale to extend beyond the life of her husband. (*Bevan* v. *Cooper*, 72 N. Y. 317; *Reynolds* v. *Reynolds*, 16 id. 257; *Lupton* v. *Lupton*, 2 Johns. Ch. 623; *Harris* v. *Fly*, 7 Paige, 423; *Myers* v. *Eddy*, 47 Barb. 263; *Taylor* v. *Dodd*, 58 N. Y. 335; *Kalbfleisch* v. *Kalbfleisch*, 67 id. 354; *Hoyt* v. *Hoyt*, 85 id. 142; *Covenhoven* v. *Schuler*, 2 Paige, 129, 130; *Trustees of Theological Seminary* v. *Kellogg*, 16 N. Y. 88, 89; 1 Jarman on Wills, 411, 412, 415, 416; *Simms* v. *Dougherty*, 5 Ves. 247; *Post* v. *Hover*, 33 N. Y. 599; *Van Nostrand* v. *Moore*, 52 id. 12.) The will took effect at the death of the testatrix, and the property must be viewed as it was at her death. The power of sale, being discretionary, did not constitute an equitable conversion of the real estate into personalty. (*Stagg* v. *Jackson*, 1 N. Y. 206; *Allen* v. *De Witt*, 3 id. 276; *Lovett's Ex'rs* v. *Gillender*, 35 id. 617; *White* v. *Howard*, 46 id. 162; *Harris* v. *Clark*, 7 id. 242, 261; *Reed* v. *Underhill*, 12 Barb. 113; *Hetzel* v. *Barber*, 69 N. Y. 1, 7; *Lucas* v. *Brandreth*, 28 Beav. 273.) There can be no presumption of any other intent than that which the words employed in a will express, and the rule which permits a construction in aid of an intent not clearly expressed never allows a disregard of plain provisions which speak positively, and which must have full effect given to them, even though the result may be to make it impracticable to execute the will as to all its provisions. (*Myers* v. *Eddy*, 47 Barb. 263; *Van Nostrand* v. *Moore*, 52 N. Y. 12; *Schauber* v. *Jackson*, 2 Wend. 13 at 33.)

Everett P. Wheeler for respondents. The court has jurisdiction at the suit of an executor upon whom a power of sale is conferred by a will, to be exercised by him for the benefit of third parties, to entertain a suit for the construction of a will, and to obtain the instruction of the court as to his duty in the premises. The power is such cases is a power of trust.

(1 Rev. Stat. 734, § 94 [Edmonds' ed., p. 684]; 1 Redfield on
Wills, 492; *Dill* v. *Wisner*, 88 N. Y. 153; *Delancy* v. *Van
Aulen*, 84 id. 16.) The directions to create certain trust funds
by investment in personal securities must fail entirely unless a
power to sell the real estate exists. When this is the case and
the directions are imperative a power of sale will always be
implied. (*Kalbfleisch* v. *Kalbfleisch*, 67 N. Y. 354; *Hoyt* v.
Hoyt, 85 id. 142; *Taylor* v. *Dodd*, 58 id. 335; *Shulters* v.
Johnson, 38 Barb. 80; *Livingston* v. *Murray*, 39 How. Pr.
102; *Connover* v. *Hoffman*, 1 Bosw. 214; *Van Vechten* v.
Keator, 63 N.Y. 52; *Tucker* v. *Tucker*, 5 id. 408, 413; *Meakings* v. *Cromwell*, id. 136; *Hoyt* v. *Hoyt*, 85 id. 142, 149;
Lupton v. *Lupton*, 2 Johns. Ch. 614.) It is the intention of
the testator expressed in the will which is to govern. (1 Redfield on Wills, 432; *DuBois* v. *Ray*, 35 N. Y. 162, 175.) If
the intention is that the real estate shall be converted into
money, it will be considered in equity as so converted, from
the time the conversion is directed to take place. (*Fisher* v.
Banta, 66 N. Y. 468, 477; *Kalbfleisch* v. *Kalbfleisch*, 67 id.
354; *Inglis* v. *Trustees Sailors' Snug Harbor*, 3 Pet. 99, 117;
Towns v. *Wentworth*, 11 Moo. P. C. 526, 543; *Abbott* v. *Carpenter*, 7 H. of L. Cas. 68; *Biddulph* v. *Lees*, 1 Ell. Bl.
& Ell. 289.) The intent of the testator as manifested by
the whole will should control and the consent of the husband required by the last clause is a limitation which expired upon his
death, leaving the executors an unlimited power to sell thereafter. (*Kalbfleisch* v. *Kalbfleisch*, 67 N. Y. 354; *Inglis* v.
Trustees S. S. H., 3 Pet. 99–117; *Towns* v. *Wentworth*, 11
Moore's P. C. 526, 543; *Abbott* v. *Carpenter*, 7 H. of L. Cas.
68; *Biddulph* v. *Lees*, E. B. & E. 289.)

FINCH, J. The courts which have construed this will were
so impressed with the necessity of a trust estate, or power in
trust vested in the executors, by force of which the real estate
could be sold and converted into money, to effect the carefully
framed and deliberately expressed purposes of the testatrix,
that they have sustained a trust power as arising by implication,

and have been ready to put a construction upon the last clause of the will somewhat different from that suggested by the order of its language. That clause is as follows: "I hereby nominate and appoint my beloved husband, John D. Phillips, and my sons, Louis, Isaac, Henry J. and Asher L., executors of this my last will and testament, hereby authorizing such and whichever of them as shall qualify, and the survivor and survivors of them to act in the like manner and with like effect as if they or he alone had been named. as such executor, and *during the life-time of my said husband,* my said executors, and such and whichever of them as shall act are authorized and empowered, *by and with the consent of my said husband,* to sell and dispose of any part of my estate, real and personal, not specifically bequeathed," etc. If the two expressions we have italicized belong together, and have been separated by accident or mistake; if they may be brought together by transposition, and if then they may be inclosed in brackets and read parenthetically, the construction of the courts below will be reached, and what seems inevitably to have been the purpose and intention of the testatrix will be preserved. The material part of the clause in question would then read thus, viz.: "and my said executors, and such and whichever of them as shall act are authorized and empowered (*during the life-time of my said husband, by and with the consent of my said husband*) to sell and dispose of any part of my estate, real and personal," etc. If such was the real meaning and intention of the testatrix; if an examination of the whole will forces that conviction; if its plain and definite purposes are endangered by inapt or inaccurate modes of expression; and we are sure that we know what the testatrix meant; we have a right and it is our duty to subordinate the language to the intention. In such a case the court may reject words and limitations, supply them or transpose them, to get at the correct meaning. (*Pond* v. *Bergh,* 10 Paige, 140; *Drake* v. *Pell,* 3 Edw. 251; *Mason* v. *Jones,* 2 Barb. 229.) But we are to construe the will, not make it anew; and the inquiry comes whether in the case at bar the actual intention has been reached in the construction adopted.

The testatrix owned a large amount of real estate but only about $16,000 in personal property. She left surviving her, besides her husband, four sons and five daughters, all of age and all of the latter married, and one grand-daughter, the sole representative of a deceased daughter. This property she sought to dispose of for the benefit of this family by a will which is long, deliberate, and characterized by distinct and definite purposes. After the payment of debts she first provided for her husband. She gave all her property, real and personal, to her executors in trust, to rent, invest and improve the same, and apply the rents, issues, income, interest, dividends, and profits thereof to the use of her husband for and during his natural life. This trust and estate of the trustees was to end at the death of the husband. All that follows in the way of bequest or devise expressly and carefully relates to the situation and period after her husband's decease. There is first a specific devise of her house and lot in Thirty-fourth street, New York, to her daughter Rachel Moeller, together with the household furniture. Then comes a series of ten carefully constructed trusts for the benefit of the nine children and the grandchild Clara, in each of which the trustees named are different, and the sum of $25,000 is to be invested for the use of the selected beneficiary. These ten trusts required $250,000 from an estate having not enough of personal property to constitute a single one of them, and show conclusively the purpose and intention of the deceased to devote to them the proceeds of her real estate. Each of these ten trust estates is created and described by itself, and they disclose a definite aim in the manner of their creation. Taking the first as an example, we find that the beneficiary is Henry, while the trustees are his three brothers, Lewis, Asher and Isaac. The latter are required to invest the sum of $25,000 and apply the interest and income to the use of Henry during his natural life, and upon his death to pay the principal to his issue, or in default of such, to his surviving brothers and sisters, and the issue of such as may be dead.

For each of the sons the trustees were his three brothers; and for each of the daughters two of the sons and the husband of the beneficiary, while for the granddaughter Clara, the four sons were made trustees. The details of these ten trusts carefully wrought out occupy five printed pages of the case, and they evince a clear and definite purpose on the part of the testatrix to carry the bulk of her estate to her grandchildren and preserve it for them, safe from the possible waste or improvidence of the sons, or the control and possession of the sons-in-law. For the married daughters the trusts were important safeguards, and for the grandchildren the sole basis of their rights. It is quite clear that the testatrix did not intend to put the bulk of her property represented by these ten shares within the absolute control of the beneficiaries, and leave the grandchildren to the chances and accidents of their parent's success or failure, if there be nothing else in the will to modify our conclusion.

The next clause in the will is a bequest of $1,000 to each of her living grandchildren at the date of her death. How many there were we are not explicitly informed, but the papers in this case and in the action of partition submitted with it, indicate that at that period they were more than forty in number; the payment of their legacies alone requiring not less than $40,000, a sum for which the testatrix must have known the personal property was totally inadequate, and, therefore, must have considered her real estate as converted into money, and providing the source of payment.

There is then a devise to Priscilla Cohen, a sister-in-law, of a house and lot on Forty-first street. This property and that previously specifically devised to Mrs. Moeller became seriously incumbered before the death of testatrix, and caused the execution of a codicil. That instrument recites that the incumbrance upon the house and lot devised to Mrs. Moeller was about $20,-000, and directs her executors to pay that off and also the incumbrances upon Mrs. Cohen's lot " from any money or assets that may come into their hands before making any other disbursements, or paying off any legacy." The personal estate was utterly insufficient even to pay off these incumbrances, and when so applied, as far as it would reach, left the ten trusts and the legacies to the grandchildren utterly valueless and hollow. It is difficult to imagine that the testatrix deliberately contemplated such a result as possibly required by the language of her will.

Two additional trusts are then framed, in which the sons are made trustees and the beneficiaries are a sister, Mrs. Isaacs, and a sister-in-law, Mrs. Cowan. To the latter is given the income of $5,000, and to the former of $3,000, during their respective lives, with remainder over to the children of testatrix, except a moiety to the husband of Mrs. Cowan. These two life estates entirely fail if the real estate cannot be sold and its proceeds be applied, and as the sister and sister-in-law could take nothing by inheritance, we are driven to the difficult conclusion, upon the appellants' theory, that the testatrix really contemplated an emergency in which these provisions should be illusory and vain.

A similar result attends the charitable bequests that follow: $4,000 are distributed among four institutions of the Hebrew faith; gifts on paper without a dollar behind them; a deceptive pretense of charity; if in truth the donor contemplated a possible emergency carrying her real estate to her heirs. In the same condition are the bequests to Mrs. Meyer of $2,000; that to the sister Sarah of the use of $1,000; those to the nephews Maurice and Isaac Simmons of $1,000 and of $500 respectively; that to the Rev. Samuels M. Isaacs of $250; and that to Henrietta Wolff, "who was named after my deceased daughter Henrietta," of $250.

Three general provisions follow which assume and require a conversion of the real estate, and the management and control of its proceeds by the executors. The first requires that all investments to be made by her trustees shall be in bonds and mortgages or government bonds, or those of the State or city of New York. The second that if any of her children, grandchildren or god-sons should " marry out of the pale of the Jewish faith " their legacies should be revoked, and the party so offending should have "$100 *only*." Was this intended as merely an idle threat, and did the testatrix contemplate that a child so offending might yet, in one event, inherit one-tenth of the whole estate, and enjoy and spend it among the Gentiles ? The third provision authorized the trustees, whenever she had given them "property," to call in, alter and change investments.

Then comes a final disposition of all the rest, residue and remainder of the estate, evincing a purpose to dispose of all her property, and die intestate as to none. The executors are directed to divide such residue into ten equal shares, and pay them over to the trustees of the ten trusts for the benefit of the nine children and the granddaughter Clara. And then follows the final clause relating to the power of sale, the construction of which is to be determined.

Such is the will. There is but one possible answer to the inferences which its elaborate provisions force upon us. That answer is not without weight and is pressed with ability, and with evident sincerity. It is said that the testatrix intended to condition the whole scheme of her will upon the consent of her husband; that unless he consented to a sale, she meant that her whole elaborate structure of trusts, and legacies, and charities, and conditions should crumble and be destroyed; and that the entire fabric was intended to be dependent upon his word. It is argued that exactly this the testatrix said, by a form of words intelligent and not in the least ambiguous, and that we have no right to dislocate and torture her words into something which she did not say. And then the theory is sought to be made more reasonable and less difficult of belief by the suggestion that the beneficiaries in the ten trusts are identical with the heirs at law who take by descent, and that what was left dependent upon the choice of the husband was merely whether the children and Clara should take absolutely or only for life with remainder over. But this suggestion takes no account of other provisions which are sacrificed. It overlooks the specific gifts to each of the grandchildren, the failure to pay off incumbrances, the total destruction of the life estates of sister and sister-in-law, the lost or imperiled charities, the ineffectual penalty for departure from the Jewish faith, and the purpose by the gift of estates for life to her children of preserving the bulk of her property for the benefit of her grandchildren. We cannot believe the theory. It does violence to the whole testamentary scheme, contradicts its every declared purpose and all its careful and thoughtful intentions, and leaves it unsubstantial and deceptive. In view of its whole structure, as we study the power of sale conferred, we find it impossible to escape the conviction that the testatrix intended to confer upon her executors a power of sale extending beyond the life of her husband, during his life to be exercised by his consent, but thereafter continuing to exist, and rendering possible of performance the terms and conditions of the will.

The judgment should be affirmed, with the costs of all parties payable out of the estate.

All concur.

Judgment affirmed.

———— ————

LEVI S. CHATFIELD, Appellant, *v.* ALFRED L. SIMONSON et al., Respondents.·

In this action by C., an attorney, to recover a compensation agreed to be paid for professional services, it appeared that W., being interested in the success of the plaintiff in an action brought for the purpose of contesting the validity of a will, in which action a verdict had been rendered sustaining the will, entered into a contract with C., by which the latter agreed to appeal and conduct the case to a final determination, W. to pay a sum specified therefor. C. was thereupon substituted as attorney for the plaintiff in said action, and performed services therein. W. having died, his executors, the defendants in this action, settled and discontinued the action. Defendants were permitted to prove, under objection and exception, that after the employment of C., and before the death of W., the former entered into a contract with the attorney for one of the defendants in said action, whereby he agreed, for the consideration of $1,500, to release certain premises from the operation of said action. C., without disclosing the fact that he was to receive compensation, applied to his

client and to the nominal plaintiff in said action to consent to such release. Neither consented. Notwithstanding this he executed in his
own name, as attorney for plaintiff, a release. *Held,* that the evidence
was properly received, and that the facts proved a violation of his professional duty on the part of C., and so constituted a good defense.

Defendants' answer contained a general denial, and also, in a separate
count, a statement of the facts above stated. The count commenced,
"Defendants, for further answer to said complaint," allege, etc. It concluded by alleging that the sum so received by C. in right, and equity belonged to W., and that "these defendants will set off the same" against
any demand established by plaintiff. *Held,* that the evidence was proper
under the general denial, as it showed non-performance of his implied
contract by plaintiff; but that if necessary to specifically set forth the
facts, this was done, and defendant could not be precluded from insisting
upon the defense, because the special use to be made of the facts was not
correctly pointed out.

Also *held,* that pleading the acts of C. by way of set-off was not a ratification thereof; that it was, at most, but the assertion of a legal conclusion
which did not operate as an estoppel

(Argued March 19, 1883; decided April 17, 1883.)

APPEAL from judgment of the General Term of the Court of
Common Pleas, in and for the city and county of New York,
in favor of defendants, entered upon an order made January 2,
1882, which overruled plaintiff's exceptions and directed judgment on an order dismissing plaintiff's complaint on trial.

The nature of the action and the material facts are stated in
the opinion.

Walter S. Cowles for appellants. To make the counter-
claim available as a defense in this action, the defendants must
show not only the existence of the demand for money had and
received, which they alleged, but that such demand existed in
favor of their testator solely in his life-time and in them as
his executors. (*Wood* v. *Mayor,* 73 N. Y. 566; *Colt* v.
Stewart, 50 id. 17; *Bates* v. *Rosekrans,* 37 id. 409; *Andrews*
v. *Artisans' Bank,* 26 id. 298; *Benedict* v. *Smith,* 10 Paige,
162.) Had this action been brought against Samuel Wood in
his life-time, he could not have sustained such a demand as a
counter-claim in his favor in such action, and no more can his
executors sustain it in this action. (*Vassear* v. *Livingston,* 13

N. Y. 248; *Merrick* v. *Gordon*, 20 id. 93; *Cummings* v.
Morris, 25 id. 628; *Baldwin* v. *Briggs*, 51 How. 477; *All-
gover* v. *Edmunds*, 66 Barb. 579; *Dale* v. *Cooks*, 4 Johns.
Ch. 11; *Campbell* v. *Genet*, 2 Hill, 290; *Hopkins* v. *Lane*, 2
Hun, 38.) No evidence offered for the purpose of proving
the claim or demand which the defendants attempted to interpose in this action was admissible. (1 Greenleaf's Ev. [13th
ed.], § 51.) The court cannot of its own motion change the
character or form of a pleading by striking out or treating as
surplusage those words which characterize and give form to
the action, because out of the facts stated by way of induce-
ment to show a right to set-off, facts can be spelled out which,
when put in proper shape, might constitute a defense in bar.
(Code of Civil Procedure, § 723; *Matthews* v. *Cady*, 61 N.
Y. 651; *Barnes* v. *Quigley*, 59 id. 265; *Bradley* v. *Aldrich*,
40 id. 504; *Wright* v. *Delafield*, 25 id. 266.) Unless an error
in the admission of evidence prejudicial to the party objecting
be shown conclusively to be innocuous, the judgment will be
reversed. (*Coleman* v. *People*, 58 N. Y. 555; *Quinn* v.
Van Pelt, 56 id. 417; *Anderson* v. *Rowe*, 54 id. 343;
Baird v. *Gillett*, 47 id. 146; *Van Deusen* v. *Young*,
29 id. 9; *Wilson* v. *Wilson*, 4 Keyes, 423; *Finney* v.
Veeder, 31 How. 15.) In the present action the setting
up a claim for the money received by the plaintiff from
Wakeman was a ratification by the defendants of plaintiff's
alleged transaction with Wakeman. (*Rodermund* v. *Clark*,
46 N. Y. 354; *Morris* v. *Rexford*, 18 id. 552; *Benedict* v.
Smith, 10 Paige, 162; *Bell* v. *Day*, 32 N. Y. 172.) The defendants can have no remedy for the alleged official misconduct
of plaintiff. (*People* v. *Randall*, 73 N. Y. 416; *Foster* v.
Townsend, 68 id. 203, 205; *Richardson* v. *Brooklyn, etc., R.
R. Co.*, 22 How. Pr. 368; *Waters* v. *Whittemore*, 22 Barb.
593; *Ray* v. *Birdseye*, 5 Denio, 627; *Seymour* v. *Ellison*, 2
Cow. 28, 29; 1 R. S. 68, § 1, subd. 3; 1 R. L. 417, § 5; 1 R.
S. [6th ed.] 403, § 97; 1 R. L. 416, § 4; 3 R. S. [6th ed.]
449, § 56; Code of Civ. Proc., §§ 14, 70; *In re Husson*, 21 Daily
Reg. 33; Code of Civ. Pro., §§ 67, 68.) A penalty cannot be

raised by implication, but must be expressly created and imposed. (*Jones* v. *Estes*, 3 Johns. 379.) If entering into the stipulations purporting to release a part of the real estate from the effect of the appeal was an act within the scope of the authority of the plaintiff under his retainer as attorney for the plaintiff in that action, then he is only liable to answer for any injury which his client may have sustained from the improvident manner in which he has exercised the power; and the motive with which the act was done constitutes no proper part of the subject-matter of inquiry. (*Harter* v. *Morris*, 18 Ohio St. 492; *Suydam* v. *Vance*, 2 McLean, 99; *Grayson* v. *Wilkinson*, 13 Miss. 268; 2 Greenleaf's Ev. [13th ed.], § 141.) If the power to release was not one of the powers incident to the retainer of the attorney, then the release was wholly nugatory, and the party dealing with him was bound to take notice that it was not within the scope of his authority. (*Foster* v. *Townshend*, 68 N. Y. 203; *Cox* v. *N. Y. C. & H. R. R. R. Co.*, 63 id. 419; *Benedict* v. *Smith*, 10 Paige, 162.)

E. Schenck for respondents. The acts of the plaintiff were such a corrupt breach of professional duty and obligation to Samuel Wood and Hewlett as to constitute an utter violation of his alleged agreement with Wood, and forfeit any claim or right to recover compensation for services rendered by him in the conduct of that case under the contract or otherwise. (*Hatch* v. *Fogarty*, 40 How. 492, 500, 501, 503, 504; 33 N. Y. Super. Ct. Rep. 166; *Herrick* v. *Catley*, 1 Daly, 512, 30 How. 208; *Von Wellhoffen* v. *Newcombe*, 10 Hun, 236, 240, 241; 1 Bouv. Law Dict. 167, subd. 6; *Pitt* v. *Golden*, 4 Burr. 2061; 2 Greenl. Ev. [10th ed.] 127, § 146; *Wilcox* v. *Plummer*, 4 Pet. 172, 181–2.) An attorney owes to his client fidelity, secrecy, diligence and skill, and he cannot, therefore, serve professionally both parties to a controversy nor take a reward from the other side. (*Herrick* v. *Catley*, *supra*. See 1 Wait's Actions and Defenses, 448, 245–249; *Hatch* v. *Fogarty*, *supra*, 503; 2 R. S. 287, § 68; 2 Greenl. Ev. 124, § 144; *Hatch* v. *Fogarty*, 40 How.

500; 2 Greenl. Ev. 127, § 147, note 7 [10th ed.]; *Case* v. *Carrol*, 85 N. Y. 385.) The relation between an attorney and client creates an unlimited confidence, and the law requires the utmost good faith in order to prevent an abuse of it. (Willard's Eq. Jur. 170, 172; *Ford* v. *Harrington*, 16 N. Y. 285, 289, 292–3; *Dutton* v. *Wilner*, 52 id. 312, 319; *Hatch* v. *Fogarty*, 40 How. 503; *Brotherson* v. *Consaulus*, 26 id. 219, and cases cited; *Brock* v. *Barnes*, 40 Barb. 528; 1 Story's Eq. Jur. [5th ed.], § 310.) The withdrawal and dismissal of the appeal in the suit of *Hewlett* v. *Samuel A. Wood* and others, and confirmation of the judgment therein, was in violation of plaintiff's alleged agreement with Samuel Wood, under which he bases his right to recover, and rendered him liable to Wood, and his estate after his death, to damages. (Story's Eq. Jur. 243, §§ 219–329, 310, 311, 334; *Brock* v. *Barnes*, 40 Barb. 521, 527; *Brotherson* v. *Consaulus*, 26 How. 213, 219; *Howell* v. *Ramson*, 11 Paige, 538; Willard's Eq. Jur. 171 to 175; *Ford* v. *Harrington*, 16 N. Y. 289.)

RUGER, Ch. J. This is an action by an attorney to recover a compensation agreed upon for professional services.

The undisputed evidence in the case shows that in January, 1878, an action was pending in the Supreme Court, between Abraham Hewlett as plaintiff and Samuel A. Wood, Samuel Wood and others as defendants, for the purpose of contesting the validity of the will of one Abraham Wood. The action had been tried and a verdict rendered sustaining the validity of the will. The defendants' testator, Samuel Wood, was interested in the success of the plaintiff in that action, inasmuch as in that event, as one of the heirs at law of Abraham Wood, he would have taken a valuable portion of his estate, which consisted, among other property, of Nos. 519 Broadway and 49 Warren street, in the city of New York.

Samuel Wood, therefore, at that stage of the case entered into a contract with the plaintiff whereby the latter was to conduct the case as attorney for Hewlett, but really for the benefit of Wood to a final determination, for which services Wood was to pay the sum of $7,500.

The plaintiff became substituted as attorney for Hewlett, and performed service therein. Samuel Wood, however, having died before any proceeding could be taken in court for a new trial, the defendants, as his executors, in April, 1878, settled and discontinued the appeal in said action. It was to recover this sum of $7,500 that the present action was brought.

It appeared from the uncontradicted evidence that intermediate the employment of the plaintiff and the death of Wood, the former entered into a contract with one Abram Wakeman, the attorney for Samuel A. Wood, one of the defendants in that action, whereby he agreed, in consideration of $1,500, which was to be paid to him by Wakeman, to release lots Nos. 519 Broadway and 49 Warren street from the operation of the action, so as to enable the defendant, Samuel A. Wood, whose right to the property was contested by the action, to mortgage the same as security for a loan of $20,000, which he then contemplated making. The plaintiff, without disclosing the fact that he was to receive a compensation for procuring such release, applied to both Abraham Hewlett and Samuel Wood to obtain their consent to its execution by him. Neither of them consented.

Notwithstanding this the plaintiff, Chatfield, proceeded to execute, in his own name, as attorney for Abraham Hewlett, and caused his son, as attorney for Samuel Wood, to execute a stipulation in the action whereby he purported to release the two lots from the operation of the action. Upon the faith of these instruments Samuel A. Wood subsequently executed mortgages upon the lots, and borrowed the sum of $20,000 upon the security thereof. It does not appear that the plaintiff ever informed Samuel Wood of the execution of such release. The proof of some of these facts was objected to by the plaintiff upon the trial upon the ground that they were inadmissible under the pleadings, and all of the evidence was objected to as immaterial, incompetent and irrelevant.

The plaintiff was examined in his own behalf as a witness, and these facts were established by his testimony and by written instruments signed by him, the execution of which he admitted, and no justification or excuse was made or offered by the plaintiff for the conduct disclosed by the evidence. Upon the close of the evidence, the court held that these facts constituted a defense to the plaintiff's action, and to this decision he duly excepted, substantially upon two grounds: *First.* For the reason that the facts did not constitute a defense, upon the merits, to the action ; and *second,* because the answer set up these facts by way of set-off, and that, therefore, they could not be made to operate as a defense to the action.

We think that the exceptions to the ruling of the court below were not well taken. The contract, which the law implies from an attorney's employment is, that he shall render faithful and honest service to his client in the conduct of the business in which he is employed, and that he shall not use the knowledge gained therein, or the position which he occupies by virtue of his relation, to the prejudice of his client, and that he will serve his client in good faith and to the best of his knowledge and ability. He had no right to use his position as an attorney to bargain for a personal advantage with his adversaries in the action, or to do any act which would tend to prejudice the rights of his clients in the event of a successful termination of the action.

The conduct of the plaintiff, as disclosed by this evidence, was a violation of his professional duty and the obligations which he owed to his client, and tended directly to defeat the object of the employment, and the sole consideration for the promise counted upon by him in this action. We are, therefore, of the opinion that the facts were established showing a breach of his agreement, and a good defense to the plaintiff's claim thereon, and it follows that they were properly received in evidence and considered in the determination of the case. The plaintiff objected to the admission of the evidence upon the ground that it was immaterial, incompetent, irrelevant and inadmissible under the pleadings. These objections were overruled by the court, and the evidence received generally in the case. By reference to the pleadings, it will be seen that there was a general denial which put in

issue the performance by the plaintiff of the contract under
which his claim to compensation arose. Under this plea it
was competent for the defendants to show any facts tending to
disprove the allegations of the complaint that the conditions
of the contract had been performed by the plaintiff. In addition to this general denial, the answer contained a special
count setting up the particular facts constituting this defense,
which commences as follows : " *Third.* These defendants, for
further answer to the said complaint, allege," etc. Then follows the statement of facts constituting said defense. After
such statement the count concludes by alleging that " Chatfield
received from said Wakeman, as the consideration for said
release, the sum of $1,000, which sum, in right and equity,
belonged to the said Samuel Wood, and these defendants will
set off the same against any demand which the plaintiff may
establish in this cause," etc. It may very properly be said
that these facts are not alleged as a counter-claim, and that
their effect as a defense is not controlled by the concluding
claim that the sum received under the agreement would be set
off as therein claimed. But however this may be, under the
liberal rule which now prevails for the construction of pleadings, it would be unjust in the extreme to defeat a meritorious
defense upon the ground here claimed, unless we could see that
the party making the claim would be seriously prejudiced
thereby. It is quite certain that the plaintiff was as well prepared to try this issue as he ever could be, the entire defense
having been made out by his own testimony; and if there had
been any answer to it, he had only to speak to have had the
benefit of it. He suggested no answer in his testimony, and
it must be assumed that none existed.

The rule has so frequently been stated in this court that the
relief demanded in a pleading is unimportant so long as the
facts stated entitle the party pleading them to some form of
relief, that no one ought now to be considered ignorant of it.
The courts now uniformly administer the relief to which the
facts set forth in a pleading seem to entitle the party, without
regard to the particular form of relief demanded. In an ac-

tion on a promissory note, where the answer alleged facts sufficient to constitute a defense of want of consideration or a
recoupment of damages, it is not necessary for defendant to
state which he will rely upon, and if he so states he will not
be precluded from insisting upon any defense which the facts
alleged will justify. (*Springer* v. *Dwyer*, 50 N. Y. 19;
Pomeroy's Remedies and Remedial Rights, §§ 724, 725.)

It is quite clear that this count in the answer would not have
been held bad on demurrer because the special use to be made
of the facts set out in the pleading was not correctly pointed
out therein. (*Emery* v. *Pease*, 20 N. Y. 62; *Williams* v.
Slote, 70 id. 601.)

It would even be the duty of the court upon this appeal
under section 723 of the Civil Code, to either disregard the
alleged defect in the pleading or make it conform to the facts
proved, if that course were necessary to support the judgment.

It has been argued that the defendants have ratified the act
of Chatfield in obtaining the $1,000 from his adversary in the
Hewlett action by pleading it by way of set-off in this suit.

This point was not raised in the court below, and might
properly be excluded from our consideration here, but there
are other answers to it which we will briefly refer to.

Authorities are cited by the appellant's counsel to the effect
that a party, being entitled to two inconsistent remedies, is
precluded by the selection of one from the pursuit of the
other; as, for instance, that a party may not sue to recover the
price agreed to be paid upon a contract of sale, and also prosecute an action to reclaim the property sold upon the ground
of fraud in the contract itself. Cases are also cited to the
effect, that where an agent has exercised his authority in
making a contract, his principal cannot claim the benefits of
the contract without also assuming its obligations. But these
principles have no application to the circumstances of this case.

The question presented here is governed solely by the rules
regulating the pleadings of parties in actions at law. The
Code expressly authorizes a party to plead as many defenses or
counter-claims, or both, as he may have, and whether they be

those formerly denominated legal or equitable. (§ 507, Code
of Civil Procedure.)

The defendants in this action, as we have seen by their general denial, have entitled themselves to prove the facts set up
in the third count of the answer as a bar to the action Assuming in their answer that they might not be entitled under the
third count to use the facts therein stated as a bar, they still
attempted to use them as the basis of a counter-claim. This
left the defendants in the position of claiming that the facts
pleaded should either constitute a bar to the action, or in the
event that this should not be permitted, they might operate as
a defense *pro tanto.*

Thus the most that can be claimed from the language used
in the third count of the answer is, that it is the assertion by
the pleader of a mere legal conclusion to be drawn from the
facts stated, or a statement of the character of the relief to
which he deems himself entitled upon such facts.

Such a claim, although erroneous, does not preclude the
court from giving the party the relief to which he is entitled
by the facts stated. It has been held by this court that the
assertion of a legal conclusion where the facts were all stated
did not operate as an estoppel upon the party making such
assertion. (*Brewster* v. *Striker,* 2 N. Y. 19; *Norton* v. *Coons,*
6 id. 33.) Even as to a fact stated in a pleading a party has
been held not to be estopped from showing another consideration for a contract than the one stated and relied on in his
complaint. (*Russell* v. *Kierney,* 1 Sandf. Ch. 34; *Day* v.
Perkins, 2 id. 359.)

A further answer to this point is furnished by the fact, that
upon the trial the only issue left in the case was that arising
upon the plaintiff's claim to recover compensation upon his
special contract with defendants' testator, and the answer
thereto. The third count of defendants' answer set up the
facts therein recited, conditionally only. They were claimed
as a set-off only in the event that the plaintiff should succeed
in establishing some valid claim in the action.

The claim of the defendants could not, therefore, be regarded as a ratification of the act of Chatfield in taking compensation from his client's adversaries, for the reason that it was to be so used only in the event that such conduct failed to furnish an absolute defense to the action upon the merits.

Under the views which we have taken of the pleadings, all of the evidence objected to by plaintiff was competent, and the exceptions to its admission taken by him were, therefore, unfounded.

The question now made, that the evidence of the unlawful agreement between plaintiff and Wakeman raised a question of fact only which should have been submitted to the jury, was not taken in the court below, and it is too late to raise it now.

Even if we should feel inclined to entertain this point, we are precluded from doing so because the facts stated in the third count of defendants' answer have been established by uncontradicted and unexplained evidence, whose conclusive force the plaintiff was not at liberty to dispute.

We are, therefore, of the opinion that the judgment of the court below should be affirmed.

All concur.

Judgment affirmed.

William A. Houghkirk, as Administrator, etc., Respondent, v. The President, Managers and Company of the Delaware and Hudson Canal Company, Appellant.

Under the statute (Chap. 450, Laws of 1847, as amended by chap. 256, Laws of 1849) authorizing an action to recover damages for death caused by negligence, the pecuniary loss which a party named in the statute is entitled to recover may consist of special damages, i. e., of actual definite loss, and also of prospective general damages.

The special damages being capable of proof and of measurement with approximate accuracy, to entitle plaintiff thereto, evidence must be given not only that the damages were sustained, but also showing their character and amount.

As the prospective damages are incapable of accurate estimate, the amount within the limit fixed by the statute is for the determination of the jury.

Such facts, however, as are naturally capable of proof, and which will give a basis for the judgment of the jury, *i. e.*, the age and sex, the general health and intelligence of the person killed, the situation and condition of the survivors and their relation to the deceased should be proved.

The General Term has power and it is its duty to review the verdict in such an action and to set it aside if it appears excessive, or the result of sympathy and prejudice.

Plaintiff's intestate was run over and killed in attempting to cross the tracks of defendant's road at a place where plaintiff claimed a right of crossing ; there was no flagman present at the scene of the accident. The court submitted it to the jury to determine whether, under the circumstances, due care required the presence of a flagman, and whether for the omission of that precaution defendant was chargeable with negligence. *Held* error.

*Houghkirk.*v. *Pres't, etc., D. & H. C. Co.* (28 Hun, 407).

(Argued March 21, 1883 ; decided April 17, 1888.)

APPEAL from judgment of the General Term of the Supreme Court, in the third judicial department, entered upon an order made December 16, 1882, which affirmed a judgment in favor of plaintiff, entered upon a verdict, and affirmed an order denying a motion for a new trial.   (Reported below, 28 Hun, 407.)

This action was brought to recover damages for alleged negligence in causing the death of Eliza Houghkirk, plaintiff's intestate.

The deceased, at the time of the accident, was riding in a wagon with the plaintiff, her father, who lived on Van Rensselaer island in the Hudson river, which was connected with the main shore by a bridge, built partly by the Albany and Susquehanna Railroad Company, whose road defendant leased and was operating.   The tracks of the road passed at the end of the bridge, and conveyances coming from the island have to cross them to reach the highway.   As the wagon was crossing the tracks it was struck by a passing locomotive and said intestate was killed.

The further material facts are stated in the opinion.

Henry Smith for appellant. The General Term was in error in holding that they could not review the question of damages and set aside the verdict as excessive. (26 Alb. Law Jour. 412; *McIntyre*, 37 N. Y. 892; *Peck* v. *Cox*, 63 id. 422; *Downing*, 37 id. 380.) The court improperly refused to charge as requested that there was no duty imposed on the company to look out for Mr. Houghkirk at that crossing that night. (*Sutton*, 66 N. Y. 243.) Negligence of the defendant cannot be predicated upon the omission of the company to do something outside of the operation of its train. (*Webber's Case*, 58 N. Y. 459; *Caton*, 51 id. 544; *Grippen*, 40 id. 34; *Beisiegel*, id. 9.) The court erred in· leaving it to the jury to determine whether the defendant should have had a flagman at this crossing. (*Grippen's Case*, 40 N. Y. 40.)

E. Countryman for respondent. The plaintiff and the deceased being lawfully on the crossing, the defendant was bound to exercise reasonable care and vigilance not to do them injury while passing at that point. (*Stinson* v. *N. Y. C. R. Co.*, 32 N. Y. 333; *Driscoll* v. *N. & R.*, etc., *Co.*, 37 id. 637; *Cordell* v. *N. Y. C. & H. R. R. R. Co.*, 70 id. 119, 124, 125; *Kay* v. *Penn. R. Co.*, 65 Penn. St. 269, 273, 274; *Corrigan* v. *Union S. R.*, 98 Mass. 577; *Dublin, etc., R. Co.* v. *Slattery*, L. R., 3 App. Cases, 1156; *Delaney* v. *Milwaukee, etc., R. Co.*, 33 Wis. 67; *Delaney* v. *Milwaukee, etc., R. Co.*, id. 70, 71; *Kay* v. *Penn. R. Co.*, 65 Penn. St. 273, 274; *Dublin, etc., R. Co.* v. *Slattery*, L. R., 3 App. Cases, 1156; *Nicholson* v. *Erie R. Co.*, 41 N. Y. 526, 529.) The court properly submitted to the jury upon the question of the defendant's negligence the circumstances of the omission to ring the bell or sound the whistle, and the absence of the flagman from his post; and all of its rulings on these subjects were proper. (*Cordell* v. *N. Y. C. & H. R. R. R. Co.*, 64 N. Y. 535, 538; *Dolan* v. *D. & H. Canal Co.*, 71 id. 285; *Casey* v. *N. Y. C. & H. R. R. R. Co.*, 78 id. 518, 523, 524; *McGovern* v. *N. Y. C. & H. R. R. R. Co.*, 67 id. 417, 423; *Kissinger* v. *N. Y. & H. R. R. Co.*, 56 id. 539,

543; *Ernst* v. *H. R. Co.*, 39 id. 61, 64, 67; *Phil., etc.,
R. Co.* v. *Killips*, 88 Penn. St. 405, 413 ; *St. Louis, etc., R. Co.*
v. *Dunn*, 78 Ill. 197.) The court properly submitted the
question of the defendant's negligence to the jury. (*Mc-
Govern* v. *N. Y. C. & H. R. R. R. Co.*, 67 N. Y. 417; *Casey*
v. *N. Y. C. & H. R. R. R. Co.*, 78 id. 518 ; *Cordell* v. *N. Y.
C. & H. R. R. R. Co.*, 70 id. 119 ; *Smedis* v. *Brooklyn, etc.,
R. Co.*, 88 id. 11, 20.) The Court of Appeals has no jurisdiction to reverse a judgment because the damages are excessive. (*Gale* v. *N. Y. C. & H. R. R. R. Co.*, 76 N. Y.
594; *Peck* v. *N. Y. C. & H. R. R. R. Co.*, 70 id. 587 ; *Maher*
v. *C. P. N. & E. R. Co.*, 67 id. 52; *Metcalf* v. *Baker*, 57 id.
662 ; *Campbell* v. *Page*, 50 id. 658; *Clark* v. *Lousie*, 82 id.
580; *People* v. *Laurence*, 81 id. 644; *Fisher* v. *Gould*, id.
228; *Snebler* v. *Conner*, 78 id. 218; *Verplank* v. *Member*, 74
id. 620; *Hewlett* v. *Wood*, 67 id. 394.) The damages were
not excessive. (3 R. S. [6th ed.] 569, § 4; *Cornwall* v. *Mills*,
12 J. & S. 45, 52; *Minick* v. *City of Troy*, 19 Hun, 253–
258; *Bierbauer* v. *N. Y. C. & H. R. R. R. Co.*, 15 id. 559,
564; *Gale* v. *N. Y. C. & H. R. R. R. Co.*, 13 id. 1 ; *Coleman* v. *Southwick*, 9 Johns. 45; *Ihl* v. *Forty-second Street
R. Co.*, 47 N. Y. 317, 320, 321 ; *Oldfield* v. *N. Y. & H. R.
R. Co.*, 14 id. 310, 318; *O'Mara* v. *Hudson R. Co.*, 38 id.
445, 450; *Prendegast* v. *N. Y. C. & H. R. R. R. Co.*, 58
id. 652, 653 ; *Chicago* v. *Hessing*, 83 Ill. 204, 207 ; *Nagel* v.
Mo., etc., R. Co., 75 Mo. 653, 666; *Gorham* v. *N. Y. C.
& H. R. R. R. Co.*, 23 Hun, 449 ; *Baltimore, etc., R. Co.* v.
State, 24 Md. 271 ; *Walters* v. *Chicago, etc., R. Co.*, 41 Iowa,
71, 80; *Quinn* v. *Moore*, 15 N. Y. 432, 436.) The loss of
the services of the child during her minority was only one of
the elements of damages. (*McGovern* v. *N. Y. C. & H. R.
R. R. Co.*, 67 N. Y. 418, 423, 424; *Drew* v. *Sixth Avenue
R. Co.*, 26 id. 49, 52, 53; *Casey* v. *N. Y. C. & H. R. R. R.
Co.*, 78 id. 518; 2 R. S. [6th ed.] 808, § 1; Code of Civ.
Pro., § 914; *Stone* v. *Burgess*, 47 N. Y. 521; *Turner* v.
Hadden, 62 Barb. 480.) The measure of damages is the
reasonable expectation of pecuniary advantage from the con-

tinuance of the life of the deceased and the probable pecuniary loss occasioned by that expectation being disappointed. (*Dalton v. S. E. R. Co.*, 4 Com. Bench [N. S.] [93 Eng. C. Law], 296; *Pym* v. *G. N. R. Co.*, 4 B. & S. [116 Eng. C. Law] 396; *Costello* v. *Landwehr*, 28 Wis. 524; *Eames* v. *Brattleboro*, 54 Vt. 471; *Potter* v. *Chicago, etc., R. Co.*, 21 Wis. 372, 376; *Penn. R. Co.* v. *McCloskey's Adm.*, 23 Penn. St. 526, 528, 531, 532; *Catawissa R. Co.* v. *Armstrong*, 52 id. 282; *Baltimore, etc., R. Co.* v. *State*, 24 Md. 271; *Costello* v. *Landwehr*, 28 Wis. 524.)

FINCH, J. The jury in this case rendered a verdict of $5,000 as their estimate of damages resulting to the next of kin from the death of a little girl killed by a switch engine of the defendant. The evidence showed that she was about six years old; an only child; bright, intelligent, and healthy; and the daughter of a market gardener. This, and the circumstances of her death, constituted the only proof bearing on the question of damages, and which served as a basis for the judgment of the jury in estimating the pecuniary loss suffered by the next of kin. The General Term declined to set aside the verdict as excessive, assigning as a reason in the opinions delivered that the doctrine of this court as to damages in such a case leaves it impossible to say in any instance that they are excessive, and involves an utter surrender of the right of the General Term to order a new trial for that reason. The defendant alleges error in this ruling, and insists that the verdict was wholly unwarranted by the evidence; that there was no proof of facts from which even a plausible conjecture of the amount of damages could be derived; that the verdict indicated partiality or prejudice; and the case should be remitted to the General Term for the consideration which has been withheld. We have quite carefully examined the authorities cited in the opinion below (*Ihl* v. *Forty-second St., etc., R. R. Co.*, 47 N. Y. 317; 7 Am. Rep. 450; *Oldfield* v. *N. Y. & H. R. R. Co.*, 14 N. Y. 310; *O'Mara* v. *Hudson R. R. R. Co.*, 38 id. 445; *McGovern* v. *N. Y. C. & H. R. R. R. Co.*, 67 id. 417);

and nearly or quite all of the other cases bearing on the subject.
Most of them recognize the difficulties inherent in suits founded
upon the statute, and seek in good faith to make operative the
will of the legislature in a new and before unknown class of
actions. None of those decisions purport in any manner to
narrow the right and discretion of the General Term to set
aside verdicts for excessive damages, but on the contrary all are
consistent with its survival, and some expressly recognize it.
(*Oldfield* v. *N. Y. & Harlem R. R. Co.*, 14 N. Y. 314; *Ihl*
v. *Forty-second St., etc., R. R. Co.*, 47 id. 321; 7 Am. Rep. 450.)
Undoubtedly there are difficulties in the way of its judicious
exercise, but so far as these exist they spring from the inherent
nature of the subject, and obedience to the command of the
legislature. The statute implies from the death of the person
negligently killed damages sustained by the next of kin.
(*Quin* v. *Moore*, 15 N. Y. 432.) Recognizing the generally
prospective and indefinite character of those damages, and the
impossibility of a basis for accurate estimate, it allows a jury to
give what they shall deem a just compensation, and limits their
judgment to a sum not exceeding $5,000. (*Tilley* v. *Hudson
Riv. R. R. Co.*, 29 N. Y. 252.) But within that range the
jury is neither omnipotent, nor left wholly to conjecture.
They are required to judge, and not merely to guess, and,
therefore, such basis for their judgment as the facts naturally
capable of proof can give should always be present, and is
rarely, if ever, absent. The pecuniary loss in any such case
may be composed of very different elements. It may consist
of special damages, that is of an actual, definite loss, capable of
proof, and of measurement with approximate accuracy; and also
of prospective and general damages, incapable of precise and
accurate estimate because of the contingencies of the unknown
future. An example of such special and actual damages occurred
in the case of *Murphy* v. *N. Y. Central, etc., R. R. Co.* (88 N.
Y. 446), where we allowed as one element of the total loss the
funeral expenses of the deceased. To such an item the doctrine
of *Leeds* v. *Met. Gas-light Co.* (90 N. Y. 26) would have a proper
application. To prove merely that there were funeral expenses,

and, without evidence of their character or amount, or even that they were usual and ordinary, to permit the jury to guess at their amount as an element of the total loss, would be to substitute conjecture for proof where proof was possible, and a proper basis of judgment attainable. But the value of a human life is a different matter. The damages to the next of kin in that respect are necessarily indefinite, prospective, and contingent. They cannot be proved with even an approach to accuracy, and yet they are to be estimated and awarded, for the statute has so commanded. But even in such case there is and there must be some basis in the proof for the estimate, and that was given here and always has been given. Human lives are not all of the same value to the survivors. The age and sex, the general health and intelligence of the person killed, the situation and condition of the survivors and their relation to the deceased; these elements furnish some basis for judgment. That it is slender and inadequate is true (*Tilley* v. *Hudson Riv. R. R. Co.*, *supra*); but it is all that is possible, and while that should be given (*McIntyre* v. *N. Y. Cent. R. R. Co.*, 37 N. Y. 289), more cannot be required. Upon that basis, and from such proof the jury must judge, and having done so, it is possible, though not entirely easy, for the General Term to review such judgment and set it aside if it appears excessive, or the result of sympathy and prejudice. A difficult duty we grant; but not for that reason to be abandoned. In its intrinsic nature it is no more difficult than to determine whether a verdict is excessive in an action for slander or libel where the injury is to reputation, or in actions where pain and suffering may be considered in ascertaining the loss. The Supreme Court has never abdicated its power of review in such cases and should not in those under the statute. The jury are compelled to judge in an atmosphere freighted with sympathy. In the General Term the deliberation may be more cool and thoughtful, and while the judgment of the trial court should not be lightly disturbed, it should not be held necessarily conclusive. But it is impossible for us to say that such error has been committed in the present case. We cannot go to the

opinions delivered to ascertain, and must assume that the order
which denied a new trial for excessive or partial damages, and
which was affirmed by the General Term, was made after due
and proper consideration, and in the full performance of the
duty of review which we have always upheld and have not at
all narrowed or infringed.

But we must reverse the judgment rendered for an entirely
different reason. The accident occurred, not at a street crossing, but upon the premises of the defendant, at a point opposite a bridge owned by the railroad company whose road defendant leased and operated, leading from Van Rensselaer
island, and where it was contended the plaintiff had a right to
cross the tracks derived from the payment of toll to the agent
of the defendant. There was no flagman present at the scene
of the accident, and this circumstance led to an erroneous
ruling. The plaintiff requested the court to "leave it to the
jury as a question of fact to say whether, under all the circumstances disclosed by the evidence, defendant should have
had a flagman at the crossing." The court answered: "I
have done so," and the defendant excepted. The court then
added: "I said I would not charge as matter of law whether
the company was or was not bound to have a flagman there.
It was a question for the jury to say under the circumstances;" and the defendant again excepted. The charge in
this respect was substantially the same as that in *Grippen*
v. *N. Y. Central* (40 N. Y. 41) for which the judgment
was reversed. In both instances the jury were allowed to
find that due care required the presence of a flagman, and
that the omission to station one at the crossing was negligence on the part of the railroad company. The last thing
said to the jury in the present case, the final impression made
upon their minds was, that even if the defendant was prudent
and careful in the running of its train, and guilty of no negligence in its approach to this crossing, yet the jury might find
that due care required the presence of a flagman, and for the
omission of that specific precaution the company was chargeable with negligence. The true rule and the proper distinc-

tions were well stated in *McGrath* v. *N. Y. C. & H. R. R.
R. Co.* (63 N. Y. 528). It was there said it would be error for
a judge to instruct a jury that it is the duty of a railroad company to keep a flagman at a crossing, or " to submit to a jury
the question whether it ought to have kept a flagman there."
And the reason was carefully pointed out. A railroad company is not bound and owes no duty so to station a flagman,
and negligence cannot be predicated of the omission. The
fact may be proven as one of the circumstances under which
the train was moved, and by which the degree of care requisite in its handling and running may be affected; so that the
question never is whether there should have been a flagman, or
one ought to have been stationed at the crossing, but whether,
in view of his presence or absence, the train was moved with
prudence or negligence. The final charge in this case left to
the jury whether the company was or was not bound to have
a flagman at the crossing, and whether the defendant should
have had one there, and so permitted the jury to predicate
negligence upon the omission. We have sought in vain to
give the language used any other construction. In the body
of the charge the question of negligence was very properly
presented, and it is quite likely that in the collision of request
and answer, at its close, the form and language used was not
closely observed; but its purport was very plain, and it is evident that the jury were liable to be misled by it. They must
have gone to their deliberations with the final impression upon
their minds that they were at liberty to find that the defendant ought to have stationed a flagman at the crossing, and that
omission constituted negligence, upon which a verdict could be
founded. For this error we think there should be a new trial.

The judgment should be reversed and a new trial granted,
costs to abide the event.

All concur, except DANFORTH, J., not voting.

Judgment reversed.

2/0 SIMEON SMITH, as Executor, etc., Respondent, v. WILLIAM D.
Burch, Appellant.

In 1877, M., plaintiff's testatrix, made her will, which contained this clause :
"I further give and bequeath to my beloved husband all the ready
money I may have, either in bank or elsewhere, at my decease." In
1879 she gave to defendant, her husband, authority to collect a legacy
due to her, which he collected during the year 1880. From January
1st of that year up to her death, which occurred in September, 1881,
the testatrix was of unsound mind and incompetent to transact business.
The money so collected was used by defendant with his own money
in defraying household expenses and in procuring nurses and medical
attendance for his wife, and none of it remained at her death. Defendant
was able to provide suitably for his family out of his own property. In
an action to recover the amount so collected, *held*, that under said clause
of the will, defendant was entitled to retain the same ; that when collected it could properly be treated as " ready money ; " it remained in his
hands as such, liable to be paid on demand, he holding it simply as a depositary, and he used it subject to this liability.
The authorities as to what is included in the word " money," as used in
wills, collated.
Smith v. *Burch* (28 Hun, 331), reversed.

(Argued March 26, 1883 ; decided April 17, 1883.)

APPEAL from judgment of the General Term of the Supreme Court, in the third judicial department, in favor of
plaintiff, entered upon an order made December 16, 1882,
which directed such judgment upon a case submitted under
section 1279 of the Code of Civil Procedure. (Reported below, 28 Hun, 331.)

The facts stated in the case submitted are substantially set
forth in the opinion.

George B. Davis for appellant. Defendant, after receiving
the legacy due his wife, by not paying it over to her, became
the depositary of the fund, and stands in the position of a
banker. (Story on Agency, 206 ; *Cowling* v. *Cowling*, 26
Beav. 449 ; *Stoll* v. *King*, 8 How. 298 ; *U. S.* v. *Inhabitants*,

etc., Davis, 154; *Giepp's Appeal,* 15 Penn. St. 428; *Parley v. County of Muskegan,* 20 Am. Rep. 645; 17 Wend. 94; 20 N. Y. 76; 6 id. 412; 1 Paige, 249; 6 Hill, 297; 5 Denio, 555.) Money deposited in a bank would pass on a bequest of " money," and this account and demand for money against the defendant presents all the advantageous features of such a claim against a banker for a deposit, and therefore comes under the same rule being a deposit elsewhere. (2 Redfield's Law of Wills, 128; *Gorden* v. *Dortrell,* 1 Mylne and Keen, 56; *Low* v. *Thomas,* 5 DeG., M. & G. 315; *S. C.*, Kay, 369; Redfield on Wills, 112, note; Wigram on Wills, 69, 70, 71; *Roberts* v. *Kuffin,* 2 Aiken, 113; *Dobney* v. *Cottrell,* 9 Gratt. 572; *Chapman* v. *Reynolds,* 6 Jur. [N. S.] 440; *Morton* v. *Perry,* 1 Metc. 446; *In the Matter of the Estate of Miller,* 48 Cal. 165; *Fryer* v. *Rankin,* 11 Sim. 55; 2 Redfield on Law of Wills, 128, 438; *Pilkington's Trust,* 6 N. R. 246.)

William Hazlitt Smith for respondent. The word " money," even if it stood alone in the will without any of the qualifying words, would not give the defendant the Stevenson legacy. (*Mann* v. *Mann,* 1 Johns. Ch. 231; *S. C.* affirmed, 14 id. 1; 2 Jarman on Wills [Randolph & Talcott's notes], 373 and note; *Williams* v. *Williams* [1876], 8 Ch. Div. 789; *Manning* v. *Purcell* [1855], 56 Eng. Ch. [7 DeG., M. & G.] 55; *Bysom* v. *Brandreth* [1873], L. R., 16 Eq. 475; *In re Mason's Will,* 34 Beav. 494; *Low* v. *Thomas* [1854], 54 Eng. Ch. [5 DeG., M. & G.] 315; *S. C.* below, Kay, 369; *Mann* v. *Mann,* 1 Johns. Ch. 231 [same affirmed, 14 Johns. 1]; 2 Jarman on Wills, 373; *Williams* v. *Williams,* 8 Ch. Div. 789; *Manning* v. *Purcell* [1855], 56 Eng. Ch. [7 DeG., M. & G.] 55; *Bysom* v. *Brandreth* [1873], L. R., 16 Eq. 475; *Re Mason's Will,* 34 Beav. 494; *Low* v. *Thomas* [1854], 54 Eng. Ch. [5 DeG., M. & G.] 315.) The word " money " has only been given a more extended meaning where the terms of the will itself required it, and especially when used in a residuary clause : as courts will so construe a will as to avoid intestacy if possible. (*Morton* v. *Perry* [1840], 1 Metc. 446; *Rogers* v. *Thomas,* 2 Keen, 8; Jarman on

Wills [R. & T.'s notes], 375, *et seq.*) The qualifying words "ready and in bank or elsewhere" are words of limitation and locality, and do not extend in the least the strict and ordinary meaning of the word. (*Stein* v. *Ritherdon*, 37 L. J. Ch. 369; *Parker* v. *Merchant* [1843], 19 Eng Ch. [1 Phillips] 355; *S. C.*, 1 Youngs and Collyer, 290; *Collins* v. *Collins*, 40 L. J. Ch. 541; *Freyer* v. *Rankin* [1840], 34 Eng. Ch. [11 Sim.] 55; *Vaisey* v. *Reynolds* [1828], 5 Eng. Ch. [5 Russell] 12; *Stein* v. *Ritherdon*, 37 L. J. Ch. 369; *Parker* v. *Marchant* [1843], 1 Youngs and Collyer [N. S.], 290; 19 Eng. Ch. [1 Phillips] 365; 49 id. 355; *Collins* v. *Collins*, 49 L. J. Ch. 541; *Vaisey* v. *Reynolds*, 5 Eng. Ch. [5 Russell] 12; *Fryer* v. *Rankin*, 34 id [11 Simons] 55.) The word "bequest" must be construed from the terms of the will itself, there being facts in the case as to the amount, character and kind ₄of property left by the testatrix. (Code, § 1281; *Feasing* v. *Irwin*, 55 N. Y. 486, 489; *Van Alstyne* v. *Van Alstyne*, 28 id. 375, 378.)

EARL, J. In December, 1877, Margery Burch, the wife of the defendant, made her will, which, after bequests of legacies to certain relatives named amounting to $1,300, contained the following provision: "I further give and bequeath to my beloved husband all the ready money I may have, either in bank or elsewhere, at my decease, before any of the foregoing legacies or bequests shall be paid," and the remainder of her estate she bequeathed to certain missionary societies for charitable purposes. She died on the 26th day of September, 1881, and in October thereafter her will was admitted to probate and the plaintiff qualified as executor.

In the year 1878 Mrs. Burch, as a legatee under the will of Jane Stevenson, became entitled to a legacy of $450, and one McChair was executor of that will, and had funds as such with which to pay the legacy. But there was delay on his part in making the payment to Mrs. Burch by reason of his financial embarrassment. In the early part of the year 1879 Mrs. Burch gave her husband instructions to collect the legacy from McChair for her. Between the 14th day of January, 1880, and the 8th day of December of the same year, he collected the legacy from McChair for his wife, and the sum collected amounted to $490.25. For some time prior to the 1st day of January, 1880, and up to the time of her death, Mrs. Burch was incompetent to transact her ordinary business and unfit to exercise any control over her property by reason of severe bodily and mental infirmities and unsoundness' of mind. As fast as the money was collected by the defendant from Stevenson, between the 14th day of January, 1880, and the 8th day of December of the same year, he used it with his own money in defraying his household expenses, and in procuring nurses and medical attendance for his sick wife, so that at her death no portion of the money received by him from McChair was on hand. During the time he thus expended the money he was able to provide suitably for his family out of his own property.

Upon these facts agreed upon for submission to the General Term, the plaintiff claims that the defendant is not entitled, under the will of his wife, to retain the sum of money collected by him of Stevenson, but that he owes this money to the estate of his wife, and he claims to recover that sum of him, with interest. On the other hand the defendant claims that he is entitled to the money received by him from Stevenson under the clause of the will above set out.

The facts stated are meager, and it would seem that other facts must have existed which would have enabled the court with greater certainty to arrive at the intention of the testatrix.

The meaning of the words "money" and "ready money," when used in a will, depends upon the context, and also to some extent upon the condition of the testator's property and the circumstances surrounding his estate; and in construing them, therefore, the courts seek for light in all the provisions of the will and in all the circumstances surrounding the testator and his estate, and it is their aim to give effect to the intention of the testator when that can be ascertained. The word "money" has sometimes been held to include securities, stocks, personal property, money in bank and money in the hands of agents, when the context and all the circumstances which were rightfully considered indicated such to be the intention of the testator. In 2 Williams' Law of Executors (7th ed.), 1188, it is said : " Where a testator gives to one person ' all his moneys in hand ' and to another 'all his moneys out on securities' the balance at his bankers will pass as money in hand. Under a bequest of all the testator's ' money ' in his house at A., bank notes and ready money will alone pass, although he may leave in it mortgages, bonds or receipts for government annuities. Where the testator bequeathed all his 'money ' in the Bank of England, and never had any cash in the bank, but was entitled to some three per cents and five per cents, bank annuities, Sir Willliam Grant, M. R., held that the stock passed. But though upon the whole context of the will stock may pass by the term 'money' yet ' money ' does not, by the force of the word, include stock." In 2 Redfield on Wills, 129, it is said: " The word 'money' in a will means that and nothing else, but when used with other words it may have much greater extension." In Wigram on Wills (O'Hare's ed.), 69, the author says : " The term ' *money* ' in America would doubtless pass all debts and annuities, stocks and securities belonging to the testator. The phrase ' ready money ' is perhaps usually different in meaning." In Roper on Legacies, it is said that " the word ' money ' unaided by the context, will include cash, bank notes, money at the bankers, notes payable to bearer, exchequer bills, and bills of exchange indorsed in blank, because they, as before observed, are not to be considered as choses in action, but money of the persons in whose possession they are. But choses in action, promissory notes not payable to bearer, government stock, long annuities and Columbian bonds will not pass under the word ' money.' " In the *Estate of Thomas Miller* (48 Cal. 165 ; 17 Am. Rep. 422), the court held that the word " money " used in making a devise in a will will be construed to include both personal and real property, if it appears from the context and on the face of the instrument that such was the intention of the testator. In *Manning* v. *Purcell* (7 DeG., M. & G. 55), it was held that under a bequest

of "all my moneys," money due on deposit notes, at the
testator's bankers, as well as on the balance of his current account, and also money in the hands of a stakeholder on a bet,
would pass. In *Parker* v. *Marchant* (19 Eng. Ch. 355), it
was held that a testator's balance at his bankers would pass
under the words "ready money." In *Fryer* v. *Rankin* (11
Simons, 55), there was a bequest in the following words: " I
give and bequeath unto my dear wife Susannah Fryer, all my
ready money at my bankers, in my dwelling-house or elsewhere; by which I mean money not invested in security or
otherwise bearing interest, but which I may have in hand for
current income and expenses, at the time of my decease; "
and it was held that cash balances in the hands of the testator's bankers and of his agent, and dividends of stock due at
the testator's death, passed by the bequest, but that the rent of
a house and the interest of a sum due on mortgage did not
pass. In *Byrom* v. *Brandreth* (Law Rep., 16 Eq. 475), there
was a bequest of " any money of which I may die possessed,"
and it was held to include cash in the house and money at the
bankers, and any money of which, at the time of her death, she
might have claimed immediate payment; but not the apportioned part of an annuity, or of interest payable to her which
had accrued from the last stated days of payment to her death,
nor a legacy due to her which had not been acknowledged as at
her disposal. In *Waite* v. *Combes* (5 De G. & S. 676), it was
held that the word "moneys" must be taken to include stock
in the funds. The vice-chancellor said: "There is no doubt
upon the authorities that the word 'moneys' may pass stock
in the funds, it being a question of construction upon the
whole will whether the testator meant to use the word in that
sense or not." In *Beck* v. *McGillis* (9 Barb. 35) it was held
that under a bequest of "all moneys" that the testator should
die possessed of, the legatee was entitled to the cash, using the
term in its proper sense, which the testator at the time of his
death had in his possession, or deposited in bank, and to nothing else. In *Mann* v. *The Executors of Mann* (1 Johns. Ch.
231) it was held, that where the testator bequeathed to his

wife all the rest, residue and remainder of the moneys belonging to his estate at the time of his decease, the word "moneys"
must be understood, in its legal and popular sense, to mean
gold or silver, or the lawful currency of the country, or bank
notes, where they are known and used in the market as cash,
or money deposited in bank for safe-keeping; and not to comprehend promissory notes, bonds and mortgages, or other
securities, there being nothing in the will itself to show that
the testator intended to use the word in that extended sense.

We have made these citations at some length to show what
scope has been given to these words, and how differently they
have been construed by the courts and text writers. We cannot perceive that they have received different construction in
this country from that which they have received in England.
Ordinarily, standing alone, they have been held to mean only
that which passes current as money, including also bank deposits. But when read with the context they may be held to
mean any kind of personal property, and it is the office of
the courts, considering every thing which may properly be resorted to for aid, in every case to give effect to the intention of
the testator in their use.

The money here in controversy was received by the defendant from McChair as the agent of his wife. After he received
it, it could fairly be treated as "ready money" in his hands
for her. At the time he received it she had become imbecile
and incompetent to do business, and therefore it remained in
his hands as a depositary. He used it, subject, however, to
his liability to account for it and pay it over whenever lawful
demand should be made upon him for it. It was not money
invested in securities, or out upon interest; but it was like
money in bank liable to be paid upon call, and held by him as
a simple depositary. She regarded money in bank, for which
the bank was simply her debtor, liable to pay her upon proper
demand, as ready money; and when she spoke of money,
"either in bank or elsewhere," she meant all her money that
was situated similarly to that which she had in bank. She
evidently did not use the words "ready money" in their

limited sense, and she did not probably mean besides the money deposited in bank simply money kept on hand by her in her house or upon her person; but she meant ready money in bank or anywhere else. Money in the possession of her husband occupying the same house with her, which was at all times subject to call, could with some propriety be called ready money.

While we do not deem this case entirely free from doubt, we think the husband should, under the circumstances, have the benefit of the doubt, and that the bequest should have effect upon the money in his hands.

The judgment of the General Term should, therefore, be reversed and judgment given for the defendant, with costs.

All concur, except FINCH, J., who took no part.

Judgment accordingly.

In the Matter of the Estate of DAVID YOUNG, deceased. HENRIETTA E. YOUNG, Appellant, *v.* WALTER D. HICKS et al., Executors, etc., Respondents.

By an ante-nuptial agreement the woman covenanted that if, after marriage, the man died first, she would accept $1,500 " in full satisfaction of her dower in his estate, and shall bar her from claiming the same, either in his real or personal estate." He covenanted to provide by will for the payment of that sum "in lieu of dower, or her rights as his widow in his estate." The parties married and the husband died, having made provision by will as covenanted. *Held,* that the agreement was valid and remained in full force after marriage (§ 3, chap. 375, Laws of 1849); that the intent was that the woman should take nothing as widow from her husband's estate ; and that, therefore, there being no children living, the issue of such marriage, she was not entitled to the specific articles given by the statute (2 R. S. 83, § 9) to a widow; that, although not to be appraised, they were part of the estate, and she, by her agreement, was estopped from claiming them.

Also *held,* that the surrogate, on application of the widow to compel the executor to set apart said articles for her, had jurisdiction to determine the question.

As to whether the matter would have been affected by the existence of minor children or others interested, *quære*.

(Submitted March 28, 1883 ; decided April 17, 1883.)

APPEAL from judgment of the General Term of the Supreme Court, in the second judicial department, entered upon an order made May 8, 1882, setting aside a decree of the surrogate of Dutchess county, which directed the executors of the estate of David Young, deceased, to set apart, for the use of his widow, the articles specified in the statute (2 R. S. 83, § 9). (Reported below, 27 Hun, 54.)

The executors refused to set aside any property of the estate because of an ante-nuptial agreement, the body of which is as follows:

" Whereas, a marriage is about to be had and solemnized between the said parties ; and the party of the first part is desirous of making provision for a fit and proper settlement to and for the use and benefit of the said Henrietta E. Tripp, his intended wife ; now, therefore, the said party of the first part doth hereby agree, that if the said marriage shall be had and solemnized as aforesaid, that the said Henrietta shall receive, have and be provided for as follows, to-wit :

" 1. She shall have, hold, retain and dispose, during her life or by will, of any and all property, real or personal, which she now has or may hereafter receive, or become entitled to as her own.

" 2. In case she should happen to survive the said David Young, he hereby agrees to make provision by his last will and testament, or otherwise, that she shall have and receive out of his estate the sum of $1,500, with interest from the day of his decease — in consideration of said marriage and also in lieu of dower, or her rights as widow in his estate ; and in case no such provision is made as aforesaid, then such sum is to be paid out of his estate, at all events by those who shall administer the same.

" 3. And the said Henrietta E. Tripp, in consideration of

the premises, hereby covenants and agrees that in case such sum of $1,500 shall be paid to her as aforesaid, in the event of her surviving said David Young, that she will accept and receive the same in full satisfaction of her dower in his estate, and shall bar her from claiming the same, either in his real or personal estate; and that she will execute and deliver any release or releases of such dower rights to his heirs at law, devisors, or legal representatives on demand thereof."

Young died leaving no children the issue of his marriage, and leaving a will in which he made provision as required by the said agreement.

Allison Butts for appellant. A testator cannot by his will defeat the provision which the law makes for the widow. (*Vedder* v. *Saxton*, 46 Barb. 188.) Under the statute the title of the widow to such exempt property when there is no minor child is absolute on the death of her husband, not only as against creditors and next of kin but against legatees. (*Vedder* v. *Saxton*, 46 Barb. 188.) A provision in the will of a husband in favor of the wife will never be construed by implication to be in lieu of dower, or any other interest in his estate given by law. The design to substitute one for the other must be unequivocally expressed. (*Sheldon* v. *Bliss*, 8 N. Y. 31; *Mills* v. *Mills*, 28 Barb. 454.) Parties about to celebrate a marriage cannot by ante-nuptial agreement deprive their children or any member of the family of this right given by the statute of exemption, and the intended wife could not make a contract which must deprive not only herself but also her family of the exempt property which the statute secures to them. (Dayton on Surrogates [3d ed.], 276; *Vedder* v. *Saxton*, 46 Barb. 188; Redfield on Surrogates [2d ed.], 409; *Kneetle* v. *Newcomb*, 22 N. Y. 249; *Harper* v. *Leal*, 10 How. 276; *Crawford* v. *Lockwood*, 9 id. 547; *Woodward* v. *Murray*, 18 Johns. 400; *Gray* v. *Hook*, 4 N. Y. 449; *Brill* v. *Leggett*, 7 id. 176.)

Daniel W. Guernsey for respondents. Contracts made between persons in contemplation of marriage remain after such marriage takes place, and will be enforced according to the obvious intent, however informally or irregularly they have been executed. (2 Hill's Ch. 3, 6; 3 Johns. Ch. 550; *Pierce v. Pierce*, 71 N. Y. 157; 1 Story's Eq. Jur., § 986; Waterman on Spec. Perf. of Contracts, 589.) An indorsement on an antenuptial agreement, subsequent to the marriage, cannot be regarded as a part of the original contract or as explanatory thereof. (Tyler on Infancy and Coverture, 460.)

Danforth, J. The parties intended by an ante-nuptial contract to avoid the effect of marriage upon their property relations, and this contract, however invalid at common law, remained in full force after marriage. (Laws of 1849, chap. 375, § 3.) Its purpose is very plain. There is first a promise that the woman shall retain as her own such property as she has when married, or which she might acquire or become entitled to after marriage, with full power of disposition. As to all that, she was to remain, as it were, a single woman. Next she agrees, if after marriage the man dies first, to accept the sum of $1,500 "in full satisfaction of her dower in his estate, and thereby be precluded from claiming the same either in his real or personal estate." On his part is a covenant to provide by will for the payment of this sum to her with interest from the day of his decease "in lieu of dower or her rights as widow in his estate," and if he fails to make such provision, that amount is to be paid to her from his estate "by those who shall administer" it.

While there is some difference in the phraseology of the covenants, the meaning is the same, and each expresses an intent that she shall take nothing as widow from his estate either as dower or any other interest given by law. Both parties were bound by this agreement, and on the part of the husband and his representatives it has been fully performed.

The question was within the jurisdiction of the surrogate and his authority " to direct and control the conduct * * * of executors" (Code, § 2472, subd. 3), and "to administer justice in all matters relating to the affairs of decedents according to the provisions of the statutes relating thereto" (Code, § 2472, subd. 6), but we think he erred in holding that the plaintiff might take the specific articles given by statute to the widow of the deceased. Although not to be appraised, they were still part of his estate, and she was, by her agreement, estopped from claiming them. How this matter would be affected by the existence of minor children, or others interested, it is not necessary to determine.

It follows that the decree of the surrogate was properly vacated, and the judgment of the Supreme Court should be affirmed, with costs.

All concur.

Judgment affirmed.

In the Matter of the Final Accounting of JAMES FRAZER et al., Executors, etc.

The will of W. gave to his widow "all of the household property in the dwelling-house and the use of the dwelling-house during her life." In the dwelling-house, at the time of the testator's death, was a quantity of coal and wood, provided for family use, and a shot-gun. Upon settlement of the accounts of the executors, *held*, that these articles were properly allowed to the widow; that the shot-gun might have been provided for the defense of the house, and in the absence of proof the court was not required to presume the contrary.

The appraisers set apart as exempt and for the use of the widow, a horse, phaeton and harness, of the value of $150. *Held*, that the gift of the household property did not preclude this allowance; that "other personal property" was available for the exemption and might be necessary.

Peck v. *Sherwood* (56 N. Y. 615), distinguished.

A claim against the estate, based upon an alleged contract with the deceased, which was presented and sworn to in the ordinary manner, was allowed and paid by the executors. *Held*, that the burden was upon the contestants to show that it was not a just debt, and in the absence of such evidence it was properly allowed.

M., the claimant, was allowed to testify as a witness to the contract. *Held* no error; as he was not a party, nor did the executors derive any title through or from him. (Code of Civil Procedure, §§ 828, 829.)

Also *held*, that it was no objection to the allowance that the executors could, had they resisted the claim, have excluded M. as a witness to personal transactions with the deceased.

The executors allowed to a widow a claim for the wages of her son P. This was objected to on the ground that she was not authorized to receive them, and that the claim was outlawed when paid. The services ended in March, 1871. P. was then eighteen years of age. His father died in 1877, the payment was made in 1879, previous to which P. had died. No administrator was appointed. *Held*, that as the payment was of a just debt and had gone to the benefit of those entitled, and as the estate could not be required to pay a second time, and so had suffered no wrong, the executors were properly credited with the payment.

The testator, having in his hands a sum of money belonging to his wife, loaned it in 1869, taking notes in the name of his wife. Afterward he included the amount in a mortgage executed to himself by the borrower. The amount, with interest, was allowed to the widow by the executors. It was claimed by the contestant that it was to be presumed that the wife did not consent; that the husband was guilty of a conversion of her money, and so the statute of limitations was set running and the claim outlawed prior to the testator's death. *Held* untenable; that it was to be presumed, in the absence of evidence to the contrary, that the security was taken by the husband, with the consent of the wife; and therefore to the extent of her interest, he held the mortgage as agent or trustee for her.

Also *held*, that interest was properly allowed, as it was earned by the investment and received by the testator.

The will directed the executors to expend a sum not exceeding $2,000 " in repair " of a cemetery lot. A sarcophagus was erected on the lot at the expense of $500, and the testator's remains placed therein. A monument on the lot was exchanged for a better one and headstones to graves erected, and coping replaced at a cost of $935.05. *Held*, that what was done was within the authority and discretion given to the executors.

The testator's residuary estate, including the homestead in which his wife was given a life estate, he gave to his wife, to H., the contestant, and to W. in equal proportions. The executors, at the request of the widow and H., expended $320 in repair to the premises, one-half of which they charged to each. It was objected that but one-third should be so charged. *Held* untenable.

Also *held*, that as the will contained no provisions excluding the widow from dower or repugnant to a claim therefor, the acceptance by her of the provisions in the will for her benefit did not deprive her of the right to make the claim.

(Argued March 26, 1883 ; decided April 17, 1883.)

APPEAL from judgment of the General Term of the Supreme Court, in the fourth judicial department, entered upon an order made the second Tuesday of June, 1882, which affirmed a decree of the surrogate of the county of Livingston upon the final accounting of the executors of the will of Harlow W. Wells, deceased.

The will, after giving various legacies, contained these provisions.

"All the rest and residue of my estate, both real and personal, I give, devise and bequeath to my beloved wife, Frances C. Wells, Henry M. McDonald and Willard Wells McDonald, to be equally divided between them; I do hereby authorize and direct my executors, hereinafter named, to sell the property in the village of Caledonia, and the farm north of said village, on such terms as they may think best. The McDonald farm is not to be sold, and my brother, Horace Wells, is to have his support out of my said property for and during the term of his natural life, and I hereby direct my executors, hereinafter named, to reserve in their hands sufficient thereof for that purpose, and to apply the same for said purpose. I hereby authorize and direct my executors, hereinafter named, to expend a sum not to exceed $2,000 in the repair of the burying lot of W. H. Smith, and that my body should be kept in a receiving vault in Leroy until such repairs can be made. I also give, devise and bequeath to Mrs. Carr, wife of William Carr, of Caledonia, the house and lot where she now resides, and direct my executors to deed the same to her. I likewise give, devise and bequeath to my wife, Frances C. Wells, all of the household property now in my dwelling-house, in the village of Caledonia, and the use of said dwelling-house for and during the term of her natural life, and direct that said dwelling-house shall not be sold during her said life."

The testator died in 1877. He owned at the time of his death two farms — one known as the McDonald farm and several lots in the village of Caledonia, on one of which was the "dwelling-house" specified in the will.

SICKELS — VOL. XLVII.   31

There was at the time of the testator's death, in an out-house, four tons of coal and four cords of wood provided for family use ; also a shot-gun ; these were allowed by the execu-tors to the widow. A horse, phæton and harness, appraised at $150, were set apart by the appraisers for the widow, and allowed by the executors.

One Mullin presented a claim, duly verified, for his personal services on the farm of the testator. The executors allowed this claim. On the final settlement Mullin was sworn, and proved a contract for such work with the testator. The con-testant excepted to such testimony.

Peter Tierney worked for the testator from May 2, 1870, to March 16, 1871. At the last mentioned date he was a minor of about eighteen years of age. His father, John Tierney, was then living in the town of Caledonia. He settled with the testator in his life-time after the 16th day of March, and about May 14, 1874, excluding from such settlement his son's wages, and made no claim then or afterward upon the testator there-for. The father died about November 1, 1877 ; the son, Peter, died before both the testator and his father; the mother, per-sonally, without being appointed administrator, presented a claim for this work for $106.92, and the executors paid her the same. Before this, Henry McDonald, the contestant, ob-jected to the payment of this claim, and asked that it be re-ferred, under the statute, which the executors declined.

Mrs. Wells had, before February 3, 1869, given her husband $380 to loan for her. On that day he, as her agent, loaned this sum to one Alexander McPherson, and took for it his note, payable to Mrs. Wells in one year, with interest. On the 1st day of February, A. D. 1870, said McPherson executed and delivered to the testator his bond and mortgage for $2,000, part of the consideration for which was said note. The executors allowed to the widow the amount of the note, with interest.

Under the power given in the will, the executors expended out of the moneys of the estate $500 in making and erecting upon the said cemétery lot mentioned in the will a sarcophagus, or walled tomb, for the remains of the testator and his wife.

They also exchanged the monument on the lot for another, and caused new head-stones to be put to all the graves, and repaired the coping around the lot. For this, in addition to the old monument exchanged, they paid out of the estate the sum of $935.65. Before the executors did any thing on the lot the contestant objected to this last expenditure.

Under the power contained in the will, the executors sold and conveyed two of the village lots of which the testator died seized. The widow joined in this deed, and out of the avails the executors paid her as and for her dower therein the sum of $300.95.

The executors expended the sum of $320 in making permanent repairs upon the homestead, the life estate of which was by the will given to the widow. This was done on the request of the widow and the contestant, and the executors charged it in their account, one-half to each.

The action of the executors in the matters above stated was approved by the surrogate, and the items so paid by them allowed.

Angus McDonald for appellants. Household property does not include coal, wood and double-barrel shot-gun, or either of those articles. (Roper on Legacies, 273 ; *Dayton* v. *Fellow*, 1 Rob. 28 ; *Cole* v. *Fitzgerald*, 1 S. & S. Eng. Ch. 189.) The executors should be charged with the horse, phaeton and harness, $150, claimed to be set apart as exempt. (*Peck* v. *Sherwood*, 56 N. Y. 615 ; *Applegate* v. *Cannon*, 2 Bradf. 119 ; *Clayton* v. *Wendell*, id. 7 ; *Applegate* v. *Cannon*, id. 119 ; *Bliss* v. *Sheldon*, 7 Barb. 152 ; affirmed, 8 N. Y. 35.) Executors are trustees for creditors and legatees. They must simply see right and justice is done, and that as between them each has his legal rights. (2 Perry on Trusts, 106 ; Tiffany and Bullard on Trusts, 483 ; 2 Story's Eq. Jur. 502 ; Redfield's Surrogate, 222–4 ; McClelland's Surrogate [2d ed.], 434 ; *Dox* v. *Blackenstose*, 12 Wend. 542 ; McClelland's Surrogate, 607 ; *Martin* v. *George*, 9 N. Y. 398 ; *Freeman* v. *Freeman*, 2 Redf. Surr. 137 ; *Bucklin* v. *Chapin*, 1 Lans. 448 ; *McLaren* v. *McMartin*, 37 N. Y. 88 ; § 829 of New Code ; 36 N. Y.

88; § 382, Rev. Stat. [3d ed.] 152; Dayton's Surrogate, 383; *Williams* v. *Purdy*, 9 Paige, 109; *Westervelt* v. *Gregg*, 1 Barb. Ch. 471; *Flagg* v. *Rœder*, 1 Bradf. 197; *Metzger* v. *Metzger*, id. 265; 2 Smith's Practice, 122; *Valentine* v. *Valentine*, 4 Redf. 265; *Westervelt* v. *Gregg*, 1 Barb. Ch. 471; 2 Perry on Trusts, 106; *McLaren* v. *McMartin*, 36 N. Y. 88.) Neither the affidavit of the claimant on his proof, nor his evidence as to personal transactions with the deceased, can be used on the final accounting in favor of the executors. (Dayton's Surrogate, 383; 6 Paige, 169; 1 Bradf. 197–205; 1 Barb. Ch. 471; § 829 of New Code; *White-head* v. *Smith*, 81 N. Y. 151; *Wilkins* v. *Baker*, 24 Hun, 32; § 829 of Code.) If, at the time the testator took the $2,000 mortgage and gave up the note his wife consented to it, then he was immediately liable to her for so much money had and received. If she did not know or consent, she might have an action for conversion, if she were alive and so elected. (*Boyce* v. *Brockaway*, 31 N. Y. 490; Angell on Limitations, § 394; *Kelsey* v. *Griswold*, 6 Barb. Sup. Ct. 436; *Boughton* v. *Flint*, 74 N. Y. 478.) In either case the cause of action then accrued, and the statute commenced to run. (Angell on Limitations, § 304; *Kelsey* v. *Griswold*, 6 Barb. Sup. Ct. 436; *Payne* v. *Gardiner*, 29 N. Y. 167; *Stacy* v. *Graham*, 14 id. 492; *Power* v. *Hathaway*, 41 id. 214–19.) The statements and verified accounts of Mrs. Wells, in which she credits interest for two years, down to Feb. 1st, 1872, are evidence. (§ 829 of Code; *Risley* v. *Wight-man*, 13 Hun, 165; Code, § 403; *Reynolds* v. *Collins*, 3 Hill, 37; *Howell* v. *Babcock's Ex'rs*, 24 Wend. 488; *Buck-ley* v. *Chapin*, 1 Lans. 499; *Sanford* v. *Sanford*, 62 N. Y. 553.) The executors were not authorized to pay the $935.65 in addition to the $500, for the sarcophagus, in exchange for monuments. (Abbott's Law Dictionary, word "repair;" 29 How. Pr. 429; 24 N. J. Eq. 373; *Emans* v. *Hickman*, 12 Hun, 425; *Owen* v. *Bloomer*, 24 id. 296; *Fenvir* v. *Sedg-wick*, 41 N. Y. 315; *Springsteed* v. *Sampson*, 32 id. 703; *Matter of Elracher*, 3 Redf. on Surr. 8; *Matter of Luckey*,

4 id. 495.) By accepting her portion under the will the widow elected to take it instead of her dower. (*Adsit* v. *Adsit*, 2 Johns. Ch. 448; *Tobias* v. *Ketchum*, 32 N. Y. 319; *Chamberlain* v. *Same*, 43 id. 444; *Canfield* v. *Sullivan*, 85 id. 159; *Tobias* v. *Ketchum*, 32 id. 327; *Savage* v. *Burnham*, 17 id. 561; *Dodge* v. *Dodge*, 31 Barb. 413; Ex. A. Fol. 137 of case; *Pearson* v. *Pearson*, 1 Brown's Ch. 292, and note; *Vernon* v. *Vernon*, 53 N. Y. 352; *Dodge* v. *Dodge*, 31 Barb. Sup. Ct. 413; 32 N. Y. 327; 17 id. 561; *Parker* v. *Somersby*, 27 Eng. Law & Eq. 154; *Herbert et al.* v. *Wren et al.*, 7 Cranch, 370–8; *Birmingham* v. *Kirwin*, 7 Sch. & Lef. 452; *Colgate's Ex'r* v. *Colgate*, 53 N. J. Eq. [8 C. E. Green] 372; *Chalmers* v. *Storel*, 2 Ves. & Bea. 223; *Mills* v. *Mills*, 28 Barb. Sup. Ct. 457; *Dickinson* v. *Robinson*, Jacob, 509; *Dodge* v. *Dodge*, 31 Barb. Sup. Ct. 413; *Burley* v. *Boyce*, 4 Strobh. [S. C.] 84; *Savage* v. *Burnham*, 17 N. Y. 577; *Wood* v. *Wood*, 5 Paige, 601.)

Lucius N. Bangs for respondent. The widow was entitled, as legatee, to the coal, wood and shot-gun in the testator's house, which were delivered to her. (*Dayton* v. *Tillow*, 1 Robt. 21.) There being nothing in the will, which by language or inference can make the provision for the widow take the place of her dower right in the property of the testator, she is not driven to an election, but takes the provision under the will in addition to her dower right. (*Jackson, ex dem. Loucks,* v. *Churchill*, 7 Cow. 287; *Bundig* v. *Bundig*, 3 Kay & Johns. 257; *Jackson* v. *Churchill*, 7 Cow. 290; *Ellis* v. *Lewis*, 3 Hare, 310; *Sanford* v. *Jackson*, 10 Paige, 266–270; *Dawson* v. *Bise*, 1 Keene, 761; *Harrison* v. *Harrison*, id. 765; *Holdrich* v. *Holdrich*, 2 Y. & C. Ch. 20; *Havens* v. *Sackett*, 15 N. Y. 365, 371, 372; *Adsit* v. *Adsit*, 2 Johns. Ch. 448; *Church* v. *Bull*, 2 Denio, 430, 431; *S. C.*, 5 Hill, 200; 1 Jarman on Wills [Bigelow's ed.], 458, n. 2; 2 Jarman on Wills [R. & T. ed.], 22–24; *Fuller* v. *Yates*, 8 Paige, 325; *Havens* v. *Havens*, 1 Sandf. Ch. 324–329–331; *Gibson* v. *Gibson*, 17 Eng. Law & Eq. 349–352; 2 Jarman on Wills

[R. & T. ed.], 29; *Gibson* v. *Gibson*, 17 Eng. Law & Eq. 349–353. See *Mills* v. *Mills*, 23 Barb. 454.) The claim of dower is favored. (*Lasher* v. *Lasher*, 13 Barb. 106; 2 Jarman on Wills [R. & T. ed.], 25, 29; *Thompson* v. *Burra*, 16 Eng. Law & Eq. 592–602; *Kenedy* v. *Nedrow*, 1 Dal. 415–417; *Leonard* v. *Steele*, 4 Barb. 20; Jarman on Wills, chap. 14, Election.)

FINCH, J. The provision of the will giving to the widow " all of the household property in the dwelling-house " is broad enough to include the coal and wood provided for the use of the family, and also the shot-gun, in the absence of proof showing that it was not kept for the defense of the house. (*Dayton* v. *Tillou*, 1 Robt. 21; *Cole* v. *Fitzgerald*, 1 Sim. & Stu. 189.) Such may have been its use and purpose, and we are not required to presume the contrary from any fact given in evidence. The ruling of the surrogate in these respects was correct.

The appraisers set apart as exempt and for the use of the widow a horse, phaeton and harness of the value of $150, which it is now said were not " necessary," since she took under the will all the household property, and the use of the house for life. If we could so decide, where the testator had given to the widow the use of all his real and personal property, except a legacy due him (*Peck* v. *Sherwood*, 56 N. Y. 615), we cannot say it where only the household property is given. In such a case " other personal property " is available for the exemption, and may be necessary. When the appraisers have so determined and the surrogate approved, there is no basis left for us, unless upon very different facts, on which to found a reversal of such conclusion.

Certain payments of alleged debts against the estate are questioned, and the executors sought to be charged with their amount. All of them are shown to have been honest debts, and honestly due. No adequate reason is given why the executors should have suspected their justice, or doubted the propriety of their payment. What is said amounts only to an assertion that the executors might possibly have resisted them with success, and were bound to make the effort. One of these claims was that of Mullin. It was based upon an alleged contract with the deceased, and presented and sworn to in the ordinary manuer. The executors having paid it and produced their voucher, the burden was on the contestants to show that it was not a just debt of the estate. They showed nothing of the kind. All the proof is the other way, and the sole point of their criticism is that the executors could have kept out proof of the contract by resisting the claim, and shutting out Mullin as a witness to personal transactions with the deceased. But that does not follow. If the executors had defended, proof of the contract might have come from some other source. And in any event there is evidence of the value of Mullin's services reaching quite to the level of his claim. We think Mullin was a competent witness. He was not a party, nor did the executors derive any title or interest from him. They neither owned the debt, nor asserted any title to it. As the contestants did not establish that the demand was unjust, and not a debt of the estate, the payment by the executors was properly allowed.

The objection to the payment made Mrs. Tierney, for the wages of her son Peter, appears to have been that she was not authorized to receive them, and they were outlawed. The services ended in March, 1871. Peter was then eighteen. The statute did not begin to run against him until 1874. (Code, § 396.) The payment was in 1879. Peter had died at some time previous, but when we do not know. His father died in November, 1877. If the wages belonged to the father it is claimed they were outlawed; but if they belonged to the son it is not claimed that they were barred by the statute, but only that the mother, not having been appointed administrator, could not lawfully discharge the debt. But the estate of Wells has suffered no wrong. It cannot be made to pay the debt a second time, for the statute is a bar. It was an honest debt, and has gone to the benefit of those entitled. The executors should not be charged with it unless by their act the estate has suffered some loss. It has suffered none and can suffer none;

and we ought not to punish executors for omitting a precaution, which would have been wise, but which time has rendered unnecessary for the safety of the estate committed to their care.

The third payment questioned was made to the widow. The fact that the testator had $380 of her money and loaned it in 1869 and afterward included the amount in a mortgage taken to himself is not disputed. But the statute of limitations is again relied on. The husband was allowed by the wife to retain the money. There was no conversion by him for which trover could have been maintained. The transaction amounted to a trust or a deposit. Originally the money was loaned to McPherson, and the notes taken in the name of the wife. In February, 1870, McPherson wanted more money on his bond and mortgage, and the testator loaned it, including in the security taken in his own name the debt due his wife. Whether this was done with the knowledge and assent of his wife we do not certainly know, but assuming that it was, unless she loaned him the money, which is not shown, he held the mortgage to the extent of her money in it as her agent or trustee. If she so consented, which is most probable, she became in equity the owner of a proportionate part of the mortgage, but was not entitled to receive the money until it was paid, and could maintain no action until her right was in some manner denied. But we are asked to presume that she did not consent in order to make her husband a wrong-doer, and guilty of a conversion of the money, and so set running the statute of limitations, and outlaw the demand before the death of the testator, and thus make the executors liable for an improper payment. The burden was upon the contestants to prove their case. We cannot relieve their failure by presuming that the husband was guilty of a conversion of his wife's money, when it is both possible and probable that he merely invested it in his own name for her benefit, and with her knowledge and consent. The relation of the parties to each other, their conduct, and all the facts disclosed indicate such to have been the truth of the transaction, and, therefore, that the claim of the wife was just, and not barred by the statute of limitations.

On that basis interest was payable to the widow because earned by the investment of her money and received by the testator for her. .

The will directed the executors to expend a sum not exceeding $2,000 in the repair of the cemetery lot of W. H. Smith, who was testator's father-in-law, and that his body should be kept in a receiving vault in Le Roy until such repairs be made. After his death a sarcophagus was erected upon the lot at a cost of $500 and his remains placed therein. After this, the monument on the lot was exchanged for a better one, headstones to graves erected, and coping replaced at a further cost of $935.05. This last expenditure is objected to on the ground that a new monument was not "in repair" of the lot, and there being a sarcophagus there was no need of a monument. It can scarcely be necessary to review a discretion exercised by the executors and kept within the limit fixed by the testator himself. What was done was plainly within the authority of the will and was reasonably and fairly executed.

Certain repairs were put upon the homestead amounting to $320, which were done at the request of the widow and Henry McDonald. One-half was, therefore, charged to each. Under the will the widow had a life estate in the homestead. The remainder in fee went to Henry and Willard McDonald. The repairs benefited both the life estate and the remainder. The executors were not bound to make them so far as the facts disclose. What they did was to advance to the widow and Henry $320 out of the estate, at their request, which was expended for their benefit and in accordance with their direction. Why they should not be charged with what they had, and why the executors should personally pay one-third of it, we are unable to perceive.

Finally, it is objected that the widow was not entitled to dower because the provisions for her benefit under the will were accepted by her, and dower was excluded by the manifest intention of the testator derived from the scope and tenor of the will. No trust estate was vested in the executors. They had simply a power of sale, with no right to rent or lease, and no control over the rents and profits. No duty relating to the real estate was imposed upon them except to sell and convey. Dower, therefore, was not excluded by the creation of a trust estate inconsistent with it, vested in the executors. (*Savage* v. *Burnham*, 17 N. Y. 561; *Tobias* v. *Ketchum*, 32 id. 327.) The provision giving the rest, residue and remainder of his property to the widow and the McDonalds is not inconsistent with dower, for it relates to the division of his estate, and does not purport to dispose of hers. The two may stand together. The intention manifested in the will was not an equal division of all his property among the three, as in *Chalmers* v. *Storil* (2 Ves. & Bea. 222), a case shaken by subsequent criticism. (*Gibson* v. *Gibson*, 17 Eng. L. & Eq. 349.) But the equal division aimed at is of a residue which may well be deemed the remainder of the property subject to the dower right. (*Havens* v. *Havens*, 1 Sandf. Ch. 324; *Mills* v. *Mills*, 28 Barb. 456.) The repugnancy, therefore, which drives the widow to an election must come, if at all, from the provision for the support of testator's brother, those directing a sale, and that devising a house and lot to Mrs. Carr. It is conceded that the support of the brother was simply charged upon the McDonald farm, which was not to be sold. The existence of such a charge does not necessarily exclude the widow's dower in the same land, especially since the executors are also directed to reserve in their hands sufficient of testator's property for the purpose of that support. The devise to Mrs. Carr and the direction to sell and convey a part of the real estate do not necessarily conflict with the right of dower in the present case. (*Jackson* v. *Churchill*, 7 Cow. 287; *Havens* v. *Havens*, *supra*; *Fuller* v. *Yates*, 8 Paige, 325.) Directions for a sale may be so expressed and the purpose to be answered of such peculiar character as to indicate an intention to exclude dower. (*Vernon* v. *Vernon*, 53 N. Y. 362.) But no unusual or peculiar state of facts exists in the present case to compel an inference that the property directed to be conveyed was to pass free and discharged from the widow's dower. There is enough in the will to produce hesitation and reflection, but not enough to establish that clear repugnancy, that manifest intention which is alone sufficient, in the absence of express words, to drive the widow to her election.

The judgment should be affirmed, with costs.

All concur.

Judgment affirmed.

MARY JANE FIESTER, Appellant, *v.* JOHN SHEPARD, Executor, etc., Respondent.

Under the Code of Civil Procedure (§§ 2717, 2718) a surrogate has no jurisdiction to entertain proceedings instituted by one claiming a legacy, to compel an executor to pay the same, when the executor " files a written answer duly verified, setting forth facts which show that it is doubtful whether the petitioner's claim is valid and legal, and denying its validity." In such a case, the surrogate must dismiss the petition.

The objection, although not raised in the Surrogate's Court or at General Term, may be taken on appeal to this court.

(Argued March 27, 1883; decided April 17, 1883.)

APPEAL from an order of the General Term of the Supreme Court, in the fourth judicial department, made December 30, 1881, which reversed an order of the surrogate of Livingston county, directing defendant, as the executor of the will of Ann Havens, deceased, to account, etc., and remitted the proceedings to said surrogate, with directions to enter an order dismissing the proceedings. (Reported below, 26 Hun, 183.)

The nature of the proceedings and the material facts are stated in the opinion.

J. A. Van Derlip for appellant. Extrinsic evidence is always competent to define or identify either the subject or the object of a testator's bounty. (1 Jarman on Wills [5th Am. ed.], 429; *Stubbs* v. *Sargon*, 2 Keen, 255; O'Hara's ed. of Wigram [2d Am. ed.], 128; see, also, Prop. V and VII of same author, 142 *et seq.*; *Petway* v. *Powell*, 1 Dev. & Bat.

Eq. 308; *Smith* v. *Smith*, 1 Edw. Ch. 188, 191; 4 Paige,
271; *Thomas* v. *Stevens*, 4 Johns. Ch. 607; *Burrell* v. *Boardman*, 43 N. Y. 254, 258; *Holmes* v. *Mead*, 52 id. 332, 343;
Leonard v. *Davenport*, 58 How. Pr. 384, 387; 3 Myl. & Cr.
507.) It is no valid objection to carrying out the obvious
intention of the testator, if it be not illegal or against good
morals, that it is strange, or unnatural, or absurd. (1 Redfield
on Wills [4th ed.], 434.)

Solomon Hubbard for respondent. Upon the filing of the
sworn answer of the executor, the petition ought to have been
dismissed by the surrogate. (*Bevan* v. *Cooper*, 72 N. Y. 318,
327; Code of Civ. Pro., §§ 2717, 2718, 2723, subd. 3; *Hurlburt* v. *Durant*, 88 N. Y. 122; Throop's note to § 2742, Code
of Civ. Pro.; *Riggs* v. *Cragg*, 89 N. Y. 479–490, etc.)

·RUGER, Ch. J. On the 1st day of November, 1880, the
petitioner presented her petition to the surrogate, requesting a
citation to be issued against John Shepard, as the executor of
the will of Ann Havens, deceased, requiring him to render an
account of his proceedings as such executor. The claim of
the petitioner was based upon the allegation that she was the
last person who took care of one Darling Havens, before his
death, and thereby became the residuary devisee and legatee of
all of the real and personal property of the testatrix. The
citation was issued and served upon the executor, and upon the
return day he appeared and filed an answer in writing to the
petition, duly verified, wherein he denied that the petitioner
was the last person who took care of Darling Havens before
his death, or that by the provisions of the will she became the
residuary devisee or legatee of all or any of the real and personal property of the testatrix.
  Upon the issue thus formed a trial was had before the surrogate, and on the 18th day of April, 1881, he rendered his
decision, holding that the petitioner was the last person who
took care of Darling Havens before his death, and, therefore,
became entitled as residuary devisee and legatee to the estate

·of the testatrix. The surrogate, thereupon, made his order requiring the executor to show cause why he should not pay the residue of the estate to the petitioner. From this order an appeal was taken by the executor to the General Term where the order of the surrogate was reversed upon the ground that the evidence given before him did not show the petitioner to be the person who was, under the terms of the will, entitled to the legacy in question. The petitioner, thereupon, appealed to this court.

The point is now made by the executor that the surrogate had no power to entertain this proceeding and adjudicate upon the question presented by the petition, that being the only question tried by him. We believe the point is well taken.

Although so far as the record shows this objection was neither raised in the Surrogate's Court nor at the General Term, yet as it lies at the foundation of the proceeding and concerns the jurisdiction of the surrogate over the subject-matter of the controversy, it is effectual and may be taken at any stage of the proceeding and must be considered and disposed of when raised.

The will of the testatrix which was put in evidence on the trial provided that after the payment of her debts and funeral expenses all of the real and personal property should be held in trust by her executor to receive the rents and profits thereof and apply the same to the benefit and support of her father, Darling Havens, during his life. The executor was authorized to convert the same, or so much thereof as might be necessary, into money, and apply the proceeds thereof to the benefit and support of the said Darling.

After the death of Darling Havens, the executor was directed to " use and dispose " of what was left as follows :

First, to pay her father's funeral expenses.

Second, to erect a suitable monument for him.

Third, to invest the sum of $200 to provide an income to take care of the graves of the father, mother, and testatrix.

Then after the devise of certain specific articles of personal property to relations and friends comes the clause of the will upon which the claim of the petitioner is founded and which reads as follows: "The residue of my estate, if any there shall be, to be paid by my executor, to the person who shall last take care of my father before his death."

Whether the surrogate would have jurisdiction to try the question presented by this provision of the will in any form of proceeding may well be doubted, but it is quite certain that he has no such power upon the invitation of the claimant alone.

It might very well happen under this provision that no one would be entitled to claim the benefit of the devise, and in any event it presents a question which can only be determined by an inquiry into circumstances extrinsic the will itself, and apparently involves the interests of all who might in any event be entitled to a distributive share in the personal or to inherit the real property of the testator. Such a controversy could properly be determined only by a tribunal authorized to bring all of the parties interested before it, and having jurisdiction to try and decide the various questions involved in determining the meaning and effect of the clause in question, and the identity of the parties claiming under it.

It has, therefore, been frequently decided that Surrogates' Courts do not possess these powers and have no jurisdiction to hear and determine such questions. Such courts have been held to be courts of limited jurisdiction and entitled to exercise only such powers as are conferred by statute, or those which are incident to the exercise of the powers expressly granted to them. (*Bevan* v. *Cooper*, 72 N. Y. 329; *Sipperly* v. *Baucus*, 24 id. 46; *Riggs* v. *Cragg*, 89 id. 479.) It has accordingly been held that they have no power to adjudicate the validity of a debt upon the petition of a creditor when the claim is disputed by the executor (*Tucker* v. *Tucker*, 4 Keyes, 136), or the question whether a legacy is a charge upon the real estate (*Bevan* v. *Cooper, supra*), or to order a set off of mutual judgments. (*Stilwell* v. *Carpenter*, 59 N. Y. 414.) But this question has recently been so extensively discussed in this court in the case of *Riggs* v. *Cragg* (89 N. Y. 479) that its further consideration, either upon principle or authority, is deemed unnecessary. These principles have now been incorporated into the Code of Civil Procedure, and this case having arisen since the 1st day of September, 1880, must be governed by its provisions. Section 2717 provides for a proceeding by a creditor or legatee before the surrogate to enforce the payment of a debt or legacy against an executor or administrator. Subdivision 2 of this section authorizes " a person entitled to a legacy " to prosecute such a proceeding. Section 2718 authorizes the surrogate to issue a citation to the executor or administrator upon a petition presented under section 2717, but further provides that he must dismiss the petition " when the executor or administrator files a written answer duly verified, setting forth facts which show that it is doubtful whether the petitioner's claim is valid and legal, and denying its validity absolutely or upon information and belief." We are unable to see how, in the face of these explicit provisions of the statute, the surrogate had any authority to hear and determine the questions involved in this proceeding.

The statute is imperative that upon the presentation of these facts affecting the jurisdiction of the surrogate, in the manner therein provided, he shall dismiss the petition without prejudice to an action or an accounting in behalf of the petitioner. (*Hurlburt* v. *Durant*, 88 N. Y. 121.) When the right of the claimants, whether arising upon a legacy or a debt against an estate, is denied by its representative, the surrogate is prohibited by the statute from hearing and deciding the issue thus formed, and the party is remitted to another proceeding or tribunal to establish and enforce his right.

We are, therefore, of the opinion that the surrogate should have dismissed the petition upon the presentation of the answer, and the order of the General Term, remitting the proceedings to him for that purpose, should be affirmed with costs, to be paid to the respondent out of the estate.

All concur.

Order affirmed.

In the Matter of the Claim of WILLIAM H. FLANDROW, Creditor, etc.

Pending a contest as to the validity of a will a special administrator was appointed. A judgment had been recovered against the decedent prior to his death. An attachment against the judgment creditor was sought to be executed upon the judgment by service of copy upon the executrix named in the will. The special administrator was then acting, and the contest was then and is still pending. *Held*, that the executrix had no power to represent the estate, and so was not the "individual holding such property" within the meaning of the provision of the Code of Procedure (§ 235*), authorizing the execution of an attachment by service of a copy; that, therefore, the judgment was not reached by the attachment; and that an order of the surrogate denying an application of the attachment creditor for the payment of the same to him was proper.

Also *held*, the fact that the attorney for the special administrator, upon being inquired of, gave information that the person named in the will was executrix, but concealed the appointment of the special administrator, did not preclude the latter from raising the objection.

(Argued March 28, 1883; decided April 17, 1883.)

APPEAL from an order of the General Term of the Supreme Court, in the first judicial department, made November 24, 1882, which affirmed an order of the surrogate of the county of New York, denying an application of William H. Flandrow, claiming to be a creditor of Tunis Van Brunt, deceased, requiring the payment of his claim by Edward Schell, special administrator, out of the assets of the estate. (Reported below, 28 Hun, 279.)

In March, 1867, during the life-time of said Van Brunt, the Marine Bank of Chicago obtained a judgment against him for $6,858.12. Van Brunt died in 1867, leaving an instrument purporting to be his will, which appointed his widow his sole administratrix. The validity of the will when presented for probate was contested, and the proceedings are still pending undetermined. In consequence of such contest, in December, 1868, said Schell was appointed special administrator, and still acts as such. In an action brought by one Hammond against

---

*See Code of Civil Procedure, § 649.

said Marine Bank an attachment was issued, and the petitioner claims title to the said judgment under said attachment and as assignee of the judgment rendered in the attachment suit. This application was based mainly upon an affidavit, stating, in substance, that on or about April 6, 1869, the person making it delivered a certified copy of the attachment with a notice showing the property levied upon, *i. e.*, the judgment, to Mary J. Van Brunt as executrix of said will.

Further facts are stated in the opinion.

Joseph H. Choate for appellant. The surrogate's power may be exercised in a case like the present in the same manner as a court of record and of general jurisdiction. (Code, § 2481, subd. 6.) The claim, being a judgment against the deceased, need not be sued over, but the surrogate has power to decree its payment. (*McNulty* v. *Hurd*, 72 N. Y. 518.) The fact that judgment has been entered does not deprive the surrogate of the power to grant a new trial or rehearing. (*Tracy* v. *Altmeyer*, 46 N. Y. 598, 604; Code, § 2481, subd. 6; *Courtney* v. *Baker*, 60 N. Y. 7.) The fact of appeal does not prevent surrogate from granting relief. (3 Code R. 69.) The order and judgment appealed from are appealable to this court. (*Tilton* v. *Beecher*, 59 N. Y. 176; *Eq. L. Ins. Co.* v. *Stevens*, 63 id. 341; *Morris* v. *Wheeler*, 45 id. 708; *Davis* v. *Clark*, 87 id. 623; *In re Ross*, id. 514; *Tracy* v. *Altmeyer*, 46 id. 598.) Service of the warrant upon the sole executrix was sufficient. Her rights and liabilities accrued on the death of the testator. (Redfield's Law and Practice of Surrogate's Court [2d ed.], 427–8, 433, 434, 435 and 436, note 4; *Valentine* v. *Jackson*, 9 Wend. 304; *Schultz* v. *Pulver*, 11 id. 364; *Dox* v. *Blackentose*, 12 id. 542; 2 R. S. 71, § 16; Willard on Ex'rs, 147; *Durlich* v. *Johnson*, 2 Vern. 48; Wms. on Ex'rs [7th ed.], 302.) Service upon Mrs. Van Brunt was service upon the "debtor" within the meaning of the Code. (*O'Brien* v. *M. & T. Ins. Co.*, 56 N. Y. 57.) A party cannot take advantage of irregularity in issuing attachment, *a fortiori* in its service. (2 Wait's Pr. 184; *Tracy* v. *Seventh*

Nat. B'k, 37 N. Y. 323; *Johnson* v. *Ketchum*, 46 Barb. 43; *Smith* v. *Mahon*, 63 How. 382–385.) The court must assume upon the General Term decision, which reversed the decree of the surrogate, that the will is valid, and will presently be admitted to probate, in which event the executrix's representative capacity will be complete and unquestionable from the beginning. (*Rockwell* v. *Saunders*, 19 Barb. 473; *Bellinger* v. *Tord*, 21 id. 311; 2 R. S. 71, § 15; 3 id. 74, § 17 [6th ed.].)

George Zabriskie for respondent. The service of the warrant upon the executrix was not valid, the will never having been proved, and a special administrator having been appointed. (2 R. S. [4th ed.] 71, § 16; id. 76, §§ 38, 39; id. 81, § 78; *Flandrow* v. *Van Brunt*, 84 N. Y. 1; *McKinney* v. *Collins*, 88 id. 216; *Pennoyer* v. *Niff*, 95 U. S. 714.)

MILLER, J. Upon the former application to the surrogate in this matter it was held, upon appeal to this court,* that an attorney for the successful party in an action, by whom a judgment was procured, is not an "individual holding such property" within the meaning of the provision of the Code of Procedure (§ 235), authorizing the execution of an attachment by service of a copy. On this appeal it appears that upon the application to the surrogate an affidavit was presented showing that the warrant of attachment was served upon Mary T. Van Brunt as executrix of the last will and testament of Tunis Van Brunt, deceased, the judgment debtor. By the affidavit sworn to as the return to the attachment, it appears that service of the said attachment was made on the attorney by whom the judgment had been entered by a different person and at a different period of time from that named in the affidavit now relied upon, which was not sworn to until some twelve years after the service mentioned therein. The length of time which has elapsed since the service may be regarded as subject to some criticism, especially as the person upon whom the alleged service was made, swore, in 1874, that no such service had been made upon her. Assuming, however, that the affidavit is to be regarded as entitled to full credit and consideration, the question arises whether it was sufficient, in view of all the circumstances presented, to establish the right of the applicant to the relief claimed.

Tunis Van Brunt, against whom the judgment which was attached was entered, died in 1867. The instrument purporting to be his will, in which his widow was named as executrix, was contested, and in 1868 Edward Schell was appointed special administrator of the estate. The validity of the will and the rights of the executrix were not determined and were the subject of controversy at the time the alleged service was made, and have not yet been the subject of adjudication. So far as the estate is concerned, the special administrator has acted in that capacity, and has never been served, nor has any effort been made to serve the attachment upon him. We think the service upon Mrs. Van Brunt was not sufficient, in view of the facts, to bind the estate of Tunis Van Brunt. The Code of Procedure (§ 235) which was in operation at the time of the alleged service required that "the execution of the attachment upon * * * any debts or other property incapable of manual delivery to the sheriff shall be made by delivering a certified copy of the warrant of attachment * * * with the debtor or individual holding such property." The judgment was due from the deceased to the bank and belonged to it. It could only be attached by a service upon the judgment debtor, or, in case of his death, upon the representative of his estate. Mrs. Van Brunt did not occupy that position. The will had not been established, and it had not then been decided that she had any right or claim to act as executrix of the estate. Although she was the widow, sole legatee and executrix named in the will, it had never been admitted to probate, and she had acquired no right by which she was authorized to act for or on behalf of the estate. So far as any such authority existed, it was, at that time, vested in the special administrator; the executrix had not qualified, nor had she taken possession of the assets of the estate; she could not have sued as a representative of the estate, nor been prosecuted by any creditor; the most which she could do was to pay the funeral expenses and preserve the assets, and she had even been deprived of this power by the appointment of the special administrator. She certainly had no power to represent the estate in reference to debts existing or claimed against it.

We are referred by the learned counsel for the appellant to numerous authorities to sustain the position that the executrix named in the will was vested with rights which entitled her to represent the estate in regard to the claim in question. The rules established by the authorities cited may well apply to cases where the will has been properly executed and no question arises as to its validity, but they cannot be invoked in reference to a case where a contest exists in regard to the due execution of the will under which the executor or executrix was authorized to act. In the case considered, it does not appear that the will was legally executed, but on the contrary a contest existed as to its execution, and hence the executrix could not be regarded as having any authority under the instrument in question. She might or she might not have, as the result might occur; as this was uncertain, she did not occupy the position of a lawful representative of the estate. The statute is directly in conflict with the right of the executrix here to represent the estate of the deceased. It confers certain rights upon the executrix for the preservation of the estate, and can have no application so long as a question existed in regard to the validity of the will under which she was appointed. So far as this estate is concerned, any power which existed in reference to its preservation must rest with the special administrator. It is no answer to the position that no person was qualified to act as executrix and upon whom service could be made, to say that the respondent cannot question the regularity and authority of the will as he has sought to establish it in another proceeding. The question here is whether a valid service has been made upon the party representing the estate, and the respondent has a right to insist that this should be done in conformity to the law and practice in similar cases.

The appellant's counsel claims that the respondent's attorneys upon being inquired of concealed the fact that a special administrator had been appointed and gave information that Mary T. Van Brunt was the executrix, and hence he is now precluded from claiming that he should be served with the attachment. It is not apparent that there was any fraudulent concealment, and it is difficult to see upon what principle the statement made by the attorneys could change the rule with regard to serving the attachment upon the party who represented the debtor, and authorize such a service upon one whose right to represent the estate was not established. There is no practice established which dispenses with the necessity of serving upon the party in interest under the circumstances claimed to exist in reference to the alleged concealment. Upon no principle do we think it can be contended that the service upon Mrs. Van Brunt was a service upon the debtor within the provision of section 235 of the Code of Procedure. There is no ground for claiming that a liberal rule should be adopted in reference to the service of the attachment as in cases where the debtor does not seek to set the attachment aside.

It is also urged that the presumption being in favor of the validity of the will and that it will be admitted to probate, that the service upon the executrix will be complete from the beginning. We do not think that this position is well founded. As the case stands, the executrix does not legally represent the estate; she may never be authorized to act in that capacity. Under these circumstances, it would be going very far to say that the service upon the executrix is sufficient because eventually the will may be proved and established. There is no rule of law which sanctions such a presumption and which can be invoked in this case.

There are other questions raised upon the argument, but inasmuch as the decision of the surrogate should be sustained for want of a sufficient service of the attachment, as already stated, a discussion of them is not required.

The order should be affirmed.

All concur.

Order affirmed.

NICHOLAS DE PEYSTER, as Executor and Trustee, etc., Appellant, *v.* HENRY W. T. MALI et al., Respondents.

O S.

In an action brought under the provision of the act of 1813 (§ 184, chap. 86, Laws of 1813), authorizing a person entitled to an award of the commissioners of estimate and assessment in the city of New York to bring an action against any other person to whom the same has been paid to recover the same, it is no defense that the award was excessive or inequitable, or that plaintiff was entitled to only nominal damages while the commissioners awarded substantial damages. The award, as to this, is "final and conclusive" (§ 178), and it is sufficient for the plaintiff to show that the award was made for lands owned by him and so that he was entitled to it.

De Peyster v. *Mali* (27 Hun, 439), reversed

(Argued March 29, 1883 ; decided April 17, 1883.)

APPEAL from judgment of the General Term of the Supreme Court, in the first judicial department, entered upon an order made June 30, 1882, which affirmed a judgment in favor of defendants, entered upon a decision of the court on trial without a jury. (Reported below, 27 Hun, 439.)

This action was brought under the act chapter 86, Laws of 1813 (§ 184), to recover from defendants certain awards, made by the commissioners of estimate and assessment in the city of New York, which awards were made to Henry W. T. Mali, now deceased, and were paid by the city to his heirs, the defendants herein.

The material facts are stated in the opinion.

James A. Deering for appellant. If this plaintiff was, at the time of the confirmation of the report of the commissioners of estimate and assessment, the owner of the parcels of land in question, he can maintain this action. (Laws of 1813, chap. 86, § 184; *Cahill* v. *Palmer*, 45 N. Y. 480; *In re Arnold*, 60 id. 26.) The report of the commissioners of estimate and assessment, awarding the sums in question, was an adjudication conclusive upon the parties to this action, and upon "all persons whomsoever," as to the interests and estate for which said awards were made, and upon every question submitted to or decided by the commissioners or the court, or necessarily involved in the decision of the court confirming the report, except as to the ownership of the land for which the awards were made. (Laws of 1813, chap. 86, § 178; *Matter of Riverside Park*, 50 N. Y. 493; *Matter of Dept. of Parks*, 73 id. 560; *Pittman* v. *The Mayor*, 3 Hun, 372; 62 N. Y. 237; *Dolan* v. *The Mayor*, id. 742; *In re Arnold*, 60 id. 26; *Swift* v. *Poughkeepsie*, 37 id. 511; *People* v. *Collins*, 19 Wend. 56; *Supervisors* v. *Briggs*, 2 Hill, 135.) The report, as confirmed, is not only final and conclusive as to the subject-matter or matters thereby determined, but as to every other matter which the parties might litigate in the cause, and which they might have had decided. (*Voorhees* v. *Bank of U. S.*, 10 Pet. 449; *La Goun* v. *Gouverneur*, 1 Johns. Cas. 436; 2 Smith's Lead. Cas., tit. "Estoppel," 455, note; *Etheringe* v. *Osborne*, 12 Wend. 399; 63 N. Y. 472; 50 id. 493; *In re Dept. of Public Parks*, 73 id. 560.) The report being conclusive as to the estate, etc., for which the awards were made, the awards in question belong to the owner of the fee of the land for which made. (*In re Dept. of Works*, 73 N. Y. 560; *Trinity Church* v. *Cooke*, 21 How. 89; *Turner* v. *Williams*, 10 Wend. 140; *Gillespie* v. *The Mayor*, 23 id. 645; *Kelsey* v. *King*, 33 How. Pr. 40; Laws relative to New York city, Valentine, 1197; *Matter of Dept. of Parks*, 73 N. Y. 560.) [1] The commissioners of estimate and assessment in the Riverside park opening matter were right in allowing substantial compensation for the fee. (*Williams* v. *N. Y. C. R. R. Co.*, 16 N. Y. 97; *Trustees* v. *Auburn R. R. Co.*, 3 Hill, 567; *Kelsey* v. *King*, 33 How. Pr. 39; *Knox* v. *The Mayor*, 55 Barb. 404; *Matter of Prospect Park & C. I. R. R. Co.*, 16 Hun, 261; Laws of 1838, chap. 223; Laws of 1847, chap. 203; Laws of 1851, chap. 183.) The plaintiff, as executor, etc., was at the time of confirmation of the report the owner in fee of the said parcel of land. (19 Wend. 679; *Jackson* v. *Hathaway*, 15 Johns. 453; *Van Amringe* v. *Barnett*, 8 Bosw.

357; *In re John & Cherry St's*, 19 Wend. 659; *Williams* v.
N. Y. C. R. R. Co., 16 N. Y. 97, 101; *Hooker* v. *Utica, etc.*,
12 Wend. 371; *Trustees, etc.*, v. *Auburn R. R. Co.*,
3 Hill, 567; *Pearsall* v. *Post*, 20 Wend. 131; *Barclay*
v. *Howell's Lessee*, 6 Peters, 498; *People* v. *B'd of Westchester*, 4 Barb. 64; *Etz* v. *Daily*, 20 id. 32; *Kelsey* v.
King, 33 How. 39; *Higgins* v. *Reynolds*, 31 N. Y. 151;
Bloomfield Gas Co. v. *Kalkins*, 62 id. 386.) The city
and " all persons whomsoever" are concluded by that adjudication. (*Matter of Dept. of Parks*, 73 N. Y. 560.) Acceptance by the council was necessary to complete the dedication
by the owners. (*Niagara Co.* v. *Bachman*, 66 N. Y. 266;
Badum v. *Mead*, 14 Barb. 328; *Fonda* v. *Borst*, 2 Abb. Ct.
of App. 155; *Holdam* v. *Coldspring*, 21 N. Y. 474; *Peck* v.
Mallins, 10 id. 509.) The "release," in any event, only granted
an easement in such land, and not the fee. (*Hunter* v. *Trustees
of Sandy Hill*, 6 Hill, 407; *Cincinnati* v. *Lessee of White*, 6
Pet. 438; *Merriam* v. *Russell*, 2 Jones [N. C.], 470; *Schuylkill Co.* v. *Homer*, 2 Grant's Pa. Cas. 462; *Pollard* v. *Maddox*,
28 Ala. 321; *Jackson* v. *Hathaway*, 15 Johns. 147; *Jamaica
Pond* v. *Chandler*, 9 Allen, 164; *Graves* v. *Amoskeag Co.*, 44
N. H. 465; *Leavitt* v. *Towle*, 8 id. 99; *Dubuque* v. *Benson*,
23 Iowa, 248; *Gedney* v. *Earl*, 12 Wend. 98; *People* v. *Kerr*,
27 N. Y. 188; *Merriam* v. *Russell*, 2 Jones [N. C. Eq.], 470;
Rogers v. *Storer*, 24 Penn. St. 186; *Schuylkill Co.* v. *Stoever*, 2
Grant's Pa. Cas. 462; *Clark* v. *Cottrell*, 63 Barb. 336.) A reservation in a grant of "a road" or "highway" reserves simply
an easement. (*Leavitt* v. *Towle*, 8 N. Y. 96; *Richardson* v.
Palmer, 38 N. H. 210; *Graves* v. *Amoskeag Co.*, 44 id. 462;
Keeler v. *Wood*, 30 Vt. 242.) The release as a grant is void
for uncertainty, unless the description of land and estate conveyed is that contended for above. (*Peck* v. *Mallins*, 10 N. Y.
509; *U. S.* v. *King*, 3 How. 773; *Jackson* v. *Parkhurst*, 4
Wend. 369.) A grant by the side of a street or road conveys
to such side only. No part of the street or road passes. The
land in the road-bed remains in the grantor. (*Jackson* v. *Hathaway*, 15 Johns. 449; *Jones* v. *Cowman*, 2 Sandf. 233; *Wet-*

more v. *Law*, 34 Barb. 515; *Van Amringe* v. *Barnett*, 8 Bosw. 367; *Anderson* v. *James*, 4 Robt. 35; *Costers* v. *Peters*, 5 id. 192; *Sherman* v. *McKeon*, 38 N. Y. 266; *Wallace* v. *Fee*, 50 id. 694; *Fearing* v. *Irwin*, 4 Daly, 385; *English* v. *Brennan*, 60 N. Y. 609; *White's B'k* v. *Nichols*, 64 id. 65; *Mott* v. *Mott*, 68 id. 246; *Patten* v. *N. Y. E. R. R.*, 3 Abb. N. C. 341; *In re Dept. of Parks*, 73 N. Y. 560; *Kings Co. F. Ins. Co.* v. *Stevens*, 87 id. 287; *Burnett* v. *Wadsworth*, 67 id. 634; *Jackson* v. *Loomis*, 18 Johns. 86; *Loomis* v. *Jackson*, 19 id. 449; *Haynes* v. *Young*, 36 Me. 557; *Gans* v. *Aldridge*, 27 Md. 294; *Thorndyke* v. *Richards*, 12 Me. 430; *McGowen* v. *Lewis*, 26 N. J. L. 451; *Smith* v. *Strong*, 14 Pick. 128; *Sherman* v. *McKeon*, 38 N. Y. 272; *Whitney* v. *Dewey*, 18 Pick. 353; *Chaplin* v. *Sword*, 7 Watts, 710; *Bissell* v. *N. Y. C. R. R. Co.*, 23 N. Y.; *Perrin* v. *Same*, 36 id. 120; *Sizer* v. *Devereux*, 16 Barb. 160; *Jones* v. *Cowman*, 2 Sandf. 233; *Van Amringe* v. *Barnett*, 8 Bosw. 367; *Costers* v. *Peters*, 5 Robt. 192; *Wallace* v. *Fee*, 50 N. Y. 694; *Fearin* v. *Irwin*, 4 Daly, 385; *White's B'k* v. *Nicholls*, 64 N. Y. 65; *Mott* v. *Mott*, 68 id. 246.) The land in the Bloomingdale road in front of "the lots conveyed" did not pass as an "appurtenance." (*Jackson* v. *Hathaway*, 15 Johns. 453; *Harris* v. *Elliott*, 10 Pet. 25; *Sherman* v. *McKeon*, 38 N. Y. 270; *Ogden* v. *Jennings*, 62 id. 526; *Woodhull* v. *Rosenthall*, 61 id. 382; *Otis* v. *Smith*, 9 Pick. 293; 19 Wend. 679; 15 Johns. 452; Laws of 1867, chap. 697, § 3; *Jackson* v. *Hathaway*, 15 Johns. 453; *Wheeler* v. *Clark*, 58 N. Y. 271.) Purchases since 1807 must be assumed to have been made with knowledge of the law regulating the extent of the easement in the highway and subject to its exercise, the effect of which would be to give the owner of the land in the road-bed the right to take absolute possession thereof upon its closing. (*Underwood* v. *Stuyvesant*, 19 Johns. 181; *Grinnell* v. *Kirtland*, 3 Abb. N. C. 386.) In the city of New York no private rights of way or streets or roads can be created by owners of land. (Laws of 1799, chap. 70, pp. 733, 737; re-enacted in 1803, 3 Webster's Laws, 232; made perpetual in 1806, 4 id. 575, § 6; Laws of 1807, chap. 115, § 1; Laws of 1867, chap.

697; *Underwood* v. *Stuyvesant*, 19 Johns. 181; *Grinnell* v. *Kirtland*, 2 Abb. N. C. 386.) To create an easement or right of way in such case, there should be a grant in express terms. (*Wheeler* v. *Clark*, 58 N. Y. 267; *Jackson* v. *Hathaway*, 15 Johns. 449; *Matter of John* v. *Anthony St.*, 19 Wend. 659; *Fearing* v. *Irwin*, 4 Daly, 385; *In re Albany St.*, 11 Wend. 149; *Bloodgood* v. *M. & H. R. R. Co.*, 14 id. 51; *Varick* v. *Smith*, 5 Paige, 137; *Robinson* v. *S. R. R. Co.*, 3 id. 45; *Taylor* v. *Porter*, 4 Hill, 140.)

Franklin Bartlett for respondents. The plaintiff, in order to maintain his action, was bound to show that he was the person to whom the awards of right belonged, and to whom they ought to have been paid. (2 Revised Laws of 1813, p. 419; *De Peyster* v. *Mali*, 27 Hun, 440, 445, 446; *Fisher* v. *The Mayor*, 57 N. Y. 344, 349; *Spears* v. *Mayor, etc., of N. Y.*, 87 id. 359, 373.) The plaintiff was not entitled to any substantial award on the land in question, as it had been previously appropriated for the purposes and uses of a public highway. (*Cook* v. *Harris*, 61 N. Y. 448; *Matter of the Comm'rs of Central Park*, 54 How. Pr. 314; *Matter of Barclay*, Daily Register of March 19, 1883.) The grantee's easement, which had become appurtenant to the land, rendered the naked fee of merely nominal value. (*Matter of Dep't of Public Works to open Sixty-Seventh St.*, opinion by DANIELS, J.; *Matter of Opening 156th, 157th, 158th and 159th Sts.*, May, 1879; *White's B'k of Buffalo* v. *Nichols*, 64 N. Y. 65, 73; *Matter of Opening Eleventh Avenue*, 81 N. Y. 457.) The plaintiff was entitled to no substantial award for the fee, because the Bloomingdale road at this point was not closed or abandoned under the act of 1867, but was retained as preserved, enlarged and continued under the name of the Riverside drive or avenue. (*Matter of Comm'rs of Central Park*, 54 How. 313; *People* v. *Asten*, MSS. op. BARRETT, J., First Dep't, Gen. Term.) The confirmation of a report of commissioners of estimate and assessment should not be held conclusive against a party to whom an award of money is made by name in such a way as to estop him from interposing any defense in an action by a third party. (2 Revised Laws of 1813, 413, 414; *Matter of the Opening of Eleventh Avenue*, 81 N. Y. 436, 447, 448; 49 id. 154.) The proper distribution or apportionment of an award is not a question which can be litigated before the confirmation of the commissioners' report by the Supreme Court. (*Matter of Dep't of Public Parks*, 85 N. Y. 463; *Matter of Dep't of Parks*, 73 id. 564; *Matter of the Opening of Eleventh Avenue*, 81 id. 436, 443; *Fisher* v. *The Mayor, etc.*, 57 id. 344, 350; *Matter of Lange*, 85 id. 310; *Spears* v. *The Mayor*, 87 id. 376.) Under the name "owner," in the report of the commissioners, every person entitled to compensation is to be recognized. (Mills' Eminent Domain, § 65; *Matter of Eleventh Ave.*, 81 N. Y. 448; *Barnes* v. *The Mayor, etc.*, 27 Hun, 236, 238, 239; *Remington Paper Co.* v. *O'Dougherty*, 81 N. Y. 489, 490; *Riggs* v. *Pursell*, 74 id. 370, 379.)

EARL, J. Under and pursuant to the provisions of the act chapter 697 of the Laws of 1867, the board of commissioners of the Central park laid out and established the Riverside drive, and also the Riverside park adjoining the same. The land taken for the park was owned in fee by the heirs of Henry W. T. Mali, and was bounded on the east by the westerly line of the Bloomingdale road. The plaintiff owned in fee the land in the westerly half of the Bloomingdale road, which land was subject to a perpetual easement for the public road and a private easement for the owners of the abutting land; and the Riverside drive was laid out in such road and took the place thereof, and the land thereof was appropriated for the same.

The commissioners of estimates and assessments awarded to the heirs of Mali for their abutting land upward of $160,000, and for the westerly half of the Bloomingdale road opposite to their land in two awards, $6,634. The latter awards were for the fee of the land in the road, were made to the heirs of Mali as the owners thereof, were confirmed and afterward paid by the city to the defendants. This action was brought to recover of the defendants the money so paid, and whether the plaintiff, upon the facts found, was entitled to recover the same is the sole question for our determination.

It is too clear for dispute that the defendants had no right whatever to these awards. They had an easement in the Bloomingdale road in front of their lot for use as abutting owners. But their easement was not taken. The road was not closed, but remained open as the Riverside drive, with undiminished usefulness as a highway; and as their abutting land was taken for the Riverside park, this easement went with that as appurtenant thereto, and they ceased to have any private interest in the road.' And such was the view of the judge at Special Term, who said in his opinion: "It is quite evident that the persons who received the awards in controversy had no right to them, for the reason that they had no interest whatever in the title to the land included within the bounds of the highway; and any possible right or interest they might have in the enjoyment of the highway itself was in no sense restricted or diminished by its incorporation within the bounds of the Riverside drive." But he held that as the plaintiff's fee in the land was subject to a perpetual easement for the highway, he was entitled to only nominal damages from the city, and that, therefore, he was not justly and equitably or of right entitled to the awards, and upon that ground he defeated the plaintiff.

By section 178 of chapter 86 of the Laws of 1813, it is provided that the award of the commissioners of estimates and assessments, when confirmed, "shall be final and conclusive as well upon the said mayor, aldermen and commonalty of the city of New York as upon the owners, lessees, persons and parties interested in and entitled unto the lands, tenements, hereditaments and premises mentioned in the said report, and also upon all other persons whomsoever." Under this provision, while these awards were undoubtedly excessive, they were final and conclusive, and this is so even if we must assume that they should have been but for nominal damages, and that the commissioners and the Supreme Court, when it confirmed their report, mistook both the law and the facts applicable to the case, and so it has frequently been decided. (*Matter of Commissioners of Central Park*, 50 N. Y. 493; *Dolan* v. *The Mayor*, 62 id. 472; *Matter of the Department of Parks*, 73 id. 560.) If, therefore, the city had been sued for the awards before their payment, it could not have resisted a recovery for the whole amount thereof. But it voluntarily paid to the defendants, and they received, the awards made for the plaintiff's land, and hence this is a case where the plaintiff is entitled to recover the amount of the money thus paid from the defendants, under section 184 of the same chapter, which provides that in every case where any sum awarded by the commissioners in favor of " any person or persons, or party or parties whatsoever, whether named or not named in the said report, shall be paid to any person or persons, or party or parties whomsoever, when the same shall of right belong and ought to have been paid to some other person or persons, or party or parties, it shall be lawful for the person or persons, or party or parties, to whom the same ought to have been paid, to sue for and recover the same, with lawful interest and costs of suit, as so much money had and received to his, her or their use, by the person or persons, party or parties respectively, to whom the same shall have been so paid." Under this provision to whom of right did these awards belong? Clearly to the plaintiff. They were made for his land, and so long as the awards remained in force the city could not dispute that the amounts awarded were just and proper; and the defendants who received the awards from the city certainly could not claim when sued for them that they were excessive or inequitable, or that the plaintiff was entitled to only nominal damages where the commissioners had awarded substantial damages. Whether the awards were just or unjust, too large or too small, was a matter of no concern to them. They held the precise money awarded for plaintiff's land and were bound to refund it to him as money they had received to his use. (*Cahill* v. *Palmer*, 45 N.Y. 480.) It was sufficient for him to show that

the awards were made for land owned by him, and that entitled him to the money paid for them.

The judgment should, therefore, be reversed and a new trial
granted, costs to abide event.

All concur.

Judgment reversed.

FREDERICK A. BUSHNELL, as Administrator, etc., Respondent,
v. CALVIN C. L. B. CARPENTER, Appellant.

The will of C. gave to two grandchildren "the sum of $1,000 each, to be
paid to them respectively as they arrive at the age of twenty-five years."
To five children he gave $1,000 each, payable one legacy each year for
five years after his decease. After certain devises and bequests, he gave
his residuary estate to defendant, his son, subject to the payment of his
debts and the legacies. In an action by the administrator of the estate
of one of said grandchildren, who died before reaching the age of twenty-
five, brought after she would have reached that age, had she lived, to
recover the legacy, *held*, that the postponement of the time of payment
did not make the gift contingent; that the testator's intent, as disclosed
by the will, was simply to postpone payment for the benefit of the estate;
that the legacy vested upon the death of the testator, and that plaintiff
was entitled to recover.

(Argued March 29, 1883; decided April 17, 1883.)

APPEAL from judgment of the General Term of the Supreme
Court, in the fourth judicial department, entered upon an order
made October 20, 1882, which affirmed a judgment in favor of
plaintiff, entered upon a decision of the court on trial without
a jury. (Reported below, 28 Hun, 19.)

This action was brought by plaintiff, as administrator of the
estate of Ellen O. Bushnell, deceased, to recover a legacy given
to her by the will of Stephen V. Carpenter, deceased. Carpenter died in February, 1864, leaving a will executed in July,
1863, of the material clauses of which the following is a copy:

" Second. I give and devise to my son Calvin G. L. B. Carpenter all and singular the real estate whereof I may die seized wherever the same may be situated, excepting, however, the house and lot in the city of Rochester, and the two houses and lots in Little Falls hereinbefore mentioned, and I give and bequeath to my said son all my personal estate of every name and kind wherever the same may be, except my household goods and furniture hereinbefore bequeathed, to have and to hold the said real and personal estate to my said son and to his heirs and assigns forever, subject, nevertheless, to the payment by him of all my debts, and further to the payment of the several legacies hereinafter made to my daughter Elvira G. and her children, Ann Maria and her children Betsey, Catherine and Nancy, hereby expressly making the said legacies a charge and lien upon the property devised to my said son.

" Third I give and bequeath to my daughter Elvira $1,000, to be paid to her one year after my decease. To my daughter Ann Maria $1,000, to be paid to her two years after my decease. To my daughter Betsey $1,000, to be paid to her three years after my decease. To my daughter Catherine $1,000, to be paid to her four years after my decease, and to my daughter Nancy $1,000, to be paid to her five years after my decease.

" The above legacies to be in full payment, satisfaction and discharge of all claims which may be made by any of my said daughters against my estate.

" Fourth. I give and bequeath to the four children now living of my daughter Elvira the sum of $3,000, as follows, to-wit: $1,000 to the son of my said daughter and $2,000 to the three girls, share and share alike, to be paid to the said children respectively as they arrive at the age of twenty-five years.

" Fifth. I give and bequeath to the two children now living of my daughter Ann Maria the sum of $1,000 each, to be paid to them respectively as they arrive at the age of twenty-five years."

Plaintiff's intestate was a daughter of the testator's daughter Ann Maria mentioned in the fifth clause of the will. She died in November, 1869, being then fifteen years old. Defendant, who is the son of the testator mentioned in the second clause

of the will, accepted the gifts to him and took possession.
The court found that " the postponement of the time of the
payment of the several legacies given in and by the will of the
testator was for the benefit of the testator's estate and for the
convenience of the defendant as devisee."

A. M. Mills for appellant.   When by express provision
the pending income is to be enjoyed or received by the legatee
it denotes an intention that the legacy shall not vest. (*Patterson* v. *Ellis*, 11 Wend. 259; *Everett* v. *Everett*, 29 N. Y. 39;
Warner v. *Durant*, 76 id: 133; *Boies* v. *Wilcox*, 40 Barb. 286.)
The fact that the legacy is not given out of the personal property or general estate of the testator, but is directed to be paid
personally by the defendant and made a charge on the farm
devised to the defendant, indicates that the legacy is not vested.
(*Birdsall* v. *Hewlett*, 1 Paige, 32.)   The legacy being by the
express terms of the will made a charge upon the real property
devised to the defendant, and the legatee having died before the
time of payment arrived, the legacy lapsed and the plaintiff
cannot recover. (*Birdsall* v. *Hewlett*, 1 Paige, 33; *Marsh* v.
Wheeler, 2 Edw. Ch. 156; *Harris* v. *Fly*, 7 Paige, 421, 429;
Delavergne v. *Dean*. 45 How. Pr. 206, 209; *Sweet* v. *Chase*,
2 N. Y. 73, 80.)

C. D. Adams ior respondent.   The legacy is a lien and can
be enforced in equity against the land. (79 N. Y. 136.)   A
purchaser from defendant must necessarily make his title
through the will, and has notice of the lien, and takes subject
to it. (7 Paige, 421.)   The scheme of the will is to give the
defendant the bulk of the estate, which is cultivated land, pro-
ducing an income, on condition he pays the defendant and his
five sisters $1,000 each, and certain grandchildren $5,000 in all.
(71 N. Y. 105.)   The legacies were given absolutely. (85 N.
Y. 142, 146, 147; 7 Paige, 429, 430; 71 N. Y. 100, 102.) If the
postponement of a legacy is for the benefit of the estate, it vests
immediately. (11 Wend. 259.)   Words directing or implying
payment preclude contingency. (Dayton on Surrogates [3d
ed.], 425; Redfield's Surrogates' Law and Pr. [2d ed.] 576
and note.)

DANFORTH, J.   It is well settled that a mere postponement of the time of payment will not make a legacy contingent, and here is nothing more. " I give," says the testator, " I give and bequeath to the two children now living of my daughter Ann Maria, the sum of $1,000 each, to be paid to them respectively as they arrive at the age of twenty-five years." And since we know that Ellen, whom the plaintiff represents, is one of those two children, we may read the will as if the testator said, " I give and bequeath to Ellen the sum of $1,000." Upon these words appellant makes no argument. They clearly signify a direct and positive gift (1 Roper on Legacies, 479; *Lister* v. *Bradley*, 1 Hare 10), and can be considered otherwise only by importing into the clause the word " if," or some other word of similar meaning, signifying a condition precedent. The learned counsel for the appellant relies on the rest of the sentence and says there is a contingency. But the testator does not say, " I give," " provided," or " if " Ellen arrives at the age of twenty-five years, but only indicates the period which must elapse before payment can be demanded. (*Manice* v. *Manice*, 43 N. Y. 303; *Livingston* v. *Greene*, 52 id. 118; *Smith* v. *Edwards*, 88 id. 92.) And when we see that the defendant takes the land of the testator, especially charged with and subject to the payment of this legacy, it is difficult to find any ground for the contention that the death of the legatee relieves him from the obligation.

So far as the learned counsel for the appellant treats the intent of the testator as a question of fact depending on outside circumstances, it is needless to follow him, for the trial court and General Term are both the other way, and we agree that the force of the argument is not all on his side.

Upon the will itself, having regard to its various provisions, we have no doubt that day of payment was postponed for the convenience of the estate.

The defendant is charged with the payment of all the debts of the testator, and his legacies; in regard to the latter, time is given, so that they are to be paid at intervals, annually, for the first five years, to his several children, to the grandchildren as they arrive at the age of twenty-five years, in each instance without interest, and as may be inferred chiefly from the land itself and its profitable tillage. Nor do the cases cited for the appellant, tend to his support. In *Loder* v. *Hatfield* (71 N. Y. 98) the legacies there in question were held to have vested upon reasons not inapplicable here. In *Patterson* v. *Ellis* (11 Wend. 260) a distinction is taken between a legacy "given to A., to be paid when he shall attain the age of twenty-one years," and one given when the legatee shall attain, or provided he does attain, the age of twenty-one, and it is said the first vests, and payment only is postponed ; the other does not, because time is the substance of the gift. But even in the latter case, if interest is in the mean time to be paid, the principal vests. And so in the other cases. (*Everitt* v. *Everitt*, 29 N. Y. 39, and *Warner* v. *Durant*, 76 id. 133). This circumstance may disclose the intent of the testator, as in these instances, but that intent may appear without, as in the case now in hand, where the legacy is a distinct gift, as appears both by a strict construction of the words, and by the general intent manifest in the will. We think the case was well disposed of in the court below.

The judgment appealed from should, therefore, be affirmed. All concur.

Judgment affirmed.

ANNIE A. GRATTAN as Administratrix, etc., Respondent, *v.* THE METROPOLITAN LIFE INSURANCE COMPANY OF NEW YORK, Appellant.

A warranty in an application for a policy of life insurance that a third person is in good health does not mean an actual freedom from illness or disease, but simply that the person has indicated in his actions and appearance no symptoms or traces of disease, and to the ordinary observation of a friend or relative is in truth well.

Where, therefore, in an action upon a policy, upon the question as to a breach of such a warranty, the court charged that if from the appearance of the person he was in good health so that anybody would so pronounce him, and there was nothing to indicate he was not in good health, the warranty was not broken although in fact the germs of a hidden and lurking disease then existed. *Held* no error.

An application contained a warranty that the answers to the questions in the report of the medical examiner were "fair and true" and the applicant signed a certificate at the foot of said report to the effect that he had given true answers to the questions and "that they agree exactly with the foregoing." He gave a truthful answer to a question by the medical examiner, but the latter wrote a different and untruthful answer in his report. The evidence authorized a finding that the applicant did not see the answer as written in the report and was ignorant of the fact that it differed from that given by him. *Held*, that this having been found, the company, not the insured, was responsible for the falsehood.

Such a certificate can only be met and answered by proof establishing either that the answer was not written or was not known to the applicant when the certificate was signed by him; the burden of the untruth must be shown to rest solely on the agent of the company.

To prove the falsity of the answer as given in the report, defendant put in evidence a portion of a letter written by the insured. Plaintiff was permitted, under objection and exception, to read in evidence the remainder of the letter, which gave a history of the transaction, showing that the writer gave a correct answer and was ignorant of the fact that an untruthful answer was written in the report. *Held*, that the ruling was proper.

The introduction by one party of part of a conversation or a writing in evidence renders admissible on the other side so much of the remainder as tends to explain or qualify what has been received; and that is to be deemed a qualification which rebuts and destroys the inference to be drawn from, or the use to be made of, the portion put in evidence.

A physician who was called upon professionally to make an examination of T., brother of the insured, was asked "what opinion did you form, based on the general sight of the man before you made an examination, or before you had any conversation with him." *Held*, that the question was properly excluded as privileged within the statute. (Code of Civil Procedure, § 834.)

Edington v. *Ætna Ins. Co.* (77 N. Y. 564), distinguished.

After a physician called by defendant had been asked if T., upon whom he attended, died of consumption, and the question had been excluded, he was asked whether, in response to questions put by plaintiff's counsel on a former trial, he had not answered that T. died of consumption. This was objected to and excluded. *Held* no error; first, what the witness had testified to could only be proved to contradict him or refresh his memory; second, the plaintiff's inquiry on the former trial did not preclude his objecting to the evidence.

Owen v. *Cawley* (36 N. Y. 600), distinguished.

(Argued March 15, 1883; decided April 24, 1883.)

APPEAL from judgment of the General Term of the Supreme Court, in the third judicial department, entered upon an order made December 16, 1882, which affirmed a judgment in favor of plaintiff, entered upon a verdict. (Mem. of decision below, 28 Hun, 430.)

This action was brought upon a policy of insurance issued by defendant upon the life of Hugh P. Grattan, plaintiff's intestate. The defense was alleged breaches of warranty contained in the application; this warranted that all the answers to questions therein and to those in the examiner's report " are fair and true, without omission, concealment or mental reservation." The answer to a question in the medical examiner's report as to the condition of health of the applicant's brothers was " good." It was claimed by the defendant that this was untrue as to the intestate's brother Terence. The answer to a question as to the disease of which a sister had died was " not known to applicant." This was claimed to be untrue. The facts in relation thereto so far as material are stated in the opinion.

William II. Arnoux for appellant. Any false, incorrect or erroneous statement made in the application upon which the contract of insurance is based avoids the policy, if by the terms of the contract such statements are made warranties. (*Barteaux* v. *Phœnix M. L. Ins. Co.*, 67 N. Y. 595; *Ætna L. Ins. Co.* v. *France*, 91 U. S. 510; *Anderson* v. *Fitzgerald*, 4 H. L. C. 484; *Goddard* v. *Monitor M. L. Ins. Co.*, 108 Mass. 56; *State M. F. Ins. Co.* v. *Arthur*, 30 Penn. St. 315; *Grattan* v. *M. L. Ins. Co.*, 80 N. Y. 281; 24 Hun, 43; *Flynn* v. *Eq. L. Ins. Co.*, 78 N. Y. 575; *Foote* v. *Ætna L. Ins. Co.*, 61 id. 571; *Swick* v. *Home L. Ins. Co.*, 2 Ins. Rep. 415; *Duckett* v. *Williams*, 2 Cr. & M. 348; Bliss on Life Ins. 48, 59; *Ritzler* v. *World Mut. L. Ins. Co.*, 1 J. & S. 409, 414; *Fitch* v. *Am. P. L. Ins. Co.*, 59 N. Y. 557, 569; *Ripley* v. *Ætna F. Ins. Co.*, 30 id. 137; *Lasher* v. *N. W. Nat. Ins. Co.*, 18 Hun, 98; *First Nat. B'k* v. *Ins. Co. of N. A.*, 50 N. Y. 45.) The court erred in charging that if the defects were not patent to general observation, even though they actually existed and were of so serious a character as when developed to cause the party's death, nevertheless it was not a breach of warranty. (*Bennett* v. *Buchan*, 76 N. Y. 386; *Bidwell* v. *N. W. Ins. Co.*, 68 id. 434; *Tallman* v. *At. Ins. Co.*, 3 K. 87; *Mayor* v. *Ex. F. Ins. Co.*, id. 436; *Rowley* v. *Empire Ins. Co.*, id. 557, 561; *Ripley* v. *Ætna Ins. Co.*, 30 N. Y. 136.) The word "good" in the answer to the question concerning the condition of the health of the insured meant that his health was, in fact, not in appearance, good. (*Smith* v. *Ætna L. Ins. Co.*, 49 N. Y. 211; *Barteau* v. *Phœnix Mut. L. Ins. Co.*, 1 Hun, 430; *Bliss on Life Ins.* 146–150; *Peacock's Case*, 20 N. Y. 293; *Conner's Case*, 6 Chic. Leg. News, 144; *Scotch's Case*, 17 Scotch Jur. 253; *Horn's Case*, 64 Barb. 82; *Water Com'rs* v. *Burr*, 2 Sweeney, 25.) The medical testimony as to Terence's health was improperly excluded. (*Grattan* v. *Met. L. Ins. Co.*, 80 N. Y. 281; *Edington* v. *Ætna L. Ins. Co.*, 77 id. 564.) The statute may be expressly waived by the protected party himself asking the objectionable questions; or it may be waived negatively by interposing no objection to the question by the adversary. (*Johnson* v. *Johnson*, 14 Wend. 641–2; *Owen* v. *Cawley*, 36 N. Y. 400; 1 Phillips on Ev. 440; *Mc-Nabe* v. *Nat. L. Ins. Co.*, 13 Hun, 144.) Defendant properly introduced and read the first part of the letter containing an admission that the deceased knew the cause of his sister's death. (1 Greenleaf on Ev. [13th ed.] 218; Stark. on Ev. 26; *North* v. *Miles*, 1 Campb. 390; *Stern* v. *R. R. Co.*, 7 Leg. Gaz. 223; *Bartlett* v. *Eillard*, 3 Russ. 156; *Davis* v. *Spurling*, 1 Russ. & M. 68.) Where a party on the trial of a cause avails himself of an admission of his adversary to sustain his action or defense, the opposite party is entitled to prove such other parts of the conversation had on his part as tend to explain, modify or even destroy the admission made by him; but is not at liberty to call for such parts of the conversation had by him as relate to assertions made operating in his favor upon the general merits of the case, but having no connection with the admission made. (*Garry* v. *Nicholson*, 24 Wend. 350;

Kelsey v. *Bush*, 2 Hill, 440; *Rouse* v. *Whited*, 25 N. Y. 170; *Dilleber* v. *Home L. Ins. Co.*, 69 id. 258.)

James Lansing for respondent. Terms in life insurance contracts, and indeed in all others, are to be construed in their popular and usual sense or signification, keeping in view the object and subject-matter of the contract. (2 Parsons on Contracts [5th ed.], 501; *Delebar* v. *Home Life Ins. Co.*, 69 N. Y. 263; *Cushman* v. *U. S. L. Ins. Co.*, 70 id. 76.) When the term " good health " occurs in the description of a living individual, it cannot denote any thing more than the absence of any ostensible or known or felt symptoms of disorder. (*Comer* v. *Phœnix Mut. L. Ins. Co.*, 6 Chicago Legal News, 144; *Hutchinson* v. *Nat. L. Ass. Soc.*, 17 Scotch Jurist, 253; Bliss on Life Ins. 148; *Scott* v. *Rose*, 16 Ct. of Sess. Cases, 1145; *Peacock* v. *N. Y. L. Ins. Co.*, 20 N. Y. 293; *S. C.*, 1 Bos. 338; *Cushman* v. *U. S. L. Ins. Co.*, 70 N. Y. 76; *Horn* v. *Amicable Mut. L. Ins. Co.*, 64 Barb. 82; Park on Insurance, 353; Angell on Fire and Life Insurance, § 313.) The term " good health " does not import a warranty against latent or imperceptible diseases, or those that can be discovered only by *post mortem* examination, or from symptoms disclosing themselves at an after period of time. (*Cushman* v. *U. S. L. Ins. Co.*, 70 N. Y. 77; *Peacock* v. *N. Y. Life Ins. Co.*, 20 id. 293.) The question whether the condition of health is misstated is one of fact, and, if there is any conflict of evidence, becomes a question for the jury. (*Swift* v. *Mass. Mut. L. Ins. Co.*, 2 T. & C. 302; *McGinley* v. *U. S. L. Ins. Co.*, 8 Daly, 394; *S. C.*, 77 N. Y. 495; *Maury* v. *The World Mut. L. Ins. Co.*, 7 Daly, 324.) The applicant having truthfully stated to the defendant's medical examiner the cause of his sister's death, and the medical examiner having inadvertently inserted the answer, " Not known to applicant," such erroneous answer must be taken as the declaration of the defendant; and in any controversy depending upon it must, as between the parties, be taken to be true. (*Grattan* v. *Mut. L. Ins. Co.*, 80 N. Y. 292; *Mowry* v. *Rosendale*, 74 id. 360; *Flynn* v. *Eq. L. Ins. Co.*,

78 id. 568; *Grattan* v. *Mut. L. Ins. Co.*, 24 Hun, 43.) This is so although the answers as written by the agent were subsequently read to " applicant," and signed by him. (*Am. Ins. Co.* v. *Mahone.* 21 Wall. 152; *Wilcox* v. *Howell,* 44 N. Y. 398.) The defendant having put in evidence the entire letter of the plaintiff's intestate, to establish by an admission in a portion of the letter that said intestate knew the cause of his sister's death, the remainder of the letter, which showed that he truly stated the cause, and which tended to destroy or modify the use which the defendant might otherwise make of the admission, was competent. (*Rouse* v. *Whited,* 25 N. Y. 170, 175; *Wailing* v. *Toll,* 9 Johns. 141; *Credit* v. *Brown,* 10 id. 365; *Kelsey* v. *Bush,* 2 Hill, 440; *Smith* v. *Jones,* 15 Johns. 229; *Forrest* v. *Forrest,* 6 Duer, 102, 122–132; *Lawrence* v. *Ocean Ins. Co.,* 11 Johns. 241; *Walden* v. *Sherburne,* 15 id. 409; *Wynants* v. *Sherman,* 3 Hill, 74; *Kelly* v. *Dutch Church of Schenectady,* 2 id. 105.) When the agent of a company, with full knowledge of the facts, instructs the applicant as to the proper answer to be made by him to any question, the company is estopped by the act of the agent where there is no collusion or fraud on the part of the insured. (*Mowry* v. *Rosendale,* 74 N. Y. 360; *Flynn* v. *Eq. L. Ins. Co.,* 78 id. 568.) The seal which the law fixes upon privileged communications remains, unless removed by the party himself or his legal representatives. (*Edington* v. *Mut. L. Ins. Co.,* 67 N. Y. 196; Code, §§ 834, 836; *Grattan* v. *Nat. L. Ins. Co.,* 15 Hun, 75.) Communication to the sense of sight is within the statute as to privileged communications as much as if it had been oral, and reached the ear. It needs not that the examination should be private. It is enough that the physician acquired the information in his character of physician, and in the due and proper exercise of his calling. (*Edington* v. *Mut. L. Ins. Co.,* 67 N. Y. 185; 5 Hun, 12; *Grattan* v. *Met. L. Ins. Co.,* 80 id. 281, 297; *Pierson* v. *People,* 18 Hun, 248.)

FINCH, J. The defendant resists the verdict rendered in this action upon numerous grounds, the first of which is, that

there was a breach of warranty by the insured as to the health
of his brother Terence ; that there was no conflict of evidence
to carry the question to the jury ; and that the charge of the
court upon the subject was erroneous.   There was much and
very strong evidence that, for a considerable period just before
the warranty of the applicant that his brother's health was
good, Terence was in fact ill, and was emaciated, weak, and
had a consumptive cough.   His employers so testify, and that,
as a consequence, they sent him to their own medical adviser,
Dr. Mareness, to be examined, upon whose report he left their
employ as unable longer to endure the labor required.   On
the other hand, witnesses were examined who testified that
during the same period he appeared to be in good health, that
he looked like a healthy man, and gave no indications to the
contrary.   The controversy, therefore, revolves about the true
meaning of good health as used in the words of warranty ;
the appellant contending that it means good, in fact, actual freedom from illness or disease, and that, so understood, there
was no dispute about the facts since the sickness of Terence
was proved, and the plaintiff's evidence never went beyond
mere appearances and raised no issue over the real fact.   But
it must be remembered that the question put and the answer
given related not to the applicant's own health but to that of a
third person.   Unless in rare and exceptional cases the insured
answering could only answer from physical appearances and
indications.   He could not have the knowledge that an individual has of his own condition, though even in such case self-
deception is not rare, and very often entirely innocent and
honest.   Such an inquiry and its answer must necessarily be
understood in a general and ordinary, and not in a strict and
rigid sense.   One who is not a doctor and speaks not of himself but of a third person, necessarily gives rather an opinion
founded on observed facts than an absolute and accurate fact
when he describes the health of such person as good.   He
means, and is understood to mean, that the individual inquired
about has indicated in his action and appearance no symptoms
or traces of disease, and to the observation of an ordinary

friend or relative is in truth well. He means that, because he cannot usually mean any thing else; and the insurer naturally and necessarily must so understand question and answer, and, considered as a warranty, the answer warrants what it means and nothing more. The authorities almost, if not quite without exception, justify this view of the scope and meaning of an answer warranting the good health of a third person. (*Cushman* v. *U. S. Life Ins. Co.*, 70 N. Y. 76; *Peacock* v. *N. Y. Life Ins. Co.*, 20 id. 293.) Upon such view of the law the plaintiff's evidence was admitted, and the question of the truth of the warranty submitted to the jury. The criticism upon the charge is that it confused the distinctions between a representation and a warranty, and substituted the honest belief of the applicant in the room of the actual fact. Some portions of the charge spoke of the answer given by the applicant as a representation, and of its falsity, if false, as a misrepresentation; but at the close of the charge its language and purport in this respect were challenged, and the court thereupon carefully explained its meaning. The learned counsel for the defendant asked the court to charge that the applicant " was bound at his peril to know the truth of every statement that he made, and whether intentionally or otherwise, if in fact any statement that he made was not true, under the warranty it vitiated the policy." The court so charged, and added by way of explanation, and to make clear the meaning intended to be conveyed, " that if from all the appearances of the brother he was in good health; in fact in good health, so that everybody would so pronounce him; and there was nothing to indicate to any person that he was not in good health," then the warranty was not broken, although in fact the germs of a lurking and hidden disease might exist. All difficulty as to the difference between representation and warranty was thus cleared away, and the meaning to be attached to the latter definitely stated, and we think correctly. A question of fact was thereby raised for the jury. While the evidence of Jeffers and of Warren showed the existence of ill health, the symptoms of which were plainly apparent, and their conduct in sending him to Dr. Mareness for examination, and his in submitting to it, and thereupon ceasing work furnishes very strong evidence of ill health, both actual and apparent, yet there is a considerable array of evidence in the contrary direction. Warren admits that he had before sworn he was not aware that Terence was a sick man until he returned with a paper from the doctor. Noelte, with whom Terence boarded, describes him as not sick and showing no such appearance; Fleming and Lewis, with whom he worked, say his health was good to their observation; Eicholz, the agent of the company, took his application for insurance, and the defendant's medical examiner certified the risk in the usual manner. Where the truth is in this contradiction it is difficult to say. Both the actual condition and the observable condition of Terence's health at the date of the warranty were put in doubt by the proofs, for the fair inference from the plaintiff's evidence, taken by itself, was not only that Terence seemed well, appeared well, but actually was in good health. The question of fact was submitted to the jury in terms quite as favorable to the defendant as the law of the case required, and their conclusion is beyond our review.

Another objection to the recovery is founded upon the answer given by the applicant to the medical examiner of the company which in the written statement denies, on the part of the insured, knowledge of the cause of his sister's death.

The question is serious. It is conceded that the sister of the insured, before his own application, died of consumption; that the insured knew the fact; that it was material to the action of the insurance company which was entitled to know the truth; that the fact was concealed and a false answer that the applicant did not know was made, either by the applicant or the medical examiner; that the false answer was in fact written down by the latter; but that the insured told him the precise truth and the actual fact. The controversy is thus narrowed to the single question, who was responsible for the falsehood; was the insured chargeable with it, or was it the sole fault of the company through its medical examiner? On the face of the papers it was the insured. His application, signed by him, and with knowledge of the contents of which he is *prima facie* chargeable, declares and warrants that his answers to the questions therein contained, " and to those in the examiner's report herewith are fair and true." The examiner's report contains the falsehood ; and appended to that is the certificate of the insured, signed by him, in these words, viz. : " I hereby declare that I have given true answers to all questions put to me by the medical examiner, that they agree exactly with the foregoing, and that I am the same person described in the accompanying application, and whose signature is appended to declaration and warrant herewith." This certificate in terms confesses that the questions appearing upon the paper to have been answered by the applicant were in truth answered by him ; that they were written out upon the paper before its signature by the applicant ; that as so written they agree exactly with the answers made ; and that the insured knew that fact and had knowledge of how they were written. Stopping at this point the case is clear. It is one in which the truth is told to the medical examiner ; where the latter, instead of the truth, writes down a falsehood ; where the applicant reads and knows the answer that is written, and with full knowledge of its falsity as written certifies that it is true and "agrees exactly" with the answers in fact made. This is the applicant's written admission. It is conclusive upon him, unless by some sufficient proof he explains and rebuts it. If he did read the answer as written, if he knew of its presence and still certified to its truth, the fraud was his. The medical examiner might write down the untruthful answer by mistake or inadvertence, but the applicant could not read it and then certify to its truth without fraud. It is evident, therefore, that no proof can explain and answer the applicant's certificate which falls short of showing either that the answer was not written when the certificate was signed, or at least was not known to the insured when he made such signature. In a former case against the same defendant the first of these facts was proved. (*Grattan* v. *Met. Life Ins. Co.*, 80 N. Y. 292 ; 36 Am. Rep. 617.) In that case the referee expressly found that the whole of the medical examiner's certificate was in blank and the cause of the sister's death was unwritten when the applicant signed it. In *Mowry* v. *Rosendale* (74 N. Y. 361) the same fact appeared. The applicant signed a blank and trusted to the agent of the company to fill it up thereafter. In *Maher* v. *The Hibernia Ins. Co.* (67 N. Y. 283) there was proof that the incorrect language of the policy was pointed out by the insured, but he was prevented from having the same corrected, or was thrown off his guard, and dissuaded therefrom by the acts or declarations of the agent of the insurer. The insured must show a state of facts indicating honesty and truthfulness on his part, and leaving the burden of having declared an untruth solely upon the agent of the company. The proof here relied upon for that purpose comes from the letter of the insured written to the company in answer to its assertion of fraud, its tender back of the premium paid, and its demand that the policy be canceled. The defendant introduced the letter and read so much of it as admitted that the applicant knew that his sister died of consumption, and the plaintiff read the rest under objection and exception. We think she had the right to do so. The whole of the letter was one connected narrative and an explanation of a single definite accusation. It was written to contradict the charge of a false representation as to the cause of the sister's death. To read part of it and suppress the rest distorts its purpose and meaning and turns a justification into a confession. The plaintiff could not have read it at all. When the defendant read a part of it he was bound to take with it all that explained or qualified what preceded. The rule appears to be firmly settled, both as to a conversation or writing, that the introduction of a part renders admissible so much of the remainder as tends to explain or qualify what has been received, and that is to be deemed a qualification which rebuts and destroys the inference to be derived from or the use to be made of the portion put in evidence. (*Rouse* v. *Whited*, 25 N. Y. 170; *Forrest* v. *Forrest*, 6 Duer, 126–7; *Gildersleeve* v. *Landon*, 73 N. Y. 609.)

Here the admission of knowledge by Hugh of the cause of his sister's death, relatively to the written answer signed by him, tended to convict him of a falsehood and a fraud. That was the use to be made of the admission and the purpose of its proof. Whatever else in the letter tended to modify or destroy that effect of the admission and change its purport from a confession of guilt to an assertion of innocence, was a qualification of the statement to which the plaintiff was entitled. The case of *Dilleber* v. *Home Life Ins. Co.* (69 N. Y. 257; 25 Am. Rep. 182), to which we are referred, was of a different character. There the plaintiff was the wife for whose benefit the husband's life was insured. She, and not he, was the owner of the policy. His declarations, not part of the *res gestæ*, could not affect her. His letter, therefore, was only evidence of his knowledge of his condition, but not of the facts constituting it, when offered against the owner of the policy. It would have been such evidence as against him or his personal representative. But here the declarations of the letter were not admissible in behalf of the plaintiff at all, because she was the personal representative of the deceased. The defendant could waive that difficulty by putting such declarations, or a part of them, in evidence, on its behalf, but when it did so, must also make equally evidence that which tended to explain or qualify the portion which was used. We recur then to the letter. It is not in all respects clear and full, but substantially asserts entire ignorance of the answer written, and one given which was truthful. It begins with an explicit denial of having made any fraudulent misrepresentation, and then proceeds to state what it calls "the true facts." It avers that the company's agent solicited the two brothers to insure; that he came to their father's house for needed information; that the father took the Bible and from it gave the family ages and deaths, and the cause of the sister's death, which was consumption; that the agent wrote all these details down upon a slip of paper; that Terence and the agent went direct to the medical examiner, to whom the agent handed the slip with the answers upon it; that the doctor asked Terence if all those answers were correct and true, to which he said "yes," but "what he put down he does not know." The recital then adds, "the same was done with me, only in this, that I did not go with the agent." Stopping at this point in the

letter we must infer from its statements that each of the brothers signed the certificate in blank, leaving the medical examiner
to fill it out afterward from the slip which was declared to be
correct. This view of the case was that which prevailed and
was held sufficient in the litigation over Terence's policy. But
some things which follow in the letter indicate that Hugh did
not sign in blank, and that the answers were written when he
appended his name. He described his interview with the medical examiner, and says he " *took* those dates of ages from the
slip, and *when he came to* the cause of my sister's death, he
said, ' your sister died of consumption?' " I answered, " yes,
sir ; in.yours " (that is, in their letter to him) " you say that my
answer was 'I did not know;' some person lies; we do not."
This version of the scene indicates that the medical examiner,
with the company's blank before him containing the list of
questions, put them in their order and wrote down the answers
as they were received. Still it does not follow that the protes-
tation of the insured that he did not know what answers the
doctor wrote is either untrue or improbable. It does not appear that he saw what was written, or read it himself, or that
it was read to him. If the transaction took this latter shape,
the medical examiner, receiving a true answer, wrote down a
false one ; and his act could not be inadvertent, but was fraudulent. If so, he would be quite sure not to read the written
answer to the insured, or permit him to read it, but procure his
signature at the end through natural confidence and trust in the
accurate statement of his answers. In any view, therefore, of
this letter it raised a question of fact. It tended to explain and
rebut the inferences flowing from the certificate of the assured
and to throw the burden of the false answer upon the company's agent alone. (*Mowry* v. *Rosendale* and *Grattan* v. *Met.
Life Ins. Co.*, *supra; Flynn* v. *Eq. Life Ins. Co.*, 78 N. Y.
568; 34 Am. Rep. 561.) Upon the question of fact thus raised
we must again be content with the verdict of the jury.

The question asked Dr. Mareness, viz.: " what opinion did
you form, based on the general sight of the man, before you
made an examination, or before you had any conversation with

him ? " was properly excluded as privileged within the statute. The doctor had never seen him before, nor seen him since. His whole knowledge came from the one interview, which was wholly and purely of a professional character.   We have distinctly held in such a case that the communication to the physician's sense of sight is within the statute, and as much so as if it had been oral and reached his ear (*Grattan* v. *Met. Life Ins. Co.*, 80 N. Y. 297; 36 Am. Rep. 617), and that information derived from observation of the patient's appearance and symptoms must not be disclosed. (*Edington* v. *Mut. Life Ins. Co.*, 67 N. Y. 185.)   The case here is not like *Edington* v. *Ætna Life Ins. Co.* (77 N. Y. 564).   There the physician had seen the patient, both before and after he attended him professionally.   He had a possible knowledge derived from observation when no professional relation existed.   Here such relation began upon the instant that Terence came into his presence and continued until he disappeared from view.   No information so acquired could be disclosed.

Dr. Halves was examined as a witness by the defendant, and testified that he was called as a witness on a former trial, but did not say by whom; and that he attended Terence in his last illness.   He was then asked if Terence died of consumption, which was excluded.   The question was then put whether upon such former trial he was not asked by the plaintiff's counsel if he attended Terence in his last illness, to which he answered in the affirmative, and that Terence died of consumption.   This and some similar evidence offered was excluded.   The appellant claims that this ruling is erroneous, upon the ground that the silence imposed upon the physician is a personal privilege which may be waived, and that the questions put on behalf of the plaintiff on the former trial amounted to such a waiver But the evidence was inadmissible for two reasons.   What the witness testified to on a former trial, he being living and present for examination on the second trial, could only be proved for the purpose of contradicting him or of refreshing his memory.   No emergency of that kind existed to justify the proof.   To establish a waiver of the right to prevent disclosure,

the only proof necessary or competent in any event was the
fact of the inquiry by the plaintiff. The answer given was not
needed for such purpose. It was the question which opened
the door. But we do not agree that the plaintiff's inquiry on
the former trial precluded his objection on the latter one. It
was an incident in the mode of trial. It waived for that occasion and under then existing circumstances an objection which
might have been relied upon. It was in no sense an admission
of the party, but proof by a witness. The party was not even
then bound by the fact, but might disprove it. *Owen* v.
Cawley (36 N. Y. 600), cited as authority, was a peculiar case.
An order had been entered by the General Term entitling
either party on the new trial to read the evidence which had
been given on the other. And it was the admission of the
party that was sought to be proved, and in that connection it
was said that where an absolute and unqualified admission is
made in a pending cause, whether by written stipulation of the
attorney, or as matter of proof on the hearing, it cannot be re-
tracted on a subsequent trial unless by leave of the court. The
case is far from establishing that, because proof which might
have been, was not, excluded on a first trial, it cannot be shut
out on the second. Such a rule would tend to perpetuate and
make incurable the errors or indiscretions or oversights of
counsel, and hamper the second trial with a study of the first.
We do not know how the plaintiff came to ask the questions.
The case does not show who called the witness. The plaintiff
may have asserted her privilege and been overruled by the
court, and so driven to these inquiries without any voluntary
waiver of her rights. We are of opinion that the evidence objected to was properly excluded.

It was claimed that the assured warranted his occupation to
be that of a soda-water "dealer," when in fact he was a
soda-water "peddler." If there was any material difference
between the phrases, it was cured by proof that the actual facts
were truthfully stated to the defendant's agent, and the expression used was the latter's choice as correctly stating the
truth.

Some other exceptions taken have been examined, but do not require special consideration.

The judgment should be affirmed, with costs.

All concur, except EARL, J., not voting.

Judgment affirmed.

JEREMIAH BARRY, Administrator, etc., Respondent, *v.* THE NEW YORK CENTRAL AND HUDSON RIVER RAILROAD COMPANY, Appellant.

In an action against a railroad company for alleged negligence, causing the death of plaintiff's intestate, it appeared that the decedent was run over and killed in attempting to cross defendant's tracks at a point where the owners of adjoining lands had a right of way, and where the public for thirty years had been in the habit of crossing. *Held*, that the acquiescence of defendant for so long a time in this public use amounted to a license or permission to all persons to cross at this point, and imposed a duty upon it as to persons so crossing to exercise reasonable care in the movement of its trains, so as to protect them from injury.

Hounsell v. *Smyth* (97 Eng. C. L. 731), *Nicholson* v. *E. R. Co.* (41 N. Y. 525), *Sutton* v. *N. Y. C. & H. R. R. R. Co.* (66 id. 243), distinguished.

The train which caused the death was backing up without a bell being rung or other signal given, in charge of a brakeman, who was on a platform between two cars, where he could not see persons on the track or have notice to apply the brakes in case of danger. Persons were at all times crossing the tracks, several hundreds crossing daily. *Held*, that the evidence justified the submission of the question of defendant's negligence to the jury.

The intestate was a boy ten years old. The train which ran over him went past the crossing followed by a freight train. The bell on the freight train was ringing and the flagman on the crossing was flagging it, paying no attention to the other. The first train was switched on to another track and backed up on the track the boy attempted to cross. There was no direct proof as to what precautions he took before crossing the track. *Held*, that the question of contributory negligence was properly submitted to the jury ; that it was competent for them to infer that the boy seeing the first train pass supposed it was going on, and his attention being attracted by the freight train, he did not observe that the first train had changed its direction and was backing up.

In the case of a child of tender years, where the circumstances would justify an inference that he was misled or confused in respect to the actual situation, and that his conduct was not unreasonable in view of those circumstances, and his age, the question of contributory negligence is for the jury, although he may have omitted some precaution which in the case of an adult would be deemed conclusive evidence of negligence. *It seems* it cannot be held as matter of law, that, under the circumstances of this case, the ringing of the bell would fulfill the whole duty resting on defendant.

(Argued March 27, 1883; decided April 24, 1883.)

APPEAL from judgment of the General Term of the Supreme Court, in the third judicial department, entered upon an order made December 16, 1882, which affirmed a judgment in favor of plaintiff, entered upon a verdict.

This action was brought to recover damages for alleged negligence causing the death of John J. Barry, plaintiff's intestate, who was run over and killed in attempting to cross defendant's tracks in the city of Troy.

The material facts are stated in the opinion.

Esek Cowen for appellant. As the deceased was, when killed, on defendant's land, by its license implied from the habit of workmen and others to cross its tracks at that spot, it owed him no duty except to do him no intentional harm, and it was error to hold that defendant was bound to give the deceased warning of the approach of its train. (*Nicholson* v. *Erie R. Co.*, 41 N. Y. 525; *Sutton* v. *N. Y. C. & H. R. R. R.*, 66 id. 243; *P. & R. Co.* v. *Hummel*, 44 Penn. St. 375; *Matze* v. *N. Y. C. & H. R. R. R.*, 1 Hun, 417; *Harty* v. *C. R. of N. J.*, 42 N. Y. 468.) It makes no difference in this respect that the deceased was of tender years. (*Penn. R. Co.* v. *Lewis*, 79 Penn. St. 33–43; *P. & R.* v. *Hummel*, 44 id. 379; *Hornsberger* v. *Second Ave. R. Co.*, 1 Keyes, 570.) The deceased was guilty of contributing negligence, and for this reason the nonsuit should have been granted. (*Haight* v. *N. Y. C. & H. R. R. R.*, 7 Lans. 11; *Davis* v. *N. Y. C. & H. R. R. R.*, 47 N. Y. 400; *Barker* v. *Savage*, 45 id. 191; *Gorton* v. *Erie R. W.*, id. 660; *Wilcox* v. *Rome, W. & O. R. R.*, 39 id. 358; *Salter* v. *Utica & B. R. R.*, 75 id. 273; *Day* v. *Flushing, etc., R. R.*,

id. 610; *Mitchell* v. *N. Y. C. & H. R. R. R.*, 2 Hun, 535.)
The burden of proof was on plaintiff to show at least that he
employed such means as a child of ten years might be expected
to employ to insure his own safety. (*Reynolds* v. *N. Y. C. &
H. R. R. R.*, 53 N. Y. 248; *Cordell* v. *N. Y. C. & H. R. R. R.*,
75 id. 330; *Hale* v. *Smith*, 78 id. 480, *Hart, Admr.*, v. *Hudson
River Bridge Co.*, 84 id. 56.) The court erred in refusing to
charge as requested, that if the bell was rung the defendant was
not bound to give any other warning. (*Grippen* v. *N. Y. C.
R. R. Co.*, 40 N. Y. 34.)

Martin I. Townsend for respondent.   Plaintiff's intestate
was, at the time he was injured, where he had a right to be.
(*Sibley* v. *Ellis*, 11 Gray, 417; Washburn on Easements, 67,
margin ; id. 73, 74, margin 76.) The plaintiff's intestate had
the right to require the defendant, its agents and servants,
to use all reasonable care and diligence proportioned to the
magnitude of the danger to avoid doing him an injury, and if
it has failed and he has been injured without his own fault
which contributed to the injury, the defendant must respond.
(*Fero* v. *Buffalo R. R. Co.*, 22 N. Y. 209; *Johnson* v. *Hudson R. R. R. Co.*, 20 id. 65; *Beiseigel* v. *N. Y. C. R. R. Co.*,
40 id. 28; *McDermott* v. *N. Y. C. & H. R. R. R. Co.*, 16
W'kly Dig. 57.) The measure and degree of care, the omission of which would constitute negligence, is to be graduated
by the age and capacity of the individual. (*Powell* v. *N. Y.
C. & H. R. R. R. Co.*, 22 Hun, 56; *Haycroft* v. *L. S. & M.
S. R. R. Co.*, 3 Sup. Ct. 49; *McGovern* v. *N. Y. C. & H. R.
R. R. Co.*, 67 N. Y. 417; *Byrne* v. *N. Y. C. & H. R. R. R.
Co.*, 83 id. 620; *Wendell* v. *N. Y. C. & H. R. R. R. Co.*, 14
W'kly Dig. 406.) The question as to whether the deceased
was, under the circumstances of the case, free from negligence,
was for the jury to determine, and the court properly denied
the motion for a nonsuit. (*Ernst* v. *H. R. R. R. Co.*, 39 N.
Y. 61; *Weber* v. *N. Y. C. & H. R. R. R. Co.*, 58 id. 451;
McGrath v. *H. R. R. R. Co.*, 32 Barb. 144; *Payne* v. *T. &
B. R. R. Co.*, 83 N. Y. 572.)

ANDREWS, J. If the absolute legal right of the intestate to be upon the track of the defendant at the place of the injury was a material question in the case, it may have been error in the court to have submitted to the jury to find whether such right existed under the deed from Cushman and Norton to Paine and Buell. But we are of opinion that the question was quite immaterial to the determination of the controversy. It is undisputed that the owners of lots abutting on the railroad at this point had a right of way across the defendant's tracks, and that for more than thirty years the public were in the habit of crossing the tracks at this point to reach Madison and other streets lying northerly and easterly of the railroad, the proof being that several hundred people crossed there every day. There can be no doubt that the acquiescence of the defendant for so long a time, in the crossing of the tracks by pedestrians, amounted to a license and permission, by the defendant, to all persons to cross the tracks at this point. These circumstances imposed a duty upon the defendant in respect of persons using the crossing, to exercise reasonable care in the movement of its trains. The company had a lawful right to use the tracks for its business, and could have withdrawn its permission to the public to use its premises as a public way, assuming that no public right therein existed; but so long as it permitted the public use, it was chargeable with knowledge of the danger to human life from operating its trains at that point, and was bound to such reasonable precaution in their management as ordinary prudence dictated to protect wayfarers from injury. It is doubtless true that the owner of the premises owes no duty to keep them in such condition that an intruder, or a person casually thereon by sufferance, shall not be injured. The quarry case (*Hownsell* v. *Smyth*, 97 Eng. Com. Law, 731) is an apt illustration. There the plaintiff in crossing the defendant's waste land, which the public had been allowed to cross, fell into an unguarded excavation, and the court held that the plaintiff had no cause of action, because the defendant was under no legal duty to fence or otherwise guard the excavation for his protection. The plaintiff there availed himself of the license to use the premises in their existing condition, and accepted it with its attendant perils. The defendant did no affirmative act at the time by which existing conditions were changed and new perils created.

In the case of the movement of a train of cars over a track at a place which the public are permitted to use as a crossing the company are necessarily apprised that it is attended with danger to life. The company is an actor at the time in creating the circumstances which imperil human life, and it would be alarming doctrine that it was under no duty to exercise any care in the movement of its trains. The cases of *Nicholson* v. *Erie Ry. Co.* (41 N. Y. 525), and of *Sutton* v. *N. Y. C. & H. R. R. R. Co.* (66 id. 243), do not sustain the defendant's contention. In neither of these cases was the movement of the cars the direct act of the party sought to be charged, but resulted from causes which could not reasonably or naturally have been anticipated. There was in fact no negligence shown on the part of the defendants. The court in these cases properly held that the circumstances did not create any duty toward the party injured, or tend to establish any culpable negligence.

The ground of liability in this case is negligence, and the duty of the defendant to exercise reasonable care, existed irrespective of the fact whether the plaintiff's intestate had a fixed legal right to cross the track, or was there simply by the defendant's implied permission. The construction of the deed was not material in determining the question of reasonable care. The circumstances known to the defendant required this, whether the plaintiff's intestate was there by right or by a mere license. The judge, upon the defendant's request, charged that if the intestate was on the track by mere license of the defendant, and having no other right, the plaintiff could not recover. The learned judge in making this charge followed what he understood to be the ruling of the General Term on the first appeal, and the charge was, we think, for the reasons stated erroneous. But the error was in favor of the defendant, and the jury having found that the defendant was guilty of negligence in the management of the train which caused the

intestate's death, this finding, if justified (in the absence of
contributory negligence), sustains the action.

It is claimed that there was no evidence to justify the submission to the jury of the question of the defendant's negligence. The court could not, we think, have properly taken
this question from the jury. The train consisted of an engine
and two passenger cars. It was, as the evidence on the part
of the plaintiff tends to show, backing up without a bell being
rung, or other signal being given, in charge of a brakeman who
was at the time on the platform between the two cars, and
where he could not see persons on the track, or have notice so
as to apply the brake in case of danger. Moving a train in
this way in a populous locality where persons were at all times
crossing the track, might very well be found by a jury to be
culpable negligence.

The point of contributory negligence is also relied upon.
The intestate was a boy ten years of age. There is no direct
proof what precautions he took before crossing the track, but
the general situation was that he was in a position before crossing to have seen, in his line of vision, without any material
change of position, the train which ran over him, going southerly on the track of the Union railroad, away from him
toward Albany. At the same time there was a freight train
also going southerly on the Union railroad track, in rear of the
other, which a flagman standing near the point of the accident was flagging, paying no attention to the first train. The
bell on the freight train was also ringing. We think it was
competent for the jury to have inferred that the boy seeing
the first train going south, supposed it was going to Albany,
not understanding that it was intending to go only so far
south as the switch on Monroe street, and then to back north
toward Madison street, and that his attention was attracted by
the freight train and the flagman, and that he did not observe
that the first train had changed its direction and was backing
up on the track which he attempted to cross. The law, as was
said in *McGovern* v. *N. Y. C. & H. R. R. R. Co.* (67 N. Y.
417), is not so unreasonable as to expect or require the same ma-

turity of judgment, or the same degree of care and circumspection in a child of tender years as in an adult, and in the case of a child, where the circumstances would justify the inference that he was misled or confused in respect to the actual situation, and that his conduct was not unreasonable under the circumstances and in view of his age, then the question of contributory negligence is for the jury, and this although he may have omitted some precaution which in the case of an adult would be deemed strong, or even conclusive evidence of negligence.

The additional point is made that the court erred in refusing to charge as requested, that if the bell was rung the defendant was not bound to give any other warning. We think it cannot be held as matter of law, under the circumstances of this case, that the ringing of the bell fulfilled the whole duty resting on the defendant.

We find no error of law in the record, and the judgment should therefore be affirmed.

All concur, except Ruger, Ch. J., dissenting.

Judgment affirmed.

Benjamin H. Hutton et al., as Trustees, etc., Respondents, v. James Benkard et al., Appellants.

In 1869 S. conveyed all of her estate to trustees, in trust, to convert into money, and keep the proceeds invested, applying the income and such portion of the principal as they should deem proper to her use during her life, and paying over the residue as she should by will appoint. In 1877 S. made a will, which made no reference to the trust, but by which she devised certain real estate, part of the trust estate, gave legacies amounting to $275,500, and gave her residuary estate, including that she might thereafter acquire or become possessed of, to seventeen beneficiaries named. At the time of the execution of the will and of her death, S., aside from the trust estate, only owned property of the value of about $25,000, which consisted principally of an undivided interest in the estate of a deceased sister. She was in the habit of spending all the income paid her by the trustees, and was well acquainted with the condition and amount of her estate. At the time of executing the will, S. was in delicate health, and was apprehensive that she might die at any moment. In an action by the trustees for an accounting and for directions as to the disposition of the trust estate, *held*, that the power of appointment reserved in the trust deed was properly and effectually executed both as to real and personal estate.

Where it appears, from the terms of a will, taken as a whole, and construed in the light of surrounding circumstances, that it was the intention of the testator in the dispositions made by him to execute a power of appointment, such intention will have effect although the power is not referred to in express words.

The provisions of the Revised Statutes in reference to powers (1 R. S., part 2, chap. 1, title 2, art. 8, p. 732 *et seq.*) apply so far as they can be made applicable to personal as well as to real estate, and the rules governing the construction of testamentary appointments in regard to real estate apply when they affect personal property.

The provision, therefore, of such statutes (1 R. S. 737, § 126), declaring that lands embraced in a power to devise shall pass by a will purporting to convey all the testator's real estate " unless the intent that the will shall not operate as an execution of the power shall appear, expressly or by necessary implication " applies to personalty.

(Argued April 16, 1883 ; decided April 24, 1883.)

APPEAL from order of the General Term of the Supreme Court, in the first judicial department, made the first Monday of October, 1882, which denied a motion made under section 1001 of the Code of Civil Procedure, for a new trial after an interlocutory judgment herein.

This action was brought by plaintiffs as trustees under a trust deed executed to them by Emma Magnin D. Collogny, afterward Emma Strecker, for the settlement of their accounts as trustees, and for the direction of the court as to the disposition of the trust estate.

The material facts are stated in the opinion.

Charles M. DaCosta & William Jay for appellants. At common law a valid execution of a power of appointment can only be effected by an instrument in which either the power or the subject-matter is specifically referred to. The want of such a reference cannot be supplied by parol, and if it be uncertain whether the act is done in execution of the power or not, it will not be construed to be an execution of the power. (Worthington on Wills, Law Lib., 44 N. S. 295, 296; Powell on Powers, 118; 2 Story's Eq. Jur. [12th ed.], § 1062 *a* ; Sugden on Powers [8th ed.], 300, 301, 317; Farwell on Powers [1874], 179; 2 Chance on Powers, 84; Powell on Devises [3d ed.], 70; Theobold on the Construction of Wills, 77, 78; O'Hara on the Construction of Wills, 208; Wigram on Wills, 67, 68; Jarman on Wills [Randolph & T.'s ed.], 272, 273; *Sir Edward Clere*, 6 Coke, 17 *b* ; *Aylesworth* v. *Chadwell*, 3 id. 38; *Molton* v. *Hutchinson*, 1 Atk. 558; *Ex parte Caswell*, id. 559; *Lowson* v. *Lowson*, 3 Brown's C. C. 372; *Standen* v. *Standen*, 2 Ves. 589; *Bucklan* v. *Barton*, 2 H. Blackst. 136; *Langham* v. *Nenny*, 3 Ves. 467; *Croft* v. *Slee*, 4 id. 60; *Nannock* v. *Horton*, 7 id. 391; *Att'y-Gen.* v. *Vigor*, 8 id. 256, 292; *Bennett* v. *Aburrow*, id. 609, 616; *Bradley* v. *Westcott*, 13 id. 445; *Hellings* v. *Bird*, 11 East, 49; *Lowes* v. *Hackward*, 18 Vesey, 168; *Webb* v. *Honnor*, 1 J. & W. 352–357; *Lewis* v. *Lewellyn*, 1 Turner & R. 104; *Denn* v. *Roake*, 5 B. & C. 720; *Nowell* v. *Roake*, 2 Bing. 497, 504; 6 id. 475; *Jones* v. *Tucker*, 2 Mer. 533; *Jones* v. *Curry*, 1 Swart, 66; *Walker* v. *Mackie*, 4 Russell, 76; *Grant* v. *Lyman*, id. 293; *Adams* v. *Austin*, 3 id. 461; *Buxton* v. *Buxton*, 1 Keen, 755; *Lempreere* v. *Valpy*, 5 Sim. 108; *Lovell* v. *Knight*, 3 id. 275; *Hughes* v. *Turner*, 3 M. & K. 666; *Napier* v. *Napier*, 1 Sim. 28; *Owens* v. *Dickinson*, 1 Craig & Phil. 53; *Innes* v. *Sayer*, 8 Eng. L. & Eq. 157; *Lake* v. *Currie*, 2 DeG., M. & G. 536; *Harvey* v. *Stracey*, 1 Drewry, 112; *In re Morgan*, 7 Irish Ch. 18; *Blagge* v. *Mills*, 1 Story, 427, 446, 454; *Willard* v. *Ware*, 10 Allen, 263; *Bangs* v. *Smith*, 98 Mass. 271; *Reilly* v. *Chouquette*, 18 Mo. 228; *Frank* v. *Egglestone*, 92 Ill. 515; *Bingham's Appeal*, 64 Penn. St. 345; *White* v. *Hicks*, 43 Barb. 64; *Wetherill* v. *Wetherill*, 18 Penn. St. 265; *Jones* v. *Wood*, 16 id. 25; *Hollister* v. *Shaw*, 46 Conn. 248; *Morey* v. *Michael*, 18 Ind. 227, 246; *Bilderback* v. *Boyce*, 14 S. C. 539.) The provisions of the article of the Revised Statutes on uses and trusts do not apply to personal property, except in the instance where it is therein specifically mentioned. (*Kane*

v. *Gott,* 24 Wend. 641, 661; *Gilman* v. *Reddington,* 24 N.
Y. 9, 12; *Graft* v. *Bonnett,* 31 id. 9, 19; *Power* v. *Cassidy,*
79 id. 602.) Where a trust is of personal estate, the execution
of the trust, upon the death of a surviving trustee, descends
to his personal representatives in accordance with the well-
known common-law rule. (*Bucklin* v. *Bucklin,* 1 Abb. Ct. of
App. Dec. 242; *Emerson* v. *Bleakley,* 2 id. 22; *Westmore* v.
Hegeman, 88 N. Y. 69, 72.) The will must specifically deal
with the property over which a power of appointment exists
if it does not in terms refer to the power itself. (*Lake* v.
Currie, 2 DeGex, M. & G. 536, 547; *Innes* v. *Sayre,* Eng. L.
& Eq. 157.)

George G. DeWitt, Jr., for the trustees, respondents. In
order to execute the powers of appointment it was not necessary for the testatrix to recite or refer to the same in her will.
The intention to execute the powers and dispose of all her
estate clearly appears. (2 R. S. [6th ed.], § 147, p. 1118;
Bolton v. *DePeyster,* 25 Barb. 564–576; *Van Wert* v. *Benedict,* 1 Bradf. 122–123.) The article of the Revised Statutes
relating to powers applies to personalty as well as to realty.
(*Cutting* v. *Cutting,* 86 N. Y. 522.) As the will in suit clearly
indicates an intention to execute the power of appointment,
although it does not refer to it, it will be deemed an execution
of the power. (*Braddish* v. *Gibbs,* 3 Johns. Ch. 523–551;
Heyer v. *Burger,* 1 Hoff. Ch. 18; *Van Wert* v. *Benedict,*
1 Bradf. 115–123; *Bolton* v. *DePeyster,* 25 Barb. 577; *White*
v. *Hicks,* 43 id. 64; 33 N. Y. 383; *Blake* v. *Hawkins,* 98 U.
S. 315; *Crane* v. *Lessee of Morris & Astor,* 6 Peters, 598;
2 Washburn on Real Prop. [4th ed.] 658; Sugden on Powers
[8th ed.], 289; *Keefer* v. *Swartz,* 11 Wright, 503; *Bishop* v.
Remple, 11 Ohio St. 277.) By the very terms of the trust
deed, it will be seen that the testatrix contemplated a disposition of her estate to charitable objects. (*Amory* v. *Meredith,*
7 Allen, 400; *Bangs* v. *Smith,* 98 Mass. 270; *Willard* v.
Waar, 10 Allen, 263.) The evidence showing the condition
of Mrs. Strecker's estate at the time she made the will was

properly admitted. (*White* v. *Hicks,* 43 Barb. 91; 33 N. Y. 383; *Blake* v. *Hawkins,* 98 U. S. 315.)

E. H. Landon for the executors, respondents. The will was a valid execution of the power of appointment reserved by the trust deeds, and the real estate passed thereby. (1 R. S. 737, §§ 124, 126; id. 732, § 73; *Cutting* v. *Cutting,* 86 N. Y. 522.) Independent of the statute, the will was a valid execution of the power, as to the personal as well as the real property. (*White* v. *Hicks,* 33 N. Y. 383.)

EARL, J. In August, 1869, Emma Strecker owned a large amount of real and personal property, and desiring to create a trust for her own benefit she made and executed a trust deed, whereby she conveyed all her estate to these plaintiffs, in trust, to convert the same into money at their discretion, to invest and keep the same invested, and to receive the income and profits of the same and apply them, and so much of the principal as they should deem proper to her use during her life; and upon and after her death, to pay and divide the principal of the estate, "to and among such person or persons, or bodies corporate or politic, and in such relative shares and proportions as she (Emma Strecker) shall by any instrument in writing in the nature of a last will and testament, executed in due form of law, limit or appoint, and in default of any such appointment, to pay and divide the same to and among such persons as shall then be her heirs at law, and in the same proportions they would by law be entitled to if the same were all real estate, and she had died intestate and possessed thereof in fee-simple, and not married." The plaintiffs as such trustees took possession of all the estate conveyed to them by the deed, and during the life-time of Mrs. Strecker, collected and received the income of the estate and from time to time paid the same over to her.

On the 24th day of October, 1877, Mrs. Strecker made and executed a last will and testament in due form of law; and on the 18th day of February, 1879, she died. The will was admitted to probate May 9, 1879, and letters testamentary were issued to the defendants Landon and Corse, as executors, who qualified and entered upon their duties as such. By her will she devised two lots of ground in Greenwood cemetery to the trustees of the cemetery; distributed her household effects among various legatees, and bequeathed to various persons and religious and benevolent institutions in all $275,500. She devised all her undivided interest in certain parcels of land situated in the city of Newburgh, which she inherited from her grandfather, to the children of her brothers and of her sister; and disposed of her residuary estate as follows: " All the rest, residue and remainder of my estate, both real and personal, whatsoever and wheresoever, as well that which I now have as that which I may hereafter acquire, or die possessed of, or entitled to, including any portion of my estate that I have not hereinbefore effectually or sufficiently disposed of, I give, devise and bequeath, in equal shares and proportions, to the following charitable and benevolent institutions and societies; " and then she named seventeen benevolent institutions and societies located in the city of New York.

The trial court found that at the time she executed her will, and at the time of her death, Mrs. Strecker did not, aside from the estate held by the trustees under the trust deed, own any property, of any kind, exceeding in value the sum of $25,000, and that that property consisted principally of an undivided interest in the estate of her deceased sister, Mary Gordon, who died in April, 1876; that at the time of making her will, and prior and subsequent thereto, she was in the habit of spending and did spend all her income paid to her by her trustees ; that at the time of making her will she was well acquainted with the condition and amount of her estate; that she could have had no reasonable expectation of increasing her estate by inheritance or accumulation, other than from the income of her estate held in trust, and her interest in her deceased sister's estate ; and that she did not, thereafter, make any accumulation from either of those sources; that at the time of making her will she was in delicate health, and was apprehensive of heart disease, complained of pains about the heart, and expressed fear that she might die at any moment; and that she intended by her will to execute, and did thereby execute, the power of appointment contained in the trust deed, and did, thereby, dispose of all her estate held by the trustees under the trust deed.

The sole question submitted for our determination is whether the power of appointment reserved to Mrs. Strecker in the trust deed was properly and effectually executed as to both real and personal estate by the will.

As to the real estate the question is easily solved by the express provision of the statute, which provides that "lands embraced in a power to devise shall pass by a will purporting to convey all the real property of the testator, unless the intent that the will shall not operate as an execution of the power shall appear expressly or by necessary implication." (3 R. S. 2193, § 126 [7th ed.].) This will purports to convey all the property of the testatrix, both real and personal, and the intention that the will shall not operate as an execution of the power does not appear, expressly or by necessary implication.

But the claim is very confidently made on the part of the appellants that there was not a valid execution of the power as to the personal property, because the will contains no reference whatever to the power, and does not purport, in its dispositions of the personal property, to be in execution of the power. If we concede the contention of the learned counsel for the appellants, that there should be a valid execution of the power as to the personal property tested by the rules of the common law, we are yet of opinion that under the common law, as expounded by the courts of this State, the power was effectually executed.

When a will is claimed to be effectual as an execution of a power, all parts of it may be considered and its language and terms construed in the light of circumstances surrounding the testator at the time of the execution of the will, and if, from all these, it can be seen that it was his intention, in the dispositions he made, to execute the power, such intention will have effect. The power need not be referred to in express

terms; no form of words need be used; but the will is to be
construed, as all wills are to be construed, so as to give effect
to the intention of the testator. If it can be seen that he intended to dispose, not only of the property which he owned in
his own right, but of property which he had the right to dispose of just as effectually as if he did own it, under the power
of appointment, then effect will be given to the intention, if
that intention can be gathered from all the terms of the will,
read in the light of such circumstances surrounding the testator at the time of its execution as are proper to be considered.
In *Braddish* v. *Gibbs* (3 Johns. Ch. 522), Chancellor KENT
said: "The rule is that if a will be made without any reference
to the power it operates as an appointment under the power,
provided it cannot have operation without the power. If the
act can be good in no other way than by virtue of the power,
and some part of the will would otherwise be inoperative, and
no other intention than that of executing the power can properly be imputed to the testator, the act, or will, shall be deemed
an execution of the power, though there be no reference to
the power. Here the will can have no effect without the
power, not even as to personal property, and if the power operates upon it at all it operates equally upon every part of the disposition." In *Heyer* v. *Burger* (1 Hoff. Ch. 1) it was held
that a will, in the execution of a power of appointment, need
.not refer to the power and was well executed without any reference thereto. In *White* v. *Hicks* (43 Barb. 64), H. gave to
his executors the sum of $100,000 in trust, to pay over the in-
come to his daughter, R., during her life, and in case she
should have no children or grandchildren living at the time of
her death, then in trust to pay over one-half of such sum to
such person or persons, whether her husband or otherwise, as
she might, by last will and testament, appoint; and R. made
a will by which she gave her husband $50,000 in general terms
and without any reference to the power of appointment given
her by the will of her father. It was held that the will was a
valid execution of the power; also that evidence as to the circumstances or condition of the property or fund in the hands

of H.'s executors, to show that R.'s own savings or property were not sufficient to answer the special legacies bequeathed by her will, and of other extrinsic facts, as distinguished from what she said at or about the time of executing her will, was properly received. That case was appealed to this court, and is again reported in 33 N. Y. 383, and the judgment of the Supreme Court was here affirmed. In that case, in a very exhaustive and learned opinion, in which the numerous English cases are cited and criticised, DENIO, J., reached the conclusion, which was unanimously adopted by the court, that a person, entitled under a power of appointment to dispose of property by deed or will, may make such disposition by a proper instrument without inserting in it a reference to the power, if it otherwise appear that the intention was to execute the power; that it was competent for the court to compare the dispositions of the will with the testator's own property, and to deduce therefrom an intention to embrace in his testamentary gifts the subject he was entitled by the power to dispose of; that the English cases decided since the American Revolution, by which it was established that the amount of the testator's property could not be inquired into to show an intention to execute a power of appointment, are not to be followed in this State, especially as the rule has been disapproved of by English judges, and has recently been abrogated by an act of Parliament; that it was competent, not only to receive evidence respecting the property owned by the testatrix, but also in reference to her expectation of approximate death, on account of the state of her health, as bearing upon the construction to be given to her will; and that her intention could be collected from the provisions of her will, applied to the state of her property, and her personal condition at the time it was made.

Further citation of authority for a rule so reasonable is not needed.

In this case it must be borne in mind that the trust property came from her, and that she alone, during her life-time, was entitled to the entire income thereof for her sole use and benefit, and also to a portion of the principal if she should need it, and that she reserved to herself the absolute, unrestricted disposal thereof by will. Hence it would not be unnatural for her, when she came to make a will, to treat this trust property, which she had the same right to dispose of by will to any person whatever, as she had to dispose of her own property, as if it were, in fact, absolutely hers. She had not more than $25,000 of property outside of the trust, and yet, making her will after for several years she had consumed the entire income of her trust property, when she could have had no expectation whatever of increasing her estate, at a time when she regarded the continuance of her life as very uncertain, and the possible approach of death very proximate, she disposed of $275,500 of personal property and yet supposed that there would be a large surplus, as she made a very careful disposition of the residue among numerous charitable and benevolent institutions. It would be quite absurd to suppose that she did not have in mind the trust property at the time she made these dispositions. Besides this, by the twenty-sixth clause of her will, it is clear that she devised real estate covered by the trust. Without referring to other indications of her intention, we think it is clear that she meant, by her will, to execute the power of appointment reserved to her in the trust deed.

In affirming the judgment of the court below we could rest here; but we go farther, and are of opinion that, even if this will would not have been a valid execution of the power of appointment as to the personal estate before the Revised Statutes, it is so now. It is provided that "powers as they now exist by law are abolished, and from the time this chapter shall be in force the creation, construction and execution of powers shall be governed by the provisions of this article." (3 R. S. [7th ed.] 2188, § 73.) This language is very broad; broad enough to include all powers, both as to real and personal property. The subsequent provisions in the same article seem in terms to relate mainly if not exclusively to real estate. But yet, by analogy, the rules for the creation, construction and execution of powers as to real estate should be applied, so far as they can be, to personal estate. There should not be two rules, one applicable to personal and the other to real estate, by which to determine whether there has been a valid execution of a power; and to have different rules would certainly be very inconvenient and perplexing where the will disposes of both real and personal estate. It is a very rational construction of section 73 to hold that it abolishes all powers theretofore existing in reference to both real and personal estate; and that as to personal estate, the creation, construction and execution of powers are to be governed by the same rules, so far as they can be applied, which govern the creation, construction and execution of powers as to real estate. The surrogate of New York, in *Van Wort* v. *Benedict* (1 Bradf. 114), said: "Nor do I think it unreasonable to apply the same rule which the legislature has adopted for the construction of testamentary appointments in regard to real estate to such appointments when they affect personal estate, and to hold that personalty covered by a power shall pass by a bequest of 'all the personal property,' just the same as lands embraced in a power pass by a devise of 'all the real estate.' I think it would be a safe rule of construction, at least in cases where the estate was a single fund of a mixed character and the design of the testator was evidently to pass the entire corpus unbroken."

In *Bolton* v. *DePeyster* (25 Barb. 539), MITCHELL, P. J., writing one of the opinions of the court, after referring to section 126 above quoted, said : "This clause was introduced to put an end to the uncertainties previously existing whether a power was intended in each particular case to be executed or not. It lays down a clear rule which (I am of opinion) the courts must apply also to personal estate." In *Cutting* v. *Cutting* (86 N. Y. 522), we held that it was the intent of the legislature to make the article of the Revised Statutes "of powers" a complete and exhaustive Code on the subject, and that it included and was applicable as well to powers concerning personalty as to those affecting real estate. FOLGER, Ch. J., writing the unanimous opinion of his brethren, said: "It would be an ill-featured anomaly in the law that there should be two so inconsistent rules in the same body of law, as that of English equity and that of the Revised Statutes, and that the revisers and the legislature intended that the rule which they declared in the article of powers should be as well the rule for the creation, construction and effect of powers concerning personal property," and that "there is certainly much force in the position that one body of law should not declare a different rule for two kinds of property when there is nothing in the nature of either kind of property, or in the nature and effect of the rule, that calls for it. Clearly in the nature of things there is no reason why a gift or bequest of personal property, with a power of disposition, should not be measured by the same rule as a grant or devise of real estate with the same power." Hence we are of opinion that the rule laid down in section 126, in reference to the execution by will of a power as to real estate, should also be applied to personal estate; and if so applied, it cannot be contended that this will was not a proper execution of the power of appointment as to the personal property, because there is certainly no intention manifested in it, expressly or by necessary implication, that the will should not operate as an execution of the power.

We are, therefore, of opinion that no error was committed in the decision below, and that the order should be affirmed, with costs.

All concur.

Order affirmed.

THE PEOPLE, ex rel. JOHN MURPHY, Appellant, v. STEPHEN B. FRENCH et al., Commissioners, etc., Respondents.

The provisions of chapter 16 of the Code of Civil Procedure in reference to appeals, do not apply to an appeal in a proceeding by *certiorari* commenced prior to September 1, 1880 (Code, § 3347, subd. 11).

It seems, the provision of said chapter (§ 2140), declaring that in such a proceeding the court, upon " *the hearing,*" shall have power to determine whether there was such a preponderance of proof against the existence of any fact found, that the verdict of a jury affirming its existence rendered in an action in the Supreme Court, " would be set aside as against the weight of evidence," has no application to appeals to this court. It only applies to the " hearing " on return to the writ, and is confined to the court in which such hearing is had.

It seems, also, that the general statutory scheme for the distribution of judicial powers does not contemplate the review by this court of disputed questions of fact, and it will not entertain such questions in the absence of express legislative authority.

(Argued April 16, 1883 ; decided April 24, 1883.)

APPEAL from order of the General Term of the Supreme Court, made May 20, 1881, which affirmed an order of Special Term affirming the proceedings of the board of police of the police department in the city of New York, which were brought up for review by *certiorari.*

In January, 1880, written charges were preferred against the relator, who was a patrolman, for conduct unbecoming an officer, with specifications for improperly demanding and receiving sums of money from houses of prostitution. The usual notice of examination was given to him. Such examination was had in May, 1880, the relator appearing by counsel, and on May 24 the relator was found guilty and removed. The writ of *certiorari* was issued in April, 1880.

John D. Townsend for appellant. . The new provision embodied in subdivision 5 of section 2140 of the Code of Civil Procedure was applicable to the relator's proceeding, although the *certiorari* was granted prior to September, 1880. (Code of Civ. Pro., §§ 2141, 3347, subd. 11 ; *People, ex rel. Hart,* v. *Bd. Fire Comm'rs,* 82 N. Y. 358.)

D. J. Dean for respondents. The order appealed from is not reviewable in this court. (*People* v. *Sup'vrs of Allegany Co.,* 15 Wend. 198 ; *People, ex rel. Agnew,* v. *The Mayor,* 2 Hill,

9; *Matter of Mt. Morris Square,* id. 14; *People, ex rel. Moore,* v. *Mayor,* 5 Barb. 43; *People* v. *Rochester,* 21 id. 656.) This court will not entertain an appeal from an order which quashes and vacates the writ. (*People, ex rel. Davis,* v. *Hill,* 53 N. Y. 545; *People, ex rel. Hudson,* v. *Fire Comm'rs,* 77 id. 605; *People, ex rel. Waldman,* v. *Police Comm'rs,* 82 id. 507; *People, ex rel. Purvis,* v. *Police Comm'rs,* 86 id. 639.) Even where it appears that the tribunal below examined the proceedings and pronounced them regular, and assigns that as the reason for its decision. (*People* v. *Stilwell,* 19 N. Y. 531.) The court will not, in this proceeding, examine into the evidence farther than to see whether there is any competent testimony to sustain the conviction. (*People, ex rel. Cook,* v. *Bd. of Police,* 39 N. Y. 506, 512, 518; *People, ex rel. Folk,* v. *Bd. of Police,* 69 id. 408; *People, ex rel. Campbell,* v. *Campbell,* 82 id. 247; *People, ex rel. Hart,* v. *Bd. of Fire Comm'rs,* id. 358.) A verdict will not be set aside where the question was one of the credibility of witnesses, that question being solely within the province of the jury. (*Morss* v. *Sherill,* 63 Barb. 21; *Honsee* v. *Hammond,* 39 id. 89, 96; *Winchell* v. *Latham,* 6 How. 682; *Culver* v. *Avery,* 7 Wend. 384; *Cheney* v. *N. Y. C., etc., R. R. Co.,* 16 Hun, 415.) It is only where, either from an overwhelming preponderance of contrary testimony, or from some other cause, the court are forced to believe that through passion, prejudice, inattention or mistake, they have failed to perform their function, and have not weighed the testimony, that they set the verdict aside. (*Cothran* v. *Collins,* 29 How. 155; *Cohen* v. *Dupont,* 1 Sandf. 260, 262; *Murphy* v. *Boker,* 3 Rob. 1, 4, 5; *People, ex rel. Hart,* v. *Fire Comm'rs,* 82 N. Y. 358, 362.)

RUGER, Ch. J. Upon conflicting evidence the relator was removed by the board of police commissioners from his position as a member of the police force of the city of New York.

The board had jurisdiction to make the order, and the charges made against the relator were sufficient to warrant his removal, if legally established. (§ 55, chap. 335, Laws of 1873.)

The Special and General Terms have both affirmed the order of the commissioners upon the merits, and we are now asked to review the evidence upon which their determinations were based.

It is claimed by the appellant that by force of section 2140 of the Code of Civil Procedure this court have the right to review the decisions of the subordinate tribunals and reverse them, if we should conclude that the weight of evidence was so decidedly against their conclusions, that a trial court would be justified in setting aside a verdict if rendered upon similar evidence, as against the weight of evidence.

It is not claimed by the appellant that there is an absence of evidence to support the order of removal, but his claim is, that the evidence of the defendant strongly preponderated over that of the relator.

For several reasons we think that the claim of the defendant as to the power of review possessed by this court is incorrect.

This proceeding was commenced previous to the 1st day of September, 1880, and must, therefore, be governed by the rule in force prior to that time.

It has been repeatedly held by this court that upon an appeal from a decision of the court below rendered upon a common-law *certiorari* it will look into the record only for the purpose of seeing whether the subordinate tribunal has kept within its jurisdiction, based its decisions upon some legal proof of the facts authorizing it, and violated no rule of law in its proceeding affecting the right of the relator. (*People, ex rel. Hart,* v. *Board of Fire Commissioners,* 82 N. Y. 360 ; *People, ex rel. Haines,* v. *Smith,* 45 id. 772 ; *People, ex rel. Folk,* v. *Board of Police Commissioners,* 69 id. 408.) It necessarily follows, unless some change has been made by the Code of Civil Procedure in the consideration of such appeals, that this order must be affirmed. Section 2140 of that Code provides among other subjects of consideration that the court should also upon the *hearing* have power to determine " whether there was upon all the evidence such a preponderance of proof against the existence of any of those facts, that the verdict of a jury affirming the existence thereof, rendered in an action in the Supreme Court triable by a jury, would be set aside by the court as against the weight of evidence."

This section would, if applicable to this case, require us to go farther than the former practice authorized and examine the record not only to see if there was any evidence to support the finding of the trial court, but also to see whether that evidence was not overborne by the contradicting evidence of the defendant.

But it is further provided by subdivision 11 of section 3347 of the Code that "so much of chapter 16 as regulates the proceedings to be taken in an action or special proceeding and the effect thereof applies only to an action or special proceeding commenced on or after the 1st day of September, 1880."

That the character of the questions presented for review upon an appeal from a decision of a trial court rendered upon a common-law *certiorari* are the necessary and logical effects of the proceedings authorized and regulated by chapter 16 of the Code cannot admit of doubt or discussion, and such effects are by the express terms of section 3347 denied application to a proceeding commenced prior to September 1, 1880.

But beyond this it is quite apparent that section 2140 has no application to appeals to this court from decisions made upon the hearing of common-law *certioraris*. The provision quoted is by its terms confined to proceedings occurring at the "hearing" upon the return of the writ and must necessarily be confined to the court in which such hearing is had.

The general scheme for the distribution of judicial powers established by the laws and practice of the State does not contemplate the review by this court of disputed questions of fact, and it will not entertain such questions in the absence of express provisions of law authorizing such review.

The order should, therefore, be affirmed, with costs.

All concur.

Order affirmed.

THE PEOPLE OF THE STATE OF NEW YORK, Appellant, v.
THE FIRE ASSOCIATION OF PHILADELPHIA, Respondent.

The act of 1865 (Chap. 694, Laws of 1865), as amended in 1875 (Chap. 60,
Laws of 1875), providing that an insurance corporation of another State
seeking to do business here shall pay to the superintendent of the insurance
department for taxes, fines, etc., an amount equal to that imposed by the
"existing or future laws" of the State of its origin, upon companies of
this State seeking to do business there, when such amount is greater than
that required for such purposes by the then existing laws of this State,
is not an unlawful delegation of legislative power.

Barto v. *Himrod* (8 N. Y. 483), distinguished.

The legislature has power to pass an act to take effect upon the happening
of some future event, certain or uncertain, which, in its judgment, affects
the expediency of the law.

The fact that the contingency upon which the operation of the act is made
to depend is the action of the legislature of another State does not invalidate the act. It does not follow, therefrom, that the legislative discretion of such other State is substituted for our own.

Clark v. *Port of Mobile, Ala.* (10 Ins. L. J. 361), disapproved.

It seems, however, that the question of expediency may not be delegated,
but must be settled definitely and finally by the legislature itself.

The said act is not repugnant to the provision of the Federal Constitution
(Art. 14), declaring that no State shall "deny to any person within its
jurisdiction the equal protection of the law." That provision relates
wholly to persons rightfully within the jurisdiction, not to the terms and
conditions on which alone they can come in.

A foreign corporation may not come or transact business within the jurisdiction except by permission, express or implied; the State may prohibit
it entirely, or may impose conditions, on compliance with which only it
may come.

Said provision, therefore, applies only to foreign insurance companies after
they have performed the conditions upon which they are entitled to
admission.

It seems that, even if the conditions were unconstitutional, the foreign corporation waives the objection when it accepts the conditions by coming
in under them, and is estopped from raising it.

The constitutional difference between the rights of non-resident individuals and foreign corporations pointed out.

Said act is not violative of the provision of the State Constitution (Art. 3,
§ 20), declaring that "every law which imposes, continues or revives a tax
shall distinctly state the tax and the object to which it is to be applied,
and it shall not be sufficient to refer to any other law to fix such tax or
object," as the condition imposed by the act is in the nature of a
license fee.

The said act is not affected by the provision of the act of 1881 (§ 8, chap. 361, Laws of 1881) in reference to taxing certain corporations, companies and associations, which declares that the organization mentioned by the act shall thereafter "be exempt from assessment and taxation for State purposes," except as therein provided, as the exemption there is only from the general taxes for State purposes.

By a law of Pennsylvania it is provided that an insurance company of another State doing business in that State shall pay into the State treasury annually three per cent of the premiums received there during the year. *Held*, that said act of 1875 required of an insurance company of that State doing business here a payment to the superintendent of such sum as, with other payments, would make a full payment of three per cent on the premiums received by it; that if it had not paid the two per cent required to be paid by the State law (Chap. 463, Laws of 1875, as amended by chap. 359, Laws of 1876, chap. 138, Laws of 1878, and chap. 153, Laws of 1879), to the treasurers of the fire departments of the cities and villages, on all premiums received on property located therein, because there was no fire department in a particular locality to receive it, such amount must be added to the sum payable to the superintendent.

(Argued March 29, 1883; decided May 1, 1883.)

APPEAL from judgment of the General Term of the Supreme Court, in the third judicial department, in favor of defendant, entered upon an order made February 3, 1883, directing such judgment on a case submitted under section 1279 of the Code of Civil Procedure.

The questions submitted were as to the constitutionality of the act chapter 694, Laws of 1865, as amended by chapter 60, Laws of 1875, and if constitutional as to the amount, defendant, a Pennsylvania insurance company, is liable to pay to the superintendent of the insurance department of this State under said act upon premiums received by it in this State.

Defendant had paid to the trustees of the Exempt Firemen's Fund in the city of New York two per cent upon the premiums received on property insured in that city, as required by the statutes. It also had paid to the State comptroller eight-tenths of one per cent on all premiums on business transacted in this State. It had also paid to the treasurers of fire departments of other cities and villages of the State $1,816.69, which as stated in the case was "all that was demanded of the defendant, there being many villages in the State in which property insured by the defendant had no fire department or fire companies." The whole amount paid was $4,036.65. The superintendent claimed that defendant was liable to pay to the State three per cent on the gross sum received by it for premiums on State business during the year aforesaid, which percentage would amount to $5,885.10, less the sum so paid.

Leslie W. Russell, attorney-general, for appellant. The legislature has the power to impose upon foreign corporations doing business in this State such terms for the privilege granted as it may deem proper. (*Liverpool Ins. Co.* v. *Mass.*, 10 Wall. 566; *Bank of Augusta* v. *Earl*, 13 Pet. 586; *Fire Dep't* v. *Noble*, 3 E. D. Smith, 440, 452; *Fire Dep't* v. *Wright*, id. 453; *People* v. *Imlay*, 20 Barb. 68; *Paul* v. *Virginia*, 8 Wall. 168; *Nathan* v. *Louisiana*, 8 How. 73; *Ducat* v. *Chicago*, 10 Wall. 410; *Conner* v. *Elliott*, 18 How. [U. S.] 591.) A State may, in its discretion, prohibit foreign corporations from exercising their corporate privileges within its jurisdiction. They are not citizens within the meaning of section 2, article 4 of the Constitution of the United States, which provides that "the citizens of each State shall be entitled to all privileges and immunities of citizens in the several States," and their right to do business in foreign States depends upon the assent of those States which may be given on such terms as they please. (*Paul* v. *Virginia*, 8 Wall. 168; *St. Louis* v. *Wehrung*, 46 Ill. 392; 48 id. 172; 92 id. 399; 94 id. 364; *Slaughter-House Cases*, 16 Wall. 36, 81.) The license to do business being a favor and not a right, the proffer of the terms, though those terms could not be compelled because interfering with the privilege of the citizen, once accepted, makes the conditions binding on the corporation, as constitutional rights created for personal benefit may be waived. (*Embury* v. *Connor*, 3 Comst. 511; *Sherman* v. *McKeon*, 38 N. Y. 267; *Phyle* v. *Eimer*, 45 id. 103.) And having waived the privilege the corporation will be estopped. (*Vose* v. *Cockroft*, 44 N. Y. 415; *Cancemi* v. *People*, 18 id. 128; *Morse* v. *Home Ins. Co.*, 30 Wis. 496; 20 Wall. 445;

State, ex rel. Drake, v. *Doyle,* 40 Wis. 175 ; *State, ex rel. Continental Co.,* v. *Doyle,* id. 220 ; *Doyle* v. *Continental Co.,* 94 U. S. 535.) The object of this tax is, under section 20, article 3, of the Constitution, sufficiently designated. (2 R. S. [7th ed.] 1447, § 7; *People* v. *Nat. F. Ins. Co. of N. Y.,* 27 Hun, 188; *People, ex rel.* v. *Davenport,* 25 id. 630–632; *Mut. Ins. Co.* v. *Mayor,* 5 Sandf. 10; affirmed, 8 N. Y. 24; *People, ex rel.* v. *Supervisors,* 17 id. 235 ; *People, ex rel.* v. *Supervisors,* 27 Barb. 575–583, note *a.*) The court below erred in deciding that the act of 1875 was unconstitutional, in that it was an improper delegation of legislative power. (*Bank of Rome* v. *Vil. of Rome,* 18 N. Y. 38 ; *Starin* v. *Town of Genoa,* 23 id. 439 ; *Clarke* v. *City of Rochester,* 28 id. 605 ; *Bank of Chenango* v. *Brown,* 26 id. 467 ; *Matter of Gilbert El. Ry. Co.,* 70 id. 361, 374 ; *Vil. of Gloversville* v. *Howell,* id. 287 ; *Home Ins. Co.* v. *Swigert,* MSS. opinion ; *Locke's Appeal,* 72 Penn. St. 491 ; *Kerrigan* v. *Force,* 68 N. Y. 381.) The law of 1881, which is confessedly a substitute for the former methods of State taxation, does not affect any tax which those former methods did not affect. (*People, ex rel.* v. *Davenport,* 25 Hun, 630, 632; Ct. of Appeals, MSS., March 13, 1883; 2 R. S. [7th ed.] 1447, § 7.)

Joseph H. Choate for respondent. The act of 1865 is void, because it involves an improper delegation of legislative power. (*Clark* v. *Port of Mobile,* 10 Ins. Law Jour. 361.) The legislature neither must nor can transfer the power of making laws to anybody else, or place it anywhere but where the people have. (2 Locke on Civ. Gov. [ed. 1766] 273; Cooley on Taxation, 48; *Burlow* v. *Himrod,* 8 N. Y. 483; *Bradley* v. *Baxter,* 15 Barb. 122; *Thorne* v. *Cramer,* id. 112; *Foss* v. *City of Chicago,* 56 Ill. 354.) The act in question is in direct conflict with article 7, section 13, of the Constitution of 1846, which provides that every law which continues, imposes or revives a tax shall distinctly state the tax and the object to which it is to be applied, and it shall not be sufficient to refer to any other law to fix such tax or object. (Cooley on Taxation, 397.) The act of 1863 is in direct conflict with the first section of the fourteenth amendment of the Constitution of the United States. (*Missouri* v. *Lewis*, 101 U. S. 22; *Pearson* v. *City of Portland*, 69 Me. 278 ; *City of Portland* v. *City of Bangor*, 65 id. 120; *Northwestern F. Co.* v. *Town of Hyde Park*, 3 Biss. 480 ; *Bank of U. S.* v. *Devereux*, 5 Cranch, 61; *Detroit* v. *D. & H. P. R. Co.*, 43 Mich. 140, 147 ; *N. Y. C. & H. R. R. R. Co.* v. *Met. Gas L. Co.*, 63 N. Y. 326 ; *Matter of Roch. Water Co.*, 66 id. 413 ; *County of San Mateo* v. *So. Pac. R. R. Co.*, 13 Fed. Rep. 722.) The legislative department has not unlimited power to prescribe a class, or what companies shall constitute a class; classification must be with equal protection to all under the same circumstances. (*Bureau Co.* v. *Chicago, etc., R. R. Co.*, 44 Ill. 229 ; *All-hands* v. *The People*, 82 id. 234 ; *Hughes* v. *City of Cairo*, 92 id. 339 ; Cooley on Taxation, 128.)

FINCH, J. The legislation of the State relating to foreign insurance companies is challenged on this appeal as a violation of constitutional right. The act of 1875 (Chap. 60) in substance provides, that an insurance corporation of another State, seeking to do business here, shall pay to the superintendent of the insurance department for taxes, fines, penalties, certificates of authority, license fees and otherwise, an amount equal to that imposed by the State of its origin upon companies of this State seeking to do business there, when such amount charged is greater than our own. The evident purpose of the act is to treat the corporations of another State seeking to transact business here precisely as such other State should treat our own corporations seeking to do business there. It rests upon the idea that the comity due from one State to another is not required to be more than equal and reciprocal, and what is wholly matter of privilege may be granted or withheld upon conditions.

This legislation is assailed, first, upon the ground that it is an unlawful delegation of the legislative power, and the General Term have so held upon the authority of *Barto* v. *Him-*

rod (8 N. Y. 483). We do not think that case at all decisive
of this. What was there denominated the school law came
from the hands of the legislature, not as a law, but as a proposition. Whether it should be a law or not was precisely the
question submitted to the popular vote. The legislature proposed the law, but left it to the people to enact. The process
carried out and applied to all bills would have resulted in a
complete abdication by the senate and assembly of their authority and functions. Instead of making laws they would
simply have suggested them, reported them for consideration,
but left the judgment upon them, the determination of their
expediency and wisdom, to an authority outside of their own.
As to the school law, the people were made the legislature, and
left to decide whether the bill proposed should or should not
become a law. This court held that the legislature, under the
Constitution, could not so delegate its power, but was bound
to determine for itself the expediency of the measure, and
either enact or reject it. But nothing in that decision denied
to the legislature the right to pass a law whose operation
might depend upon, or be affected by, a future contingency.
The opinions expressly conceded the existence of such power.
It was not denied that a valid statute may be passed to take
effect upon the happening of some future event, certain or
uncertain. And this was said as to the character of such
event, viz.: "The event or change of circumstances on which
a law may be made to take effect must be such as, in the judgment of the legislature, affects the expediency of the law; an
event on which the expediency of the law in the judgment of
the law-makers depends. On this question of expediency the
legislature must exercise its own judgment definitively and
finally." The statute before us fully answers this description.
It came from the hands of the legislature a complete and perfect law, having at once a binding force of its own, and dependent upon no additional consent or action for its vitality
and existence. The question of expediency involved in it
was not delegated to any other tribunal, but settled definitively
and finally by the legislature itself. It determined, as a con-

clusion proper and expedient, that foreign insurance companies, as the price of admission to our territory, should pay in taxes, license fees and the like precisely what the States which created them should impose upon our companies in excess of our usual rates as the price of admission to the foreign territory. That was the whole question involved. Nothing else in the proposed law remained to be settled as expedient or otherwise, and that question the legislature determined for itself, upon its own reasons and its sole responsibility. Neither the law nor its expediency depended upon the legislation of another State. It remained the law and its expediency was the same, whether other States legislated or not. If they did, the contingency arose which the law stood ready to meet; if they did not, it remained none the less the law, although no fact occurred to set it in operation. This court has steadily declined to push the doctrine of *Barto* v. *Himrod* beyond the point which it decided. In *Bank of Rome* v. *Village of Rome* (18 N. Y. 39) we sustained as constitutional an act conferring upon municipal authorities certain powers not to be exercised until the act had been approved by two-thirds of the tax payers. The distinction taken was that the law took effect immediately, and conferred the necessary power, but did not compel the village to act under it unless the tax payers so determined. The law was complete, although its operation depended upon a contingency, which might or might not happen. A similar distinction was taken in other cases. (*Starin* v. *Town of Genoa*, 23 N. Y. 439; *Bank of Chenango* v. *Brown*, 26 id. 467; *Clarke* v. *City of Rochester*, 28 id. 605.) While there were differences of opinion in these cases as to the precise grounds which distinguished them from *Barto* v. *Himrod*, there was an entire concurrence in the construction put upon the latter case, a construction which makes it inapplicable to the statute under consideration.

But it is argued that this act offends, although not in the same manner as the school law, by leaving the amount of the tax or fine to the legislative discretion of another State. The argument is, that the nature of the attempted legislation is vicious; that what the amount of a tax, fine, penalty or license shall be is essentially the direct and immediate effect of statutory enactment; that the act in question does not determine it; that it remits it to the legislature of another State by its enactments to create or change the tax.   Authority for this criticism is found in a decision in Alabama (*Clark & Murrell* v. *The Port of Mobile,* 10 Ins. Law Jour.) and in one in Indiana (id. 361). But the whole argument rests on the single point that the amount of the tax or fine imposed is not definitely fixed by the terms of the statute, but depends above a certain rate upon foreign legislation.   Is it true that a fine or tax cannot be imposed unless its amount be stated in the law?   And that, if left to be determined by some other tribunal, thereby the legislative power has been delegated?   Laws define a multitude of forbidden acts and impose fines and penalties not exceeding certain amounts, but below those amounts left wholly uncertain and committed to the discretion and judgment of judicial officers or tribunals.   It is quite certain, therefore, that the legislature does not abdicate its functions and delegate its authority when it imposes a fine or penalty without itself fixing the amount, or when it leaves it to be fixed by some other tribunal.   But in the statute before us nothing is left to anybody's discretion.   That is certain which can be rendered certain, and the act fixes the tax by reference to an extrinsic fact which determines its amount in excess of a fixed and established rate.   Because that extrinsic fact is the legislation of another State, it does not follow that the legislative discretion of such other State is in any manner substituted for our own.   The opinion in the case decided in Alabama turns upon what appears to us to be this error.   It asserts that the law of which it speaks "authorizes in effect the legislature of Mississippi, speaking through its statutes, which are the subjects of extrinsic proof and not of judicial knowledge in our courts, to fix by law the amount which the treasurer of Alabama shall demand of appellants as a license tax to do business in this State."   A similar inference from our own statute is pressed upon us in the case at bar.   But if, when our

statute was passed, there had been in existence a law of Pennsylvania, imposing upon New York companies a license fee of three per cent, and because of that fact our legislature had enacted that all Pennsylvania companies should pay a license fee of three per cent, would that law have been a delegation of legislative authority to the State of Pennsylvania? Most clearly not, although the fact of the foreign law lay at the foundation of our legislative judgment and discretion. And if, within a month, the foreign law changed the impost to four per cent, and our own legislature, again ascertaining the fact, and because of it should change our tax to four per cent, would that be Pennsylvania legislation and not our own? And what would be certainly constitutional if done *seriatim*, by several and separate acts, does it become unconstitutional when the same precise and identical result, founded upon exactly the same legislative discretion, is accomplished by one? If so, a grave constitutional question is made to turn upon the bare form instead of the substance of legislative action. It seems to us that the whole difficulty arises from a failure to regard the foreign law, relatively to our own legislation, as simply and purely an extrinsic and contingent fact. Such fact, like any other, may justly influence and even occasion legislative action, without at all changing its nature, destroying its discretion or abridging its duties or its judgment. Most laws are made to meet future facts. They are complete when passed, but sleep until the contingency contemplated sets them in operation. A law which defines and punishes murder is none the less complete and authoritative although no murder be committed, and so the contingency it was framed to meet does not occur. Such contingency may sometimes be, instead of a certain and definite fact, one which is variable and changeable. The legislation suited to such a fact and adapted to such a future emergency may properly recognize its movable character, and be itself made flexible to the changing emergency, and this very characteristic is the product of legislative will and discretion rather than a surrender of it. If a foreign nation should impose upon American shipping onerous and severe harbor dues, with

a view of crippling our commerce and gaining for itself our
carrying trade, and because of this Congress should pass an act
imposing upon the vessels of such nation coming into our
ports such and the same harbor dues as by their laws should
be at the time charged upon our shipping, the act would be one
of retaliation; deliberately intended to operate according to
the measure of the foreign law, treated as an existing or contingent fact; but could not justly be said to amount to an abdication by Congress of its legislative discretion and judgment.

Possibly we may get nearer to the ultimate point of the objection urged. That would seem to be that, while the legislature might, by a series of separate acts, each passed because of
a then existing foreign law, follow its changes, yet it cannot do
so by one act which adopts and enacts such future and contingent mutations. This doctrine requires us to hold that a law,
so framed as to follow and recognize the changes of foreign
legislation, and thereby incorporate such changes into its own
operation, is a delegation of the legislative power and therefore inadmissible. We have found no authority for such a
broad and general proposition. What has been said upon the
subject is to the contrary, except, perhaps, inferentially by the
ruling in specific cases. In *State* v. *Parker* (26 Vt. 365)
the general subject was discussed and it was said : "If the
operation of a law may fairly be made to depend upon a future
contingency, then, it makes no essential difference what is the
nature of the contingency, so it be an equal and fair one, a
moral and legal one, not opposed to sound policy, *and so far
connected with the object of the statute as not to be a mere idle
and arbitrary one.*" And it was added : "One may find any
number of cases, in the legislation of Congress, where statutes
have been made dependent upon the *shifting* character of the
revenue laws, or the navigation laws, or commercial rules,
edicts, or restrictions of other countries." How true this is,
and how dangerous would be a denial of the power to legislate
in such manner, may be made more apparent by examples.
The non-intercourse acts of the three years beginning with

1809 were made in terms dependent upon the action of France and England toward this country, and were to be revived or revoked according to the course of the foreign law, the effect of which was to be determined by the president and declared by his proclamation. This instance is cited in *Bull* v. *Read* (13 Gratt. 90) as a law depending upon an uncertain future contingency, and an objection taken in the Federal courts that the power of legislation was transferred to the president was disregarded. (*Cargo of Brig Aurora* v. *United States*, 7 Cranch, 386.) In *Williams* v. *Bank of Michigan* (7 Wend. 540) it appeared that by an ordinance of Congress, passed in 1787, the governor and judges of the north-western territory were authorized to adopt and publish in the district such laws of the original States, both civil and criminal, as might be necessary and best suited to the circumstances of the district. In 1805 Michigan was made a separate territory with a government "in all respects similar" to that provided for the north-western territory. Under this legislation it was held that the governor and judges of Michigan could legally incorporate a banking institution. The duty of making laws for the territory was saved only to the national legislature by its power of disapproval. Congress has legislative power over the formation and procedure of the Federal judiciary. It is provided (§ 914, U. S. R. S.) that the practice, pleadings, and forms and modes of proceeding in civil causes, other than equity and admiralty causes, in the Circuit and District Courts shall conform as near as may be to those existing at the time in like causes in the courts of record of the State within which such Circuit and District Courts are held. And more specifically it is ordained that jurors to serve in the Federal courts shall have the same qualifications and be entitled to the same exemptions, and shall be designated by ballot, lot or otherwise, according to the mode of forming such juries then practiced in the State courts. Coming to our own legislation, we notice that affidavits taken in another State may be effectual here if taken before any officer authorized by the laws of such State to take affidavits. (3 R. S. [6th ed.] 657, § 27.) A deed may be recorded or

read in evidence in this State when made by a person residing
without the State and in some other State or territory if proved,
or acknowledged before any officer "authorized by the laws
thereof" to take the proof and acknowledgment of deeds.   (2
R. S. [6th ed.] 1140, § 5.)   And wills of personal estate, duly
executed by persons residing out of this State, "according to
the laws of the State or country in which the same were
made," may be proved and established and become valid and
effectual here.   These illustrations are not strictly analogous,
but they tend to show how a law may be made to fit a changing event, and follow it, and adjust itself to it, through a
series of future mutations, and those, too, made by foreign
legislation, or the voluntary action of other bodies; and they
indicate also the dangers of forbidding such discretion.   But
it is said the doctrine thus asserted would permit one State to
adopt the law of another State together with its future
changes by one sweeping enactment; and, for an example, that
New York might enact that the rate of interest here for the
loan of money should be such and the same as that which
should be from time to time prescribed by the law of
Maine.   These are seeming, but in reality false analogies.
They are pure cases of an abdication of its functions by the
legislature and of an unwarranted delegation of its authority.
But that is so because there is no dependent or causative connection between the domestic and the foreign law, as was said
in *State* v. *Parker* (*supra*); and because, as was explained in
Barto v. *Himrod*, the event upon which the law is made to
take effect is not one on which the expediency of the law in
the judgment of the law-makers depends.   In other words, no
legislative judgment is involved.   Perhaps we can test the distinction in another way.   We may compare the law as to interest above-mentioned, and the one before us, in respect to
their capacity, to be debated on the merits.   The former would
have no merits and could not be debated.   The only discussion
on its merits would be in Maine, and there it would be over its
law, and that when enacted would become our law.   The debate upon the expediency of the particular rate to be charged

would be all there, and our legislature would form no judgment upon it and could not debate it. The only thing they could debate would be whether they should thus abdicate their own judgment and authority. But the law before us could be debated on the merits, and passed or rejected as the result of legislative judgment and discretion. On one side it could be argued that the proposed law was just and wise; that it gave needed protection to our own corporations going beyond our borders; that it aimed to produce equality of privilege; that unless the legislature remained in continual session the law must be adjusted to meet emergencies occurring during its recess; that the bill was framed to meet that emergency and was expedient on its own merits. On the other side it could be said that the measure would be inherently vicious because in the nature of retaliation; and a change might be made in the foreign State which we should be reluctant to follow. And to this the reply would come that as the tax involved did not touch or interfere with our general system of taxation, and was merely a license fee or price of admission to our jurisdiction, that it could properly be adjusted to the prices charged, and follow them whenever in excess of our established rates; and, if such excess should be taken away entirely, precisely the good result arrived at would be accomplished; corporations would freely pass both borders, paying only the equal rates of ordinary and just taxation. There is thus developed the clear and wide difference between the two laws. One has merits of its own; the other has none. The expediency of one is debatable; that of the other is not. The one is enacted *because* of the foreign law; the other only *according* to the foreign law. The one is passed for legislative reasons and out of a legislative discretion which the foreign law and its possible mutations engender; the other without any such reasons and with no reason whatever, but only through trust in a foreign reason. It seems to us that the difference is plain and decisive. The law before us preserves our normal and ordinary rate of taxation in any event and operates only when the foreign rate rises above it, and cannot be justly held unconstitutional as involving a delegation of the legislative discretion. We should not so determine except in a very clear and certain case, and be careful not to restrain or hamper, without obvious necessity, the scope and range of the legislative authority. Legislation which retaliates is not inevitably vicious. It may sometimes be just, and often be necessary and even indispensable. In its inherent nature it is founded upon and adapts itself to the foreign law as a fact or contingency to be met. In any given instance it may be wise or unwise, but we are not ready to adopt a doctrine which denounces it as unconstitutional because it openly professes and declares itself to be precisely what it is, and fails to disguise itself in the form of separate acts following the mutations of the foreign law without confessing the fact. And that such legislation is not necessarily vicious, and may be in a given case entirely just and perfectly fair, will appear as we proceed to consider some further questions.

A second objection to the constitutionality of the act is founded upon article 14 of the Federal Constitution, and especially upon its final clause which commands that no State shall " deny to any person within its jurisdiction the equal protection of the laws." The argument here takes a wide range, and touches upon questions of supreme and vital importance as to the relations of the States to each other, and of each to the United States. Corporations are claimed to be "persons" within the meaning and protection of the clause referred to; its force and operation is carried beyond the limit indicated by the emergency from which it sprang; and it is asserted to forbid unequal taxation and condemn such legislation as that under consideration. But we think these grave questions are not before us, and the clause relied upon has no application to the rights of the defendant. It is a corporation, organized and existing under the laws of Pennsylvania; a creature of those laws, and beyond their jurisdiction, carrying its corporate life and existence only by sufferance and upon an express or implied consent. It could not come within our jurisdiction, or transact business within our territory except by our permission either express or implied. The right of a State to exclude foreign corporations is perfectly settled and not open to debate. (*Paul* v. *Virginia*, 8 Wall. 168; *Bank of Augusta* v. *Earle*, 13 Pet. 586; *Liverpool Ins. Co.* v. *Massachusetts*, 10 Wall. 566; *Co. of San Mateo* v. *S. P. R. Co.*, 13 Fed. Rep. 722, FIELD, J.) Out of comity between the States has grown a right founded upon implied consent. Where a State does not forbid, or its public policy, as evidenced by its statutes, is not infringed, a foreign corporation may transact business within its boundaries and be entitled to the protection of its laws. But this right is still founded upon consent which is implied from comity and the absence of prohibition. But a State may prohibit. This State did prohibit and has steadily continued to prohibit the transaction of business within its limits by foreign fire insurance companies except upon certain express terms and conditions. By the act of 1853 as amended (2 R. S. [5th ed.] 762, § 54), fire insurance companies incorporated by any other State were forbidden "directly or indirectly to take risks or transact any business of insurance in this State," unless upon compliance with certain specified conditions. In 1871 (Chap. 388, § 5) the prohibition was repeated except upon the fulfillment of all the requirements of the laws then in force together with those named in that act. The law now under consideration was then in force, having been passed in 1865 (Chap. 694). The amendment of 1875 simply added a provision authorizing the superintendent to remit certain fees and charges. The situation then is this : The State, having the power to exclude foreign corporations, determines to do so unless they will submit to certain conditions. It meets the applicant on the border, forbidding admission, as it has a right to do, except on condition that it will fulfill all of the requirements of our statutes relating to foreign corporations, one of which is the very law here assailed. When the corporation comes in it agrees to the conditions. They become binding by its assent. The tax or license fee charged by the act of 1865 is one of these conditions. It is imposed as the price of permission to come within the jurisdiction, and not as a tax upon one already within the jurisdiction. The fourteenth amendment, therefore, has no application. It can apply to foreign insurance companies only after they have performed the conditions upon which they are entitled to admission. Any other view of the case involves this absurdity: that the foreign company may agree to pay the tax charged by the act of 1865 so as to get within our jurisdiction, and then refuse to pay it while insisting upon the right to remain. It cannot agree to conditions as the price of admission, and after having been admitted turn around and dispute them. Even if the conditions were unconstitutional, which cannot be said of the terms of the act of 1865, considered as conditions, the foreign company could waive the objection (*Embury* v. *Conner*, 3 N. Y. 511; *Sherman* v. *McKeon*, 38 id. 267; *Phyfe* v. *Eimer*, 45 id. 103); and does do so when it accepts the conditions by coming in under them, and is estopped from raising the question. (*Vose* v. *Cockcroft*, 44 N. Y. 415.) Even where the condition was a violation of the Federal Constitution and the Supreme Court of the United States so declared, they refused to prevent the State from excluding the offending company and revoking its license. (*Doyle* v. *Continental Ins. Co.*, 94 U. S. 535.) By that process, even in such a case, obedience could be compelled, at the peril of removal from the State. But in the case before us the condition imposed is not a violation of the Federal Constitution upon any construction of the final clause of the fourteenth article, for that relates wholly to persons within the jurisdiction, already there in fact and of right, and their treatment thereafter, and not at all to the terms and conditions on which alone they can come in. This view of the case renders of no importance the argument founded on the word "tax," and the distinction sought to be drawn between that and a license fee. Grant that it is properly denominated a tax, yet the payment of a specific tax may be imposed as a condition of assent to fire insurance within the State, and, as we have seen, has been so imposed by express and positive law. Its nature as a condition precedent is not altered by its name. The constitutional difference between the rights of non-resident individuals and foreign corporations is fundamental and apparent. The citizen of another State has a constitutional right to come within our jurisdiction. The charter of the nation has secured him that right, and we cannot exclude him nor clog his right with conditions, unless in exceptional cases under the police power. But foreign corporations, artificial beings, the product of a law not our own, have no constitutional right to pass their own borders and come into ours. The Federal Constitution has neither granted nor secured any such right. We may exclude absolutely, and in that power is involved the right to admit upon such conditions as we please. Until they are within our jurisdiction, the final clause of article 14, by its own terms, does not apply. While they stand at the door bargaining for the right to come within, they may decline to come, but cannot question our conditions if they do. How then is the legislation vicious which proposes to treat them precisely as their own State treats our corporations similarly situated? Is exact equality unfair? Must comity become magnanimity or injustice? If we owe courtesy to sister States, do we not also owe protection to our own corporations, formed and fostered under our law? Is it vicious to insist for them upon precise equality of·treatment? These questions our legislature answered. The inquiry was within the just range of their discretion. This court, at least, is bound to assume, and finds no difficulty in assuming, that they answered it wisely and justly.

A third ground of objection may be more briefly dismissed. Reference is made to article 3, section 20 of the State Constitution, which provides that "any law which imposes, continues or revives a tax shall distinctly state the tax and the object to which it is to be applied, and it shall not be sufficient to refer to any other law to fix such tax or object." We are of opinion that this provision does not relate to a tax imposed as a condition upon a foreign insurance company, and, therefore, in fact in the nature of a license fee, and that the tax covered by the constitutional provision is one general in its provisions and co-extensive with the State. (*People* v. *Supervisors of Chenango*, 8 N. Y. 326.)

The point taken as to the effect of the law of 1881 (Chap. 361, § 8) is substantially disposed of by our decision in *People, ex rel. Westchester F. Ins. Co.*, v. *Davenport* (91 N. Y. 574). We there held that the exemption under the law of 1880 was from the general taxes levied for the general purposes of the State. The same construction must apply to the act of 1881.

The final question raised is over the amount to be collected. We think the act requires, in the present case, a full payment of three per cent upon the premiums received, and if any part of it has not been paid, because there was no fire department in a particular locality to receive it, such amount must be added to the sum payable to the superintendent. He must receive such sum as with the other payments will equal the three per cent required.

The judgment of the General Term should be reversed and judgment entered for the plaintiffs for $1,848.45, with interest from January 15, 1882, with costs.

All concur.

Judgment accordingly.

THE PEOPLE OF THE STATE OF NEW YORK, Respondents, *v.* THE HOME INSURANCE COMPANY, Appellant.

577

The statement in the act (Chap. 542, Laws of 1880, as amended by chap. 361, Laws of 1881) providing for the taxation of certain corporations and associations, that the taxes imposed thereby "shall be applicable to the payment of the ordinary and current expenses of the State," is a sufficient compliance with the requirement of the State Constitution (Art. 3, § 20) that every law imposing a tax "shall distinctly state * * * the object to which it is to be applied."

The taxes upon corporations, imposed by said act, are taxes upon franchises, not upon property, and the fact that dividends, a portion of which is derived from securities exempt from taxation, furnish the basis for computing the amount of the tax, does not invalidate it.

In taxing corporations under the act the State authorities are not required to deduct the amount of stock which the corporation holds in United States bonds from the total amount of its capital stock and to compute the tax only upon dividends derived from the remainder.

The legislature has, by virtue of its jurisdiction over corporations organized under its laws, authority to impose such a tax.

In performing the duty of levying taxes the legislature may, in its discretion, impose unequal or double taxes, and in determining the question of legislative power the courts are precluded from considering that question.

It seems, however, that the corporations affected by said act are not thereby subjected to unequal or double taxation.

The authorities showing the distinction between franchise and property taxes collated.

(Argued March 29, 1883 ; decided May 1, 1883.)

APPEAL from judgment of the General Term of the Supreme Court, in the third judicial department, in favor of the plaintiff, entered upon a case submitted under section 1279 of the Code of Civil Procedure.

The facts stated in the case submitted are substantially as follows. Defendant, a domestic fire insurance company, in the year 1881, had a capital stock of $3,000,000. On January 1 and July 1, of that year, it declared semi-annual dividends of five per cent each. On January 1, of that year, it had $3,300,000 invested in United States bonds, and on July 1, it had $1,940,-000 so invested ; on November 15, it made its report to the State comptroller, as required by the act chapter 542, Laws of 1880, as amended by chapter 361, Laws of 1881, and it tendered to that officer a tax at the rate of one and one-quarter mills upon $1,060,000, which tender was rejected, the comptroller claiming $7,500, " being a tax of one-quarter of a mill upon defendant's capital stock for each one per centum of dividend." The question presented for determination was as to whether any, and if so how much, tax should be aid by defendant under said act.

Benjamin H. Bristow for appellant. A tax law must state its object distinctly. (Const., art. 3, § 20.) The object stated in a tax law must be either a defined expenditure, a defined class of expenditures, or a defined fund for future expenditures. (*Sun Mut. Ins. Co.* v. *City of New York.* 5 Sandf. 10; *People* v. *Sup'vrs of Orange*, 17 N. Y. 235.) "The ordinary and current expenses of the State" is an indefinable object. (R. S., part 1, chap. 9, tit. 1, § 16 [8]; Laws of 1882, chap. 362.) The statement of object in the tax law in question is a delegation of legislative duty, and is, therefore, unconstitutional. (*People* v. *Sup'rs of Kings*, 52 N. Y. 556, 7, 69; Cooley's Const. Lim. 116.) A tax invalid under one name is invalid under any other. (*Macbeth* v. *Ashley*, L. R., 2 Sc. App. 352, 352, 358; *Passenger Cases*, 7 How. 283, 458; *People* v. *Draper*, 15 N. Y. 532, 539; *Inman St'shp Co.* v. *Tinker*, 94 U. S. 238–244; *R. R. Co.* v. *Husen*, 25 id. 465, 472; *Almy* v. *California*, 24 How. 169; *Bank Tax Case*, 2 Wall. 200; *Henderson* v. *Mayor of N. Y.*, 92 U. S. 259, 268; *People* v. *Allen*, 42 N. Y. 404, 413; *Monroe Sav. B'k* v. *Rochester*, 37 id. 365, 7; *New Hampshire* v. *Louisiana*, U. S. Sup. Ct., March 5, 1883.) It is true in particular of so-called franchise and business taxes. (*Cook* v. *Pennsylvania*, 97 U. S. 566; *Webber* v. *Virginia*, 103 id. 344, 350; *Tel. Co.* v. *Texas*, 105 id. 460, 465.) The tax in question was not a franchise or business, as contra-distinguished from a property tax. (*Monroe Sav. B'k* v. *Rochester*, 37 N. Y. 365, 7; *Burke* v. *Bodlam*, 57 Cal. 594, 601; *Porter* v. *Rockf., R. I. & St. L. R. R. Co.*, 76 Ill. 561, 578; *Veazie B'k* v. *Fenno*, 8 Wall. 543, 547; *State R. R. Tax Cases*, 92 U. S. 575, 602–607; *San Jose Gas Co.* v. *January*, 57 Cal. 614; *Lane County* v. *Oregon*, 7 Wall. 71, 77.) The tax in question impedes and burdens the operations of the United States and is in so far invalid. (*McCullough* v. *Maryland*, 4 Wheat. 316, 436; *Lane County* v. *Oregon*, 7 Wall. 71, 77; *Bank* v. *Sup'vrs*, id. 26, 30.) A general tax on property, when United States bonds form part of the property, is in so far a tax on the bonds, and in so far invalid. (*B'k of Commerce* v. *N. Y. City*, 2 Black, 620; *Weston* v. *Charleston*, 2 Pet. 349.) Any thing equivalent to a tax on capital stock is a general tax on the property of the corporation taxed. (*B'k of*

Commerce v. *N. Y. City*, 2 Black, 620 ; *People* v. *Comm'rs, etc.*, 23 N. Y. 192, 193–5 ; *Bank Tax Case*, 2 Wall. 200, 207 ; *Chadwick* v. *Crapsey*, 35 N. Y. 196, 202 ; *Lackawanna Co.* v.* B'k of Scranton*, 94 Penn. St. 221 ; *New Haven* v. *City B'k*, 31 Conn. 106 ; *Trustees of Connersville* v. *B'k of Indiana*, 16 Ind. 105 ; *Burrall* v. *Bushwick R. R. Co.*, 75 N. Y. 211, 216 ; *Wynhamer* v. *People*, 13 id. 378, 433 ; *People, ex rel. Leonard*, v. *Comm'rs, etc.*, 90 id. 63.) The tax in question is a tax on capital stock at its actual value, and a further tax on any item of the property of a company taxed under this law would be double taxation. (*Lackawanna Iron Co.* v. *Luzerne Co.*, 42 Penn. St. 424, 30 ; *Westchester Gas Co.* v. *County of Chester*, 30 id. 232 ; *Coatesville Gas Co.* v. *County of Chester*, 97 id. 476, 81 ; *Phœnix Iron Co* v. *Commonwealth*, 59 id. 104 ; *Lehigh Crane Iron Co.* v. *Comm.*, 55 id. 448, 451.) The tax in question is a tax on capital stock at a valuation varying as the dividends vary. (*Comm.* v. *C. P. & A. R. R. Co.*, 29 Penn. St. 370 ; *Lehigh Crane Iron Co.* v. *Comm.*, 55 id. 448 ; *Oswego Starch Factory* v. *Dolloway*, 21 N. Y. 449.) Holding the tax in question not to be a tax on property would make it unequal, oppressive and unconstitutional. (*People* v. *Comm'rs*, 76 N. Y. 64, 71 ; *People* v. *Sup'vrs of New York*, 16 id. 424, 439 ; *S. C.*, 20 Barb. 81, 88 ; R. S., part 1, chap. 13, tit. 1, §§ 1, 3, 7 ; Laws of 1881, chap. 361, § 8 ; Cooley on Taxation, 165 ; *Mygatt* v. *Washburn*, 15 N. Y. 316, 319 ; U. S. Const., 14th amendment, § 1 ; Const. of N. Y., art. 1, § 6 ; *Co. of San Mateo* v. *So. Pac. R. R. Co.*, 13 Fed. Rep. 722 ; *Society, etc.*, v. *Town of New Haven*, 8 Wheat. 464, 489 ; *U. S.* v. *Amedy*, 11 id. 392, 412 ; 1 Blackst. Comm. 123 ; 2 Kent's Comm. 267 ; *People* v. *Utica Ins. Co.*, 15 Johns. 358, 382 ; *Detroit* v. *Detroit & H. P. R. Co.*, 43 Mich. 140 ; *Sinking Fund Cases*, 99 U. S. 700, 720, 721 ; *Comm.* v. *Essex Co.*, 13 Gray, 239, 253 ; *Stuart* v. *Palmer*, 74 N. Y. 183, 189, 195 ; *Gordon* v. *Comes*, 47 id. 608, 612 ; *City of Lexington* v. *McMillan's Heirs*, 9 Dana [Ky.], 513 ; *Howell* v. *Bristol*, 8 Bush [Ky.], 498 ; *Parish of Orleans* v. *Cochran*, 20 La. Ann. 373 ;

Burroughs on Taxation, 68; *Portland B'k* v. *Apthorp*, 12 Mass. 252, 258.)

S. B. Brownell, Julien T. Davies, George Richards, John O. Heald and Edward Lyman Short for companies similarly situated with appellant. The statutes fail to state the object of the tax. (*Sun Mutual* v. *Mayor*, 5 Sandf. 10; 8 N. Y. 241; *People* v. *Sup'rs*, 17 id. 235; *Black River B'k* v. *Sup'rs*, 27 Barb. 583; *People* v. *Sup'rs*, 52 N. Y. 556.) The tax is on the property and not on the franchises or business. (*B'k* v. *Tax Comm'rs*, 2 Blatchf. 620; *People* v. *Comm'rs*, 23 N. Y. 192; *People* v. *Pacific Mail S. S. Co.* v. *Tax Comm'rs*, 5 Hun, 200; 64 N. Y. 541; *Lehigh Crane Iron Co.* v. *Comm'rs*, 55 Penn. St. 457; *Comm'rs* v. *P., Ft. W. & C. R. R.*, 74 id. 83; *Catawissa R. R. Co.'s Appeal*, 78 id. 59; *Hamilton Co.* v. *Comm'rs*, 12 Weekly N. C. 328.) The use of "franchise" in the act of 1881 is without avail. (*People* v. *Compagnie, etc.*, 2 Sup. Ct. Rep. 87; *U. S.* v. *Erie Ry.*, 5 Mo. St. 836.) A franchise tax is different from the present one. (*Spring Valley* v. *Schottler*, 10 Pac. Coast L. J. 430; *Williams* v. *Rees*, 9 Biss. 405; *Atlantic, etc., R. R. Co.* v. *Comm'rs*, 87 N. C. 129; *R. R. Co.* v. *Comm'rs*, id. 426; *Oliver* v. *Mills*, 11 Allen, 273.) Capital stock invested in United States bonds cannot be taxed by the State. (*Weston* v. *Charleston*, 2 Pet. 449; *B'k of Commerce* v. *New York*, 2 Black, 620; *Monroe B'k* v. *Rochester*, 37 N. Y. 365; *People, ex rel. Leonard*, v. *Tax Comm'rs*, 15 W'kly Dig. 299.) The court will look beyond mere words. (*Memphis R. R. Co.* v. *Nolan*, 14 Fed. Rep. 532.) The acts are void because there is no reasonable rule of apportionment. (*State* v. *Auditor*, 46 Mich. 231; *Olcott* v. *Sup'rs*, 16 Wall. 689; *People* v. *Comm'rs*, 76 N. Y. 71; *People* v. *Salem*, 20 Mich. 452; *Gordon* v. *Carnes*, 47 N. Y. 608; Cooley, 60; Burroughs, § 26; *Loan Ass'n* v. *Topeka*, 20 Wall. 655.) The principle of equality of taxation is violated by section 3, chapter 371, Laws of 1881. (*Penn. R. R. Co.* v. *Comm'rs*, 94 Penn. St. 474; *Hamilton Co.* v. *Ivan*, 6 Wall. 641; *Comm'rs*

v. *Hamilton*, 12 Allen, 308; *Penn. R. R. Co.* v. *Comm'rs*, 94 Penn. St. 479; *Lehigh, etc., Co.* v. *Comm'rs*, 55 id. 451; *Comm'rs* v. *P., Ft. W. & C. Ry. Co.*, 74 id. 92; *Howell* v. *Bristol*, 8 Barb. 498; *Comm'rs* v. *Sav'gs B'k*, 5 Allen, 437.) Equality of burden does not exist as between corporations liable to taxation under section 3 and those not liable to taxation under that section, but where capital stock is liable to local taxation, and where real estate is taxed. (*Oswego* v. *Holloway*, 21 N. Y. 45; *People* v. *B'd of Assessment*, 39 id. 81; *People* v. *Harland*, 61 Barb. 273; *B'k* v. *Tennessee*, 104 U. S. 695; *R. R. Co.* v. *Comm'rs*, 87 N. C. 426.) The State has denied to the defendant the equal protection of the laws. (*San Mateo* v. *South. Pac. R. R. Co.*, 13 Fed. Rep. 722.) The State has deprived the defendant of the property for public use, without just compensation. (*Gordon* v. *Caines*, 47 N. Y. 612; *City of Lexington* v. *McMillan's Heirs*, 9 Dana, 513; *Howell* v. *Bristol*, 8 Bush, 498.) In this State the principle of equality is a constitutional one. (*Baldwin* v. *Mayor*, 2 Keyes, 396; *Farmers' Loan & Trust Co.* v. *Mayor*, 7 Hill, 299; *Colonial Life Ass. Co.* v. *B'd of Sup'rs*, 4 Abb. 88; *People* v. *B'd of Sup'rs*, 16 N. Y. 439; *People* v. *Comm'rs of Taxes*, 23 id. 196; *Stuart* v. *Palmer*, 74 id. 189; *People* v. *B'd of Sup'rs*, 20 Barb. 88; *Cowen* v. *Folsom*, 13 Minn. 222.)

Leslie W. Russell, attorney-general, for respondent. The statement in chapter 542 of the Laws of 1880, as amended by chapter 361 of the Laws of 1881, that the taxes derived " shall be applicable to the payment of the ordinary and current expenses of the State," was a sufficiently distinct statement of the tax and the object to which it was to be applied under section 20 of article 3 of the Constitution. (*People, ex rel. Burroughs,* v. *Supervisors of Orange Co.*, 17 N. Y. 235, 240, 241; *Sun Mut. Ins. Co.* v. *The Mayor*, 5 Sandf. 10, 14, 15; 8 N. Y. 241; *People* v. *Nat. Ins. Co.*, 27 Hun, 188; Laws of 1871, chap. 717; Laws of 1877, chap. 341; Laws of 1879, chap. 372; Laws of 1881, chap. 453; 1 R. S. [7th ed.] 494; id. 495,

§§ 4, 5, 16, subd. 8; *People* v. *Superv'rs of Chenango Co.,* 8 N. Y. 317, 326, 327.) The franchise of a corporation is equally subject to taxation as its property. (*Provident Inst.* v. *Massachusetts,* 6 Wall. 611, 622; *Soc. for Svgs.* v. *Coite,* 6 Wall. 594; *Portland B'k* v. *Apthorp,* 12 Mass. 252; *Comm.* v. *Five Cent Svgs. B'k,* 5 Allen, 431; Burroughs on Taxation, 164, 165, § 83; *Hamilton Co.* v. *Massachusetts,* 6 Wall. 632; *Monroe Svgs. B'k* v. *City of Rochester,* 37 N. Y. 365.) The objection of the defendant's counsel that if the tax in question is not a property tax, the statute imposing it was repugnant to the fourteenth amendment to the United States Constitution, is untenable. (*St. Louis* v. *Wehrung,* 46 Ill. 392; *Ducat* v. *Chicago,* 48 id. 172; *S. C.,* 10 Wall. 410; *Hughes* v. *City of Cairo,* 92 Ill. 339; *Co. of San Mateo* v. *So. Pac. R. R. Co.,* MSS. opinion; *Youngblood* v. *Sexton,* 32 Mich. 406; *Litchfield* v. *Vernon,* 41 N. Y. 124; *People* v. *The Mayor,* 4 id. 419; Cooley on Taxation, 175, 179; *State R. R. Tax Cases,* 92 U. S. 575, 611; *Comm.* v. *People's Five Cent Svgs. B'k,* 5 Allen, 428, 436, 437; *Slaughter-House Cases,* 16 Wall. 36, 81; *B'k of Chenango* v. *Brown,* 26 N. Y. 467; *State Tax on Foreign Held Bonds,* 15 Wall. 314, 319; *Davidson* v. *New Orleans,* 96 U. S. 97; *Kelly* v. *Pittsburg,* 104 id. 78.)

Ruger, Ch. J. It is claimed by the appellant that the law under which the tax involved in this action was imposed is obnoxious to the provisions of section 20 of article 3 of the Constitution, in that it does not state distinctly the object to which the tax is applicable.

The statement is, that it is "applicable to the payment of the ordinary and current expenses of the State." (§ 9, chap. 542, Laws of 1880.) It was admitted upon the argument, by the learned counsel raising the objection, that it would be impracticable to state the object of a prospective tax in all cases without more or less indefiniteness, and that the question actually to be considered was the degree to which such indistinctness might constitutionally extend. It was further conceded that a provision which defined the object of a tax to be the replenishment of the general or any other specified and legally recognized fund of the State treasury, or a provision for any one of these funds, or for " unforeseen contingencies," would be a sufficient compliance with the requirement of the Constitution.

We think these concessions are fatal to the contention of the appellant.

To sustain his position it would be necessary for the appellant to demonstrate that the specification of some, out of many, items legally chargeable upon a certain fund is a less distinct statement of the object of a tax than a statement that it is to be applied to replenish the undivided fund itself. It is obvious that this cannot be done. These concessions were of course involuntary, and such as counsel was, by force of controlling adjudications in this court, constrained to make. Even in the absence of such admissions, the decisions referred to would lead to the same result.

The system by which the finances of the State are classified, and the purposes to which their moneys may be applied, is embodied in numerous acts of the legislature creating various distinct and separate funds. Among them is a so-called general fund, which is also recognized by the Constitution. (§ 2, art. 7 of Constitution ; 1 R. S. 493 *et seq.*) Each of these several funds aside from the general fund is devoted to some special object, and payment therefrom for any other purpose than that to which it is specifically devoted is prohibited by law. The most, if not all of the ordinary and current expenses of the State, are specifically chargeable to the general fund. (1 R. S. [7th ed.] 496 to 500.) In addition to these special provisions it is further enacted that any appropriation made by the legislature not specially charged to any other fund shall be paid from the general fund. (1 R. S. 500, 501.) It is thus apparent not only that the payment of all the current and ordinary expenses of the State government is chargeable upon the general fund, but also that of various other necessary expenditures. It seems to follow that if the specification of the replenishment of this fund be held to be a sufficiently distinct statement of the object of a tax within the constitutional requirement, the designation of one or more of the several classes of expenditures lawfully chargeable to that fund would be equally sufficient and distinct. This question has been before this court on several occasions, and the effect of each decision is adverse to the claim made by the appellant.

The first time it was raised, was in the case of *The Sun Mutual Ins. Co.* v. *The City of New York* (reported in 5 Sandf. 10). The statute under which that case arose empowered the board of supervisors of New York county to raise by tax upon the real and personal property subject to taxation in said county the sum of $1,606,525, and described the object of the tax; that it was " to be applied toward defraying the various contingent expenses legally chargeable to the said city and county, and such expenses as the mayor, aldermen and commonalty of the city of New York may in any manner sustain or be put to by law." It was held, Chief Justice OAKLEY delivering the opinion, that the statement of the object of the tax was a sufficient compliance with the constitutional provision. This case was affirmed upon appeal to this court, although the particular question referred to was not discussed in the opinion, and did not even appear to have been mooted. (8 N. Y. 241.) The opinion upon this point, as reported in 5 Sandford, was, however, expressly approved by this court in *The People, ex rel. Burrows,* v. *Supervisors of Orange County* (17 N. Y. 235). The law authorizing that tax directed its proceeds to be paid into the State treasury " to the credit of the general fund." It was held that the description of the object of the tax was as distinct as was reasonably practicable and was a sufficient compliance with the requirement of the Constitution. Mr. Justice HARRIS, delivering the opinion of the court, says : " The sum of the whole argument is this: the general fund is a thing long and well known by every intelligent citizen of the State. Its existence is recognized by the Constitution itself. It is an object to which money has often been and may now lawfully be appropriated. The legislature thought fit to make an appropriation to this fund. For this purpose it directed a tax to be levied.   It is distinctly stated in the law that this was the object for which the tax was imposed.   The constitutional requirement in this respect was thus satisfied."   We regard the description of the object of the tax in the law of 1880 to be at least as definite and precise as that considered in either of these cases.

It is quite significant that the framers of the clause, as well as of the Constitution of 1846, designated the general fund as the object of a tax laid by that instrument, and thus gave a practical construction by its authors of the meaning of the language under consideration.   The financial operations of the State have now been carried on for nearly thirty-seven years under this provision of the Constitution, and during each of those years questions involving its practical construction have been presented to each branch of the State government, and have been necessarily considered and decided by the various departments.

The almost uniform description of the object of the annual tax levies in the laws authorizing their imposition has been to require their application " to the purposes of the general fund, and for the payment of those claims and demands which constitute a lawful charge upon that fund."   Taxes have been levied by the legislature, collected by the State officers, and disbursed by its authorized agents during this long period without objection as to the sufficiency of such statements or the legality of the method by which these acts were performed, and it would now seem too late to raise a question of such importance and fraught with such dangerous consequences to those engaged in the enforcement of the laws.

If this question were at all doubtful upon authority this constant and uniform construction by every department of the State government for so long a period would have great if not controlling weight upon the interpretation of this provision. We are, therefore, of the opinion that this objection to the constitutionality of the act cannot be sustained.

The only remaining question in the case is whether the State authorities, in taxing corporations under the statutes of

1880 and 1881, are obliged to deduct the amount of stock
which such corporations hold in bonds of the United States
from the total amount of their capital stock and compute the
tax only upon the dividends derived from the remainder of
such capital. The agreed statement of facts in this case shows
the total capital stock of the appellants to be $3,000,000, of
which the sum of $1,940,000 was, on the 1st day of Novem-
ber, 1881, invested in United States bonds. The annual dividend declared by the corporation for the year preceding that
date was ten per cent upon its entire capital stock. The tax
imposed under these acts, computed upon such dividend,
aggregated $7,500. A statement of some of the propositions
of law, undisputed or conceded by the respective parties, will
limit the range of citation and discussion. No question was
made upon the argument as to the correctness of the propositions that a State legislature has no power to levy a tax directly
either upon United States bonds held by individuals or corporations, or upon the property represented by such bonds, or the
income derivable therefrom; and that a legislature could not
indirectly accomplish an object which it was prohibited from
attaining by direct and positive legislation. It was also undisputed that a State, in the exercise of its legislative power, has
the right to impose taxes upon the business privileges and
franchises of a corporation organized under its laws and from
which alone it derives its corporate existence and secures protection in the prosecution of its business. In other words, it
is admitted that among the legitimate subjects of State taxation is not only the property of individuals and corporations,
but in the case of corporations the very right of exercising the
privileges granted to them by the State. These several propositions are also abundantly sustained by the authorities. It
thus appears that the only question presented for our consideration under this branch of the appeal is whether the tax in
question was in fact levied upon the franchises of the defendant, which would be undeniably lawful, or upon the property
of the corporation invested in the securities of the general government, which would be unlawful. It is not claimed that this

law in terms assumes to authorize the taxation of the exempted
securities, but it is asserted that it effects this result indirectly,
and, therefore, amounts to the exercise of a prohibited power.

This involves an inquiry into the real intention of the legislature in passing this statute.   The appellant claims that we
must go behind the object declared by that body, and, from
the language and effect of the act as well as from other sources
of information, hold its real object to be different from its declared intent.   Waiving for the present a consideration of the
question whether the court has the right by judicial construction to determine that the legislature has in fact exercised a
prohibited power, instead of one which it legally might and
which it expressly declared it did exercise, we will proceed to
examine the question presented upon the theory advanced by
the appellant.   In the determination of questions involving
the construction of statutes and their validity as depending
upon legislative intent, we may doubtless legitimately examine
the history of the legislation as well as the act itself and acts
in *pari materia*.   By such examination we are enabled to see
the general nature of the scheme inaugurated by the legislature and its relation to prior and existing laws concerning taxation.   The statutes in question left the corporations still
subject to the payment of local taxes (*The People, ex rel.
Westchester F. Ins. Co.*, v. *Davenport et al., Trustees*, 91 N.
Y. 574), always constituting the great bulk of taxation in the
State, and attempted by a new system to collect only so much
of the burdens laid upon them as inured exclusively to the
use of the State, by tax upon their franchise alone.   They
were expressly exempted from the customary tax laid for
State purposes upon their property by the general law and
thus secured some compensation for this franchise tax by a
partial exemption from the usual property tax.   Not only the
object but also the method contemplated by the legislature
were new in many respects.   Among other things the law
enumerates certain distinct and specified classes of corporations
to whom its various provisions shall respectively apply, and for
the first time in the history of State taxation the State, as dis-

tinguished from the local authorities, intervened directly not only in the assessment of the tax but also in its collection and the transfer to the State treasury of the funds thus collected. It is also believed to be the first time in the practice of the State that an attempt has been made by a general scheme to impose taxes exclusively upon the franchises and business of corporations organized under its laws and to exact their payment as a condition upon the exercise of the privileges granted them by the State. The tax complained of was levied under section 3 of chapter 542 of the Laws of 1880, as amended by chapter 361 of the Laws of 1881, and which, after describing the corporations subject to its provisions, continues as follows : " shall be subject to and pay a tax upon its corporate franchise or business into the treasury of the State annually to be computed as follows : " " If the dividend or dividends made or declared by such corporation, joint-stock company or association during any year ending with the 1st day of November amount to six or more than six per cent upon the par value of the capital stock, then the tax to be at the rate of one-quarter mill upon the capital stock for each one per centum of dividends so made and declared." When the dividends are under six per cent another method of computation is provided which it is not here essential to describe. By section five of the same act a further tax of eight-tenths of one per centum upon the gross amount of their receipts for premiums, also as a tax upon their corporate franchise and business, was required to be paid by fire and marine insurance companies annually into the State treasury. The act further provides that such corporations shall be exempted from all further taxation for State purposes except upon their real property. In case of the intentional neglect or refusal of the corporations bound to report their condition or pay the taxes, as therein required, it was provided that an action to recover the tax might be brought by the attorney-general and also that their respective charter and corporate privileges should be forfeited and terminated. We have before seen that the State legislature had an undoubted right by virtue of its jurisdiction over corporations organized under its laws, to levy such tax upon their business and privileges, aside from all property taxation, as in its discretion it might deem just and proper in order to provide revenues for the State. Conceding this the appellant claims that because the legislature has directed the amount of this tax to be arrived at in a particular way, *i. e.*, by requiring payment of a percentage upon declared dividends and because such computation may be based in part upon interest derivable from funds invested in United States bonds, such method necessarily invalidates the tax to the extent of dividends accrued from the capital so invested.

We are unable to see why this precise proposition has not been determined adversely to the appellant both by this court and by the Supreme Court of the United States. The question was substantially involved in *Monroe Savings Bank* v. *City of Rochester* (37 N. Y. 365), where it was held that a tax upon the entire surplus of a savings bank levied as a tax upon the franchises of the corporation was not void although it had a portion of its property invested in United States bonds, and although such bonds were estimated as property in computing the sum upon which the tax was levied. The franchises of a corporation were held to be proper subjects of taxation, the court saying : " It follows that if such taxation falls within the scope of legislative power, that power may also prescribe a rule or test of value." " It can hardly be denied that a fair measure of the value of the franchises of corporations would be the profits resulting from their use, and in adopting such a rule of estimate no one could justly complain of its being unequal in its effects upon different corporations or unjust in its general operation." In *Society for Savings* v. *Coite* (6 Wall, 59); *Provident Institution* v. *Massachusetts* (id. 611); *Hamilton Company* v. *Massachusetts* (id. 633), the point here involved was also decided. In the Coite case a law of the State of Connecticut had imposed a tax of three-fourths of one per cent on the total amount which savings banks had on deposit on a day certain in lieu of all other taxes upon them. The bank had on the day specified upwards of half a million dollars of its deposits invested in United States government bonds, and claimed that such amount should be deducted from its gross deposits by the State authorities in levying the tax. Although the law did not in terms purport to levy a tax upon the franchises or business of the corporation, yet the court held that it was a tax upon the franchise, and was a legitimate exercise of the taxing power of the State. The criticism is made upon this case that the law authorized a tax upon the liabilities of the bank; even if this were so, it would not impair the force of the case as an authority. But the criticism, we think, is not well founded; for, admitting that the deposits of a savings bank represent the amount of its indebtedness, they also indicate its ability to pay, as well as its financial condition. It would be difficult to devise a more accurate test of the value of the franchise of a savings bank than by taking the amount of its deposits as the measure of its prosperity. The case of *Provident Institution* v. *Massachusetts*, immediately following, reaffirmed the proposition laid down in the case of Coite and declared that a tax levied upon the gross deposits of a savings bank was not susceptible to the objection that it was a tax upon government securities.

Mr. Justice CLIFFORD in his opinion says: "It is the corporation that is to make the payment, and if it fail to do so it is liable not only to an action for the amount of the tax, but what is more significant, it may be enjoined from the future exercise of its franchises until all taxes shall be fully paid." And further, discussing the differences existing between franchises and property taxes, he says, in language particularly applicable to this case: "Franchise taxes are levied directly by an act of the legislature, and the corporations are required to pay the amount into the State treasury. They differ from property taxes, as levied for State and municipal purposes, in the basis prescribed for computing the amount, in the manner of assessment and in the mode of collection." "Comparative valuation in assessing property taxes is the basis of computation in ascertaining the amount to be contributed by an individual, but the amount of a franchise tax depends upon the business transacted by the corporation and the extent to which they have exercised the privileges granted in their charter." This case was followed by the *Hamilton Company Case* in which the conclusions before reached were again affirmed.

The legislature of Massachusetts had enacted a statute by which corporations in that State having a capital stock divided into shares were required to pay a tax of one-sixth of one per cent upon each dollar of the excess of the market value of all such stock over the value of its real estate and machinery. The Hamilton Company had invested $300,000 of its capital in the bonds of the United States. Some of the questions considered involved the construction of constitutional provisions and statutes not applicable here, but the broad doctrine was announced that a law which apportioned a tax upon the franchise of a corporation according to the value of its capital stock, although such capital stock was partially invested in securities exempt from taxation, was not for that reason invalid. The main question argued was, that inasmuch as no express authority existed under the State Constitution to tax the business or franchises of a corporation, unless comprehended in the word "commodities," whether that word conferred the necessary power, and it being held under the long-settled decisions of the State courts that the term did confer such power, the Supreme Court affirmed the validity of the tax as a tax upon franchises and not upon property.

Mr. Justice CLIFFORD, who also wrote in this case, says: "All trades and avocations by which the citizens acquire a livelihood may also be taxed by the State for the support of the State government. Power to that effect resides in the State independent of the Federal government, and is wholly unaffected by the fact that the corporation or individual has or has not made investments in Federal securities."

In neither of the three cases cited was it claimed or suggested upon the argument that if the State legislature had in terms laid the tax upon the business or franchise of the corporation any question as to the validity of the tax could have been successfully raised, but on the contrary it was clearly held

that the State having power to tax the franchise of corporations
and having exercised the power, the court would ascribe such
exercise to the power which authorized it, although the act
levying the tax did not specially designate its character.

Applying the tests derived from these authorities it seems
conclusively established that the act under which this tax was
levied must be held to have imposed a franchise and not a
property tax, and that its enactment constituted a lawful exercise of legislative power. It is levied upon corporations alone,
and one of the penalties provided for its non-payment is the
forfeiture of their charter. The amount of the tax is dependent upon their business prosperity, as evidenced by their capacity to declare dividends instead of upon the value of the corporate property, and it is made payable by the corporations
affected, directly to the State authorities. The income of these
corporations is referred to only as a means of arriving at the
measure of their liability. As was said in the *Provident Institution Case :* " The subject-matter to be taxed is the corporation, and the average amount of the deposits within the period
named furnishes the basis of computing the amount." It was
conceded on the argument that neither by statutory nor judicial authority had any fixed basis for computing the taxable
value of a corporate franchise been established either by the
State or Federal government. It necessarily follows that this
question must be decided according to the judgment and discretion of the bodies having authority to tax such privileges,
as the occasion for such a decision may from time to time arise.
Having this power and having professed to exercise it in a
given case, it is not easy to see upon what principle a court
can judicially ascribe the legislative action to another power
which the legislature is prohibited from exercising. The contention is that we should hold that the legislature has really
imposed a tax upon property, while professing only to tax a
franchise. In other words, the rule of construction claimed is,
that we should impute to the legislature an unlawful intent in
a case where its action is plainly sustainable upon justifiable
grounds. Well and long-settled rules forbid us from placing

such an interpretation upon statutory enactments, and re-quire us to make every reasonable intendment to uphold rather than to nullify the exercise of legislative authority. The authorities cited would seem to require us to hold this law valid as a tax upon franchise, even though that character had not been expressly ascribed to it by the terms of the act.

The case of the Hamilton Company goes much farther than we need go to sustain the judgment appealed from. There although the value of exempted bonds held by a corporation entered directly into the computation of the amount of a pro-posed tax, no portion of the tax was deemed to have been in-validated thereby. If the principal of such bonds can be considered as a basis for computing the amount of a franchise tax, the partial consideration of the income of such bonds for a similar purpose must be equally unobjectionable.

We have examined the Pennsylvania cases cited by the appel-lant in support of the proposition that a tax like the one in ques-tion had there been judicially decided to be a tax upon capital stock. They do not appear to us to support that proposition. The cases arose under local statutes and were controlled by special provisions therein contained. It is true some of them hold that in a case where the State officers were authorized to tax capital stock alone, the imposition of a tax by them, in which the amount of the tax was determined by the amount of cor-porate dividends declared, was a tax upon capital stock. This conclusion was reached by force of the rule contained in the maxim "*ut res magis valeat, quam pereat;*" the court holding that the dividends which were there made the basis of the tax were merely referred to as a means of arriving at the value of the capital stock, which was in fact the subject of taxation. If these cases can be assumed to hold beyond this, they conflict with *Hamilton Company* v. *Massachusetts and Monroe County Bank (supra).*

It is further strenuously contended by the appellant that because the amount of the tax authorized to be levied upon corporations dividing less than six per cent annually shall be graduated by the appraised value of their capital stock, it necessarily follows that the tax in question must be held to be a tax upon capital stock and not upon the franchise. The cases above cited hold directly the contrary. We also think it may safely be assumed that so long as a corporation continues business under its charter the privilege of so doing is of some pecuniary value to it, and that there is no valid reason why the value of the capital stock may not be used as an element for determining the amount of tax levied upon franchise, and why it will not in each year approximate its variable taxable value quite as accurately as any other method. In the present case the dividends are used to determine the value of the corporate franchise, and there is no inconsistency in these modes of estimating the respective values of capital stock and of corporate franchises. The prosperity of a corporation will affect equally the value of its franchises and the market value of its capital stock, or in other words, what enhances the value of the franchise will raise the value of its capital stock, and while the one may in the aggregate be more greatly enhanced than the other, yet they may equally afford a just method of arriving at the taxable value of the respective subjects. The operation of the same law determines the relative value of both stock and franchise.

The title to the stock involves the ownership of the property of a corporation, including its franchise, and variations in the value of such stock, as affected by its prosperity, indicate by necessary relation the comparative variations in the value of its franchise.

We are unable to see any force in the objection raised to this law that various corporations subjected to its provisions are thereby subjected to unequal or double taxation. Corporations are of course alone subject to the payment of franchise taxes, and they may be divided into as many classes as the different pursuits followed by them may require. (*State Railroad Tax Cases*, 92 U. S. 575.) The rate of taxation provided by the act seems to be justly and equitably apportioned and to bear equally upon each of the classes named therein who stand in similar relations to each other.   Absolute equality in laying the burdens of taxation as shown by experience is impossible of attainment, and it is not an insuperable objection to a law that it does not accomplish that result. (*Commonwealth* v. *The People's Five Cent Savings Bank*, 5 Allen, 428; *Bank of Chenango* v. *Brown*, 26 N. Y. 467.) In the consideration of the effect and meaning of laws imposing taxes it would undoubtedly be the duty of the court to so construe them, if possible, as to avoid unequal and double taxation, but in determining the question of legislative power we are precluded from entertaining such considerations and must be governed by the constitutional authority conferred upon the legislative body.   In performing the duty of levying taxes for the support of government, State legislatures may, in the exercise of their undoubted power, impose double taxes or lay burdens beyond the financial capacity of the classes taxed, and however impolitic or unwise such a course would be, the courts have no right to interfere with the exercise of the legislative discretion. (*The People, ex rel. Griffin*, v. *The Mayor of Brooklyn*, 4 N. Y. 419; *Gordon* v. *Cornes, infra.*) Such questions properly belong to the legislative branch of the government, whose exclusive duty it is to apportion and impose the taxes required for the use of the government. (*Monroe County Bank* v. *Rochester, supra; Gordon* v. *Cornes*, 47 N. Y. 608; *Litchfield* v. *Vernon*, 41 id. 124.) If this question were open for examination in this court upon principle, we think the plan adopted by this law for determining the taxable value of corporate franchises is fair and equitable and affords no reasonable cause for complaint.

The tax is governed by actual results, and is measured exclusively by the prosperity of the corporation taxed, as shown by the profits voluntarily distributed among its shareholders. The mode of assessment seems to be governed by just principles and to adapt itself to the variable character of the property.   The amount is so graded that it rises and falls with the fluctuations in the prosperity of the corporation.   The various processes which are so essential in securing equality and fairness in distributing the burdens of property taxes are rendered inapplicable and unnecessary by a rule which refers the valuation of the thing taxed to the owner of the property without reference to the actual value of his invested or accumulated property, and is based upon the principle by which a business tax alone is supported. It must be borne in mind that this tax is a fractional tax, for which an equivalent property tax has been surrendered, and thereby substantial equality of taxation may be presumed to have been produced even as between individuals and the corporations taxed. In this case the propriety of the method is made apparent from the fact that although nearly two-thirds of the capital of the defendant is invested in government bonds, but about one-quarter of its income is derived from that source.

It would seem that these corporations could not fairly claim exemption for more than the proportionate amount of income which is derived from investment in exempted securities, but we feel constrained to hold, in accordance with the principles laid down in the cases cited, that the tax in question was a tax upon franchises alone, and was, therefore, within the exercise of legitimate legislative power.

The judgment should be affirmed.

All concur.

Judgment affirmed.

THOMAS J. CHAMBERLAIN et al., Appellants, *v.* HASCAL L. TAYLOR et al., Respondents.

The provision of the Revised Statutes (2 R. S. 691, § 5) making it a misdemeanor to accept a conveyance of lands, which, to the knowledge of the grantee, are at the time held adversely, and the title to which is in litigation, does not affect the previous title of the grantor in a deed executed in violation thereof, and the conveyance is no defense to an action of ejectment brought by him.

If the deed be utterly void, the grantor may recover as owner of the legal title; if void only as to the defendants, the action is authorized by the

Code of Civil Procedure (§ 1501) in the name of the grantor for the benefit of the grantee.

Chamberlain v. *Taylor* (26 Hun. 601), reversed.

(Argued April 16, 1883; decided May 1, 1883.)

APPEAL from judgment of the General Term of the Supreme Court, in the fourth judicial department, in favor of defendants, entered upon an order made at the April term, 1882, which overruled plaintiffs' exceptions, denied a motion for a new trial, and directed judgment upon a verdict. (Reported below, 26 Hun, 601.)

The nature of the action and the material facts are stated in ·the opinion.   ·

E. Darwin Smith for appellants. The plaintiffs, having duly established on the trial title in themselves, were entitled to a verdict finding and asserting such title in fee, and to the possession of said premises, which were wrongfully withheld from them by the defendants. (Civil Code, §§ 1502, 1519.) The will of Chamberlain with the probate thereof, which devised all his real and personal estate to the plaintiffs, with directions to convert the same into money and divide same, vested the whole undisposed real estate of the testator, including the premises in question, in the plaintiffs. (*Chamberlain* v. *Chamberlain*, 43 N. Y. 425, 431 441; *Dodge* v. *Pond*, 23 id. 69; *Powers* v. *Cassidy*, 79 id. 603, 614; *Shumway* v. *Harman*, 6 T. & C. 626; *Stagg* v. *Jackson*, 1 N. Y. 212; *Forsyth* v. *Rathbone*, 34 Barb. 388, 405; Leigh & Dalzell on Equitable Conversion, 5, 109.) The proof that the executors had conveyed the premises in question to Ensign and others for $400 did not impair the plaintiffs' title or the right to maintain their action for the benefit of such grantees. (*Hamilton* v. *Wright*, 37 N. Y. 502; *Towle* v. *Remson*, 70 id. 310, 313; *Ward* v. *Reynolds*, 62 How. 183; *Hasbrouck* v. *Bunce*, 62 N. Y. 482; Code of Civil Proc., § 1501; *Brinley* v. *Whiting*, 5 Pick. 348; *Stephens* v. *Deming*, 60 Ind. 486.) The statute allows an action in all such cases in the name of the grantor in

a deed, when the same would be void under the statute as against
such grantee because of adverse possession. (Code, § 1501;
Towle v. *Smith*, 2 Rob. 493.) If Ensign was nonsuited in a previous action erroneously commenced in his own name, such nonsuit cannot affect this action, or preclude a recovery in an action
in the name of his grantors, the plaintiffs in this action. It was
at least a mere nonsuit. (*Williams* v. *Tibbits*, 5 Johns. 489;
Jackson v. *Vredenbergh*, 1 id. 159; *Jackson* v. *Leggett*, 7 Wend.
377; *Jackson* v. *Demont*, 9 Johns. 55; *Livingston* v. *Proseus*,
2 Hill, 528; *Hamilton* v. *Wright*, 37 N. Y. 506; 4 Kent, 448;
Williams v. *Jackson*, 5 Johns. 489, 501; *Vanhosen* v. *Ben-
ham*, 15 Wend. 164; *Towler* v. *Kelly*, 9 Bosw. 494.)

D. H. Bolles for respondents. The action cannot be sustained unless the deed executed by the plaintiffs to William H.
Ensign and others is valid and effectual. (Code of Civil Proc.,
§ 541; *Hamilton* v. *Wright*, 37 N. Y. 507.) The deed from
the plaintiffs to William H. Ensign and his associates was
executed in contravention of the statutes of champerty and
therefore void. (R. S., § 5, tit. 3, chap. 1, part 4 [2d ed.], p.
718; 2 Kent's Com. 466 [marg.]; *Dewitt* v. *Brisbane*, 16
N. Y. 508, 573.) The plaintiffs had no power, authority or
right to execute the deed in question, and it was therefore void.
(R. S. [1st Edm. ed. 678], §§ 56, 76, 94, art. 2, tit. 2, chap. 1,
part 2.)

FINCH, J. This is an action of ejectment. The plaintiffs
sue as executors of the will of Benjamin Chamberlain, deceased.
They allege title in themselves and right of possession; a conveyance by them to one Ensign and others; an adverse holding
of the premises at the delivery of such deed; and claim to recover for the benefit of their grantees. The defendants deny
the material allegations and put in issue the title asserted.
Upon the trial the plaintiffs showed title in the testator by a
patent from the State; proved his death, his will, its due probate, their letters testamentary and their conveyance to Ensign
and others, during an adverse holding by the defendants; and

rested. There was no motion for a nonsuit. The defendants gave evidence, for the most part under objection, consisting of the judgment finally construing the will of Chamberlain, and the decrees of the surrogate, settling the accounts of the executors. It was also proved that at the time of the execution of the deed, an action was pending, brought by said grantees against the defendants, to recover possession of the same premises. At the close of the evidence the defendants requested the court to direct a verdict in their favor. No ground of the request was assigned, but it was granted and the plaintiffs excepted. The judgment thereupon entered was affirmed by the General Term, but for reasons in which we do not concur.

If we assume, as was asserted, that both grantors and grantees were guilty of a misdemeanor, the former for conveying and the latter for accepting a deed of land held adversely, and the title to which was at the time involved in litigation, still the conclusion of the General Term does not follow. The criminal law affects the deed given in violation of its command, but not the grantor's previous title. The former may be void, but if it is the grantor's title has neither been extinguished nor transferred, and remains valid and effectual. Upon it the grantors may rely as against trespassers and occupants without title. Upon it they do rely in this action. They are the sole plaintiffs here and we can recognize no others. Their action is not founded upon the illegal deed, but upon a disaffirmance of it. It is the legal title of the grantors which has in it no vice born of the violation of the criminal law which the defendants are called upon to answer. The grantees are not before us. That they may and will reap a benefit from the recovery of the grantors does not deprive the latter of their title or serve to weaken or defeat it. That is an after question between grantors and grantees, with the solution of which the defendants have no concern. If the deed is utterly void, an absolute nullity, because it was a crime to give and receive it, then certainly the plaintiffs may recover, as owners of the legal title, which has never passed from them. If, on the contrary, it is only void as to the defendants, and good between the other

parties, then the Code permits the action, in the name of the
plaintiffs, for the benefit of the grantees. In either event the
grantors' title can be asserted and established. Similar actions
have always been sustained. Under the old practice, before
the Revised Statutes, the plaintiff could count upon different
demises from different lessors and recover upon the title of
the grantor when that of the grantee was rendered void by an
adverse holding. (*Jackson* v. *Vredenbergh*, 1 Johns. 159;
Jackson v. *Demont*, 9 id. 55; *Jackson* v. *Leggett*, 7 Wend.
377.) The same mode of pleading was sustained after the use
of fictitious names was abolished, and counts were permitted in
the names both of grantor and grantee. (*Ely* v. *Ballantine*,
7 Wend. 470; *Livingston* v. *Proseus*, 2 Hill, 528.) In the
case last cited the correct doctrine was thus stated: "As against
the person holding adversely the deed is utterly void; a mere
nullity. There was an attempt to convey, but the parties
failed to accomplish the object. The title still remains in the
original proprietor, and he may, indeed must, sue to recover
the land. It is true that the recovery will inure to the benefit
of the grantee in the deed, but that is a matter between him
and the grantor and with which the person holding adversely
has nothing to do. It is enough for him that the deed does
him no injury." When the Code enacted that actions should
be brought in the name of the real party in interest, the new
difficulty was removed by the special provisions allowing the
action, although for the benefit of the grantee to be brought in
the name of the grantor. (Code, § 111; Code of Civil Procedure,
§ 1501.) If there is any jar between the civil and criminal law
upon this subject, it can only occur in some action founded
upon the illegal deed, and not in one which concedes its
illegality and rests upon a valid title. It cannot be that a mere
trespasser can defeat the grantee of the true owner, because
his deed is void, and then defeat the grantor because the same
deed is good.

But the judgment is defended upon the further ground that
under the will of Chamberlain and its construction by the
courts, the executors took no title, but the fee descended to the

heirs at law, subject only to the execution of the power of
sale; and that such power is spent and dead because all its.
purposes are accomplished. The point appears to be serious,
and strikes us as worthy of careful consideration. But it does
not appear to have been suggested on the trial; it has not been
considered by the General Term, and the complete provisions
of the will are not before us. There may be something in
them which would modify the inference to be drawn from the
brief extracts furnished in the printed case. We, therefore,
express no opinion upon it, but leave it to be considered on a
new trial and in the light of the full and complete facts which
will doubtless be supplied.

The judgment should be reversed and a new trial granted,
costs to abide the event.

All concur.

Judgment accordingly.

CYNTHIA A. TOLMAN as Administratrix, etc., Respondent, v.
THE SYRACUSE, BINGHAMTON AND NEW YORK RAILROAD COM-
PANY, Appellant.

Where an order of Special Term recited that it was made "on reading
and filing the decision of the court," referring to an opinion which was
the only decision filed, and the minutes of the General Term on affirmance of such order stated that it was affirmed on opinion of the judge at
Special Term, *held*, that the opinion was thus made part of the record
and could be referred to to ascertain the grounds of the decision; and, it
appearing therefrom that the decision was based upon the ground of a
want of power, *held* that the order, although a discretionary one, was reviewable here.

Under the provision of the Code of Civil Procedure (§ 3271) giving to the
court discretionary power to require the plaintiff in an action brought by
or against an executor, administrator, etc., in his representative capacity,
to give security for costs, the court has power to require such security
of one bringing suit in such capacity, although there is no evidence of
mismanagement or bad faith, and aside from the question of his personal liability for costs as prescribed by the Code (§ 3246).

Darby v. *Condit* (1 Duer, 599), overruled.

9
16
—
92
e167

Appeal from order of the General Term of the Supreme Court, in the fourth judicial department, made January 9, 1883, which affirmed an order of Special Term denying a motion on behalf of defendant, that plaintiff be required to file security for costs.

Louis Marshall for appellant. This court will, upon appeal, review the determination of the courts below even upon a discretionary order where it appears that the decision was based on the ground of a want of power to grant the application. (*Tilton* v. *Beecher,* 59 N. Y. 176; *Beech* v. *Chamberlain,* 3 Wend. 366; *Russell* v. *Conn,* 20 N. Y. 81; *Tracy* v. *Altmeyer,* 46 id. 598; *Brown* v. *Brown,* 58 id. 609; *Allen* v. *Meyer,* 73 id. 1; *Matter of Duff,* 41 How. 350; *Eq. L. Ass. Co.* v. *Stevens,* 63 N. Y. 341; *Dunlop* v. *F. Ins. Co.,* 74 id. 145; *Jamison* v. *Citizens' Savings B'k,* 85 id. 546; *Matter of Atty.-Gen.* v. *Cont. L. Ins. Co.,* 88 id. 77; *Salmon* v. *Gedney,* 75 id. 481; *Hewlett* v. *Wood,* 67 id. 399.) The Supreme Court has the statutory power of requiring security for costs to be given in any one of the cases specified in section 3271 of the Code of Civil Procedure, even in the absence of evidence of mismanagement or bad faith, and independent of the question of personal liability. (*More* v. *Durr,* 45 N. Y. Supr. Ct. 154; *Reade* v. *Waterhouse,* 52 N. Y. 587.) The exercise of the power to require security for costs rests in the discretion of the Supreme Court. (*Briggs* v. *Vanderbergh,* 22 N. Y. 467; *Gedney* v. *Purdy,* 47 id. 676; Code of Civil Pro., § 3271; *Murphy* v. *Travers,* 60 How. Pr. 301.)

C. V. Kellogg for respondent. The court will not require security for costs to be filed, except for mismanagement or bad faith in commencing or prosecuting this action. (*Darby* v. *Condit,* 1 Duer, 509; *Norris* v. *Greed,* 1 Sheldon, 27; *S. C.,* 12 Abb. Pr. [N. S.] 185; *Wilbur* v. *White,* 56 How. 321-2; *Kimberly* v. *Stewart,* 22 id. 443; *Ryan* v. *Potter,* 4 Law Bulletin, 62; Code Civ. Pro., vol. 2, p. 33; *Sheppard* v. *Burt,* 8 Duer, 645; *Hall* v. *Waterbury,* 5 Abb. N. C.

356.) The court will not require security for costs merely upon the ground that the estate which an executor or administrator represents has no funds except the claim in litigation. (*Darby* v. *Condit*, 1 Duer, 599; *Ryan* v. *Potter*, 4 Law Bulletin, 62; *S. C.*, Code Civ. Pro., vol. 2, p. 33.) If this court should be of the opinion that the court of original jurisdiction has not exercised its discretion, and should have exercised such discretion, and either require security to be filed or not, then the respondent claims that the motion should have been denied. (*Putnam* v. *N. Y. C. & H. R. R. R. Co.*, 16 N. Y. W'kly Dig. 114; *Earnst* v. *H. R. R. Co.*, 33 N. Y. 9; *Renwick* v. *N. Y. C. & H. R. R. R. Co.*, 36 id. 132; *Kellogg* v. *N. Y. C. & H. R. R. R. Co.*, 79 id. 72; *Massoth* v. *N. Y. C. & H. R. R. R. Co.*, 64 id. 524; *Roach* v. *Flushing, etc., R. R. Co.*, 58 id. 626; *Smedis* v. *Brooklyn & R. B. R. R. Co.* 32 Hun, 279; 88 N. Y. 13; *Waldile* v. *N. Y. C. R. R. Co.*, 19 Hun, 69, 72–3; *Johnson* v. *Hudson R. R. Co.*, 20 N. Y. 65.) The order appealed from is not appealable. It is a discretionary order, and not reviewable here. (*Gedney* v. *Purdy*, 47 N. Y. 676; *Cushman* v. *Brunditt*, 50 id. 296; *Paul* v. *Munger*, 47 id. 469; *People* v. *Schoonmaker*, 50 id. 499.)

MILLER, J. This is an appeal from an order of the General Term, affirming an order of the Special Term, denying a motion to compel the plaintiff to file security for costs. It appears from the opinion of the judge at Special Term that the motion was denied upon the sole ground that a case did not arise under section 3271 of the Code of Civil Procedure for the court to exercise its discretion in requiring security for costs, unless it appeared from the papers presented that the court would be likely at the proper time to require the plaintiff to pay costs for mismanagement or bad faith in the prosecution of the action under section 3246. The minutes of the General Term show that the order was affirmed on the opinion of the judge at Special Term, and the order entered states that fact. It thus appears that only a single question was decided at the General Term, as the courts below refused to exercise their discretion, upon the sole ground that they did not possess the power to do so unless a case was made out under section 3246 of the Code of Civil Procedure. We think the order is reviewable on this appeal. This court will review upon appeal the determination of the courts below, even upon a discretionary order where it appears that the decision was based on the ground of a want of power to grant the application. (*Tilton* v. *Beecher*, 59 N. Y. 176; 17 Am. Rep. 337; *Russell* v. *Conn.*, 20 N. Y. 81; *Tracey* v. *Altmyer*, 46 id. 598; *Brown* v. *Brown*, 58 id. 609; *Allen* v. *Meyer*, 73 id. 1.)

The order at Special Term recites that it is made " on reading and filing the decision of the court," thus referring to the opinion which was the only decision made and which forms a part of the record. The order is not intelligible without reading the opinion, and it constitutes a part of the record, as much as the affidavits and notice of motion which are referred to in the earlier part of the order, and shows that the motion was denied upon the grounds stated in the opinion. The order of the General Term is also very specific and expressly states that the order of the Special Term was affirmed upon the opinion of the judge at such term.

In view of these facts we think the opinion must be considered as a part of the several orders referred to and as incorporated therein. There can be no doubt, therefore, as to the ground upon which the decision was based. While the opinion cannot ordinarily be referred to to show the ground upon which an order is made, this case is not brought within any such rule. The reason for the rule is, it forms no part of the record, and, therefore, cannot be referred to to explain the meaning of the record. (*Salmon* v. *Gedney*, 75 N. Y. 481.) Here the opinion constitutes an important and material part of the record and is expressly referred to in the orders.

The order not being discretionary, and the motion being disposed of for want of power, we are called upon to consider whether the courts committed an error in denying the motion upon the grounds stated. We think that the Supreme Court had the power to require security for costs under section 3271 of the Code of Civil Procedure, even although there was no evidence of mismanagement or bad faith and aside from the question of personal liability.

The provisions of the Code relating to the subject are sections 3246 and 3271, and each is independent of the other and contained in different titles and separated from each other by other provisions which do not bear any special relation to the subject-matter of the sections cited. The former section, 3246, relates to the awarding and enforcement of the payment of costs, and the latter section, 3271, to security for costs. Neither one refers to the other and it does not appear that they are in any way connected. It is only by inference that it can be claimed that the latter section is controlled or limited by the former. Section 3246 provides that, "In an action by or against an executor or administrator in his representative capacity, or the trustee of an express trust, or a person expressly authorized by statute to sue or be sued * * * costs are exclusively chargeable upon and collectible from the estate, fund or person represented, unless the court directs them to be paid by the party personally for mismanagement or bad faith in the prosecution or defense of the action." This section is applicable to both plaintiffs and defendants acting in a representative capacity, and it also refers to costs in a final judgment rendered in an action. Section 3271 provides that, "In an action by or against an executor or administrator in his representative capacity, or the trustee of an express trust, or a person expressly authorized by statute to sue or to be sued, or by an official assignee, the assignee of a receiver, or the committee of a person judicially declared to be incompetent to manage his affairs, the court may, in its discretion, require the plaintiff to give security for costs." This section refers to three classes of parties not included in section 3246, viz.: First, an official assignee; second, the assignee of a receiver, and third, the committee of a person judicially declared to be incompetent to manage his affairs. The effect of construing the two sections together would be to apply the condition of section 3246 to these cases, which could not have been intended. Section 3271 is applicable to plaintiffs alone, without regard to the question whether they act in a representative capacity or not. There is no ground for claiming that the plaintiff could not be compelled to give security for costs unless the court would require him to pay them personally on the ground of bad faith or mismanagement. The term "mismanagement," under section 3246, could have no meaning when applied to a person not acting in a representative capacity. Section 3271 declares the terms upon which security may be required and the limitation placed upon the right to impose it, which is in the discretion of the court. The meaning of the section last cited is very manifest, and it would be going very far to hold that it is directed and controlled by a previous section with which it has no distinct connection and which cannot affect it except by a constrained construction. Section 3271 refers to a proceeding during the pendency of an action, while, as we have seen, section 3246 has reference to costs in the final judgment.

We think these sections very evidently are to be construed separately and independently of each other; they apply to different cases, and upon no sound principle can it be held that section 3271 is to be limited in its operation by section 3246. Some authorities are cited and relied upon to sustain the position contended for by the respondent's counsel, and the principal case referred to is that of *Darby* v. *Condit* (1 Duer, 599), which has been followed by several decisions at Special Term. This case is claimed by the appellant's counsel to be overruled by a decision in the same court in *More* v. *Durr* (45 N. Y. Super. Ct. 154) and a contrary rule laid down. Without considering the question whether there is a conflict in these decisions we cannot resist the conclusion that the case of *Darby* v. *Condit* (*supra*) is not a well-considered case and should not be followed.

We do not deem it necessary to examine more at length the authorities cited in this connection, and we are satisfied that, under a fair construction of the sections cited, both the Special and General Terms erred in their decision.

The orders of the Special and General Terms should, therefore, be reversed, without costs, and the proceeding remitted to be heard at Special Term that its discretion may be exercised upon the merits.

All concur, except RUGER, Ch. J., who did not sit.

Ordered accordingly.

THOMAS MURTHA, Appellant, *v.* MICHAEL CURLEY, Impleaded, etc., Respondent.

Where a plaintiff is entitled to costs, under the Code of Civil Procedure (§ 3228), upon entry of judgment in his favor, and such judgment is reversed and new trial granted by the General Term " with costs to appellant to abide the event," but is affirmed on appeal by plaintiff to this court, he is entitled, of course, to the costs of the appeals to the General Term and to this court. (Code, § 3238.)

(Submitted April 17, 1883; decided May 1, 1883.)

APPEAL from order of the General Term of the Superior Court of the city of New York, made the first Monday of February, 1883, which reversed an order of Special Term retaxing plaintiff's costs.

The facts are sufficiently stated in the opinion.

Adolphus D. Pape for appellant. Plaintiff is entitled to the costs at General Term. (*Sanders* v. *Townsend*, 11 Abb. N. C. 217; Code of Civ. Proc., §§ 3228, 3230, 3237, 3238.) The order is appealable. (*Sturgis* v. *Spofford*, 58 N. Y. 103; 3 Abb. [N. S.] 183; 49 N. Y. 660.)

Starr & Hooker for respondent. The first appeal to the General Term being from a final judgment the costs thereof were in the discretion of the General Term, under section 3238 of the Code of Civil Procedure, because a new trial was directed. (Subd. 1, last clause of § 3238.) Also because the action was in equity. (Subd. 2 of § 3238; *Black* v. *O'Brien*, 23 Hun, 82, 84; *Taylor* v. *Root*, 48 N. Y. 687; *Palmer* v. *Ranken*, 56 How. 354; *Chipman* v. *Montgomery*, 63 N. Y. 222, 238; *Matter of Prot. Epis. School*, 86 id. 397, 398.) Where, as in the present cause, there was a reversal by the Court of Appeals "with costs," the costs of the Court of Appeals only are intended. (*Sisters of Charity* v. *Kelly*, 68 N. Y. 628; *Post* v. *Doremus*, 60 id. 372, 380.) As the Court of Appeals did not give to Murtha the costs of the appeal to the General Term, the Special Term had no authority, either original or delegated by the *remittitur*, to review a discretion in the matter of costs of appeal to a General Term already exercised by that General Term. (*Matter of N. Y. Prot. Epis. School*, 24 Hun, 369.) It is only where costs are given generally "to abide the event," that whichever party is successful eventually is entitled to tax the costs of such appeal to the General Term. (*First Nat. B'k of Meadville* v. *Fourth Nat. B'k of N. Y.*, 22 Hun, 563; *Howell* v. *Van Sichen*, 8 id. 525.)

EARL, J. In this action a money judgment was recovered against the defendant. From that judgment he appealed to the General Term of the New York Superior Court, where the judgment was reversed and a new trial granted, "with costs to the appellant to abide the event of such new trial." From the order of the General Term the plaintiff appealed to the Court of Appeals, which reversed the order of the General Term and affirmed the judgment of the Special Term, "with costs." Upon the taxation of costs, plaintiff sought to tax the costs of the appeal to the General Term. Upon objection on behalf of the defendant, the clerk disallowed such costs, and plaintiff then appealed to the Special Term, which reversed the ruling of the clerk and directed him to tax the costs of the appeal to the General Term. The defendant then appealed from the order of the Special Term to the General Term, which reversed the order of the Special Term and affirmed the ruling of the clerk, and this appeal is from that order of the General Term.

Section 3228 of the Code provides for the cases in which a plaintiff is entitled to costs of course; and subdivisions 1, 2 and 3 of that section provide for costs in what are commonly called actions at law. Subdivision 4 gives costs to the plaintiff in "an action other than one of those specified in the foregoing subdivisions of this section, in which the complaint demands judgment for a sum of money only." Under this subdivision it does not matter whether the action be legal or equitable, the sole condition being that the judgment demanded must be for money only. Section 3229 provides that the defendant shall have costs, of course, in the same actions specified in the preceding section, unless the plaintiff is entitled to costs as therein prescribed. Section 3230 provides that, except as prescribed in the preceding two sections, the court may, in its discretion, award costs to any party upon the rendering of a final judgment. Section 3237 provides that the preceding sections "do not affect the recovery of costs upon an appeal;" and then section 3238 provides that "upon an appeal from the final judgment in an action the recovery of costs is regulated as follows: 1st. In an action specified in section 3228 of this act the respondent is entitled to costs upon the affirmance, and the appellant upon the reversal of the judgment appealed from; except that where a new trial is directed costs may be awarded to either party, absolutely or to abide the event, in the discretion of the court. 2d. In every other action, and also where the final judgment appealed from is affirmed in part and reversed in part, costs may be awarded in like manner, in the discretion of the court."

It does not appear in the record before us what judgment was demanded in the complaint. From the fact a money judgment was rendered we may infer that a money judgment only was demanded in the complaint; and such from records in our possession we know to be the fact. (90 N. Y. 372.) Therefore this is a case where the plaintiff was entitled to costs of course under section 3228, upon the entry of the judgment in his favor; and as his judgment was finally affirmed in this court, he was of course entitled to his costs of the appeals to the General Term and to this court, under section 3238.

It follows from these views that the order of the General Term should be reversed, and that of the Special Term affirmed, with costs of the appeal to the General Term and to this court.

All concur.

Ordered accordingly.

THE ALBANY CITY NATIONAL BANK, Respondent, *v.* THE CITY OF ALBANY, Appellant.

/27

Certain accounts for repairs to the " City Building," and for articles furnished defendant were presented to and audited by its common council, and by resolution ordered to be paid. The common council had power to make the repairs and to purchase the articles. In an action upon the accounts, *held*, that the action of the common council not having been rescinded, it was conclusive recognition of the liability of the city, and precluded it from defending on the ground that it was not originally bound to pay because the indebtedness was incurred without previous authority.

The work was done and articles furnished by direction of individual members of the common council, who were not authorized to bind the city or contract debts on its behalf. The accounts, when presented, were referred to the proper committee, and were reported back with a certificate to each to the effect that the committee had examined the account, that the prices charged were reasonable, and that the expenditure " was duly authorized by the common council," and thereupon that body audited the accounts. *Held*, that assuming the city could only be charged on proof or ratification, the evidence justified a finding of such ratification ; that the common council was chargeable with knowledge of its own records, and this although there had been a change in the individuals composing that body ; and, therefore, it was to be assumed that, in acting upon the bills, it knew the indebtedness had not been authorized by any resolution, and that it acted independently of the statement in the certificates, and in auditing and directing payment of the bills, intended to adopt the transactions out of which the indebtedness arose.

Also *held*, that a clause in the city charter (§ 16, chap. 805, Laws of 1877), prohibiting any member of the common council from incurring any expense in behalf of the city for repairs or supplies unless previously ordered by the common council, did not limit the legislative power of that body, or prevent the city from paying a debt so incurred.

(Argued April 19, 1883 ; decided May 1, 1883.)

APPEAL from judgment of the General Term of the Supreme Court, in the third judicial department, entered upon an order made February 10, 1882, which affirmed a judgment in favor of plaintiff, entered upon the report of a referee.

This action was brought by the plaintiff as assignee upon certain bills for services rendered and materials furnished by different persons for the city of Albany, in making repairs on the "City Building," to fit it for use as a city hall, after the City Hall had been consumed by fire.

It was admitted on the trial that the services were rendered and articles furnished, and it was found by the referee that they were rendered and furnished in putting in repair the "City Building" and furnishing it for use, and that the prices charged were reasonable.

In May, 1878, the common council, by resolution, authorized and directed the committee on public buildings to cause necessary repairs to be made to the City Building, and in February, 1880, said committee was authorized to fit up rooms for the city officers, who were left without office room by the burning of the City Hall. Most of the work was done and materials furnished prior to the last resolution. Each of the bills in question had been presented to the common council and referred to the committee on public buildings, and reported on favorably, and a certificate of the committee was indorsed on each bill in the following words:

"This is to certify that we have examined the within account, and find that the prices charged therein are reasonable, and that the expenditure was duly authorized by the common council."

On the 7th, 9th, 12th and 14th days of June, 1880, resolutions were severally passed by the common council ordering the bills to be paid, which order of payment was duly certified on each bill and signed by the clerk of the common council. Each of the resolutions ordering payment was subsequently approved by the mayor.

It appeared that the committee on public buildings did not, as a body, order the work done or the articles charged to be furnished, but that they were ordered by individual members of the committee, in some cases against the protest of other members.

Further facts appear in the opinion.

R. W. Peckham for appellant. The acts of one member

of a committee were incapable, in this instance, of ratification by the common council. (*Peterson* v. *Mayor*, 17 N. Y. 449 ; *Martin* v. *Zellerbach*, 38 Cal. 300.) If it be conceded that a ratification of the void act of the committeeman could be made, the facts in this case utterly fail to show any legal ratification. (Dill. on Mun. Corp. [3d ed.] 296, § 283, note; *Astor* v. *Mayor*, 62 N. Y. 567, 580; *Seymour* v. *Wyckoff*, 10 id. 213, 224 ; *Peterson* v. *Mayor*, 17 id. 449 ; *Ritch* v. *Smith*, 82 id. 627 ; *Adair* v. *Brimmer*, 74 id. 539 ; *Van Schaick* v. *Ins. Co.*, 68 id. 434; *Partridge* v. *Ins. Co.*, 17 Hun, 95; *Lancey* v. *Bryant*, 30 Me. 463.) There is no liability attaching to the city by reason of using the materials, etc., in the building. (*McDonald* v. *The Mayor*, 68 N. Y. 23; 1 Hun, 719 ; *Parr* v. *Greenbush*, 72 N. Y. 463; *Dickinson* v. *Poughkeepsie*, 75 id. 65 ; *Alexander* v. *Cauldwell*, 83 id. 480.)

Amasa J. Parker for respondent. It was not necessary to the validity of this claim that it should have been previously authorized by the common council. (*McCloskey* v. *City of Albany*, 7 Hun, 472; *Peterson* v. *Mayor of New York*, 17 N. Y. 449 ; *Nelson* v. *Mayor*, 63 id. 536.) If the work was done and materials furnished, it would be enough to present their bills, and if the common council audited and approved them and ordered them paid, and the mayor also approved, it would be a binding ratification. A mere irregularity in a previous step would be immaterial. (*Moore* v. *Mayor*. 73 N. Y. 238 ; *Brown* v. *Mayor*, 55 How. Pr. 11.)

Per Curiam. We think the judgment should be affirmed.

First. It is conceded that the common council had power to make the repairs and to purchase the articles, the making and furnishing of which constitute the claims in this action, and to contract debts therefor, binding upon the city. The several bills were presented to the common council, and were duly audited, and by resolution approved by the mayor, they were ordered to be paid. This was a legislative act within the legislative power of the common council. It is also conceded that the work and materials specified in the bills of particulars to which the audit related was done and furnished, and that the prices charged were reasonable. The defense is based upon the ground that the work was done and the materials furnished without any previous authority of the council, but (as appears) under the authority of individual members of the council, not authorized to bind the city or to contract debts in its behalf. The action of the city in auditing the accounts and directing their payment, not having been rescinded, is we think a conclusive recognition of the liability of the city, and precludes it from defending on the ground that it was not originally liable to pay the debts in question.

Second. Assuming that the city can only be charged upon proof of ratification of the unauthorized acts of the individual members of the council who ordered the work and made the purchases constituting the claims in question, we think the evidence justifies the finding that the city ratified the unauthorized transactions. The bills were presented to the council and were referred, as may be assumed, to the proper committee, and were reported back with a certificate of the committee indorsed on the bills respectively, to the effect that the committee had examined the account to which the certificate related, and found that the prices charged were reasonable, and that the expenditure " was duly authorized by the common council." The council thereupon audited the bills and by resolution directed their payment as above stated. It is claimed that this did not constitute a ratification, for the reason that it was not true, as reported by the committee, that the expenditure had been authorized by the council, and that, so far as appears, the council acted in ignorance of this fact.

The defendant relies upon the rule that to constitute a ratification by a principal of the act of an assumed agent acting without authority, it must appear that all the material facts were known to the principal at the time of the alleged ratification. The difficulty in the application of this rule here is that there is no reason to infer that the council, in auditing the bills and directing their payment, relied upon the fact stated in the report of the committee that the expenditure had been duly authorized by the council, but on the contrary it is a just inference from the circumstances that it acted independently thereof and without reference thereto. It is claimed by the learned counsel for the defendant that no part of the indebtedness had been authorized by any resolution of the council. This is not, perhaps, true, to the full extent of the claim. But it is true as to a part of the work and materials constituting the indebtedness claimed, and this was ascertainable at the time by a comparison of the resolutions of the council appearing on its records, with the items in the bills. The common council was chargeable with knowledge of its records. A mere change in the individuals which compose the common council does not destroy the continuity of the body, or relieve it from the presumption of knowledge of the official acts appearing of record of a former council. It is clear, therefore, that as to the part of the indebtedness, for the creation of which no authority whatever had been given by the council, the council is chargeable with knowledge of the fact, and cannot be deemed to have relied upon the statement mistakenly made in the certificate.

The other part of the indebtedness was authorized by the resolution of May 27, 1878, that is to say, that resolution authorized and directed the committee on public buildings to make repairs of the same character as those which the claimants were employed to make. The defect was that the work, instead of being ordered by the committee collectively, was ordered by one or more members thereof, without any action of the committee as such, and in some cases against the protest of other members. In a sense the certificate of the auditing committee as to the fact of the indebtedness was true. The expenditure was ordered to be made by the common council, but the requirement that it should be made under the direction of the committee, as such, was not followed. It is a reasonable inference from the circumstances that the council, in auditing the bills and directing their payment, intended to adopt the transactions out of which the indebtedness arose, and that

it did not rely upon the particular fact stated in the report of
the auditing committee, that the expenditure had been previously authorized by the council. As to part of the bills, the
council, as has been said, is chargeable with knowledge that
the fact was not true, and as to the other bills it was true *sub
modo*. It appears, moreover, affirmatively, that when the bills
were reported back by the committee, the only thing said was
that the committee reported the bills and recommended payment. The clause in the charter, prohibiting any member or
members of the common council to incur any expense in behalf
of the city for repairs or supplies, unless previously ordered by
the common council, does not limit the legislative power of
the council, or prevent the city from paying a debt for work,
labor or supplies of which it has received the benefit, although it was originally created under the direction of a member or members of the council, in excess of his or their authority. (*Peterson* v. *The Mayor*, etc., 17 N. Y. 449.)

We think the judgment should be affirmed.

All concur.

Judgment affirmed.

———

2 368
6 872

PATRICK FLEMING, Respondent, *v.* THE VILLAGE OF SUSPEN-
SION BRIDGE, Appellant.

Where the trustees of an incorporated village organize into a board of
water commissioners for the purposes and as prescribed by the act of 1875
(Chap. 181, Laws of 1875), and as such enter into a contract for erecting
water-works for the village, they act simply as agents for, and the contract is binding upon it, and an action is maintainable against it thereon.
It is immaterial whether the contract is made in the name of the village,
or in the names of the trustees as water commissioners, or as a board.
Said statute confers upon such water commissioners general power to
contract, and the entire control of the work for procuring a water supply ;
and where a contract has been regularly let as prescribed, if in the substantial performance thereof slight variations or changes are necessary.
they may be made by their direction without a new letting, and for the
extra expense the village is liable.

In an action to recover for such extra work it did not appear that it was formally ordered by the board at any regular meeting thereof, or that any formal action was taken in reference to it. It appeared, however, that some one or more of the commissioners were upon the work nearly every day, and sometimes all of them, supervising and inspecting the same. It was provided in the contract that the work should be at all times under their control. *Held,* it was to be presumed they all had knowledge of what was being done and assented to the extra work ; and so, a finding that such work was ordered by the board was justified.

(Submitted April 19, 1883 ; decided May 1, 1883.)

APPEAL from judgment of the General Term of the Supreme Court, in the fourth judicial department, entered upon an order made October 28, 1881, which affirmed a judgment in favor of plaintiff, entered upon the report of a referee.

The nature of the action and the material facts are stated in the opinion.

H. N. Griffith for appellant. The defendant could not be made liable except by the provisions of the act of 1875 (Chap. 181), and by this the liability essential to sustain this action is not imposed upon the defendant. (*King* v. *City of Brooklyn,* 42 Barb. 627 ; *Van Valkenburg* v. *Mayor, etc., of N. Y.,* 33 id. 109 ; *Theall* v. *Yonkers,* 21 Hun, 265 ; *Donovan* v. *Bd. of Education of the City of New York,* 85 N. Y. 117 ; *Maximilian* v. *Mayor,* 62 id. 160 ; *N. Y. & B. S. M. & L. Co.* v. *City of Brooklyn,* 71 id. 580.) The commissioners had no authority to make any contract for any work or materials except that given them by the act of 1875, and in the manner and form therein prescribed, and as found by the referee. (*Bigler* v. *Mayor,* 5 Abb. N. C. 51 ; *McDonald* v. *The Mayor,* 68 N. Y. 23 ; *Dickson* v. *City of Poughkeepsie,* 75 id. 65, 74, 75 ; *Smith* v. *City of Newburgh,* 77 id. 130, 136.) Acts could not be treated as the acts of the board unless all were present, or those absent had notice to be present. By such act only, in any event, could the defendant be bound. (2 R. S. 575, § 27 ; *People* v. *Batchelor,* 22 N. Y. 146 ; *People, ex rel.* v. *Nostrand,* 46 id. 375, 383 ; *Olmstead* v. *Dennis,* 77 id. 379 ; 1 Dillon on Municipal Corporations, § 224.)

C. H. Piper for respondent. The water commissioners are not a corporation, and are not liable to be sued as such for work done and materials furnished at their request. (*Appleton* v. *Water Commrs. of N. Y.*, 2 Hill, 432; *Bailey* v. *The Mayor*, 3 id. 531; 2 Denio, 433; *Conrad* v. *Vil. of Ithaca*, 16 N. Y. 158.) The work which plaintiff performed has been accepted, acquiesced in, used and enjoyed by defendant, and being for its benefit, defendant is now estopped from claiming that the work was done without authority. (*Messenger* v. *City of Buffalo*, 21 N. Y. 196; *Hoyt* v. *Thompson*, 19 id. 207; *Alexander* v. *Brown*, 9 Hun, 641; *Lord* v. *City of Rochester*, MSS. Opinion, Fourth Dept.; *Castle* v. *Lewis*, 78 N. Y. 131, 134; *Le Grand* v. *M. M. Assn.*, 80 id. 638; *Hooker* v. *Eagle B'k of Rochester*, 30 id. 83; *Landers* v. *Frank. St. Church*, 15 Hun, 340; *Argus Co.* v. *The Mayor*, 7 Lans. 273.)

EARL, J. In 1876 the trustees of the village of Suspension Bridge, under the act chapter 181 of the Laws of 1875, organized themselves into a board of water commissioners. Afterward, in the same year, the board entered into a contract with the plaintiff to build for the village certain water-works for conducting into and through the village water from the Niagara river for a compensation of $5,185. He completed the work required by the contract and received the stipulated consideration, except a small balance.

During the performance of his contract the plaintiff was requested by the water commissioners to perform some extra work; and to recover for such work and the balance due him under his contract, he commenced this action. The action was referred to a referee, who found there was due the plaintiff a balance of $110, under the contract, and three items, $35, $600 and $70.20, for extra work ordered by the water commissioners.

During the progress of the trial the counsel for the defendant took many exceptions to the rulings of the referee upon questions of evidence, and he also filed exceptions to the findings of the referee; and he now claims that there were errors which call for the reversal of the judgment.

It is objected on the part of the defendant that the board of water commissioners had no power under the act of 1875 to make any contract for or binding upon it. The objection is not well founded. The act provides that the trustees of any incorporated village in this State may hereafter organize into a board of water commissioners, in the manner provided in the act; that it shall be the duty of the commissioners to examine and consider all matters relating to supplying the village with water; and for that purpose that they shall have power to employ engineers, surveyors and such other persons as shall be necessary; that they shall adopt such plans as in their opinion shall be most feasible for procuring the water supply, and that they shall have power to contract for and purchase and take by deed in the name of the village all lands, rights or privileges whatever which may be required for the purpose, and to contract for the execution of the work and the supply of any necessary material. The act further provides for acquiring the title of lands in all cases where the water commissioners shall be unable to agree with the owners, and that the title of the land thus taken shall vest in fee in the village; that the commissioners shall have power to borrow from time to time upon the credit of the village a sum not exceeding ten per cent of the assessed value of the real and personal estate of the village as shall appear by the last assessment-roll, upon such term of credit, not exceeding thirty years, as shall seem to them for the best interests of the village; and that to secure the payment of the money thus borrowed they may execute bonds, certificates or other obligations, to be signed by them, which shall be a valid liability against the village, and the credit of the village is pledged for the payment of the same. Other portions of the act provide for the rents to be charged for the use of water; that the proceeds of such rents shall be used to pay the expenses of repairing the water-works and the interest and principal of the money borrowed; that in case the water rents shall not be sufficient to pay the interest on the loans or the principal of the bonds as they fall due, the deficiency may be imposed by tax upon the property of the village, and that judgments against the commissioners in their name of office, and judgments against them where the transaction upon which the action was brought shall have been in the performance of their duties as commissioners, shall not be enforced against the individual property of either of the commissioners.

It will thus be seen from this analysis of the act that the board of water commissioners is not a corporation. There is no provision in the act authorizing the commissioners to sue or to be sued as a board. The board is at all times composed of the trustees of the village, and the water commissioners are manifestly the agents of the village. The water-works are a local improvement, exclusively for the benefit of citizens of the village. They are to be constructed upon the credit of the village, are to belong to it when constructed, and the title to all the land taken is vested in it. The rents received for the use of the water belong to it, and the entire expense of constructing the water-works is a charge upon it. It was, therefore, immaterial whether in making this contract the water commissioners made the same in the name of the village, as they did, or in their own official names as water commissioners, or as a board of water commissioners. The village became bound by their act, and for this conclusion the cases of *Appleton* v. *The Water Commissioners* (2 Hill, 432), *Bailey* v. *The Mayor, etc., of New York* (3 id. 531; *S. C.*, 2 Denio, 433), and *Sage* v. *The City of Brooklyn* (89 N. Y. 189), are ample authority. Any other construction of the act might practically leave a contractor performing the work without any remedy. It is expressly provided that he shall have no remedy to be enforced against the individual property of either of the commissioners, and if he has no remedy against the village it would be quite difficult to see how payment for work done under the act could be enforced. It is clearly to be inferred, from the fact that the commissioners are exempted from individual liability, that it was the intention of the legislature to impose the liability upon their principal, the village.

It is further claimed on behalf of the defendant, that it was never made liable for the extra work not included within the contract, because the act requires that all work should be let by contract. The only provision contained in the act upon the subject· is in the tenth section, which, after conferring upon the water commissioners power to make all necessary contracts for labor and material, provides that three weeks public notice shall be given in one or more newspapers " of the times and places at which sealed proposals will be received for entering into contracts, and the commissioners shall have full discretion as to the acceptance or rejection of all sealed proposals; and in case any materials and labor shall then remain uncontracted for, the like notice for sealed proposals and like proceedings may be had as above provided; and so from time to time, as said commissioners may direct, for work or materials." The three items of extra work for which the referee allowed were of the following description : The plaintiff had laid pipe upon the grade given by the commissioners, and had filled the trench over it in accordance with his contract; and then, by the direction of the commissioners, he opened the trench, took up the pipe over a space of about one thousand two hundred feet, and dug the trench deeper. He then relaid the pipe, and by the direction of the commissioners he took up about three hundred feet of the pipe a second time, and dug the trench still deeper and relaid the pipe therein and refilled the trench; and for the extra labor thus performed the referee allowed the sum of $600. He also, by direction of the commissioners, furnished and delivered twenty-six feet of cast-iron pipe of the value of $70.20, which was not embraced in his contract; and he furnished two hundred feet of pipe which was of larger diameter than was required by the contract, and for this the referee allowed an extra compensation of $35. The statute confers upon the water commissioners the entire control of the work for procuring the water supply. It gives them general power to contract for the performance of the work. It directs them to give public notice for proposals, but does not bind them to let the work to the lowest bidder. It gives them full discretion as to the acceptance or rejection of all sealed proposals.

Acting in good faith, exercising their best judgment for the interests of the village, they could accept the highest proposal instead of the lowest. They let the work to the plaintiff upon the proposal made by him. So far the statute was literally complied with. There is nothing in its letter or the spirit which required them, if, in the prosecution of the work, they found it was essential to dig a trench a little deeper, or to change its route, or to procure a little larger pipe than the contract required, to advertise for new proposals. The work was still in the substantial performance of the same contract, and these slight variations could be made under the general authority conferred upon them by the statute without a new letting.

It did not appear upon the trial of this case that these items of extra work were formally ordered by the board of water commissioners at any regular meeting of the board, or that any formal action was taken in reference to them. But it appeared that some one or more of the water commissioners were upon the work nearly every day supervising and inspecting the .same. It was provided in the contract that the work should, at all times, be under the control of the commissioners during its progress, and that it should be commenced and prosecuted at such points as they should direct. Sometimes one and sometimes several, and sometimes all of them, were upon the work, directing and supervising it, so that it is clearly inferable that they all had knowledge of what was being done; that they all knew of the directions which were given by either, and that they all assented to the extra work, and hence we think the finding of the referee was justified by the evidence that the extra work was ordered by the board of water commissioners.

We have now noticed the principal grounds of objection to the recovery by the plaintiff. Many other exceptions were taken. They have all been carefully considered, and we do not think any of them require a reversal of the judgment.

We are, therefore, of opinion that the judgment should be affirmed, with costs.

All concur, except MILLER, J., absent.

Judgment affirmed.

James R. Wood et al., Executors, etc., Respondents, *v.* Viola
Yates Mitcham et al., Appellants.

/3 ¥

. .
92
161
-

R. died, leaving a will, prior to the execution of which, C., a married daughter, had died, leaving four children, a son and three daughters. Her
husband had remarried and had by the second marriage two children,
daughters, who were of no kin to R. All of said children survived him.
By his will he directed a seventh part of his residuary estate to be subdivided into four equal shares, to be held in trust, one for each of the
four children of C. during their respective minorities, and then to be
paid over. Substantially similar provisions were made for the disposition of each of said shares in case the beneficiary died before coming of
age. The direction as to the share of E., one of the testator's said grandchildren, was that in case of such death and in default of issue "living
at her death, then to pay over the same with its accumulations to her
then living brother and sisters and the issue of any deceased brother or
sister who shall have died having lawful issue then living, each then
living brother and sister taking one equal share thereof, and the issue of
any deceased brother or sister taking by representation the share the parent of such issue would have taken if then living." E. died before
coming of age leaving no issue, but leaving her brother and two sisters
and her two half sisters surviving. In an action for a construction of
the will, *held*, that her share went to her brother and sisters of the full-
blood, and that her sisters of the half-blood were not entitled to any
portion thereof; that as the contrary construction would result in diverting a portion of the testator's estate from his lineal descendants to
strangers to his blood, the burden was upon them to establish that the
testator in using the word "sisters" intended to include them; that the
presumption to the contrary could only be overcome by clear and unequivocal language; and, therefore, the fact that in the direction as to
the disposition of the shares of two of the other of his said grandchildren
in case of such death the word "brothers" was used instead of "brother"
as in the clause quoted, did not show such an intention.
Where a will is capable of two interpretations that one should be adopted
which prefers those of the blood of the testator to strangers.

(Argued March 22, 1883; decided May 8, 1883.)

Appeal from judgment of the General Term of the Supreme Court, in the first judicial department, entered upon
an order made the first Monday of October, 1881, which af-

firmed a judgment entered upon a decision of the court on trial at Special Term.

This action was brought by plaintiffs as executors and trustees under the will of James Rowe, deceased, to obtain a construction of said will.

The substance of the portions of the will in question and the material facts are stated in the opinion.

Geo. G. De Witt, Jr., for appellants. The intention of the testator, if not inconsistent with the rules of law, must govern ; and this intention must be ascertained from the whole will taken together. (*Hone* v. *Van Schaick*, 3 Comst. 536, 540, 541 ; *Scott* v. *Guernsey*, 48 N. Y. 106, 120–121 ; *Quinn* v. *Hardenbrook*, 54 id. 83, 86.) If there are two probable interpretations of the will, that one is to be adopted which prefers the kin of the testator to strangers. (4 Kent's Comm. [11th ed.] 535 ; *Quinn* v. *Hardenbrook*, 54 N. Y. 86 ; *Van Kleek* v. *Dutch Church*, 20 Wend. 457 ; *Scott* v. *Guernsey*, 48 N. Y. 106 ; 60 Barb. 163 ; *Areson* v. *Areson*, 3 Denio, 461 ; *Kelso* v. *Lorillard*, 85 N. Y. 182 ; *Gazlay* v. *Cornwell*, 2 Redf. 139 ; *Valentine* v. *Wetherill*, 31 Barb. 635.) The testator is presumed to have used words in the primary or ordinary sense, unless the contrary appears from the context. (*Cromer* v. *Pinckney*, 3 Barb. Ch. 475 ; *Mowatt* v. *Carow*, 7 Paige, 328 ; *Lawrence* v. *Hebbard*, 1 Bradf. 252 ; *Hone* v. *Van Schaick*, 3 N. Y. 538 ; *Kiah* v. *Grenier*, 56 id. 220 ; *Palmer* v. *Horn*, 84 id. 516 ; *Clark* v. *Pickering*, 16 N. H. 284 ; *Wheeler* v. *Clutterbuck*, 52 N. Y. 71.) No change of one word for another can ever be made, unless it becomes necessary to carry into effect the "clearest intent" of the testator, or the word used conflicts with his plainly expressed intention. (Redfield on Wills, 471, 491, 492, *n.*)

Samuel Hand for respondents. By the absolute and unqualified direction to sell and convert into money all the testator's real and personal property, and invest the proceeds for the uses and purposes therein specified, the real estate was converted into money. (*Moncrief* v. *Ross*, 50 N. Y. 431, 436, 437.) The intent of the testator is to be gathered from the words of the will itself. (*Mann* v. *Mann*, 14 Johns. 1; *Arcularius* v. *Geisenheimer*, 3 Bradf. 64; id. 114; *Westcott* v. *Cody*, 5 Johns. Ch. 334; *Hone* v. *Van Schaick*, 3 Barb. Ch. 506; *Lovett* v. *Kingsland*, 44 Barb. 560; *Lovett* v. *Gillender*, 35 N. Y. 617, 621; *Cramer* v. *Pinckney*, 3 Barb. Ch. 466, 475.)

Rapallo, J. The will of James Rowe was dated February 19, 1868, and he died October 18, 1871. Before the date of this will, viz.: in 1856, the testator's daughter, Cordelia Yates, wife of Charles Yates, had died, leaving four children, the issue of her marriage with said Charles Yates, viz.: one son, Henry Yates, and three daughters, Viola, Adelaide and Catharine, all of whom survived the testator.

Charles Yates, the father of these children, had, after the death of his wife Cordelia, and during the life-time of the testator, viz.: in 1860, remarried, and by his second marriage had two children, viz.: Frances Yates, born in 1864, and Stella Yates, born in 1866. These two children also survived the testator. They were, however, of no kin to him.

The testator by his will, after providing for his widow and son, directed that the residue of his estate be divided into seven equal parts. Six of these parts he directed to be held in trust for six daughters named in the sixth clause of his will, and the remaining one-seventh part he disposed of by the seventh clause of the will for the benefit of his four above-named grandchildren, the issue of his deceased daughter, Cordelia Yates. The construction of this seventh clause is the subject of the present controversy.

By this clause he directed his executors to subdivide the said seventh part into four equal sub-shares, and to invest and accumulate one of said sub-shares for the benefit of each of said four grandchildren, Henry, Viola, Adelaide and Catharine Yates, during their respective minorities, and to pay over to each of them his or her share, with its accumulations, on his or her arriving at age. Provision was made for the disposition of the shares of any of said four grandchildren who might die before attaining the age of twenty-one years. The direction as to the share of each of said grandchildren is substantially the same, with some verbal differences to which importance has been attached, and which will be remarked upon hereafter. The direction in respect to the sub-share of his granddaughter, Catharine, is the one immediately under consideration, and is in the following words:

"And to invest and accumulate the remaining one equal fourth 'part until the arrrival at full age, or death, whichever shall first happen, of my granddaughter, Catharine Yates, child of my deceased daughter, Cordelia Yates, and upon her arrival at the age of twenty-one years, to pay over the same, with its accumulations, to her, and in case of her death prior to attaining said age, to pay over the said fourth part, with its accumulations, to her lawful issue. And in default of issue of my said granddaughter, Catharine, living at her death, then to pay over the same, with its accumulations, to her then living brother and sisters, and the issue of any deceased brother or sister who shall have died leaving lawful issue then living, each then living brother and sister taking one equal share thereof, and the issue of any deceased brother or sister of hers taking by representation the share the parent of such issue would have taken if then living."

After the death of the testator, viz.: November 30, 1874, Catharine Yates died, being then a minor and without issue, leaving her surviving her brother, Henry, and her two sisters, Viola and Adelaide, and also her two half-sisters, or sisters of the half-blood, Frances and Stella Yates, and the question now presented is whether it was the intention of the testator that upon the death of his granddaughter, Catharine, under age and without issue, her share should go to his surviving grandchildren, Henry, Viola and Adelaide, and their issue, or whether he intended that Frances and Stella Yates, the children of Charles Yates by his second marriage, and strangers to the blood of the testator, should participate therein. It is claimed on their behalf that they answer the description of sisters of Catharine, and are entitled to take as such, and that the clause in question, read in connection with other parts of the will, shows that the testator so intended. Bouvier's Law Dictionary defines " sister " as " a woman who has the same father and mother with another, or one of them only. In the first case she is called sister simply; in the second, half-sister." Worcester defines "sister" as "a female born of the same parents." The word is defined by Webster as "a female whose parents are the same as those of another person." Blackstone (vol. 2, p. 227) defines a kinsman of the whole blood as " he that is derived, not only from the same ancestor, but from the same couple of ancestors." (*Clark* v. *Pickering*, 16 N. H. 284; *Wheeler* v. *Clutterbuck*, 52 N. Y. 71.)

The statute of descents (1 R. S. 752, § 6) does not apply to a case like the present, but only to the case of relatives inheriting from the same ancestor, or from each other, and recognizes the distinction between relatives of the full blood and of the half-blood.

It is not necessary to enter into a discussion whether, in view of the definitions referred to, the primary meaning of the word "sister" is to be regarded as confined to a sister of the full blood, or whether it includes a sister of the half-blood, for we have a well-settled rule, applicable to the present case, which is more satisfactory than mere definitions, viz.: that where a will is capable of two interpretations, that one should be adopted which prefers those of the blood of the testator to strangers. (Kent's Com. [11th ed.] 535; *Van Kleeck* v. *Dutch Church*, 20 Wend. 457; *Quinn* v. *Hardenbrook*, 54 N. Y. 86; *Scott* v. *Guernsey*, 48 id. 106; *Kelso* v. *Lorillard*, 85 id. 182.)

Inasmuch as the construction claimed by the respondents would result in diverting the property left by the testator, from his lineal descendants, to strangers to his blood, the burden is upon them to establish that in using the term " sisters," the testator intended to include the half-sisters of his grandchildren named in the seventh clause. The presumption is to the contrary, and this presumption can be overcome only by clear and unequivocal language. It cannot be contended that if the direction, "and in default of issue of my granddaughter Catharine, living at her death, then to pay over the same with its accumulations to her then living brother and sisters," stood alone, her half-sisters, who were of no kin to the testator, could be deemed to be included. The rule before referred to would require us so to construe this provision as to prefer her brother and sisters of the full blood, who alone were of the blood of the testator. But it is contended that the words next following manifest a different intent. The words are, " and the issue of *any deceased brother or sister* who shall have died leaving lawful issue then living, *each then living brother and sister* taking one equal share thereof, and *the issue of any deceased brother or sister* of hers taking by representation the share the parent of such issue would have taken if then living." Stress is laid upon the words italicised as showing that the testator contemplated that more than one brother of his granddaughter might survive her, or one might have died leaving issue, and another might survive, but inasmuch as she had but one brother at the date of the will, and her mother had long been dead, she could have no other brother unless it were a half-brother thereafter born, an event which was possible, as her father, Charles Yates, was then living. From this it is argued that the testator intended that such after born half-brother should participate in her share, in the contingency mentioned, and that this shows an intention that her half-sisters should participate in like manner.

In our judgment this circuitous mode of reasoning, depending on such close verbal criticisms, falls far short of that clear demonstration of intention which is necessary to authorize a construction of the will which will divert the testator's property from his own lineal descendants for the benefit of strangers to his blood. The language is the ordinary verbiage of a conveyancer, and though perhaps not the most accurate which might have been used, is quite consistent with the interpretation that all it was intended to express was that if either or any of the persons to whom the contingent remainder was limited, and who consisted of a brother and three sisters, should die without issue, the property should go to the survivors or survivor, and to the issue of any of those deceased, such issue taking by representation. It could not be known whether the deceased might be the brother or one or more of the sisters, and the language was designed to fit either case. As the limitation was in the first instance to the brother and the sisters, it cannot be supposed that it was intended to provide for the issue of any brother other than the one first referred to.

It is claimed, however, that the construction contended for by the respondents is fortified by reference to the provisions in favor of Viola and Adelaide Yates, contained in the same seventh clause. These are identical in form with the provision for Catharine, except that the contingent remainders limited upon their shares respectively, instead of being given to their surviving *brother* and sisters, is given to their surviving brothers and sisters. From the use of the word *brothers* in the two provisions last referred to, it is argued that the intent of the testator must have been, as to the shares of those two granddaughters, to provide for any half-brother they might subsequently have, and consequently to include their half-sisters; and that it is to be presumed that his intentions were the same in regard to the share of Catharine.

The use of the word "brother" in the case of Catharine, and "brothers" in the cases of Viola and Adelaide, indicates either that the testator had some different intention in the one case than the other, or that the difference in language occurred through inadvertence. It would certainly seem extraordinary that, if he entertained different intentions, he should select such an obscure method of manifesting them; and it is equally difficult to comprehend why he should design that the two half-sisters should participate in the succession to the shares of some of his grandchildren and not of the others. If any significance is to be attached to the difference between the term "brother" and "brothers" the argument is of course open that the term "brother" may have been inadvertently used in

the case of Catharine ; but we are of opinion that the difference has no significance and was accidental. And we are confirmed in this conclusion by reference to the provision as to
the share of Henry Yates. His share was limited to his surviving "sisters" only, showing clearly the intention of the
testator, in that case at least, to confine his dispositions to his
own descendants. And it is not reasonable to suppose that, if
he had intended to make nice distinctions between those who
were to succeed to the shares of his different grandchildren, he
would have left them to depend upon the ingenious course of
reasoning resorted to by the respondents.

A more substantial guide to the intentions of the testator is,
we think, afforded by recurring to the primary provision which
he makes for the children of his daughter Cordelia. If he
had entertained any idea of including in that provision the
half-sisters of those grandchildren, the issue of the second
marriage of their father, he would naturally have included
them in the original bequest. They were living when the
will was made, and yet no provision is made for them, but the
share which would have gone to his daughter Cordelia is carefully limited to her children and their issue, and the issue of
the second marriage of their father are in no way recognized.

The whole frame of the will seems to us to indicate that the
testator intended to bestow his property upon his own descendants. Notwithstanding this general intent it was still possible,
however, that by some convolution of events parts of his
estate might have drifted out of that current. And upon
these possibilities an argument is sought to be constructed.
But notwithstanding the ingenuity and ability of that argument we are of opinion that the mere omission of the testator
to guard against every such contingency, even if it were possible to do so, cannot be construed as indicating an intention
that his estate should go out of the natural course. To so hold
would reverse the ordinary rules of construction applicable to
such cases.

We are, therefore, of opinion that on the death of Catharine
Yates, her portion of the testator's property (which under the

provisions of the will must be taken as converted into person-alty), was under the will distributable to her brother Henry and her sisters Viola and Adelaide. And that her half-sisters Frances and Stella Yates were not entitled to share therein.

The judgments below should, therefore, be reversed and judgment entered for the appellants, according to the forego-ing views, the costs of all the parties to be paid out of the estate.

All concur.

Judgment accordingly.

THE PEOPLE OF THE STATE OF NEW YORK, Respondent, *v.* THE SPRING VALLEY HYDRAULIC GOLD COMPANY, Appel-lant.

Under the act of 1880 (Chap. 542, Laws of 1880), providing for "raising taxes for the use of the State upon certain corporations," etc., the first report required to be made by the officers of the corporation included in the act was to be made in November, 1880, and the first tax paid in Janu-ary, 1881 ; and this, although at the latter date the corporation had not been in existence for a year.

This construction does not give to the act a retroactive effect, as the tax so imposed was to pay the prospective expenditure for the fiscal year com-mencing October 1, 1880.

(Argued April 23, 1883 ; decided May 8, 1883.)

APPEAL from judgment of the General Term of the Su-preme Court, in the third judicial department, entered upon an order made November 22, 1882, which affirmed a judgment in favor of plaintiff, entered upon a decision of the court on trial without a jury.

This action was brought to recover the amount of a tax alleged to be due from defendant, a domestic corporation, on January 1, 1880, under the act chapter 542, Laws of 1880.

The material facts are stated in the opinion.

Ro. L. Harrison for appellant. The tax levied under the statute in question is a tax on the franchise in contradistinction to a tax on the property of the company. (*Prov. Inst.* v. *Massachusetts,* 6 Wall. 361, 630, 632; *Soc. for Savings* v. *Coite,* id. 608, 609; Laws of 1881, chap. 361.) It is a tax upon the enjoyment of the franchise for the period of a year. (*Park B'k* v. *Wood,* 24 N. Y. 93; *Susq. B'k* v. *Supervisors of Broome,* 25 id. 312.) Statutes are to have a prospective and not retrospective operation. (Broom's Legal Maxims, 14; *Dash* v. *Van Kleeck,* 7 Johns. 447; *Warren M'f'g Co.* v. *Ætna Ins. Co.,* 2 Paige, 501; *People, ex rel.* 23d *St. R. R. Co.,* v. *Commrs. of Taxes,* 81 N. Y. 593; 14 N. Y. W'kly Dig. 464; *Drexel* v. *Comm.,* 46 Penn. St. 31; *People* v. *N. Y. Floating Dry Dock Co.,* Sept. Term, 1882.) Under the most favorable construction for the plaintiff, the tax in question should be apportioned, and the defendant should be taxed on its franchise during that portion only of the year that it existed after the act had become a law. (*Ebervale Coal Co.* v. *Commw.,* 91 Penn. St. 47.)

Leslie W. Russell, attorney-general, for respondent. Defendant, in all the essentials of its actual existence and the right to exercise the powers conferred upon it, is conclusively within the jurisdiction of this State, and for the purposes of taxation it does not matter where its actual business is carried on or where its tangible property is situated. Its capital stock is property, and so are its franchises, either or both of which are legitimate subjects of taxation. (*Soc. for Savings* v. *Coit,* 6 Wall. 594, 606, 607; *State Tax on Foreign-held Bonds,* 15 id. 300, 419; *People* v. *The Mayor,* 4 N. Y. 419.) Uniformity of taxation is a question governed entirely by the Constitution and laws of the State. The legislature in the exercise of the taxing power is supreme unless limited by the Constitution. (*B'k of Chenango* v. *Brown,* 26 N. Y. 467; *State Tax on Foreign-held Bonds,* 15 Wall. 314; *State R. R. Tax Cases,* 92 U. S. 575, 611; Cooley on Taxation, 129, note 1; *St. Louis* v. *Wehrung,* 46 Ill. 392; 48 id. 172; 92 id. 339;

94 id. 364; *Youngblood* v. *Sexton*, 32 Mich. 406; *Litchfield* v. *Vernon*, 41 N. Y. 124; *People* v. *The Mayor*, 4 id. 419; *Slaughter-house Cases*, 16 Wall. 36, 81.) The power of the legislature to apportion taxation and to classify the subjects and persons which are to be taxed is identical with, and inseparable from, the power to tax. (*People* v. *Mayor, etc.*, 4 N. Y. 419, 426, 427; Cooley on Taxation, 175, 179; *Comm.* v. *People's Five Cent Savings B'k*, 5 Allen, 428, 436, 437.) The rules cited as to the repugnancy of the courts to a construction which would favor retroactive legislation do not apply in this case. (Cooley on Taxation, 169, and note 2, 221; *Locke* v. *New Orleans*, 4 Wall. 172; *Comm.* v. *People's Five Cent Savings B'k*, 5 Allen, 428; Cooley on Taxation, 170; Burroughs on Taxation, § 86; *Soc. for Savings* v. *Coit*, 6 Wall. 608; *Drexel* v. *Comm.*, 46 Penn. St. 31, 40.) The objection that the act of 1880 is unconstitutional in that it requires no assessment of the value of the property taxed is untenable. (Laws of 1880, chap. 542, § 1; *People* v. *Hays*, 7 How. Pr. 248; *Smith* v. *The Mayor*, 37 N. Y. 518, 520.) The act in question is not unconstitutional as violative of section 20, article 3 of the Constitution. (*People, ex rel. Burroughs*, v. *Supervisors of Orange Co.*, 17 N. Y. 235; *Sun Mut. Ins. Co.* v. *Mayor, etc., of N. Y.*, 5 Sandf. 10, 14, 15; *People* v. *Nat. Ins. Co.*, 27 Hun, 188.)

ANDREWS, J. The defendant, a corporation incorporated and organized on the 12th day of February, 1880, under the laws of this State, on the 16th day of November, 1880, by its treasurer, made a report in writing to the comptroller, under oath, setting forth the capital of the corporation paid in, and that no dividend had been declared during the year ending with the 1st day of November. On the same day the secretary and treasurer, after having been duly sworn, estimated and appraised the capital stock of the corporation at $800,-000, which was declared to be its actual value in cash, not less than the average price which the said stock sold for during the year ending November 1, 1880, and forwarded to the comptroller a certificate of such estimate and appraisal, together with a copy of the oath by them signed, duly attested by the officer before whom it was taken. This action is brought in the name of the people to recover of the defendant a tax at the rate of one and a half mills on each dollar of the valuation of its corporate stock, so made by its secretary and treasurer, amounting in the aggregate to the sum of $1,200, which is alleged in the complaint to have become due and payable to the State from the defendant on or before the 15th day of January, 1881, pursuant to the provisions of chapter 542 of the Laws of 1880.

It is conceded that the defendant is a corporation liable to taxation under the third section of the act. It is claimed, however, by the counsel for the defendant that by the true construction of the act no tax became payable thereunder by the defendant until January, 1882, and this is the only question presented on this appeal.

The act in question is entitled " An act to provide for raising taxes for the use of the State, upon certain corporations, joint stock companies and associations." It inaugurates a new system for the taxation of a certain specified class of corporations for general and State purposes, but as construed, leaves them subject to taxation for local purposes under the pre-existing law. (*People, ex rel. Westchester Fire Ins. Co.,* v. *Davenport,* 91 N. Y. 574.) The general scheme of the act is to impose a tax on corporations paying dividends exceeding six per cent per annum on the basis of dividends declared during the year preceding the imposition of the tax. But when no dividends have been declared, or have been less than six per cent on the par value of the capital stock during such annual period, the tax is based on the cash value of the capital stock, to be ascertained as provided in the act.

To carry out the system it was necessary to provide a method of ascertaining the amount of dividends declared by the corporations liable to taxation under the act, and where no dividends had been declared, or were less than six per cent per annum, the value of the capital stock, and it was manifestly important that this information should be communicated to the State officers. The first section, therefore, which commences with the word "hereafter," makes it the duty of corporations liable to taxation under the third section, "annually on or before the 15th day of November," to make a report to the comptroller, stating the amount of capital paid in, the date, amount and rate per centum of each and every dividend declared "during the year ending with the first day of said month." And in the case of non-dividend paying corporations, and of corporations whose dividends declared "during the year ending as aforesaid," were less than six per cent on the par value of the capital stock, it provides that "the treasurer or secretary thereof * * * shall between the 1st and 15th days of November in each year in which no dividend has been made or declared as aforesaid * * * estimate and appraise the capital stock of such company upon which no dividend has been made or declared at its actual value, not less, however, than the average price which said stock sold for during said year." The third section imposes the liability to taxation, and declares that the corporations specified "shall be subject to and pay a tax into the treasury of the State annually," to be computed either on the dividends or on the value of the capital stock as the case may be, in the one case the tax to be at the rate of one-quarter mill on the capital stock for each one per centum of dividend, and in the other a half mill on each dollar of valuation.

It is contended that the act does not contemplate that corporations shall make a report under the first section, until the year succeeding that in which it was passed, to-wit: November, 1881, and that no tax was required to be paid under the provisions of the third section, until after that time. This contention rests mainly upon the supposed implication arising from the word "annually" in the first and third sections, and from the requirement that the report to be made under the first section is to state the dividends declared during the year prior thereto, or in case of non-dividend corporations, that the capital stock shall be valued at "not less than the average price which said stock sold for during the year."

It is said that the act having been passed in June, 1880, a report made in November, 1880, is not an annual report, and that
the requirement that the report shall state the dividends declared during the year before the report is made, and that
when a valuation of the capital stock is to be made, it is to be
at a sum not less than the average price for which the stock
sold during the same period, indicates that it was the intention
of the legislature to allow corporations at least a year after the
passage of the act to ascertain the value of their franchise before subjecting them to taxation under the new system. The
intention of the legislature in passing a statute, and its true
meaning is to be collected from its language, applied to the
subject-matter, and in view of the general scope and purpose
of the enactment, and the construction of a particular clause
or section of a statute, if obscure or doubtful, is to be determined by a consideration of all its parts. A clause or section
which, considered separately, may be obscure, or justify one
construction, may be made clear by reference to other clauses
or sections, or may be subordinated to another and paramount
intention derived from other parts of the statute. It is to be
observed that the time when the first report is to be made is
not stated in terms in the first section, nor does the third section fix the time for the payment of the tax imposed thereby.
The time of payment is, however, specifically prescribed in
the *fourth* section, which makes it the duty of the corporation
upon which a tax is imposed by the preceding sections, " to
transmit the amount of said tax to the treasury of the State
within fifteen days from the first day of January *in each and
every year.*" This language is explicit and can be satisfied
only by a payment in each January after the passage of the
act. In no other way can there be a compliance with the direction that the tax shall be paid within fifteen days from the
first day of January in " each and every year." By the construction claimed by the defendant no tax would be payable until
January, 1882, nineteen months after the passage of the act,
and this would not be a payment " annually," as provided in
the third section. The claim that it was not intended to tax

corporations which had not been in existence a year at the time of the passage of the act, is not a reasonable one. The act does not exempt from taxation corporations which have paid no dividends, or of which no sales of stock have been made. If dividends have been declared, or sales of stock made, these facts constitute elements in the valuation, but not otherwise. It could not be claimed that a corporation organized in 1881, or in any year after the passage of the act, would be exempted from making a report the succeeding November, or from paying a tax in the January following, on the ground that it had not been in existence for the period of a year, and the defendant stands in no better position, unless on the ground that as to it, the statute, if construed as imposing a tax in January, 1881, would be retrospective, a point which will be considered hereafter. There is another cogent reason for the construction that by the act the first report is to be made in November, 1880, and the first tax paid in January, 1881. The last section declares that the act shall take effect immediately. The *eighth* section declares that the capital stock of corporations liable to taxation under the act, "shall hereafter be exempt from assessment or taxation, except as in this act prescribed." It may be safely assumed that it was not the intention of the legislature to exempt the corporations mentioned in the third section, from taxation for State purposes for the fiscal year commencing October 1, 1880. But such would be the effect of the construction insisted upon by the defendant. The act exempts such corporations from assessment and taxation "hereafter," except as in the act prescribed. Under the system of taxation which prevailed before the act of 1880 was passed, the tax levied in each year for State purposes (commonly called the State tax) in each of the counties of the State (other than the county of New York) was levied and collected to pay the State appropriations and expenditures for the fiscal year commencing October 1st and ending September 30th. The tax was levied in advance of the expenditures, that is to say, a State tax levied in the fall of any year, was levied to pay State charges and appropriations for the fiscal year commencing the first day of October of the same year. The tax imposed by the act of 1880, is a substitute for the tax collected in the several counties of the State under the former system. When the act was passed, the assessment of property liable to taxation for that year under the then existing laws, including the property of corporations (in counties other than New York), had not been completed, nor had the assessment-rolls been made, nor had the State tax been apportioned. (Laws of 1859, chap. 312, § 8.) The *eighth* section of the act of 1880, abrogated the old system of taxation for State purposes, as to counties where the assessment had not been made, and substituted the system prescribed by that act, and that system was made exclusive from the time of its passage. A construction which would relieve corporations from all taxation for State purposes, for the fiscal year commencing October 1, 1880, could only be allowed where the statute was incapable of any other construction, and such a construction is not required in respect to the statute in question.

It is claimed by the defendant that if the statute is construed as requiring corporations to make a report in November, 1880, and to pay a tax under the act in January, 1881, it necessitates giving a retrospective effect to the act, which is contrary to principle and the accepted canons of construction. But we are of opinion that this objection is not well founded. It must be borne in mind that the tax which corporations become liable to pay under the act of 1880, is a tax for State purposes only, and takes the place of the tax for State purposes under the former system. Corporations have been relieved from the one and are required to pay the other, and in paying the first tax under the act of 1880, in January, 1881, they are simply paying their share of a prospective expenditure of the State for the current fiscal year. The tax was in no just sense the imposition of a burden for past transactions, or a tax on franchise or business prior to June 1, 1880. The fact that the amount of the tax may in some cases be fixed by reference to the business of the company during the year, does not make the act retrospective. The burden it imposes is future, and for future expenditures. It is competent for the legislature to adopt such method of valuing the franchise or property of corporations for the purpose of taxation, as it deems proper.

The defendant we think was liable to pay the tax sued for, and the judgment should, therefore, be affirmed,

All concur.

Judgment affirmed.

THE BOARD OF SUPERVISORS OF THE COUNTY OF MONROE, , Respondent, *v.* FREEMAN CLARK, Impleaded, etc., Appellant.

The imposition by the board of supervisors of a county upon the county treasurer, during his term of office, of the duty of raising, keeping and disbursing large sums of money, in addition to the usual and ordinary duties of his office, for instance the raising and disbursing money, during a war, for bounty purposes, does not discharge the sureties upon his bond from all liability.

Conceding no liability is imposed upon them on account of such increased duties, their obligations having reference to the usual and ordinary duties of the treasurer remain unaffected.

Pybus v. *Gibb* (6 E. & B. 902), disapproved.

In an action upon a county treasurer's bond, the defendants are properly chargeable with interest upon an amount which it appears it was the duty of that officer to pay, but which he failed to pay over at the expiration of his term of office, to his successor.

(Argued April 18, 1883 ; decided May 8, 1883.)

APPEAL from judgment of the General Term of the Supreme Court, in the fourth judicial department, entered upon an order made October 28, 1881, modifying, and affirming as modified, a judgment in favor of plaintiff, entered upon the report of a referee.

The nature of the action and the material facts are stated in the opinion.

Joseph A. Stull for appellant. The imposition of new duties on the treasurer discharged the sureties thenceforth from all liability on the bond absolutely for all future conduct of the office. (*Ward* v. *Stahl,* 81 N. Y. 406–408 ; *Ludlow* v. *Simons,* 2 Cai. Cas. 1 ; *Miller* v. *Stewart,* 9 Wheat. 702 ; *Mc-Clusky* v. *Cromwell,* 11 N. Y. 598 ; *People* v. *Pennock,* 60 id. 426 ; *U. S.* v. *Boyd,* 15 Peters, 187 ; *U. S.* v. *Kilpatrick,* 9 Wheat. 720 ; *Martin* v. *Stewart,* id. 680 ; Burge on Surety, 214 ; *Whiston* v. *Hall,* 5 B. & C. 269 ; *Bangs* v. *Strong,* 4 Comst. 315 ; *People* v. *Vilas,* 36 N. Y. 460 ; Fell on Guaranty and Suretyship, 191, and note, 517 ; *Franklin B'k* v. *Cooper,* 36 Me. 197 ; *Glass* v. *Stimson,* 2 Sumner, 453 ; *Grocers' B'k* v. *Kingman,* 15 Gray, 473 ; *Manufacturers' B'k* v. *Cole,* 39 Me. 188 ; *Leggett* v. *Humphreys,* 21 How. 66 ; *Welch* v. *Bailey,* 10 Johns. 180 ; *Henderson* v. *Marvin,* 31 Barb. 297 ; *St. Albans B'k* v. *Dillon,* 30 Vt. 22 ; *Bonar* v. *McDonald,* 3 H L. Cases, 226 ; *Pybus* v. *Gibbs,* 6 E. & B. 902 ; 88 Eng. Com. L. 902, 911, 912, 914, 917 ; *Bartlett* v. *Att'y-Gen.,* Parker, 277 ; *Napier* v. *Bruce,* 8 C. & F. 470 ; De Golyer on Guarantee and Principal and Surety, 268 ; *U. S.* v. *Hillegas,* 3 Wash. C. C. 70 ; *U. S.* v. *Tillotson,* 1 Paine's C. C. 305 ; *Postmaster-Gen.* v. *Reeder,* 4 Wash. C. C. 178 ; *Mahew* v. *Boyd,* 5 Ind. 102 ; *Wells* v. *Grant,* 4 Yerg. 491 ; *Pickering* v. *Day,* 3 Houst. [Del.] 474 ; *Webb* v. *Cuspalk,* 3 Ohio, 522 ; *Crandall* v. *Crawford,* 59 Penn. St. 196 ; *Governor* v. *Ridgeway,* 12 Ill. 14, 17 ; *Compher* v. *People,* id. 290 ; *Comm.* v. *Holmes,* 25 Gratt. 774 ; *U. S.* v. *Kirkpatrick,* 9 Wheat. 720 ; *People* v. *Vilas,* 36 N. Y. 459 ; *Mayor* v. *Ryan,* 35 How. 408 ; *S. C.,* 3 Abb. Rep. Am. Cases, 226 ; *People* v. *Pennock,* 60 N. Y. 421, 427.)

William F. Cogswell for respondent. Defendant was not released from liability on account of the increase of duties imposed upon the county treasurer after the execution of the bond in suit, and during the term mentioned therein. (1 R. S. 369, §§ 20, 21, 23, 24, 25 ; *People* v. *Vilas,* 36 N. Y. 459, 469.) Assuming that new duties were imposed upon the treasurer not appropriate to his office, and not within the purview of his sureties when they signed the bond, the bond is not avoided thereby, but is still good as to his appropriate duties, and secures his official faithfulness in reference thereto. (*Gaussen* v. *U. S.*, 97 U. S. 584; *Commonwealth* v. *Holmes*, 25 Gratt. 771; *Inhabitants of Attleborough* v. *Hatch*, 97 Mass. 533.)

RUGER, Ch. J. This action was against the surety upon a treasurer's bond to the county of Monroe. The term of Baker, the treasurer, whose faithful performance of the duties of the office the bond was designed to secure, extended from October, 1861, to October, 1864. Many questions which were litigated before the referee and some of those discussed at General Term have been eliminated from the case by the acquiescence of the parties against whom they were determined, and this opinion will be confined altogether to the discussion of the remaining points.

It was claimed on the trial by the defendant that by reason of the imposition upon the treasurer during his term of office by the plaintiffs of the duty of raising, keeping and disbursing large sums of money during the war for bounty purposes, which was in addition to the usual and ordinary duties of his office, that the contract of suretyship was so changed by the obligees, that the surety was discharged not only from liability on account of such increased duties, but from his entire obligation upon the bond. This claim was based upon the well-settled principle that a change in the terms or obligations of a contract by the principal without the consent of the surety operates to discharge him from his liability.

The referee held that the surety was not liable for the acts of the treasurer concerning the moneys received by him by reason of the additional duties imposed upon him, but decided that his obligations upon the bond having reference to the usual and ordinary duties of the treasurer remained unaffected by the increase of the duties enjoined upon him. The plaintiff did not appeal from that part of the decision which relieved the surety from responsibility for the treasurer's default in accounting for the enlarged receipts of the office, and can, therefore, raise no question as to its correctness. The defendant appealed, alleging that he should have been altogether discharged from liability upon his bond.

The General Term having affirmed the referee's views of the liability of the surety, the defendant now comes to this court and asks for such total exemption from liability. No claim is made, that any change was attempted in the literal terms of the contract between the parties or the general nature of the duties or subject to which it applied, but it is argued that because the always indefinite sum of money which is liable in any year to come into the treasurer's hands has been increased beyond the supposed contemplation of the parties when they entered into it, that, therefore, the party is relieved *ipso facto* from his contract liability as a surety.

We think that the decisions of the courts below were quite as favorable to the defendant upon this question as he could justly have expected upon the evidence. They held that the statutes authorizing the issue of bounty war bonds by the county of Monroe did not, under the circumstances of this case, impose any additional legal duty upon the treasurer, and that, therefore, the surety was not liable for a defalcation by the treasurer in the funds so raised. The proof showed that the treasurer acted in conjunction with a committee of the board of supervisors in raising moneys and disposing of a large amount of bonds. Many of the bonds (the amount not appearing) were issued and delivered directly to recruits in payment of bounties, while others, the amount of which is equally uncertain, were negotiated, and the money realized was paid to recruits by the treasurer and other agents of the county. It is safe to assume, however, that the moneys passing through the treasurer's hands on account of these transactions were much larger in amount than those which he would usually have manipulated, and the question arises whether the possession and disbursement of these moneys by the treasurer with the knowledge and consent of the supervisors vitiated the obligation of the surety upon his bond. A well-settled distinction between the obligations assumed by sureties upon the bonds of public officers and by those liable upon private contracts is recognized. In the case of the former, the parties' contract, having reference to the acknowledged power of the legislature to vary and change the power and duties of such officers.

It has been repeatedly held in our courts that unless the territorial jurisdiction of such officer has been enlarged or the general nature or functions of his office changed, a surety upon his bond will not be discharged on account of changes made in the official duties after the execution of the contract. This point was considered in *People* v. *Vilas* (36 N. Y. 459), where it was held that the sureties upon the bond of a public officer were not discharged by the subsequent imposition through an act of the legislature of new duties similar in their nature and character to those which the officer originally performed. In that case a loan commissioner was required by an act passed subsequent to the execution of his bond to take charge of an additional sum of money which had previously been in the custody of another commissioner. This decision goes further than we need go, for here we are to consider the effect merely of such additional duties upon the original obligation of the bond.

We are referred to a large number of authorities upon this question and with few exceptions they support the proposition that a surety is responsible for default in the performance of the duties of his principal as they existed at the time of his assumption of liability. *Gaussen* v. *United States* (97 U. S. 584) is directly in point. There Mr. Justice STRONG, in his opinion, said: " If it be conceded, as it may be, that the addition of duties different in their nature from those which belonged to the office when the official bond was given, will not impose upon the obligor in the bond, as such, additional responsibilities, it is undoubtedly true that such addition of new duties does not render void the bond of the officer as a security for the performance of the duties at first assumed. It will still remáin a security for what it was originally given to se-cure."

Not only does the case of *People* v. *Vilas* (*supra*) sustain the same doctrine, but such is the uniform course of decisions in the United States, and the rule is now too well settled to be controverted. (*Commonwealth* v. *Holmes*, 25 Gratt. 771; *Hatch* v. *Inhabitants of Attleborough*, 97 Mass. 533; *United States* v. *Kilpatrick*, 9 Wheat. 720; *White* v. *Fox*, 9 Shepley [Me.], 341; *Colter* v. *Morgan's Adm'rs*, 12 B. Monr. 278.)

The case of *Pybus* v. *Gibb* (6 Ell. & Bl. 902), which supports the contrary rule, has been uniformly repudiated in this country whenever it has been cited as an authority.

The further point, is made that the referee included in the amount charged to the defendant the sum of $29,127.11, which had been collected by the treasurer during his previous term, and which he had omitted in his accounts, but which in October, 1863, by agreement between the supervisors and the treas-urer was brought forward and charged against him. There are several answers to this claim. A careful reading of the case has failed to disclose to us any evidence to sustain it; on the contrary, it quite conclusively appears that although this discrepancy was discovered as existing in 1863, and it was agreed between the supervisors and Baker that he should be charged with that amount as of that date, yet it did not enter into the account by which the referee ascertained the amount awarded by his report. In stating his account the referee sus-taining the defendant's claim that the plaintiffs were bound by the amount fixed by Baker and the supervisors in October, 1861, as the true amount then on hand, excluded all items of account arising prior to that date, and in arriving at the balance of $77,328.06, which he finds to have been in the treasurer's hands on the 4th day of October, 1864, he assumes the cor-rectness of that balance and then states the specific items of cash received and paid out during the treasurer's term, which make up both the debit and credit sides of the account. This process excludes the possibility of the admission of the item of $29,000, or any part of it into the referee's account, and no such item appeared therein. It may also be said that no exception was taken upon which to raise the question. The point involves a question of fact upon which the referee has neither passed nor has a finding been requested thereon by the appellant. This court will not examine the evidence to determine such questions for the purpose of discovering grounds upon which to reverse a judgment. (*Fabbri* v. *Kalbfleisch*, 52 N. Y. 28; *Van Slyke* v. *Hyatt*, 46 id. 259.)

The claim of the appellant that the referee erred in allowing interest upon the amount which he found that Baker or his executor failed to deliver to his successor on the expiration of his term of office is untenable. The condition of the bond was that the treasurer shall pay according to law all moneys which shall come into his hands as such county treasurer. The statute provides that at the termination of his office, " all books and papers belonging to his office and all moneys in his hands by virtue of his office shall be delivered to his successor in office upon the oath of the preceding county treasurer, or in case of his death, upon the oath of his executors or administrators." He is also required "to keep a just and true account of the receipts and expenditures of all moneys which shall come to his hands by virtue of his office." (§§ 21 and 24, 1 R. S. 369.) The statutory provisions impose an active duty upon the treasurer, and a failure to perform it constitutes a breach of the conditions of his bond.

The necessary and legitimate damages arising from this breach is the amount of money which the treasurer failed to pay over and the interest thereon from the day when the obligation matured. (*Adams* v. *Fort Plain Bank*, 36 N. Y. 255; *Stay* v. *Graham*, 14 id. 492.)

It was held that a county treasurer is chargeable with interest on all sums in his hands which he omits to account for at the annual meeting of the supervisors. (*Supervisors of Chenango* v. *Birdsell*, 4 Wend. 453.) The case seems to be decisive upon this point. The other questions discussed on the argument are necessarily controlled by the conclusions we have reached as above.

The judgment should be affirmed.

All concur, except DANFORTH, J., not sitting.

Judgment affirmed.

EUGENIA ROCHE, Respondent, *v.* JAMES M. MARVIN et al., Appellants.

Plaintiff's complaint alleged, in substance, that defendants, as trustees, held the legal title to certain hotel property situate in the county of Saratoga, and as such issued to plaintiff a certificate showing him to be entitled to an interest therein and in the rents and profits; that as such trustees defendants had declared a dividend on said certificate, which he claimed to recover. The answer averred payment of the dividend. The venue was laid in the county of New York; on motion to change the place of trial to Saratoga county, *held*, that the action was not to determine or affect any interest in land within the meaning of the provision of the Code of Civil Procedure (§ 982), requiring such action to be tried in the county where the subject of the action or some part thereof is situated; but that the action was in the nature of one for moneys had and received, and so was triable in New York.

(Argued May 1, 1883; decided May 8, 1883.)

APPEAL from an order of the General Term of the Supreme Court, in the first judicial department, made January 9, 1883, which affirmed an order of Special Term, denying a motion to change the place of trial of this action from the county of New York, where the venue was laid, to the county of Saratoga.

The complaint herein alleged in substance, that in the year 1875 the defendants were appointed trustees of the United States Hotel of Saratoga Springs, in the county of Saratoga, and that they thereafter delivered to the plaintiff a certificate stating that she was entitled to a beneficial interest in said hotel, its furniture and appurtenances, the legal title of which was then held in trust by James M. Marvin and John Tayler Hall, to a specified amount, and was entitled to share in the net rents and profits thereof, or a proportionate share of the net proceeds of a sale thereof; that a dividend of eight per cent had been .declared on said certificate, for which amount the plaintiff demanded judgment besides costs. The answer alleged payment.

Charles C. Lester for appellants. The language of section 982 of the Code of Civil Procedure includes actions of an equitable nature as well as actions at law. (*Fliess* v. *Buck-ley*, 22 Hun, 551; *Bush* v. *Treadwell*, 11 Abb. [N. S.] 27.) The certificate attached to the complaint is in no sense an obligation. It contains no covenant, promise or agreement of any kind. (2 Blackstone's Comm. 840.) It is a declaration of trust. (Hill. on Trustees, 64; Tiffany & Bullard, 354.)

G. F. Beakley for respondent. A dividend is a severance from the common fund of the company of so much for the use and benefit of each corporator in his individual right, which may be demanded by him, and if refused, become the subject of an action for money had and received to his use. (*Keppell* v. *Petersburgh R. R. Co.*, Chase's Dec. 167; *Stoddard* v. *Shetucket F. Co.*, 34 Conn. 542; *Kane* v. *Bloodgood*, 7 Johns. Ch. 90; *Jones* v. *T. H. & R. R. R. Co.*, 57 N. Y. 196; *Carpenter* v. *N. Y. & N. H. R. R. Co.*, 5 Abb. Pr. 277.)

MILLER, J. The only question arising upon this appeal is whether the action was a local one, and being such, the place of trial should have been in the county of Saratoga. The appellants claim that the plaintiff in this action seeks to establish an equitable interest in real estate in the county of Saratoga, the legal title of which is vested in the defendants, which entitles her to a share of the rents and profits of said real estate, and that the action is within the letter and spirit of section 982 of the Code of Civil Procedure, which provides, among other things, that an action must be tried in the county in which the subject of the action, or some part thereof, is situated, and where the action is "to procure a judgment establishing, determining, defining, forfeiting, annulling, or otherwise affecting an estate, right, title, lien or other interest in real property or chattel real."

We think that this position cannot be maintained. This action is brought on a certificate signed by the defendants, which certifies that the plaintiff is entitled to an interest in certain property known as the United States Hotel at Saratoga Springs, the legal title to which is held in trust by the defendants, and in the net rents and profits thereof, and the plaintiff claims to recover the dividend declared by the defendants as such trustees on said certificate and payable to the plaintiff. The answer of the defendants sets up payment as a defense, thus admitting the validity of the certificate set forth in the complaint. The complaint alleges that a certain portion of the profits received had been set apart and appropriated from the entire fund in the hands of the trustees for the use and benefit of the plaintiff. The action being brought to recover the sum which the plaintiff claims, does not relate to real estate, nor is it commenced to enforce any lien against real estate, but to recover a dividend declared on the certificate set forth in the complaint. It appearing from the pleadings that such demand is due from the defendants to the plaintiff, an action lies in the nature of assumpsit to recover the dividend as a demand due from the defendants to the plaintiff as the holder of such certificate. The certificate is an obligation on the part of the defendants to pay in a certain contingency, which has occurred, and by means thereof the defendants became liable for the amount claimed. It is in the nature of an agreement or a promise which bound the defendants. The action is for moneys received by the defendants which they were bound to apply upon the certificate. It was a contract on their part, and upon the trial of the action no equitable right would be involved. The right of the plaintiff under the certificate was admitted by the pleadings, and the burden of proof would be upon the defendants to show that the demand had been paid. On the part of the plaintiff she had nothing to prove, and her case was established as the pleadings stood.

Under these circumstances there is no foundation for the claim that the action is of an equitable character which affects real estate and comes within the provisions of the Code to which reference has been had.

The order should be affirmed.

All concur.

Order affirmed.

HUGH CONAUGHTY, Appellant, *v.* THE SARATOGA COUNTY BANK, Respondent.

128
135-

The provision of the Code of Civil Procedure (§ 3253), in reference to extra allowances of costs, simply authorizes such an allowance in an action wherein rights of property are involved and a pecuniary value may be predicated of the subject-matter; the importance of a litigation in any other than its pecuniary aspect affords no basis for the allowance, and when no money judgment is asked or rendered and the "subject-matter involved" is not capable of a money value, or the value is not shown, the allowance is not authorized.

The term "subject-matter involved" refers simply to property or other valuable thing, the possession, ownership or title to which is to be determined by the action, it does not include other property although it may be directly or remotely affected by the result.

Within the limitations fixed by said provision the power of the court below to make allowances is not subject to review here; but the question whether an allowance exceeds those limitations is one of law, proper to be considered by this court.

In an action, therefore, brought to restrain a corporation from the exercise of its corporate franchises, *held*, that the subject-matter involved was simply the corporate franchises, not its capital and moneyed assets, that in the absence of any evidence as to the money value of those franchises, an extra allowance was improper, and that an order allowing it was reviewable here.

Conaughty v. *Saratoga County Bank* (28 Hun, 373), reversed.

(Argued May 1, 1883; decided May 8, 1883.)

APPEAL from order of the General Term of the Supreme Court, in the third judicial department, made November 21

1882, which affirmed an order of Special Term granting to defendant an extra allowance. (Reported below, 28 Hun, 373.)

This action was brought to restrain defendant from the further exercise of its franchises and privileges on the ground of certain specified violations of the law under which it was organized. The defendant succeeded in the action. The value of the moneyed assets of the defendant after payment of its debts was found to be $100,000; aside from this no evidence was given as to the value of the franchises; an extra allowance of $1,000 was granted.

Esek Cowen for appellant. An extra allowance can only be granted on the value of the subject-matter involved, where the title to some tangible property is controverted in the action, and the judgment vests or confirms such title either as to the absolute ownership or as to use and enjoyment in the successful party. (*Potter* v. *Farrington*, 24 Hun, 521; *Struthers* v. *Pearce*, 51 N. Y. 365; *Browning* v. *Vanderhoven*, 55 How. 97; *Weaver* v. *Ely*, 83 N. Y. 89; *Rothery* v. *N. Y. Rubber Co.*, 24 Hun, 172.) When the action affects only intangible rights of the parties having no definite, ascertainable value, the value of the property over, or as to which those rights have been, or are to be exercised, is not the proper basis of an allowance of costs. (*Atlantic Dock Co.* v. *Libby*, 45 N. Y. 499; *People* v. *N. Y. & S. I. Ferry Co.*, 68 id. 72; *People* v. *A. & S. R. R. Co.*, 5 Lans. 25.) The franchise of a corporation is like any other mere right to do business and make a profit if you can, incapable of a money measurement, and if it were so capable there is no proof on the subject in this case. (*State R. R. Tax Cases*, 92 U. S. 575.)

Nathaniel C. Moak for respondent. The order is not appealable to this court, no appeal having been taken from the judgment. (*Comins* v. *Board*, 64 N. Y. 626; *People* v. *Boardman*, 41 id. 362; *People* v. *Lewis*, 28 How. Pr. 470; *McClure* v. *Supv'rs*, 4 Abb. Pr. [N. S.] 202.) The court properly granted the extra allowance. (2 R. S. 463–464, §§

39–42; 2 Edm. St. 484; 1 R. S. 589, §§ 1, 2, 3, 4; 1 Edm. Stat. 547–8; Laws of 1838, p. 252, §§ 27–8; Laws of 1841, p. 357; Laws of 1843, p. 300, § 4, as amended by Laws of 1847, p. 520, § 2; Code of Civil Procedure, §§ 1207, 3253; *Durand v. Hankerson,* 39 N. Y. 287; *Wright* v. *Wright,* 54 id. 437; *Murtha* v. *Curley,* 15 W'kly Dig. 561.) The value of the property directly to be affected by the result of an action is the proper basis for an extra allowance. (*People* v. *Albany, etc.,* 16 Abb. 465.) The word "involved" means "affected," and where the question was whether certain property should be taken from defendant, the value of such property was involved. (*Williams* v. *West. Union, etc.,* 1 Civ. Pro. R. 194; 61 How. Pr. 305; *Burke* v. *Candee,* 63 Barb. 552, 553–4; *Sickels* v. *Richardson,* 14 Hun, 110; *Latimer* v. *Livermore,* 72 N. Y. 174, 183; *Comins* v. *Board, etc.,* 64 id. 626; Affirming 3 T. & C. 296, 298, note; *Howes* v. *Garrison,* 1 N. Y. Monthly Law Bulletin, 83; *Saratoga, etc.,* v. *McCoy,* 9 How. Pr. 339, 341; *Morrison* v. *Agate,* 20 Hun, 23, 25; *Backus* v. *Hathorne,* 17 id. 87, 90–1.) No one of the stockholders, nor all combined, as such, had any individual interest in or title to the property and assets of the corporation. (*Mickles* v. *City B'k,* 11 Paige, 119, 127–8; affirmed, id. 129, note; *Central, etc.,* v. *Walker,* 66 N. Y. 428; *Darlington* v. *Mayor,* 31 id. 197; *Detroit* v. *Mutuals, etc.,* 43 Mich. 594, 600–3; Field on Corporations, §§ 127–8; *Bank* v. *Bank U. S.,* 7 Penn. L. J. 129; 4 id. [Clarke's], bottom paging; *McCulloch* v. *Moss,* 5 Denio, 567, 575; *Bradley* v. *Bauder,* 36 Ohio St. 35.)

RUGER, Ch. J. Extra allowances to the successful party in a litigation are regulated by statute, and must be governed strictly by the provisions of the law authorizing them. Among the cases in which it is provided that they may be granted are " difficult and extraordinary cases," and in this respect this case is within the provisions of the statute. The amount of such allowance cannot in any case exceed the sum of $2,000, and is further limited to a sum not exceeding five per centum "upon the sum recovered, or claimed, or the value of the subject-matter involved." (§ 3253, Code of Civil Pro.) This section plainly contemplates a litigation wherein rights of property are involved and values may be predicated of the subject and limits the allowance to a percentage upon the pecuniary value of the subject. Within these limitations the power of the court below to make allowances is not subject to review in this court, but when they exceed them, an appeal presents a question of law for our consideration.

In the present case no sum having been claimed or recovered by either party, the right to an allowance is based altogether upon the value of the subject-matter involved in the action.

In the determination of this question the pleadings furnish the sole evidence as to what was the subject-matter involved, and the value of such matter can be arrived at only by competent evidence tending to establish the fact.

The language of the statute is plain and unambiguous and cannot be strained by construction to cover cases not within its terms. The importance of a litigation in any other than its pecuniary aspects does not afford the basis of an extra allowance, and although a litigation may seem to come within the spirit of the provisions if the subject involved is not capable of a money value, or the value is not shown, an allowance is not authorized. (*People* v. *Albany and Susquehanna R. R. Co.*, 5 Lans. 35.) It is apparent that the word involved is used in a legal sense, and means the possession, ownership or title to property or other valuable thing which is to be determined by the result of the action. It does not mean the property which may be either directly or remotely affected by the result, as such a rule would from its vagueness, and uncertainty be impracticable in application. The cases uniformly seem to sustain this view.

Thus in an action to determine the validity of a lease of a railroad, which involved the right to its possession and use, it was held that the subject-matter involved was the value of the lease and not of the railroad or its rental value. (*O. & L. C. R. R. Co.* v. *Vt. C. R. R. Co.*, 63 N. Y. 176.) In an action by

a legatee to compel an accounting by an executor and the distribution of the estate, it was held that the value of the
legatee's interest was the subject-matter involved, and as the
estate proved to be insufficient to pay more than the debts, an
allowance was held unauthorized. (*Weaver* v. *Ely*, 83 N.
Y. 89.)

Where a party instituted an action to establish his right to
one-quarter of the value of a lease of real estate belonging to
a firm of which he claimed to be a member, it was held that
the value of the quarter sued for was the only basis for an
allowance. (*Struthers* v. *Pearce*, 51 N. Y. 365.) A case
which seems to be particularly in point occurred in the *Atlantic Dock Co.* v. *Libby* (45 N. Y. 499). The action was to
prevent the use of certain premises in Brooklyn for the prosecution of a certain business, and to recover $1,000 damages.
The premises were appraised as of the value of $50,000, and
an allowance of $500 was granted. It was held that the value
of the premises affected by the action was not the subject-
matter involved, and the order making the allowance was reversed. The value of an easement to " freedom of air, light,
and vision " for certain premises were held to be the subject-
matter involved in an action to sustain the infringement of
such a right secured by covenant. (*Lattimer* v. *Livermore*,
72 N. Y. 174.) These authorities seem controlling in this
case. The action was brought to restrain the defendant from
continuing in the exercise of its corporate functions on account
of certain alleged violations of law committed by it. The
effect of a recovery by the plaintiff would have been the forfeiture of its chartered privileges and the distribution of its
property among those who were then and are now legally entitled to it upon dissolution. It contemplated a present instead
of a future distribution. It sought only to accomplish the
extinguishment of its right to continue business in a corporate capacity. It did not ask for or contemplate any change
in the eventual proprietary rights existing in the property held
in the corporate name. While the naked legal title was in the
corporation, all rights of ownership in equity belonged to its

creditors and stockholders. The retention of the corporate franchise simply continued the right to carry on its corporate ·business. This right might or might not have been valuable. There is no evidence on the subject. We are not aware of any rule of presumption as to the value of a corporate franchise. It is a thing capable of appraisal, and ascertainable by evidence, and is frequently made the subject of taxation by the sovereign power. It is a right separate and distinct from the capital and moneyed assets of a corporation, and as to the value of which they furnish no evidence. It was this franchise alone which was the subject-matter involved in this litigation, and which was thereby determined, and whose value can be used in determining the amount of an allowance of costs.

The order granting an extra allowance in the absence of proof as to any value in such franchise was erroneous, and it should be reversed, with costs.

All concur.

Order reversed.

---- - - ———

WILLIAM H. DORRANCE, as Administrator, etc., Appellant, *v.*
WILBUR M. HENDERSON, as Sheriff, etc., Respondent.

After defendant, as sheriff, had levied upon property and advertised it for sale under executions issued to him, proceedings in bankruptcy were commenced against the judgment debtors : and, with the usual order to show cause, an order was issued by the clerk, as of course, without direc. tion of the court as required by the Bankruptcy Act (U. S. R. S., § 5023), staying defendant from any transfer or disposition of the property. The sale was adjourned by defendant by direction of the attorneys for D., the judgment creditor, who before the adjourned day intervened by petition in the bankruptcy proceedings, setting forth these facts, and the consideration for his judgments, and alleging that they were recovered without collusion with the judgment creditors. The petition asked for a modification of the stay so as to allow defendant to sell under the executions. The application was opposed by affidavits tending to show that the debts and the judgments thereon were in fraud of the bankrupt law. After a hearing the bankrupt court denied the application, but directed the assignee in bankruptcy to sell the property levied upon free from the lien of the executions, which lien the order declared should attach to the proceeds of sale, and gave to D. permission, within a time named, to apply for an order requiring the assignee to apply the proceeds in payment of the judgments. Defendant thereupon returned the executions *nulla bona.* D. failed to make such application and brought this action for an alleged false return. Thereafter the assignee in bankruptcy filed a bill in equity against D. and the judgment debtors to determine the validity of the judgments, and who was entitled to the proceeds of sale. D. appeared therein and answered averring, among other things, that " the property was taken from the sheriff by the assignee in obedience to the order of the court and by him in like manner disposed of." After trial had in such action, the court decreed the judgments and executions were obtained in fraud of the Bankrupt Act, that the levy was null and void as against the assignee and that he was entitled to said proceeds. *Held,* that conceding the injunction accompanying the order to show cause was without force, the voluntary appearance of D. made him a party to the bankruptcy proceedings, and gave effect from that moment not only to the subsequent orders but to the one already made, that the United States courts had jurisdiction over the subject-matter and D.; also that D., having appeared in and contested the action brought by the assignee, could not now object that that court had no authority as to him to take the proceedings; and that, therefore, the orders and judgment were a protection to defendant; also that it was immaterial that the decree was made after the commencement of this action; and that it was properly set up by supplemental answer. (Code of Civil Procedure, § 544.)

(Argued April 30, 1883 ; decided May 11, 1883.)

APPEAL from order of the General Term of the Supreme Court, in the third judicial department, made May 2, 1882, which reversed a judgment in favor of plaintiff, entered upon the report of a referee. (Reported below, 27 Hun, 206.)

This action was brought against defendant, as sheriff of the county of Madison, to recover damages for alleged false returns to two executions issued to him as such.

The material facts are stated in the opinion.

Edwin H. Risley for appellant. The fact that the clerk docketed the judgment against "Thomas Downs, Jr., impleaded," did not affect the regularity of the judgment or executions. (*Northern B. of K.* v. *Wright,* 5 Robt. 604 ; *Lahey* v. *Kinyon,* 13 Abb. 192.) It was an irregularity not affecting the judgments, executions or levies, and one that the defendant could not avail himself of. (*Cable* v. *Cooper*, 15 Johns. 153; *Jones* v. *Cook*, 1 Cow. 309 ; *Hinman* v. *Brees*, 13 Johns. 529.) The stay contained in the order to show cause, issued by the District Court on filing the petition in bankruptcy, having been inserted by the clerk without authority, did not stay the defendant in making sale on the plaintiff's judgments and executions. (U. S. R. S., § 5022; *Roderigas* v. *E. R. S. Ins. Co.*, 76 N. Y. 316; *Cromy* v. *Hughes*, 2 Bk. Reg. 61; *Creditors* v. *Cozzens*, 3 id. 281; *Clark* v. *Binninger*, 38 How. Pr. 341.) The rights of a prior execution can only be determined by suit brought by the assignee against the execution creditor. (*Smith* v. *Mason*, 14 Wall. 419; *Marshall* v. *Knox*, 16 id. 551 ; *Doyle* v. *Sharpe*, 74 N. Y. 154.) The decree in the District Court, procured long after the defendant had made the false return on the executions and after this action was commenced, is not a bar to the plaintiff's recovery in this action; defendant was not a party or privy to the record. (2 Smith's Lead. Cas. 626, 627; 1 Greenleaf on Evidence, §§ 523, 524; *Godard* v. *Benson*, 15 Abb. Pr. 191.) It is only questions, necessarily determined that conclude parties and their privies. (*Campbell* v. *Consalus*, 25 N. Y. 614; *Mason* v. *Alston*, 9 id. 28; *Luska* v. *O'Brien*, 68 id. 446.) The judgments and executions did not create a lien on the personal property of the bankrupt. The lien was created by force of the levy. (U. S. R. S., § 5128.) The levy by the defendant on personal property belonging to the defendants in the execution operated *per se* as a satisfaction of the judgments, and his unauthorized release of the same, and his return on the executions will not revive the judgments, so as to make them valid against the defendants. (*Ex parte Lawrence*, 4 Cow. 417; *Jackson* v. *Brown*, 7 id. 13.) The decree of the District Court did not vacate the judgments or executions. The levy, if preferential, was simply voidable at the election of the assignee; as to all others the lien of the levy was valid. (*Cragen* v. *Thompson*, 12 N. B. R. 81; *In re Pierce*, 3 id. 258; *Reed* v. *Taylor*, 37 Iowa, 209; 4 N. B. R. 710; *Mattie* v. *Hotchkiss*, 5 id. 485;

Hass v. *O'Brien*, 66 N. Y. 597.) The defendant cannot litigate or show by the decree or otherwise the invalidity of his levy as being made in violation of the bankrupt law, as a defense to this action. (*Cable* v. *Cooper*, 15 Johns. 158 ; *Ontario B'k* v. *Hottell*, 8 Cow. 192 ; *Ames* v. *Webster*, 8 Wend. 546; *Hinman* v. *Brees*, 13 Johns. 529 ; *Ginochio* v. *Oser*, 1 Abb. 433 ; *Watson* v. *Brenan*, 7 J. & S. 81 ; *Dunford* v. *Weaver*, 84 N. Y. 445 ; Crocker on Sheriffs, §§ 860, 862.) The same rule applies to a property as to a body execution. (*Renick* v. *Oser*, 4 Bosw. 384 ; *French* v. *Willett*, id. 649 ; *Bacon* v. *Cropsey*, 7 N. Y. 195 ; *Benson* v. *Lynch*, 44 id. 162 ; *Carble* v. *Cooper*, 15 Johns. 753 ; *Hutchinson* v. *Bumb*, 6 How. 74 ; 9 N. Y. 208; 57 How. 151; 16 Wend. 568 ; *Wisner* v. *Ocumpaugh*, 71 N. Y. 113.) The decree of the District Court is not competent evidence in mitigation of damages. (*Bowman* v. *Cornell*, 39 Barb. 69 ; *Ledyard* v. *Jones*, 7 N. Y. 550 ; *Colwell* v. *Blakeley*, 1 Abb. Ct. of App. Dec. 400 ; *Keer* v. *Hoys*, 35 N. Y. 331 ; *Stedman* v. *Patchin*, 34 Barb. 218.)

Louis Marshall for respondent. A party who has had notice of and has been heard upon a motion is bound by the decision, and this is true *a fortiori* if he himself invokes the interposition of the court. (*Acker* v. *Ledyard*, 8 N. Y. 62 ; *Barstow* v. *Randall*, 5 Hill, 518 ; *Martin* v. *Kanouse*, 2 Abb. Pr. 390 ; *O'Brien* v. *Weld*, 2 Otto, 81 ; *S. C.*, 15 Bank. Reg. 405 ; *People, ex rel. Jennys*, v. *Brennan*, 3 Hun, 666 ; *Swain* v. *Seaman*, 9 Wall. 274 ; *O'Brien* v. *Weld*, 2 Otto, 81.) The judgment in the action between the assignee in bankruptcy as plaintiff, and Thomas Downs, Jr., was a valid and binding adjudication upon the parties thereto and their privies, and estopped them from questioning any of the facts thereby determined. (*Castle* v. *Noyes*, 14 N. Y. 329 ; *Goddard* v. *Benson*, 15 Abb. Pr. 191 ; *Ansonia Brass & C. Co.* v. *Babbitt*, 74 N. Y. 402, 405 ; *Root* v. *Wagner*, 30 id. 9 ; *People* v. *Reeder*, 25 id. 302 ; *Castle* v. *Noyes*, 14 id. 329 ; *White* v. *Philbrick*, 5 Greenl. 147 ; *Tate* v. *Hunter*, 3 Strobh. Eq. 136 ; *Tuska* v. *O'Brien*, 68 N. Y. 446 ; *Gates* v. *Preston*, 41 id. 113 ; *Gel-*

ston v. *Hoyt*, 13 Johns. 570; *Cornell* v. *Barnes*, 7 Hill, 35; *McDonald* v. *Bunn*, 3 Den. 48; *Inman* v. *McNeil*, 57 How. Pr. 51; *Forsyth* v. *Campbell*, 15 Hun, 236; *Albee* v. *Ward*, 8 Mass. 78; *Jones* v. *Hope*, 1 Saund. 37; *Josuez* v. *Conner*, 7 Daly, 448; *Earl* v. *Camp*, 16 Wend. 567; *Horton* v. *Hendershot*, 1 Hill, 118; *Dr. Drury's Case*, 8 Coke, 142; *McDonald* v. *Bunn*, 3 Denio, 48.) Any fact which annuls, avoids or vacates a judgment and an execution issued thereon operates as an excuse to the officer to whom the execution is issued in an action for a false return. (*McGuinty* v. *Herrick*, 5 Wend. 240; *Brown* v. *Feeter*, 7 id. 301; *Wood* v. *Colvin*, 2 Hill, 566; *Ruckman* v. *Cowell*, 1 Comst. 505; *Carpenter* v. *Stilwell*, 11 N. Y. 71; *Craft* v. *Merrill*, 14 id. 456; *Stilwell* v. *Carpenter*, 59 id. 415; *Tiffany* v. *St. John*, 65 id. 314; *Terrett* v. *Brooklyn Imp. Co.*, 18 Hun, 6; *Ocean Nat. Bank* v. *Olcott*, 46 N. Y. 12; *Frost* v. *Yonkers Savings Bank*, 70 id. 560.) The judgments and executions upon which plaintiff founds his action having been annulled, he has, therefore, sustained no injury by their non-enforcement. (*Wehle* v. *Conner*, 69 N. Y. 546; *Stephens* v. *Rowe*, 8 Denio, 333; *Warren* v. *Tenth Nat. Bank*, 7 Bank. Reg. 481; *Traders' Bank* v. *Campbell*, 14 Wall. 87.) The proof of the debt evidenced by the two judgments by plaintiff's intestate in the bankruptcy proceedings as an unsecured debt constitutes a bar to a recovery by the plaintiff. (*Ansonia Brass Co.* v. *Babbitt*, 74 N. Y. 404.)

DANFORTH, J. On the 8th of August, 1876, Thomas Downs, Sr., obtained two judgments in the Supreme Court of this State, against Joseph D. Case and Thomas Downs, Jr. (partners in trade under the name of Case & Downs); and issued executions for their enforcement, to the defendant, then sheriff of Madison county. He levied them on property of the value of $2,000, and advertised it for sale, but on the 22d day of December, 1876, made return that he found nothing to satisfy the executions. This action was brought on the 31st of August, 1877, by the plaintiff's intestate, upon the theory that the return was false. It was sustained by proof of these facts. It was competent, however, for the sheriff in defense of the action to show that the judgment debtors were bankrupts, and that the property, or its proceeds, belonged to their assignees. This was held in *Brydges* v. *Walford* (6 M. & S. 42), where it also appeared by the sheriff's return that he had levied and even sold the debtor's goods; all the judges of the King's Bench agreed "that on every ground both of law and fair dealing," he should prevail, and Lord ELLENBOROUGH said the plaintiff's claim " was against both law and morals." This defense was relied upon in the case before us, and relates to the same matter. On the part of the defendant it was proven that after the levy and on the 15th day of August, 1876, other creditors of Case & Downs commenced proceedings against them in the District Court of the United States in bankruptcy, and with the usual order to show cause, procured an order staying the defendant, "and all other persons from making any transfer or disposition of any of the property of the said Case and Downs * * * and from any interference therewith, except for its security and preservation."

On the 22d day of August they were adjudged bankrupts, and the matter sent to a register. The advertised day of sale was the 16th, but on the 15th the sheriff was directed by the attorney in the executions to adjourn the sale to the 18th, and in the meantime the order in bankruptcy and stay having been served, that attorney on the 17th of August notified him that he (the attorney) might have " to apply to the court for an order in the matter," and unless heard from before a certain hour on the next day, he wished the sheriff " to adjourn the sale to August 23." This was done, and afterward a further adjournment, and on the 30th of August the attorney directed him to adjourn the sale to Wednesday, September 6, also saying, he "hoped to get the injunction dissolved" on the Tuesday before that day.

By petition dated September 4, entitled " *In the Matter of Case and Downs, Jr.*, against whom a petition for adjudica-

tion of bankruptcy was filed on the 15th day of August,
1876," duly subscribed and verified by the judgment creditor,
and by the same attorney who issued the executions. Downs,
Sr., intervened in the bankruptcy proceedings. After representing by his petition to the District Court among other
things, the recovery of his judgments, the issuing of executions,
and levy, and advertisement for sale thereunder, the order to
show cause, the injunction order, and its service upon the sheriff,
and that " he deemed himself thereby restrained from selling
the property levied on," he stated the consideration of his
judgments, asserted that they were recovered without collusion
with the judgment debtors, that a speedy sale was desirable,
not only for his own interest, but that of all their creditors,
"prayed that said order may be so far modified as to allow
the sheriff of Madison county to sell said property upon and
by virtue of said executions, or that such other or further order.
in the premises be made and granted, as shall be just and
equitable."

A copy of this petition, with notice that upon it, the order
to show cause of August 15, and all other papers in the matter, he should apply to the District Court in bankruptcy for the
relief asked for in the petition, was duly served on the attorneys for the creditors in bankruptcy, and at the time named
was opposed by them upon an affidavit, tending at least to
overcome the statements of the petitioner as to the consideration of the judgment debts, and the absence of collusion with
the judgment debtors, and sufficient, if credited, to show that
both the debts and judgments were in fraud of the bankrupt
law, 'and invalid, and thereupon the bankrupt court, after hearing both parties, made an order dated September 19, 1876, by
which the specific relief asked for was denied, but directing
the assignee in bankruptcy, when appointed, to sell the assets
so levied upon, "free and discharged" from the lien of the executions, "which lien," it declares, "shall attach to the moneys
realized upon such sale, with the same effect as it now exists
upon the property," and further ordered that the judgment
creditors might, within a time named, apply upon petition and

upon notice to the assignee, for an order requiring him to apply the proceeds in payment of the judgments.

The judgment creditor, Downs, Sr., procured several extensions of time within which to present this petition, but finally omitted to do so, and on the 27th day of September, 1877, the assignee in bankruptcy filed his bill of complaint in equity against the judgment creditor and the judgment debtors, setting up the transactions before referred to, and asking that the judgments and executions be vacated, and the moneys arising from the sale of the property levied on, be adjudged to belong to the assignee in bankruptcy, and not to the judgment creditor. Downs, Sr., appeared in the suit and answered; among other things alleging that " the property was taken from the sheriff by the assignee in obedience to the order of the court, and by him in like manner disposed of, and that he still holds the proceeds." After trial had, the court decreed that the judgments and executions were obtained in fraud of the Bankruptcy Act, "that the said levy of said executions and the seizure of said goods and property by virtue thereof are null and void as against the complainant, and that the moneys arising from the sale of said property so levied on, and seized by virtue of said levy, and now in the depository of this court, belong to the complainant herein (the assignee in bankruptcy), and that the same be delivered over to him, free and discharged from all claims of said Thomas Downs, Sr., under said judgments and executions, or any order of this court heretofore made." Evidence of these things was rejected by the referee.

It may be conceded to the appellant that the injunction accompanying the order to show cause was without force in the first instance because issued by the clerk, and as of course without direction from the court. (U. S. R. S., § 5023.) But the voluntary appearance of the judgment creditor made him a party to the bankruptcy proceedings, and gave effect from that moment not only to subsequent orders therein but to the one already made. (*Acker v. Ledyard*, 8 N. Y. 62.) The defendant's case, however, does not rest on that alone. The order of September 19 was invited by the judgment creditor,

who by his petition invoked the summary interference of the
bankrupt court and its adjudication as to the validity of his
executions, and although he neglected to avail himself of the
privilege accorded by the District Court, yet he acquiesced in
the order, and if, as the learned counsel for the appellant now
claims, the orderly and proper mode of determining the conflicting claims for money made from the debtor's goods was by
bill in equity, that method also was tendered to, and accepted
by, him. The bill filed by the assignee was, as already shown,
for that very purpose. Upon trial the issue was found against
him. It has not been denied that the United States court had
jurisdiction over the subject-matter of the controversy, and
the consent of the judgment creditor was enough to bring him
within its jurisdiction. But he not only consented — he took
his chances of success in obtaining a favorable order and judgment, and cannot now object that as to him the court had no
authority to take the proceedings.

They are, therefore, a protection to the sheriff. A similar
question was presented in *O'Brien* v. *Weld* (92 U. S. Sup.
Ct. 81), and in *People, ex rel. Jennys*, v. *Brennan* (3 Hun,
666); and under like circumstances it was held, that the sheriff
was justified in paying over the money collected to the
assignee. Nor is it material that the decree in question was
made after the commencement of this action. The Code
(§ 544) allowing a supplemental answer expressly includes such
a case, and it is enough that the money, proceeds of the levy,
is adjudged to belong to the assignee. It is not necessary to
determine whether the decree also vacates the judgments and
executions.

The order appealed from should be affirmed, and judgment
absolute, dismissing the complaint with costs, should be rendered in favor of the respondent.

All concur, except RUGER, Ch. J., not sitting.

Order affirmed, and judgment accordingly.

1883.]   PEOPLE, ex rel. SHERWIN, v. MEAD.   **415**

Statement of case.

THE PEOPLE, ex rel. FRANK R. SHERWIN, Appellant, v. MICHAEL
L. MEAD, Respondent.

A warrant issued after indictment found may briefly state the offense, and
need not be more precise and accurate than is sufficient to apprise the
prisoner of the charge against him.

A warrant so issued by a district attorney as authorized by the statute
(Chap. 338, Laws of 1847) for the arrest of the relator, stated that he
stood indicted " for contempt " ; on *habeas corpus*, issued on the petition
of the relator. *Held*, that this was a sufficient specification of the
offense ; that as the statement was of a contempt which has already
served as a basis of an indictment, it necessarily implied a willful contempt, of a character constituting a misdemeanor.

Also *held*, that as the indictment was found prior to the enactment of the
Code of Criminal Procedure the provisions therein (§§ 301, 302) as to the
form of bench warrants did not apply (§ 962), nor was it a case of a commitment for contempt specified in the provision of the Revised Statutes
(2 R. S. 567, § 40) in relation to *habeas corpus*.

Also *held*, that it was not essential to the validity of the indictment that
the accused should first have been adjudged guilty of contempt by the
court whose process he disobeyed.

The relator was served with a subpœna, requiring him to appear before
the Court of Oyer and Terminer in the county of Albany. He was
called, and omitted to appear. *Held*, that he was properly indicted for
contempt in that county ; that the offense was there committed.

The indictment was found by the Court of Sessions of Albany county ;
the application for the writ of *habeas corpus* was made to a justice of the
Supreme Court in New York. At the time of the hearing thereon the
Court of Oyer and Terminer in and for Albany county was in session.
Held, that the Oyer and Terminer had authority to try the prisoner (2 R.
S. 205, §§ 29, 30), and so that the justice had no authority to let the
prisoner to bail. (2 R. S. 728, §§ 56, 57.)

(Argued May 1, 1883; decided May 11, 1883.)

APPEAL from an order of the General Term of the Supreme
Court, in the first judicial department, made the first Monday
of May, 1882, which affirmed an order of a justice of that
court, dismissing a writ of *habeas corpus* and refusing to
admit the relator to bail. (Reported below, 28 Hun, 227.)

On the 4th day of February, 1882, the relator was in custody in the city of New York, by virtue of a bench warrant,

issued by the district attorney of the county of Albany, dated the
3d day of February, 1882, wherein defendant was commanded to
take into custody the relator, " Who (the warrant stated) stands
indicted by the Court of Sessions of the county of Albany, for
contempt, and bring him before said court, at the City Hall, in the
city of Albany, in said county, if the said court shall then be in
session, together with this warrant, but if the said court be not
in session, you are hereby commanded to deliver him, together
with this warrant, to the keeper of the Albany county jail," etc.
On the day aforesaid, a justice of the Supreme Court in the
city of New York, on the petition of the relator, issued
a writ of *habeas corpus*, commanding the person having
the custody of the relator to bring him before the justice
that he might be discharged, the petitioner claiming that
he was illegally arrested and detained, and if it should
appear that he was lawfully in custody, that he might be let
to bail.   An immediate return was made by Mead, wherein he
stated that he had arrested the prisoner, and held him pursuant
to the said warrant, a copy of which was annexed, and by no
other process.   The proceedings were adjourned until the 8th
day of February.   The hearing proceeded from day to day until
the 1st day of March, when said justice dismissed the proceedings,
and remanded the relator to the custody of Mead.   It was
made to appear that the Court of Oyer and Terminer in and
for the county of Albany commenced a term of its court on
the 6th of February, and was in session during the pendency
of the proceedings.   The indictment charged in substance that
the prisoner had been duly and lawfully subpœnaed to attend
a term of the Court of Oyer and Terminer in and for the
county of Albany, at the City Hall, in the city of Albany, on
the 18th day of May, 1874, at three o'clock in the afternoon
of that day, then and there to testify and give evidence on
behalf of the people, concerning a certain indictment, then to
be tried in said court; that said writ of subpœna was on the
1st day of May, 1874, at the city of New York, State of New
York, exhibited to the said prisoner, and duly served upon
him, and that the prisoner, with an intent to impede and ob-

struct the due course of justice, unlawfully and willfully disobeyed the writ of subpœna, and did not appear before the
Court of Oyer and Terminer at the time and place specified
in the writ of subpœna, to testify as by said precept he was
commanded, to the great hindrance and delay of public justice,
and in contempt of said court.

Henry Edwin Tremain for appellant. If a court had not
the power and authority to send forth such process as it has
issued, and in the manner in which it did issue it, then there
was no competent court, and therefore no process. All is
coram non judice and void. (*People* v. *Liscomb*, 60 N. Y.
568, 571 ; 5 Hill, 164.) When a relator appears charged with
contempt of any kind or nature whatsoever, in all cases the
charge of contempt shall be so far inquired into upon the
habeas corpus proceedings as to ascertain its details and the
limitations, authority and jurisdiction of the court or officer
undertaking to pursue a citizen on such an allegation. (3 R. S.
[6th ed.] 887, §§ 55–57, marg. p. 567, §§ 40–42 ; Code of Civil
Pro., § 2032 ; id., § 2016, re-enacting 3 R. S. 563, § 22.) The
law of this State never has permitted an indictment as for a
criminal contempt until some contempt shall have been declared to have been committed by some court or officer competent to make such a judicial declaration. (3 R. S., marg. p.
693, § 14 ; id. 278 ; Code of Civil Pro., §§ 8, 9, 10, 11, 12,
13, 14 ; Penal Code, §§ 143, 680 ; 3 R. S. 534 ; Code of Civil
Pro., title 2, §§ 852, 853, 857 ; Code of Crim. Pro., §§ 615–
619.) Our jurisprudence assumes every man innocent until
he is adjudged guilty ; therefore, a person who "is guilty."
of criminal contempt and therefore liable to indictment under
the above section must be a person who has been adjudged
guilty. (Penal Code, 407, 412, 413 ; 3 R. S., §§ 56 [68], p.
449, marg. p. 286 ; id., §§ 11 [12], p. 441, marg. p. 278 ; id. [6th
ed.] 442, marg. p. 278, §§ 14 [15].) No man who has simply
failed to respond to a subpœna served upon him in a distant
part of the State can, with any reason or by any authority, be
designated as a criminal, and be indicted in the first in-

stance, without even an opportunity to be heard before the court whose process he is alleged to have disregarded. (Cowp. 386; Dougl. 561; 2 Caines, 92; Code of Civil Pro., § 853; Code of Crim. Pro., § 619; *In re Clements*, 36 L. T. R. [N. S.] 332; *Kobourne* v. *Thompson*, 13 Otto, 168.) Until a witness not attending under a sub- pœna shall have been brought before the court or magis- trate issuing such subpœna, he is liable only civilly, not crimi- nally. (*Reg.* v. *Rendle*, 11 Cox's Cr. Cas. 209; *Rex* v. *Lord Assulston*, Andrews, 310; *Ex parte Langdon*, 26 Vt. 682; *State* v. *Matthews*, 37 N. H. 450; N. Y. Code of Crim. Pro., § 619; N. Y. Code of Civ. Pro., § 853; *State* v. *Newton*, 1 Grant, 454 [Penn. 57]; *People* v. *Nevins*, 1 Hill, 158; *Mack* v. *People*, 82 N. Y. 236.) No man can be proceeded against for a criminal contempt arising from his alleged disobedience of a subpœna until after he shall have been given the oppor- tunity to explain to the court issuing the subpœna, his am- biguous act. (*People* v. *Few*, 2 Johns. 290; *People* v. *Van Wyck*, 2 Caines, 334; *Reg.* v. *Russell*, 7 Dowl. 693; 1 Gab- bett's Cr. L. 287; *Reg.* v. *Lefroy*, L. R., 8 Q. B. 134; 11 Mod. 59; 2 Bish. Cr. L., § 268; Wharton's Cr. Pl. & Pr., § 968 [8th ed.]; *State* v. *Nixon*, Wright [Ohio], 763; *McConnell* v. *State*, 46 Ind. 298; *Whitten* v. *State*, 36 id. 211–213; *Pitt* v. *Davison*, 37 N. Y. 239; *People* v. *Wilson*, 64 Ill. 205; *Scholes* v. *Hilton*, 10 M. & W. 15.) Every warrant is to recite accurately the accusation, and that no man can be ar- rested or held to answer before a jury "for contempt" unless the court offended and the time, place and method of offense be stated in the warrant of apprehension. (*Pratt* v. *Bogardus*, 39 Barb. 92; Barb. Cr. L. 535; *People, ex rel. Greeley*, v. *N. Y. Oy. & T.*, 27 How. Pr. 14.) A warrant in derogation of personal liberty is to be strictly construed, and is "not to be varied or enlarged by any intendments or presumptions." (*People* v. *Bergen*, 6 Hun, 268.)

Nathaniel C. Moak for respondent. The indictment in question having been found in 1874, section 301 of the Code of Criminal Procedure does not apply. (Code of Crim. Pro., § 962; *Willett* v. *People*, 27 Hun, 469, 470–1; *People* v. *Sessions*, 10 Abb. N. C. 192; 62 How. Pr. 415.) The Albany Oyer and Terminer having been commenced February 6, 1882, and continued in session until after the termination of the proceedings, that court had jurisdiction to try the indictment against Sherwin, even though the indictment was found in the Court of Sessions and had not been sent by that court to the Oyer. (2 R. S. 205, §§ 29, 30; 2 Edm. Stat. 214; *People* v. *Myers*, 2 Hun, 6, 26; *People* v. *Gay*, 10 Wend. 509, 511; *People* v. *Gen. Sessions*, 3 Barb. 144, 147; *People* v. *Quimbo Appo*, 20 N. Y. 544.) A justice of the Supreme Court may let to bail after indictment, provided it shall appear that the court having cognizance of the offense and jurisdiction to try the same is not sitting at the time the application for bail was made. (*People* v. *Clews*, 14 Hun, 90, 92; *S. C.*, 77 N. Y. 39, 40; *Babcock's Case*, 2 Abb. Pr. [N. S.] 204, 210.) The bench warrant was properly issued by the district attorney. (2 Laws of 1847, p. 444; 1 Laws of 1872, pp. 728, 729, § 25.) The indictment charged an offense. (2 R. S. 278, § 10, subd. 3; 2 Edm. Stat. 288, 289, 715; 2 R. S. 692, § 14; id. 278, § 15; Code of Civ. Pro., § 13; *People, ex rel. Negus,* v. *Dwyer*, 2 Civ. Pro. Rep. 379, 382–4; *People* v. *Gilmore*, 88 N. Y. 627.)

FINCH, J. The application for the relator's discharge from arrest was properly denied.

1. The statement of the offense charged contained in the warrant was sufficient. That commanded the officer to "take Frank R. Sherwin, who stands indicted in the Court of Sessions of the county of Albany for contempt." It was issued after indictment found (2 R. S. 728, § 55), and by the district attorney, who was duly authorized to issue it (2 Laws of 1847, p. 444); and sufficiently specified the offense charged in the indictment. That was for "contempt." While it is true that an act or omission may be in the nature of a contempt and properly described as such without constituting a crime, yet it is also true that a contempt may be such as to fall within the

criminal law and subject the offender to indictment. The statement in the warrant was of a contempt which had already served as the basis of an indictment, and necessarily implied a willful contempt ·and of a character which constituted a misdemeanor. The person arrested could not be misled by it, and was fairly apprised of the nature of the pending accusation. A warrant issued after indictment found may briefly state the offense, and need not be more precise and accurate than is sufficient to apprise the prisoner of the charge against him. (*Pratt* v. *Bogardus*, 49 Barb. 92.) The Code of Criminal Procedure does not apply (§ 962), nor is this a case of commitment for contempt within 2 Revised Statutes, 567, section 40.

2. It was not necessary to the validity of the indictment that the accused should first have been adjudged in contempt by the court whose process he disobeyed. The two proceedings are wholly independent of each other. One who disobeys the lawful order of a court not only offends against the dignity of the particular tribunal, but also against the public law. The particular court may pass over the contempt and suffer its order to be spurned, but the offense against the people remains. Their authority has been contemned, the administration of public justice assailed, and its power despised. For such an offense the guilty party may be punished by indictment, although the court whose order has been disobeyed may take the indignity in silence. The statute has made such disobedience, when willful in its character, an offense against the people, and not left it dependent upon the action or non-action of the specific judge or court. The statute contemplates that both remedies, or either may be pursued. If the court has first moved and proceeded against the offender by attachment and inflicted punishment, he may nevertheless be indicted for the same wrong, but in that event the sentence is to be affected by the previous punishment. (3 R. S. [6th ed.] 442, § 14.) We have considered the argument very elaborately stated, founded upon the phrase in the criminal statute, " every person who shall be guilty of a criminal contempt," and construing the word "guilty" to mean adjudged guilty by the court whose

process has been disobeyed, without being convinced by it. We have no doubt that the language means guilty in fact of the willful disobedience which constitutes a criminal contempt, although not so adjudged by the court whose process has been disregarded.

3. It is said the offense was not committed in the county of Albany. The relator was served with a subpœna requiring him to appear before the Court of Oyer and Terminer at Albany. He did not so appear. The disobedience and the contempt were there, and could be nowhere else. The order, if obeyed, was to be obeyed in Albany, and, if disobeyed, could only be disobeyed there. The witness was called in Albany, and omitted to appear and answer in Albany. We have no doubt that the offense for which he was indicted was committed there; if, indeed, it shall be shown upon the trial that any offense was committed at all.

4. There was no error in refusing to take bail when the application was made. At that time the Albany Oyer and Terminer was in session, and in such case the justice of the Supreme Court to whom the application was made in New York had no power to let the prisoner to bail. (2 R. S. 728, §§ 56, 57.) The Albany Oyer and Terminer had authority to try the prisoner, although the indictment was found in the Court of Sessions. (2 R. S. 205, §§ 29, 30.) The very object of bail is to cover an interval before the session of the next court at which the trial can be had. It takes the place of the imprisonment during such interval. When, therefore, there is no such interval, and the court being in session, the presence of the prisoner is due at once, there is no necessary occasion or proper cause for bail, unless by the court sitting, and the statute, therefore, denied the authority in such event to any tribunal except the court in session before which the indictment was triable. (*People* v. *Clews*, 77 N. Y. 39.) There is no difficulty in harmonizing the provisions of title 2 and title 4. The first relates to arrest before indictment found and the last to the indictment and proceedings thereafter. The whole subject was

considered in the *Clews' Case*, and its argument does not need to be repeated.

Some other objections have been considered but do not require discussion.

The order of the General Term should be affirmed, and it should be "ordered and adjudged that said Frank R. Sherwin appear at the next General Term of the Supreme Court, to be held in the first judicial department, on the first day of said General Term, at the opening of said General Term, or as soon thereafter as counsel can be heard, and on such other days and times as may be fixed by it, and abide by and perform its judgment or order in the premises."

All concur.

Ordered accordingly.

————————

THOMAS A. R. WEBSTER, Plaintiff in Error, *v.* THE PEOPLE OF THE STATE OF NEW YORK, Defendant in Error.

Upon a writ of error no exception lies to a refusal to postpone a criminal trial by reason of the absence of witnesses.

An indictment for false pretenses averred in substance, that the accused having contracted to sell to B., the complainant, certain premises, fraudulently exhibited to B., who was illiterate and unable to read, a deed which he falsely represented to be a deed of the premises, when in fact the description covered other premises, etc. What purported to be a copy of the deed was set forth in the indictment. The deed offered in evidence on trial showed that in the copy in the indictment the easterly and westerly boundary lines were omitted. The copy, however, showed inferentially the length of these two lines. *Held*, that the variance was not material.

The indictment did not allege that the deed was under seal. It was so stated, however, in the attesting clause, a copy of which was set forth. *Held*, this, with the averment that the instrument was a deed, amounted to a substantial averment that it was under seal.

Where such an indictment sets forth various pretenses alleged to be false, if one or more are proved to be false, and are sufficient *per se* to constitute the offense, a conviction is proper, notwithstanding the failure of the prosecution to prove the other alleged pretenses to be false.

(Submitted May 2, 1888; decided May 11, 1888.)

ERROR to the General Term of the Supreme Court, in the first judicial department, to review judgment, entered upon an order made November 24, 1882, which affirmed a judgment of the Court of General Sessions in and for the county of New York, entered upon a verdict convicting the plaintiff in error of the crime of obtaining money by false pretenses.

The indictment charged, in substance, that the accused, with intent to cheat and defraud one Breen, who was an illiterate man, unable to read writing, falsely represented that he owned four lots of land in the town of Brookhaven, north of the Long Island railroad, free and clear of incumbrances, and that a certain deed which he then and there exhibited was a deed and conveyance of said lots, that said Breen, believing the said representations and induced thereby, agreed to purchase said lots, and delivered to the accused $175 for the said conveyance, whereas in truth and in fact there was an incumbrance, by mortgage, upon the said lots, and the said deed did not convey and did not set forth or describe the same. What purported to be a copy of the deed was set forth in the indictment. The land was described therein as follows : " Beginning at a point in the east side of Coats avenue, distant two hundred and seventy-five feet south of the center of the Long Island railroad ; thence running easterly, parallel with the railroad, two hundred and eighteen feet, to the west side of Locust avenue, fifty feet ; thence westerly, parallel with the south line, two hundred and eighteen feet, to the east side of Coats avenue, fifty feet to the point or place of beginning, making, as staked out, four lots of land each twenty-five feet front and rear, and one hundred and nine feet deep.''

Upon moving the indictment for trial, a motion was made to adjourn because of the absence of a material witness, which motion was denied.

When the deed was offered in evidence, it was objected to on the ground of variance between it and the one set forth in the indictment in that in the copy set forth no easterly and westerly boundary lines were given which were contained in the deed, also that the deed was under seal, which was not alleged in the indictment.

Other facts are stated in the opinion.

William F. Kintzing for plaintiff in error. When an application for an adjournment is made in good faith and upon proper facts shown, and not for the purpose of delay, it is error at law to refuse same, and such refusal is reviewable. (*B'klyn Oil Works* v. *Brown,* 38 How. 451; *Onderdonk* v. *Ranlet,* 3 Hill, 323; *Ogden* v. *Payne et al.,* 5 Cow. 15; *Hooker* v. *Rogers,* 6 id. 577; *People* v. *Vermilyea,* 7 id. 383; *Pulver* v. *Hiserodt,* 3 How. 49; 2 Tidd, 708; 1 Arch. 210; 1 Chitt. Cr. Law, 492; *King* v. *D'Eon,* 1 Bl. Rep. 510; 3 Burr. 1513.) The court erred in imposing the condition upon defendant that the testimony of the absent witness be taken upon interrogatories. (*People* v. *Vermilyea,* 7 Cow. 368; 1 Stark. Ev. 129–30.) The object of setting out an instrument in an indictment is to inform the accused of the offense of which he is charged, and must be an exact copy of the original instrument. The deed offered should have been excluded. (*Kingsley* v. *People,* 2 Cow. 522; *People* v. *Shall,* 9 id. 778; *People* v. *Harrison,* 8 Barb. 560.) Where a mortgagee assigns to the mortgagor and another there is a merger. (*Beal* v. *Miller,* 1 Hun, 390; *Angel* v. *Boner,* 38 Barb. 425.) The evidence was insufficient to justify the judge in submitting the question to the jury, and the court should have granted the motion of prisoner's counsel and directed an acquittal. (*Bennet* v. *People,* 49 N. Y. 137.)

John Vincent for defendant in error. A motion for an adjournment is wholly addressed to the discretion of the court, and its refusal to grant the motion is not reviewable. (*People* v. *Horton,* 4 Park. Cr. 222; *Eighmy* v. *People,* 79 N. Y. 546.) The term " deed," used in the indictment, imports, *per se,* a seal, and it is unnecessary to allege, when that term is used, that the instrument is sealed. (*Page* v. *People,* 6 Park. Cr. 684.) The only object of setting out an instrument in an indictment is to inform the accused of the offense with which he is charged, and this is answered, even where the instrument

is directly charged upon by describing it with sufficient definite-
ness to enable the defendant to identify it without setting it
forth fully or exactly. (*Tomlinson* v. *People*, 5 Park. Cr.
313; *People* v. *Holbrook*, 13 Johns. 90; *People* v. *Jackson*, 8
Barb. 637.) The place where the money was obtained and the
transaction completed determines the place of the commission
of the offense and of the indictment therefor. (*People* v. *Sully*,
5 Park. Cr. 142, 170.) Where several pretenses are alleged in
an indictment it is sufficient to establish one to the satisfaction
of the jury to sustain the indictment. (*Wood* v. *People*, 34
N. Y. 351; *Bellschofsky* v. *People*, 3 Hun, 40.)

MILLER, J. Upon the application to postpone the trial of
the indictment against the prisoner, there were circumstances
to excite suspicion in the mind of the court that the application was not made in good faith. There had been a long delay, as appears from the facts, stated by the public prosecutor,
which were not contradicted, and the proposition of the court
to take the testimony of the absent witness at his residence
was a fair one, and would have given the prisoner the benefit
of the testimony and should have been acceded to by the
prisoner's counsel. Although it is always desirable that a
witness should be present instead of his testimony being taken
in writing, yet under the circumstances presented we do not
think any just ground of complaint exists for refusing to postpone the trial on the ground of the absence or the inability
to procure the personal attendance of the witness. It is enough
to justify the condition imposed that the judge had reason to
suspect the application was not made in good faith. It
may be added that upon a writ of error no exception lies to a
refusal to postpone a criminal trial by reason of the absence
of witnesses. (*Eighmy* v. *People*, 79 N. Y. 546.)

There was no error in admitting in evidence the deed offered by the prosecution. The objection is that the boundary
lines easterly and westerly contained in the deed were left out
of the indictment, and that there was no seal. The indictment, it is true, does not in terms allege that the deed was

sealed. It is so stated, however, in the attesting clause of the deed as set forth in the indictment, and the allegation that it was a deed was a substantial averment that it was under seal. Such a conveyance imports a seal, and it may be assumed, therefore, that the deed set out in the indictment contained all that was required to constitute a valid conveyance The omission of two of the boundary lines from the description in the deed set forth in the indictment did not constitute a material variation and was not important, inasmuch as the copy in the indictment shows inferentially that the northerly and southerly lines were fifty feet in length, and as the easterly and westerly points were correctly given the description was not radically deficient. The indictment stated that the lands had been staked out, and the length and breadth were given as stated in the deed itself. No mistake could have been made by the prisoner by reason of the omission, as the copy was in substance and effect the same as the one he had executed.

It is claimed by the appellant's counsel that the court erred in refusing to take the case from the jury. This position is based upon the ground that the evidence established the mortgage was assigned to the prisoner and his wife on the 23d day of October, 1872; that it was conceded the prisoner's wife owned the fee of the land that was purchased at the time the representations were made; that the mortgage and fee in the land having merged the property was free and clear. Assuming the correctness of this position, we think there was sufficient evidence to authorize the court to submit the case to the jury.

It was alleged in the indictment as one of the false representations made by the prisoner, to one John Breen, who was an illiterate person and unable to read writing, that he owned four lots of land north of the Long Island railroad, that a deed purporting to be executed by him and wife to the said Breen was a deed and conveyance of the said four lots, that the four lots were set forth and described therein, and that Breen, believing the representations and that the instrument was a conveyance of said four lots, and being deceived thereby, paid to the prisoner the sum of money mentioned in the indictment.   The evidence shows that the witness was not able to read the deed and that the prisoner read it to him falsely, in that the property was situated one hundred and seventy-five feet north of the center of the Long Island railroad, and the prosecutor testified that he would not have paid the money if he had not believed the deed to contain a description of the property which had been exhibited to him by the prisoner as the property to be sold and which was situated on the north side of the railroad.   There was proof to show the representations, in regard to the location of the property, were false, and that the allegation set forth in the indictment concerning the same was true.   Where one or more pretenses are proved to be false, and the pretenses thus proved to be false are sufficient *per se* to constitute the offense, the accused will be convicted notwithstanding that the public prosecutor fails in proving to be false other pretenses alleged in the indictment.   (*Butler* v. *Maynard*, 11 Wend. 552; *Bielschofsky* v. *People*, 3 Hun, 40.)   Whether the land was free and clear from all incumbrances was, therefore, of no consequence, if the intentional misreading of the deed induced the prosecutor to part with his money, and a case was made out independent of the false representations alleged to have been made in this respect.

It follows that there was no error in refusing to take the case from the jury or in refusing to direct the acquittal of the prisoner.

The judgment should be affirmed.

All concur.

Judgment affirmed.

———————

JAMES LANGDON, Appellant, *v.* THE MAYOR, ALDERMEN AND COMMONALTY OF THE CITY OF NEW YORK, Respondent.

A regular clerk in a department of the government of the city of New York, whose services are no longer needed, may under the charter of that city of 1873 (Chap. 335, Laws of 1873) be removed by the head of the department without any previous trial, hearing or notice; the provision of said charter (§ 28) declaring that "no regular clerk * * * shall be removed until he has been informed of the cause of the proposed removal, and has been allowed an opportunity of making an explanation," does not apply to such a case.

(Argued May 3, 1883; decided May 11, 1883.)

APPEAL from judgment of the General Term of the Supreme Court, in the first judicial department, entered upon an order made June 10, 1882, which affirmed a judgment in favor of defendant, entered upon an order dismissing plaintiff's complaint on trial.

This action was brought to recover a sum alleged to be due plaintiff as salary. In 1875 the plaintiff was employed as a regular clerk in the bureau of the commissioners of taxes in the finance department of the city of New York, at a salary of $1,200 a year; on the 23d of June, 1875, he received a notice from the comptroller informing him that said officer proposed removing him from his office; the alleged cause of removal being a diminution of business in the department; and he was advised that he would be allowed an opportunity to make any explanation to the comptroller on the 24th of June, at an hour named. He appeared before the comptroller, and was then informed that his removal was on account of the diminution of business, by reason of which his services were no longer required. On the same day he was discharged, by notice in writing announcing that his removal was to take place on the 1st of July following.

Charles P. Miller for appellant. Plaintiff was a regular, not a temporary, clerk, and as such could only be removed for cause. (Laws of 1873, chap. 335, § 28; *People, ex rel. Munday,* v. *Fire Commissioners,* 72 N. Y. 445.)

David J. Dean for respondent. The plaintiff held his office for no fixed term, and was subject to removal at the pleasure of the appointing power, provided the conditions and method of removal prescribed by the legislature were observed. (*Gillespie* v. *Mayor*, 6 Daly, 286; *People* v. *Comptroller*, 20 Wend. 595.) The plaintiff might have been lawfully removed for the reason that his services were no longer required on account of the diminution of public business, without any prior notice of cause. (*People, ex rel. Evans,* v. *Commissioners of Parks*, 61 How. 130; *Phillips* v. *Mayor*, 88 N. Y. 246; *Dunphy* v. *Mayor*, 8 Hun, 479.)

EARL, J. The plaintiff was a regular clerk in the finance department of the city of New York, and was removed because his services were not needed. There was no contract, express or implied, to retain him in the service of the department for any definite time. He held his place subject to the power of the comptroller to remove him at any time under the provisions of the city charter. (Laws of 1873, chap. 335, § 28.) That power was unlimited, except that it was provided that "no regular clerk or head of bureau shall be removed until he has been informed of the cause of the proposed removal, and has been allowed an opportunity of making an explanation." That limitation does not apply to a case like this. Its purpose was fully explained in the cases of *People, ex rel. Munday,* v. *Fire Commissioners* (72 N. Y. 445), and *Phillips* v. *Mayor, etc.* (88 id. 245). In the latter case it was held not to apply to a case where a regular clerk was discharged, not to make way for another, but because there was no further need of his services, or because there were no funds provided for his payment. Here the business of the department had so diminished that the plaintiff's services were not needed. For such cause the comptroller had the absolute power of removal, without any previous trial, hearing or notice, and hence the judgment should be affirmed, with costs.

All concur.

Judgment affirmed.

92 430
17   85

The People, ex rel. The Brooklyn City Railroad Company, Appellant, *v.* The Board of Assessors of the City of Brooklyn et al., Respondents

The act of 1865 (Chap. 453, Laws of 1865), providing, where property has been omitted in an assessment-roll, for its assessment and taxation for the omitted year, in the year next succeeding, is to be construed in connection with the general system of taxation of which it forms a part, and so is not subject to the constitutional objection that it does not provide for notice or a hearing.

The relator. a corporation liable to taxation for State purposes under the act of 1880 (Chap. 542, Laws of 1880), was omitted from the assessment-roll by the assessors of the city of Brooklyn, where it was taxable, and no tax upon its personal property for city and county purposes was imposed for that year. In 1881 it was assessed for that year, and, in addition, for the omitted year, under said act of 1865, the valuation for the year 1879 being taken. Notice was given as prescribed by the statute also calling attention to the laws of both years. *Held*, that the act of 1865 was adjustable to the change made by the act of 1880, and that the assessment was valid.

(Submitted May 4, 1883 ; decided May 11, 1883.)

Appeal from judgment of the General Term of the Supreme Court, in the second judicial department, entered upon an order made September 12, 1882, which affirmed an order of Special Term dismissing a writ of *certiorari* brought to review the proceedings of the board of assessors of the city of Brooklyn and of the board of supervisors of the county of Kings in assessing in 1881 a tax for the year 1880 for city and county purposes upon the personal property of the relator.

The material facts are stated in the opinion.

Benjamin K. Silliman for appellant. The assessors, having made no assessment on the relator in 1880 for that year, could not in 1881 assess and impose a tax on it for 1880. (Laws of 1865, chap. 453, §§ 1, 2, p. 818 ; *People* v. *Goff*, 52 N. Y. 434.)

John A. Taylor for respondents. The capital stock and personal property of the relator having been liable to taxation for city and county purposes for the year 1880, and having been omitted from the assessment-roll of that year, it became the duty of the assessors, upon the application of three tax payers, to enter said property in the assessment-roll of the year 1881. (*People, ex rel. Oswald,* v. *Goff,* 52 N. Y. 434.)

FINCH, J. The relator was a corporation, to which the law of 1880 (Chap. 542) applied, and liable to taxation under its provisions. The assessors of Brooklyn, through an erroneous construction of the law (*People, ex rel. Westchester Fire Ins. Co.,* v. *Davenport,* 91 N. Y. 574), treated the relator as exempt from taxation for city and county purposes upon its personal property for the year 1880 and omitted to assess it. In 1881 the mistake was discovered; the relator was assessed for that year, and in addition for the omitted year under the provisions of the act of 1865 (Chap. 453). The relator sued out a writ of *certiorari* to test the validity of that assessment. The only open questions are the construction of the act of 1865, and its constitutionality. By the first section the assessors are required to enter the omitted property at the valuation of the year of omission, or, if not then valued, at the valuation of the preceding year, and in a separate line on the roll, upon the application of any three tax payers. Then section second provides that the board of supervisors, on the petition of the assessors, "shall proceed to levy a tax on the same at the rate per cent of tax imposed upon land or property in said town, city or ward in the preceding year." It is now claimed that these provisions cannot be adjusted to the new legislation; that the relator having already paid the State tax of 1880 must be assessed at the rate per cent of that year or not at all; and since such rate per cent was founded on an aggregate which included the State tax, it is impossible to apply it to a case in which the State tax cannot be included because it has been paid. The difficulty does not seem to us serious. The rate per cent of 1880 consisted really of three several rates per cent, one for the city, one for the county, and one for the State, aggregated for convenience, but easily separable whenever necessary. The valuation of the property assessed for the year remained a constant factor, while the several amounts to be raised for the three different purposes varied greatly. It was, therefore, as easy to ascertain the rate per cent of the city and county taxes by themselves as such rate when aggregated with the State tax. And when the relator was charged with its proportion of the city and county tax at the same rate imposed upon other property, the precise purpose of the law was accomplished, and it was easily adjusted to the change made by the law of 1880.

The constitutional objection raised to the act of 1865 is that it does not provide for notice or a hearing. It must be read and construed in connection with the general system of which it forms a part. If the property was valued in 1880 there was notice and opportunity to be heard provided by the law. If not then valued the assessors are required to enter the valuation of the preceding year. That, of course, was made upon notice. But the valuation of 1879 might not be identical with the proper value of 1880. Still, notice was required to be given in 1881. We must assume it was given. It warned everybody that the assessors had finished their rolls and they were open for examination. It was the privilege and the duty of this relator to see what they had done and object if any thing was wrong. As matter of fact the notice was given. It was specific and particular. It called attention to the taxes of both years. It does not appear that any objection was made to the valuation as applied to 1880. Probably the value in that year was greater than in 1879, and if so, the relator was certainly not harmed. The statute provided for notice; it was given; and no objection was made to the valuation. If it had been, a question might have been raised as to the right of the assessors to make a correction according to the facts shown. Even if they could not, if their duty to enter the property at a fixed valuation taken from a previous assessment-roll, was not only purely ministerial (*People, ex rel. Oswald,* v. *Goff,* 52 N. Y. 434), but so fixed and absolute as to exclude correction, which may be doubted, still the requirement of notice would not be violated so as to annul the act of 1865.   Public notice was given in 1880 as required by law.   The relator had opportunity to know that its personal property was not valued for that year, and was bound to know that if not so valued then it might be entered the next year at the valuation of 1879.   If it was not satisfied with that, because of an actual decrease of value, its duty was to object to the omission and show the real value.   Not doing so it must be held to have accepted the valuation of 1879 as, at least, no larger than the actual fact in 1880.   It cannot be said, therefore, that the act of 1865 requires that the property of the relator be taken without notice or an opportunity to be heard.

The judgment should be affirmed, with costs, not exceeding $50 and disbursements.

All concur.

Judgment affirmed. ·

ROBERT R. STEPHENSON et al., Respondents, *v.* SPENCER D. SHORT et al., Respondents, THE ONTARIO ORPHAN ASYLUM et al., Appellants.

92

A devise or bequest to a corporation organized under the act of 1848 (Chap. 319, Laws of 1848), providing for the incorporation of "benevolent, charitable, scientific and missionary societies," contained in a will made within two months of the testator's death, is, by the terms of the exception in the provision of said act (§ 6) authorizing such corporations to take by devise or bequest, invalid ; and this, although the testator leaves no wife, child or parent.

Lawrence v. *Elliott* (3 Redf. 285), overruled.

Where by the charter of a missionary society (§ 2, chap. 41, Laws of 1862) it was authorized to take by bequest or devise "subject to the provisions of law relating to bequests and devises to religious societies," *held*, that said exception in the provision of the act of 1860 applied ; and that a bequest to the society, in the will of one who died within two months after the execution of the will, was invalid.

(Argued March 10, 1883 ; decided June 5, 1883.)

APPEAL from judgment of the General Term of the Supreme Court, in the fourth judicial department, entered upon an order made the second Tuesday of June, 1882, which reversed in part a decree of the surrogate of the county of Ontario, upon the final accounting of the executors of the will of James Stephenson, deceased. Reported below (27 Hun, 380).

The material facts are stated in the opinion.

John E. Parsons for appellants. All the provisions of section 6 of the act of 1848 (Chap. 319) are limited to the case of a person leaving a wife, child or parent. (*Squire's Case,* 12 Abb. Pr. 38; *Jackson* v. *Lewis,* 17 Johns. 475; *People* v. *N. Y. C. R. R. Co.,* 13 N. Y. 78; *Waller* v. *Harris,* 20 Wend. 555, 562; *Lawrence* v. *Elliot,* 3 Redf. 235; *Levy* v. *Levy,* 33 N. Y. 97; *White* v. *Howard,* 52 Barb. 294, 314; *Chamberlain* v. *Chamberlain,* 3 Lans. 348, 355; 43 N. Y. 424, 440; Willard's Eq. Jur. 576; *Currin* v. *Fanning,* 13 Hun, 458, 473; *Kerr* v. *Dougherty,* 79 N. Y. 327, 351; Redfield's Surr. Ct. Prac. 185.) The provision is in derogation of the common-law right of a testator to dispose of his property by will and should be strictly construed. (4 Kent, 501; 1 Redfield on Wills, 1; *Newell* v. *Wheeler,* 48 N. Y. 486; *Kerr* v. *Dougherty,* 79 id. 327, 355; 9 Bacon's Abr. 246; Story's Com. on Eq., § 1165.) It was the intention of the legislature in enacting this statute to restrain charitable donations only in favor of lawful heirs. (Code Theodos. Lib. 16, title 2, § 4; Story's Eq., § 1137, citing 2 Domat; id., §§ 1139, 1141; Civ. Law, B. 4, tit. 2, § 6, art. 1, §§ 2, 7; *Williams* v. *Williams,* 4 Seld. 525; Essays in Anglo-Saxon Laws, 107, 108; 2 Bl. Com. 268, 269; *Magna Carta,* 9 Hen. 3, chap. 36, A. D. 1225; Westminster, 3; 18 Edw. I, chap. 3; 2 Bl. Com. 271, 272, 273; *Atty.-Gen.* v. *Day,* 1 Ves. Sen. 218; 1 Jarman on Wills, 449; Shelford on Mortmain, 120.) The policy of our State has not been to restrict benevolent institutions in acquiring property, but it has uniformly encouraged them, and restrictive provisions were made almost wholly for the benefit of the heirs and near relatives of the deceased. (*Levy*

v. *Levy*, 33 N. Y. 97, 112; *Yates* v. *Yates*, 9 Barb. 324, 339;
1 Greenl. Laws 71; 2 Van Ness and Woodworth's N. Y. Laws,
212; Laws of 1840, chap. 318; Laws of 1846, chap. 74;
Laws of 1849, chap. 273; Laws of 1862, chap. 302; Laws of 1860,
chap. 360; Willard's Eq. Jur. 577.) The desire to benefit the relations of the testator, and not the feudal policy of the
English statutes, as far as they existed, was the *animus* which
prompted our mortmain laws in the United States. (Story's
Eq. Jur., § 1194; *Atty.-Gen.* v. *Stewart*, 2 Mer. 143, 163;
2 Kent's Com. 282; *Perin* v. *Carey*, 24 How. [U. S.] 465;
Gen. Laws, § 235; Ill. R. S., chap. 23, § 1; Missouri Genl. Stat.,
chap. 70; Minn. Stat. at L., chap. 17, § 150; R. S. 472,
§ 4; 1 R. S., chap. 19, § 10; Mass. Pub. Stat., 656, § 7; R.
I. Pub. Stat., chap. 160, § 6; Code of Iowa, § 1101; California Code, § 6313; Ohio R. S., § 5915; Georgia Code, § 2419;
Reynolds v. *Bristow*, 37 Ga. 283.) The surrogate erred in
holding that the void legacies lapsed and went to the next of
kin. They go to the Presbyterian Board of Home Missions
as residuary legatee. (2 Jarman on Wills, 365; 2 Redfield on
Wills [3d ed.], 115; *Bernard* v. *Minshull*, 1 Johns. [Eng.
Ch.] 276; *King* v. *Strong*, 9 Paige, 94; *Floyd* v. *Barker*, 1
id. 480; *Roberts* v. *Cooke*, 16 Ves. 451; *Allen* v. *White*, 97
Mass. 504; *Kerr* v. *Dougherty*, 79 N. Y. 327; Dayton on
Surr. [3d ed.] 476; *Bernard* v. *Minshull*, 1 Johns. [Eng. Ch.]
276, 279; *Banks* v. *Phelan*, 4 Barb. 80; *King* v. *Woodhull*,
3 Edw. Ch. 79–82; *Moreton* v. *Fossick*, 1 B. &. Ad. 186;
Cambridge v. *Rous*, 8 Ves. 12, 25; *Bland* v. *Lamb*, 2 J. &
W. 399; *King* v. *Strong*, 9 Paige, 94; *Banks* v. *Phelan*, 4
Barb. 80; *Waring* v. *Waring*, 17 id. 553; *Shanley* v. *Baker*,
4 Ves. 732; *Roberts* v. *Cooke*, 16 id. 451; 2 Jarman on Wills,
365; *James* v. *James*, 4 Paige, 115; *Van Kleeck* v. *Dutch
R. Church*, 6 id. 600; 20 Wend. 457; *Youngs* v. *Youngs*,
45 N. Y. 254; *Kerr* v. *Dougherty*, 79 id. 327.)

H. L. Comstock for Ontario Orphan Asylum, appellant.
The restriction contained in the last clause of section 6 of
chapter 319 of the Laws of 1848 applies only to devises or

bequests of a person leaving a wife, child or parent (*Lawrence* v. *Elliott*, 3 Redf. Surr. 335; Willard on Real Estate, 501; Willard's Equity Jurisprudence, 576; *Beekman* v. *The People*, 27 Barb. 305.)

John S. Morgan for the Baptist Missionary. Convention, appellant. This corporation had full power to receive the bequest, under the first section of its charter. (Laws of 1862, chap. 41, § 1; Laws of 1817, chap. 128, p. 116; Laws of 1825, chap. 170; Laws of 1841, chap. 131; *Sherwood* v. *Am. Bible Soc.*, 40 N. Y. 564; *Williams* v. *Williams*, 8 id. 515; *In re Howe*, 1 Paige, 214; Angell & Ames on Corporations, § 177; 1 Jarman on Wills [R. & T. ed.], 388, note.) The court below erred in assuming that section 6 of the act of 1848 (Chap. 319) was general in its application. (*Lefevre* v. *Lefevre*, 59 N. Y. 447; *Kerr* v. *Dougherty*, 79 id. 336.) The law of 1848 does not apply to this case, where the decedent left no wife, child or parent him surviving. (*Lawrence* v. *Elliott*, 3 Redf. Surr. 235; *Kerr* v. *Dougherty*, 79 N. Y. 327.)

E. A. Nash for Robert R. Stephenson *et al.*, respondents. A devise or bequest to a corporation formed under the act of 1848 (Chap. 319, § 6) is void where the will is made within two months of the death of the testator. (*Marx* v. *McGlynn*, 88 N. Y. 358; *Lefevre* v. *Lefevre*, 59 id. 447, 448; *Lawrence* v. *Elliott*, 3 Redf. 235, 243; Willard's Equity Jurisprudence [Potter's ed.], 576; 27 Barb. 305; 2 T. & C. 339; McClellan's Surr. Pr. 104; *Areson* v. *Areson*, 3 Den. 458; *Arcularius* v. *Sweet*, 25 Barb. 403; *Beekman* v. *Beekman*, 27 id. 304, 305.) The Baptist Missionary Convention and the Board of Home Missions of the Presbyterian Church are both within the law of 1848. (*Kerr* v. *Dougherty*, 79 N. Y. 327; *People* v. *Utica Ins. Co.*, 15 Johns. 381.) The sums bequeathed to the Sunday schools were properly distributed by the Surrogate's Court as in case of intestacy. (*Kerr* v. *Dougherty*, 79 N. Y. 328.)

Elihu M. Morse for Sibley Stephenson *et al.*, respondents. The bequest to the Ontario Orphan Asylum is void. (*Lefevre*

v. *Lefevre,* 59 N. Y. 443 ; *Kerr* v. *Dougherty,* 79 id. 328 ; *Marx* v. *McGlynn,* 88 id. 357 ; *Stephenson* v. *Ontario Orphan Asylum,* 27 Hun, 380.) The same principle governs as to the bequest to the Presbyterian Board of Home Missions. The act of incorporation subjects it to all the provisions of law relating to devises and bequests by last will and testament. The act of 1848 is a general law controlling this society. (*Kerr* v. *Dougherty,* 79 N. Y. 328.)

RAPALLO, J. The act of 1848, entitled "An act for the incorporation of benevolent, charitable, scientific and missionary societies" (Chap. 319 of the Laws of 1848) contains the following provision :

"§ 6. Any corporation formed under this act shall be capable of taking, holding or receiving any property, real or personal, by virtue of any devise or bequest contained in any last will or testament of any person whatsoever, the clear annual income of which devise or bequest shall not exceed the sum of $10,000 ; provided no person leaving a wife or child, or parent, shall devise or bequeath to such institution or corporation more than one-fourth of his or her estate, after the payment of his or her debts, and such devise or bequest shall be valid to the extent of such one-fourth, and no such devise or bequest shall be valid in any will which shall not have been made and executed at least two months before the death of the testator."

James Stephenson, the testator, a resident of Ontario county, died November 27, 1878, leaving a will which was executed only two days before his decease, wherein he made bequests to the Ontario Orphan Asylum, a corporation formed under the before-mentioned act of 1848, and to certain missionary societies. He left no wife, child or parent, but left him surviving several brothers and sisters, nephews and nieces, his next of kin.

On a final accounting of the executors of the will before the surrogate of Ontario county, the next of kin of the testator contested the validity of the bequests before mentioned, on the ground that the will was executed within less than two months

before the death of the testator, viz., within two days before
his death. The surrogate, however, decided that the bequests
were valid, holding that the two months clause in section 6 of
the act of 1848 applied only to cases where the testator left a
wife, child or parent, and he delivered a very able opinion in
support of this view.

The Supreme Court, at General Term in the fourth department, reversed the decree of the surrogate and held that the
two months clause applied to all wills, and was not confined to
cases where the testator left a wife, child or parent.

The sixth section of the act of 1848 has been frequently before this court, but the precise point now presented has never
before been specifically raised, or been passed upon. It has
been elaborately argued here, and we have given to it the ma-
ture consideration which the importance of the question demands.

After a careful examination of the act and of the exhaustive
briefs of counsel, we are satisfied that the point taken by the
appellant's counsel cannot be sustained, and that the true construction of the last provision of section 6 is that no devise or
bequest to any corporation formed under the act shall be valid
in any will which shall not have been made and executed at
least two months before the death of the testator.

The section contains three distinct provisions. The first
confers upon the corporations referred to, the power to take
" by devise or bequest," by the will of any person, limiting the
amount which they may so take.

The second restricts the power of testators to devise or bequeath to such corporations, in certain cases, and prohibits a
testator who leaves a wife, child or parent from devising or
bequeathing to such a corporation more than one-fourth of his
estate; but for the purpose of preventing an entire failure of a
devise or bequest to such a corporation, in case the limit should
be transgressed, it provides that " *such devise or bequest* "
shall be valid to the extent of such one-fourth.

The third and last provision is that " *no such devise or be-*

quest shall be valid in any will which shall not have been executed at least two months before the death of the testator."

The appellants contend that, inasmuch as the second provision refers to a devise or bequest to a corporation formed under the act, made by a person leaving a wife, child or parent, and the saving clause refers to "*such devise or bequest,*" these words, when repeated in the next succeeding third provision, must be construed as referring, not merely to a devise or bequest to a corporation formed under the act, but the word "such" carries with it the limitation contained in the second provision, and that it refers only to a devise or bequest to such a corporation made by a person leaving a wife, child or parent.

We cannot agree to this reasoning. It must be observed that all three provisions relate to a devise or bequest to one of these corporations. The first, to such devises and bequests when made by any person whomsoever; the second, to such devises and bequests when made by certain persons, and the third declares that "no such devise or bequest" shall be valid in any will which shall not have been made within the time specified, without reference to the person by whom made, unless the word "such" be regarded as having been introduced for the purpose of restricting its operation to wills made by persons referred to in the second provision.

We do not think that the word "such" was inserted with that view. It is apparent that it was necessary to the sense of the sentence, for without it the provision would declare invalid every devise or bequest in every will not executed two months before the death of the testator. We think the word "such" was inserted for the purpose of connecting the provision with the subject of the section, which was, devises and bequests to corporations formed under the act. The same idea might have been conveyed by resorting to repetition, and saying that no devise or bequest to any corporation formed under the act should be valid, etc.; but as such devises and bequests were the subject of the whole section, the word "such" was doubtless adopted for the sake of brevity. We think it very clear that the first provision related to the power of the corporations to take, the second to the power of testators, in certain cases, to give to them, and the third to the time which in all cases must elapse between the execution of the will and the death of the testator to render the gift valid.

The appellants, however, contend that this construction is not consistent with the intent of the act, and that the sole purpose of the two months clause was to protect the *wife, children* or *parents* of the testator against his inconsiderate acts when *in extremis.*

Counsel refer to numerous *dicta* and authorities relating to the English statute of mortmain (9 Geo. II, chap. 36), which prohibited the giving of land for charitable uses, unless by deed executed twelve months before the death of the donor.

The preamble of this act and the cases cited, show that the mischief aimed at by that statute was the making of large and important alienations and dispositions by languishing or dying persons, or by other persons, to charitable uses, to take effect after their deaths, to the disherison of their heirs, and the counsel cites the comments of Judge STORY upon that statute (Story's Eq. Jur., § 1194), where that eminent jurist suggests that it deserves the consideration of every wise American legislator, whether provisions similar to those of that celebrated statute are not proper to be enacted in this country, with a view to prevent undue influence upon pious and feeble persons in their last moments, and check the unfortunate propensity to acquire fame as a religious devotee and benefactor, at the expense of the natural claims of blood and parental duty. The observations of distinguished jurists of our own State upon the sixth section of the act of 1848 are cited as indicating their opinion that the purpose of the two months clause was to protect wives, children and parents from improvident testamentary dispositions to charitable or religious institutions, made *in extremis,* but it will be found on examination that these observations were intended to refer to the portion of the sixth section which limits the power of the testator to give more than one-fourth of his estate, and to the act of 1860, which increases the amount to one-half of his estate. The only case in which the two months clause is directly passed upon is *Lawrence* v. *Elliott* (3 Redf. 235), where the surrogate sustained the construction contended for by the appellants, while in *Beekman* v. *People* (27 Barb. 260, 305), Judge DAVIES expressed a contrary opinion.

Conceding that the purpose of the two months clause is to prevent the testator when *in extremis* from devoting his estate to charitable or religious purposes to the disinheriting of his kindred and heirs, and that it is intended for their protection, we find nothing to indicate that it ever was the policy of the legislature of this State to confine that protection to the wife, children, or parents of the testator. These are especially protected by the provisions limiting his power of disposition to one-quarter, even if the will is executed more than two months before his decease. There is nothing in the course of legislation on this subject, which sanctions the idea that it has been the policy of the legislature to confine the protection of the two months clause to wives, children and parents, but so far as appears, its policy has been quite the reverse. The act incorporating the "Presbyterian Committee of Home Missions," etc. (Laws of 1862, chap. 340), of which corporation the present Board of Home Missions, one of the appellants, is one of the successors, contains the following provision:

"§ 5. No inhabitant of this State *who shall die leaving a wife, child or parent,* shall devise or bequeath to the corporation hereby created more than one-half of his or her estate, after the payment of his or her debts, but a devise or bequest *by such inhabitant* shall be valid to the extent of such one-half; in *no case*, however, shall *any devise* or bequest to such corporation be valid in any will made by *any inhabitant of this State* which shall not have been made and executed at least two months before the death of the testator or testatrix."

This provision was evidently intended for the purpose of incorporating in the special charter then being granted the second and third provisions of the general act of 1848, with the modifications only, of confining their restrictions to wills made by inhabitants of this State, and of increasing the limit of one-quarter, in the second provision, to one-half. But the two months clause is too explicit to be capable of being misunderstood, and clearly shows that the policy of the legislature was to invalidate all devises and bequests by any inhabitant without reference to the circumstance of his having a wife, child or parent.

The counsel for the appellants refers to the case of *Reynolds* v. *Bristow* (37 Ga. 283), and claims, on the strength of that case, that notwithstanding the definite and clear language of section 5 of the act of 1862, above cited, it would not, even if applicable to the Board of Home Missions, invalidate the bequest in controversy. Perhaps the Georgia case does go that length; but if it does, we could not follow it.

Section 5 of chapter 189 of the Laws of 1862, incorporating the Mutual Aid Society of the East Genesee Annual Conference, provides that the corporation may take by devise or bequest, etc., provided " that such corporation shall not take by the last will and testament of any person leaving a husband, wife, child, or parent more than one-half of his or her estate remaining after his or her debts are paid, nor shall it take *any thing* by *any* last will and testament which shall be made within two months of the death of the testator."

Section 5 of chapter 458 of the Laws of 1862, incorporating the American Missionary Association, contains the same provision as is contained in the charter of the Presbyterian Committee of Home Missions, before cited, and invalidates any devise or bequest to the corporation by *any inhabitant* of this State, made within two months before his or her death.

We have not been referred to any act of the legislature of this or any other State, containing the two months clause, or any similar provision, in which the operation thereof is confined to wills made by persons leaving a wife, child or parent (unless it be the State of Georgia as its statute was construed in *Reynolds* v. *Bristow, supra*), nor can we see any reason for so confining it. Provisions of this character, wherever we have found them in the statutes of other States, are of general application to the wills of all persons, whoever their heirs may be. In Pennsylvania the act of 1855 provides that "No estate, real or personal, shall hereafter be bequeathed, devised or conveyed to any body politic or to any person, in trust for religious or charitable uses, except the same be done by deed or will, attested by two credible witnesses, at least one calendar month before the decease of the testator or alienor, and all dispositions of property contrary hereto shall be void, and go to the residuary legatee or devisee, next of kin or heirs," etc.

In California the Pennsylvania statute is adopted in substantially the same language, except that, instead of referring to religious or charitable uses, it refers to benevolent or charitable societies and to charitable uses, and restricts the power of the testator to giving more than one-third of his estate to such uses, if he leaves legal heirs. The statute of Georgia, which has been referred to and which was construed in *Reynolds* v. *Bristow*, reads as follows (Code of 1882, § 2419): "No person leaving a wife or child, or descendants of a child, shall by will devise more than one-third of his estate to any charitable, religious, educational or civil institution, to the exclusion of such wife or child; and *in all cases* the will containing such devise shall be executed at least ninety days before the decease of the testator, or such devise shall be void."

The policy and purposes of the statute of mortmain are declared by Lord HARDWICKE, in *Atty.-Genl.* v. *Day* (1 Ves. Sr. 218), to have been

First. To prevent the locking up land and real property from being aliened; and

Second. To prevent persons in their last moments from being imposed on to give away their real estate from their families.

Shelford attributes the same policy and object to the act, enlarging the second by declaring it to have been to prevent testators in their last moments from being imposed upon by mistaken notions of religion, in giving away their estates from their heirs and families. (Shelford on Mortmain, 120.)

Judge STORY, in suggesting the enactment of similar provisions in this country, states the purpose to be "with a view to prevent undue influence and imposition upon pious and feeble minds in their last moments, and to check an unfortunate propensity (which is sometimes found to exist under a bigoted fanaticism), the desire to acquire fame as a religious devotee and benefactor at the expense of all the natural claims of blood, and parental duty." The statutes which have been enacted in this State on the subject are doubtless founded on the policy of the statute of mortmain, and if the policy of that statute was to prevent testators from being imposed on to give away their estates from their heirs and families, it is impossible to assign any reason for limiting that policy to testators leaving a wife, child or parent. The statute itself did not so limit it, but on the contrary the preamble, as has been seen, speaks of improvident alienations by languishing and dying persons, to take effect after their death, to the disherison of their *heirs*. Brothers and sisters, nephews and nieces are very near kindred and certainly entitled to be considered in guarding against undue influence over a testator, yet not only they, but even grandchildren would, on the theory of the appellants, be without the protection of the statute. Those standing in a still closer relation to the testator, his wife, children and parents, receive greater and especial protection from the statute, for even though the will be made more than two months before the death of the testator, he is disabled from devoting to charitable purposes more than one-fourth (and by the act of 1860, one-half) of his estate. But we think that the two months clause was intended to protect, not only them, but all the heirs and kindred of the testator, and even the testator himself, against the influences which might be brought to bear upon him in his last moments, and the mistaken notions which might govern him, and, to use the language of the opinion of the surrogate, "his inconsiderate acts during the brief interval when he would be more impressible to the idea of charitable donation as a means of tranquilizing a disturbed conscience, in apprehension of a speedy dissolution."

Many cases may occur where devises and bequests, which are free from all imputation of imposition or undue influence, mistaken notions of religion, improvidence, vanity, weakness, or any of the evils at which it is said that the statute was aimed, may be made to worthy and useful religious bodies and charitable institutions, and yet be invalidated solely by the circumstance of their having been made within the prescribed time. When such instances occur, it is greatly to be regretted that the pious and benevolent intentions of the testator should be frustrated, and that the intended recipients should be deprived of the benefit of his bounty. But it is beyond the power of human wisdom to frame a general law of this description which may not in some cases so operate as to inflict hardship.

A separate point is made by the appellant, "The Baptist Missionary Convention of the State of New York." That appellant is not organized under the act of 1848, but under a special charter, and claims that it is not subject to the provisions of section 6 of that act. Its charter has been several times renewed, and the last renewal was by chapter 41 of the Laws of 1862. Its charter contains no restriction upon its right to take by devise or bequest, or upon the power of testators to devise or bequeath to it, except the following: "The corporation shall have authority to take and hold by gift, bequest, devise or grant, any real or personal property subject to the provisions of law relating to bequests and devises to religious societies, and to use and dispose of the same." (Laws of 1862, chap. 41, § 2.)

The appellant concedes that this section subjects it to the provisions of the act of 1860 (Laws of 1860, chap. 360), because that act in terms names "religious" societies, and prohibits any person having a husband, wife, child or parent, from devising or bequeathing to any such society more than one-half of its estate, but it contends that the act of 1848 does not mention religious societies, but only " benevolent, charitable, scien tific and missionary societies," and treats of devises and bequests to them — that "religious societies" *per se* and *eo nomine* are recognized by our statutes as something separate and distinct from any or either of those named in the act of 1848 (even missionary societies), and that the clause in its charter subjecting it to the provisions of law relating to bequests and devises to "religious societies," is not sufficient to subject it to section 6 of the Laws of 1848.

We concur with the General Term in holding that a missionary society is a religious society, and are of opinion that the clause subjecting the appellant to the provisions of law relating to devises and bequests to religious societies, is sufficient to extend to it all provisions on the subject relating to any kind of religious society, and that consequently section 6 of the act of 1848, must on the authority of *Kerr* v. *Dougherty* (79 N. Y. 327) and *Lefevre* v. *Lefevre* (59 id. 434), be held to apply to the bequest to this last-named appellant.

The judgment of the General Term should be affirmed, with costs to the respondents, the executors, and the next of kin to be paid out of the estate.

.All concur.

Judgment affirmed.

GEORGE D. PURDY et al., Appellants, *v.* SAMUEL A. HAYT et al., Respondents.

Where the construction of a will is necessary to determine questions arising on the accounting of the executors, the surrogate has jurisdiction to pass upon the construction; this attaches as incident to the proceeding. The provision of the Revised Statutes (1 R. S. 723, § 17) declaring that "where a remainder shall be limited on more than two successive estates for life, all the life estates subsequent to those of the two persons first entitled thereto shall be void, and upon the death of those persons the remainder shall take effect," refers only to vested, not to contingent remainders, and executes the remainders in possession only in favor of such ascertained persons as, except for the void life estate, would under the will or deed be entitled to the immediate possession.

Where, therefore, the gift in remainder is upon a contingency which has not happened at the time of the death of the second life tenant, the provision does not apply, and the gift is invalid.

The will of D gave his real estate to his sisters J. and C. "during their respective lives," and after their deaths directed it to be sold by the executors, the proceeds to be invested, and the income to be paid by them to E., "during her life, and at her death the principal to be divided equally between any children she may leave ;" in case of her "not leaving lawful issue," the principal was given to other parties named. The two sisters named and E. survived the testator.' The sisters have since died, J. dying first, and thereafter the executors sold the real estate. E. is still living and has two children. On final accounting of the executors, *held*, that the devise to the testator's sisters vested in them a life estate in the land with cross remainders, that they took as tenants in common, not as joint tenants ; each taking a distinct and several freehold for life in one-half of the farm ; that the remainder given to the children of E. was contingent; that upon the death of J. and the consequent termination of her life estate, a second life estate vested in C., and upon her death the limit of the statute, as to that share, was reached, the third life estate in E., attempted to be created, was void, and as the remainder could not then take effect, because it could not be ascertained until the death of E., who would be entitled to take, it was void and the title to the undivided half of the land descended to the testator's heirs at law, subject to the power of sale, and they were entitled to one-half the proceeds of sale and to the subsequently accruing income ; but that the devise to E. was valid as to the share of C., as upon her death but one life estate therein had run, and she was entitled to the income from one-half the proceeds of the sale during life ; also that the remainder, as to this share, was valid.

It is no objection to the validity of a remainder in fee that it is limited in favor of persons not in being when the limitation is created, or who are not ascertainable until the termination of the precedent estate, provided the contingency upon which it depends must happen within or not beyond the prescribed period for the vesting of estates.

Where the precedent or particular estate is given to several persons as tenants in common, the remainders limited upon the estates of part of the tenants in common may fail without affecting the remainders limited upon the estates of the others.

(Argued March 19, 1883 ; decided June 5, 1883.)

APPEAL from judgment of the General Term of the Supreme Court, in the second judicial department, entered upon an order made September 12, 1882, which affirmed a decree of the surrogate of the county of Dutchess, made upon the final accounting of the executors of the will of Chauncey Delevan, deceased.

Delevan died in 1864, leaving a will, by which he gave his real estate, consisting of a farm at Fishkill, to his sisters, Jane and Catharine, " during their respective lives," and after their deaths he directed it to be sold by his executors, the proceeds to be invested and the income to be paid by them to his niece, Elizabeth Brinkerhoff, daughter of his sister Betsey, " during her life, and at her death the principal to be divided equally between any children she may leave, or if but one such child, the whole to be paid to that one." But should said " niece, Elizabeth, die, not leaving lawful issue," then the principal was given to other parties named in the will.

The two sisters of the testator, Jane and Catharine, survived him. His sister Jane died in 1865, and his sister Catharine in 1867. His niece, Elizabeth Brinkerhoff, also survived him and is still living. She has two children, but it does not appear when she was married or whether the children were born before or after the death of the testator's sisters, Jane and Catharine. The executors, on the 8th day of February, 1868, sold the farm, the net proceeds being $19,617. They invested the proceeds of the sale, and thereafter paid the net income thereof, so far as received up to the time of the accounting, to the testator's niece, Elizabeth Bartow (formerly Brinkerhoff), and they now have in their hands the principal of the fund. On the 15th of June, 1881, the executors applied to the surrogate for a final accounting, and a citation was issued and served on all the parties interested. The appellants, who are some of the heirs at law, appeared on the accounting and objected to the credits in the account to the executors for income paid to Mrs. Bartow, on the ground that the provision in the will directing the executors to pay the income from the sale of the farm to her was void, and that the estate of the testator descended, on his death, to his heirs at law, as in case of intestacy. The surrogate declined to pass upon the construction of the will for want of jurisdiction, and made a decree, allowing the accounts as presented. The General Term, on appeal, affirmed the decree on the ground that, assuming that the life estate given to Mrs. Bartow was invalid, the only consequence would be that the remainder to her children vested immediately on the death of the testator's sisters, Jane and Catharine, and that, therefore, the appellants had no interest in the disposition of the income.

Thomas Nelson for appellants. The clause of the will of the testator making Elizabeth Bartow, during her life, the beneficiary of the income of the proceeds of the sale of the real estate and the limitation of the estate over, at her death, to her children is void, being in violation of the statute against perpetuities. (1 R. S. 723, §§ 14, 15; *Amory* v. *Lord,* 5 Seld. 404.) It makes no difference that there are two life estates in the land and one life estate in the proceeds of the sale of the land. (*Savage* v. *Burnham,* 17 N. Y. 572.) Remainders limited upon a limitation which suspends the power of alienation for more than two lives in being at the death of the testator are void. (*DeBarante* v. *Gott,* 6 Barb. 492; *Vail* v. *Vail,* 7 id, 241; *McSorley* v. *Wilson,* 4 Sandf. Ch. 515; *Hones' Ex'rs* v. *Van Schaick,* 20 Wend. 564; *Knox* v. *Jones,* 47 N. Y. 397, 398; *Smith* v. *Edwards,* 88 id. 92; *Chipman* v. *Montgomery,* 63 id. 233; *Woodruff* v. *Cook,* 61 id. 641; *Schettler* v. *Smith,* 41 id. 347.)

Milton A. Fowler for guardian *ad litem, et al.,* respondents. The decision of the surrogate that he had no jurisdiction to determine the validity or invalidity of a trust was erroneous. (*Riggs* v. *Cragg,* 89 N. Y. 479.) The gift of the use and occupation of testator's farm to his two sisters during their respective lives was valid, however the gift of the use of the proceeds to testator's niece may be determined to have been. (*Woodruff* v. *Cook,* 61 N. Y. 638.) The remainder of the estate, whether it be in the land or its proceeds, vested on the death of the testator, Chauncey Delevan, in the children of his niece, Elizabeth Bartow, whether such children were born or unborn. (*Livingston* v. *Greene,* 52 N. Y. 118; *Ackerman*

v. *Gorton*, 67 id. 63 ; *Monarque* v. *Monarque*, 80 id. 321 ;
Harrison v. *Harrison*, 36 id. 543 ; *Smith* v. *Edwards*, 88 id.
92 ; 29 id. 39, 75.)

Thomas J. Swift for executors, respondents. The trustees
and executors cannot be held to the exercise of greater fore-
thought than that of a man of ordinary prudence at that time
and under the circumstances. (*McCabe* v. *Fowler*, 34 N. Y.
818 ; *Ormiston* v. *Olcott*, 84 id. 839 ; *Lansing* v. *Lansing*, 45
Barb. 182.)

ANDREWS, J. The surrogate erred in declining to entertain
jurisdiction to construe the will. The construction of the will
was necessary to determine the questions arising on the accounting, and in such a case jurisdiction to construe a will
attaches as incident to that proceeding. (*Riggs* v. *Cragg*,
89 N. Y. 479; *In re Verplanck*, 91 id. 439.) It becomes
necessary, therefore, in deciding this appeal, to consider the
dispositions of the real estate made by the testator, and to determine as to their validity.

It is claimed on the part of the appellants that by the will
three successive life estates were created in the testator's farm,
viz., one to continue during the joint lives of the testator's
sisters, Jane and Catharine, another for the life of the survivor,
and a third in the proceeds for the life of Elizabeth Brinkerhoff. If this claim is well founded it is, we think, impossible to resist the conclusion that both the life estate given to the
testator's niece, Elizabeth Brinkerhoff, and the remainder to
her children, are void, the life estate by force of the express
terms of section 17 of the article of the Revised Statutes relating to the creation and division of estates, and the remainder because it suspends the power of alienation beyond the
period allowed by law. How far the claim of the appellants
can be sustained will be now considered.

It is provided by the seventeenth section of the article of the
Revised Statutes, before referred to, that " successive estates for
life shall not be limited unless to persons in being at the crea-

tion thereof; and where a remainder shall be limited on more than two successive estates for life all the life estates subsequent to those of the two persons first entitled thereto shall be void, and upon the death of those persons the remainder shall take effect in the same manner as if no other life estates had been created." (1 R. S. 723, § 17.) The prohibition against the creation of more than two successive life estates in the same property has no necessary connection with the law of perpetuities. There is no suspense of the power of alienation of land by the creation of successive life estates therein unless they are contingent. Any number of successive vested life estates may be created without violating the statute of perpetuities. The prohibition against creating more than two successive life estates in the same property applies to such estates, whether vested or contingent. The policy of the prohibition, where applied to vested and therefore alienable interests, need not be considered. It is sufficient to say that it was regarded by the legislature as not imposing an undue restraint upon the owner of property, and the provision is in harmony with the general rule prescribing the period during which the power of alienation of land may be suspended, viz., two lives in being at the creation of the estate. The statute, however, does not avoid the whole limitation where more than two successive life estates are limited. It permits the first two to take effect, avoiding those only which are in excess of the permitted number.

So also the seventeenth section preserves a remainder limited on more than two successive estates for life. But we apprehend that the section must be construed as referring to vested, and not to contingent remainders. It cannot in reason, or by its true construction, be held to apply to the latter. Where the right of the remainderman is vested, and the right of possession only is postponed, the statute, in case of three or more precedent estates for life, accelerates the period fixed by the will or deed for the vesting of the remainder in possession, and vests it immediately upon the termination of the two estates for life first created. The statute so far overrides the precise intention of the grantor or testator, as expressed in the will or deed, but as the possession in the remainderman was postponed, presumably ·for the purpose of allowing an intermediate life estate to run, and that purpose being defeated by section 17, the statute, by accelerating the remainder, gives effect as near as may be to the intention of the creator of the estate. But where the gift in remainder is upon a contingency, which has not happened at the time of the death of the second life tenant, so that it cannot then be known who will be entitled in remainder according to the terms of the instrument creating the estate, the statute, we conceive, can have no application.

The construction that section 17 applies only to vested remainders, is moreover, sufficiently plain upon its language. The remainder, the section says, is to take effect in the same manner *as if* no other life estate had been created. Where the remainder was contingent when the life estate commenced, and remains so at the death of the tenant of the second life estate, it would not vest, although no other life estate had been created, and the statute gives effect to remainders only in the same manner as if limited upon two life estates instead of three. It is plain we think that the statute only executes the remainder in possession in favor of such ascertained persons as, except for the void life estate, would under the terms of the will or deed, be entitled to the immediate possession. (See *Knox* v. *Jones*, 47 N. Y. 397; *Smith* v. *Edwards*, 88 id. 104.)

We are now prepared to consider the nature and character of the several estates for life, and in remainder, created by the will. We are of opinion that by the true construction of the will, the devise to the testator's sisters, Jane and Catharine, vested in them a life estate in the farm as tenants in common, with cross-remainders. That they took the estate devised, as tenants in common, is declared by the express language of the statute. The statute declares that "every estate granted or devised to two or more persons in their own right, shall be a tenancy in common, unless expressly declared to be a joint tenancy." (1 R. S. 727, § 44.) By the common law a

grant or devise to two or more persons, without more, created
a joint tenancy. (*Lorillard* v. *Coster*, 5 Paige, 228.) This rule
of the common law was abrogated by the legislature at an
early period (1 Green. Laws, 207, § 6), and the rule as then enacted, and re-enacted in the Revised Statutes, has ever since been
the law of this State. It was said by NELSON, J., in his opinion
in the Court of Errors, in the case last cited, that in order to
create an estate in joint tenancy, since the Revised Statutes, it
was not necessary that the words *joint tenancy* should be used,
but that any other expression clearly imputing such an intent,
would be sufficient. (*Coster* v. *Lorillard*, 14 Wend. 342.) In
that case the real estate of the testator was devised to his brother
and twelve nephews and nieces *in trust* to pay over and divide
the rents and profits of his real estate " to and among the twelve
nephews and nieces during their natural lives, and to the survivor and survivors of them equally, to be divided between
them, share and share alike," and Judge NELSON was of
opinion that this language created a joint tenancy in the beneficiaries, basing his opinion upon the words of survivorship in
the will, the right of survivorship being the principal incident
of that estate. (4 Kent, 360.) The chancellor held, when
the case was before him, that the interests of the nephews
and nieces was in the nature of a tenancy in common for
life, with cross remainders. (5 Paige, 229.) It is not
material to consider what view of the limitation in that
case was the correct one. In this case there are no words of
survivorship, and no words from which the intention to create
a joint tenancy in the estate devised to the two sisters clearly
appears, and nothing short of this at least will satisfy the
language of the statute. But it was manifestly the intention
of the testator that the survivor of the two sisters should succeed for life to the interest of the sister first dying. The
testator gives to the two sisters the use and occupation of the
farm during their respective lives, and the intent that the surviving sister should have the use of the whole farm after the
death of the other is clearly indicated by the restriction of the
power vested in the executors to sell the farm, to a sale to be

made "after the decease of my sisters, Jane and Catharine," and a sale before that time would have been unauthorized. But the purpose of the testator, that his surviving sister should enjoy the whole estate after the death of the other, can be accomplished without construing the original estate in the two as a joint tenancy. There seems to be no objection to a limitation to two as tenants in common for life, and of the share of the one first dying to the survivor for life. (See cases cited by NELSON, J., 14 Wend. 338, *et seq.*) The raising of cross remainders by implication is not unusual, and where such an implication is justified by the language of the will and will accomplish the purpose of the testator, it is the duty of the court so to construe the will as to give effect both to the statute and to his intention. (1 R. S. 748, § 2.)

The remainder given to the children of the testator's niece Elizabeth is contingent, both within the rule of the statute and of the common law. It is inferable from the facts stated that no children of the testator's niece were born until after his death, nor, so far as appears, until after the death of his two sisters. The remainder is limited to any children of the testator's niece, which " she may leave," and the gift over takes effect in case of her death, " not leaving lawful issue." The remainder is not to the children of the testator's niece, as a class, but to such children as she may leave at her death. The children now living may not survive their mother, and whether they will ever be entitled to take under the will depends upon that contingency, and whether any of her present children will survive her cannot, of course, be known until her death. This brings the remainder precisely within the statute definition of a contingent estate, which declares that future estates are contingent whilst the person to whom, or the event upon which they are limited to take effect, remains uncertain, and within the fourth class of contingent remainders mentioned by Mr. Fearne. (1 R. S. 723, § 13 ; Fearne on Contingent Remainders, 9.) In this case the remainder, when created, depended upon a double contingency, viz.: the birth of children to the testator's niece and their survivorship of the mother. One of these contingencies has happened, the other is still uncertain. That the remainder in this case is contingent, is, we think, settled by decisions in this State upon similar language, in cases arising since the Revised Statutes. (*In re Ryder*, 11 Paige, 185; *Savage* v. *Burnham*, 17 N. Y. 571; *Carmichael* v. *Carmichael*, 4 Keyes, 346.)

Having thus ascertained the nature of the estates for life and in remainder given by the will, it only remains to apply the test of the statute to determine their validity. The law permits, as we have seen, the creation of only two successive estates in the same property. The two sisters of the testator took, as we have held, an estate in the farm as tenants in common with cross remainders for life. The life estate of his sister Jane, who first died, terminated on her death, and her enjoyment constituted one life estate in her share. A second life estate in that share then vested in her sister Catharine, and was spent at her death. The limit of the statute as to that share was then reached, and no subsequent life estate therein could be limited either in the land or the proceeds. The third life estate in the proceeds of that share attempted to be created in the testator's niece Elizabeth was therefore void, and the *corpus* of the share vested in the children of Elizabeth then living by force of the gift in remainder, and the seventeenth section of the statute, or descended on the death of the testator's sister Jane to the testator's heirs at law, as in case of intestacy. The remainder could not take effect for the reason that it was contingent, and the remaindermen were not ascertained, and could not be until the death of the testator's niece. The other alternative alone remained, viz.: the devolution of the title in the undivided half of the farm upon the testator's heirs, subject to the power of sale vested in the executors. The result, therefore, is that there was no valid disposition of the fee in the undivided half of the farm, and it descended to the testator's heirs, who, upon the sale under the power, became entitled to one-half of the proceeds of the sale, and consequently to the subsequently accruing income therefrom.

But the devise to the testator's niece of a life estate in the proceeds of the farm, with remainder to her children, though void as to the share devised for life to the testator's sister Jane was, nevertheless, valid as to the share of his sister Catharine. When his sister Catharine died, but one life estate in her original share had run. On the death of the testator she took a distinct and several freehold estate for life in one-half of the farm, although her particular share was not set off or partitioned, and of that share, though undivided, she was solely and severally seized. (1 Co. Litt. 875 ; 4 Kent, 368 ; *Collumb v. Read,* 24 N. Y. 505.) There was no devolution of her share upon her sister, for the plain reason that her sister first died. There was, therefore, no objection to a limitation of an additional life estate in the share of the one of the testator's two sisters who should survive, for this would be simply giving a second life estate in that share ; and as it is the duty of a court to carry out the intention of a testator so far as is consistent with the rules of law, we think the devise to the testator's niece Elizabeth for life should be held valid to the extent of entitling her to the income from the half of the proceeds of the sale of the farm. The validity of the remainder as to this share may also, we think, be sustained. Whether we regard the limitation as one of real or personal property, the absolute title will vest at the expiration of two life estates, viz. : the life estates of the testator's sister Catharine, and of his niece Elizabeth. The death of the latter will point out and ascertain the persons entitled in remainder, and this satisfies the statute.

It is no objection to the validity of a remainder in fee that it is limited in favor of persons not in being when the limitation is created, or not ascertainable until the termination of a precedent estate, provided only that the contingency upon which the remainder depends must happen within, or not beyond the termination of the prescribed period for the vesting of estates.

(*Gilman* v. *Reddington*, 24 N. Y. 9; *Manice* v. *Manice*, 43 id. 303.)

The question as to whether the remainder can be sustained as to the share of the sister of the testator, last dying, in view of the statute of perpetuities, is in one aspect a novel one. It is apparent that the power of alienation was suspended by the contingent limitation in remainder, and such suspense could not lawfully exceed two lives, and in a single case, a minority in addition. There was, under the will, a limitation for three lives as to the share of one of the two sisters of the testator, but upon which share that limitation would operate, could not be known until one of the sisters should die, and that event would render it certain that the unlawful limitation in remainder, was of the share of the sister so first dying. The question therefore arises, whether it wholly defeats the remainder, that it could not be ascertained, until one life estate was spent, which of the shares would be unlawfully suspended. We perceive no good reason why such a result would follow. The rule is well settled that where by the terms of the instrument creating an estate, there may be an unlawful suspension of the power of alienation, the limitation is void, although it turns out by a subsequent event, as by the falling in of a life, no actual suspension beyond the prescribed period, would take place. (*Hawley* v. *James*, 16 Wend. 121.) But this rule relates to cases where, if the limitations take effect, in their order, as contemplated by the grantor or devisor, some of the estates limited will not vest within the prescribed period, and they are cut off as too remote, although it may happen that the estates so cut off, would, by events subsequently happening, take effect within two lives.

The case here is not, we think, within this principle. In the one case the vice affects the whole limitation, and in the other, the limitation of a part only of the property devised, the only uncertainty being as to the part the title of which will be unlawfully suspended, and this will be ascertained within the period of a single life. Where the precedent or particular estate is given to several persons as tenants in com-

mon, the remainders limited upon the estates of a part of the
tenants in common, may fail, without affecting the remainders
limited upon the estates of the others. (Fearne on Rem. 193;
Hawley v. *James, supra.*) We think, therefore, the unlawful
suspension under the will in question, affected only the share
of the estate given for life to the testator's sister Jane.

For these reasons, the judgment of the General Term and
the decree of the surrogate should be reversed, and the case
remitted to the surrogate to take the accounting upon the principles stated in this opinion.

All concur, except Ruger, Ch. J., not voting.

Judgment accordingly.

The People of the State of New York, Respondent, *v.*
The Albany Insurance Company, Appellant.

The acts providing for the taxation of the franchises of certain corporations
and associations (Chap. 542, Laws of 1880, as amended by chap. 361,
Laws of 1881) are prospective in their character; the tax thereby imposed is not for the past, but for the future enjoyment of the franchises,
and the amount of the dividends made or declared during the year are
made simply the measure of the annual value of the franchises.

Defendant, a corporation, taxable under said act, and having a capital of
$200,000, in January, 1881, declared a dividend of six and one-fourth per
cent from the earnings and profits of the company for the current year.
In February, 1880, having on hand a large surplus fund, all of which
had been earned and acquired before January 1, 1880, and in contemplation of the expiration of its charter, which would take place in June, 1880,
it was resolved by the company that $100,000 should be taken from such
surplus and paid to and divided among its stockholders, and it was at
the same time resolved that the charter should be extended. Upon
a case submitted under the Code of Civil Procedure (§ 1279), *held,*
that this division, even if a dividend within the letter, was not such
within the meaning or for the purposes of the act; that the accumulation of earnings was no measure of the value of the enjoyment of the
franchises during the year 1880 or 1881, and was not within the contemplation of the framers of the act; and that the corporation was not liable
to taxation thereon.

It seems that should a corporation, for the purpose of evading taxation under the act, divide six per cent or more, but less than its actual earnings in any one year after the passage of said act, and thus create a surplus, the division of such surplus in a subsequent year may be treated as a dividend within the act.

(Argued March 30, 1883 ; decided June 5, 1883.)

APPEAL from judgment of the General Term of the Supreme Court, in the third judicial department, entered upon an order made February 3, 1883, which directed judgment in favor of plaintiff, upon a case submitted under section 1279 of the Code of Civil Procedure.

The questions submitted were whether any, and if so, what amount of tax the defendant was liable to pay, for the current year ending November 1, 1881, under the act chapter 542, Laws of 1880, as amended by chapter 361, Laws of 1881.

The facts stated in the case submitted, so far as material, are set forth in the opinion.

Leonard G. Hun for appellant.   The return to and division among the stockholders of the appellant of the $100,000 taken from its surplus fund in contemplation of the termination of its corporate existence was not the making or declaring of a dividend within the meaning of those terms as used in section 3 of the act of 1881 (Chap. 361). (*Lockart* v. *Van Alstyne*, 31 Mich. 76 ; *Traft* v. *Hartford, etc., R. R. Co.*, 8 R. I. 310 ; *Atty.-Genl.* v. *State B'k*, 1 Div. & B. Eq. 545.)

Leslie W. Russell, attorney-general, for respondent.   The distribution of the surplus funds of the company was a dividend in the full sense of the term. (Burroughs on Taxation, 160 ; *Lehigh Iron Co.* v. *Commonwealth*, 5 P. F. Smith, 448.)

RAPALLO, J.   The only question in this case which remains open, in view of our recent decisions, is whether the $100,000 divided among the stockholders of the defendant in February, 1881, was a dividend made or declared during the year ending November 1, 1881, within the intent and meaning of those words, as used in section 3 of chapter 361 of the Laws of 1881.

It appears from the agreed statement of facts, and the report thereto attached, that the capital of the company was $200,000; that on the 30th of June, 1880, it had a surplus fund of $179,-437.16, being an accumulation of past earnings; that on the 1st of January, 1881, this fund had increased to $201,942.64; that the charter of the company was to expire by lapse of time in June, 1881; that in January, 1881, the company declared a dividend of $12,500, being six and a quarter per cent on its capital stock, and that in February, 1881, it was resolved that the sum of $100,000 should be taken from its surplus fund and paid to and divided among the stockholders. It is admitted that such division was made in contemplation of the expiration of the company's charter, it being at the same time resolved that such charter should be extended. It is further admitted in the statement of facts that the whole of the said $100,000 so paid to and divided among the stockholders was earned and acquired by the said company before the 1st of January, 1880, and was the result of the accumulation of the profits of the company for several years prior to that time, and that the dividend of six and one-quarter per cent declared in January, 1881, was paid from the earnings and profits of the company for the current year, and was the only one so declared or made in the year beginning November 1, 1880.

The tax sought to be recovered is computed on the basis of dividends having been made or declared during the year ending November 1, 1881, to the amount of fifty-six and one-quarter per cent on the par value of the stock of the company.

As we have held in the tax cases lately decided, the tax in question is not upon the dividends declared, nor upon the property of the company, but upon its franchise of carrying on business as a corporation. Former laws provided for the taxation of the property of corporations, but this tax upon their franchise was a new tax first created by chapter 542 of the Laws of 1880, of which the act of 1881 is an amendment. These acts are prospective in their operation, and the tax thereby imposed is payable annually, not for the past, but for the future enjoyment of the franchise. The framers of the act had to solve the problem of ascertaining the value of such enjoyment, and for that purpose alone was reference made to dividends. The act provides that every corporation (with certain exceptions) shall pay annually into the treasury of the State, a tax upon its corporate franchise, to be computed as follows: If the dividend or dividends made or declared by such corporation, etc., during any year ending with the first day of November, amount to six or more than six per centum upon the par value of its stock, then the tax to be at the rate of one-quarter mill on the capital stock for each one per centum of dividends so made or declared; or, if no dividends be made or declared; or, if the dividends made or declared do not amount to six per centum upon the par value of the capital stock, then the tax to be at the rate of one and one-half mill upon each dollar of the valuation of the said capital stock, etc.

The amount of dividends made or declared during the year are thus made simply the measure of the annual value of the franchise upon which the tax is to be annually paid. As dividends can be legally made only out of earnings or profits, and cannot be made out of capital, they are assumed to approximate as nearly as practicable the just measure of the tax which should be imposed upon the corporation for the enjoyment of its franchise. Should a corporation earning six per cent or more withhold all dividends or pay less than six per cent and accumulate its earnings, or employ them as capital to improve its property, it would not thereby escape taxation, for it would then be taxable according to the actual value of its capital stock, and that value would be increased by the amount of surplus thus accumulated, and it would be taxable at the rate of one and one-half mills upon each dollar of the valuation of such stock, which will be found by computation to be substantially the same amount for which it would have been taxable had the profits been divided. But should a corporation, for the purpose of evading taxes under the act, divide six per cent or more, but less than its actual earnings in any one year after the passage

of the acts of 1880 and 1881, and thus create a surplus, there
would be no injustice in treating the division of such surplus
in a subsequent year as a dividend within the meaning of the
act, for it would be the statutory measure of the value of the
franchise which the corporation had enjoyed since the time
when such franchise was subjected to the tax.

But the present is a very different case from that supposed.
The surplus here in question was all acquired prior to the passage even of the act of 1880, and was the accumulation of earnings of several previous years. It had constituted part of the
property of the corporation, and been taxable as such, during
those years. It might have been the measure of the enjoyment of the franchise during those previous years when the
franchise was not taxable, but was no measure of the value of
such enjoyment during the year 1880 or 1881, and these aggregated earnings of several years were certainly no criterion of
the value of such franchise during any single year. A division of property thus previously acquired could not have been
within the contemplation of the framers of the act, in fixing
upon the annual dividends as a measure of the value of the
franchise of the corporation, and even if a dividend within
the letter of the act, to construe it as a dividend for the purposes of the act would be so contrary to its spirit and intent,
that such a construction is inadmissible.

The decision of the Supreme Court of the United States
in *Bailey* v. *Railroad Co.* (106 U. S. 109) is very much in
point. Section 122 of the Internal Revenue Act of 1864 (13
Stat. at Large, 284) provided that any railroad company that
declared any dividend in scrip or money, due or payable to its
stockholders as part of the earnings or profits of such company,
should be subject to a duty of five per cent on all such dividends, whenever payable. The railroad company, in 1868,
issued certificates which were decided to be a scrip dividend,
of $23,000,000, to its stockholders, as representing earnings of
the company which had been expended in the construction and
equipment of the road and the purchase of real estate and
other property. It was contended on the part of the plaintiff,

that by the express terms of section 122, these certificates, being a declaration of a dividend, as part of the earnings of the company, were taxable upon the amount thereof without deduction; that the policy as well as the language of the act fixed the charge upon the declaration itself, and for the purposes of taxation, concluded both, as to the amount subject to the tax, and that such a rule was reasonable as furnishing an obvious standard, and the only safe criterion of the tax, to avoid fraudulent evasions. The court, however, held that the tax provided for in the act was an annual income tax, the scheme of the statute being to levy the tax upon the income for each year ending the 31st of December next preceding the assessment of the tax, and that the defendant might show what portion of the earnings represented by these certificates accrued prior to the passage of the act imposing the income tax, and those earnings should be deducted from the amount of the scrip dividend.

We are of opinion that the dividend of fifty per cent, or $100,000, should not be considered in assessing the tax in question, and that it should be computed on the basis of the dividend of six and one-quarter per cent, made in January, 1881.

The judgment appealed from should be reversed, with costs.

All concur.

Judgment reversed.

Upon motion, subsequently made, the remittitur was amended so as to read as follows:

Judgment modified by striking therefrom the sum of $2,500 and interest thereon from January 15, 1882, without costs to either party.

HIRAM SMITH et al., Appellants, *v.* THE CITY OF ROCHESTER, Respondent.

The riparian owners of lands adjoining fresh-water, non-navigable streams, take title to the thread of the stream, and as incident to the title acquire

129
134

the right to the usufructuary enjoyment of the undiminished and undisturbed flow of said stream.

This is so also as to the fresh water navigable streams and small lakes within this State where the tide does not ebb and flow; save that the public has an easement in such waters for the purpose of travel, as on a public highway, which easement, as it pertains to the sovereignty of the State, is inalienable and gives to the State the right to use, regulate and control the waters for the purposes of navigation.

This public easement gives the State no right to convert the waters or to authorize their conversion to any other uses than those for which the easement was created, *i. e.*, for the purposes of navigation.

The right to divert the waters for other uses, although public in their nature, can only be acquired under and by virtue of the sovereign right of eminent domain, and upon making " just compensation."

Plaintiffs are the owners of certain premises, on the banks of Honeoye creek, used and occupied by them for milling purposes, and their mills are operated by the waters of the stream; said creek is a fresh-water, non-navigable stream, formed by the junction of the surplus waters of three small inland lakes; one of these, Hemlock lake, is about seven miles in length, and one-half mile in width; it is to a certain extent navigable and has for many years been navigated for local purposes by those living upon its shores. Said lake and the lands adjoining and the plaintiffs' premises are included in the territory of which the proprietorship was ceded by this State to Massachusetts by the treaty of 1786. Under the authority of the act chapter 754, Laws of 1878, defendant constructed a conduit from the said lake to the city, for the purpose of furnishing water for the inhabitants of the city, which conduit draws from the lake 4,000,000 gallons of water daily. In an action to restrain the continued diversion of the surplus waters of the lake from said creek, *held*, that, conceding the lake was part of the navigable waters of the State and subject to all the rules pertaining to such waters, and that the State by the act aforesaid conferred upon the defendant all of the rights in the lake which remained in the State subsequent to the treaty, it imposed the same liability to those who might be injured by defendant's use of such waters as the State itself would have incurred for a similar use; that the diversion of the waters for the purpose specified was for an object totally inconsistent with their use as a public highway or the common right of all the people to their benefits; that the State had no right, and by the said act did not attempt to grant a right to such use to the detriment of the riparian owners upon said creek and without making compensation; and that, as the evidence tended to show plaintiffs were injured by the diversion complained of, a dismissal of their complaint was error.

The rights of the riparian owners upon the Hudson (aside from its tidal character) and the Mohawk rivers are affected by the doctrines of the civil law, prevailing in the Netherlands from whose government they were derived, and are distinguishable from the rights of riparian owners upon other navigable waters of the State.

People v. *Canal Appraisers* (33 N. Y. 461), distinguished and limited.

Gould v. *H. R. R. R. Co.* (6 N. Y. 522) and *People* v. *Tibbetts* (19 id. 527), distinguished.

It seems that the doctrine above stated, as to the rights of riparian owners, does not apply to the vast fresh-water lakes or inland seas of this country, or to the streams forming the boundary lines of States.

(Argued April 20, 1883; decided June 5, 1883.)

APPEAL from judgment of the General Term of the Supreme Court, in the fourth judicial department, entered upon an order made the second Tuesday of June, 1882, which affirmed a judgment in favor of defendant, entered upon a decision of the court on trial at Special Term.

This action was brought by plaintiffs, as owners and lessees of mills and manufactories situated upon the banks of Honeoye creek, to restrain defendant from diverting the waters of Hemlock lake from said creek.

The court found in substance these facts: Hemlock lake is a body of water situate in Livingston county, N. Y., about seven miles long and one-half mile wide. The outlet of said lake is at the northerly end of the lake, and, within a mile, it unites with the outlet of Canadice lake, which is a stream of nearly the same size. After flowing in a northerly direction about five miles, the waters of the two lakes above mentioned unite with Honeoye creek, the outlet of Honeoye lake, and these united waters flow into the Genesee river about sixteen miles above the city of Rochester. Plaintiffs severally own, or operate as lessees from the owners, mills and manufactories of various kinds, situate upon the Honeoye creek, below its junction with the waters of Hemlock lake, and operated by the waters of said creek; which mills and manufactories were so in operation for more than twenty years before the construction by the defendant of the water-works hereafter mentioned. The waters of Hemlock lake are part of the navigable waters of the State, and have actually been

SICKELS — VOL. XLVII.   59

navigated by citizens of the State, with scows, steamboats and other craft, for over thirty years.

An act was passed by the legislature of this State in June, 1873, entitled "An act to define and restrict the powers of the board of water commissioners of the city of Rochester" (Chap. 754, Laws of 1873), in and by the third section of which it is provided that the board of water commissioners of the city of Rochester, appointed under the provisions of act chapter 387 of the Laws of 1872, are authorized to enter upon, control and use, as the agents of the city of Rochester, the waters of Hemlock and Canadice lakes, for the purpose of procuring a water supply for the city of Rochester, and also have the power to raise the surface of the water in said lakes not to exceed two feet, and to draw down the said water below low-water mark not to exceed eight feet, also the right to take such measures and make such constructions as should be necessary to secure said waters for the purposes intended, and to protect the same from improper obstruction or pollution from any cause, and also to perform any and all acts relating thereto which may be necessary for the purposes for which the said commissioners were appointed; and in and by said third section it is further provided, that all the powers thereby granted are to be exercised with due regard to the rights of owners of property adjacent thereto or dependent thereon, and that the city of Rochester shall be liable to pay to such owners any and all damages caused to said property by the performance of said act or the exercise of the powers thereby granted. Before the passage of the last-mentioned act, an artificial channel had been constructed by other parties than defendant or its agents at the point near where the outlet from Hemlock lake commenced, the bed of which was six feet lower than the bed of the natural outlet from the lake. For many years before the passage of said law, the Hoppough mills, situate upon the outlet a short distance below the lake, had been in operation and were supplied with water from the lake, which was retained by a dam across the outlet below the junction with the outlet of Canadice lake, the crest of

which dam was two feet lower than the bed of the natural outlet of Hemlock lake at the point where the same leaves said lake.
After the passage of said act the board of water commissioners of the defendant, claiming to act under the authority
therein given, constructed a bulk-head, and placed gates
therein to enable them to control the flow of water from
Hemlock lake. They also laid an iron pipe of three feet
internal diameter, extending from said lake ten miles toward the city of Rochester, where the size of the pipe was
reduced to two feet interior diameter, and the same was continued of that size to said city, for the purpose of conveying
through the same the waters of said lake to the city of Rochester, and thus supply the residents thereof with pure and wholesome water. The size of such pipe will enable the defendant
to draw through the same nine million gallons per day, if the
wants of the city require that quantity, and the waters of
Hemlock lake may be drawn through such pipe until the surface of the lake is reduced six feet below the bed of the natural outlet thereof. It has not been necessary thus far to draw
from said lake for the use of the city to the full capacity of said
pipe, and for the year past the defendant has diverted from
the water of said lake through said pipe four million gallons
daily to the city of Rochester; but the defendant claims the
right, and when the necessities of the city require the same,
intends to divert the waters of said lake to said city to the
full capacity of said pipes for that purpose. Defendant
has used so much of the water of Hemlock lake so by it
taken to the city of Rochester as was necessary for the
domestic use of the inhabitants thereof for that purpose, and
has allowed divers manufacturing establishments in said city
to use the residue not used for domestic purposes, and has received pay from such establishments for the use thereof.
The three lakes and Honeoye creek, with the lands adjoining.
are located within that portion of the territory of the State
of New York which was the subject of dispute between the
States of New York and Massachusetts, and which is described
in the compact or agreement made by the commissioners of

said States at Hartford, in the State of Connecticut, on the
16th day of December, 1786, by which said territory was ceded
to Massachusetts.

As conclusions of law, the court found in substance that the
people of the State were, at the time of the passage of the
said act of 1873, in their sovereign capacity, the absolute
owners of Hemlock lake, including the waters therein and the
land under the same, and had full right at their pleasure to
grant and convey the same to the defendant.   That in and by
said act the State granted to the board of water commissioners of the city of Rochester, and to defendant, full
power to enter upon, control and use the waters of Hemlock
lake for the purpose of procuring a water supply for the city
of Rochester, and by virtue thereof the defendant had full
power and authority and legal right to divert the waters of
Hemlock lake as fully as it has diverted the same, and thereupon directed judgment dismissing the complaint.

Other facts appear in the opinion.

Theodore Bacon for appellants.   All valid individual title
to land is derived from the grant of our own local government or from the crown or royal chartered governments
established here prior to the revolution.   (3 Kent's Comm.
377–8; *Jackson* v. *Ingram*, 4 Johns. 163; *Jackson* v. *Waters*,
12 id. 365.)   By several distinct grants the English crown had
divested itself of all proprietary right, although unquestionably
reserving to itself certain rights of " government, sovereignty
and jurisdiction " over the territory in which the water-courses
now in question are situated (1 U. S. Charters and Const. 921–
931; id. 932, 954, 257.)   The Constitution adopted in 1777
confirmed the royal patents granted before the revolution.
(*People* v. *Clark*, 5 Seld. 349, 360; 10 Barb. 120, 142; *People*
v. *Van Rensselaer*, id. 291, 320; 2 U. S. Charters and Const.
1337–8, §§ 35, 36; 1 Greenl. 13, 31; 1 N. Y. R. S. [2d ed.]
31, 32; Stat. 1779, chap. 25, §14.)   Land under the water of the
streams and lakes was capable of being the subject of a grant
from the sovereign; was, therefore, included in the grants from

the British crown, and confirmed to Massachusetts by the treaty of cession. And this was true of the navigable as well as the non-navigable streams and lakes. (*People* v. *Platt*, 17 Johns. 195; *Rogers* v. *Jones*, 1 Wend. 237; *Canal Appraisers* v. *Tibbits*, 17 id. 571, 609–614; *Commrs. Canal Fund* v. *Kempshall*, 26 id. 404; *Brookhaven* v. *Strong*, 60 N. Y. 56, 71–2; *Gould* v. *H. R. R. R. Co.*, 2 Seld. 522, 531–2, 534; *Burbank* v. *Fay*, 65 N. Y. 57–62; *Marshall* v. *Ulleswater Steam Nav. Co.*, 41 L. J. Q. B. 41; L. R., 7 Q. B. 166; 25 L. T. [N. S.] 793; *Bristow* v. *Cormican*, L. R., 3 App. Cas. H. L. [I.] 641, 652–3, 666–7; *S. C.*, Ir. Rep., 10 Com. L. 418; *Munson* v. *Hungerford*, 6 Barb. 263; *Ledyard* v. *Ten Eyck*, 36 id. 172; 1 R. L. 293, § 4; Laws of 1815, chap. 199; Laws of 1824, chap. 30; 1 R. S. 208, § 67.) Incident to the ownership of the soil contiguous to and under the non-navigable streams like Honeoye creek is the right to have the water of the streams flow in the channel of the stream, rendering such service as it can be made to render in passing the owner's premises. (*Ledyard* v. *Ten Eyck*, 36 Barb. 102, 124–5; *Burbank* v. *Fay*, 65 N. Y. 57, 62; 2 R. L. 289, § 15.) This right is not limited, either in character or extent, to any present or prior use by the owners of the water, but extends to any useful purpose to which it can now or may in the future be applied. (Angell on Water-Courses, §§ 90–96; *Gardner* v. *Newburgh*, 2 Johns. Ch. 162; *Reid* v. *Gifford*, Hopk. 416; *Corning* v. *Troy Iron and Nail Factory*, 34 Barb. 485; *S. C.*, 39 id. 311; 40 N. Y. 191.) The flow to which they are entitled is the natural flow of the stream, whether more or less free even from casual obstructions, although brought in by the operation of natural processes. (Hale's Com. Law [ed. 1779], "Analysis," 96, § xlvi; *Brown* v. *Best*, 1 Wils. 174; *Hodges* v. *Raymond*, 9 Mass. 316; *Prescott* v. *White*, 21 Pick. 341; *Prescott* v. *Williams*, 5 Metc. 429; *Mayor of Lynn* v. *Turner*, Cowp. 86; Woolrych on Waters, 274–5, 281–2.) The plaintiffs' right to the flow of water by their premises is property within the meaning of that constitutional provision which forbids the taking of property without compensation; and of that which forbids the deprivation of property without due process of law. (*Gardner* v. *Newburgh*, 2 Johns. Ch. 162 ; *Pumpelly* v. *Green Bay Co.*, 13 Wall. 166; *Comm'rs Canal Fund* v. *Kempshall*, 26 Wend. 404; *Colter* v. *Lewiston R. R. Co.*, 36 N. Y. 217.) Private right to the use of water upon streams is inconsistent with the public right of "government, sovereignty and jurisdiction;" is exercised, if at all, only by the sufferance of the sovereign, and may be determined by the arbitrary will of the sovereign. (Webster's Dict., sub. voc.; Bouv. Law Dict., *Ibid.;* 2 Kent's Com. 339; *Beekman* v. *S. & S. R. R. Co.*, 3 Paige, 45, 72-3.) There was in the State, for public use, a right to insist that all streams and bodies of water capable of use as highways should always be kept open for that purpose, although, for every other than the purpose of public passage, such streams and ponds might be the subject of private ownership. (*People* v. *Platt*, 17 Johns. 195; *Comm'rs* v. *Kempshall*, 26 Wend. 404; *Varick* v. *Smith*, 9 Paige, 547; *Morgan* v. *King*, 35 N. Y. 454.) The rights of the plaintiffs in this non-navigable stream are as clear and as independent of the State as any man's title to his farm can be. (*Pearsall* v. *Post*, 20 Wend. 111; *Post* v. *Pearsall*, 22 id. 425; *Lyon* v. *Fishmongers' Co.*, L. R., 1 App Cas. 662; *Chen. Bridge Co.* v. *Paige*, 83 N. Y. 178; *Ex parte Jennings*, 6 Cow. 518; *Morgan* v. *King*, 35 N. Y. 454, 458; *Dutton* v. *Strong*, 1 Black, 23; *Yates* v. *Milwaukee*, 10 Wall. 497; *Morrill* v. *St. Anthony's Falls Water Power Co.*, 26 Minn. 222; *Simickson* v. *Johnson*, 2 Harr. [N. J.] 129; *Crittenden* v. *Wilson*, 5 Cow. 165; *Pumpelly* v. *Green Bay Co.*, 13 Wall. 166; Angell on Tide-Waters, *passim; In re Townsend*, 39 N. Y. 171.) The rights of some of the plaintiffs to their water privileges, granted by one State and confirmed by another, had also become established as against both States, by more than forty years adverse use. (*Comm'rs* v. *Kempshall*, 26 Wend. 404, 421; *People* v. *Clarke*, 5 Seld. 349; *Chad.* v. *Tilsed*, 2 Brod. & Bing. 403.) These rights may properly be protected by a court of equity; and the plaintiffs, having a common interest in the object of the action, and not seeking to recover damages in regard to which their rights are entirely distinct, have properly joined in bringing it. (*Reid* v. *Gifford*, Hopk. 416 ; *Murray* v. *Hay*, 1 Barb. Ch. 59 ; *Brady* v. *Weeks*, 3 Barb. 157 ; *Fort* v. *Bronson*, 4 Lans. 47 ; 3 Blackst. Comm. 433–439 ; *Garwood* v. *N. Y. C. R. R.*, 83 N. Y. 400, 406 ; Kerr on Injunctions, 4–7 ; Angell on Water-Courses, § 449 ; *Gardner* v. *Newburgh*, 2 Johns. Ch. 162 ; *Webb* v. *Portland Manufacturing Co.*, 3 Penn. 189 ; *Bonaparte* v. *C. & A. R. R. Co.*, 1 Bald. C. C. 205 ; *Ballou* v. *Hopkinton*, 4 Gray, 324 ; *Belknap* v. *Trimble*, 3 Paige, 577 ; *Olmsted* v. *Loomis*, 5 Seld. 423 ; *Corning* v. *Troy I. & N. Factory*, 34 Barb. 485 ; *S. C.*, 39 id. 311 ; *S. C.*, 40 N. Y. 191 ; *Crooker* v. *Bragg*, 10 Wend. 260 ; *Garwood* v. *N. Y. C. & H. R. R. R.*, 17 Hun, 356 ; *S. C.*, 83 N. Y. 400 ; *Lyon* v. *McLoughlin*, 32 Vt. 425 ; *Wilts. & Berks. Canal Nav. Co.* v. *Swindon Water-Works Co.*, L. R., 9 Ch. App. 451 ; L. R., 7 H. of L. 697, 714 ; *Acquackanonck Water Co.* v. *Watson*, 29 N. J. Eq. 366.) Chapter 754 of the Laws of 1873, under which plaintiff's rights were invaded, is void under the provisions of the Constitution. (Constitution, art. 8, § 16 ; art. 1, § 6 ; art. 1, § 7 ; *People* v. *O'Brien*, 38 N. Y. 193 ; *Fishkill* v. *Plankroad Co.*, 22 Barb. 634 ; *People* v. *Allen*, 42 N. Y. 404, 419 ; *Smith* v. *Mayor*, 34 How. Pr. 508 ; *People* v. *Com., etc., of Palatine*, 53 Barb. 70 ; *Huber* v. *People*, 49 N. Y. 133 ; *People* v. *Brooklyn*, 13 Abb. [N. S.] 121 ; *Watertown* v. *Fairbanks*, 65 N. Y. 588 ; *Matter of Lands in Flatbush*, 60 id. 398, 407 ; *Matter of Sackett, etc., Streets*, 74 id. 95, 102– 103 ; *Ives* v. *Norris* [Nebraska], 13 N. W. Rep. 276 ; *White* v. *White*, 5 Barb. 474, 482–5 ; *Stuart* v. *Palmer*, 74 N. Y. 183 ; U. S. Constitution, 14th Amendment, § 1 ; *Bloodgood* v. *M. & H. R. R. Co.*, 18 Wend. 9 ; *People* v. *Haydon*, 6 Hill, 361 ; *Bohlman* v. *Green Bay R. R.*, 30 Wis. 105 ; Constitution U. S., art. 1, § 10 ; *People* v. *Platt*, 17 Johns. 195.) The defendant's acts in erecting bulk-heads, obstructing the flow of water and making reservoirs of the lakes, not for the purpose of using the water at those points, but to facilitate the diversion of it into a new channel thirty miles long, are no defense to this action. (*Clinton* v. *Myers*, 46 N. Y. 511 ; *Webb* v. *Portland*

Manuf. Co., 3 Sumn. 189; *Gerrish* v. *N. M. Manuf. Co.*, 10 Foster, 478; *Harding* v. *Stamford Water Co.*, 41 Conn. 87.)

William F. Cogswell for respondent. The injury to the defendant by the granting of the relief sought being immeasurable and irreparable, involving great public interests, while the injury to the plaintiffs is one that can be compensated by money, a decree for injunction will not be granted. (*Wood* v. *Sutcliff*, 2 Simons [N. S.], 163; *Bankhart* v. *Houghton*, 27 Beav. 425; *Durell* v. *Pritchard*, L. R., 1 Ch. App. 244; Kerr on Injunction, 225, 231-2.) Defendant's structure, having been completed before the suit was commenced, the injunction prayed will not be granted, especially in view of the fact that the same was constructed without remonstrance on the part of the plaintiffs, and that their damages may be compensated by the payment of a sum of money. (*Deere* v. *Guest*, 1 M. & C. 516; *Jacomb* v. *Knight*, 32 L. J. Ch. 601; *Wickes* v. *Hunt*, Johnson [Eng. Rep.], 372; Kerr on Injunctions, 231-233.) The law in reference to the right of riparian proprietors in running streams has no applicability to the case on hand. (*Haldin* v. *Brockhart*, 45 Penn. St. 514; Angell on Water-Courses [6th ed.], § 112.) As Hemlock lake is a navigable lake, its waters belong to the State, the State had the right to take the waters thereof, or grant them to the defendant without making compensation to the plaintiffs. (*Cohn* v. *Wason Boom Co.*, Alb. L. J., Nov. 8, 1879, p. 375; *People* v. *Canal Appraisers*, 33 N. Y. 461; *Crill* v. *City of Rome*, 47 How. Pr. 398; *Morgan* v. *King*, 35 N. Y. 454; *People* v. *Tibbets*, 19 id. 523; *Gould* v. *H. R. R. R. Co.*, 2 Seld. 522; *Susq. C. Co.* v. *Wrights*, 9 W. & S. 9; 3 Kent, marg. p. 430; Angell on Water-Courses, §§ 41-43, 537, 542, note 1, 546, 550 *a;* Woolrych on Waters, 40; *Martin* v. *Waddell*, 16 Peters, 367, 410; Houck on Navigable Rivers, chap. 5, p. 78; *People* v. *Canal Appraisers*, 33 N. Y. 461; *Morgan* v. *King*, 35 id. 425; *Canal Comm'rs* v. *People*, 5 Wend. 423; *People* v. *Tibbits*, 19 N. Y. 523.) By the treaty between New York and Massachusetts of 1786, the right of the State in the navigable waters did not pass to Massachusetts with the proprietary right to the soil, but is one of those public rights or rights of sovereignty which were ceded to and reserved by the State of New York. (*People* v. *Vanderbilt,* 26 N. Y. 287–292; 38 Barb. 286; *Williams* v. *Wilcox,* 3 N. & P. 606; *Lansing* v. *Smith,* 4 Wend. 9, 20.)

RUGER, Ch. J. The State by virtue of its sovereignty is deemed the original grantor of all titles to real estate, and a conveyance by it of riparian rights upon non-navigable streams vests its grantees, both mediate and remote, with all the rights which such owners can acquire against any grantor.

The riparian owners of lands adjoining fresh water, non-navigable streams, take title, "*ad usque filum aquæ,*" to the thread of the stream, and thereby acquire the right as incident to such title to the usufructuary enjoyment of the undiminished and undisturbed flow of such water. "Fresh rivers of what kind soever do of common right belong to the owners of the soil adjacent," is the expressive language of the common law and is of universal application. (*Clinton* v. *Myers,* 46 N. Y. 511; 7 Am. Rep. 373; *Chenango Bridge Co.* v. *Paige,* 83 N. Y. 178; 38 Am. Rep. 407.)

The plaintiffs have shown title to the several premises occupied and enjoyed by them as mill-owners upon the banks of a non-navigable stream, which entitles them to the uninterrupted flow of its waters in the channel of the stream contiguous to their respective premises as it had been accustomed to flow. (*Gardner* v. *Vil. of Newburgh,* 2 Johns. Ch. 162; *Reid* v. *Gifford,* Hopk. 416; *Brown* v. *Bowen,* 30 N. Y. 519; *Pixley* v. *Clark,* 35 id. 520; *Varick* v. *Smith,* 5 Paige, 137.) Their right to maintain an action to restrain the infringement of any rights of property which they possess as riparian owners is unquestionable. (*Gardner* v. *Vil. of Newburgh, supra; Corning* v. *Troy Iron and Nail Factory,* 40 N. Y. 191; *The West Point Iron Co.* v. *Reymert,* 45 id. 703; *Garwood* v. *N. Y. C. & H. R. R. R. Co.,* 83 id. 404; *Yates* v. *Milwaukee,* 10 Wall. 504.)

Honeoye creek, upon which the mill privileges of the several plaintiffs are situated, is á fresh-water, non-navigable stream, formed by the junction of the surplus waters of the Hemlock, Canadice and Honeoye lakes flowing through their respective outlets and affords valuable water privileges, which have been used and enjoyed by the respective owners of lands on the creek for a long series of years. It is not claimed that the creek was ever made a public highway, or that it is capable of navigation, neither is it denied that the riparian proprietors own the bed of the stream. It necessarily follows that such owners possess all the rights in the running water of this stream that belong to the riparian owners of any stream or watercourse.

This action is brought to restrain the continued diversion by the defendant of the surplus water of Hemlock lake from this creek, such diversion being effected by means of a conduit constructed by the city of Rochester from the lake to the city, and which now draws from the lake four million gallons of water and has the capacity for carrying upward of nine million gallons daily. The conduit was constructed about the year 1875 for the purpose of furnishing for the use of the citizens of Rochester a supply of water for domestic and other purposes, and was authorized by chapter 754 of the Laws of 1873.

The defense proceeds upon the theory that Hemlock lake being a navigable body of water, as such with its bed belongs to the State, and that the State possessed the consequent right of authorizing the appropriation of the water by its agents or grantees for any public use without regard to the rights of individuals who may have previously acquired proprietary interests therein.

The proofs and the finding of the court below establish that this lake was to a certain extent navigable, and that for many years it had in a limited way and for local purposes been actually navigated by those living upon its shores. It was a small inland lake, about seven miles in length and one-half mile in width, lying about thirty miles south-easterly from Rochester. It may be assumed, then, that this lake formed a portion of the navigable waters of the State, and was, therefore, subject to all of the rules pertaining to such waters, and further, that the State conferred upon the defendant all of the rights in the lake which remained in it, subsequent to the original grant of the lands on Honeoye creek. Section 3 of chapter 754 of the Laws of 1873, under authority of which said conduit was built, reads as follows: " The board of water commissioners of the city of Rochester appointed under the provisions of act chapter 387 of the Laws of 1872 are hereby authorized to enter upon, control and use as the agents of the city of Rochester the waters of Hemlock and Canadice lakes, situated in the county of Livingston, for the purpose of procuring a water supply for the said city of Rochester, and shall also have the power to raise the surface of water in said lakes, not to exceed two feet, and to draw down the said water below low-water mark not to exceed eight feet; also, the right to take such measures and make such constructions as shall be necessary to secure said waters for the purposes intended." "All of the above powers hereby granted to be exercised with due regard to the rights of owners of property adjacent thereto and dependent thereon. And the city of Rochester shall be liable to pay to such owners any and all damages which may be caused to such property by the performance of said act or the exercise of the powers hereby granted." This act does not infringe any constitutional provision and was enacted in substantial conformity with the requirements of the fundamental law.

The provision quoted undoubtedly grants to the city of Rochester the right to make such use of the waters of the lake as the State itself might have made and imposes with it the same liability to those who might be injured by its use of such waters as the State itself would have incurred for a similar use.

It seemed to be assumed upon the argument that the rights of the State in the waters of Hemlock lake depended upon the ownership of the soil under its bed, and the question whether the title of riparian owners by the rules of common law in-

cluded the land to the center of the bed of the adjoining navi-
gable-body, or was restricted to the water's edge. We do not
think this is necessarily so, but conceding the claim for the
present let us examine that position. This question has occasioned some diversity of opinion in this country and has led to
conflicting and apparently irreconcilable decisions in our courts.
It would be a vain and useless effort to attempt to harmonize
the divergent views on the subject, but we believe that a
doctrine may be evolved from the authorities which will accord
with the great weight of judicial opinion in this country, and
still preserve such property rights as have been acquired and
have grown up under the authority of diverse decisions. We
have arrived at the conclusion that all rights of property to
the soil under the waters of Hemlock lake were acquired by
and belong to its riparian owners, while such rights only over
its waters belong to the State as pertain to sovereignty alone.

The ownership and jurisdiction over the lands in the south-
western part of the State in which Hemlock lake is located,
were, in the earlier history of this country, the subject of
much controversy between the sovereign States of Massachusetts and New York. These differences were finally adjusted
by a treaty executed between the respective States, in December, 1786, whereby the State of New York did "cede, grant,
release and confirm to the said Commomwealth of Massachusetts, and to the use of the Commonwealth, their grantees and
the heirs and assignees of such grantees forever, the right of pre-
emption of the soil from the native Indians, and all other the
estate, right, title and property (the right and title of government sovereignty and jurisdiction excepted), which the State
of New York hath, of, in or to" the lands in question; on the
other hand, the State of Massachusetts ceded to New York all
claim to the government, sovereignty and jurisdiction of the
lands described.

Subsequent to this treaty there remained in the State of
New York only such rights of property in these lands as necessarily pertained to its sovereignty and were inalienable by the
sovereign. All such rights of property in or to the territory in

dispute as could by the most comprehensive and absolute conveyance be granted to another were, by this treaty, conferred upon the Commonwealth of Massachusetts and its grantees. (*Burbank* v. *Fay*, 65 N. Y. 57; *Commr's of Canal Fund* v. *Kempshall*, 26 Wend. 404.) The settlers in this territory derive the title to their lands from the Commonwealth of Massachusetts and have become possessed of all of the rights which that State acquired in such lands by virtue of the treaty of cession or otherwise.

It now remains to consider the nature of the rights of property which pertain exclusively to sovereignty and which do not pass to the grantee under a conveyance of the soil bordering upon and adjoining fresh-water navigable lakes and rivers. It may be premised that the mere right of eminent domain always and from necessity resides in the sovereign. It is declared by statute that the State, by virtue of its sovereignty, is deemed to possess the original and ultimate property in and to all lands within the jurisdiction of the State. (3 R. S. [7th ed.] 2162, § 1; *People* v. *Fulton F. Ins. Co.*, 25 Wend. 219; *People* v. *Denison*, 17 id. 312; *De Peyster* v. *Michael*, 6 N. Y. 467; *People* v. *Van Rensselaer*, 9 id. 319.) This right confers upon the State the title to such property as may be forfeited or escheated, or the title to which for any reason fails, and also the right to resume the ownership and possession of such property as may be required or rendered necessary for public purposes. (*Varick* v. *Smith*, 5 Paige, 143, 159; *Matter of Albany St.*, 11 Wend. 149; *Morgan* v. *King*, 35 N. Y. 454.) Among other rights which pertain to sovereignty is that of using, regulating and controlling for special purposes the waters of all navigable lakes or streams, whether fresh or salt, and without regard to the ownership of the soil beneath the water. This right is known as the *jus publici* and is deemed to be inalienable.

Judge EDMONDS, in his learned opinion in *Gould* v. *Hudson River Railroad Co.* (6 N. Y. 546), says: " When regarding the rights of the State in respect to lands, we must not be unmindful that it has two interests, one governmental and the other proprietary. Or as it is divided by M. Prudhon in his *Traité du Domain Public*, the public domain, which is that kind of property which the government holds as mere trustee for the use of the public, such as public highways, navigable rivers, salt springs, etc., and which are not, of course, alienable; and the domain of the State, which applies only to things in which the State has the same absolute property as an individual would have in like cases." Although this quotation is from a dissenting opinion, yet, so far as the principle announced is concerned, it met with no dissent and is supported by universal authority. (6 N. Y. 555; *U. S. B'k* v. *B'k of Metropolis,* 15 Pet. 387; *Doe dem Knight* v. *Nepean,* 5 B. & A. 91; *Hoyt* v. *Sprague,* 12 Pick. 407; 3 Kent's Com. 537; *Pollard's Lessee* v. *Hagan,* 3 How. [U. S.] 222.)

In the examination of any of the numerous questions relating to water-courses that may arise, no discussion would be complete which failed to refer to the ancient and learned treatise *De jure Maris,* by Sir Matthew Hale, and which, after the lapse of two centuries, remains the most concise, comprehensive and reliable work on the subject of which it treats. As appears from the learned note of Judge COWEN to *Ex parte Jennings* (6 Cow. 537), under the following title " Of the right of prerogative in private or fresh rivers," it reads : " The king, by an ancient right of prerogative, hath had a certain interest in many fresh rivers, even where the sea does not flow or reflow, as well as salt or arms of the sea, and those are these which follow :

" 1st. A right of franchise or privilege that no man may set up a common ferry for all passengers, without prescription time out of mind or a charter from the king.

" 2d. An interest as I may call it of pleasure or recreation.

" 3d. An interest of jurisdiction.

" And another part of the king's jurisdiction in reformation of nuisances is to reform and punish nuisances in all rivers, whether fresh or salt, that are a common passage not only for ships and greater vessels, but also of smaller as barges and boats, to reform the obstructions or annoyances that are therein to such common passage for as the common highways on the land are for the common-land passage, so these kind of rivers, whether fresh or salt, that bear boats or barges are highways by water, and as the highways by land are called *altæ viæ regiæ*, so these public rivers for public passage are called *fluvie regales* and *streomes le Roy*, not in reference to the propriety of the river but to the public use."

The doctrines of this treatise so far as relate to the jurisdiction of the sovereign over navigable waters, have been frequently cited with approval in our reports and are now indisputable. (*People* v. *Platt*, 17 Johns. 210; *Hooker* v. *Cummings*, 20 id. 100; *Commissioners* v. *Kempshall*, *supra*; *Canal Appraisers* v. *People*, 17 Wend. 570.)

The rule of common law is concisely stated in the note above referred to as follows: "Rivers not navigable, that is, fresh rivers of what kind soever, do of common right belong to the owners of the soil adjacent to the extent of their land in length. But salt rivers, where the tide ebbs and flows, belong of common right to the State. That this ownership of the citizen is of the whole river, viz., the soil and the water of the river, except that in his river where boats, rafts, etc., may be floated to market, the public have a right of way or easement."

It may, however, be stated in passing, that it is generally conceded that this doctrine is inapplicable to the vast freshwater lakes or inland seas of this country or the streams forming the boundary line of States. (*Canal Commissioners* v. *People*, 5 Wend. 446; *Tibbetts Case*, *supra*.) Whatever conclusion may, therefore, be reached with reference to the ownership of the bed of Hemlock lake, it still remains that the State had certain rights in its waters and so far as the same were alienable the defendant has succeeded to them. It may, also, be affirmed that if the term "navigable water" as used in England was ever there for any purpose wholly restricted to the waters which were affected by the ebb and flow of the tide, it has by common consent a more enlarged signification in this country and is here held to mean all such waters as are actually naviga-

ble, whether fresh or salt. When it is considered that the
rights and interests of the public, such as fishing, ferrying and
transportation, are preserved in all navigable waters by the inherent and inalienable attributes of the sovereign, it would
seem to follow that the controversies which have arisen over
the nominal ownership of the soil under such waters have been
magnified beyond the real interests involved. This becomes
still more apparent when we consider the character and extent
of the property which may in the nature of things be acquired
and enjoyed in running water. *"Aqua curret debet currere."*
Neither sovereign nor subject can have any greater than a usufructuary right therein, and even this is subject to the temporary enjoyment by the riparian proprietors over whose lands it
passes while on its way to its final destination, undiverted and
undiminished, save for domestic or manufacturing purposes.
(3 Kent's Com. 439; *Tyler* v. *Wilkinson*, 4 Mason, 397.) Thus
all land covered by running water is subject to a servitude,
either dominant or servient, and all interest in such water is
simply an easement, incapable of fixed appropriation or conversion. (1 Stephens' Blackst. 169; Washb. on Easements, 200.)
The rule of the common law of England has been uniformly
deemed to apply in this country to the affluents of all navigable waters as well as to all those which are non-navigable, and
the only serious controversy arises over its application to its
inferior fresh-water navigable streams and lakes. These rules
were made the fundamental law of this State by its original
Constitution and have been readopted upon every subsequent
revision of that instrument.

Section 25 of the Constitution of 1877 reads: "And this
convention in the name and by the authority of the good people of this State ordain, determine and declare that such parts
of the common law of England and of the statute law of England and Great Britain and of the acts of the legislature of
the colony of New York as together did form the law of the said
colony on the 19th day of April, in the year of our Lord one
thousand seven hundred and seventy-five, shall be and continue the law of this State, subject to such alterations and pro-

visions as the legislature of this State shall from time to time make concerning the same." (§ 13, art. 7, Const. of 1821; § 17, art. 1, Laws of 1846.)

It is not claimed that the legislature has ever changed or modified the common-law rules on the subject under consideration by express legislation or direct action looking to their limitation. The only grounds for a denial of their application to the subject in this country is on. account of their alleged inapplicability to the larger bodies of water possessed by our people and the action of the legislature in assuming the owner-ship of the lands under the waters of the Mohawk and the Hudson rivers above tide-water. (DAVIES, J., opinion, *People v. Canal App.*, 33 N. Y. 478.)

Peculiar reasons have governed the action of the State as to the lands under the Mohawk and Hudson rivers as we shall see hereafter. We do not think the reasons given justify the court in disregarding the positive requirements of the fundamental law to the extent claimed by some of the . cases. In addition to the apparently conclusive force of the constitutional provision, we also think the decided preponderance of judicial authority in the State favors the application of the common-law rule to the navigable waters of this State. It would be unprofitable to go into an extended discussion or citation of the numerous cases treating of this question, and, therefore, but few of them will be referred to and those only in our State which illustrate the views commending themselves most strongly to our judgment. (*People* v. *Platt*, 17 Johns. 195; *Hooker* v. *Cummings*, 20 id. 90; *Rogers* v. *Jones*, 5 Wend. 237; *Commissioners* v. *Kempshall*, 26 id. 404; *Ex parte Jennings*, 6 Cow. 518; *Gould* v. *H. R. R. .R. Co.*, 6 N. Y. 522; *Trustees of Brookhaven* v. *Strong*, 60 id. 56; *Chenango Bridge Co.* v. *Paige*, 83 id. 178; 38 Am. Rep. 407.) These decisions show a course of authority extending from an early period of our history to the most recent times, and although they do not constitute an unbroken chain, yet they are fortified by a wealth of learning, reason and illustration that render them irresistible as authority.

We can hardly omit to refer particularly to the learned note by Judge Cowen in *Ex parte Jennings*, the opinion of Judge Edwards in *Gould* v. *H. R. R. R. Co.*, and that of Senator Verplanck in the *Kempshall Case.* Neither is it deemed necessary to refer to all of the cases which apparently sustain conflicting views upon this question. These cases nearly all relate to the river Hudson above tide-water and to the Mohawk, and the remarks made with reference to one, therefore, apply to all. Undoubtedly the leading case on that side in our courts is *The People* v. *Canal App.* (33 N. Y. 461), in which the late Judge Davies delivered a learned and elaborate opinion. The head-note shows precisely the questions there involved and the extent of the doctrine announced : " The Mohawk river is a navigable stream, and the title to the bed of the river is in the people of the State. Riparian owners along the stream are not entitled to damages for any diversion or use of the waters of the Mohawk by the State."

It will be observed that the case relates to the Mohawk river and an appropriation of its water for the purpose of navigation alone — that being one of the uses which universally pertain to the rights of the sovereign in all navigable streams. The case is not, therefore, an authority for the appropriation of navigable waters for other public uses. We think this and similar cases might properly have been decided for reasons peculiar to the Mohawk and Hudson rivers upon the grounds stated in the *Commissioners* v. *Kempshall* (*supra*), by Senator Verplanck and by the chancellor and Senator Beardsley in *Canal Appraisers* v. *People* (17 Wend. 572). The titles granted to the original settlers in the Hudson and Mohawk valleys, as construed by the rules of the civil law prevailing in the Netherlands, from whose government they were derived, did not convey to their riparian owners the banks or beds of navigable streams. Upon the surrender of this territory the guaranty assured by the English authorities to its inhabitants of the peaceable enjoyment of their possessions simply confirmed the right already possessed, and the beds of navigable streams, never having been conveyed, became, by virtue of the right of eminent domain, vested in the English government as ungranted lands, and the State of New York, as a consequence of the Revolution, succeeded to the rights of the mother country.

As to the lands under these rivers, the people of this State have, from the earliest times, asserted their title, however acquired, and have assumed to grant and convey them like other unappropriated lands belonging to the State. (3 Greenl. Laws, 13 [Dec., 1792]; *Palmer* v. *Mulligan*, 3 Caines, 308.) It is stated in *People* v. *Canal Appraisers* (*supra*), that when the possession of these waters subsequently became necessary to the State for the purposes of navigation, they reacquired the rights formerly granted by them from the Western Inland Navigation Company by purchase, and they then appropriated them by virtue of their original proprietorship. We think the authority of these cases should be confined to the waters of the Hudson and Mohawk rivers, rights in which were alone necessarily involved in their determination. However this may be, we are clearly of the opinion that Hemlock lake is not such a body of water as under any rule entitles the State to claim the ownership of its bed, and that the only rights, if any, which the defendant acquired by virtue of chapter 754 of the Laws of 1873 were those which the State possessed by virtue of its sovereignty over the territory in question. Those rights are quite distinct from such as the State would have possessed as a riparian owner. Such rights would have entitled her to the same uses and subject to the same liabilities as other owners of property. (*People* v. *Vanderbilt*, 26 N. Y. 292; *Commissioners* v. *Kempshall, supra*.) We have before seen that the sovereign right grew out of and was based upon the public benefits in promoting trade and commerce, supposed to be derived from keeping open navigable bodies of water as public highways for the common use of the people.

We have also seen that they constituted an easement over the lands of the riparian owners for limited purposes, and embracing no right to convert the waters to any other uses than those for which the easement was created. It is an element-

ary principle that all easements are limited to the very purpose for which they were created, and their enjoyment cannot
be extended by implication. This right, being founded upon
the public benefit supposed to be derived from their use as
a highway, cannot be extended to a different purpose inconsistent with its original use. The diversion of these waters
for the purposes of furnishing the inhabitants of a large city
with that element for domestic uses, and especially to lease
them for manufacturing and other purposes, is an object totally
inconsistent with their use as a public highway or the common
right of all the people to their benefits.

We concede that such a use is a public one in the sense that
enables a municipal corporation to procure the lawful condem-
nation of property for that object, but we deny that it is consistent with the purpose upon which the sovereign right is
based.

The exercise by a ruler of the right of eminent domain is always subject to the obligation of making compensation for the
property taken. (*Gould* v. *Hudson River R. R.*, *supra.*)
Due regard for the distinctions existing between a public
right and a public use, and also those between a sovereign
and a proprietary right is essential to a just consideration
of the rights of parties in navigable water-courses. While a
sovereign may convey its proprietary rights, it cannot alienate
its control over navigable waters without abdicating its sovereignty. (*Martin* v. *Waddell*, 16 Peters, 367.) A neglect to
observe these distinctions has been the cause of much error in
treating of these rights.

In *Comm'rs* v. *Kempshall*, Senator VERPLANCK says: "I
cannot assent to the position that the conceded common-law
authority of the State over such rivers, for the purposes of
navigation, comprehends the right to divert the waters to other
purposes of artificial navigation, wholly distinct from that of
the river itself." He then proceeds to state rules in apt and
pertinent language, which we consider decisive of this case in
its various aspects. "The proprietor of the bed and bank of
the stream has himself no absolute property in the waters, but

strictly a usufructuary interest appurtenant to his freehold. He can use the waters for his own benefit; but he may not divert them to the injury of his neighbors, or lessen their quantity, or detain them unreasonably. If such be the strict limitation of the proprietary right, can it be that the State, as the trustee of a special public servitude, has a much less restricted right, and can divert or detain the waters for other uses? By its sovereign right of eminent domain, it undoubtedly may do so," * * * * " but all these exercises of sovereign authority are alike ' the taking of private property for public use,' which the Constitution pronounces may not be done ' without just compensation.' "

It is said by the court in *Ex parte Jennings*, that "individual property cannot be taken, or which is the same thing, individual rights impaired for the benefit of the public without just compensation."

" The public right is one of passage and nothing more, as in a common highway. It is called by the cases an easement, and the proprietor of the adjoining land has a right to use the land and water of the river in any way not inconsistent with this easement. If he make any erection rendering the passage of boats, etc., inconvenient or unsafe, he is guilty of a nuisance, and this is the only restriction which the law imposes upon him. It follows that neither the State nor any individual have a right to divert the stream, or render it less useful or valuable to the owner of the soil."

It was also said by Judge EARL in the *Chenango Bridge Case, supra:* " The legislature, except under the power of eminent domain, upon making compensation can interfere with such streams only for the purpose of regulating, preserving and protecting the public easement. Further than that it has no more power over the fresh-water streams than over other private property." (See, also, *Morgan* v. *King*, 35 N. Y. 457; *Hooker* v. *Cummings*, 20 Johns. 99; *Gardner* v. *Village of Newburgh, supra.*)

The case of *Gould* v. *The Hudson River R. R. Co.* (6 N. Y. 522) has been cited as holding a contrary doctrine, but we do not so regard it. The question there related solely to the ownership of the lands between low and high-water mark on the Hudson river. This was at the point in dispute, a tidal river, and by the conceded doctrine of the common law the titles of its riparian owners were bounded by the line of high-water mark. The property there taken for a public use was acquired from the State, who was its lawful owner (see *Gould Case*, p. 539).

The case of *People* v. *Tibbetts* (19 N. Y. 527) also involved the rights of riparian owners upon the Hudson river, and was put upon the express ground that by the common law the State was the owner of the bed and waters of that stream so far as the tide ebbed and flowed.

These cases, therefore, cannot be considered as authority upon the question here presented. We are, therefore, of the opinion not only that the State had no right to grant to the city of Rochester the use of the waters of Hemlock lake, to the detriment of the riparian owners upon the banks of the stream formed by its outlet, but that their rights were recognized and provided for by the act under which the defendant assumes to justify its acts.

Evidence was given to support the theory that the improvements made by the defendant in the outlets of Canadice and Hemlock lakes furnished a more uniform and constant supply of water to the plaintiff's mills than before existed. It was claimed from this fact that they were, therefore, uninjured by the alleged diversion of water. No express finding upon this issue was made by the court below, and no grounds for its consideration here are now presented. The evidence upon the issue was conflicting, and we have no means of determining the question of fact involved.

Upon proceedings being taken to condemn this property by the city of Rochester, such a consideration would have great weight in determining the extent of the injuries to the plaintiffs' property, occasioned by an unlawful interference with their water privileges, and it might bear also upon the question of the propriety of an injunction herein, but it is altogether, in its present aspect, a question for the consideration of the court below.

The evidence in this case tended to show that the plaintiffs were injured by the act of the defendant in diverting the water of Honeoye creek, which had theretofore been accustomed to flow in its channel to the benefit of the mill-owners on that stream. This court must assume that some damage occurred to the parties who were illegally deprived of their property. The extent of this injury has not been tried and determined. We cannot look into the evidence to determine that question. That is exclusively a question for the consideration of the trial court. It is enough that the plaintiffs have a clear legal right which has been invaded, and the right to try the question of the extent of their injury has been denied them. It is possible that, upon all the circumstances of the case, the court below may, in the exercise of their discretion, deny a remedy by injunction, or grant it upon terms and conditions such as in their judgment will best preserve the rights and interests of the parties. But the plaintiffs have an undoubted right to the exercise of such discretion by that court. This has been refused them, and for that reason a new trial must be ordered.

The judgments of the General and Special Terms should, therefore, be reversed and a new trial granted.

All concur.

Judgments reversed.

THE PEOPLE OF THE STATE OF NEW YORK, Respondent, *v.* THE NEW YORK FLOATING DRY-DOCK COMPANY, Appellant.

The defendant was incorporated for the purpose, as expressed in its charter, (Chap. 170, Laws of 1843) " of constructing, using and providing one or more dry-docks or wet-docks or other conveniences and structures for building, raising, repairing or coppering vessels and steamers of every description." In an action to recover taxes alleged to be due for the year 1881, under the act of 1880 (Chap. 542, Laws of 1880), *held*, that

defendant was not " a manufacturing corporation " within the meaning of the clause in said act (§ 3) which exempts such corporations
from its provisions; and that it was liable to taxation under the act.

(Argued April 23, 1883; decided June 5, 1883.)

APPEAL from judgment of the General Term of the Supreme
Court, in the third judicial department, entered upon an order
made November 21, 1882, which affirmed a judgment in favor
of plaintiff, entered upon a decision of the court on trial without a jury.

The nature of the action and the material facts are stated in
the opinion.

E. N. Taft for appellant.

Leslie W. Russell, attorney-general, for respondent. Defendant was not a manufacturing corporation within the provision of the act of 1880 (Chap. 542, § 3), exempting such
corporations from its provisions. (Laws of 1843, chap. 170,
§ 1; Potter's Dwarris on Statutes, 193.)

MILLER, J. This action was brought to recover the taxes
imposed upon defendant under chapter 542 of the Laws of
1880, for the year ending November 1, 1880. Defendant was
incorporated under chapter 170 of the Laws of 1843 " for the
purpose of constructing, using and providing one or more dry-
docks, or wet-docks, or other conveniences and structures for
building, raising, repairing and coppering vessels and steamers
of every description." The act under which the defendant
was incorporated was of a special character, and the specification of the business which the defendant was authorized to
carry on, under its charter, which states the general purpose
and object of the incorporation, does not bring it within the
provision of section 3 of said act of 1880, which exempts manufacturing corporations from its provisions as to taxation. The
term, "manufacturing corporation," cannot, we think, be considered as comprehending the business of the defendant, if the

words employed are interpreted according to the common understanding of such language.

While the act provides for the constructing, using and providing one or more dry or wet-docks or other conveniences and structures for the purposes named, its main object evidently is building, raising, repairing and coppering vessels. The principal portion of the work which the corporation is authorized to perform relates to the improvement of vessels which have already been constructed, and not to the construction of the same, and taking all the parts enumerated together they cannot be considered as embraced within the term " manufacturing," and, if regarded separately, we think, they do not come within the definition of the term employed. According to Webster a manufacturer is one who works raw materials into wares suitable for use. The constructing, using and providing of one or more docks, as used in the act of 1880, is no more a manufacturing within the meaning of that word than would be the building of warehouses and elevators for the carrying on of the business of warehousemen or the erection of buildings or residences. If the building of residences could be regarded as coming within the definition of the term "manufacturing," there would be no necessity for the enactment of chapter 117, Laws of 1853, which authorizes the formation of corporations for the erection of buildings. By this act the legislature gave a construction to the manufacturing law which indicates that it was not regarded as embracing the objects which were thereby provided for. The same remarks would apply to the act under which the defendant was incorporated. The legislative interpretation, thus given, is entitled to much weight in construing the act in question.

Considering the object of the act in question, and the purpose for which it was intended, and looking at it in all its bearings, we are brought to the conclusion that it cannot be regarded as incorporating a manufacturing corporation within the true intent and meaning of that term, and that the defendant was liable to pay the tax imposed according to its provisions.

The point made that said act is in violation of the Constitu. tion of the State is disposed of by the recent decision in this court in the case of *People* v. *Home Ins. Co.** (See opinion of RUGER, Ch. J.)

Also the point urged that the defendant was not liable for taxes until after November 1, 1881, is fully covered by the opinion of ANDREWS, J., in the case of *People* v. *Spring Valley Hydraulic Gold Company.*†

The question as to the application of the Fourteenth Amendment of the Constitution of the United States is decided adversely to the appellant's claim in the case of *People* v. *Fire Association of Philadelphia.*‡ (See opinion of FINCH, J.)

The judgment should be affirmed.

All concur.

Judgment affirmed.

MARY WOHLFAHRT, as Administratrix, etc., Respondent, *v.* CHARLES A. BECKERT, Appellant.

Where, upon the sale by a druggist of a poisonous medicine he, fully and fairly warns the purchaser of its character, and gives accurate informa- tion and directions as to the quantity which may be safely taken, and the customer is injured or killed by taking an overdose in disregard of such direction, the druggist is not liable for negligence or tort, simply be- cause of an omission on his part to put a label marked "poison" upon the "parcel in which the sale is made" as required by the statute. (2 R. S. 694, § 23.) The customer may not disregard the warning and direction and charge the consequences of his own negligence or recklessness upon the druggist.

Wohlfahrt v. *Beckert* (27 Hun, 74), in this respect overruled.

In an action against a druggist for alleged negligence in the sale of a poisonous medicine without attaching a label marked poison, thus caus- ing the death of W., plaintiff's intestate, it appeared, that W., having been advised to take a comparatively harmless preparation known as "black draught," and that he could take a small wine glass thereof, which he could procure at any drug store for ten cents, went to defendant's drug store, where, according to the testimony of defendant's clerk, he asked

---

* *Ante,* p. 323. † *Ante,* p. 388. ‡ *Ante,* p. 311.

defendant for ten cents worth of "black drops;" defendant told him that was a poison, and advised him to take another preparation; this W. refused, and defendant thereupon directed the witness to give him black drops, but informed him that he should only 'take ten or twelve drops for a dose; witness gave W. two drachms of the medicine asked for in a vial upon which was a label marked "black drops;" the label did not have the word "poison" thereon. W. took nearly the whole of the contents of the vial and died in consequence. *Held*, that if the testimony of the clerk was to be taken as the truth, a verdict for defendant was properly directed; but that the jury were at liberty, under the circumstances, to disbelieve such testimony, as the witness was interested, having violated the law by omitting the prescribed label; and that, therefore, the question as to whether the warning testified to was in fact given was one for the jury, and the direction was error.

(Argued April 24, 1883; decided June 5, 1888.)

APPEAL from an order of the General Term of the Supreme Court, in the second judicial department, made February 15, 1882, which sustained plaintiff's exceptions and granted a new trial; a verdict having been rendered in favor of defendant by the direction of the court, on trial, and exceptions having been ordered to be heard at first instance at General Term. (Reported below, 27 Hun, 74.)

This action was brought to recover damages for alleged negligence in causing the death of Matthias Wohlfahrt, plaintiff's intestate.

The evidence on the trial was to this effect: Wohlfahrt being temporarily troubled with diarrhœa or some bowel complaint, was informed by one Silberstein, a peddler, that a preparation known as "black draught," a vegetable non-poisonous mixture, of which he could take a small glassful, would relieve him, and that he could get ten cents worth of this "black draught" in any drug store. Wohlfahrt went to defendant's drug store, and according to the testimony of defendant's clerk what occurred there was as follows: At the door Wohlfahrt met the defendant, and said to him, "I wish to buy black drops." Defendant said, "For what do you wish black drops?" Wohlfahrt replied, "I want it for cramps in my stomach." "Why, that is a poison," defendant said, "I would advise you to take cholera drops for your sickness." "No," said Wohl-

fahrt, "I want black drops." " Well," said defendant, " that
is a poison, and you cannot take more than ten or twelve drops
of that medicine for a dose." " Yes," said Wohlfahrt.
Whereupon defendant turned to the witness and told him to
give Wohlfahrt a diluted preparation of the medicine called
for. The witness gave deceased two drachms in a vial, simply
labeled "black drops." The quantity to be taken at a dose
was not written nor was the word "poison" written or
printed upon the label, nor was any word or phrase to indicate the poisonous character of the drug. Upon his return
home, the wife of deceased took the medicine, poured it in
a little glass and gave it to him; he took all of it with the
exception of a few drops and he died within a few hours thereafter.

William C. De Witt for appellant. Where the facts are
uncontroverted, the question of negligence is one of law. (*Gon-
zales* v. *N. Y. & H. R. R. R. Co.*, 38 N. Y. 440; *Clarke* v.
Union Ferry Co., 35 id. 48; *Morrison* v. *Erie R. R. Co.*, 56 id.
302; *Riceman* v. *Havemeyer*, 84 id. 647; *Tonawanda R. R.
Co.* v. *Meyer*, 5 Denio, 255; 56 N. Y. 630; 49 id. 177; 36 id.
153.) Not every violation of a criminal provision in the
statutes gives a right of civil action *per se* against the wrong-
doer, and a person may be punishable criminally for having
violated the law and still not be liable civilly to one injured by
such violation. (*Connelly* v. *N. Y. C. & H. R. R. R. Co.*, 88 N.
Y. 346; *Pakalinski* v. *N. Y. C. & H. R. R. R. Co.*, 82 id.
424; *Riceman* v. *Havemeyer*, 84 id. 647; *Wilds* v. *H. R.
R. R. Co.*, 24 id. 430; 34 id. 9; *Cordell* v. *N. Y. C. & H. R.
R. R. Co.*, 75 id. 330.)

Samuel Greenbaum for respondent. All the inferences that
the jury might properly have drawn from all the facts are to
be held in favor of plaintiff. (*Sheridan* v. *B. C. & N. R. R.
Co.*, 36 N. Y. 39.) Defendant having sold a most virulent
poison, in violation of the express provisions of law, was guilty
of the grossest negligence and of a wrongful act. (2 Statutes

at Large, 717; 2 R. S. 662, § 19; *Thomas* v. *Winchester*, 6 N. Y. 409; *Regina* v. *Swindall*, 2 C. & K. 232–3; id. 368, 571; *Loop* v. *Litchfield*, 42 N. Y. 358; *Wellington* v. *Downer Kerosene Oil Co.*, 104 Mass. 64; *Norton* v. *Sewell*, 106 id. 143; *Binford* v. *Johnston*, 26 Alb. L. J. 353; *Ernst* v. *H. R. R. R. Co.*, 35 N. Y. 9; *Cordell* v. *N. Y. C. & H. R. R. R. Co.*, 64 id. 532; *Renwick* v. *N. Y. C. R. R. Co.*, 36 id. 132; *Gorton* v. *Erie R. R. Co.*, 45 id. 660; *Knupfle* v. *Knickerbocker Ice Co.*, 84 id. 488; *Congreve* v. *Smith*, 18 id. 79; *Creed* v. *Hartman*, 29 id. 591; *Davenport* v. *Ruckman*, 37 id. 568; *Clifford* v. *Dam*, 81 id. 56.) It is a matter of right in the plaintiff to have the issue of negligence submitted to the jury when it depends upon conflicting evidence or on inferences to be drawn from circumstances in regard to which there is room for a difference of opinion among intelligent men. (*Payne* v. *T. & B. R. R. Co.*, 83 N. Y. 574; *Wolfkiel* v. *Sixth Ave. R. R.*, 38 id. 49; *Weber* v. *N. Y. C. & H. R. R. R. Co.*, 58 id. 451; *Massoth* v. *D. & H. C. Co.*, 64 id. 524; *Sewell* v. *City of Cohoes*, 75 id. 53: *Casey* v. *N. Y. C. & H. R. R. R. Co.*, 78 id. 518; *Hart* v. *H. R. Bridge Co.*, 80 id. 622; *Ernst* v. *H. R. Bridge Co.*, 35 id. 9; *Hume* v. *York*, 47 id. 639; *Miner* v. *S. S. Co.*, 50 id. 23; *Totten* v. *Phipps*, 52 id. 354; *Keating* v. *N. Y. C.*, etc., 49 id. 673; *Barton* v. *Same*, 56 id. 660.) Although one or more witnesses may have testified to a certain state of facts, without being contradicted by other witnesses, it is nevertheless for the jury to determine, from all the facts, circumstances and inferences of the case, whether such witnesses are to be believed or not. (*Stillwell* v. *Carpenter*, 2 Abb. N. C. 238; *Nicholson* v. *Connor*, 8 Daly, 212; *Elwood* v. *W. U. Tel. Co.*, 45 N. Y. 553; *Kavanagh* v. *Wilson*, 70 id. 177; *Gildersleeve* v. *Landon*, 73 id. 609; *Ernst* v. *H. R. R. R. Co.*, 35 id. 28.) The defendant having been guilty of a wrongful act, of gross negligence, the contributory negligence of the deceased is no bar, and constitutes no defense to an action for damages. (*Kenyon* v. *N. Y. C. & H. R. R. R. Co.*, 5 Hun, 479; *Clifford* v. *Dam*, 81 N. Y. 56–57; *Lannen* v. *Alb. G. L. Co.*, 44 id. 439; *Nashville R. R. Co.* v. *Trowlin*, 1 Lea, 523; *R. R.*

Co. v. *Wilke*, 11 Heisk. 383 ; *Rowell* v. *R. R. Co.*, 57 N. H. 132 ; *Ernst* v. *Hud. R. R. R. Co.*, 35 id. 28.) The question of contributive negligence under any circumstances was for the jury. (*Massoth* v. *D. & H. C. Co.*, 64 N. Y. 524; *Poler* v. *N. Y. C. & H. R. R. R. Co.*, 16 id. 476 ; *McIntyre* v. *Same*, 37 id. 287 ; *O'Mara* v. *H. R. R. R. Co.*, 38 id. 445 ; *Mangan* v. *B. R. R. Co.*, id. 455 ; *Wolkfiel* v. *Sixth Ave. R. R. Co.*, id. 49 ; *Filer* v. *N. Y. C.*, etc., 49 id. 47 ; *Keating* v. *Same*, id. 673 ; *Eaton* v. *Erie R. R. Co.*, 51 id. 666 ; *Delafield* v. *Union Ferry Co.*, id. 671 ; *Hackford* v. *N. Y. C. & H. R. R. R. Co.*, 53 id. 654 ; *Spooner* v. *B'klyn City R. R.*, 54 id. 230 ; *Morrison* v. *N. Y. C.*, etc., 63 id. 643 ; *Hays* v. *Miller*, 70 id. 112 ; *Dyer* v. *Erie R. R. Co.*, 71 id. 228 ; *Dolan* v. *D. C. Co.*, id. 285 ; *Rexter* v. *Starin*, 73 id. 601 ; *Harris* v. *Velrelhoer*, 75 id. 169 ; *Terry* v. *Jewett*, 78 id. 338 ; *Kellogg* v. *N. Y. C.*, etc., 77 id. 72 ; *Stackus* v. *Same*, 79 id. 469 ; *Burckhardt* v. *R. & S. R. R. Co.*, 1 Abb. Dec. 131.)

FINCH, J. Whether this case should have been submitted to the jury depends upon the inquiry whether the testimony of the defendant's clerk is to be taken as the truth of the transaction, or may be questioned or doubted. If he is to be believed the druggist who sold the poison was guilty of no wrong or negligence toward the deceased, for he warned him that the "black drops" asked for was a strong poison, of which he should only take ten or twelve drops for a dose. Notwithstanding the warning, he took probably ten times the prescribed quantity, in reliance upon the previous statement of the peddler, Silberstein, that he had taken half a glass of what he called "black draught," and that it had cured him. On such a state of facts a verdict against the defendant would not be justified. Although no label marked " poison " was put upon the phial, and granting that by such omission the defendant was guilty of a misdemeanor and liable to the penalty of the criminal law, still that fact does not make him answerable to the customer injured, or his representative in case of his death, for either a negligent or wrongful act when toward that customer

he was guilty of neither, since he fairly and fully warned him
of all, and more than could have been made known by the
authorized label. The statute requires the ringing of the bell
or sounding of the whistle by an engine approaching a railroad
crossing, but one who sees the train coming has all the notice
and warning which these signals could give, and though they
are omitted, takes the risk of the danger which he sees and
knows if he attempts to cross in front of the train. (*Paka-
linsky* v. *N. Y. C. & H. R. R. R.*, 82 N. Y. 424; *Connelly*
v. *N. Y. C. & H. R. R. R.*, 88 id. 346.) So here, if the warning was in truth given, if the deceased was cautioned that the
medicine sold was a strong poison and but ten or twelve drops
must be taken, he had all the knowledge and all the warning
that the label could have given, and could not disregard it and
then charge the consequences of his own negligent and reck-
less act upon the seller of the poison. But if no such warning
was in fact given, its omission was negligence, for the results
of which the vendor was liable both at common law and by
force of the statute. (*Thomas* v. *Winchester*, 6 N. Y. 409; *Loop*
v. *Litchfield*, 42 id. 358; 1 Am. Rep. 543; *Wellington* v. *Downer
Ker. Oil Co.*, 104 Mass. 64; 3 R. S., part 4, chap. 1, title 6, § 25.)
By the statute it is made a misdemeanor for any person to sell
"any arsenic, corrosive sublimate, prussic acid, or any other
substance or liquid usually denominated poisonous, without
having the word "poison" written or printed upon a label
attached to the phial, box or parcel in which the same is so sold."
The liquid sold to the deceased was in fact a poison, and death
resulted from taking a trifle less than the quantity sold. The
evidence showed that the black drops in both forms of the
preparation was "deadly," and that it was usually denominated
poisonous is to be inferred both from its well-known character
and from the evidence given by the pharmacist who said that,
unless selling upon the prescription of a physician, he would
mark upon the medicine the dose, or label it poison, or do both.
Indeed, the learned counsel of the defendant concedes all this, for
he says, "if any third party unacquainted with the real contents
of the phial had been injured, then an action would lie against

this defendant," and the defense interposed rests wholly upon
the fact asserted, that full warning of the poisonous nature of
the liquid was given, and the quantity which might be safely
taken was stated to the purchaser. So that the question here
whether the nonsuit ordered by the trial judge can be sus
tained or not turns solely upon the inquiry whether the warning was in fact given, and that again upon the question whether
the jury would have been at liberty to disbelieve the evidence
of the defendant's clerk. His story in itself was not improbable, so far as the defendant's action was concerned. A druggist selling for ten cents a medicine which was a poison, and
in a quantity capable of killing an incautious or ignorant purchaser, would be quite likely, we should suppose, to give the
brief information needed to protect his customer and shield
himself from grave danger and disaster. Nor was the witness
impeached by what are called the contradictions in his testimony
drawn out on cross-examination. They were very slight and
utterly immaterial. But two facts disclosed by the proofs
opened his testimony to doubt and possible disbelief. He was
an interested witness. He had violated the law by omitting
the label required. The medicine he delivered had killed its
victim. The consequences of the act upon himself, upon his
future, and upon his employer were certain to be disastrous in
the absence of explanation or justification. The motive to avert
the danger, even by falsehood, was plain and powerful. The
label was not on the phial. No such defense was possible. The
only other one was to swear to the verbal warning given to the
customer. The witness, therefore, stood in a position such as
to provoke suspicion, arouse doubt, and justify watchful and
rigid criticism. And then joined to that came the facts of the
conduct of the deceased. If the evidence was true he took the
poison in a deadly dose and from the hands of his wife, with
knowledge that it was a poison and that he was largely exceeding the prescribed quantity. Nothing in the case permits us
to imagine that he did so purposely and intended suicide. What
can be said and all that can be said is that he relied upon the
peddler's story of his experience in taking without injury one-

half of a glass rather than upon the druggist's warning that
the medicine was a strong poison. That is possible, but has
about it some doubtful elements. A man even of ordinary intelligence and very moderate prudence, who had been told by
a friend that he had been cured by a particular medicine, taken
in the quantity of half a glass, and thereupon went to a druggist, who was also a doctor, to purchase it, and was then distinctly told that the medicine was a poison, and but ten or twelve
drops must be taken, would naturally be somewhat startled.
We should expect him to speak and manifest surprise, or at least
seek the truth out of the contradictions. But this customer
manifested none; he showed no curiosity; he asked no natural
question; he did not say that a friend had taken ten times the
doctor's dose with safety, and ask who was right or who was
wrong, or if there was not somewhere a mistake as to the medicine. On the contrary, with the warning ringing in his ears,
he quietly receives the medicine without surprise, allows his
wife to pour nearly the whole contents into a spoon, and says
not a word to her of the information he has received, does not
tell her what the doctor said, does not heed his warning, relies
upon the advice of an unskilled peddler, discarding that of the
druggist and physician, and takes the fatal dose. It cannot be
denied that this conduct matches naturally and exactly the line
of action we should expect if no warning had been in fact given,
and does not appear so perfectly natural when confronted with
the opposite theory. It tends, therefore, to throw doubt upon
it, and to make one hesitate as to the truth, and when combined with the palpable interest of the clerk to shield himself
and his employer, makes a case in which there is a possibility
of different and debatable inferences from the evidence given,
and so develops a question of fact, rather than one of law. In
Elwood v. *Western Union Tel. Co.* (45 N. Y. 553; 6 Am.
Rep. 140), it was said that the rule that where unimpeached
witnesses testify positively to a fact and are uncontradicted,
their testimony must be credited, is subject to many qualifications, and among them this, that the interest of the witness
may affect his credibility, and it was added upon the facts of

that case: "such evidence as there is proceeds wholly from
parties having an important interest in the question. Each of
them, if guilty of the negligent act, would have the strongest
motive to deny it, as the admission would subject him or her
to severe responsibility for the consequences. This is a controlling consideration in determining whether the statements
of these witnesses should be taken as conclusive." To a similar
effect are other cases. (*Kavanagh* v. *Wilson*, 70 N. Y. 177;
Gildersleeve v. *Landon*, 73 id. 609.) The General Term were
therefore, right in saying that the case should have been submitted to the jury.

Their judgment should be affirmed and judgment absolute
rendered in favor of the plaintiff upon the stipulation, with
costs.

All concur.

Order affirmed and judgment accordingly.

WALTER CARTER et al., Executors, etc., Respondents, *v.*
ALMIRA E. HOLAHAN, Impleaded, etc., Appellant.

D. purchased certain premises, upon which was a mortgage, the payment
whereof was guaranteed by K., plaintiff's testator. The conveyance was
by the deed made subject to the mortgage. D., in making the purchase,
acted as agent for K., who advanced the money therefor. D. subsequently conveyed the premises to K., the deed containing the same provision as to the mortgage. After K.'s death plaintiffs, as his executors,
purchased the mortgage, with accompanying bond, and took an assignment thereof. In an action to foreclose the mortgage, in which the
mortgagor was sought to be charged with any deficiency, *held*, that K.,
by the acceptance of the deed, did not become primarily liable to pay the
mortgage, and that the relief sought was properly granted.

It was claimed that K. acted as agent for the mortgagor in making the purchase of the premises. *Held*, that conceding this to be so, as neither D.
nor K. received any consideration which would support a contract to
pay the mortgage, the mortgagor was not discharged from liability.

By the will of K. no disposition was made of the premises. *Held*, that as
the legal title on his death went to his heirs, and, therefore, there was
no union of the equitable and legal estates in the same person, the mortgage was not merged upon its transfer to plaintiffs.

Defendants offered in evidence on the trial a number of receipts for moneys paid by the mortgagor to K., during his life-time; which were alleged to have been payments upon the mortgage; these were excluded. *Held* no error; that as, at the time the payments were made, K. was neither the holder nor owner of the bond and mortgage, they would not operate as payments thereon; that they were not available as a counter-claim to a demand acquired by plaintiffs after the death of their testator.

(Argued April 24, 1883 ; decided June 5, 1883.)

Appeal from judgment of the General Term of the Court of Common Pleas in and for the city and county of New York, entered upon an order made June 5, 1882, which affirmed a judgment in favor of plaintiffs, entered upon the report of a referee.

The nature of the action and the material facts are stated in the opinion.

B. F. Watson for appellant. This action cannot be maintained if Mrs. Holahan is the equitable owner of the premises, subject to the claim of Kerr's estate, as thereby the deed (Drake to Kerr) in form is treated as a mortgage in effect, and Kerr, or his representatives, will not be permitted to purchase the prior mortgage and foreclose it, and thereby cut off the equity of redemption of the mortgagor, Mrs. Holahan. (Dayton on Surrogates, 262 ; Williams on Executors, 819 ; *Moffatt* v. *Milligan*, 2 B. & P. 124, note *c ; S. C.*, 2 Chitty, 539 ; *Fitzgerald* v. *Boehm*, 6 B. Monroe, 332 ; *Rose* v. *Pulton*, 2 B. & Ald. 822.) If the plaintiffs are correct in their contention that the testator did not die intestate as to any portion of or interest in the mortgaged premises, then the purchase by the executors, through the funds of the testator, of the mortgage sought to be foreclosed merged said mortgage in the superior title, both titles belonging to said estate. (*Knickerbocker* v. *Boutwell*, 2 Sandf. Ch. 319 ; *Burnett* v. *Dennison*, 5 Johns. Ch. 35 ; *Gardner* v. *Astor*, 3 id. 53 ; 6 id. 393 ; *Angel* v. *Bonar*, 38 Barb. 425 ; *Moore* v. *Hamilton*, 48 id. 120.) If the deed from Drake to Kerr was a mortgage, then the accounting called for by the reply, and entered upon by the defend-

ant's offer to prove the amount of the payments of the interest
by Mrs. Holahan, the fact of which payments of interest was
admitted by the reply should have been permitted. (*Niagara
B'k* v. *Roosevelt*, 9 Cow. 409 ; *Breese* v. *Brangs*, 2 E. D. Smith,
486.) The transaction was, in effect and in the intention of
the parties, a conveyance of the title in fee in the mortgaged
premises to Henry A. Kerr, to hold absolutely, subject only
to resale and reconveyance to Mrs. Holahan, at her option.
(*Holmes* v. *Grant*, 8 Paige, 243 ; *Glover* v. *Pain*, 19 Wend.
518 ; *Robinson* v. *Granger*, 6 Paige, 480 ; *Barbour* v. *Thurston*, 4 Denio, 493 ; *Quesch* v. *Rodman*, 5 id. 285 ; *Grinstone*
v. *Carter*, 3 Paige, 421 ; *Whitney* v. *Townsend*, 2 Lans. 249 ;
1 Hilliard on Mortgages, 2.) To maintain the defense it was
only necessary to prove that Henry A. Kerr became legally
bound to the holder of the mortgage by the delivery to and acceptance by him of Drake's deed to pay off and discharge the
mortgage in question. (*Burr* v. *Beers*, 24 N. Y. 178 ; *Comstock* v. *Drohan*, 71 id. 9 ; *S. C.*, 8 Hun, 373 ; *Morris'
Appeal*, Supreme Court, Penn., 19 Alb. L. J. 257.) The
agreement for the assumption of the mortgage contained in
the recital in the deed from John J. Drake to Henry A. Kerr
was an agreement made with Drake, and in his name, for the
benefit of said defendant Holahan, and as her agent, and
Drake thereby became a trustee of an express trust. (Code of
Civil Procedure, § 449.) A parol promise from one person to
another, for the benefit of a third person, will enable that third
person to maintain an action on such promise. (*Schermerhorn*
v. *Vanderheyden*, 1 Johns. 140.) A principal may, under
sections 111 and 113 of the Code, sue in his own name, upon
a simple contract in writing, made with his agent, and in the
agent's name, of which the principal is the sole owner.
(*Erickson* v. *Compton*, 6 How. Pr. 471 ; *Pitney* v. *Glens
Falls Ins. Co.*, 65 N. Y. 6 ; *Simson* v. *Brown*, 68 id. 535 ;
Story on Agency, 3 ; Bouvier's Law Dict. 100.) By virtue of
the agreement in the deed, thus made with said Drake, as the
agent of said defendant, Holahan was in contemplation of law
Henry A. Kerr's grantor, and he was personally liable to pay

the mortgage debt. (*Comstock* v. *Drohan*, 71 N. Y. 9; 8 Hun, 373.) This was not merely a promise to indemnify, but to pay. (*Rawson* v. *Copland*, 2 Sandf. Ch. 278.) If the money is advanced by one whose duty it is by contract, or otherwise, to pay and cancel the mortgage, and relieve the mortgaged premises of the lien, a duty in the performance of which others have an interest, it shall be held to be a release and not an assignment, although in form it purports to have been an assignment. (2 Washburn on Real Property, 179; *Mills* v *Watson*, 1 Sweeney, 374; *Riccard* v. *Sanderson*, 41 N. Y. 179; *Kellogg* v. *Ames*, id. 259; *Angel* v. *Bonar*, 38 Barb. 425; *Moore* v. *Hamilton*, 48 id. 120; 1 Hilliard on Mortgages, 447, 500–502; *Tice* v. *Annin*, 2 Johns. Ch. 125; *Sems* v. *Crawford*, 2 Denio, 595.) The defense or counterclaim is not in any sense a plea of set-off. (Code of Civil Procedure, § 506.) It secures to the defendant the full relief which a separate action at law, or a bill in chancery, or crossbill, would have secured him on the same state of facts. (*Gleason* v. *Moen*, 2 Duer, 642.) Even if Henry A. Kerr's guaranty of the bonds in suit, and his assumption and agreement in the deed to pay it failed to make it his duty and that of his executors, to pay it, certainly he, in contemplation of law, contracted to indemnify Mrs. Holahan from paying any thing besides the land under that bond and mortgage. (*Kellogg* v. *Ames*, 41 N. Y. 259.)

George De Forest Lord for respondents. As the deed to Drake, although made subject to, did not contain any covenant on his part to assume this mortgage, the defendant could not have claimed any benefit from Kerr's covenant, even if it had been supported by a good consideration. She was not privy to Kerr's covenant, and no principle of law can be invoked to secure to her the benefit of it. (*King* v. *Whitley*, 10 Paige, 465; *Trotter* v. *Hughes*, 12 N. Y. 74; *Vrooman* v. *Turner*, 69 id. 280; *Garnsey* v. *Rogers*, 47 id. 233.) Should a grantee who assumes payment of a mortgage convey to a third party, taking a similar covenant for his indemnity against the obligation so assumed by him, his grantor (the original mortgagor) would be entitled to the benefit of that contract. (*Halsey* v. *Reed*, 9 Paige, 446.) If a break however occurs in the chain of successive covenants, its foundation is destroyed. The person to whom the covenant is given is not a debtor to the one who seeks its benefit. (*King* v. *Whiteley*, 10 Paige, 465 ; *Vrooman* v. *Turner*, 69 N. Y. 281.) Even if Mr. Kerr died intestate as to his property, that would not alter the plaintiff's obligations or enlarge the defendant's rights. No process of mere inheritance could give her any new rights. (*Halsey* v. *Reed*, 9 Paige, 446.) The receipts offered in evidence were properly excluded, as they only show that Mrs. Holahan paid those sums to Mr. Kerr on account of some preexisting debt. (3 Phillips' Ev. 427, and note.) A claim against a testator cannot be a subject of set-off or counterclaim against a claim coming to his executors after his death. (*Paterson* v. *Paterson*, 59 N. Y. 574.) If Kerr held the title only for Mrs. Holahan, his covenant in the Drake deed would bind her and not him. (*Garnsey* v. *Rogers*, 47 N. Y. 233.)

RUGER, Ch. J. On the 18th day of August, 1871, the defendant, Almira E. Holahan, who owned, and Susan Lyons, who had a dower interest in, the premises known as No. 146 West Fourth street, New York, mortgaged them to one Socarras for $9,000 to secure the payment of their bond for the same amount.

The payment of this bond and mortgage was subsequently, on May 2, 1874, guaranteed by Henry A. Kerr, the plaintiff's testator. In June, 1877, and after the death of Kerr, the plaintiffs, by purchase and assignment, became the owners of these securities and have brought this action to foreclose the mortgage, claiming judgment for any deficiency which might arise against the defendant Holahan.

The entire defense is based upon the claim that the plaintiffs' testator, during his life-time, became primarily liable to pay this bond and mortgage by reason of certain transactions between himself and the defendants relating to the title to the mortgaged premises.

This defense is attempted to be established in two ways, viz.: first, by the claim that Kerr assumed the payment of the mortgage in accepting a deed of the mortgaged premises in May, 1872, from one John J. Drake and wife, containing a provision for its payment by him ; second, by inferences sought to be drawn from evidence relating to certain transactions occurring between Kerr, the defendant, and others, respecting the title to this property.

The facts having been found against the defendant upon both of these claims, it is now also incumbent upon her to show that the referee has, upon request, refused to find as claimed by the defendant, and that the uncontradicted evidence establishes the facts as claimed.

Appropriate requests were made to the referee, and exceptions were duly taken, which enable the appellant to raise the questions. This necessarily involves the examination and consideration of the evidence taken on the trial. Certain facts in addition to those already stated were undisputed and were briefly these:

Prior to the execution of the mortgage in suit, the defendant Holahan was the owner in fee of the mortgaged premises, subject, however, to a right of dower therein in favor of Susan Lyons, her mother, who was then in possession. On the 20th day of October, 1871, the defendant Holahan conveyed an equal undivided half of these premises to one John J. Drake. Thereafter Drake commenced an action to procure a partition or sale of the premises, and under the decree rendered the premises were sold, and Drake became the purchaser thereof. The referee appointed in the partition proceedings, on April 30, 1872, conveyed the premises to Drake by deed, containing a provision making it subject to the payment of the mortgage in suit, and on May 20, 1872, Drake and wife conveyed the same to Henry A. Kerr by deed containing this clause: " Subject, nevertheless, to a certain mortgage made by Almira E. Holahan and Susan Lyon, bearing date the 18th day of Au-

gust, 1871, to secure the payment of $9,000, and interest,"
"the payment of which said mortgage, with the interest
thereon from the 18th day of February last, is hereby assumed
by the party of the second part." Kerr accepted this deed
and retained the title of the premises until his death in December, 1876. It does not appear that he ever took possession
of them, or that he received any benefit from their use or occupation.

It could not be claimed upon these facts that Kerr, by virtue of the clause contained in Drake's deed to him, became
liable to the defendant upon such covenant. That deed evidenced a contract between the parties to it alone and created
no right in favor of third persons. The only ground upon
which a liability has been sustained between others than the
immediate parties to such a contract is that growing out of
the relation of principal and surety, whereby one becomes entitled to the benefit of any security received by the other from
a party primarily liable for the payment of the debt. (*King* v.
Whitley, 10 Paige, 465; *Curtis* v. *Tyler*, 9 id. 432.) In order
to avail himself of the benefit of such a security, the party
must show that the person acquiring it owes some debt or obligation in respect to the subject of the covenant to the person claiming its benefit. In this case, Drake never became
personally liable for the payment of the mortgage debt, and
therefore owed no duty or obligation to his grantor, Mrs.
Holahan, by which she became entitled to the benefit of a
security taken by him. There was no privity between Mrs.
Holahan and Drake, and she was a stranger to the transaction
out of which this covenant grew, and was not affected by the
form which it took or the promises therein made. It was not
entered into for her benefit, and she has paid nothing to induce
or support its obligations. Drake never having been personally liable for the payment of any part of the mortgage debt,
the covenant taken by him from Kerr did not inure either to
the benefit of his grantor or to that of the holder of the mortgage. (*Trotter* v. *Hughes*, 12 N. Y. 74; *Garnsey* v. *Rogers*,
47 id. 233; *King* v. *Whitley, supra*; *Vrooman* v. *Turner*,

69 N. Y. 280 ; 25 Am. Rep. 195.) The appellant impliedly, if not directly, conceding the correctness of these positions, attempted to evade their effect by showing that Drake acted as her agent in the transactions relating to this real estate, and claimed that the rights of the parties should, therefore, be determined as though the conveyance containing the covenant of payment had been made by her directly to Kerr. The referee, upon a request by the defendant, refused to find that Drake acted as the defendant's agent, either in purchasing the property on the partition sale or in deeding it subsequently to Kerr. It might well be questioned whether the defendant has requested such a finding in form from the referee as enables her to raise this question. The requests to the referee were to find certain evidence from which Drake's agency might possibly be inferred. The fact of agency was requested to be found as a question of law alone.

The referee might have found all of the evidence as requested by the defendant, and still have properly found that in fact no agency existed. But treating the case as though there had been a proper request to find as a fact that Drake acted as defendant's agent in buying and conveying the real estate, and that an exception was duly taken to the referee's refusal to find such fact, we think the evidence was not such as entitled the defendant, as matter of right, to this finding.

It did not appear that there had been any direct communication or agreement between Holahan and either Drake or Kerr with reference to the office which either should perform in the several transfers of this real estate. Their relations to each other and to these transfers can only be inferred from their acts and their subsequent conduct. Mrs. Holahan's object in procuring a transfer of the real estate to Kerr through the process which was adopted is evident enough, and that was to dispose of her mother's right of dower and to acquire the exclusive ownership and possession of the premises. It is evident that in some way Kerr and Drake were both made use of to accomplish this object. It is equally evident that neither of them expected to reap any benefit from the transaction or

incur any responsibility in its performance. Every thing that
was done was for the exclusive benefit and advantage of Mrs.
Holahan. It is true that Kerr received the title to the property, but it was the mere naked legal title (as is even now
claimed by the appellant), and subject to Mrs. Holahan's right
to claim reconveyance upon rembursing Kerr for his advances.
In this transaction it does not appear that Drake was any more
an agent than Kerr, and neither of them received any consideration from Mrs. Holahan or otherwise which would support a
contract to pay this mortgage. If the correctness of the appellant's theory be conceded, neither Drake nor Kerr have received
any benefit from the transaction, they have simply consented
to be used as Mrs. Holahan's instruments for retransferring
this property freed from some of the incumbrances existing
upon it into her possession.

We do not think in performing this office that either Drake
or Kerr can be termed her agent in such a sense as to entitle
her to all the benefits of the contracts entered into between
them in transacting her business and at the same time to discharge her from all her liabilities with reference to the subject-
matter of said contract. We have thus far regarded this
question from the standpoint taken by the appellant, but going
further and considering the defendant and Kerr as occupying
independent positions with reference to this property, we think
the referee properly declined to find that Drake acted as the
agent of Mrs. Holahan in purchasing the property.

It may be conceded that Drake was pointed out or selected
by Mrs. Holahan or her attorney as a proper person to hold
the title of the real estate temporarily to accomplish the result
intended, but inasmuch as a certain trust was to be reposed by
all parties in some one this did not conclusively indicate whose
agent he was. It appears, nevertheless, that Drake received
from Kerr not only the funds with which to purchase the property on the partition sale, but also his authority and instructions
for making such purchases. It is unimportant that Mrs. Holahan subsequently repaid Kerr for the advances made by him

in the purchase of the property. The money when advanced was Kerr's money, and it was in accordance with the whole theory of the transaction that it was conducted for Mrs. Holahan's sole benefit and she was under obligation to repay all expenses incurred in its execution. This fact did not preclude Kerr from holding the property as security for his advances or from appointing and controlling the agencies by which his connection with the affair was to be manifested. We think, therefore, that there was evidence to show that Drake acted as Kerr's agent in buying and deeding the property, and the referee properly refused to find as requested.

There is no foundation for the claim that the mortgage merged upon its transfer, by its holders, to Kerr's executors. This portion of Kerr's real estate having been undisposed of by the will the title on his death went to his heirs; there was never a union of the equitable and legal estates in the same person. We are, therefore, of the opinion on the whole case that Kerr never became liable to Mrs. Holahan to pay and discharge the mortgage in suit.

The defendant on the trial offered in evidence a number of receipts for moneys paid by Mrs. Holahan to Kerr during his life-time.

Their admission in evidence was objected to by the plaintiffs and they were excluded by the referee, to which decision the defendant excepted. These moneys were alleged in the answer to have been, and the receipts were apparently offered to prove payments by Mrs. Holahan to Kerr between the years 1872 and 1876 upon the bond and mortgage in suit. At the time they were paid, Kerr being neither the holder nor the owner of the mortgage, they could not possibly operate as payments thereon. There was no offer to give any evidence to connect these payments in any way with the mortgage, nor was there any claim made to prove them as a counter-claim thereto. Even if such claim had been made they were not properly the subject of a counter-claim to a demand acquired by the executors after the death of the testator. (*Patterson* v. *Patterson*, 59 N. Y. 574; 17 Am. Rep. 384.)

The evidence as offered was in effect to show that the defendant had made payments to Kerr upon some pre-existing liability, the nature of which did not appear.

We think the referee properly rejected the proof.

The judgment should, therefore, be affirmed.

All concur.

Judgment affirmed.

JOSEPH M. PRAY et al., Executors, etc., Appellants, *v.* JOSEPH HEGEMAN, Executor and Trustee, etc., et al., Respondents.

The provisions of the Revised Statutes (1 R. S. 726, § 37; id. 773, § 3), authorizing an accumulation of the income of real and personal property for the benefit of minors, require that the accumulation shall be for the benefit of a minor solely and during his minority, and that, when the period of accumulation ceases, the accumulated funds shall be released from further restraint and paid over to the person for whose benefit the accumulation is directed.

A direction for accumulation during a minority, accompanied with a gift of the income of the accumulated fund after the expiration of the minority, to the minor for life, and of the principal, upon his death, to other persons, is void. (1 R. S. 726, § 38.)

The will of M. gave his residuary estate to his executors, to be divided into shares as specified, a share to be held in trust during the life of each child of the testator who should survive him. After authorizing an expenditure of an amount, not exceeding a sum specified, out of the rents and profits of the share of each child for its support and education, the will directed that " the balance of such income shall from time to time be added to the share or sub-share from which the same proceeded, and accumulated as principal until he or she arrives at the age of twenty-one years, after which period the whole of such income shall be paid over, quarter-yearly, to such child. *Held*, it was the intention of the testator that during the minority of each child the surplus income of his or her share should be capitalized and thereafter the beneficiary should be entitled only to the income during life on the original share as augmented by the accumulations, and upon the death of the child the share, together with the accumulations, should go to the remaindermen as provided; that the direction for accumulation was void, and so was to be regarded as stricken out of the will, thus leaving to each child a gift of a life estate in the share held for him or her, which would carry all the accruing income ; and it appearing that the surplus income of the share of A., a son of the testator, had accumulated during his minority, *held*, that the accumulation belonged to him and could be reached by a judgment creditor of his in an action brought for that purpose.

Also *held*, that the same result would be reached if the right to the accumulated fund was to be governed by the provision of the statute (1 R. S. 726, § 40), providing that where, in consequence of a valid limitation of an expectant estate, there is a suspense of the power of alienation or ownership, during which the rents and profits are undisposed of, they "shall belong to the persons presumptively entitled to the next eventual estate ;" that the provision of the will might be treated as creating an equitable expectant life interest or estate in the son after his arrival at majority, and so constituting the "next eventual estate" within the meaning of the statute.

Meserole v. *Meserole* (1 Hun, 66), *Barbour* v. *De Forest* (28 id. 615), overruled.

Pray v. *Hegeman* [Mem.] (27 Hun, 603), reversed.

(Argued April 26, 1883 ; decided June 5, 1883.)

APPEAL from judgment of the General Term of the Supreme Court, in the second judicial department, entered upon an order made September 12, 1882, which affirmed a judgment in favor of defendants, entered upon a decision of the court on trial at Special Term. (Mem. of decision below, 27 Hun, 603.)

This action was in the nature of a creditor's bill. It was originally brought by John Dikeman, the judgment creditor, against Austin D. Moore, Jr., the judgment debtor, and Joseph Hegeman, as executor and trustee under the will of Austin D. Moore, Sr., its object being to reach a fund in the hands of Hegeman as such executor and trustee, which plaintiff claimed belonged to the judgment debtor, the original plaintiff and Moore having died during the pendency of the action, the executors of the former and those claiming the fund in question, on the death of the latter, were substituted as parties.

The will of Austin D. Moore, Sr., by the fourth clause thereof, gave his residuary estate to his executors in trust, a share to be held for each of his three children who should survive him, for the life of such child, and after providing for the disposition of each share upon the death of the child for whom it was held in trust, which provisions were considered and their validity determined in the case of *Moore* v. *Hegeman* (72 N. Y. 376). The will contained the following as subdivision six of said fourth clause :

" 6. When, by any of the foregoing provisions, property is held in trust for any of my children, such property shall be under the exclusive management and control of my executors, who shall receive the rents, issues and profits of the real estate, and collect the income of the personal estate; which rents, issues, profits and income of the share or sub-shares held in trust for each child shall be disposed of as follows: While such child remains under eighteen years of age, such an annual sum as his or her guardians shall think necessary, not, however, to exceed $700, shall be applied to his or her education and support; and while such child remains between the ages of eighteen and twenty-one years, such an annual sum as his or her guardian shall deem necessary, not exceeding $1,000, shall be applied to his or her education and support; and the balance of such income shall, from time to time, be added to the share or sub-share from which the same proceeded and accumulated as principal until he or she arrives at the age of twenty-one years; after which period the whole of such income shall be paid over, quarter-yearly, to such child; such income of my daughters to be paid to them, to their sole and separate use, free from all authority and control of their husbands."

Acting under this provision Hegeman, as executor and trustee, accumulated from income of the share of said Austin D. Moore, Jr., one of the children referred to in the will, during his minority, a sum of over $27,000. This amount, plaintiff claimed, belonged to the said son when he became of age, and the action was brought to reach and apply it in payment of plaintiff's judgments. Defendants claimed that the accumulations became part of the principal, and that the son was only entitled to the income upon the whole fund during life. Further facts appear in the opinion.

I. T. Marean for appellants. Upon a true construction of

the will the accumulations were payable to Austin D. Moore, Jr., upon his attaining his majority. (Evans' Statutes, 245; 40 Geo. 3, chap. 98; R. S., Creation and Division of Estates, §§ 37, 38, 39, 40; R. S., Accumulations of Personal Property, §§ 3, 4, 5 : R. S., Uses and Trusts, § 55; *Forsyth* v. *Rathbone,* 34 Barb. 401, 403–404; *Bolton* v. *Jacks,* 6 Robt. 229, 230; *Manice* v. *Manice,* 43 N. Y. 377; *Vail* v. *Vail,* 4 Paige, 317; *Stagg* v. *Jackson,* 2 Barb. Ch. 95, 96.) Every direction for accumulation for the benefit in whole or in part of any person other than the infant whose minority defines the period of accumulation, and who is presumptively entitled to the next eventual estate is void. "For the benefit of" means "for the sole benefit of." (*Vail* v. *Vail,* 4 Paige, 331; *Hawley* v. *James,* 16 Wend. 62, 64, 65, 116, 117, 162, 210; *Harris* v. *Clark,* 7 N. Y. 242; *Boynton* v. *Hoyt,* 1 Denio, 53; *Lang* v. *Ropke,* 5 Sandf. 371; *Kilpatrick* v. *Johnson,* 15 N. Y. 325, 326; *Manice* v. *Manice,* 43 id. 377; *Whitehouse* v. *Whitehouse,* opinion by GILBERT, J. ; *Barbour* v. *De Forest,* Daily Reg., May 27, 1881; *Matter of Healy,* per LIVINGSTON, surrogate; *Riggs* v. *Cragg,* 89 N. Y. 486–7.) If the direction for accumulation is void then the income as received was immediately payable to Austin D. Moore, Jr., who was presumptively entitled to the next eventual estate in the share from which it proceeded, and the plaintiffs were entitled to the relief demanded. The rule is the same as to both personal and real estate. (R. S., Creation and Division of Estates, § 40 ; R. S., Accumulations of Personal Property, § 2 ; *Manice* v. *Manice,* 43 N. Y. 385; *Bolton* v. *Jacks,* 6 Robt. 230; *Haxton* v. *Corse,* 2 Barb. Ch. 518; *Lang* v. *Ropke,* 5 Sandf. 371; *Kilpatrick* v. *Johnson,* 15 N. Y. 326; *Robinson* v. *Robinson,* 5 Lans. 167, 168.) The person presumptively entitled to the next eventual estate in the present case is the person presumptively entitled to the income from and after the period of accumulation. (*Manice* v. *Manice,* 43 N. Y. 385.)

William C. De Witt for respondents. The will did not give the surplus income accumulated to Austin D. Moore, but incor-

porated it permanently with the principal of the trust fund.
(*Vail* v. *Vail*, 4 Paige, 330.) The statute would exclude the
provision for accumulation in this case. (*Baucus* v. *Stover*,
89 N. Y. 7.) Courts have upheld a gift of the income already
accumulated, in the event of the minor's death, as a lawful
limitation upon the minor's property in the accumulations.
(*Manice* v. *Manice*, 43 N. Y. 377; *Hetzel* v. *Barber*, 69 id. 8;
Willetts v. *Titus*, 14 Hun, 556; *Boulton* v. *Jacks*, 6 Robt. 229;
Vail v. *Vail*, 4 Paige, 317; *Meserole* v. *Meserole*, 1 Hun, 66,
72.)

ANDREWS, J. The explicit language of the fourth clause of
the will leaves no doubt that it was the intention of the testator
that during the minority of his children, the surplus income of
their several shares should be capitalized, and that thereafter
they should be entitled only to the income on the original
share, as augmented by the accumulations, and that upon the
death of any child, the whole of the original share of the one so
dying, together with the accumulations, should go to his or
her issue, or in default of issue, as otherwise provided in the
will. The sixth subdivision of that clause, after directing
that a specified annual sum out of the income should be applied
to the support and education of each child during minority,
further directs that the balance of such income shall be added
to the several shares, and accumulated as principal, until he or
she arrives at the age of twenty-one years, "after which period
the whole of such income shall be paid over quarter yearly to
such child." The accumulations are to constitute a part of the
principal of the shares from which they arise, and there is not
only an absence of any direction that they should be separated
therefrom and paid over to the respective children on reaching
their majority, but such intention is excluded by the direction
that thereafter the whole income should be paid to them in
periodical payments. No other payments are provided for,
and the direction manifestly contemplates that the payments
are to be made from income accruing during the quarter-yearly
periods preceding the time of payment.

It becomes necessary, therefore, to consider the principal question in the case, viz.: Whether a direction for the accumulation of the income of real and personal estate during a minority, accompanied with a disposition of the accumulated fund by giving the income arising therefrom, after the expiration of the minority, to the minor for life, and the principal on his death, to his issue, or over to other persons, is valid. The determination of this question depends upon the construction of the statute defining when an accumulation of the rents and profits of real estate, or the income of personal property, may be lawfully directed. (1 R. S. 726, §§ 37, 38 ; id. 773, § 3.)

By the thirty-seventh section, above cited, an accumulation of the rents and profits of land for the benefit of one or more persons, may be directed by will or deed for the benefit of minors in being when the accumulation commences, and to terminate with their minority, subject to the proviso in the second subdivision of the section, that when the accumulation is directed to commence at any time subsequent. to the creation of the estate, it shall commence within the time permitted by the statute for the vesting of future estates. By the thirty-eighth section all directions for the accumulation of the rents and profits of real estate, except as allowed by the thirty-seventh section, are declared to be void. Under the will in question, the accumulation was to commence on the creation of the estate, that is, on the death of the testator. If the accumulation directed by the testator was for the benefit of his minor children, within the statute, the direction was valid. If it was not a direction for accumulation for their benefit according to the true meaning of section thirty-seven, it was void by the express terms of section thirty-eight.

The statute regulating the accumulation of the income of personal property, is substantially the same as that relating to the accumulation of the rents and profits of land, and need not be more particularly referred to. (1 R. S. 773, § 3.) If the accumulation directed in this case is valid or void as to one species of property, it is valid or void as to the other.

It is manifest that the infant son of the testator would derive a benefit from the accumulation directed by the will, for
it would enlarge the fund to the income of which he would be
entitled after his majority. It is equally plain that the accumulation would not be for his sole benefit, because on his
death the remaindermen would be entitled to both the capital
of the original share, and the accumulations. In determining
the question whether the partial benefit resulting to the minor
from the accumulation is an accumulation for his benefit
within the statute, it is important to consider the law on the
subject of accumulations, antecedent to the Revised Statutes,
and the change effected thereby. It was the settled law in
England, prior to the statute 39 and 40 George III (Chap.
98), that accumulations of the rents and profits of land, or the
income of personal property, could be lawfully directed for the
same period allowed for the suspension of the power of alienation, viz., lives in being, and twenty-one years thereafter.
(*Thellusson* v. *Woodford*, 11 Ves. 112.) This case led to the
enactment of that statute which restricted accumulations of the
income of real and personal estate by will or deed, (1) to the
life of the grantor or settler, or (2) the term of twenty-one
years from the death of such grantor, devisor, etc., or (3) during the minority of any person or persons living or in *ventre
sa mere* at the death of any such grantor, devisor, etc., or (4)
during the minority or respective minorities only of any person
or persons who, under the instrument directing such accumulation, would, for the time being, if of full age, be entitled to
the rents, profits, interest, dividends or annual produce so directed to be accumulated.

The revisers, as they declare (5 Edm. Stat. 572), intended by
section thirty-seven to limit the power of accumulation to one of
the four cases specified in the statute of George III, viz., "during
the minority of any person who, under the deed or will directing the accumulation, would then, if of full age, be entitled to
such rents and profits." Under the English statute, in the
first three cases specified, an accumulation was authorized for
the benefit of adults as well as of minors. The age or non-age of

the beneficiary had nothing to do with the lawfulness of the accumulation. It was only necessary that the period of accumulation should be measured by life or lives of the grantor or settlers, or by minorities, or by an absolute term, not exceeding twenty-one years. If the real intention of the revisers was embodied in the thirty-seventh section, it is quite plain that it was the general purpose to permit an accumulation of the estate of minors, that is, of persons who, except for their infancy, would, under the deed or will, be entitled to the rents and profits directed to be accumulated. The statute does not permit an accumulation of the rents and profits of land, or the income of personal property for the benefit of adults for any period of time, however short. The general policy of our law favors the greatest freedom of alienation of property consistent with the necessities of families, and the making of reasonable provision for the various contingencies which may be expected to arise, requiring the postponement of the vesting of estates, and the suspense of the power of alienating the *corpus* of property is permitted only within narrow limits. But the right to direct the accumulation of the fruits and profits of property is much more restricted than the right to control the property itself. It is permitted only in a single case and for a single purpose, viz., during minority, and for the benefit of the minor during whose minority the accumulation is directed. The main purpose of the thirty-seventh section of the statute was not to limit the term of accumulation previously permitted. The legislature intended to uproot the doctrine that the rents and profits of property might be accumulated and the enjoyment postponed, with a single exception. This was accomplished by sections thirty-seven and thirty-eight. The exception in section thirty-seven must be construed in view of the general policy of the legislature, and the particular policy upon which the exception proceeded.

There can be no reasonable doubt that the object of the legislature in creating the exception to the general rule was to provide for a case not within the reason of the rule, that is, the case of minors who, during the period when the judgment

is immature, or their necessities are limited, do not require and
might not be safely entrusted with a large income. In that case
the legislature authorized it to be retained and accumulated until
their majority, for their benefit. Section thirty-seven enables a grantor or testator to direct an accumulation of rents
and profits in cases where a court of equity, independently of
the statute, in the exercise of its inherent jurisdiction over the
persons and estates of minors, might direct such accumulation,
although we do not intend to say that the section may not
cover cases not strictly within the principle governing this
equitable jurisdiction. The proper construction of the provision
in section thirty-seven, that the accumulation must be for the
benefit of the minors, requires, we think, that when the period
of accumulation ceases, the accumulated fund shall then be
released from further restraint and paid over to the person for
whose benefit the accumulation was authorized. The thirty-ninth
section strengthens this construction. It treats rents and profits,
authorized to be accumulated under section thirty-seven, as the
property of the minor, the enjoyment of which has been postponed. It authorizes the chancellor, in case the minor is des-
titute of other means of support and education, to direct a
suitable sum out of the rents and profits to be applied to his
maintenance and education.

The argument that the words of the statute are satisfied by
a limitation to the minor of the use of the accumulated fund,
after his majority, for life, with remainder over, or, in other
words, that it is not necessary that the accumulation should be
for the sole benefit of the minor, if allowed to prevail would
introduce great uncertainty and confusion. Under that construction the benefit of the infant might be the mere
pretext and not the real reason for accumulation. The
answer made is that a mere nominal benefit to the minor
would be an evasion of the statute, and would so be held.
But the difficulty with this view is that there is no principle by
which to determine whether the limitation is evasive or not.
The principle which would sustain a limitation of the use of
the accumulated fund to the minor after majority, for life, as

an accumulation for his benefit, would sustain such a limitation for a term of years only. The accumulation in either
case might be almost wholly for the benefit of the remainderman, depending upon the duration of the life of the person to
whom the use was given after majority, or the term of years
upon which the use was limited. It would be an equally uncertain rule to make the validity of the direction for accumulation depend on the consideration whether the minor's benefit
was the primary object of the limitation, and the benefit of
the remainderman only incidental and secondary. We are satisfied that the policy and language of the statute require, in
order to sustain a direction for accumulation under section
thirty-seven that the accumulation must be for the sole benefit
of the minor, and that this can only be true where the accumulated fund is given over to him absolutely when the period of
accumulation ceases.

This precise question does not seem to have been finally
determined, but the result we have reached is sustained by
cases involving the construction of section thirty-seven.
In *Hawley* v. *James* (5 Paige, 318), the trust term under
the will there in question was to continue until the youngest
child or grandchild of the testator, living at his death, attaining the age of twenty-one years, should attain that age.
Meanwhile, as the court construed the will, the surplus rents,
profits and income of the real and personal estate were to be
accumulated, and to constitute a part of the estate, to be divided
at the termination of the trust, and on the division, each of the
respective beneficiaries were to take a life estate in his or her
share, with power of appointment by will, and in default of
appointment, the share was to go as in the will provided. It
will be seen that the precise question we have considered was
involved in the limitation for life of the shares in the capital
and accumulations of the estate on the division. The learned
reporter states in the syllabus of the case, as one of the propositions decided, that to render a trust for an accumulation of
the rents and profits or income of an estate valid, the accumulation must be for the sole benefit of an infant, and must be

payable to him, absolutely, if he survive his majority. The chancellor, in his opinion, referring to the direction for accumulation, after stating that the testator probably acted upon the erroneous supposition that the accumulation was valid if one or more infants, in being were to be benefited thereby, and without reference to the beneficial interests they would take in the accumulated fund, said that if such a construction should be put on the statute, the accumulation of an estate for twenty years could always be secured by selecting several infants upon whose minorities a trust term should be limited, and giving them mere nominal limited interests in the accumulated fund. The chancellor then proceeds : " The only way to prevent this is to give that construction to the statute, which, from the notes of the revisers, it is evident, they intended should be given to the language employed to convey the meaning of the legislature. That is, to allow an accumulation of the rents and profits only in those cases where the accumulated fund is for the sole benefit of one or more minors, if they live until they are of age, who are in existence at the time the accumulation is directed to commence, and who will continue such minors, if they live, until the accumulation ceases." We do not find in the opinion of the chancellor a statement, in precise terms, of the proposition contained in the head-note of the reporter to which we have referred. The trust for accumulation in the will, there considered, was subject to several objections. Some of the beneficiaries were adults when the accumulation was to commence, and others might reach their majority before the period prescribed for the accumulation, would expire, and the same feature of a gift of a use only to the beneficiaries after the accumulation should cease with a gift over on their death was in that will as in this. But the principle of construction stated by the chancellor, sustains the view we have taken of the statute. The Court of Errors reversed the decree of the chancellor so far as it sustained, in part, the validity of the trust term, but all the judges, who gave opinions, concurred with the chancellor in holding the trust for accumulation void. (*Hawley* v. *James*, 16 Wend. 114, 147,

183.)   In *Boynton* v. *Hoyt* (1 Denio, 54) it was held that a trust for the accumulation of rents and profits of land for the benefit of a testator's wife and minor children was void, the court saying: " Such a trust must be for the benefit of minors only." In *Kilpatrick* v. *Johnson* (15 N. Y. 326) it was held that a direction for accumulation for the benefit of minors and adults was unauthorized and void, although it was contingent merely, *i. e.*, where it was uncertain whether, after applying the current income as directed, there would be any surplus to accumulate. In *Manice* v. *Manice* (43 N. Y. 303) it was held that a direction for accumulation could not be lawfully made for the benefit of minors to whom a contingent interest only, in the estate, was given by the will. (See, also, *Lang* v. *Ropke*, 5 Sandf. 363, and *Vail* v. *Vail*, 4 Paige, 331.)

A direction for accumulation similar to that in this case was sustained by the general term of the first Department in *Meserole* v. *Meserole* (1 Hun, 66), and that case has been followed by the same general term in *Barbour* v. *De Forest* (28 id. 615) by a divided court. The opposite construction seems to have been reached by other courts, in cases referred to on the argument, not reported. The question is an important one, and may well give rise to diverse opinions, but, we think, upon reason and the general course of authority, the direction for accumulation, in this case, must be held to be unlawful.

The direction for accumulation being void, but the income having been, in fact, accumulated during the minority of Austin D. Moore, Jr., to the amount of $27,000, the question arises as to the persons entitled to the accumulated fund. We are of opinion that the rents and profits, illegally directed to be accumulated, belonged to Austin D. Moore, Jr., from whose share in the estate of the testator they were derived. The direction for accumulation being void, it must be treated as stricken out of the will. (*Williams* v. *Williams*, 8 N. Y. 538.) There then remains a plain devise of an equitable life estate to Austin D. Moore, Jr., in the share given to him, which would carry all the accruing rents and profits. The same result would follow if the right to the accumulated fund is governed by the fortieth section of the statute. (1 Rev. St. 726, § 40.) The testator directs that during minority a certain fixed sum shall be applied out of the rents, profits and income of the share of the son, for his education and maintenance, and on his majority he gives the whole income to the son for life. This may be treated as creating an equitable expectant life interest or estate in the son, in the share devised to his use, from and after his arrival at majority, and as constituting the next eventual estate within the fortieth section, in the property out of which the income arises. It can scarcely be doubted that this disposition of the rents and profits would accord more nearly than any other with the wish of the testator if he had contemplated that the direction for accumulation could not be supported.

The final question raised, is as to the estoppel of the former judgment in the suit of *Moore* v. *Hegeman.* We think the facts are too imperfectly presented, to enable us to pass upon this question. Neither the pleadings nor judgment in that suit, are set out in the case. The only information in respect to that action of which we can take notice, is contained in the twenty-first finding of the court. By that finding it appears that the action was brought by Austin D. Moore, Jr., in his life-time, against the defendant Hegeman, in his individual capacity, and not otherwise, for a conversion of his share, under the will of his father, and the accumulations. What issues were presented by the pleadings, or upon what issues the parties went to trial, do not appear. It is stated that it was adjudged that the trusts in the will of Austin D. Moore, Sr., were valid, but whether the question here involved was considered, or could under the pleadings have been considered, we have no information. Upon a new trial the facts bearing upon the alleged estoppel of the former judgment, may be more fully presented, and we think that no opinion in respect thereto should now be expressed.

The conclusion is that the judgment of the Special and General Terms should be reversed, and a new trial ordered.

All concur.

Judgment reversed.

EDWARD D. MOORE, an Infant, by Guardian, etc., Respondent, *v.* JOSEPH HEGEMAN, Executor and Trustee, etc., Appellant.

92
124

The wife of M., a resident of this State, procured a divorce from him on account of his adultery; the judgment forbade him from marrying again. He thereafter went into the State of New Jersey, and there married during the life of his first wife, returning with his second wife to this State, and continuing to reside here. The statute law of New Jersey declares that "all marriages, where either of the parties shall have a former husband or wife living at the time of such marriage, shall be invalid, * * * and the issue thereof shall be illegitimate." In an action to test the right of plaintiff, a son born of the second marriage, to inherit, as the lawful heir of M., *held*, that at the time of the second marriage the latter had no former wife living within the meaning of said statute; that the laws of this State and the provision of the judgment prohibiting marriage had no effect, and M. had a right to marry in another State whose laws did not prohibit a second marriage by one divorced; and that plaintiff was legitimate and so entitled to inherit.

Also *held*, that as there were statutory provisions on the subject, there was no presumption that the rule of the common law still existed in New Jersey; that the statute superseded and took the place of such rule.

The distinction between the New Jersey statutes upon this subject and those of this State pointed out.

Cropsey v. *Ogden* (11 N. Y. 234), distinguished.

After the dissolution of the first marriage M. and his first wife were again married, but in an action brought by her it was adjudged that the second marriage was prohibited by the statutes of this State, and was void; after the entry of this judgment the marriage in New Jersey took place. It was urged here that such re-marriage was valid. *Held*, that the judgment not having been reversed, and having been made by a competent court having jurisdiction of the parties and the subject-matter, was conclusive.

As to whether after a judgment of divorce on the ground of the adultery of one of the parties, and the consequent prohibition against another marriage by the guilty party, a second marriage of the parties in this State will be valid, *quære*.

(Argued April 26, 1883; decided June 5, 1883.)

APPEAL from judgment of the General Term of the Supreme Court, in the second judicial department, entered upon an order made May 8, 1882, which affirmed a judgment in favor

of plaintiff, entered upon a decision of the court on trial at
Special Term. (Reported below, 27 Hun, 68.)

The nature of the action and the material facts are stated in
the opinion.

Frederic R. Coudert, for guardian *ad litem,* appellant.
Austin D. Moore, Jr., was at liberty to marry his former wife
after the decree. (*Van Voorhis* v. *Brintnall,* 86 N. Y. 25.)
The wife being the injured party, and the judgment being
rendered in her favor, she could waive the benefit of it, except
in so far as it prevented the delinquent husband from marrying any person other than herself. (*Williamson* v. *Williamson,* 1 Johns. Ch. 491; Poynter on Marriage and Divorce, 170, note *d; People* v. *Hovey,* 5 Barb. 117.) The
marriage, or alleged marriage, between Austin D. Moore, Jr.,
and Carrie Maynard, in New Jersey, was void. (R. S. [Edm.
ed.], art. 3, tit. 1, pt. 2, chap. 8, § 20, p. 147; *Cropsey* v. *Ogden,*
11 N. Y. 233, 234; 2 R. S. [Edm. ed.], tit. 1, pt. 2, chap. 8,
§ 5, p. 144; *Van Voorhis* v. *Brintnall,* 86 N. Y. 25; *Smith* v.
Woodruff, 44 Barb. 198; 2 Bishop on Marriage and Divorce,
§ 727; *Williamson* v. *Parisien,* 1 Johns. Ch. 393; *Fenton* v.
Reed, 4 Johns. 52; *People* v. *Hovey,* 5 Barb. 117.) The
common law is particularly to be considered here, as New
Jersey has clung with great fidelity and consistency to the
common-law rules, and even where we find a statute upon a
given subject, that was theretofore exclusively governed by the
common law, the latter is still very important as a measure and
test. (Poynter on Marriage and Divorce, 9, 182, note 1 and
appendix 2; Bishop on Marriage and Divorce, § 727; *Colvin*
v. *Colvin,* 2 Paige's Ch. 385.)

Henry M. Whitehead for appellants. The whole, or a
material part of the marriage contract, was made in the State
of New York, and therefore void. (R. S., title 1, part 2,
chap. 8, § 1; 2 R. S. [Edm. ed.] 144.) The marriage of Austin D. Moore and Carrie Maynard, viewed as a contract in the
State of New Jersey, was unlawful and void under the statute

of that State. (*Cropsey* v. *Ogden*, 11 N. Y. 228.) The courts
of this State will not entertain an action in furtherance of,
or based upon a contract in ·direct violation of the statute
law of the State and the decree of the court in which the
action is brought, although the contract was made in a State
where it was lawful. (2 Kent's Com. 457 ; Story on Confl. of
Laws, § 244 ; *Varnum* v. *Camp*, 1 Green, 326 ; *Watson* v.
Murray, 8 N. J. Eq. 257.)

William C. De Witt for respondent. A judgment of absolute divorce for adultery dissolves and extinguishes the marriage relation altogether. (*People* v. *Hovey*, 5 Barb. 117 ; *Cropsey* v. *Ogden*, 11 N. Y. 232 ; *Kade* v. *Leonber*, 16 Abb. Pr.
[N. S.] 288 ; *Dickson* v. *Dickson*, 1 Yerg. 110.) The statute
and decree prohibiting the marriage of the inculpated
party during the life-time of the successful party thereto
is not a qualification or limitation upon the divorce, but
is in the nature of a distinct penalty or prohibition. (*Van
Voorhis* v. *Brintnall*, 86 N. Y. 18, 28 ; *Thorp* v. *Thorp*, 90
id. 602.) The laws of New Jersey did not interdict the marriage of the plaintiff's father and mother. (Revision of New
Jersey Statutes [1877], 215.) The New Jersey statute had in
view another wife clothed with all her marital rights. (*Vandegrift* v. *Vandegrift*, 3 Stewart [N. J.], 76 ; *Zule* v. *Zule*, 1
Saxton [N. J.], 96.) The word "former" was not used in the
statute in the pluperfect sense, denoting a person who had
formerly been a wife or husband, although not presently such,
but referred to a legal existing husband or wife by virtue of a
former marriage. (*Dickson* v. *Dickson*, 1 Yerg. [Tenn.] 110 ;
2 Bishop on Marriage and Divorce, § 701.)

MILLER, J. This action was brought for the purpose of determining whether plaintiff is the lawful issue of Austin D.
Moore, Jr., deceased, and as such is entitled to a share in the
estate of his grandfather, the testator, now in the hands of the
defendant, Joseph Hegeman, as executor of said estate.

The right of the plaintiff depends upon the validity of the mar-

riage entered into by his father and mother on the 17th day
of November, 1877, at Jersey City in the State of New Jersey.
Prior to that time and on the 21st of November, 1871, the
plaintiff's father was married to one Elizabeth Rowe, who, on
the 8th day of November, 1875, obtained a divorce from him
on the ground of adultery. On the 9th of December, 1876,
the same parties were, in form, remarried, and shortly after and
on the 26th day of June, 1877, in an action for divorce commenced by Elizabeth, it was adjudged that the second ceremony
of marriage was wholly void on the ground that such attempted marriage was prohibited and made void under the
statutes of the State of New York. The judgment in the
first action for divorce prohibited the plaintiff's father from
marrying again during the life-time of Elizabeth Rowe.

The main question which is presented upon this appeal is,
whether the marriage in New Jersey was legal and valid so as
to authorize the plaintiff to claim as a lawful heir of his deceased father. In *Van Voorhis* v. *Brintnall* (86 N. Y. 18;
40 Am. Rep. 505), it is held that the validity of a marriage
contract is to be determined by the law of the State where it
was entered into; if valid there, it is to be recognized as such
in the courts of this State, unless contrary to the prohibitions of
natural law or the express prohibitions of a statute. In the case
cited a divorce had been granted to the wife on the ground of
the husband's adultery, and it was decreed that it should not
be lawful for him to marry again until after her death. He
afterward and during her life married again in the State of
Connecticut. By the laws of that State the marriage was valid,
and the decision in the case cited holds that the marriage being
valid by the laws of Connecticut, a child born from such marriage is legitimate and entitled to inherit. This case was followed by the case of *Thorp* v. *Thorp* (90 N. Y. 602), where
the same rule is upheld. (See, also *Cropsey* v. *Ogden*, 11 N.
Y. 232; *Dickson* v. *Dickson*, 1 Yerg. 110.) The statute and
decree prohibiting the marriage of the guilty party can have
no effect beyond the territorial limits of this State. Where
the laws of another State do not prohibit such marriage by a

party divorced its validity cannot be questioned in this State. The first inquiry which arises in this case is, whether the marriage of Austin D. Moore, Jr., which took place in New Jersey, was valid according to the laws of that State. The statutes of New Jersey relating to divorces contain the following provision : "Divorces from the bonds of matrimony shall be decreed when either of the parties had another wife or husband living at the time of such second or other marriage; and that all marriages where either of the parties shall have a former husband or wife living at the time of such marriage shall be invalid from the beginning and absolutely void, and the issue thereof shall be deemed to be illegitimate and subject to all the legal disabilities of such issue." This statute provides for the dissolution of the marriage where another husband or wife is living at the time of the second or other marriage, and that such marriage shall be void and the issue thereof illegitimate. It has particular reference to divorces granted by the courts. It speaks of "another" husband or wife, and subsequently in the same sentence of a "former" husband or wife. The word "former" was evidently intended to relate to the language that preceded it in the same section and not to extend beyond that; it is in fact as used synonymous with the word "another." The legislature intended to distinguish between a legal wife or husband and a person claiming to be a subsequent wife or husband, whose marriage was in contravention of law, and the expression was employed to discriminate between the lawful wife or husband and a wife or husband who had subsequently and illegally married. It is very clear that the statute cited had in contemplation a wife or husband who had not been divorced and who was invested with all the marital rights conferred by a lawful marriage. This construction is fully supported by the decisions in the courts of the State of New Jersey.

In *Vandegrift* v. *Vandegrift* (3 Stewart [N. J.], 76), the plaintiff asked for a divorce upon the ground that his wife had a "former" husband living at the time of their marriage from whom she had not been divorced. The word "former" was considered as applying to such husband. (See *Zule* v. *Zule,* 1 Saxton [N. J.], 96, and *Dickson* v. *Dickson,* 1 Yerg. [Tenn.] 110.)

If the marriage of Austin D. Moore, Jr., with Elizabeth Rowe was dissolved then he had no former wife living at the time of his marriage in New Jersey, and no provision of the statutes of that State was violated. Elizabeth Rowe, the first wife, was freed from the marital relations and had a perfect right to marry anywhere and the husband had a right to marry in any other State where such a marriage was not prohibited by law. The interpretation we have placed upon this statute is also supported by the statutes of New Jersey in regard to bigamy, which declare as follows: "If any person being married, or who hereafter shall marry any person, the former husband or wife being alive, then the person so offending shall be deemed guilty of a high misdemeanor and on conviction thereof shall be punished by * * *. But neither this act nor any thing therein contained shall extend to any person * * * who is or shall be at the time of such marriage divorced by the sentence or decree of any authority or court having cognizance thereof, nor to any person where the former marriage hath been, or shall be, by the sentence or decree of any such authority or court, declared to be void and of no effect."

This statute, while using the words "former husband or wife," expressly exempts such a marriage as the one under consideration from the inhibition contained in the statute. It may also be remarked that the effect of the construction contended for by the appellant would be to prevent marriages, by the innocent parties, in many cases where divorces have been granted for legal causes. Without enumerating the different cases where such an interpretation would render the marriage unlawful, it is sufficient to say that it would have prevented the lawful marriage in the State of New Jersey of the wife of Austin D. Moore, Jr., who had obtained a divorce from her husband on the ground of adultery, and this clearly could never have been intended by the legislature. The counsel for the appellants further claims that at common law the marriage

which is now claimed to be valid would be null and void, and
that inasmuch as the State of New Jersey has with great
fidelity and consistency adhered to and followed common-law
rules, and its legislature has enacted a statute upon the subject,
it is very important to consider the common law as it previ
ously existed, in the interpretation of the statute. The object of
a statutory enactment is sometimes to change the common-law
rule, and where that is the case such rule is not a proper subject of consideration in the interpretation of the statute, and
it cannot be said in this case that the common law is presumed
to exist, for there is no absence of statutory provision on the
subject. As the statute has superseded and taken the place of
such rule and established another and a different one, it should
be considered in accordance with its intention and the purpose
which it was designed to accomplish.

The appellant's counsel insists that the same language which
is contained in the statutes of New Jersey (*supra*) is used in
this State in 2 Revised Statutes, 147, § 20, which provides
that a marriage contract may be declared void for this among
other causes: " That the former husband or wife, or one of
the parties was living, and that the marriage with such former
husband or wife was still in force." The New Jersey statute
which is cited must be considered without regard to the statute
of this State. The two statutes are entirely independent of
each other, and there is no such similarity in their language as
would authorize the same construction to be placed upon each
of them. The latter stands by itself and does not contain the
word "another," which is employed in the New Jersey statute,
and in its construction the same question is not presented.
There is, therefore, no analogy between these different statutes
which would make the interpretation of the one applicable to
the other.

The appellants also rely upon the case of *Cropsey* v. *Ogden*
(11 N. Y. 234), which involved the construction of the statute
prohibiting certain marriages in this State. The statute referred to provides that "No second or other subsequent marriage shall be contracted by any person during the life-time of

any former husband or wife of such person." We are unable to perceive how the decision of the court in this case can affect the construction to be given to the statute of the State of New Jersey, which is entirely different in its language from the statute which was the subject of consideration in the case cited, and hence we think it is not applicable. It may also be remarked that the case of *Van Voorhis* v. *Brintnall* (*supra*) is not, we think, inconsistent with *Cropsey* v. *Ogden*.

It is also urged that the second marriage of Austin D. Moore, Jr., to Elizabeth Rowe was a valid marriage, and that the prohibition contained in the decree obtained against him applied only to marriages with persons other than the complainant, and that section 1761 of the Code of Civil Procedure does not prevent the remarriage of the parties to the action. The argument of the learned counsel is that neither the statute nor public policy prevents a remarriage between parties who have been divorced upon the ground of adultery, even although the inculpated party is prohibited from marrying again. Whether the innocent party, who has the right to marry again, can resume the marriage relation with the husband from whom she has been divorced, who is prohibited from marrying again, and such marriage be legal and valid, presents a serious question which has not been decided in the courts of this State. In *Colvin* v. *Colvin* (2 Paige's Ch. 385), where the decree of divorce was set aside upon the consent and application of the parties, the chancellor expressed an opinion that the decree should be set aside before the reunion of the parties. The question presented did not arise, and the remarks of the chancellor were a mere *dictum*, which cannot be regarded as a controlling authority. The point, therefore, remains undetermined and is open for consideration when it shall properly arise. It is not presented in this case, for it appears, as we have seen, that in this action for divorce between the parties it was adjudged that the second marriage was void by reason of the prohibition of the statute and of the decree made by a competent court, having jurisdiction of the parties and of the subject-matter, and that this decree was in full force at the time Moore married Carrie

Maynard, and the decree not having been reversed, as the case stands, there was no valid second marriage between Moore and his former wife Elizabeth Rowe.

We are, therefore, in view of ,the facts, not called upon to decide the question whether a party who is divorced on the ground of adultery can marry his former wife.   There is no force in the position that the marriage contract between Austin D. Moore, Jr., and Carrie Maynard was made in the State of New York.   The agreement of the parties to marry, made within the State of New York, was not of itself sufficient to establish a valid contract of marriage.   The ceremony which was performed in the State of New Jersey was the marriage contract between the parties, and the declarations of the parties which preceded it cannot be considered in this case as a legal marriage. This was the interpretation placed upon it by the parties themselves by their subsequent action in causing the marriage ceremony to be performed between them, and in law this constituted the contract of marriage.

The judgment should be affirmed.

All concur.

Judgment affirmed.

AUGUSTUS D. JUILLIARD, as Receiver, etc., Appellant, v. ZECHARIAH CHAFFEE, as Trustee, etc., Respondent.

99
114

99
122

92
124

[92
145

The rule excluding evidence of parol negotiations and undertakings, when offered to contradict or substantially vary the legal import of a written agreement, does not prevent a party to the agreement, in an action between the parties thereto, from proving, by way of defense, the existence of an oral agreement made in connection with the written instrument, where the circumstances would make the use of the latter, for any purposes inconsistent with the oral agreement, dishonest or fraudulent.

As also the consideration of an agreement is open to inquiry. a party may show that the design and object of the written agreement were different from what its language, if alone considered, would indicate.

He may also show that the written instrument was executed in part performance only of an entire oral agreement, or that the obligation of the instrument has been discharged by the execution of a parol agreement collateral thereto.

In an action to recover a sum of money, alleged to have been loaned by H. S. & Co. to defendant, plaintiff put in evidence a written instrument executed by defendant, which stated that he had " borrowed and received " of S. M. & Co. the sum claimed, and that the same was " payable to them or order on demand, with interest." Defendant offered and was permitted to prove, as a defense, that the instrument was executed as part of a prior oral agreement by the terms of which the payees were to advance the money in anticipation, upon debts owing by them and on the defendant's promise that it should be applied in discharge of those debts, and that the writing should be executed, but when the money was so applied that it should be returned to the defendant; also, that the latter had applied the money as agreed. *Held* no error; that the paper was but evidence of part of the agreement, and it was proper to show in defense the whole transaction.

Hoare v. *Graham* (8 Camp. 57), distinguished.

Plaintiff sued, as receiver of said firm of S. M. & Co. It appeared that the form of the writing was adopted at the request of the payees, so that if creditors, other than those benefited by the advance, should make inquiry, they might suppose the transaction was as the paper indicated. Plaintiff claimed that this was fraudulent as to other creditors represented by the receiver. *Held* untenable; that in providing beforehand for the payment of one rather than another obligation, the firm violated no duty, although insolvent; also, that it could not be said as matter of law that any fraud was intended by either, it was a question of fact for the jury.

It seems that if a creditor was here, who, on the faith of the security apparently afforded by the instrument, had either sold goods or given credit, or in any way changed his position to his detriment, a different question would arise.

It seems, also, that if the agreement was against the spirit of the bankrupt or insolvent laws, or otherwise contrary to public policy, plaintiff's position was no better than that of defendant and he could not avail himself of the objection.

(Argued April 27, 1883; decided June 5, 1883.)

APPEAL from judgment of the General Term of the Supreme Court, in the first judicial department, entered upon an order made January 30, 1883, which affirmed a judgment in favor of defendant, entered upon a verdict and affirmed an order denying a motion for a new trial.

The nature of the action and the material facts are stated in the opinion.

William Allen Butler for appellant. The parol agreement, having been prior to, and inconsistent with, the terms of the writing, should have been excluded. (1 Greenleaf on Ev., §§ 275, 277; *Hoare* v. *Graham*, 3 Campb. 57; *Mosely* v. *Hanford*, 10 B. & C. 729; *Woodbridge* v. *Spooner*, 3 B. & A. 233; *Free* v. *Hawkins*, 8 Taunt. 92; *Foster* v. *Jolly*, 1 Cr. M. & R. 70; *Adams* v. *Wardley*, 1 M. & W. 374, 380; *B'k of U. S.* v. *Dunn*, 6 Peters, 51, 57; *Billings* v. *Billings*, 10 Cush. 178; *Erwin* v. *Saunders*, 1 Cow. 249; *Payne* v. *Ladue*, 1 Hill, 116; *Brown* v. *Hull*, 1 Denio, 400; *B'k of Albion* v. *Smith*, 27 Barb. 489; *Thomas* v. *Hall*, 45 id. 214; *Dudley* v. *Dole*, 4 N. Y. 486, 491; *Ely* v. *Kilborn*, 5 Denio, 514.) The written instrument in question was plain and unambiguous, and could not be contradicted or its terms cut down by a prior or contemporaneous oral agreement in contradiction of those terms. (*Mumford* v. *McPherson*, 1 Johns. 414; *Van Nostrand* v. *Reed*, 1 Wend. 424, 432; *La Farge* v. *Rickert*, 5 id. 187, 190; *Cleves* v. *Willoughby*, 7 Hill, 83; *Mayor of N. Y.* v. *Price*, 5 Sandf. 542; *Colwell* v. *Lawrence*, 38 N. Y. 71; *Renard* v. *Sampson*, 12 id. 561; *Johnson* v. *Oppenheim*, 55 id. 280, 293; *Van Bokkelen* v. *Taylor*, 62 id. 105; *Wilson* v. *Deen*, 74 id. 531, 534, 535, 538; *Chapin* v. *Dobson*, 78 id. 74, 79; *Adams* v. *Wardley*, 1 M. & W. 380.) The rule is the same in equity as in law. (*Wilson* v. *Dean*, 74 N. Y. 531, 535.) The defense was wholly without merit, as it involved a deceptive transaction in fraud of the rights of creditors represented by the plaintiff as receiver. (*Hoppough* v. *Struble*, 60 N. Y. 430, 435.) The defendant cannot base an equitable defense upon a confessed fraud or concealment where the parties affected by the fraud or concealment, both as its perpetrators and its victims, are all before the court in the person of their representative trustees. (*McKewan* v. *Sanderson*, L. R., 20 Eq. Cas. 65, 72; *Jackman* v. *Mitchell*, 13 Ves. 581, 587; *More* v. *Sandford*, 1 Giff. 288, 295; Willard's Eq. Jur. 210; *Williams* v. *Schreiber*, 14 Hun, 38; *Russell* v. *Rogers*, 10 Wend. 473; *Breck* v. *Cole*, 4 Sandf. 79; *Lawrence* v. *Clark*, 36 N. Y. 128; *Harloe* v. *Foster*, 53 id. 385.) Equity

will not permit the defendant to destroy his negotiable written
obligation by showing that it was a sham contrived between
himself and the insolvents to give a false appearance to the
transaction. (*Bolt* v. *Rogers*, 3 Paige, 154, 157; *Gale* v. *Gale*,
19 Barb. 250; 1 Story's Eq. Jur., § 194; *Delamater* v.
Bush, 63 Barb. 168.) If the defendant had brought his action
to cancel the instrument in question, equity would have denied
relief on the facts proved, because *melior est conditio defen-
dentis;* but the law will not interfere to protect either party.
(*Burrill* v. *M. S. & N. J. R. R. Co.*, 22 N. Y. 285, 304.)

Luther R. Marsh for respondent. Evidence may be given
by parol to show that a paper in form a note or other contract
was intended and delivered to accomplish some other purpose
than that which the paper purports by its terms; and that
when such a verbal arrangement is made, and a note even given
in fulfillment of it, the party making the note has a right, if
sued on it, to prove the entire agreement, and show that the
note was not intended to be a note. (*Grierson* v. *Mason*, 60
N. Y. 394; 1 Hun, 113; 3 T. & C. 185; 60 N. Y. 394;
De Lavallette v. *Wendt*, 75 id. 579; *Smith* v. *Rowley*, 34 id.
367; *Slade* v. *Halsted*, 7 Cow. 322; *Benton* v. *Martin*, 52
N. Y. 570, 574; *Bookstaver* v. *Jayne*, 60 id. 146; *Meyer* v.
Lathrop, 73 id. 315; *Chapin* v. *Dobson*, 78 id. 74; *Seymour*
v. *Cowing*, 1 Keyes, 532, 535; *Clever* v. *Kirkham*, 33 L. T. C.
P. 672.) The parol evidence established the payment and discharge of the note. (*Lawrence* v. *Fox*, 20 N. Y. 68; *Gurn-
sey* v. *Rogers*, 47 id. 233–240; *Vrooman* v. *Turner*, 69 id.
280–284.)

DANFORTH, J. The firm of Hoyt, Spragues & Co. was dissolved by the death of one of its members, and on the application of his executors, the plaintiff, on the 30th of June, 1874,
was appointed, by the Supreme Court, receiver of its effects.
The defendant is the voluntary assignee of the A. & W.
Sprague Manufacturing Co., for the benefit of their creditors.
The action is to recover $100,000, alleged in the complaint to

have been loaned on the 7th of May, 1874, by Hoyt, Spragues
& Co. to the defendant as such assignee, upon his promise to
repay the same on demand, with interest.

The defendant by answer denied the allegations on which
the claim rests, and by way of affirmative defense, stated that certain outstanding obligations of the Manufacturing Company, on
which the firm of Hoyt, Spragues & Co. were also liable to the
holders, had been extended by the defendant's notes, indorsed
by that firm, upon an agreement that their liability should
cease on payment by them of forty per cent of the amount of
the notes, and interest. That the money named in the complaint was received by him in pursuance of this agreement, to
be paid over to the holders of the notes, in discharge, so far
as it would go, of interest which the firm had agreed to pay,
and that he so applied it.

Upon the trial the plaintiff put in evidence a written instrument in these words :

"Borrowed and received of Hoyt, Spragues & Co., the sum
of $100,000 payable to them or order on demand, with interest
at the rate of seven per cent per annum from May 7, 1874.

$100,000.   "A. & W. SPRAGUE MFG. CO.
"Z. CHAFFEE, *Trustee under their mortgage deed.*"

The defendant then gave evidence tending to prove the matters alleged in his answer, and that it was at the same time
agreed between Hoyt, Spragues & Co. and himself that the
receipt to be given for the money so advanced should be
held by them until July 1, and then returned to the defendant; that the paper upon which the plaintiff relied was the
receipt referred to, and was put in that form at the request of
Hoyt, Spragues & Co.; that the money named therein was at
its date furnished by the payees in pursuance of the aforesaid
agreement, and on account of what they would otherwise be
bound to pay July 1, 1874; and that it was applied by defendant under this agreement upon their obligations. It was conceded, however, that this arrangement was by parol made "a
day or two before the writing was signed," and the plaintiff in

due time objected to proof of it upon the general ground that it was inconsistent with the writing, and at the close of the case he move the court to strike out the evidence of parol negotiations or communications prior to the making of the paper of May 7, 1874, as contradicting the written instrument. The motion was denied and the case submitted to the jury as one proper for their consideration, the trial judge saying:

"If, as between this defendant and Hoyt, Spragues & Co., the fact really was that the $100,000 was not in truth a loan, but was an anticipation of interest, and the defendant received it as such and applied it to the purpose for which it was given to him, and in fact to the purpose to which a similar sum would have had to be applied on the 1st of July—then, in law the defendant would be entitled to your verdict, because it was not the real transaction, not what it appears to be upon the face of the instrument, but was really an advance of money for a special purpose (to which it was duly applied), and was put in the form expressed by the instrument for the reason to which I have referred."

The jury found for the defendant, and upon this appeal the learned counsel for the plaintiff contends that the defense was inadmissible "as resting solely upon a parol agreement prior to the written obligation and inconsistent therewith." Certainly the general rule which excludes evidence of parol negotiations and undertakings, when offered to contradict or substantially vary the legal import of a written agreement, is not to be questioned or disturbed. In this State it has been thought to be so well settled in reason, policy and authority, as not to be a proper subject of discussion. It has full application, however, within very narrow limits. In the first place it applies only in controversies between parties to the instrument (*New Berlin* v. *Norwich*, 10 Johns. 229), and between them is subject to exceptions, upon allegations of fraud, mistake, surprise, or part performance of the verbal agreement. Nor does it deny the party in whose favor that agreement was made, the right of proving its existence by way of defense in an action upon the written instrument, under circumstances which would make the use of it for any purpose, inconsistent with that agreement, dishonest, or fraudulent. (*Martin* v. *Pycroft*, 2 De.G., M. & G. 785, 795 ; *Jervis* v. *Berridge*, L. R., 8 Ch. App. 351.)

A party, sued by his promisee, is always permitted to show a want or failure of consideration for the promise relied upon, and so he may prove by parol that the instrument itself was delivered even to the payee to take effect only on the happening of some future event (*Seymour* v. *Cowing*, 1 Keyes, 532 ; *Benton* v. *Martin*, 52 N. Y. 570 ; *Eastman* v. *Shaw*, 65 id. 522), or that its design and object were different from what its language, if alone considered, would indicate. (*Denton* v. *Peters*, L. R., 5 Q. B. 474 ; *Blossom* v. *Griffin*, 3 Kern. 569 ; *Hutchins* v. *Hebbard*, 34 N. Y. 24 ; *Seymour* v. *Cowing*, *supra* ; *Barker* v. *Bradley*, 42 N.Y. 316 ; 1 Am. Rep. 521 ; *Grierson* v. *Mason*, 60 N. Y. 394 ; *De Lavallette* v. *Wendt*, 75 id. 579 ; 31 Am. Rep. 494.) He may also show that the instrument relied upon was executed in part performance only of an entire oral agreement (*Chapin* v. *Dobson*, 78 N. Y. 74 ; 34 Am. Rep. 512), or that the obligation of the instrument has been discharged by the execution of a parol agreement collateral thereto (*Crosman* v. *Fuller*, 17 Pick. 171), or he may set up any agreement in regard to the note which makes its enforcement inequitable.

The case before us comes within the principle upon which those exceptions to the general rule rest, or the limitations which have restrained its application. The apparent obligation incurred by the defendant under the paper put in evidence by the plaintiff, was to pay the sum named upon demand in consideration of so much money then borrowed ; but the evidence disclosed that it was only part of a prior parol arrangement, by the terms of which the payees were to advance money in anticipation upon debts owing by them, and on the defendant's promise that it should be so paid in discharge of those debts, and which also provided for a return of the paper to the defendant when the money was so applied. The note did not constitute the agreement, nor is it set out in the complaint as the foundation of the action. It is evidence of part of the agreement, and when relied upon by one party, the other might properly show in defense, the whole transaction (1 Greenl. Ev., § 284*a; Hutchins* v. *Hebbard,* 34 N. Y. 24; *Hope* v. *Balen,* 58 id. 381; *Jervis* v. *Berridge, supra*), and when that was shown, the defense was made out, not by controlling the contract indicated by the writing, but by a collateral agreement with which it was incidentally connected, the execution of which inured as payment of the note in a manner directed by the payees, and upon faith in which the note was given. (*Crossman* v. *Fuller, supra.*)

The cases cited by the learned counsel for the appellant in support of his contention (among others, *Hoare* v. *Graham,* 3 Camp. 57; *Moseley* v. *Hanford,* 10 B. & C. 729; *Woodbridge* v. *Spooner,* 3 B. & Ald. 233; *Bank of U. S.* v. *Dun,* 6 Peters, 51; *Erwin* v. *Saunders,* 1 Cow. 249) seem inapplicable to the facts before us, and are not opposed to this decision. Thus in *Hoare* v. *Graham,* the note was payable by its terms in two months. The defendants were payees and indorsers to Grill & Son, through whom plaintiff made title. The defense had two branches: first, that the note had been drawn as collateral security for certain advances made by plaintiff to Grill & Son; second, that the defendants indorsed on condition that it should be renewed when due. The court held the first branch of the defense admissible, but the second not, recognizing a distinction between an agreement collateral to the note, or one showing the purpose of its delivery to be different from the purpose apparent from its terms, and an agreement in contradiction of the terms of the note. This case, therefore, and the others cited, are in harmony with those which recognize a distinction between an agreement for the legal discharge of a contract and one which destroys its original legal effect, either by contradicting its terms or substituting a distinct and independent agreement.

It also appeared that the form of this instrument was adopted at the request of the payees, so that if creditors, other than those benefited by the advance of interest, should make inquiry, they might suppose the transaction was what the paper indicated — a loan, and the learned counsel for the plaintiff argues that this was fraudulent, as to parties represented by the receiver, and for that reason the defense should be rejected. But the payees, although insolvent, were carrying on business in their own names, and were at liberty to do so according to such methods as they might think most likely to promote success. By the one adopted they undertook no payment to which they were not bound, and in providing beforehand for the discharge of one rather than another obligation, they violated no duty. If a creditor was here who, on the faith of the security apparently afforded by the instrument signed by the defendant, had either sold goods or given credit, or in any way changed his position to his detriment, a different question would arise. No such person is here. Nor was the arrangement in contravention of any bankrupt or insolvent act. The payees were not subjected to either. But, if the contract was against the spirit of those acts, or otherwise contrary to public policy, I do not see that the plaintiff's position would be better than that of the defendant; he stands in the place of the payees. It cannot, however, be said, as matter of law, that any fraud was intended by either, nor was the court asked to submit that question to the jury. If there was ground for it, it was for that body as one of fact, and not for the court as one of law.

We think the judgment should be affirmed.

All concur.

Judgment affirmed.

GEORGE W. Dow et al., Appellants, *v.* JAMES DARRAGH, Respondent.

.

The provision of the Code of Civil Procedure (§ 3301, as amended by chap. 399, Laws of 1882), providing that the stipulation of the attorneys for parties to an action may take the place of a clerk's certificate to a copy of a paper whereof a certified copy is required, was not intended to alter the effect of the provision (§ 1315) requiring a return to this court to be certified by the clerk of the court from which the appeal is taken, or of the rule of this court (Rule 1) making the same requirement.

Returns to this court should be made by a responsible officer, under sanction of his official oath, and attorneys for parties cannot, by stipulation, make up a case for the court.

MOTION to compel the clerk to file a return without the certificate of the clerk of the court below attached.

EARL, J. Section 1315 of the Code requires that the return to this court shall be certified by the clerk of the court from which the appeal is taken, and that the appeal must be heard upon such certified return. Rule 1 of this court makes the same requirement.

Section 3301 of the Code provides for the compensation to be made to clerks of courts of record for services to be rendered by them. That section was amended by chapter 399 of the Laws of 1882 by adding to the end thereof as follows: " Where the attorneys for all the parties interested, other than parties in default or against whom a judgment or a final order has been taken and is not appealed from, stipulate in writing that a paper is a copy of any paper whereof a certified copy is required by any provision of this act, the stipulation takes the place of a certificate, as to the parties so stipulating, and the clerk is not required to certify the same or entitled to any fee therefor."

We do not think that this was intended to alter the effect of section 1315 or the rule of this court. When the parties to such a stipulation alone are interested, the stipulation will take the place of the clerk's certificate. But they cannot by stipulation make up a case for this court, until the law shall be further changed. The returns to this court should be made by a responsible officer under the sanction of his official oath, and his responsibility to the law. Any other practice would be extremely unwise and mischievous.

The motion should be denied.

All concur.

Motion denied.

HENRY A. MOTT, as Administrator, etc., Respondent, v. WARREN ACKERMAN, Appellant.

132

The will of M. devised his real estate to his executors in trust, to hold one-third part thereof for the benefit of each of his three daughters during life. Upon the death of a daughter, leaving a husband and lawful issue living, it was declared that the executors should stand seized of her third "from and immediately after her death, upon trust for the sole use and benefit of such issue;" in case of the death of a daughter single and un-married, "upon such trust, and for such purpose as she shall or may ap-point by her last will;" in default of such appointment "for the sole use and benefit of her next of kin." *Held*, that the power of appointment related to the remainder in fee; that in each event provided for, the trust in the executors upon the death of the daughter would be purely passive, the remainder vesting in the beneficiaries; that the phrase in the clause giving such power of appointment "upon such trust" meant, not a trust to be created by the daughter and so limiting the power of disposition, but related to the trust in the executors.

As to one of the daughters who was married at the time of the execution of the will, it provided that in case she should give to her husband any part of her income from the estate or pay any of his debts she should thereupon forfeit all right and interest in and to such income. *Held*, that this did not affect the conclusion above stated; it did not show any intent to limit the power of appointment.

One of the daughters died unmarried, leaving a will by which she gave all of her estate, real and personal, after payment of debts, to her two sisters who survived her, "and to the survivor of them," and to the heirs, executors and administrators of such survivor. *Held*, that this was a valid execution of the power of appointment and the title to one-third of the real estate passed under it; that the limitation in the devise to the survivor did not work an unlawful suspension of the power of alienation (1 R. S. 724, § 24); that the estate upon the death of the testatrix passed to her two sisters as tenants in common, each taking a fee, that of the one dying first being defeasible by such death, and thereupon the entire absolute estate vested, which, therefore, could be aliened after two lives at most.

It seems that the two sisters took legal estates which were alienable, and their deed immediately on the death of the testatrix would have conveyed an absolute fee in possession.

The two surviving sisters purchased and owned as tenants in common certain other real estate; one of them subsequently died, leaving a will by which she gave to her executors a power of sale, to be exercised during the life of the surviving sister with her concurrence, and (the will then proceeds) "on the death of my said sister Maria, or as soon afterward as they may think advisable * * * and within three years from the proof of this will," the executors were empowered and directed to convert into money the real estate, etc. Maria lived more than three years after probate of the will. After her death and about twelve years after such probate the surviving executors contracted to sell the real estate to defendant, who refused to complete the purchase, claiming, among other things, that the power of sale could only be exercised within the three years. *Held* untenable ; that as the purposes of the will required a sale the power was imperative (1 R. S. 734, § 96), and was so intended by the testatrix, and the neglect to sell within the time specified did not destroy the authority conferred.

The executor before bringing this action tendered a deed which was refused. Pending the appeal to this court said executor died and the present plaintiff was appointed administrator, with the will annexed, and the action was revived in his name. *Held*, that the deed so tendered could not now be delivered or treated as delivered with the effect of passing the title ; but that plaintiff could make the conveyance. (2 R. S. 72, § 22.)

Where a power of sale is given to executors for the purpose of paying debts or legacies, and especially where there is an equitable conversion of land into money for the purpose of such payment and for distribution, and the power is imperative and does not grow out of a personal discretion confided to the individual, such power belongs to the office of the executor and under the statute passes to and may be exercised by an administrator with the will annexed.

(Argued April 27, 1883 ; decided June 5, 1883.)

Appeal from judgment of the General Term of the Supreme Court, in the first judicial department, entered upon an order made January 11, 1882, which affirmed a judgment in favor of plaintiff upon a decision of the court on trial at Special Term.

This action was brought to compel a specific performance of a contract for the purchase of two pieces of real estate in the city of New York, the one being No. 545 Broadway, and 116 Mercer street, the other No. 23 West Thirty-fourth street.

No question is made as to the validity or sufficiency of the contract of purchase. The property was sold at auction on the 25th day of February, 1880, by William H. Onderdonk, as executor of the two estates of Eliza Mott and Maria M. Hobby. The defendant, who was the purchaser, paid ten per cent of the purchase-money, according to the terms of sale, but declined to accept the deeds of the premises, or either of them, or to pay the purchase-money, on the ground that a satisfactory title could not be given by the vendor as executor under the said wills.

The property described as No. 545 Broadway, and No. 116 Mercer street, was originally owned by Henry Mott, the father of said Eliza Mott and Maria M. Hobby. Henry Mott died in the year 1839, leaving a will by which he devised to his wife the use of No. 545 Broadway and its rear in Mercer street, together with an annuity during her natural life. He then devised as follows : " All my real estate, and the residue and remainder of my personal estate charged with the said annuity, and the life use of my house in Broadway, No. 545, and my stable in Mercer street, No. 94 " (now 116), " on the payment of my debts aforesaid, to my executors and executrixes hereinafter named, and their heirs and assigns forever, as joint tenants and not as tenants in common, in trust, nevertheless, to and for the uses and purposes hereinafter mentioned and declared, and to and for no other use, intent or purpose, that is to say : First, that my said trustees shall and do with all convenient speed, after my decease, collect and convert into money such part of the residue of my personal estate bequeathed to my said trustees as will not consist of money at my decease, and that they in-vest and keep invested the net proceeds thereof remaining after paying my debts and funeral expenses * * * and when-ever the said real estate above devised to my trustees shall be sold, which my said trustees are authorized, but not enjoined, to sell until such sale becomes expedient or necessary for the final settlement and distribution of the said trust property or estate, the net proceeds thereof shall be invested and kept in-vested in the like. manner.'' The will then proceeds, " my said trustees shall and do stand seized and possessed of one equal third part of the said trust property and estate, and all securities in which the same may become invested, subject to the aforesaid annuity to my wife, upon the following trusts, for the benefit of my daughter, Esther W. Mott, that is to say, upon trust to pay to my said daughter yearly, and every year during her natural life, the whole net annual income or product of the said one-third part of the said trust property or estate, for her sole and separate use, independent of any husband she may hereafter have or take, and if my said daughter shall marry and afterward die in the life-time of her husband, leaving lawful issue living at her decease, then, from and immediately after her death, upon trust for the sole use and benefit of such issue; and if my said daughter shall be single and unmarried at her death, then, from and immediately after her decease, upon such trust and for such purposes as she shall or may appoint by her last will and testament, or any codicils thereto, and in default of such appointment, then, from and immediately after her death, upon trust for the sole use and benefit of her next of kin, and if such next of kin shall consist of more than one person, then the same shall be divided among them agreeably to the provisions of the statute of distributions." The next clause gives another third to Eliza Mott in identical terms, and the fourth clause of the will gives the remaining third to Maria M. Hobby, another daughter, who was then the wife of Seth M. Hobby, in the same terms, except so far as they are modified in consequence of her having a husband then living, and excepting that it was provided in case she should give to her said husband any part of the income from the estate, or pay any of his debts, "she shall thereby and for the same forfeit all her right and interest in and to" said income. Henry Mott's wife, died during his life-time. He executed two codicils to his will. By the last codicil he appointed his three daughters, Esther W. Mott, Eliza Mott and Maria Mott Hobby his sole executors and trustees, giving to them and each of them full power and authority. The three daughters all survived the testator. Esther W. Mott died first, without issue and unmarried, in the year 1853. She left a will by which, after ordering the payment of her debts, she devised as follows: "All the rest, residue and remainder of my estate, both real and personal, of every nature, whatsoever and wheresoever, I give, devise and bequeath unto my two sisters, Eliza Mott and Maria Mott Hobby, and to the survivor of them, and to the heirs, executors, administrators and assigns of such survivor." She appointed Eliza Mott and Maria Mott Hobby executrices of her will. Eliza Mott next died, without issue and unmarried, about the 1st day of April, 1866. She left a will by which she refers to and recites the will of Henry Mott, the power it contains, the death of Esther W. Mott and her will, and the devolution of the title to the property affected by these wills. The will proceeds as to all the sixth part of the estate coming to her on the death of her sister Esther, and the third part, which she had power to dispose of by will, on her own death, and such part as might come to her on the death of her sister Maria, should she survive Maria, and all other real and personal estate which she may have power to dispose of, she bequeaths and devises the same ; first, to her sister Maria M. Hobby, for her natural life, after her death to William Underhill, in fee, subject to the payment of the legacies in the will specified. These legacies amount to about $38,000 independent of a residuary bequest ; Eliza Mott left personalty only to the amount of $1,500. Her will contained the following power of sale : " I authorize my executors, my sister Maria concurring, to make any devises, leases, sales and conveyances of all and singular the real estate, and to retain investments as they may be at my decease, and to make investments as they may think fit in real securities or in security of public debt of all moneys which shall come to their hands, and on the death of my said sister Maria, or as soon afterward as they may think advisable, taking into view the condition of the country and the probable increase of value of property, and within three years from the proof of this will, I authorize, empower and direct them to convert into money all my real and personal estate, which conversion shall be treated in law as if it had happened at the time of my sister's decease." She appointed as executors her sister, Maria M. Hobby, William Underhill and William H. Onderdonk.

Maria M. Hobby made a will identical with the will of her sister, *mutatis mutandis*, containing the same power of sale, and appointing her sister, Eliza Mott, and the same William Underhill and William H. Onderdonk to be the executors of her will. These wills were both executed on the 24th of April, 1862.

After the death of Eliza Mott, her will was proved, and the executors, Underhill and William H. Onderdonk, the original plaintiff herein, qualified. William Underhill afterward died during the year 1871. No consent appears to have been given by Mrs. Hobby during her life, and no sale was made by Eliza Mott's executors before her death. On the 8th of February, 1877, Mrs. Hobby died. Previous to her death, she executed a codicil to her will, by which she changed and increased the amount of legacies to be paid out of her personal estate, and the proceeds of the sales of her real estate, and also appointed Robert R. Willetts executor in the place of William Underhill, who had died. Robert R. Willetts and William H. Onderdonk qualified as executors under her will. The personal estate left by Mrs. Hobby amounted to about $15,000. The legacies in her will and codicil amount to nearly $80,000. Robert R. Willetts died in February, 1879. After his death Mr. Onderdonk was the sole executor, both of the will of Eliza Mott and of the will and codicils of Maria M. Hobby. Subsequent to the judgment of affirmance by the General Term herein, on the 12th day of December, 1882, said William H. Onderdonk died. Letters of administration with the will annexed upon the estate of Eliza Mott and Maria M. Hobby were issued by the surrogate of the county of New York in March, 1883, to Henry A. Mott, and the action was, by order of this court, revived in his name as such administrator. The property, No. 23 West Thirty-fourth street, was purchased by and conveyed to Eliza Mott and Maria M. Hobby during their lives.

J. Harvey Ackerman and *Isaac L. Miller* for appellant. No power is given by the will to the testator's daughters to dispose of the fee of any of .his real estate. (*Taggart* v. *Murray,* 53 N. Y. 237; *Giles* v. *Little,* 14 Otto, 298.) The will of Esther W. Mott is no execution of the power of appointment given by the will of Henry Mott; it lacks all indication of intention to execute such power of appointment, which is indispensable. (*White* v. *Hicks,* 33 N. Y. 383; 2 Story's Eq. Jur., § 1062*a,* and notes.) Assuming that Esther W. Mott had the power to devise some interest in the real estate of her father, and that it was her intention to make such devise by this will, then her devise is inoperative and void, because it attempts to unlawfully suspend the power of alienation of such interest. (1 R. S. 723, § 15; id. 737, §§ 128-129.) Where a power is given to executors to sell and convey real estate, and they fail to exercise the power within the period limited by the will, they cannot execute the power afterward so as to give a good title to a purchaser. (*Richardson* v. *Sharpe*, 29 Barb. 222.) It is enough for a defendant to show that, upon the whole case presented, the title is not free from suspicion, but is, to say the least, doubtful. (*McCahil* v. *Hamilton*, 20 Hun, 393.) Defendant should be relieved from his purchases and reimbursed all expenses incurred by him in connection therewith, particularly the expenses incurred in the examination of the title. (*Jordon* v. *Poillon*, 77 N. Y. 522; *Bigler* v. *Morgan*, id. 312.)

James M. Varnum for respondent. In an action to enforce a contract of purchase it is sufficient if the title can be made good at the time of the trial, even if it should turn out that the vendor was not competent to convey or able to make a perfect title at the time of the sale. (Willard's Equity, 295; *Seymour* v. *Delancey*, 5 Cow. 74; *Heartburn* v. *Auld*, 4 Cranch, 263; *Fagan* v. *Davison*, 2 Duer, 153; *Rigney* v. *Coles*, 6 Bosw. 479; *Schermerhorn* v. *Niblo*, 2 id. 161; *Ex parte Browning*, 2 Paige, 64; *Jenkins* v. *Fahey*, 73 N. Y. 355.) The provisions of the will of Henry Mott created a separate and distinct trust and estate for the benefit of each of his daughters, as to one-third of his lands, each independent of the other. (*Moore* v. *Hegeman*, 72 N. Y. 376; *Stevenson* v. *Leslie*, 70 id. 515; *Rooner* v. *Meiggs*, 64 id. 516; *Everitt* v. *Everitt*, 29 id. 39; 1 R. S. 732, §§ 77, 79, 81, 82, 84; *Grady* v. *Ward*, 20 Barb. 544; *Marvin* v. *Ward*, 56 id. 603; *Woodgate* v. *Fleet*, 64 N. Y. 573.) A construction which would be legal and feasible in its consequences will be preferred. (*Taggart* v. *Murray*, 53 N. Y. 236; *Quin* v. *Skinner*, 49 Barb. 134.) The will of Esther W. Mott was a valid execution of the powers conferred by her father's will. (*White* v. *Hicks*, 33 N. Y. 383; 1 R. S. 737, § 126 ; *Cutting* v. *Cutting*, 86 N. Y. 522; 1 R. S. 727, § 44; id. 724, §§ 24, 25, 27 ; id. 725, § 35.) There is no illegal suspension of the power of alienation by the provisions of any or all of these wills. (8 Bosw. 465 ; *Van Vechten* v. *Voator*, 63 N. Y. 55 ; *Crittenden* v. *Fairchild*, 41 id. 239 ; Jarman on Wills, chap. 16.) The power of sale contained in the will of Eliza Mott was not defeated or destroyed, nor its exercise rendered invalid, by the lapse of the three years spoken of in the will as the period within which the executors must sell. (*Bogert* v. *Hoertel*, 4 Hill, 495 ; *Fisher* v. *Banta*, 66 N. Y. 470 ; *Skinner* v. *Quinn*, 43 id. 105 ; *Kinnier* v. *Rogers*, 42 id. 503.) The courts, upon the application of a legatee or party beneficially interested in the residue, would compel executors or trustees in such a case to execute the power, although the time within which they were directed to sell had passed. (*Wild* v. *Bergen*, 16 Hun, 127.) The court will determine the issue presented in this action and decide as to the validity of this title, without requiring the heirs of Henry Mott or the heirs of William Underhill either to be brought into this suit or to be made parties to a distinct action. (*Jenkins* v. *Fahey*, 73 N. Y. 355 ; *Taggart* v. *Mooney*, 53 id. 233 ; *Kinnier* v. *Rogers*, 42 id. 531 ; *Chittenden* v. *Fairchild*, 41 id. 289 ; *Grady* v. *Ward*, 20 Barb. 545 ; *Jarvis* v. *Babcock*, 5 id. 139 ; *Skinner* v. *Quinn*, 43 N. Y. 99 ; *Ackerman* v. *Gorton*, 69 id. 63.) The Court of Appeals should pass upon the preliminary objections of the appellant. (*Roome* v. *Phillips*, 27 N. Y. 357.) A delivery need not be absolute, it may be conditional. (*Hunter* v. *Hunter*, 17 Barb. 25–82 ; *Nottbeck* v. *Wilkes*, 4 Abb. 315 : *Hathaway* v. *Payne*, 34 N. Y. 92 ; 25 Wend. 43 ; Gerard's Titles [2d ed.], 516, 518 ; *Worrell* v. *Munn*, 1 Seld. 229 ; *Fisher* v. *Hall*, 41 N. Y. 417 ; *Dietz* v. *Farrish*, 44 J. & S. 190 ; *Sonnerlye* v. *Arden*, 1 Johns. Ch. 240 ; *Scrugham* v. *Wood*, 15 Wend. 545 ; 16 Barb. 264 ; *Ruslin* v. *Shield*, 11 Ga. 636 ; *Tooley* v. *Dibble*, 2 Hill, 641 ; *Wheelwright* v. *Same*, 2 Mass. 447 ; *Jackson* v. *Catlin*, 8 Johns. 120 ; Bouvier's Law Dic., title Escrow.) A delivery of a deed by a grantor in escrow, to be delivered on the death of the grantor, is good. (34 N. Y. 92.) This is one of the cases where an administrator, with the will annexed, succeeds to the power of sale given to the executors by the will. (2 R. S. 72, § 22.) The provisions of the wills affected an equitable conversion of the real estate into personalty at the time the wills took effect. (*Horton* v. *McCoy*, 47 N. Y. 21 ; *Bogart* v. *Wertell*, 4 Hill, 492; 2 Story's Eq. Jur. 790, §§ 115, 116.) Where a testator directs something to be done by his executors which is imperative, or which is not clearly a personal trust or confidence, and which is legitimately connected with his duties as executor, it can be exercised by an administrator, even if it does relate to real estate. (*De Peyster* v. *Clendening*, 8 Paige, 296; *Bain* v. *Mattersen*, 54 N. Y. 663; *Bingham* v. *Jones*, 25 Hun, 6.) The court will not allow any trust or power in trust to fail through the lack of a person to administer or execute it. (*De Peyster* v. *Clendening*, 8 Paige, 296–311 ; 1 R. S. 730, §§ 70, 71 ; *King* v. *Donnelly*, 5 Paige, 46 ; 5 Wend. 224; 2 R. S. 72 ; *Roome* v. *Phillips*, 27 N. Y. 357, 4 Paige, 345, 353.)

Finch, J. The validity of the title tendered to the purchaser in performance of the contract of sale depends, primarily, upon the construction of the will of Henry Mott, and those, respectively, of his three daughters. As to that of the father it is objected that the power of appointment by will, conferred upon such of them as should die unmarried and without issue, did not extend to and embrace the fee of any of his real estate. It had that effect or none. The daughters had each a life estate under a trust vested in the executors. Upon their deaths, or that of any one of them, the remainder in fee was left for ultimate disposition. An appointment by will could not relate to their life estates, for those would be ended by the same fact which made the appointment operative and at the same moment of time. The power, therefore, must naturally be a power in gross, and relate not to the life estate, but to the remainder in fee ; and that it did so is evident from the three provisions which contemplate the death of the daughters.

Those are adapted to three emergencies, viz.: (1) the death of
a daughter married and leaving issue and a husband surviving;
(2) the death of a daughter unmarried and without issue; (3)
and, in the latter event, her death, without exercising the power
of appointment. In the first event the executors were to
stand seized for the use and benefit of the issue; in the second,
for the purposes which the daughter should by will appoint;
and in the third, for the use and benefit of such daughter's
next of kin. In each event the trust in the executors would be
purely passive, and the remainder vest in the beneficiaries.
The criticism upon this construction is founded upon the words
"upon such trust and for such purposes as she shall or may
appoint by her last will and testament." It is quite evident
that the phrase "upon such trust" means not a trust to be
created by the daughter and so limiting her power of disposition,
but relates to the trust in the executors; the same trust twice
before mentioned and once afterward; in each instance held
for different beneficiaries; and in the second of the three contingencies, for such purposes as the appointee should provide.
The slight change of phrase from "upon trust" to "upon such
trust" cannot be held to import the wide difference of intention
asserted. No trust to be created by the will of Esther is fore-
shadowed or indicated by any apparent intention of the testator.
If she sought to make one, it could not introduce a third life
estate before the vesting of the fee, and it is difficult to see any
useful purpose operating upon the testator to induce such a
limitation. It seems to us quite plain that he meant for each
of his daughters very nearly an estate in fee, by giving them
not only an estate for life, but a power of disposition by will
in case of their remaining unmarried; and a limitation confining that power to the creation of some trust, not defined, not
intimated, left wholly at large, has no reason to support it, and
is not forced upon us by the language of the will. The
inquiry why the testator forfeited only the income of the
married daughter in case she paid any of her husband's debts
does not affect our conclusion. The obvious answer to the
suggestion is that she had only that to be forfeited which

could be supposed to influence or affect her action. To strike instead at her power of appointment would have been not only ineffectual as a restraint, but would have pushed the consequences beyond her death.

It is next objected that the will of the unmarried daughter Esther, who died before her sisters, was not a valid execution by her of the power of appointment as to one-third of the estate. But the statute provides that lands embraced in a power to devise pass by a will which purports to convey the whole real property of the testator, unless a contrary intention is manifested. Esther's will directs the payment of debts and funeral expenses, and then gives to her sisters all the rest, residue and remainder of her estate, both real and personal, of every nature whatsoever and wheresoever. (1 R. S. 737, § 126.) The language is broad and brings the case clearly within the rule prescribed by the statute.

But it is further said that the disposition by Esther's will is invalid because it suspends the absolute power of alienation beyond the permitted lives ; that the computation must run from the creation of the power in the will of her father ; and so there is an estate for life in Esther ; then a devise to the two sisters, Eliza and Maria ; then one to the survivor of the two ; and lastly one to the heirs, executors, administrators and assigns of such survivor. The last alleged limitation is very certainly not such. It is intended merely to characterize as a fee or absolute estate in the land or its proceeds, if converted, the interest vested in the survivor. The devise to Esther herself must be counted as one life. Then the estate passes to Eliza and Maria, but they take as tenants in common and not as joint tenants. (1 R. S. 727, § 44 ; *Purdy* v. *Hayt*, June, 1883*) Each became the owner of an undivided half of Esther's one-third, and would have owned such one-sixth absolutely but for the further limitation to the survivor. That, it is argued, adds a second life. But it is a fee limited upon a fee, which may lawfully be done, where the contingency, if it should occur, must happen within two lives. (1 R. S. 724, § 24.)

The fee given to the one who shall first die is defeasible by such death, and thereupon the entire absolute estate vested, and could be aliened after two lives, at most. But the suspension did not exceed the life of Esther. Her sisters took legal estates in her one-third since the trust in her father's executors, after her death, was passive, and did not prevent the vesting of the entire title. While each held her fee in one-sixth defeasible upon a contingency, and each had a contingent remainder in the one-sixth of the other, these estates were alienable, and the deed of the two sisters, immediately upon Esther's death, would have conveyed an absolute fee in possession.

These are all the objections affecting the Broadway property by itself, but others are taken to the validity of the title to the property on Thirty-fourth street, and to the power to make any conveyance of any of the property by reason of the death of the sole surviving executor of the sisters pending the present litigation.

The property on Thirty-fourth street was purchased by and conveyed to Eliza and Maria, who owned it as tenants in common. Eliza died after Esther but before Maria. By her will she gave to her executors a power of sale to be exercised during the life of the latter with her concurrence. The will then proceeds: " and on the death of my said sister Maria, or as soon afterward as they may think advisable, taking into view the condition of the country, and the probable increase in the value of the property, and *within three years from the proof of this will*, I authorize, empower and direct them to convert into money all my real and personal estate, which conversion shall be treated in law as if it had happened at the time of my sister's decease." Maria lived more than three years after the probate of Eliza's will and no sale was made until after her death, and about twelve years after the probate of Eliza's will; and that was the sale to these defendants. It is now said that the power of sale could only be exercised within the three years, and that the deed of the executors tendered long after that period was invalid. But the testatrix added to her authority a command. She not only empowered her executors to sell, but directed them to do so. The purposes of the will required such sale, and the power was imperative. (1 R. S. 734, § 96.)

The neglect or misconduct of executors ought not to defeat the purposes of the testator, or destroy the rights which depend upon their proper performance of duty. We are not justified in supposing that any such result was within the contemplation of Eliza, and should, therefore, read the provision for a sale within three years as not limiting the authority, but qualifying the command. The meaning is, I "authorize" you to sell, and I "direct" you to do so within three years after probate. It was an injunction to promptness in the exercise of the authority. Neglect to obey the command did not destroy the authority conferred. Nothing in the frame of the will indicates an intention to narrow or hamper the power to sell, but on the contrary the very provision as to time indicates a purpose to have the power exercised, and that promptly and without delay. Any other construction would force us to say that the power was not imperative, and that the testatrix intended to make the whole purpose and plan of her disposition contingent upon the discretion of her executors in selling or not selling within three years.

During the life of Maria, her assent was essential to a lawful sale. While she lived her interest and welfare was the paramount consideration. She lived longer than the three years and it must be presumed withheld her assent to a sale. The executors, therefore, could not literally obey the direction of the will, and were not even blamable for the delay. Probably, just that emergency was not expected, but whether anticipated or not, the power of sale was and was intended to be imperative, and was not limited by the injunction as to time which qualified the command.

The remaining difficulty suggested by the appellant is one which has arisen since the commencement of the litigation and upon which we pass out of deference to the serious interests involved. It is conceded that since the tender of the deeds by the sole surviving executor and the judgment of the Special Term pronouncing them sufficient, and its affirmance by the General Term, the executor has died; that, thereafter, Henry A. Mott was duly appointed administrator with the will annexed of the estates both of Eliza and Maria; and that the action has been revived in the name of such administrator. The questions thus raised are whether the deeds executed by the deceased executor in his life-time and tendered to the purchaser can be now delivered, or be treated as delivered with the effect of passing the title; if not, whether the administrator with the will annexed can make the conveyance; or whether a trustee must be appointed by the Supreme Court for the purpose of an effective deed.

It is argued that the tender by the executor amounted to a conditional delivery of the deed; that the refusal to accept put solely upon the ground of doubt about the title, amounted to an acceptance upon condition that the title should be adjudged good; and that the decision of the Special Term performed the condition. We are not able to go so far as that. There was a tender but no delivery, for a delivery which vests title implies an acceptance, and here there was a refusal. We can say that a good title was offered but not that the deed was delivered. A delivery now, after the death of the executor, would be ineffectual.

But we are of opinion that the administrator with the will annexed has authority to make the necessary deed. The question has been left by the disagreement of the courts in some uncertainty which should be dispelled so far as it is possible to do so. The statute provides that administrators with the will annexed " shall have the same rights and powers and be subject to the same duties as if they had been named executors in such will." (2 R. S. 72, § 22.) In construing this statute great differences of opinion have arisen. (*De Peyster* v. *Clendining*, 8 Paige, 296; *Conklin* v. *Egerton*, 21 Wend. 430; 25 id. 224; *Roome* v. *Philips*, 27 N. Y. 357; *Bain* v. *Matteson*, 54 id. 663; *Bingham* v. *Jones*, 25 Hun, 6.) The debate has turned mainly upon the inquiry what were the distinctive duties of an executor as such, and when they were to be regarded as not appertaining to his office, but as personal to the trustee. Where the will gives a power to the donee in a capacity distinctively different from his duties as executor, so that as to such duties he is to be regarded wholly as trustee and not at all as executor ; and where the power granted or the duty involved imply a personal confidence reposed in the individual over and above and beyond that which is ordinarily implied by the selection of an executor, there is no room for doubt or dispute. In such case the power and duty are not those of executors, *virtute officii*, and do not pass to the administrator with the will annexed. But outside of such cases the instances are numerous in which by the operation of a power in trust authority over the real estate is given to the executor as such and the better to enable him to perform the requirements of the will. It will not do to say, in the present state of the law, that whenever a trust or trust power is conferred upon executors, relating to real estate, some personal confidence distinct from that reposed in executors is implied. An executor is always a trustee of the personal estate for those interested under the will. We have recently so decided where the trust character could only be derived from the office and its relation to rights claimed through it. (*Wager* v. *Wager*, 89 N. Y. 161.) And we have held, also, that, where a will devised and bequeathed to the executors the residue of real and personal estate, in trust, to sell and convert the same, to divide the balance into shares, to invest it in bond and mortgage, and to pay over the income for a time and finally the principal, the proceeds of the land sold became legal assets in the hands of the executor, for which he was liable officially, and for which his sureties were responsible ; and that an objection that he held the proceeds as trustee, and not as executor, and could only be made accountable in equity, was not well taken. (*Hood* v. *Hood*, 85 N. Y. 571.) We have no doubt, therefore, that where a power of sale is given to executors for the purpose of paying debts and legacies, or either, and especially where there is an equitable conversion of land into money for the purpose of such payment and for distribution, and the power of sale is imperative and does not grow out of a personal discretion confided to the individual, such power belongs to the office of executor, and under the statute, passes to and may be exercised by the administrator with the will annexed. That is the case before us, and the deed of the administrator with the will annexed will be as effectual as would have been that of the executor if he had survived.

We have given no attention to the questions relating to the possible interest of the heirs of Underhill, since a release from them was tendered upon the trial and must accompany the delivery of the administrator's deed.

The judgment should be affirmed, with costs.

All concur.

Judgment affirmed.

THE PEOPLE OF THE STATE OF NEW YORK, Respondent, *v.* EDWARD HOVEY, Appellant.

In the absence of exceptions on a criminal trial this court has no power to review the case upon the facts.

The provision of the Code of Criminal Procedure (§ 527), as amended in 1882 (Chap. 360, Laws of 1882), providing that "the appellate court may order a new trial if it be satisfied that the verdict against the prisoner was against the weight of evidence or against law, or that justice required a new trial whether any exceptions shall have been taken or not," applies only to appeals to the Supreme Court.

An exception to a charge taken after a criminal trial has terminated does not present any question for the consideration of an appellate court.

Where, therefore, after a criminal trial, and when the prisoner was before the court for sentence, his counsel moved for a new trial for an alleged error in the charge, and upon denial of the motion took an exception, *held*, that no question was thereby presented here for review.

It seems that where, upon such a trial, upon objection of the prisoner, his wife, who was an eye-witness to the transaction in question, is excluded as a witness, the jury has a right to infer that her evidence would not have been favorable to him, and a submission of that question to them is not error.

(Argued April 30, 1883; decided June 5, 1883.)

APPEAL from judgment of the General Term of the Supreme Court, in the first judicial department, entered upon an order made March 22, 1883, which affirmed a judgment of the Court of General Sessions in and for the city and county of New York, entered upon a verdict convicting defendant of the crime of murder in the first degree. (Reported below, 29 Hun, 382.)

The facts material to the questions discussed are stated in the opinion.

William F. Kintzing for appellant. The court erred in charging that the failure of the prisoner to call his wife as a witness was a circumstance for the jury to consider. (*Wilkie* v. *People*, 53 N. Y. 525; 1 Hale's P. C. 301; 1 Greenleaf on Evidence [13th ed.], §§ 334–343 and note; *Houghton* v. *People*, 24 Hun, 501; 22 Alb. L. J. 81; *People* v. *Briggs*, 60 How. Pr. 17; 1 Starkie on Ev., § 24; 2 id. [6th Am. ed.] 685; 1 Phillips on Ev. 172; 1 id. [Cowan & Hill's Note] 459–460; 3 Blackstone's Com. 371; *People* v. *Gordon*, 33 N. Y. 501; *People* v. *Dyle*, 21 id. 578; *People* v. *Mc Whorter*, 4 Barb. 438; *People* v. *Bodine*, 1 Denio, 281; *People* v. *Armsby*, 53 N. Y. 475; *People* v. *Kennedy*, 39 id. 254; *People* v. *Tweed*, 5 Hun, 388; *Brooks* v. *Steen*, 6 id. 517; *Bleeker* v. *Johnson*, 69 N. Y. 313; Laws of 1869, chap. 678; *Ruloff* v. *People*, 45 N. Y. 213.) The court erred in permitting the prosecuting officer, upon the cross-examination of the defendant, to ask him how often he had been in prison and for what. (Laws of 1869, chap. 678; *Brandon* v. *People*, 42 N. Y. 265; *Connors* v. *People*, 50 id. 240; *People* v. *Casey*, 72 id. 392; *Perry* v. *People*, 86 id. 353; *McGloin* v. *People*, 91 id. 291; *Newcomb* v. *Griswold*, 24 id. 298; 1 Greenleaf on Ev., § 457; *King* v. *Inhabitants of Castell Careinion*, 8 East, 77; *People* v. *Herrick*, 13 Johns. 82; *Hilts* v. *Calvin*, 14 id. 182; *Jackson* v. *Osborn*, 2 Wend. 555; 1 Greenleaf on Ev., §§ 457, 460, 461, 463; 1 Taylor on Ev. 292; 1 Phillips on Ev. 291 [Cowan & Hill's Note], 530, p. 766; *Worrell* v. *Parmelee*, 1 N. Y. 519; *People* v. *Wiley*, 3 Hill, 194–214; *Comm.* v. *Kinnison*, 4 Mass. 646; *State* v. *Zeller*, 2 Halstead, 220; *West* v. *State*, 2 Zab. 212;

Davis v. *State*, 17 Ala. 415; *Com.* v. *Thompson*, Thatcher's Crim. Cas. 28; *U. S.* v. *Gilbert*, 2 Sumner, 19; *Queen's Case*, 2 B. & B. 293; *Lee* v. *Chadry*, 3 Keyes, 225; *Crapo* v. *People*, 15 Hun, 272; *People* v. *Crapo*, 76 N. Y. 785; 2 Phillip on Ev. 943 [5th Am. ed.]; *People* v. *Gay*, 7 N. Y. 378; *People* v. *Genung*, 11 Wend. 19; *Parkhurst* v. *Louton*, 2 Swanst. 216; *Jackson* v. *Osborn*, 2 Wend. 555; *People* v. *Brown*, 72 N. Y. 571; 8 Hun, 562.) A verdict of guilty of murder in the first degree upon the evidence was erroneous. (Laws of 1873, chap. 644, p. 1014; Laws of 1862, chap. 197, p. 369; *Fitzgerald* v. *People*, 37 N. Y. 413; *People* v. *Clark*, 7 id. 385; *Kennedy* v. *People*, 37 id. 245; *Sullivan* v. *People*, 1 Park. Cr. 347; *People* v. *Johnson*, id. 291; *Wilson* v. *People*, 4 Park. Cr. 305; *Lowenburg* v. *People*, 5 id. 444; *Walters* v. *People*, 6 id. 15; *O'Brien* v. *People*, 48 Barb. 274; *Lannergan* v. *People*, 6 Park. Cr. 209; *People* v. *Austin*, 1 Parker; *People* v. *Enoch*, 13 Wend. 159; *People* v. *White*, 24 id. 524.) A new trial will be granted where error appears, except where by no possibility the error could have produced injury. (*Stokes* v. *People*, 53 N. Y. 165; *Coleman* v. *People*, 58 id. 561; *People* v. *Wiley*, 3 Hill, 194; *Worrall* v. *Parmelee*, 1 N. Y. 519; *Vandervoorst* v. *Gould*, 36 id. 639.)

John Vincent, assistant district attorney, for respondent. The proof and surrounding circumstances were sufficient to uphold the finding of the jury as to the premeditation and deliberation. (*Leighton* v. *People*, 10 Abb. N. C. 261; *Sindram* v. *People*, 88 N. Y. 196; *People* v. *Majone*, 91 id. 211.) The defendant having put himself upon the stand, he placed himself in the same position as any other witness, subject to the same rules. (*People* v. *Crapo*, 76 N. Y. 288; *Brandon* v. *People*, 42 id. 265; *Connors* v. *People*, 50 id. 240; Code of Civ. Pro., § 832.) The wife was competent as a witness if the prisoner chose to call her. (*People* v. *Houghton*, 28 Hun, 501; *Gordon* v. *People*, 33 N. Y. 516; Laws of 1876, chap. 182, § 2.)

RUGER, Ch. J. The defendant was convicted in the Court of General Sessions in the county of New York, of murder in the first degree, for killing one Fanny Vermilyea, on the 26th day of April, 1882. It is not denied that the deceased met her death at the hands of the defendant, but it was attempted to be shown on his behalf that the killing was accidental and un-premeditated.

No exceptions were taken upon the trial by the defendant either to the rulings of the court in the admission or exclusion of evidence, or to the various propositions contained in the charge to the jury.

It is claimed by the appellant that, by virtue of section 527 of the Code of Criminal Procedure, this court has the power to review the case upon the facts, and if, upon such review, it finds that the verdict was either against the weight of evidence or against law, or that justice requires a new trial, such trial should be directed although no exceptions were taken in the court below.

We are of the opinion that this section does not apply to appeals to this court.

It is contained in chapter 1 of title 11 of the Code, which embraces seventeen sections, some of which treat exclusively of appeals to the Supreme Court, and others of appeals to this court, while still others apply indiscriminately to appeals to both.

Section 527 is entitled " Stay of proceedings on appeal to Supreme Court from judgment of conviction, new trial, when granted," and contains not only the provision in question, but also others made applicable to the Supreme Court alone.

Section 528, immediately following, is entitled "Stay upon appeal to Court of Appeals from judgment of Supreme Court affirming judgment of conviction." It refers exclusively to appeals to this court and contains no provision for a review by us of the case upon the evidence.

Section 527 is nowhere made expressly applicable to this court and the provision for a review upon the facts being confined to that section, and omitted from the section expressly treating of appeals to this court, forbid the inference that it was intended to be applicable to the Court of Appeals. (*In the Matter of Ross*, 87 N. Y. 518.) This construction also accords with the general theory of the law as to the powers and duties of the various courts, and assigns to each the determination of those questions for the consideration of which it was especially organized and adapted. The review of questions of fact arising upon conflicting evidence is beyond the general powers of this court, and the consideration of such questions can only be entertained either in civil or criminal cases by force of express provision of law requiring it. (*In the Matter of Ross, supra.*)

The general object and design of the Code of Criminal Procedure was to collect the various statutes relating to the subject and to furnish a uniform, harmonious and comprehensive system of criminal practice, to apply to and govern all criminal proceedings thereafter instituted in any of the courts of the State. (§ 962, Code of Criminal Procedure.)

We should have been more reluctant in arriving at the conclusion that we had no power to review the facts in a criminal case if a perusal of the evidence given upon this trial had left any doubt in our minds as to the justice of the result attained in the courts below.

That evidence tended to prove a homicide committed under circumstances showing a wanton disregard of the sanctity of human life and the obligations of care and protection, which, as master of a household, the defendant owed to those belonging to his family circle.

The evidence tended to show that he was a person of idle and dissolute habits, and regardless of the feelings or interests of others. On the day of the homicide he visited the rooms occupied by himself and family at about noon and requested his wife to wash his feet. The wife, who was then in attendance upon her child lying dangerously sick in the room, neglected to comply with this request, and the deceased, who was present, remarked to the defendant that he ought to have more thought for his dying baby. The defendant replied to this remark with some profanity and with apparent anger.

He soon thereafter left the house, and having pledged his coat to purchase a pistol, loaded it and returned to the house where the deceased was employed in her work. Soon after entering the room where the deceased and his wife were sitting he fatally shot the deceased with the pistol he had just purchased and loaded, and then tried to conceal himself under the bed.

The conduct of the defendant immediately after the shooting was marked with great levity and indifference and his conversation immediately thereafter indicated that the act of shooting was intentional and premeditated. We cannot doubt that the jury arrived at a correct result upon the evidence and we feel no disposition to interfere with their verdict.

We have not omitted to observe that a week after the trial, when the defendant was brought before the court for sentence, his counsel moved for a new trial upon the evidence, and for an alleged error in the charge to the jury, and upon the refusal of the court to grant a new trial took an exception to such refusal.

An exception to a charge taken after the trial had terminated and where, if erroneous, the jury could not have been instructed to disregard the erroneous instructions, does not present any question of law for the consideration of an appellate court. (*Matthews* v. *Meyberg*, 63 N. Y. 656.) Even if this exception had been taken at the proper time it would have been unavailing for the reason that we think the charge was unexceptionable.

It was in reference to the testimony of the prisoner's wife, who, when offered as a witness on the part of the prosecution, was excluded, on the objection of the prisoner's counsel. The learned judge, in charging the jury, said:

" There is no eye-witness who has testified to the occurrence, except the defendant. The people claim, however, and the uncontradicted evidence established that there was another eye-witness to this occurrence, namely, the wife of the defendant. You remember when the wife was offered as a witness on behalf of the people, the court would not allow her to be examined as a witness against her husband, for, in my judgment, the law does not permit it, but while that is so, the law does allow the wife to be a witness in her husband's behalf, and the people claim that inasmuch as it appeared in evidence that she was an eye-witness to the occurrence, accessible to the defendant, and the defendant allowed by the law to call her as his witness, and having neglected to do so, that that is a circumstance which the jury have a right to consider on coming to a conclusion. And the people claim, moreover, that the prisoner's omission to call her as a witness under the above circumstances should be taken as a matter of evidence against him, and they claim that the fair presumption is that if she was called her testimony would not be favorable to the defendant."

A jury would have the right to infer that the evidence of an eye-witness to a transaction would not be favorable to a party who voluntarily excluded such witness from testifying in the case. (*Gordon* v. *People*, 33 N. Y. 508.)

The judgment should be affirmed.

All concur.

Judgment affirmed.

THE PEOPLE OF THE STATE OF NEW YORK, Appellant, *v.*
HENRY BOAS, Respondent.

The provision of the Code of Criminal Procedure (§ 527) providing that "the appellate court may order a new trial if it be satisfied that the verdict against the prisoner was against the weight of evidence, * * * or that justice requires," is applicable only to the Supreme Court and gives that court a discretionary power. When in the exercise of that discretion it refuses or grants a new trial its determination is not reviewable here.

Under the provision of said Code (§ 519), authorizing an appeal to this court by the people from a judgment of the General Term reversing a judgment of conviction, such an appeal brings up for review only questions of law.

In determining whether the reversal was solely upon questions of law, the record only can be examined; the opinion of the General Term forms no part thereof and may not be looked at.

Unless, therefore, the order of the General Term shows that the Supreme
Court has exercised its discretion and refused a new trial upon the facts
and granted it only for errors of law, there is nothing for this court to
review on appeal to it.

(Argued April 30, 1883 ; decided June 5, 1883.)

APPEAL from judgment of the General Term of the Supreme Court, in the first judicial department, entered upon an
order made March 20, 1883, which reversed a judgment of the
Court of General Sessions, in and for the city and county of
New York, entered upon a verdict convicting defendant of a
violation of the law (Chap. 675, Laws of 1872) making it felony
for an inspector of election to willfully exclude the vote of an
elector, lawfully entitled to vote. (Reported below, 29 Hun,
377.)

The material facts are stated in the opinion.

John Vincent, assistant district attorney, for appellant.
An intentional and conscious act is all that was required to
justify the verdict. Willfully means intentionally, and is distinguished from maliciously in not implying an evil mind.
(2 Bouvier's Law Dict. 817 ; L. R., 2 Cr. Cas. Res. 161 ; Penal
Code, §§ 78, 224, 639, 718.) The facts disclose a willful intent
to defy the law. (Election Laws, § 67 ; *Leighton* v. *People*, 10
Abb. [N. S.] 261; *Sindram* v. *People*, 88 N. Y. 396 ; *In re
Majone*, opinion by DANIELS, J.) The inspector's duties were
simply ministerial. (*People* v. *Pease*, 30 Barb. 588.) The
testimony of the witness Ruckert was properly admitted as
bearing upon the question of intent. (*Mayer* v. *People*, 80
N. Y. 364–373 ; *Weyman* v. *People*, 4 Hun, 511.) The recorder in his charge properly defined the word "willful" as
meaning a felonious or malicious act. (*People* v. *Hall*, 90
N. Y. 498.)

William F. Kintzing for respondent. The court erred in
refusing to advise the jury, as requested, to acquit at the close
of the testimony. (*Bennett* v. *People*, 49 N. Y. 137 ; Laws of
1872, chap. 675.) The law makes the inspectors the judges of
the qualifications of a voter, his right to vote, and in the exer-

cise of their deliberate judgments upon that question they cannot be held responsible, either civilly or criminally without
proof of malice. (Bishop on Statutory Crimes, § 806; *Byrne*
v. *State*, 12 Wis. 519; *State* v. *Daniels*, 44 N. H. 383; *State*
v. *McDonald*, 4 Harr. [Del.] 555; *State* v. *Porter*, id. 556;
Harman v. *Tappenden*, 1 East; *Jenkins* v. *Waldron*, 11
Johns. 114; *People* v. *Coon*, 15 Wend. 227; *People* v. *Norton*,
7 Barb. 477; *King* v. *Barron*, 3 Barn. & Adolph. 452; 1
Russell on Crimes, 136; 1 Chitty's Cr. Law, 873; Whart. on
Am. Cr. Law [2d ed.], 1732.) To do an act " willfully " in
contemplation of law is to do it " maliciously, criminally, with
knowledge aforethought and wicked design." (Worcester's
Dict.; Webster's Dict.) Testimony as to the defendant's guilt,
or participation in the commission of a crime wholly uncon-
nected with that for which he is put on trial, cannot be admitted. (1 Roscoe's Crim. Ev. [7th ed.] 20, 21, 57, 92, note;
Conn v. *Call*, 31 Pick. 215; *Dunn* v. *State*, 2 Ark. 229;
Bottomly v. *U. S.*, 1 Story, 135; 1 Leigh, 574; Barbour's
Crim. Law [2d ed.], 395; 2 Russell on Crimes [6th ed.], 776;
3 Greenleaf's Ev. 13; *Rex* v. *Farrington*, Russ. & Ryan, 207;
Regina v. *Phelps*, 1 Moody, 263.)

EARL, J. The defendant was an inspector of election in the
city of New York at the election held in the fall of 1881, and
he was subsequently indicted and convicted in the General
Sessions of the same city for declining to receive the vote of
an elector at that election, under section 67 of chapter 675 of
the Laws of 1872, which provides that " every inspector of
election who shall willfully exclude any vote duly tendered,
knowing that the person offering the same is lawfully entitled
to vote at such election," shall, upon conviction thereof, be adjudged guilty of a felony and be punished by imprisonment in
a State prison for not more than two years. He appealed
from the judgment against him to the General Term of the
Supreme Court, and there the judgment was reversed and a
new trial was ordered. The General Term order does not state
upon what ground or for what reason the judgment was re-

versed, and we have now to determine whether there is any thing before us for review upon this appeal.

This court is strictly an appellate court, and its general jurisdiction is confined to the correction of `errors of law presented in the records brought before it. Unless it is otherwise specially provided, it will never review mere questions of fact depending upon conflicting evidence, or the exercise of a discretion confided to the inferior courts.

Section 527 of the Code of Criminal Procedure provides that " the appellate court may order a new trial if it be satisfied that the verdict against the prisoner was against the weight of evidence or against law, or that justice requires a new trial, whether any exceptions shall have been taken or not in the court below." We have just decided that this section is confined in its operation to the Supreme Court, and that it has no application to this court. (*People* v. *Hovey.**) The section clothes the Supreme Court with power, in the exercise of its discretion, to order a new trial when it shall be satisfied that the verdict is against the weight of evidence, or that justice requires a new trial; and when, in the exercise of its discretion, it shall, under the section, refuse or grant a new trial, its determination is not reviewable here.

Under section 519, the people may appeal to this court from a judgment of the General Term reversing a judgment of conviction; but such an appeal brings before us for review only questions of law. How are we to ascertain, when the people have appealed, that the reversal was upon questions of law only ? Simply by looking at the record. The opinion of the General Term forms no part of that, and we cannot look at it for the grounds of the reversal. We must look for them in the order of the General Term, and that must show that the Supreme Court has exercised its discretion, and that the new trial was ordered for errors of law only. In a case like this, the appeal comes before us substantially in the same way that an appeal comes here from an order of the General Term of the Supreme Court granting a new trial in a civil action, after the verdict of

* *Ante,* p. 554.

a jury, in a case where that court had the power to grant a new trial in the exercise of its discretion, on the ground that the verdict was against the weight of evidence. In such cases, we have uniformly held that there was nothing for this court to review, unless it appeared that the Supreme Court had exercised its discretion and had refused a new trial on the ground that the verdict was against the weight of evidence and had granted it solely for error of law. (*Wright* v. *Hunter*, 46 N. Y. 409; *Harris* v. *Burdett*, 73 id. 136; *Snebley* v. *Conner*, 78 id. 218.)

We cannot say, therefore, that the court below committed any error of law, as the new trial may have been ordered, in the exercise of its discretion, under section 527, and its order must, therefore, be affirmed.

All concur.

Judgment affirmed.

THE FISHKILL SAVINGS INSTITUTE, Appellant, *v.* HENRY BOSTWICK, Receiver, etc., et al., Respondents.

By an agreement between plaintiff, a savings institute, and the F. N. Bank, all of the business of the two corporations was to be done in the same office and over the same counter, by the same individuals, the only separation being in the books of account. Plaintiff as such was to receive no money, but all of its funds were to be deposited in the bank, and corresponding credits were to take the place of actual payments by the bank. The business of the institute and the bank was carried on under this arrangement, the former keeping no cash-drawer or safe for the deposit of money. One C. delivered over the counter of the bank to B., who was treasurer of the institute and also cashier of the bank, a sum of money, which she desired deposited with the institute to her credit. B. received the money, entered it in C.'s pass-book, as deposited with the institute, and, as he testified, placed it in the cash-drawer of the bank: it was not entered on the bank cash-book or credited to the institute, and, in some manner unexplained, it disappeared. In an action to recover, among other things, the amount of this deposit, *held*, that while as between C. and the institute B. received the money as its treasurer, as between the bank and the institute at the same instant he received it as cashier, it became the money of the bank, and the bank was liable to the plaintiff therefor ; also, that this was so, although the money did not go into the cash-drawer but was embezzled by B.

Bartow v. *The People* (78 N. Y. 377), distinguished.

A check was presented at the bank and received by B. to pay money due plaintiff; it was payable to him as treasurer; was indorsed by him as such, and then by him as cashier of the bank, and remitted for collection. No credit was given plaintiff therefor on the bank-books. *Held*, that under the general arrangement, the check, when received, became at once the property of the bank ; the institute was entitled to credit for the amount and could recover the same of the bank.

A check drawn upon the bank by a depositor, payable to the order of B. as treasurer, was indorsed by him as such, charged to the drawer in the bank accounts, but not credited to plaintiff. *Held*, that it was entitled to recover the amount.

(Argued May 2, 1883 ; decided June.5, 1883.)

APPEAL from order of the General Term of the Supreme Court, in the second judicial department, made September 12, 1882, which reversed a judgment in favor of plaintiff, entered upon the report of a referee.

The nature of the action and the material facts are stated in the opinion.

Milton A. Fowler for appellant. In the absence of proof, on the face of the papers, that the judgment was reversed and a new trial granted upon questions of fact, the reversal will be presumed to have been on questions of law only. (Code, § 1338; *Davies* v. *Leopold*, 87 N. Y. 620.) Plaintiff having shown the course of business and an ordinary manner of dealing, and the fact that the Carrigan deposit went into the bank, defendants must show that it went elsewhere, to defeat the claim. (*Bartow* v. *People*, 78 N. Y. 377–381.)

John Thompson for respondents.

FINCH, J. The Fishkill Savings Institute brought an action against the National Bank of Fishkill and its receiver, to recover the amount of certain deposits and a balance of interest payable under a special contract. The trial was before a referee, who awarded judgment in favor of the plaintiff. On appeal the General Term reversed this judgment, and ordered a new trial, but without stating in the order that the reversal was upon the facts. Exceptions were taken to the findings of the referee as to three separate items allowed, and which were sufficient to raise the questions argued at the General Term, and present for the consideration of that tribunal questions of law, which may be reviewed on this appeal.

Each of the three charges disallowed by the General Term depended upon the action of Bartow, who was treasurer of the institute and cashier of the bank. The marvelous manner in which the business of the two corporations was transacted invested him at the same moment of time with a double capacity, and made him concurrently the representative of two separate principals. The proof shows, without the least doubt or contradiction, a general arrangement by which the business of both corporations was to be done in the same office, at the same counter, by the same individuals, the only separation being in the books of account. The institute received no money as such. All its funds were to be deposited in the bank, and from that institution corresponding credits were to take the place of the actual payments. The institute, under the business arrangement agreed upon, had no cash drawer and no safe for the deposit of money, since none was needed, and no money was to be received and retained by it. Under this mode of transacting business, events happened which occasioned the questions now to be considered.

On the 7th of April, 1875, one Joanna Carrigan appeared at the counter of the bank with $3,500 in money, which she desired to deposit with the institute to her own credit. Behind the counter stood Bartow, representing both institutions, as treasurer of the one and cashier of the other. He received the money and entered it in the pass-book of Mrs. Carrigan as deposited with the institute. He testifies that thereupon he placed the money in the cash-drawer of the bank. What became of it we do not know. Neither of the litigants entered upon an inquiry. What we do know is only that the money so received was not entered upon the cash-book of the bank, nor in any manner credited to the institute. When, at night, the cash was counted and compared with the books, it balanced very nearly, and no large surplus seems to have been disclosed. The value of this test as a basis for an inference is badly damaged by disclosures affecting the accuracy of the cash account of the bank. Balances were often forced; erasures and changes were frequent and unexplained; and at one time for several days there was a difference of about $6,000 between the cash on hand and the balance shown by the books. In addition another circumstance appeared. On the 25th of April, 1876, the same depositor appeared to withdraw a portion of her money. Bartow paid her from the money of the bank $2,000 and entered it in her pass-book, but no entry was made upon the books of either the bank or the institute, and yet at night no shortage appeared. This remarkable cash account adjusted itself to the situation without betrayal of the deficiency. Upon this state of facts the General Term held that there was no proof of a deposit in the bank. The opinion indicates a belief that the money was taken by Bartow while it remained the money of the institute, and before risk and responsibility attached to the bank. We do not concur in that conclusion. The arrangement between the two corporations about which there is no dispute precludes such a theory. Out of the double agency of Bartow, and under the agreed manner of business, it necessarily resulted that while as between Mrs. Carrigan and the institute Bartow received the money as its treasurer, yet as between the bank and the institute at the same instant and at the moment it reached his hands, he received it as cashier and on deposit with the bank. Under the arrangement no possible interval could exist between the receipt of the money and the deposit in the bank, during which Bartow, the individual, could stand between Bartow, the treasurer, and Bartow, the cashier, and by a novel sort of "stoppage *in transitu*," prevent the money from passing at once into the ownership of the bank. Even though he formed the intention of converting the money to his own use, the moment it was placed upon the counter and did so convert it immediately after having placed it in the cash-drawer, and when the depositor was gone and nobody observed, still it had become the money of the bank at the instant of its receipt. By the same identical act he received it as treasurer and held it as cashier, and if he embezzled it, he took the money of the bank for which it was responsible, whether the responsibility was confessed by a proper entry in the books, or not. The case is not altered if we disbelieve Bartow's statement that the money went primarily into the cash-drawer. There is no reason for doubting that statement, except such general distrust of Bartow as his conduct quite justifies. But admitting that it did not go into the drawer, still the general agreement as to the course of business made it the money of the bank on deposit for the institute the moment it passed from the control of the depositor, for the officer who took it as treasurer upon the instant retained it as cashier. The suggestion of the learned counsel for the respondent of a delivery of the money to Bartow as treasurer in the street, and the conclusion then to be drawn need not trouble our judgment, for such a transaction might prove to be outside of the agreed arrangement and possibly not controlled by it. In the case of *Bartow* v. *People* (78 N. Y. 377) such an outside delivery occurred, but under circumstances which led this court to decide that it was received by Bartow as cashier, and as the money, not of the institute, but of the bank. We see no just reason why we should not give effect in the present case to the agreement of the parties dictating the mode of business. Under it no formal delivery and no separate act was needed to transfer title from the treasurer to the cashier. Under it, title passed at once, and the money received for the institute at the same moment became a deposit in the bank.

The second item rejected by the General Term grew out of a different state of facts. A check for $5,000, drawn by E. and A. C. Kent on Chase & Atkins, and which belonged to the institute was presented at the bank and received by Bartow. It was payable on its face to him as treasurer. He indorsed it as such and then indorsed it as cashier, but gave no credit for

it to the institute.   Under the general arrangement above described this check became at once the property of the bank.
The indorsements were made accordingly, and the institute
was, at once, entitled to credit for the amount.   But the further
history of the check was developed.   On the 5th of April,
Bartow remitted it to Wilmerding & McCanliss, brokers in
New York, who had an account with the defendant bank, in a
letter signed by him as cashier and stating it was for credit.
They received and collected it and put it to the credit of the
bank in their account.   The receiver denounces this account
as a fraud, and as being merely a convenient depository for
Bartow's plunder.   The directors of the bank knew nothing of
it, but that does not relieve the corporation from the act of
the officer within the general scope of his authority.   To some
extent the account did represent actual transactions with the
bank.   To some extent also it probably served as a cover for
Bartow's diversion of the funds intrusted to his care.   The
evidence indicates that the check as a credit balanced two drafts
of $2,000 and $3,000, respectively, which were drawn for the
benefit of the bank, but this inference is made questionable by
Bartow's admission, made under oath in 1877 to the bank examiner that the $5,000 was used by him.   It is not necessary
to study and attempt to unravel the contradictions and difficulties which surround this branch of the case.   Enough appears
to show that this check, like Mrs. Carrigan's money, was received by Bartow as treasurer, but held and indorsed and
remitted by him as cashier, and under the general arrangement
determining the mode of business became at once a deposit in
the National Bank, for which the institute was entitled to
credit.

For similar reasons we think the General Term were wrong
in rejecting the Fowler check.   This was drawn upon the
defendant bank to the order of Bartow, treasurer, indorsed by
him as such, the check charged to Fowler in the bank accounts
but no credit given for it to the institute.   At the moment of
the receipt of this check and its indorsement by Bartow, treasurer, it became the property of the bank and entitled the insti-

tute to a corresponding credit. The construction of the respondent is that the check was paid to Bartow, treasurer. As between the bank and Fowler the check was paid, but the proceeds on the instant were re-deposited to the credit of the institute. The proceeds of the check were not drawn out by Bartow as treasurer. If he took its amount from the cash-drawer he took the money of the bank ; but took it as a wrong-doer. The check, when indorsed by him as treasurer, became at once, under the existing arrangement, the voucher of the bank, and represented so much money deposited to the credit of the institute, and any conversion thereafter either of the check or its proceeds was a conversion of the property of the bank for which it was accountable to the institute.

The order of the General Term should be reversed, and the judgment of the referee affirmed, with costs.

All concur.

Order reversed and judgment affirmed.

———————

JEREMIAH BRIDGES, as Supervisor, etc., Appellant and Respondent, *v.* THE BOARD OF SUPERVISORS OF THE COUNTY OF SULLIVAN, Appellant and Respondent.

Under the provision of the act (Chap. 296, Laws of 1874) subjecting the property of the N. Y & O. M. R. R. Co. to taxation, and appropriating the amount of the county taxes thereon, in any town which has issued bonds in aid of the construction of the road of said company, to such town, to be devoted to the payment of its bonds, after any such tax has been collected, the moneys belong to the town, and any diversion thereof from their lawful object is an injury to the rights of the town, which may be protected by an appropriate action in its behalf.

The town is not confined to the remedy given by the act (§ 4), *i. e.*, an action against the collector and the sureties upon his bond.

The action on behalf of the town might, under the Revised Statutes (2 R. S. 473, § 92), have been properly brought by the supervisor of the town, and may be so brought under the Code of Civil Procedure (§ 1926).

Where, therefore, the warrant issued to the collector of such a town required him to pay over the moneys so collected to the county treasurer, which command the collector obeyed, instead of paying the amount collected to the railroad commissioners of the town, as prescribed by the act (§ 3), *held*, that an action as for moneys had and received was properly brought by the supervisor of the town against the board of supervisors of the county to recover the amount so paid.

People, ex rel. Martin, v. *Brown* (55 N. Y. 180), distinguished.

Also *held*, that it was no defense to the action that the county had received no more money from the town for taxes than it was entitled to receive under the general statutes of the State; that it was the duty of the board of supervisors, in making an apportionment of the taxes for county purposes, after the passage of said act, to lay out of view the amount so withdrawn by the act and to assess generally, upon the county at large, a sufficient sum to cover the county charges, in addition to the tax for county purposes levied upon the property of the railroad, in the towns specified.

But *held*, that the act only appropriated to the towns that portion of the taxes in question known and described as county taxes; that they were not entitled to receive the portion collected for State purposes.

(Argued May 2, 1883 ; decided June 5, 1883.)

APPEAL from judgment of the General Term of the Supreme Court, in the third judicial department, entered upon an order made May 2, 1882, which modified, and affirmed as modified, a judgment in favor of plaintiff, entered upon a decision of the court on trial without a jury. (Reported below, 27 Hun, 175.)

This action was brought by plaintiff, as supervisor of the town of Liberty, in the county of Sullivan, to recover, in behalf of the town, the county taxes assessed upon the property of and collected from the New York and Oswego Midland Railroad Company, during the years 1874 to 1878 inclusive, under the act chapter 296, Laws of 1874, to which the town claimed a right under said act.

The collector of said town, obeying the direction of the warrants issued to him, paid over said taxes to the county treasurer, who refused to pay the same over to the railroad commissioners of the town, as did also defendant, the board of supervisors.

The amount of taxes for State and county purposes so collected and paid over, during the years specified, was $2,303.26, of which sum $745.93 was for State purposes. The trial court decided that plaintiff was entitled to recover the full amount, with interest from the time of the demand. The General

Term modified the judgment by deducting therefrom the amount collected for State purposes, with interest.

Samuel Hand for appellant. As a corporation the town of Liberty has no right to or interest in the money raised or appropriated to pay interest or principal on said bonds, and, of course, cannot sue for it as for money had and received. (*People, ex rel. Martin,* v. *Brown,* 55 N. Y. 180, 187; *Lorillard* v. *Town of Monroe,* 11 id. 399; *Gaillor* v. *Herrick,* 42 Barb. 79–85; *Gallatin* v. *Loucks,* 21 id. 578; *Murdock* v. *Aiken,* 29 N. Y. 67; *Ross* v. *Curtis,* 31 id. 606; *First Nat. B'k* v. *Wheeler,* 72 id. 201; Laws of 1866, chap. 398, §§ 4, 7, 8; Laws of 1874, chap. 296, § 2.) When a statute creates a new right unknown to the common law, and gives a remedy, he who would claim the right of the statute must pursue the remedy given by it. In such case the remedy given by the statute is exclusive. (*Durant* v. *Supvrs. of Albany Co.,* 26 Wend. 90; *Dudley* v. *Mayhew,* 3 N. Y. 9, 16; *McKean* v. *Caherty,* 3 Wend. 495; *Renwick* v. *Morris,* 7 Hill, 575; *Alma* v. *Harris,* 5 Johns. 175; *Stafford* v. *Ingersoll,* 3 Hill, 39; *Weyburn* v. *White,* 22 Barb. 83; *Bevens* v. *Rood,* 2 Sandf. 436; *Fowler* v. *Van Surdam,* 1 Denio, 557; *First Nat. B'k* v. *Whitehall,* 57 Barb. 429; *Smith* v. *Lockwood,* 13 id. 209–217; *Matter of B'k of Buffalo,* 2 Keyes, 249; *Handley* v. *Moffat,* 21 W. R. 231; *St. Pancras* v. *Battenbury,* 2 C. B. [N. S.] 477; 3 Jur. [N. S.] 1106; 26 L. J. C. P. 243; *Miller* v. *Taylor,* 4 Burr. 2305.) If the remedy provided by the fourth section of the act of 1874 is not exclusive, there can be no doubt that the remedy should have been by *mandamus* to compel the town collectors to pay the money to the railroad commissioners, and the proceedings should be in their favor. (*People* v. *Brown,* 55 N. Y. 180; Moses on Mandamus, 99; *Adsit* v. *Brady,* 4 Hill, 630.) The duties imposed by the tax laws upon boards of supervisors, of examining the assessment-rolls and equalizing the valuations of real estate, and setting down in the assessment-roll the respective sums to be paid as taxes, are judicial. (*Bellinger* v. *Gray,* 51 N. Y. 610; *Barhyte* v.

Shepherd, 35 id. 238; *Hill* v. *Selick,* 21 Barb. 207; 1 R. S. [Banks' 6th ed.] 942; *People* v. *Supv'rs of Schenectady,* 35 Barb. 408; *Swift* v. *City of Poughkeepsie,* 37 N. Y. 511.) The board of supervisors have received no money belonging to the town, and have done nothing which they not only had no right, but which they were not compelled by direct statute to do. (Laws of 1874, chap. 296; 1 R. S. [Banks' 6th ed.] 135, 942, 948; *People* v. *Hillhouse,* 1 Lans. 87; *Bellinger* v. *Gray,* 51 N. Y. 619; *Swift* v. *City of Poughkeepsie,* 37 id. 511; *City of Rochester* v. *Town of Rush,* 80 id. 302.) The railroad property in the county and in the town of Liberty, because it is subject to assessment and has been returned by the town officer himself as part of the assessable property of the town, could not be left out of a levy by the supervisors. (1 R. S. [Banks' ed.] 929, § 11; id. 943, §§ 49–53; id. 396, § 37.) The acts of 1866 and 1874 are in *pari materia,* and should be construed together. (*Smith* v. *People,* 47 N. Y. 330; *Rogers* v. *Bradshaw,* 20 Johns. 735; *Rexford* v. *Knight,* 15 Barb. 627.) The decision of the board of supervisors could only be reversed by appeal to the State assessors or perhaps by *certiorari.* (*Halsey* v. *Mancius,* 7 Johns. Ch. 174; *People* v. *City of Brooklyn,* 49 Barb. 136; *White* v. *Coatsworth,* 6 N. Y. 137; *Embrey* v. *Conner,* 3 Comst. 511; *People* v. *Sturtevant,* 15 Seld. 263–266; *Wilcox* v. *Jackson,* 13 Peters, 511; 1 R. S. [Banks' 6th ed.] 946–949.) The moneys sought to be recovered having been received in good faith by the county treasurer, under the direction of the board of supervisors, and in the discharge of his duty, and paid out by him under provisions of law, cannot be recovered back. (1 R. S. [6th ed.] 957; *Shotwell* v. *Murray,* 11 Johns. Ch. 512; *Lyons* v. *Richmond,* 2 id. 51; *Clark* v. *Dutcher,* 9 Cow. 674; *Champlin* v. *Taylor,* 18 Wend. 407.)

T. F. Bush for respondent. By force of the act of 1874 (Chap. 296), the amount of county taxes collected from the railroad property in plaintiff's town became the property of the town as soon as it came to the hand of the collector.

(*Newman* v. *Supvrs. of Liv. Co.*, 45 N. Y. 676.) The money having been paid to the county treasurer and by him used for the benefit of the county, a cause of action accrued to the town for money had and received to its use. (*B'k of Commonwealth* v. *Mayor*, 43 N. Y. 186; *Chapman* v. *City of B'klyn*, 40 id. 372; *Hill* v. *B'd of Supvrs.*, 12 id. 61; *Newman* v. *Supvrs. of Liv. Co.*, 45 id. 676; *Dewey* v. *Supvrs. of Niagara Co.*, 2 Hun, 392; *Union Nat. B'k* v. *Mayor*, 51 N. Y. 637; *Town of Lewis* v. *Marshall*, 56 id. 663; *Town of Chautauqua* v. *Gifford*, 8 Hun, 152; *Hathaway* v. *Town of Cincinnatus*, 62 N. Y. 434.) The action was properly brought in the name of the supervisor. (*Hathaway* v. *Town of Cincinnatus*, 62 N. Y. 434; *Hathaway* v. *Town of Homer*, 54 id. 655; 5 Lans. 267; *Town of Chautauqua* v. *Gifford*, 8 Hun, 152; *Town of Guilford* v. *Cooley*, 58 N. Y. 121.) The amount required from the county by the State each year for general State purposes is charged to the county and becomes a county debt. (*Merchants' Nat. B'k* v. *Supvrs. of N. Y.*, 3 Hun, 156; Affirmed, 62 N. Y. 629; 1 Statutes at Large, 359.) The intention of the law-maker is to be sought, first of all, in the language employed, and if the letter of the statute is free from ambiguity there is no occasion to resort to other means of interpretation. (*People* v. *N. Y. C. R. R. Co.*, 13 N. Y. 78; *Jackson* v. *Lewis*, 17 Johns. 477; *Benton* v. *Wickwire*, 54 N. Y. 226; *McCluskey* v. *Cromwell*, 11 id. 602.) The acts of 1874 and 1871 (Chap. 283) are in *pari materia*, and may be examined together to ascertain the intention of the legislature. (Bacon's Abr., title Stat., 1, 5, 10; *People* v. *Utica Ins. Co.*, 15 Johns. 358; *Dresser* v. *Brooks*, 3 Barb. 429; *Goodrich* v. *Russell*, 42 N. Y. 177; *Plummer* v. *Murry*, 51 Barb. 201; *Smith* v. *People*, 47 N. Y. 330; *Rogers* v. *Bradshaw*, 20 Johns. 735.) The fact that this statute prevents these moneys from going into the State treasury, or under its management, is quite different from an act taking money " out of the treasury of the State" or from under its management. (*Wallack* v. *Mayor of N. Y.*, 3 Hun, 84; *Darlington* v. *Mayor*, 31 N. Y. 164.) The general right to make exemptions is involved in the right to tax and to apportion taxes, and must be understood to exist wherever it is not forbidden. (Cooley on Taxation, 145.)

RUGER, Ch. J. This action was properly brought in the name of the supervisor of the town. Section 92 of article 4, title 4, chapter 8 of the third part of Revised Statutes expressly gives a right of action to the supervisors of towns for any injuries done to the property or rights of such officers or of the bodies represented by them. This right of action was continued in such officers by section 1926 of the Code of Civil Procedure upon the repeal of the provisions of the Revised Statutes. The action having been commenced prior to the adoption of the Code, the existing legal rights of the parties were by express provision preserved, and will, therefore, be governed by the provisions of the Revised Statutes if upon examination it appears that any injury has been done to the rights of the town represented by the plaintiff.

The supervisor of a town is in a general sense its treasurer. He is entitled to receive all moneys raised for town purposes except those which are expressly directed to be paid to the town officers having charge of highways and bridges, schools and the support of the poor. (1 R. S. [7th ed.], § 1, p. 826.) He is also directed to pay all judgments recovered against the town from any moneys in his hands which are not otherwise specially appropriated. (3 R. S. [7th ed.], § 106, pp. 2403–4.) The statute thus assumes that he is the legal custodian of the moneys of the town and chargeable with the duty not only of receiving and keeping them, but also of guarding their disbursement, and also recognizes to a certain extent the corporate existence of towns and their capacity to hold property, to protect its possession, and to enforce their *quasi* corporate rights by appropriate action.

It has been urged that the case of *People, ex rel. Martin,* v. *Brown* (55 N. Y. 180) is an authority against this position. That was an application by the railroad commissioners of the town of Hancock against the town collector, who had received the taxes assessed upon its tax payers, to compel him to pay over a part thereof to them for application upon the town bonds. The act under which such taxes were collected (§ 4, chap. 398, Laws of 1866), as well as the warrant of the supervisors authorizing such collection expressly directed the collector to pay a certain portion of such tax to the railroad commissioners for the purpose of satisfying the claims of the bondholders of the town for current interest on its obligations. The act gave the town, as such, no interest in the moneys collected and they were levied and gathered by agencies beyond its direction or control. It was held that such moneys did not become the property of the town, and, therefore, their payment to the supervisor of the town by the collector was a violation of his duty as prescribed by the warrant of the supervisors. Judge ANDREWS, delivering the opinion of the court, says: "The supervisor of the town has, under the act of 1866, no duty to perform in respect to the disbursement of the money raised for railroad purposes in the town." "The money does not belong to the town. It was not collected out of its corporate property or by its direction, nor is it liable for the act either of the board of supervisors or of the collector in levying or collecting it."

This case as well as all others cited on this point are clearly distinguishable from the present one. Here the warrant of the supervisors required the collector to pay the sum collected from the railroad corporation to the county treasurer instead of the railroad commissioners. This was an unauthorized direction. The act authorizing the imposition of the tax (Chap. 296, Laws of 1874) expressly gives to the town in its capacity as a *quasi* corporation the right to and benefit of money so collected. Section 2 of said act reads: "All moneys to be collected upon the real or personal property of the said corporation in any of the towns or municipalities by which bonds have been issued in aid of the construction of the New York and Oswego Midland railroad *are hereby appropriated to said towns or municipalities respectively.*" Although such moneys are by the act specially devoted to the purpose of paying the principal and interest upon the bonds of the town and cannot be legally diverted from such purpose, yet the equitable if not the legal title of the town to them, until they are finally applied to such object, cannot be questioned. After their collection, such moneys, whether in the hands of the collector, supervisor or railroad commissioners are the property of the town, and any diversion from their lawful object and purpose by any person occasions an injury to the rights of the town which may be protected by an appropriate action in its behalf, brought in the name of the officer authorized to institute the same. Whatever question might arise upon a conflict of authority between the supervisor and railroad commissioners over the custody and possession of such moneys, it is immaterial in this case to discuss. It is enough to say here that the rights of the town have been invaded and that the supervisor is a proper person to bring an action for the protection of such rights. (*Hathaway* v. *Town of Cincinnatus*, 62 N. Y. 434.) It was also claimed that this statute created a new right unknown to the common law, and having given a remedy for the protection of such rights, that it was exclusive and none other could be pursued in case of the invasion of this right. The grounds upon which this argument was attempted to be supported were that the exemption from taxation of the property of the New York, Oswego and Midland Railroad Company, created by the act of 1866, having been removed by the act of 1874, and that act having extended the liability of the sureties on the bond of a town collector to failure to pay over the taxes collected from such corporation, in addition to their liability on account of a default in paying over the general taxes of the town, that a new right was created, and the only remedy for a violation of such right arose upon the collector's bond. It is perhaps sufficient to say in answer to this claim that the new right, if any, which was created related to the enforcement of the payment of taxes against the railroad corporation alone, and not to the liability of the collector to account for the property of the town after it had come into his possession. That was not a right created by the statute, but existed at common law and the remedy provided had no reference to the rights which the town had previously acquired in the moneys so collected. (*Almy* v. *Harris*, 5 Johns. 175; *Stafford* v. *Ingersol*, 3 Hill, 38.)

The right of the town to the moneys collected having become perfected upon their receipt by the collector from the railroad corporation it became entitled to the same remedies for the protection of its rights of property as exist for the enforcement of similar rights in the case of individuals. The rules regulating the rights of owners of property attached to these moneys when they came into the collector's hands, and the town was authorized to pursue any remedies, which any property-owner lawfully might, to establish its interest in such property. The embezzlement of such funds would be punishable criminally, and the moneys themselves could be pursued into the hands of third persons and reclaimed by appropriate civil action. The principle contended for would apply only in favor of the party as against whom the new right was created; it certainly could not be invoked by a wrong-doer as against the party whose right under the statute had ripened into a vested interest.

It is further argued that this action cannot be maintained for the reason that the county of Sullivan has received no more money from the town of Liberty for taxes than it was justly entitled to receive under the general statutes of the State. In other words, it is claimed that being entitled to assess upon the tax payers of the town of Liberty their proportionate share of the taxes required to be raised in the county of Sullivan for county purposes, and having collected and received no more than such share from the collector of that town, they are not liable to refund to the town any part of the moneys so received by them.

This action was brought to recover from the defendant the amount collected from the New York and Oswego Midland Railroad Company in the town of Liberty as taxes for county purposes which had been paid over to the county treasurer during the years 1874, 1875, 1876, 1877 and 1878 by the collector of such town. The right of the town to this money was claimed to have been conferred by chapter 296 of the

Laws of 1874.   That statute provides in the first place for the
repeal of the law exempting the property of the New York
and Oswego Midland Railroad Company from the operation of
the general laws of the State imposing taxation upon property; it then proceeded to appropriate a portion of the taxes
thereafter to be levied and collected from the property of such
railroad to the several towns and municipalities respectively
which had issued bonds in its aid.   Then follows this section :
"It shall be the duty of the collector of taxes of each such
town or municipality to pay over to the said commissioners of
his town or municipality the amounts of the county taxes collected by him from the said corporation on the real and personal property thereof within five days from the time the same
is collected, and the said commissioners shall give to the said
collectors a receipt for the amount of county taxes so received,
which said receipt shall be returned to the treasurer of the
county in which the said collector shall reside."

This act is not assailed as being unconstitutional, and no reason is alleged by the appellant justifying any disobedience to
its provisions by any person or officer who is thereby required
to perform any duty.   The language of the act is plain and
unambiguous, and there seems to be no insuperable difficulty in
the way of carrying out its provisions.

The object of the act was, evidently, to confer exclusively upon
the several towns in the State who have aided in the construction of this railroad the benefit of the taxes from the increased
value given to property by its appropriation and use for railroad purposes and which was derived by means of their liability.   That portion of the tax authorized to be levied upon
such property for county purposes was in each year expressly
directed by the act to be withheld from the county where it
would otherwise have gone, and paid over to the railroad commissioners of the several towns respectively entitled thereto for
their use and benefit.

The plain duty of the board of supervisors was, therefore,
in making an apportionment of taxes among the several towns
of the county for county purposes in each year subsequent to

the passage of the act, to lay out of view the several amounts thus withdrawn from them by the act of 1874 and to assess generally upon the county at large a sufficient sum to cover the county charges in addition to the taxes for county purposes levied upon railroads.

The statute not only authorized but enforced this upon the board of supervisors in the several counties through which this railroad was laid and wherein towns were bonded in its aid, and authorized the insertion in their warrants issued for the collection of taxes appropriate provisions to carry out the object of the act. Thus it was held in *People, ex rel. Martin,* v. *Brown* (*supra*), that chapter 398 of the Laws of 1866, authorizing the collection of taxes for the payment of interest upon bonds issued by the several towns of the State in aid of the New York and Oswego Midland railroad, and the payment of such taxes to town railroad commissioners, gave authority to the board of supervisors to change the general form of their warrants as prescribed by the Revised Statutes and to insert therein a direction to the collector to pay such moneys to the railroad commissioners of the towns.

The defendants here, instead of requiring the collector of the town of Liberty to pay the taxes in question to their railroad commissioners as the statute imperatively demanded, directed him to pay such moneys to their own treasurer, and the town collector for the years specified has obeyed such direction and paid these moneys into the county treasury. The moneys thus specifically given to the town by the statute have been appropriated by the county to its own use, and it is no answer to an action to recover them back to plead that the county has received no more money than the law entitled it to levy upon and collect from the county at large. The question relates to these specific moneys. The county is neither entitled to these moneys nor to an equivalent amount from the town of Liberty. It is entitled to receive from the tax payers of that town only that proportion of such amount which its assessed valuation bears to the aggregate valuation of the taxable property of the whole county, and this amount is collectible only through the general tax levy. The only question here is to whom, " *Ex æquo et bono*," do the specific moneys levied from the railroad corporations for county taxes during the years named belong. We think that they unquestionably belong to the town. The county has simply failed to collect a sufficient sum to pay its county charges for the several years during which it has unlawfully appropriated the moneys of the town to its own uses. It should now refund them to the town to whom the statute gave them, and an action for money had and received is the appropriate remedy to accomplish this result. (*Hill* v. *Board of Supervisors*, 12 N. Y. 52; *Newman* v. *Supervisors of Livingston Co.*, 45 id. 676; *Dewey* v. *Board of Supervisors of Niagara Co.*, 62 id. 294.)

The question raised by the plaintiff as to the amount of the recovery was correctly disposed of by the General Term. The statute under which this action is brought recognizes and describes four purposes of taxation, viz.: State, county, town and municipal. When it appropriates to the town that portion described as county taxes it obviously means to distinguish the sum given from the other objects of taxation described in the same act.

There is no reason for supposing that the legislature intended to use the same word in the same act to convey two manifestly different meanings.

We are, therefore, of the opinion that the judgment should be affirmed, and as each party has failed in his appeal, no costs should be awarded to either in this court.

All concur.

Judgment affirmed.

MORRIS MOREY, Respondent, *v.* FRANCIS W. TRACEY, Appellant.

An action may be brought under the Code of Civil Procedure (§ 1937), after the recovery of a judgment against joint debtors, by the judgment creditor "against one or more of the defendants who were not summoned in the original action," although the defendants served have appealed and have given the security, which under said Code (§ 1810) "stays all proceedings to enforce the judgment appealed from."

The second action is not brought to enforce the judgment but to establish the liability of the defendants not served, which is not determined by such judgment.

(Submitted May 8, 1888 ; decided June 5, 1888.)

APPEAL from judgment of the General Term of the Superior Court of the city of Buffalo, entered upon an order made March 27, 1882, which affirmed a judgment in favor of plaintiff, entered on the report of a referee.

This action was brought under section 1937 of the Code of Civil Procedure, after a judgment upon a joint undertaking to charge the defendant here, who was a defendant in the prior action, but who was not served with the summons.

The defendant who was served appealed from the judgment giving the undertaking required to stay proceedings. Pending the appeal this action was brought. The defense, among other things, was that plaintiff was stayed by the undertaking from bringing the action.

Further facts are stated in the opinion.

Bowen, Rogers & Locke for appellant. The undertaking given by the defendant Tifft, in the action by this plaintiff against Tifft and Tracy, stays all proceedings to enforce the judgment pending the appeal in that case. (Code, §§ 1310, 1937, 1940, 1941; *Butchers & Grocers' B'k* v. *Willis*, 1 Edw. Ch. 645.)

E. C. Sprague for respondent. The statute of limitations does not run against a cause of action where an appeal has been perfected and an undertaking given to stay proceedings. (Code of Civ. Pro., §§ 406, 1309 ; Code of Procedure, §§ 105, 348 ; *Maples* v. *Mackey*, 89 N. Y. 146. ; The stay granted on the undertaking given by Tifft in the original action is not a bar to this action. (Code of Civ. Pro., §§ 1310, 1935.) This

is not an action upon the former judgment in any such sense
as claimed by defendant. (*Oakey* v. *Aspinwall*, 4 N. Y. 513,
535, 540; *Lane* v. *Salter*, 51 id. 1; *Brum* v. *Brooker*, 4 Denio,
56; *Foster* v. *Wood*, 1 Abb. [N. S.] 150; 30 How. Pr. 284.)

ANDREWS, J.   The judgment against George W. Tifft and
Francis W. Tracy, rendered upon their joint undertaking as
sureties upon the successive appeals in the suit of *Davis* v.
Read et al., was in form against both defendants, upon service of process upon Tifft alone.   The defendant Tracy was
not served with the summons, nor did he appear in the action.
Tifft appealed from the judgment and gave the requisite undertaking to stay proceedings.   The plaintiff, pending the
appeal by Tifft brought this action against Tracy, under section 1937 of the Code, and the sole question is whether the
provision of section 1310, that, when an appeal is perfected
and security given, " the appeal stays all proceedings to enforce
the judgment appealed from," is a defense.   The answer is
plain.   The action is not brought to enforce the original judgment.   The original judgment bound the defendant served and
authorized execution to go against his separate property or the
joint personal property of both defendants.   These are the
only rights flowing from the judgment, and their enforcement
was stayed by the appeal.   The present action is not an action
to enforce the plaintiff's rights under the original judgment,
or to obtain the fruits of it.   Its sole object is to establish
Tracy's liability on the original contract, which was not determined by the original judgment, and of which it was no
evidence.   If there had been no stay, the plaintiff would have
been compelled to proceed against Tracy by action, to enforce his
personal liability.   It is not material whether this action is regarded as an action in form on the judgment, or upon the
original contract.   It is not an action to enforce the judgment,
and this is all that the stay prevents.   The plaintiff could not
rest on the judgment, to maintain his action.   The liability of
Tracy could only be established by evidence *aliunde*, and Tracy
could interpose any defense which he might have made in the

original action. (Code, § 1039.) The primary object of section 1310, was to protect the party appealing from having the judgment enforced against him while the right was in controversy, on condition of giving security for the final judgment. The defendant is not in a position to interpose the stay secured by Tifft, as a defense to a proceeding instituted to determine rights not adjudicated by the former judgment.

The judgment should be affirmed.

All concur.

Judgment affirmed.

MARGARET A. DICKINSON, Appellant, *v.* THE MAYOR, ALDERMEN AND COMMONALTY OF THE CITY OF NEW YORK, Respondent.

Plaintiff's complaint alleged that defendant "improperly, carelessly, negligently and unlawfully suffered ice and snow to be and remain upon the crosswalk," at the intersection of two streets in the city of New York ; that in consequence thereof, plaintiff, while passing over said crosswalk, was thrown to the ground and injured, and plaintiff asked to recover the damages sustained. *Held*, that the action was "to recover damages for a personal injury resulting from negligence" within the meaning of the provision of the Code of Civil Procedure (§ 383), limiting the time for the commencement of such action to three years.

Irvine v. *Wood* (51 N. Y. 228), *Clifford* v. *Dam* (81 id. 56), *Sexton* v. *Zett* (44 id. 431), *Creed* v. *Hartmann* (29 id. 591), *Congreve* v. *Smith* (18 id. 82), distinguished.

The provision of said Code (§ 410) providing that where "a demand is necessary to entitle a person to maintain an action, the time within which the action must be commenced must be computed from the time when the right to make the demand is complete," is applicable to actions against the city of New York.

Such an action is not saved from the operation of said provision by the provision (§ 3341) declaring that "any special provision of the statutes remaining unrepealed * * * which is applicable exclusively to an action" against said city shall not be affected by the Code.

The provision of the charter of said city of 1873 (§ 105, chap. 335, Laws of 1873) providing that no action shall be maintained against the city "unless the claim upon which the action is brought has been presented to the comptroller and he has neglected for thirty days after such presentment to pay the same" was intended for the benefit of the city, not of claimants, and does not deprive the city of the benefit of the said provision as to the time when the statute of limitations begins to run.

Accordingly, *held*, that, as it was set forth in the complaint that the accident happened in January, 1877, and that the claim was presented to the comptroller in April, 1881, the action was barred.

Fisher v. Mayor, etc. (67 N. Y. 76), distinguished.

(Submitted May 3, 1883; decided June 5, 1883.)

APPEAL from judgment of the General Term of the Supreme Court, in the first judicial department, entered upon an order made at the November term, 1882, which affirmed a judgment entered upon an order sustaining a demurrer to a count of the defendant's answer. (Reported below, 28 Hun, 254.)

The complaint in this action among other things alleged that the Eighth avenue, in the city of New York, is a public thoroughfare, and that it was and is the duty of the defendant to keep and maintain the streets and avenues of said city, including the said Eighth avenue, in good order and repair, and not to suffer ice or snow to be or remain in such a rough and uneven condition on the crosswalks thereof as to be unsafe and dangerous to foot passengers. That the defendant "improperly, carelessly, negligently and unlawfully suffered ice or snow to be and remain upon the crosswalk on the east side of Eighth avenue, at the intersection of Eighteenth street, in the city of New York, in such a rough and uneven condition that a person could not walk over it without danger of falling down," and by reason thereof "the plaintiff, on or about the 10th day of January, 1877, while lawfully passing over and upon said crosswalk, and without any fault on her part, was suddenly precipitated, cast and thrown upon the ground, thereby fracturing her left thigh or hip." It then alleges the damages suffered by her, for which she claims to recover, to be $15,000, and that on the 28th day of April, 1881, the plaintiff presented the claim on which this action is brought, in writing, to the comptroller of the city of New York, and demanded payment thereof, but that he has neglected for thirty days after such presentation to pay the same.

To this alleged cause of action the defendant, for its fourth answer, alleged " that more than three years have elapsed since the cause of action set forth in the complaint accrued, and that the right of the plaintiff to make the demand necessary to entitle her to maintain an action therefor was complete more than three years before the commencement of this suit."

Clifford A. H. Bartlett for appellant. The continuance of a defect or obstruction in a public street, which it is the duty of the city to remove, is a nuisance. (Dillon on Mun. Corp., §§ 520, 541, 764; *King* v. *Russell*, 6 East, 430; *Hines* v. *Lockport*, 5 Lans. 19; Angell on Highways, §§ 223, 225; *West* v. *Brockport*, 16 N. Y. 172; *Brower* v. *Mayor*, 3 Barb. 258; *Robinson* v. *Chamberlain*, 34 N. Y. 389, 390; *Hutson* v. *Mayor*, 9 id. 169; *Ham* v. *Mayor*, 37 Sup. Ct. 468.) Ice or snow suffered to remain for a long time in a rough and uneven condition on a public street is a nuisance. (9 Md. 178; *Kirby* v. *Boylston Market Assoc'n*, 80 Mass. 249, 251, 252; *Cook* v. *City of Milwaukee*, 24 Wis. 274; *McAuley* v. *Boston*, 113 Mass. 505; *Street* v. *Holyoke*, 105 id. 85; *Stone* v. *Hubbardston*, 100 id. 56, 57; *Luther* v. *Worcester*, 97 id. 272; *Hutchins* v. *Boston*, 94 id. 572, note; *Stanton* v. *Springfield*, id. 569; *Savage* v. *Bangor*, 40 Me. 179; *Smyth* v. *Bangor*, 72 id. 251; *Collins* v. *Council Bluffs*, 32 Iowa, 328; *McLaughlin* v. *City of Corry*, 77 Penn. St. 113; *Hubbard* v. *Concord*, 35 N. H. 69; *Hodges* v. *Hodges*, 46 Mass. 211; *Wenzlick* v. *McCotter*, 87 N. Y. 128; *Swords* v. *Edgar*, 59 id. 34; *Billings* v. *Worcester*, 102 Mass. 333.) In cases of nuisances no question of negligence is involved. (Shearman and Redfield on Negligence, §§ 84, 363; *Muller* v. *McKesson*, 73 N. Y. 204; *Woolf* v. *Chalker*, 31 Conn. 130; *Irvine* v. *Wood*, 51 N. Y. 228; *Clifford* v. *Dam*, 81 id. 56; *Sexton* v. *Zett*, 44 id. 431, 432; *Creed* v. *Hartman*, 29 id. 597; *Congreve* v. *Smith*, 18 id. 82;

Dygert v. *Schenck*, 23 Wend. 447; *Nichols* v. *Marshland*, L. R., 10 Exch. 259, 260; 22 Hun, 61, 62; *Eakin* v. *Brown*, 1 E. D. Smith, 45, 46.) The right of action did not accrue until demand was made upon the comptroller. (Laws of 1873, chap. 335, § 105; *Fisher* v. *The Mayor*, 67 N. Y. 76; *Taylor* v. *The Mayor*, 52 How. 78; *Moser* v. *Mayor*, General Term, May, 1879; Code of Civ. Pro., § 3341.)

D. J. Dean for respondent. In the case at bar the alleged injury sustained by the plaintiff has been occasioned by the negligence of the defendant in omitting to perform the duty resting upon it in relation to caring for the streets, and is within the six years' limitation. (Code, § 382.) The period within which the plaintiff's action must be commenced under the statute began to run against the plaintiff when the right to make the demand was complete. (Code, § 3341; *Meehan* v. *Mayor*, 28 Hun, 642.) The statutes requiring demand to be made upon the city, prior to the commencement of an action, do not, upon principle, postpone the operation of the statute of limitations until such demand has been made. ·(Laws of 1873, chap. 335, § 105; *Fisher* v. *The Mayor*, 67 N. Y. 73; *Van Wart* v. *The Mayor*, 52 How. 78; *Brust* v. *Barrett*, 16 Hun, 409; *Stafford* v. *Richardson*, 15 Wend. 302; *Lyle* v. *Murray*, 4 Sandf. 590; *Palmer* v. *Palmer*, 36 Mich. 487; *White* v. *Southland*, 2 Alb. Law Jour. 50; *Sweet* v. *Irish*, 36 Barb. 467; *Payne* v. *Gardner*, 29 N. Y. 146.)

MILLER, J. The complaint in this action alleges, mong other things, that the defendant improperly, carelessly, negligently and unlawfully suffered ice or snow to be and remain upon the crosswalk on the east side of Eighth avenue at the intersection of Eighteenth street in the city of New York, and that, by reason thereof, plaintiff sustained injuries for which she seeks to recover damages in this action. The appellant's counsel claims that the limitation within which the action must be brought is six years for the reason that the continuance of a defect in the public street is a nuisance which it is the duty of the city to remove; that being such no question of negligence is involved, and that the legislature has provided different limitations for actions for personal injuries resulting from negligence and actions for personal injuries otherwise than from negligence. In this case it appears that the snow and ice were formed on the crosswalk from causes over which the defendant had no control. The allegations in complaint tend to establish that the defendant neglected to perform a duty by not removing the ice and snow from the walk. This was not an averment for keeping, maintaining and suffering a nuisance, but merely for negligence in not removing the ice and snow. The complaint was not for a positive wrong committed by the defendant, but for an injury sustained by reason of defendant's negligence. The authorities establish a distinction between an action for wrong and an action for negligence. (*Muller* v. *McKesson*, 73 N. Y. 204; 29 Am. Rep. 123; *Irvine* v. *Wood*, 51 N. Y. 228; 10 Am. Rep. 603; *Clifford* v. *Dam*, 81 N. Y. 56; *Sexton* v. *Zett*, 44 id. 431; *Creed* v. *Hartman*, 29 id. 591; *Congreve* v. *Smith*, 18 id. 82.)

In the cases cited no question of negligence was presented and the causes of action arose from a wrongful act of the defendants, which produced the injury aside from the negligent act or conduct of the defendants.

Some authorities are cited by appellant's counsel to sustain the doctrine that any obstruction or act, which unnecessarily incommodes or impairs the lawful use of the highway by the public, is a nuisance. Conceding the correctness of the rule laid down we do not think it is applicable to a case where the gist of the action, as alleged here, is the carelessness and negligence of the defendant and where the alleged obstruction is the mere casual existence of snow and ice which was not caused by any act of the defendant or allowed to remain by a positive wrongful act. We have examined the authorities cited by the appellant's counsel in regard to the liability of municipal corporations to keep their streets in repair and to prevent and remove obstructions, but we think that none of them go to the extent of holding that mere negligence in failing to remove a temporary obstruction of itself constitutes a nuisance which renders the defendant liable for a wrong, where such obstruction is only claimed to have been carelessly and negligently caused. A case may arise where, if ice and snow are suffered to remain for a long time in a rough and uneven condition on a public street, it may constitute a nuisance. (*Mayor, etc.,* v. *Marriott,* 9 Md. 178.) No such cause of action is alleged in the complaint in this case. It is evident that the injury to the plaintiff, as alleged in the complaint, was caused by the negligence of the defendants in omitting to perform the duty imposed upon it in relation to taking care of the streets. The plaintiff, to establish her case, must show that the defendant has failed to use ordinary diligence. It is not alleged that any act of the defendant caused the accumulation of the ice or snow, and the action is founded upon the negligence alone in omitting to perform a public duty and not upon a wrongful act in constructing an obstacle which created a nuisance. It is plain, therefore, that the cause of action alleged in the complaint is for a personal injury resulting from negligence.

The action being based upon negligence solely and not maintainable unless brought within three years, the next question which arises is whether the statute of limitations commenced to run against the plaintiff before the demand was made upon the comptroller. Section 105 of the charter provides that " no action shall be maintained against the mayor, aldermen and commonalty of the city of New York unless the claim on which the action is brought has been presented to the comptroller, and he has neglected for thirty days after such presentment to pay the same," and it is urged that the right of action did not accrue until such demand was made. The Code (§ 410) provides that " where a right exists, but a demand is necessary to entitle a person to maintain an action, the time within which the action must be commenced must be computed from the time when the right to make the demand is complete ;" and by section 3341 it is declared that " each provision of this act is to be construed as not affecting any special provision of the statutes remaining unrepealed after the former provision takes effect, which is applicable exclusively to an action against the mayor, aldermen and commonalty of the city of New York, including the recovery, entry and collection of a judgment in such action." It is insisted that under this saving clause the provisions of section 410 do not apply to actions against the city. We think that this construction of the statute cannot be maintained, and that this provision relates to and is intended to enforce the special statutory provision which authorizes and regulates actions against the city, and the application of the statute of limitations is not thereby affected. The intent and purpose of section 105 of the charter was mainly to enable the comptroller to settle claims against the city and thereby save unnecessary costs and expenses in the litigation which must ensue. We think that it was not intended to indefinitely extend the time in all cases within which an action might be brought against the city and thus put in the power of the claimant to delay, without any limitation whatever, and thereby in some instances to deprive the corporation of the benefit of testimony which otherwise might have been adduced in defense against an action brought. The statute was for the benefit of the city and not for the benefit of the claimant. It was not designed to repeal the statute of limitations as to the city and thus deprive it of a defense which belongs to and is the inherent right of ordinary litigants except in cases where it is specifically otherwise provided. The rule insisted upon might operate very oppressively against a municipal corporation whose means of knowledge of claims against it of the nature of the one in controversy could only be acquired through its officers and then generally after a presentation of the same. This construction has been upheld in the Supreme Court in case of *Meehan* v. *Mayor, etc.* (28 Hun, 642). The appellant's counsel relies upon certain authorities cited, which it is claimed sustain the doctrine that the statute of limitations does not begin to run until demand made upon the comptroller. The principal case relied upon is *Fisher* v. *Mayor, etc.* (67 N. Y.

76), which is we think clearly distinguishable from the case at bar. In that case the action was brought to recover the amount of an award for lands taken by virtue of chapter 86 of the Laws of 1813, section 183. That statute provided that the award should be payable to the parties after application to the mayor, etc., thus giving to the plaintiff a cause of action upon strict fulfillment of all the conditions therein prescribed. It will thus be seen that the right of action depended upon the statute, and an adherence to its requirements was essential to maintain it; a demand, therefore, was a part of the cause of action and necessary to be alleged and proven, and without this no cause of action existed.

Under the section of the charter cited (§ 105) the demand required was a condition of maintaining the action and not an essential part of it, upon which the inception of a right is based and the cause of action founded. It is thus manifest that in the case cited the statute gave the cause of action and that it did not exist at common law alone. In the case at bar the cause of action arose upon the principles of the common law and was perfect and complete when the injury occurred to the plaintiff by reason of the negligence of the defendant. It is obvious that there is a plain distinction between the two cases and that the former is not in point.

We have examined the other cases to which our attention has been called, and none of them we think sustain the position contended for by the appellant's counsel.

The judgment should be affirmed.

All concur.

Judgment affirmed.

In the Matter of the Application of MARY CLEMENTI, Respondent, *v.* THEODORE F. JACKSON, Registrar, etc., Appellant.

The act of 1882 (Chap. 363. Laws of 1882) validating (so far as the same remain unpaid) certain taxes in the city of Brooklyn, which were invalid because of the omission of the assessors to verify the assessment-rolls as prescribed by the city charter (§ 31, title 4, chap. 384, Laws of 1854, as amended by § 21, chap. 63, Laws of 1862) did not validiate a sale, made prior to its passage because of non-payment of such a tax ; nor did it validate the penalties by way of interest and expenses, imposed by statute for the non-payment of a tax ; it simply validated the tax with interest at the rate specified (§ 2) from the date of confirmation, on condition that the property owner might discharge it by paying the amount specified.

The acts chapter 348, Laws of 1882, and chapter 448, Laws of 1881, have no application to such a case.

A payment by a purchaser at a tax sale, prior to the passage of the act, is not a payment of the tax. Notwithstanding the sale the tax " remains unpaid" within the meaning of the act, and the property owner is entitled to the benefit of said condition, and upon refusal of the registrar of arrears of the city to accept the amount specified, is entitled to a *mandamus* to compel the acceptance thereof and the discharge of the tax.

The purchaser at the tax sale is not a necessary party to the proceeding by *mandamus.*

(Argued May 4, 1888 ; decided June 5, 1888.)

APPEAL from order of the General Term of the City Court of Brooklyn, made December 28, 1882, which affirmed an order of Special Term directing the issuing of a peremptory writ of *mandamus* directed to defendant as registrar of arrears in the city of Brooklyn, requiring him to receive of the petitioner the amount of taxes imposed upon her premises in said city for the years 1868 and 1869, with interest thereon from the time of the original confirmation of said taxes at the rate specified in the act chapter 363, Laws of 1882, and to discharge and cancel the lien of said taxes.

Prior to the passage of the said act the petitioner's property had been sold for the payment of said taxes, the purchase-money paid and leases had been executed to the purchaser. In October, 1882, the petitioner tendered to defendant the amount of the taxes with interest at the rate of six per cent from the date of the original confirmation by the board of supervisors, which he refused to accept.

Alfred E. Mudge for appellant. The taxes were not unpaid within the meaning of section 2 of chapter 363 of the Laws of 1882. (Laws of 1862, chap. 63, § 26, p. 196 ; *Brevoort* v. *City of Brooklyn*, 89 N. Y. 128.)

Nicholson P. O'Brien for respondent. The remedy of the relator for the grievance complained of is by writ of *mandamus* to compel the registrar of arrears of the city of Brooklyn to discharge and perform the statutory duties of the municipal department under his charge. (*Swift* v. *Mayor*, 83 N. Y. 535; *Francis* v. *Common Council of Troy*, 78 id. 36–7; *People* v. *Board of Supvrs.*, 64 id. 604; 73 id. 175; *Frey* v. *Canal Appraisers*, id. 443.) The relator has shown herself legally and equitably entitled to the writ, having done every thing required as a condition precedent to the right demanded. (*Stevens* v. *Hoyt*, 66 N. Y. 606; Code, §§ 2082 and 452, 1204; *People* v. *Supervisors*, 73 N. Y. 175; *People* v. *Board of Apportionment*, 64 id. 627; *Albany Inst.* v. *Burdick*, 87 id. 40; *Derham* v. *Lee*, id. 599.) The omission of the assessors, in verifying the corrected assessment-roll, to insert an averment to the effect that they have together personally examined within the year past each and every lot or parcel of land, house, building or other assessable property within the ward, as required by the statute (charter of 1854), rendered the assessment-roll defective, and failed to give jurisdiction to the board of supervisors to impose a tax. (*Van Rensselaer* v. *Wisbeck*, 7 N. Y. 517; *Westfall* v. *Preston*, 49 id. 349; *Billinger* v. *Gray*, 51 id. 610; *Bradley* v. *Starr*, 58 id. 401; *People* v. *Suffern*, 68 id. 321; *Merritt* v. *Vil. of Port Chester*, 71 id. 309; *Brevoort* v. *City of Brooklyn*, 89 id. 128.) Moneys received by an unauthorized sale cannot be considered a payment. (*Chapman* v. *City of Brooklyn*, 40 N.Y. 372, 8–9; *Peyser* v. *Mayor*, 70 id. 500; *Beekman* v. *Brigham*, 7 id. 366; *Rathbone* v. *Hooney*, 58 id. 463.) The conveyance to Brower was illegal and void, even if the tax and sale were legal, as he never served the notice required by section 27, or complied with section 28 of the charter. (*Williams* v. *Townsend*, 31 N. Y. 414; § 27, title 5 of charter.) The statute of 1882 (Chap. 363) was a remedial act, and must be read and construed according to the natural and obvious import of the language contained in it and the object to be obtained by its enactment. (*People* v. *Supvrs.*, etc., 43 N.Y. 132; *Goillotel* v. *Mayor of N. Y.*, 87 id. 445; *Astor* v. *Mayor*, 62 id. 575–8; *Dannat* v. *City of New York*, 77 id. 50; *Risley* v. *Smith*, 64 id. 576.)

RAPALLO, J. Under the decision of this court in *Brevoort* v. *The City of Brooklyn* (89 N.Y. 128), the taxes in question were illegally assessed and the assessment was void. This is not disputed by the appellant. The sales of respondent's property for the non-payment of these taxes were consequently also void, and the purchaser acquired no right or title to respondent's property by virtue of those sales or of the leases subsequently granted.

Chapter 363 of the Laws of 1882 did not validate those sales. It validated the taxes, but only *sub-modo*. It did not validate the penalties by way of interest and expenses, which would have been a lien on respondent's property, and for non-payment of which, as well as the original taxes, the property was sold, but the validating act was accompanied by the condition that the taxes thus validated and remaining unpaid should be payable with interest at the rate of six per cent per annum, from the date of the original confirmation thereof by the supervisors, provided such payment be made before the 1st of December, 1882, and if not so paid, then that interest should be collected thereon at the rate of nine per cent per annum from the date of such original confirmation. This was the extent to which the taxes were validated. All the provisions of the act must be read and construed together, and thus read and construed, it appears that these void taxes were made valid only on condition that property owners might discharge them by paying the reduced amount specified in the act. It could not have been the intention of the act that if the city had attempted to enforce payment of these void taxes, by sales and leases, the validation should stand and the landowners be deprived of the provision for their benefit, which was one of the terms upon which the legislature cured the defect in the assessment of the taxes.

Chapter 348 of the Laws of 1882 has no bearing on this case. That was not an act to validate void taxes or assessments, but a gratuitous rebate from taxes and assessments supposed to be valid, made for the purpose of inducing prompt payment. It permitted " any person *owing* the city of Brooklyn any taxes, assessments or water-rents," to pay the same at any time before the 1st of December, 1882, with interest at six per cent per annum from the date of confirmation.

Chapter 443 of the Laws of 1881 also assumed the taxes to be valid, and provided for their collection. It was not passed for the validation of void taxes or assessments.

It is contended by the appellant that the respondent was not entitled to the benefit of the portion of the act of 1882 (Chap. 363) which was beneficial to her, because that provision applied only to such of the void taxes validated by the act as *remained unpaid*, and that in her case the taxes did not remain unpaid, as the purchaser at the tax sale had paid them.

We do not think that the payments made by the purchaser were payments of the taxes. He did not make the payments for the benefit of the relator, or in her behalf, nor for the purpose of discharging the property from the lien of the taxes, but made them in his own behalf, for the purpose of acquiring an interest in the property by virtue of the sales made by the city to enforce that lien, in consequence of the non-payment of the taxes and penalties. The payments made by him were no more a payment of the taxes than would a payment made by an assignee to an assignor of a bond, in consideration of the assignment thereof, be a payment of the bond.

We are of opinion, therefore, that it was the duty of the appellant to accept the sum tendered to him by the respondent, pursuant to section 2 of the act of 1882 in discharge of these taxes.

The further point that the purchaser at the tax sales was a necessary party to this proceeding is not, we think, tenable. He had no right or title to the property if the sales were void, and if they were valid, or were made so by the act of 1882, the payment of the taxes by the relator would not affect him. This proceeding is not for an adjudication upon the title, but is a matter wholly between the relator and the respondent, to compel the latter to perform a statutory duty, the effect of which, in case of dispute, must be determined hereafter. The purchaser at the sales is no more proper a party to such a proceeding than would an adverse claimant of title to land be to a proceeding by *mandamus* to compel a county clerk to record a deed or satisfaction piece affecting the title.

The question whether the purchaser can recover back the sums paid on the tax sales is one between him and the city and does not concern the relator.

The order should be affirmed, with costs.

All concur.

Order affirmed.

BURR B. ANDREWS, Appellant, *v.* THE ÆTNA LIFE INSURANCE COMPANY OF HARTFORD, Respondent.

In an action to recover back premiums paid upon certain policies of life insurance issued by defendant, each of which when delivered contained a provision that the policy would "be good at any time, after three payments, for its equitable value," the complaint, after alleging the issuing of the policies and the payment of more than three years premiums, averred, in substance, that plaintiff, having concluded not to continue to pay premiums, demanded of defendant the equitable value of the policies, and on its refusal to allow the same, commenced an action to recover such equitable value ; that thereafter defendant notified plaintiff that said provision was inserted in the policies without its authority or consent, and set up such claim in the answer. Whereupon the plaintiff discontinued the said action, and paid the taxable costs thereof. *Held*, that assuming the first action was discontinued in consequence of said averments in the answer, defendant was not estopped, as it did not damage plaintiff, because whether the clause was part of the contract or not the former action could not have been sustained ; that the clause if binding upon defendant imposed no obligation upon the company to pay any thing until plaintiff's death ; it simply continued the policies in force for their equitable value in case no further payments were made.

It appeared upon the trial of this action that the notice referred to was a letter written to defendant's secretary, which, while it asserted that the clause was written in the policies without authority, stated that defendant was willing to perform it, and the answer in the former action which asserted that the clause was inserted without authority denied that defendant had refused to pay the equitable value. *Held*, that this was an unequivocal election on the part of defendant to affirm or ratify the alleged unauthorized act, and so the proceedings in the former action furnished no basis for an equitable estoppel.

The court refused to submit to the jury the questions as to the original validity of the policies, and whether they had been affirmed by defendant. *Held* no error; because, *first*, no such issue was tendered by the complaint; *second*, the evidence of ratification was so conclusive there was no question for the jury.

A principal upon being informed of an unauthorized act of an agent has a right to elect whether he will adopt it or not, and so long as the condition of the parties is unchanged, cannot be prevented from such adoption by the fact that the other party prefers to treat the contract as invalid.

An election once made, however, is irrevocable.

(Argued May 4, 1883; decided June 5, 1883.)

APPEAL from judgment of the General Term of the Supreme Court, in the third judicial department, entered upon an order made May 2, 1882, which affirmed a judgment in favor of defendant, entered upon an order nonsuiting plaintiff on trial.

This action was brought to recover back money paid by the plaintiff to the defendant for premiums on four policies of insurance on the life of the plaintiff, issued by the defendant November 17, 1866.

It is reported upon a former appeal in 85 N. Y. 334.

The policies when delivered, each contained the following clause: "And it is agreed that this policy shall be good at any time after three payments for its equitable value." The complaint after alleging the issuing of the several policies, and the payment by the plaintiff of cash premiums thereon to the amount of $875.25 on each policy, further alleged that prior to the 26th day of December, 1876, the plaintiff, having concluded not to continue the payment of premiums, demanded of the defendant the equitable value of the policies, which the defendant refused to allow further than to surrender the notes of the plaintiff, had by the defendant, for the part of the premiums not paid in cash, being four notes of $491 each; that the plaintiff thereupon, on the 26th day of December, 1876, commenced an action in the Supreme Court to recover the equitable value of the policies; that after the commencement of said action the defendant notified the plaintiff that the clause in the policies, in respect to the payment of equitable value, was inserted without the consent or authority of the defendant, and plaintiff alleged that this was the first notice he had of such claim; that the defendant, in its answer in said action, alleged that the agent, who took the application of the plaintiff for insurance, inserted said clause without the knowledge or consent of the defendant, and without authority, " whereupon " (the complaint continues) " the plaintiff discontinued the said action, and paid the defendant the taxable costs thereof." The complaint concludes by demanding judgment for $5,061.11 (the amount of premiums paid in cash), with interest thereon, besides the costs of the action

Further facts appear in the opinion.

R. A. Stanton for appellant. If the policies had been altered without the knowledge or consent of the company, then they were not the contract of the company as they stood. The plaintiff never accepted any other contract than the policies as they stood with the non-forfeiture clause in them. (1 Parsons on Contracts, Book 2, chap. 2, § 1; *Barlow* v. *Scott,* 24 N. Y. 40; *White* v. *Continental Nat. B'k,* 64 id. 319; *Day* v. *N. Y. C. R. R. Co.,* 51 id. 591; *Eben* v. *Lorillard,* 19 id. 302; *Utter* v. *Stewart,* 30 Barb. 20; *Delavigne* v. *United Ins. Co.,* 1 Johns. Cas. 310; *Murray* v. *United Ins. Co.,* 2 id. 171.) A fact necessarily implied from the facts stated forms a part of the pleading as much as if specifically alleged, and a direct allegation of such fact is never necessary. (2 Wait's Pr. 315; *Farron* v. *Sherwood,* 17 N. Y. 230; *Prindle* v. *Caruthers,* 15 id. 426; *Hosley* v. *Black,* 28 id. 443; *Allen* v. *Patterson,* 7 id. 476.) Every element exists in the evidence upon which to base an estoppel against the defendant as to the insertion of the clauses in question. (*Finnegan* v. *Carraher*, 47 N. Y. 493; *Abeel* v. *Van Gelder*, 36 id. 514; *Trustees of Presbyterian Congregation* v. *Williams*, 9 Wend. 147; *Hall* v. *White*, 3 C. & P. 135; *Frost* v. *S. Mut. Ins. Co.*, 5 Denio, 157; Coke's Lit. 352, A.; *Pickard* v. *Sears*, 6 A. & E. 469; *Muller* v. *Pondir*, 55 N. Y. 334; *Cont. Nat. B'k* v. *Nat. B'k Commw.*, 50 id. 575; *Mooney* v. *Elder*, 56 id. 233; *Bradner* v. *Howard*, 75 id. 417; *Glackin* v. *Zeller*, 52 Barb. 152; *Lambertson* v. *Van Buskirk*, 4 Hun, 628; *O. & M. R. R. Co.* v. *McCarthy*, 6 Otto, 258; *Brown* v. *Bowen*, 30 N. Y. 519, 540.) The doctrine of relation is an equitable fiction to protect and effectuate substantial rights. It is not a doctrine to be applied to cut off equities and to further wrongs, or cover up frauds or promote injustice. (*Gilbert* v. *Sharp*, 2 Lans. 414; *Bliss* v. *Cottle*, 32 Barb. 325; *Clark* v. *Peabody*, 22 Me. 530; *Fiske* v. *Homes*, 41 id. 442; *Gorham* v. *Gale*, 7 Cow. 737.) It was properly a question of fact for the jury, as to whether or not the company had affirmed or disaffirmed the policies with these clauses in them. (*Ritch* v. *Smith*, 82 N. Y. 627; *First Nat. B'k* v. *Morgan*, 73 id. 593; *Jellinghaus* v. *N. Y. Ins. Co.*, 8 Bosw. 282; *Justice* v. *Lang*, 52 N. Y. 323; *Harris* v. *N. Ind. R. R. Co.*, 20 id. 232; *Downs* v. *Sprague*, 2 Keyes, 60; *Le Roy* v. *Park F. Ins. Co.*, 39 N. Y. 56; *Hart* v. *Hudson R. B. Co.*, 80 id. 622; *First Nat. B'k* v. *Dana*, 79 id. 108; *Quick* v. *Wheeler*, 78 id. 300; *Newberry* v. *Wall*, 84 id. 576; *Backus* v. *Shipherd*, 11 Wend. 634; *Foot* v. *Wiswell*, 14 Johns. 304; *White* v. *Hoyt*, 73 N. Y. 506.) It was error to exclude proof of the advice which plaintiff's counsel gave him after the receipt of the letter of January 15, 1877, from the company in reference to the continuance of the action, by way of showing the object of continuing that action. (*Norton* v. *Mallory*, 63 N. Y. 434, 438; Abbott's Trial Evidence, 602, 655, 741; *Hall* v. *Suydam*, 6 Barb. 83.) It is too late on appeal for the defendant to raise the objection that the policies should have been surrendered by the plaintiff. (*Thayer* v. *Marsh*, 75

this act is to be construed as not affecting any special provision of the statutes remaining unrepealed after the former provision takes effect, which is applicable exclusively to an action against the mayor, aldermen and commonalty of the city of New York, including the recovery, entry and collection of a judgment in such action." It is insisted that under this saving clause the provisions of section 410 do not apply to actions against the city. We think that this construction of the statute cannot be maintained, and that this provision relates to and is intended to enforce the special statutory provision which authorizes and regulates actions against the city, and the application of the statute of limitations is not thereby affected. The intent and purpose of section 105 of the charter was mainly to enable the comptroller to settle claims against the city and thereby save unnecessary costs and expenses in the litigation which must ensue. We think that it was not intended to indefinitely extend the time in all cases within which an action might be brought against the city and thus put in the power of the claimant to delay, without any limitation whatever, and thereby in some instances to deprive the corporation of the benefit of testimony which otherwise might have been adduced in defense against an action brought. The statute was for the benefit of the city and not for the benefit of the claimant. It was not designed to repeal the statute of limitations as to the city and thus deprive it of a defense which belongs to and is the inherent right of ordinary litigants except in cases where it is specifically otherwise provided. The rule insisted upon might operate very oppressively against a municipal corporation whose means of knowledge of claims against it of the nature of the one in controversy could only be acquired through its officers and then generally after a presentation of the same. This construction has been upheld in the Supreme Court in case of *Meehan* v. *Mayor, etc.* (28 Hun, 642). The appellant's counsel relies upon certain authorities cited, which it is claimed sustain the doctrine that the statute of limitations does not begin to run until demand made upon the comptroller. The principal case relied upon is *Fisher* v. *Mayor, etc.* (67 N. Y.

76), which is we think clearly distinguishable from the case at bar. In that case the action was brought to recover the amount of an award for lands taken by virtue of chapter 86 of the Laws of 1813, section 183. That statute provided that the award should be payable to the parties after application to the mayor, etc., thus giving to the plaintiff a cause of action upon strict fulfillment of all the conditions therein prescribed. It will thus be seen that the right of action depended upon the statute, and an adherence to its requirements was essential to maintain it; a demand, therefore, was a part of the cause of action and necessary to be alleged and proven, and without this no cause of action existed.

Under the section of the charter cited (§ 105) the demand required was a condition of maintaining the action and not an essential part of it, upon which the inception of a right is based and the cause of action founded. It is thus manifest that in the case cited the statute gave the cause of action and that it did not exist at common law alone. In the case at bar the cause of action arose upon the principles of the common law and was perfect and complete when the injury occurred to the plaintiff by reason of the negligence of the defendant. It is obvious that there is a plain distinction between the two cases and that the former is not in point.

We have examined the other cases to which our attention has been called, and none of them we think sustain the position contended for by the appellant's counsel.

The judgment should be affirmed.

All concur.

Judgment affirmed.

In the Matter of the Application of MARY CLEMENTI, Respondent, v. THEODORE F. JACKSON, Registrar, etc., Appellant.

The act of 1882 (Chap. 363, Laws of 1882) validating (so far as the same remain unpaid) certain taxes in the city of Brooklyn, which were invalid because of the omission of the assessors to verify the assessment-rolls as

were insufficient to establish it. The court on the second trial
nonsuited the plaintiff on the ground that the case was controlled by the decision of this court on the first appeal.

It is claimed that the nonsuit was erroneous, upon two
grounds; *first*, that the case upon the point of estoppel was
changed in material respects on the second trial, so as to obviate
the objections to the former judgment on that ground; and
second, that the court erred in refusing to submit to the jury
the question whether the equitable value clause was authorized,
and further, whether if inserted without authority, the company had affirmed the policies after having been informed of
its existence. Upon the point of estoppel we are of opinion
that the case has not been materially changed. 1. The discontinuance of the first action, assuming that it was discontinued
in consequence of the defendant's assertion in the answer in
that suit, that the provision for equitable value was inserted
without authority, did not damage the plaintiff, although in
fact the assertion was untrue. Whether the clause was a part
of the contract, or not, that action could not be supported.
The clause if valid and binding upon the defendant, imposed
no obligation upon the company to pay any thing on the policies, except in the event of the plaintiff's death. It simply
continued the policy in force after three payments of premiums had been made, for its equitable value, in case no further payments should be made. The words "at any time,"
were inserted apparently to negative a possible construction
that the election to discontinue further payments, in order to
give the insured the benefit of the clause, must be made after
three payments and before any further payments were made,
and cannot reasonably be construed as imposing an obligation
to pay the equitable value during the life of the insured. The
plaintiff, therefore, never had a cause of action to recover the
money, or equitable value of the policies, assuming that the
company was bound by the provision in question. He had
elected to discontinue the payment of premiums . before any
question arose as to the validity of the policies. His only
right was to await the maturing of the contract, and leave to

his representatives after his death to demand its performance. Whatever reason, therefore, may have influenced the plaintiff to discontinue the first action, its discontinuance occasioned no legal damage.

.2. The first authoritative declaration on behalf of the company, that the equitable-value clause was inserted in the policies without authority, was made in the letter of January 15, 1877, written by the defendant's secretary to the plaintiff. But this assertion, as we construe the letter, was accompanied by an unequivocal election on the part of the company to affirm and ratify the alleged unauthorized act. The letter, after asserting that the claim was inserted without authority, and stating that the company knew nothing of the matter "until recently," proceeds: " But this is a point we do not wish to sustain here. We wish simply to convince you that the company is willing to grant all that you claim under that provision, even if it had been written at this office as a part of the policy." The letter then proceeds to argue the only question which up to that time had occasioned any controversy between the parties, viz.: whether the clause bound the company to pay the equitable value " in cash," as claimed by the plaintiff, or " in insurance," as claimed by the defendant. It is impossible to see how the commencement of the second action, and the incurring of expense and trouble in bringing it, can furnish a basis for an equitable estoppel, when the company, before it was commenced, although denying the original validity of the policies, nevertheless accompanied the denial with an election to affirm and ratify the disputed clause. It is unnecessary to refer to the other considerations bearing upon the alleged estoppel, presented on the argument. They are considered in our former opinion.

The exception to the refusal of the court to submit to the jury the question of the original validity of the policies, and whether they had been affirmed by the company, was not well taken. (1) No such issue was tendered by the plaintiff in his complaint. (2) The evidence of ratification is so clear and conclusive that a verdict to the contrary could not stand. The company ratified the policies, by the letter of January 15, 1877, by its retention of the premiums after knowledge of the alleged alterations, and it has never repudiated its liability. It is true that the answer in the first action sets up that the equitable-value clause was inserted without authority, and constituted no part of the policies, but the same answer denies that it has refused to pay their equitable value, and also sets up the outstanding notes as counter-claims. But if the answer may be deemed to contain an absolute denial of the validity of the policies, the prior conduct of the company effectually precluded it from questioning their validity. The principal, upon being informed of an act of an agent in excess of his authority, has the right to elect whether he will adopt the unauthorized act, or not, and so long as the condition of the parties is unchanged, he cannot be prevented from such adoption because the other party to the contract may for any reason prefer to treat the contract as invalid, and his election, once made, is irrevocable.

We think the nonsuit was properly granted, and the judgment should, therefore, be affirmed.

All concur.

Judgment affirmed.

THE MAYOR, ALDERMEN AND COMMONALTY OF THE CITY OF NEW YORK, Appellant, *v.* IRA DAVENPORT, Comptroller, etc., Impleaded, etc., Respondent.

The action of the State board of equalization in the discharge of the duty imposed upon it of equalizing " the State tax among the several counties of this State " (Chap. 312, Laws of 1859), is judicial in its character, and when it has acquired jurisdiction any error in its judgment or mistake in its conclusions can be asserted only in some direct proceeding for review.

The fact that said board did not have before it at its meeting a written digest of facts required by the statute (§ 7) to be prepared by the State assessors is not a jurisdictional defect, and is immaterial.

The fact that the board increased the valuation of a county without swearing and examining witnesses is immaterial ; that is the duty of the State assessors, and upon the information given by them to the board, it is authorized to act.

Nor does the fact that the board after a short secret session adopted a schedule of equalization prepared by one of the assessors affect the validity of its decision.

Losses from taxes for State purposes assessed in the city of New York, but not collected, are to be borne by the city, not the State, which is entitled to the whole amount.

Under its system of taxation the State deals not with individuals, but with counties as representing divisions or areas of taxation. The share or quota of each county is charged against it, and it is for it to make up any deficiency in the collections, save that the counties outside of New York are credited for uncollected taxes on non-resident lands. (Chap. 117, Laws of 1886 ; chap. 312, Laws of 1859; 1 R. S. 419, § 5 ; chap. 427, Laws of 1855.)

As to whether an action may be maintained by the city of New York against the State comptroller to recover alleged over-payments on account of taxes for State purposes, *quære*.

(Argued May 5, 1883 ; decided June 5, 1883.)

APPEAL from judgment of the General Term of the Supreme Court, in the first judicial department, entered upon an order made the 2d day of February, 1883, which affirmed a judgment, entered upon an order sustaining a demurrer to plaintiff's complaint.

The averments of the complaint, so far as material, are substantially stated in the opinion.

Francis Lynde Stetson and *James W. M. Newlin* for appellant.   The plaintiff is invested with both the power and the duty to protect its custody of all moneys in its treasury, or to be received therein, and to test the legality of all attempts to interfere therewith. (*U. S. v. R. R. Co.*, 17 Wall. 322–329 ; *People v. Ingersoll*, 58 N. Y. 34 ; *People v. Fields*, id. 491 ; *Webb v. The Mayor*, 64 How. Pr. 10 ; *People, ex rel. Root*, v. *Tappan*, 67 N. Y. 580.)   The board of equalization did not act within its powers.   Its power is solely that of reviewing the several county assessments for the purpose of apportioning the State tax. (*Nat. B'k of Chemung v. City of Elmira*, 53 N. Y. 53 ; *Bellinger v. Gray*, 51 id. 610 ; *Thompson v. Bur-*

hans, 61 id. 52; *Dorn* v. *Backer*, id. 261; *Avering* v. *Foote*, 65 id. 263; *People, ex rel. Hotchkiss*, v. *Burnham*, id. 223–226; *Phillips* v. *City of Stevens Point*, 25 Wis. 594; *Meek* v. *McClure*, 49 Cal. 624; *Wells, Fargo & Co.* v. *State Bd. of Equalization*, 56 id. 195; *Royce* v. *Jenny*, 50 Iowa, 676; *Dundy* v. *Richardson*, 8 Neb. 508; *Commrs. of Leavenworth* v. *Long*, 8 Kans. 284; *Paul* v. *P. R. R. Co.*, 4 Dill. C. C. 85; *Cummings* v. *Nat. B'k*, 11 Otto, 153.) The provisions of the statute relating to the duties of the State assessors and board of equalization are mandatory. (Laws of 1859, chap. 312, § 7; *Torry* v. *Millbury*, 21 Pick. 64–67; *Commw.* v. *Blair Co.*, 2 Pearson [Penn.], 419; *Davis* v. *Van Arsdale*, 59 Miss. 367; *Meek* v. *McClure*, 49 Cal. 624; *L. Assn. of Am.* v. *Bd. of Assessors of St. Louis County*, 49 Mo. 512; *Sharp* v. *Johnson*, 4 Hill, 92; *Young* v. *Joslin*, 26 Alb. L. J. 398; *Brevoort* v. *City of Brooklyn*, 89 N. Y. 128.) The law of 1874 (Chap. 147, § 1), requiring the plaintiff's chief financial officer, in advance of the receipt of taxes, to issue the plaintiff's bonds to the full amount of the State tax, and to pay the proceeds thereof into the State treasury, is a violation of the fundamental principles of constitutional law, and is of doubtful validity. (*People, ex rel. Auditor-Gen.*, v. *Supvrs. of Monroe Co.*, 26 Mich. 70, 76; *City of Phila.* v. *Cochran*, 4 W'kly Notes of Cases, 223; *Commw.* v. *Blair Co.*, 2 Pearson, 415.) Plaintiff is authorized to maintain an action for the redress or prevention of wrongs to its property. (*Jackson* v. *Hartwell*, 8 Johns. 425; *Todd* v. *Birdsall*, 1 Cow. 260; *Hempstead* v. *Hempstead*, Hopkins, 288; *Davidson* v. *Mayor*, 2 Robt. 256; *People* v. *Ingersoll*, 58 N. Y. 34; *Darlington* v. *Mayor*, 31 id. 164; *People* v. *Ingersoll*, 58 id. 21; *Wood* v. *Mayor*, 73 id. 556.) The action to redress or prevent the wrongs to the property of the plaintiff specified in the complaint may properly be brought against the defendants, including the comptroller of the State of New York. (*Belknap* v. *Belknap*, 2 Johns. Ch. 463; *Livingston* v. *Livingston*, 6 id. 467; *M. & H. R. R. Co.* v. *Archer*, 6 Paige, 83; *West. R. R. Co.* v. *Nolan*, 48 N. Y. 515; High on Ex. Leg. Remedies, chap. 2; *People* v. *Owen*,

· 17 How. Pr. 375; *Osborn* v. *Bank of U. S.*, 9 Wheat. 738; *Davis* v. *Gray*, 16 Wall. 220; *Arlington's Cases*, 5 Morrison's Transcript, 269.) The subjects of the action are within the jurisdiction of the court. (*Chegary* v. *Jenkins*, 5 N. Y. 376; *Wilson* v. *The Mayor*, 1 Abb. 15; *Nat. B'k* v. *City of Elmira*, 53 N. Y. 49; *Matter of N. Y. Cath. Protectory*, 77 id. 342; *Union Stmbt. Co.* v. *City of Buffalo*, 82 id. 357.) Plaintiff's second cause of action is not defective because it concerns moneys already paid by officers of the plaintiff. (*B'k of Comm.* v. *The Mayor*, 43 N. Y. 188; *Dewey* v. *Supvrs.*, 2 Hun, 395; *Peyser* v. *The Mayor*, 70 N. Y. 502; *Nash* v. *The Mayor*, 9 Hun, 220; *People* v. *Fields*, 58 N. Y. 491–505; *Suprs.* v. *Ellis*, 59 id. 620–625; *McGinnis* v. *The Mayor*, 6 Daly, 416.) The remedy as to both causes of action is by injunction. (*Hartwell* v. *Armstrong*, 19 Barb. 166; *Leigh* v. *Westervelt*, 2 Duer, 618; *Phœnix* v. *Commrs.*, 1 Abb. 466; *Gillespie* v. *Broas*, 23 Barb. 370; *Mace* v. *Trustees*, 15 How. 161; *Blake* v. *B'klyn*, 26 Barb. 301; Kerr's Injunctions in Equity, 181, *x*, *y*; High on Injunctions, §§ 493, 494; Bispham's Eq., § 424; *Torry* v. *Milbury*, 21 Pick. 64; *Cummings* v. *Nat. B'k*, 11 Otto, 153; *Wiley* v. *Hournoy*, 30 Ark. 609; *Chicago, etc., R. R. Co.* v. *Cole*, 75 Ill. 501; *Commrs., etc.,* v. *Long*, 8 Kans. 284; *Darling* v. *Gunn*, 50 Ill. 425; *Fratz* v. *Mueller*, 35 Ohio, 397; *Porter* v. *R. R. Co.*, 76 Ill. 564; *Paul* v. *R. R. Co.*, 4 Dill. 35; *R. R. Co.* v. *Sunnell*, 88 Ill. 535; *State R. R. Tax Cases*, 2 Otto, 575; *Kelly* v. *Pittsburgh*, 14 id. 78.)

Leslie W. Russell, attorney-general, for respondent. The State exercises no direct control over the local assessing or collecting officers, but intrusts the supervision of their conduct to the various counties, making the county authorities responsible for the amount of the tax to be paid by that subdivision. (Duke of York's Laws, published by authority of the secretary of Pennsylvania, in the year 1879, pp. 10, 47–49; chap. 133 of Laws of the Colony of New York by James Parker, printer, 1752; 2 R. S. [7th ed.] 1032; id. 1022, § 25; id. 996,

§ 37; Laws of 1855, chap. 427, § 8; Laws of 1862, chap. 456; Laws of 1867, chap. 670; Laws of 1870, chap. 705; Laws of 1874, chap. 462; Laws of 1879, chap. 372; Laws of 1881, chap. 453; *Union Ins. Co.* v. *Hoge*, 21 How. [U. S.] 35, 66; *State* v. *Vanderbilt*, 37 Ohio St. 641; *Easton* v. *Pickersgill*, 55 N. Y. 310; *People, ex rel.* v. *Dayton*, id. 367.) The city of New York has no interest whatever in the subject of this suit, and has no legal capacity to sue. (*City of Rochester* v. *Town of Lush*, 15 Hun, 239; *S. C.*, 80 N.Y. 302; *Sanders* v. *Vil. of Yonkers*, 63 id. 489; *Town of Guilford* v. *Cornell*, 18 Barb. 615; affirmed, 13 N. Y. 143; *Shoemaker* v. *Bd. of Commrs.*, 36 Ind. 175–183, 184.) The defendant cannot be sued for the cause of action set forth in the complaint. (*People* v. *Dennison*, 84 N. Y. 272; *Shoemaker* v. *Bd. of Commrs.*, 36 Ind. 175, 186; *State, ex rel. Drake,* v. *Doyle*, 40 Wis. 175, 176; *Carr* v. *U. S.*, 98 U. S. 433; Laws of 1859, chap. 312, § 8.) The courts in this case have no power of review of the legislative action on the subject of taxation. (Cooley on Taxation, 32; *People* v. *Mayor, etc., of B'klyn*, 4 N. Y. 419, 420; *Co. of Schuylkill* v. *Commw.*, 36 Penn. St. 524; Cooley on Taxation, 4; *Veazie B'k* v. *Fenno*, 8 Wall. 533, 548.) The courts have no power to review the action of the State board. (Laws of 1859, chap. 812, §§ 4, 7, 8; *St. Louis & V. R. R. Co.* v. *Surrell*, 88 Ill. 535; Cooley on Taxation, 291; *Porter* v. *R. R. Co.*, 76 Ill. 564; *Swift* v. *City of Poughkeepsie*, 37 N. Y. 511, 513; *Barhyte* v. *Shepherd*, 35 id. 238; *Weaver* v. *Devendorf*, 3 Denio, 117; *A. & W. S. R. R. Co.* v. *Town of Canaan*, 16 Barb. 244; *B., etc., R. R. Co.* v. *Supvrs. Erie Co.*, 48 N. Y. 93; *People* v. *Trustees of Ogdensburg*, id. 513, 518; *Bellinger* v. *Gray*, 51 id. 610, 618; *Genesee Val. N. B'k* v. *Supvrs. Liv. Co.*, 53 Barb. 223; *Western R. R. Co.* v. *Nolan*, 48 N. Y. 513, 519; *Strusburgh* v. *Mayor*, 87 id. 455; *Susquehanna B'k* v. *Supvrs. Broome Co.*, 25 id. 313.) It is of no avail to urge that the board of equalization violated its duty as to property in one section of the State, and that to do justice it should, therefore, have reduced the valuation in the city and county of New York, for New York is confessedly not assessed enough. (*People, ex rel. Youmans*, v. *Supvrs.*, 60 N. Y. 381, 385 ; *Wagoner* v. *Loomis*, 37 Ohio St. 571, 580–583 ; *Sanders* v. *Village of Yonkers*, 63 N. Y. 489.) The plaintiff was given a full opportunity to appear and be heard. It had ample notice of the time and place of meeting, and if it desired to be heard, or to prevent any action which might be deemed hostile to itself, it should have been represented in the only place open for review of unjust assessments between the different counties of the State. (Cooley on Taxation, 266 ; *State R. R. Tax Cases*, 92 U. S. 609 ; *Porter* v. *R. R. Co.*, 76 Ill. 561, 598 ; *Matter of Hermance*, 71 N. Y. 481–488.) The second cause of action set forth in plaintiff's complaint is, in effect, an attempt to recover from the State a specific sum of money. No such action could be maintained against the State directly. (*People* v. *Dennison*, 84 N. Y. 273 ; *Shoemaker* v. *Bd. of Commrs. of Grant Co.*, 36 Ind. 175, 186 ; *State, ex rel. Drake*, v. *Doyle*, 40 Wis. 175, 176 ; 1 R. S. [7th ed.] 463, § 1, subd .9 ; *Com. B'k of Rochester* v. *City of Rochester*, 41 Barb. 341 ; affirmed, 41 N. Y. 619 ; *Bonnell* v. *Griswold*, 68 id. 294 ; *Kinnier* v. *Kinnier*, 45 id. 535 ; *Bailey* v. *Buell*, 50 id. 602 ; *Drake* v. *Shurtleff*, 24 Hun, 422 ; *R. R. Commrs.*, 98 U. S. 541.) If the city of New York has a claim for moneys overpaid, there is only one remedy open to her. She may have, equally with other corporations and with natural persons, the equitable right of presenting her claim against the State. (Constitution of N. Y., art. 3, § 19 ; chap. 211, Laws of 1881.)

FINCH, J. The causes of action pleaded were tested by a demurrer, which the courts below have sustained. The city alleged two wrongs inflicted by the State. The first was an unjust and incorrect determination of taxable values by the board of equalization, which imposed upon the city more than its due share of the aggregate State tax. The second was a compulsory payment by the city, running through a period of twenty years, of taxes which could not be collected from the persons assessed. Such deficiencies exceeded two millions of dollars, for which the city claimed credit as against the State.

Both causes of action encounter preliminary difficulties before the merits are reached. The right of the city to sue is denied, upon the ground that, as a municipal corporation, it has no actual interest which can be affected; that it neither owns the money which may be, nor that which has been, collected from the tax payers; that its right to receive the State tax is solely for the purpose of paying it over, and it cannot turn its agency into an ownership; and that its issue of revenue bonds is authorized only for the purpose of enabling payment to be made to the State at the same time with the other counties, and in no respect confers new or different rights upon the city. It is further objected that the relief sought, though in form against the comptroller, is in fact against the State; that the latter is in reality the substantial defendant, and cannot thus be sued; and that equity will not interpose to prevent the collection of a tax, basing its refusal upon grounds of public policy and a due regard for the necessities of the State.

These questions are all interesting, and have been elaborately argued on both sides. But we deem it better to waive their consideration, since upon other grounds we have reached the conclusion that neither cause of action can be maintained.

The first is a collateral attack upon the decision of the State board of equalization, and rests wholly upon the theory that the action of that tribunal was without adequate foundation, and both unjust and erroneous. Whether in this collateral way, through a complaint against the comptroller, to which the board is not even a party, its conclusions can be reviewed, is the primary question to be determined. The process of equalization begins with the separate counties, and through the action of their boards of supervisors. The assessors of the several towns first make out their rolls and determine the valuations. In this respect they act judicially, and any erroneous decision can only be corrected by a direct review of their proceedings, whenever they have kept within their jurisdiction. If they have so acted, their conclusions cannot be assailed either by a suit at law against them, or against those who take the further steps toward collection based upon their action. (*Barhyte* v. *Shepherd*, 35 N. Y. 238; *Swift* v. *City of Poughkeepsie*, 37 id. 511; *Buffalo & S. L. R. R. Co.* v. *Supervisors of Erie Co.*, 48 id. 93; *People* v. *Trustees of Ogdensburgh*, id. 890.) The assessors deliver their rolls to the supervisors, who are thereupon required to equalize the valuations between the several towns so that they shall bear a just relation to each other. This duty is also judicial. The precise question was determined in *Bellinger* v. *Gray* (51 N. Y. 610). And what their duty is as between the towns of their county is exactly the duty of the State board as between the several counties. That duty is, therefore, of a judicial character, and if they have acquired jurisdiction, any error in their judgment, or mistake in their conclusions can be asserted only in some direct proceeding for a review.

The State board is composed of the State assessors and the commissioners of the land office. (Laws of 1859, chap. 312.) The former are required to visit every county in the State once in two years for the purpose of ascertaining the character of the valuations, and the real value of lands assessed. They are authorized to swear and examine witnesses; all papers and records are open to their scrutiny; and local officials are required to furnish them every needed information. The knowledge thus acquired they are directed to put in the form of a written digest for the use of the board of equalization, and the latter, acting upon its own knowledge, and that thus obtained, is required, on the first Tuesday in September in each year, to meet in the city of Albany, for " the purpose of examining and revising the valuations of the real and personal estate of the several counties as returned to the office of the comptroller, and fixing the aggregate amount of assessment for each county, on which the comptroller shall compute the State tax." The board, legally constituted, met at the appointed date. The county valuations returned to the comptroller were before them, and they thus had jurisdiction to revise and examine the valuations so returned. The defects pointed out by the complaint were in no respect jurisdictional, and the action of the board was not even shown to be irregular. It was alleged that the board " had before it no written digest of facts prepared by the State assessors." The law did not so require. It did command that the assessors should make such a digest ; and the complaint does not allege that it was not made. The purpose of it is declared to be to " aid " the board " in the discharge of its duties." Clearly this could not be a condition precedent to jurisdiction, for it assumes a duty entered upon in the performance of which the written digest may assist. Nothing in the complaint forbids the presumption that the digest was in fact made ; that the assessors who made it were familiar with its details ; that the other members of the board had seen and studied it, and thus prepared themselves for their duties ; and that it gave to each member of the board precisely the aid which the statute contemplated. Assuming these things, as we must, the absence of the written digest at the meeting of the board was not a matter of the least consequence.

It is further alleged that the board increased the valuation of the city without evidence. If this means that they did not swear and examine witnesses upon the subject, that is true but immaterial. The law did not require it, and contemplated no such means of information. The State assessors had been doing that, and exhausting in each county the knowledge thus obtainable. The board came to the performance of its duty with adequate preparation, and exactly of the character and from the sources which the statute contemplated. If the complaint means that such information was wanting, the allegation is neutralized by the distinct admission that they had " the general information possessed by members of the board in their acquaintance with the property contained in the State, and such oral general information as was conveyed to them by the State assessors, who had previously visited the various counties of the State," and by the legal presumption of the proper performance of official duty. It is thus sufficiently apparent that the board had and acted upon the kind of evidence and information which the law contemplated.

But it is said they adopted a schedule of equalization prepared by one of the assessors, and accepted it after a ten minutes secret session. Somebody had to prepare it. Often, and in many boards, some one willing shoulder lifts more than its proportion of the common burden. When, or how this schedule was made; how much of labor and patience it represented; and how many of the other members had impressed upon it the results of their own knowledge we do not know. It is our duty to assume that it was carefully framed, and being so, we have no warrant to measure its wisdom by the brief minutes allotted to its adoption. Such a test might make havoc with the last day's work of many legislatures.

But it is finally said, and that is the only important averment, that the assessed values of the city were more than sixty per cent of the actual and market value; while those of the other counties were less than sixty per cent of such real value; and yet the board of equalization added to the injustice by increasing the city valuation. If this is true, a great wrong was done, but it cannot be redressed in this action. The accusation touches not the jurisdiction of the board but the correctness of its judgment. Town assessors may, and possibly sometimes do, make very wrong estimates of the value of specific items of property, but it would hardly do to omit all complaint on the day of hearing, and neglect a direct review, and then ask for an injunction against the collector to prevent his levy. What is said in the case at bar is a criticism upon judicial action. It is the defendant in a judgment, who has taken no appeal, seeking to enjoin the execution because the court ought to have decided differently on the facts. It seems clear to us that we cannot heed such complaint in a collateral action. When this board met the doors were open, and the city could have been heard. Other counties appeared, and made their objections; New York did not. If dissatisfied, the injured county could have sued out a *certiorari*, but no such effort was made. At all events, whatever might have been or may hereafter be a proper remedy, we cannot in this action review the judgment of the appointed tribunal having jurisdiction and acting within its authority, but must treat its decision while unreversed as conclusive.

We come now to the second cause of action pleaded. The question in the end is whether the State is to bear the loss from taxes assessed but uncollected. For twenty years the city has paid them from the proceeds of its revenue bonds issued in advance of the tax collections, and then has failed, without fault or negligence on the part of its officers, to collect the equivalent amount and reimburse its treasury. But the revenue bonds have themselves been paid by the tax payers within the area or division denominated the city. Those bonds and their ultimate payment threw what are called, and what we may call, the deficiencies upon the tax payers of the city. What has occurred, therefore, is no more than this, that such tax payers have paid in full the tax of the city as they should have done, although not at one time and through one immediate process. What are called deficiencies are not such. They grow out of the process of distribution and apportionment. They represent a fraction of the tax due to the State and paid to the State, and to every dollar of which the State is entitled, but which, from one cause and another, cannot be collected of the persons liable, and so there is required a new distribution of burden upon the remaining tax payers. The State does not deal with individuals but with counties, as representing divisions or areas of taxation. It endeavors to throw upon each its proper and just share of the public burden. It reaches this result as well as it can under a system which tries the temper of the courts and the patience of the people. The share or " quota " of each county is thus ascertained, and the amount charged against the county considered as the responsible representative of a given area of taxation. That area must pay so much money, for that is its share. If, for any reason, it does not, then it fails to pay its share, and by as much as it fails it either unjustly increases the shares of other areas, or escapes with less than its proper burden, unless it is compelled to make up the deficiency. The State, therefore, must and does so compel. If more than two millions is to be credited to the city of New York, what will result? Two things evidently: *first*, that the city, as an area of taxation, will have borne less than its due share of the common burden by that large amount; and *second*, that the State in replacing it will be obliged to impose it as a part of a succeeding tax upon all the counties, and so shift the burden of the city to the rest of the State. If to avoid that plain injustice the legislature should reimpose it upon the city, we reach the absurdity of paying a sum one year only to reclaim it the next. These general considerations will enable us to gather the purpose and effect of the statutes relating to taxation, so far as they bear upon our inquiry.

The boards of supervisors are required to transmit to the comptroller a certificate or return of the aggregate valued amount of real and personal estate as corrected by them. (Laws 1836, chap. 117.) After these have been examined and revised by the State board of equalization, the comptroller is required to ascertain from such assessment the proportion of State tax each county shall pay, and send a statement of the amount to the county clerk and chairman and clerk of the board of supervisors of each county. (Laws 1859, chap. 312, § 8.) It is then provided that the amount of State tax which each county is to pay, as so fixed and certified by the comptroller, shall be raised and collected by the annual collection of taxes in the several counties in the manner prescribed by law. (Id., § 9.) In the general act (1 R. S. 419) the contingency of a failure to pay over taxes collected is met by a provision (§ 5) that all losses sustained by the default of any collector of a town or ward " shall be chargeable on such town or ward," and those arising from the default of a county treasurer, upon his county, and all such losses may be added to the next year's taxes. The comptroller is required to charge the treasurer or other financial officer of the county with the amount of its proportion of the State tax (Laws of 1855, chap. 427, § 8); but no credit is to be given to the county of New York, except for cash paid and fees of the disbursing officer. In the other counties credit is given for uncollected taxes on non-resident lands; but that is done because the State takes such collections into its own hands. And even in that case where the descriptions are not sufficient the amount is charged back to the county, and if no sufficient descriptions are made, is required to be reassessed upon and paid by the tax payers of the county. (2 R. S. [7th ed.] 1032.) The tax levies specifically require the county treasurers to pay the State tax into its treasury, and the city of New York is allowed to add three per cent to its levy to meet deficiencies in the actual product of the tax imposed.

There is thus disclosed in the action of the legislature the outlines of the system of taxation intended. The State annually needs a certain amount of money to sustain its organization and execute its purposes. Since those purposes relate to the common benefit, the necessary expense should be made a common burden. Justice requires that such burden should be borne in equal and fair proportion by all the property of the State. To reach such a distribution effectively and justly, the State may and does divide its area into convenient districts of taxation. These may, or may not correspond with existing political or governmental divisions, but as such require for their own purposes the complete machinery of local taxation, the State finds it convenient to adopt the counties as districts of taxation, and to avail itself of their machinery for its own purposes. It may do this in one of two ways. It may make the county officers its officers, and so deal directly with the tax payers; or it may make the county responsible as the representative of such tax payers, arming it with all necessary powers to perform the duty imposed, and giving that duty the character of an obligation. It has chosen the latter method. It makes each county as the representative of the tax payers within its area debtor to its share of the general tax. From each it must require payment in full, and does so require it. Not to do so would throw the whole system into a jangle of discord and inequality. In any given case a failure to collect a fraction of the tax does not diminish the debt due to the

State. It affects only the distribution of the full amount among the tax payers of the district. The apportionment is first made among them on the hypothesis that all will pay. If all do not pay, and some cannot be compelled to pay, to that extent the apportionment proves inaccurate and founded on an incorrect basis, and each tax payer owes in addition his own proportionate share of the deficiency which occurs. In the city of New York this is paid by each tax payer when the debt secured by the revenue bonds is discharged; in the other counties by such reassessments as are necessary. In the present case the State has received simply its just due, and no more than that. The county has paid it, as it was bound to pay, and the burden has fallen upon the tax payers of the district, where it properly belonged.

Very much more of an interesting character might be added to this discussion, but enough has been said to indicate the principal reasons for our concurrence in the disposition which has been made of the case.

The judgment should be affirmed, with costs.

All concur.

Judgment affirmed.

JOHN KEARNEY, Appellant, *v.* THE MAYOR, ALDERMEN AND COMMONALTY OF THE CITY OF NEW YORK, Respondent.

A party alleging the loss of a material paper, to make out a case authorizing secondary evidence of its contents, must show that he has in good faith exhausted, to a reasonable degree, all the sources of information and means of discovery which the nature of the case would naturally suggest and which were accessible to him.

The person last known to have been in possession of the paper must be examined as a witness to prove the loss; if out of the State his deposition must be procured or some good excuse given for not doing so.

The determination of the trial judge of the fact as to the loss cannot be reviewed here, unless the proof of loss was so clear and conclusive that it was error of law to find against it.

Where the only witness called to prove the loss is the party claiming it, the trial court is not bound as matter of law to credit his statements, although they are not contradicted by any other witness.

(Argued May 8, 1883 ; decided June 5, 1883.)

APPEAL from judgment of the General Term of the Court of Common Pleas in and for the city and county of New York, entered upon an order made at the May term, 1882, which affirmed a judgment in favor of defendant, entered upon an order dismissing plaintiff's complaint on trial.

This action was brought by plaintiff, as assignee of one Scanlon, to recover for publishing the election notice for the year 1870 in *The Irish Republic* newspaper, which, plaintiff claimed, was given to Scanlon, the publisher of said newspaper, for publication, by the then sheriff of the county of New York, as authorized by chapter 480, Laws of 1860.

The facts material to the questions discussed are stated in the opinion.

James M. Lyddy for appellant.

D. J. Dean for respondent. Secondary evidence is only admissible where the writing cannot be produced. Proof must be given of the exercise of reasonable diligence in the effort to procure the original. The circumstances must be indeed exceptional which would warrant the assertion that the efforts of the plaintiff in this case to produce the original were reasonably diligent. (*Boyle* v. *Wiseman*, 29 Eng. L. & Eq. 473; *Deaver* v. *Rice*, 2 Ired. [N. C.] 280; *Dickinson* v. *Breeden*, 25 Ill. 186; *Ralph* v. *Brown*, 3 W. & S. 395; *Shepherd* v. *Giddings*, 22 Conn. 282; *Wood* v. *Cullen*, 13 Minn. 394; *Johnson* v. *Arnwine*, 13 Vroom [N. J.], 451; 36 Am. Rep. 527; *Bunch's Adm'r* v. *Hurst*, 3 Desaur. Eq. [S. C.] 273; *Floyd* v. *Minstey*, 5 Rich. [S. C.] 361; *Turner* v. *Yates*, 16 How. [U. S.] 14; *Simpson* v. *Dall*, 3 Wall. 460, 475; *Blackburn* v. *Crawford*, id. 175, 183; *Jackson* v. *Frier*, 16 Johns. 193; *Parkins* v. *Cobbet*, 1 C. & P. 282; *Taunton B'k* v.

Briggs, 5 Pick. 436; *Empire Trans. Co.* v. *Steele*, 70 Penn.
St. 188.) The rule requiring proof of diligence, preliminary
to admitting secondary evidence, should in this case be strictly
enforced. (1 Greenleaf's Evidence, § 87; *Quilter* v. *Jorss*, 14 C.
B. [N. S.] 747; *Gully* v. *Bishop of Exeter*, 4 Bing. 290; *Brewster* v. *Sewell*, 3 B. & Ald. 296; *Freeman* v. *Arkill*, 2 B. &
C. 495; *Graham* v. *Chrystal*, 2 Abb. App. Dec. 264.) The
question whether the absence of a document is sufficiently
accounted for is addressed to the trial judge, and the court on
appeal will not reverse his decision of that question, except
when he is clearly wrong. (*Jackson* v. *Frier*, 16 Johns. 193;
Quilter v. *Jorss*, 14 C. B. [N. S.] 747; *Graham* v. *Chrystal*,
2 Abb. App. Dec. 264; *Regina* v. *Hill*, 16 Eng. L. & Eq. 358;
Nicholson v. *Conner*, 8 Daly, 215; *Sheridan* v. *Mayor*, 68 N. Y.
30; *Gildersleeve* v. *Landon*, 73 id. 609; Stephen's Digest of
the Law of Evidence, articles 71, 79, and notes; *Mason* v.
Libbey, 64 How. 267.)

RAPALLO, J. The alleged employment by the sheriff, pursuant to chapter 480 of the Laws of 1860, of Scanlon, the
plaintiff's assignor, to publish the election notice in the newspaper entitled "*The Irish Republic*," lay at the foundation of
the plaintiff's supposed cause of action. The fact of such employment was put in issue by the answer. The plaintiff was
the only witness called to prove it, and he testified that, at the
request of Scanlon, he called upon the sheriff and asked him
for the election notice. That the sheriff gave it to him with a
written indorsement thereon, which indorsement, the plaintiff
claims, contained an authorization to Scanlon to publish the
notice. The plaintiff then endeavored to give parol evidence
of the contents of the written indorsement, but on objection
being made, the court excluded such parol evidence. The plaintiff then attempted to prove that the paper was lost, but the
court held the proof insufficient, and excluded parol evidence
of its contents. The plaintiff was then asked what was said
by the sheriff at the time, and answered that he did not
remember that he said any thing. After this the witness was

repeatedly pressed to state the contents of the writing indorsed on the notice, and to state what the sheriff said at the time, but all these questions were excluded, and the answers given by witness to some of them were stricken out.

There can be no doubt that the defendant had the right to insist on the production of the paper, and to object to parol evidence of its contents without proof of its loss. It is no answer to this objection to say that the law did not require the authority or contract of employment to be in writing.

The proof of loss of the paper was addressed to the trial judge, and presented a question to be determined by him as matter of fact. His determination of the fact cannot be reviewed here, unless the proof of loss was so clear and conclusive that it was error of law to find against it. (*Jackson* v. *Frier*, 16 Johns. 193; Stephens on Evidence, article 71; *Mason* v. *Libbey*, 64 How. Pr. 267.) The proof in this case fell far short of that standard. According to the testimony of the witness he gave the paper to Scanlon. That is the last trace we have of it. The witness says that afterward, when the business of the newspaper was being wound up, he remembers making search among the records of " *The Irish Republic* " for the election notice; that he has made earnest and diligent search among his own papers, as well as among the papers of " *The Irish Republic* " for that purpose; that he and Mr. Scanlon together searched all over for it, but were not able to find it, and that Mr. Scanlon told witness he was unable to find it. He does not say where they searched, except among the papers of " *The Irish Republic.*" It does not appear that search was made among Scanlon's papers. The witness says that he is quite positive that at the time of the assignment of the claim to him, and before that, the search for this notice was made in the archives of the newspaper office, that both he and Scanlon searched for it and it could not be found.

This is all the evidence in the case on the subject of the loss of the paper, and it is apparent at the first glance that it is any thing but conclusive. The first glaring defect is that although the paper was last seen in Scanlon's possession, and although the witness says that Scanlon subsequently assisted in the search for it, he was not examined as a witness. The only excuse offered for this omission is the testimony of the plaintiff that since the assignment of the claim to him, Scanlon has not been living in the city, county and State of New York. It was not shown, however, that there was any difficulty in reaching him, and it has repeatedly been held that the person last known to have been in possession of the paper must be examined as a witness, to prove its loss, and that even if he is out of the State, his deposition must be procured if practicable, or some good excuse given for not doing so. (*Deaver* v. *Rice*, 2 Ired. [N. C.] 280; *Dickinson* v. *Breeden*, 25 Ill. 186; *Bunch's Adm'r* v. *Hurst*, 3 Desaur. Eq. [S. C.] 273; *Turner* v. *Yates*, 16 How. [U. S.] 14; *Parkins* v. *Cobbet*, 1 C. & P. 282.) And the general rule is that the party alleging the loss of a material paper, where such proof is necessary for the purpose of giving secondary evidence of its contents, must show that he has in good faith exhausted, to a reasonable degree, all the sources of information and means of discovery which the nature of the case would naturally suggest, and which were accessible to him. (*Simpson* v. *Dall*, 3 Wall. 460, 475.)

The question being one of fact, it is not necessary to show that it would have been error in the trial judge to hold the proof of loss sufficient, and admit the parol evidence offered. The point which the appellant must establish is that the proof was so conclusive that it was error of law not to hold it sufficient, and if there were nothing else in the case, the fact that the only witness called to testify to the loss was the plaintiff himself, was enough to preclude this court from reviewing the decision of the trial judge and General Term. For the court below was not bound as matter of law to credit the statements of a witness thus interested, given in his own behalf, though uncontradicted by any other witness. (*Elwood* v. *Western U. Tel. Co.*, 45 N. Y. 549; 6 Am. Rep. 140; *Nicholson* v. *Conner*, 8 Daly, 215.)

The judgment should be affirmed.

All concur.

Judgment affirmed.

THE PEOPLE OF THE STATE OF NEW YORK, Appellant, .*v.*
THE MUTUAL ENDOWMENT AND ACCIDENT ASSOCIATION
of BATH, Respondent.

To give the court cognisance of a case submitted under the provision of
the Code of Civil Procedure (§ 1279), providing for the submission of controversies upon facts admitted, the facts stated must show that there
was, at the time the submission was made, a controversy or question of
difference between the parties on the point presented for decision, and
that a judgment can be rendered thereon; the court may not pass upon
a mere abstract question.

Where in a controversy sought to be submitted between the State and a
corporation the only relief to which the former is entitled, if any, is to
restrain the corporation from exercising franchises unlawfully, the proceeding should be dismissed, as that relief may not be given therein.
(Code, § 1281.)

(Argued May 8, 1883; decided June 5, 1883.)

APPEAL from judgment of the General Term of the Supreme Court, in the third judicial department, in favor of
defendant, entered upon a case submitted under section 1279
of the Code.

The facts stated were substantially these:

Defendant is a corporation organized under the act providing
"for the incorporation of societies or clubs for certain lawful
purposes" (Chap. 267, Laws of 1875, as amended by chap. 58,
Laws of 1876, and chap. 93, Laws of 1880). By its constitution and by-laws, which were set forth in the case, it appeared
that defendant contemplated to aid its members in case of accident, "to advance to them means during their life-time, and to
pay to their widows, child, children or legatees, in case of their
deaths," such sums as the articles provided for.

The association issued two certificates of membership. Those
issued in class "A" provide that the member, or such person
as he shall by his will name, shall be entitled, upon his death,
to one dollar for every member, not exceeding a sum specified,
deducting therefrom any amount the member may have received at the expiration of two-thirds of his life expectancy.

By the by-laws it is provided that upon the expiration of two-thirds of the life expectancy of any member, if he require it, he is entitled to one-half the amount provided for at his death.   The further facts are stated in the opinion.

Leslie W. Russell, attorney-general, for appellant.

M. Rumsey Miller for respondent.

Per Curiam.   It does not appear by the agreed statement that there is any controversy or question in difference between the parties.   The submission sets forth the articles of association of the defendant and the by-laws of the association, and the form of the certificate issued to its members, comprising class "A," and states that the company have issued to such members a certificate in the form as set forth, and that the defendant has never deposited $100,000, or any other sum, with the insurance department for any purpose whatever.

The question submitted is, "whether the defendant has the right to insert in the certificate of membership a provision for the payment of a sum not to exceed one-half of the amount stated in such certificate, upon the expiration of two-thirds of the life expectancy of the member, without depositing with the insurance department $100,000 for the protection of those members holding such certificates."

There is no statement that there is any controversy or question of difference between the parties upon the point presented for decision.   The only statement is that the plaintiff insists that the defendant has no right to issue certificates in the form stated, and that such certificates are illegal.   It is not alleged that the defendant asserted such right at the time when the submission was made, or did not yield to the claim of the plaintiffs.   It is not inconsistent with the statement that the company had abandoned its use of the certificates.   The question propounded may, so far as appears, be a mere abstract one not involving any actual difference or controversy.   If the defendant is exercising franchises not conferred, or without complying with statutory conditions, it may be restrained by application to the court, but that relief cannot be given by any judgment which may be rendered in this proceeding. (Code, § 1281.)

The judgment should be reversed and the proceeding dismissed, without costs. (*Dickinson* v. *Dickey*, 76 N. Y. 602.)

All concur, except MILLER, J., absent.

Judgment reversed.

MEMORANDA

OF THE

CAUSES DECIDED DURING THE PERIOD EMBRACED IN THIS
VOLUME, WHICH ARE NOT REPORTED IN FULL.

CHARLES F. TAG, Respondent, *v.* EUGENE M. KETELTAS et al.,
Executors, etc., Appellants.

(Argued February 6, 1883; decided March 20, 1883.)

Stephen P. Nash for appellants.

Edward Solomon for respondent.

Agree to affirm.   No opinion.
All concur.
Judgment affirmed.

MARIA METZGER, Administratrix, etc., Respondent, *v.* HENRY
HERRMANN, Appellant.

(Submitted March 7, 1883; decided March 20, 1883.)

James M. Smith for appellant.

Chauncey Shaffer and *Peter Cook* for respondent.

Agree to affirm.   No opinion.
All concur.
Judgment affirmed.

DANIEL J. NOYES, as Executor, etc., Respondent, *v.* LEWIS H
BAILEY, as Executor, etc., Appellant.

(Argued March 7, 1883 ; decided March 20, 1883.)

Joseph H. Choate for appellant.

William Fullerton for respondent.

Agree to affirm.   No opinion.
All concur, except RAPALLO, J., dissenting.
Judgment affirmed.

HARVEY HUNTER, Appellant, *v.* JANE HERRICK et al., Executors,
etc., Respondents.

(Argued March 7, 1883 ; decided March 20, 1883.)

REPORTED below, (26 Hun, 272.)

D. Cady Herrick for appellant.

Samuel Edwards for respondents.

Agree to affirm order and for judgment absolute on stipu-
lation.   No opinion.
All concur.
Order affirmed and judgment accordingly.

JANE CROZIER, Administratrix, etc., Respondent, *v.* CORNELL
STEAMBOAT COMPANY, Appellant.

(Argued March 12, 1883 ; decided March 20, 1883.)

S. L. Stebbins for appellant.

John J. Linson for respondent.

Agree to affirm.   No opinion.
All concur.
Judgment affirmed.

MARY LANCTOT, Administratrix, etc., Appellant, *v.* THE TROY AND LANSINGBURGH RAILROAD COMPANY, Respondent.

(Argued March 12, 1883; decided March 20, 1883.)

Rufus W. Peckham for appellant.

Esek Cowen for respondent.

Agree to affirm.   No opinion.
All concur.
Judgment affirmed.

———————

JOHN D. FISH et al., Administrators, etc., Respondents, *v.* HENRY A. COSTER, Appellant.

(Argued March 13, 1883; decided March 20, 1883.)

Coles Morris and *Michael H. Cardozo* for appellant.

Oliver W. West for respondent.

Agree to affirm on opinion of DAVIS, Ch. J., at General Term.
All concur.
Judgment affirmed.

———————

JAMES E. DELANEY, Appellant, *v.* WILLIAM C. VAN AULEN, Individually, and as Trustee, etc., Respondent.

(Argued March 13, 1883; decided March 27, 1883.)

THIS case is reported on a former appeal in 84 N. Y. 16.
The court state that no new facts were presented on the second trial, and that the former decision must control.

D. P. Barnard for appellant.

Samuel Hand for respondent.

DANFORTH, J., reads for affirmance.
All concur.
Judgment affirmed.

JOHN WHITMORE et al., Appellants, *v.* THOMAS E. PATTERSON et
al., Executors, etc., Respondents.

(Argued March 14, 1888 ; decided March 27, 1888.)

PLAINTIFFS' complaint was dismissed on trial and the promi-
nent question here was as to whether, under the evidence, the
order was justified.

William W. Niles for appellants.

John L. Logan for respondents.

EARL, J., reads for affirmance.
All concur.
Judgment affirmed.

———————

BRIDGET JONES, as Administratrix, etc., Respondent, *v.* THE
NEW YORK CENTRAL AND HUDSON RIVER RAILROAD COM-
PANY, Appellant.

(Argued March 15, 1888 ; decided March 80, 1888.)

REPORTED below (28 Hun, 364).

Samuel Hand for appellant.

E. Countryman for respondent.

Agree to affirm ; no opinion.
All concur.
Judgment affirmed.

———————

In the Matter of the Final Accounting of SAMUEL A. HAYT
et al., Executors, etc.

(Argued March 19, 1888 ; decided March 80, 1888.)

Milton A. Fowler for appellant.

Thomas J. Swift for respondent.

Agree to affirm; no opinion.
All concur.
Judgment affirmed.

HUBBARD FOSTER et al., Respondents, *v.* THE CITY OF BUFFALO,
Appellant.

(Argued March 20, 1888 ; decided March 80, 1888.)

THIS was an appeal from an order of General Term, affirming an order of Special Term granting a preliminary injunction.
Held, that the order was in the discretion of the court below
and so not appealable.

The court cited *Van Dewater* v. *Kelsey* (1 N. Y. 533); *Paul*
v. *Munger* (47 N. Y. 469); *People* v. *Schoonmaker* (50 id. 499);
Young v. *Campbell* (75 id. 525).

Giles E. Stillwell for appellant.

E. J. Plumley for respondents.

DANFORTH, J., reads for dismissal of appeal.
All concur.
Appeal dismissed.

In the Matter of the Opening of LEXINGTON AVENUE.

(Argued March 20, 1888 ; decided March 80, 1888.)

REPORTED below (29 Hun, 303).

Herbert A. Shipman for appellant.

D. J. Dean for respondent.

Agree to affirm ; no opinion.
All concur.
Order affirmed.

In the Matter of the Petition of CAROLINE C. BISHOP to Vacate
an Assessment.

(Argued March 20, 1883 ; decided March 30, 1883.)

Samuel Hand for appellant.

D. J. Dean for respondent.

This case presented the same questions and was argued and
decided with *In re Righter* (*ante*, p. 111).

ROBERT T. SMITH et al., Appellants, *v.* JOHN B. DAVIS,
Respondent.

(Argued March 20, 1883 ; decided March 30, 1883.)

E. Moore for appellants.

Wm. L. Royal for respondent.

Agree to dismiss appeal ; no opinion.
All concur.
Appeal dismissed.

MARY O'DAY, as Administratrix, etc., Respondent, *v.* THE
SYRACUSE, BINGHAMTON AND NEW YORK RAILROAD COMPANY,
Appellant.

(Argued March 23, 1883 ; decided March 30, 1883.)

Hamilton Odell for appellant.

Samuel Hand for respondent.

Agree to affirm ; no opinion.
All concur.
Judgment affirmed.

GEORGE CRAWFORD, Respondent, *v.* THE WEST SIDE BANK, Appellant.

The complaint herein set forth a demand for $398.71 ; the answer denied liability and set up a counter-claim for $301.29. The trial court found with defendant and gave judgment against plaintiff for the counter-claim. The General Term reversed the judgment. *Held*, that the amount of the two claims constituted " the matter in controversy," within the meaning of the Code of Civil Procedure (§ 191, subd. 3), and that this court had jurisdiction on appeal.

(Argued March 20, 1883 ; decided March 30, 1883.)

THIS was a motion to dismiss an appeal.

The opinion, which is given in full, states the facts.

" The plaintiff sought to recover from the defendant $398.71, as money due. The defendant denied liability therefor, and asked judgment upon a counter-claim, for $301.29, as money theretofore advanced to the plaintiff at his request. The two sums make $700, and represent the amount of a check alleged by the plaintiff to have been wrongfully paid by the defendant from his money. The trial court held with the defendant that it was properly paid, and gave judgment in its favor against the plaintiff for the counter-claim, $301.29. On the other hand the General Term went with the plaintiff, reversed the judgment and ordered a new trial. The controversy at the General Term necessarily involved the demands on both sides, and in case of a new trial, a recovery by the plaintiff will not only charge the defendant with the payment of $398.71, but extinguish the claim made by it. These two amounts, therefore, constitute ' the matter in controversy,' and give this court jurisdiction. (Code of Civil Proc., § 191, subd. 3.)

" The motion to dismiss the appeal should, therefore, be denied, with costs."

D. M. Porter for motion.

John C. Shaw opposed.

DANFORTH, J., reads for denial of motion.

All concur.

Motion denied.

ANN REESE, Respondent, *v.* THOMAS BOESE, as Receiver, etc.,
et al., Appellants.

(Argued March 20, 1888 ; decided March 30, 1888.)

THESE were motions to dismiss appeals. The opinion, which
is given in full, shows the grounds of the motion.

"The attorney for the respondent makes a motion to
dismiss the appeal of Boese on the ground that he has not
served ' a proper case or appeal-book.'

"It appears that upon the appeal of Boese a case was prepared and settled by the consent and acquiescence of the parties,
and filed in the clerk's office, and that that case was used at the
General Term. Even if the General Term, in considering the
appeal of Boese, used other papers, it had no right to. The
return to this court is properly certified according to section
1315 of the Code. If the plaintiff desired to have other
papers or evidence contained in the cases, she should have proposed amendments to the case served on the part of Boese and
procured their insertion in that way in the case. It is too late
now for her to complain of the case as it appears before us.
The motion against Boese must, therefore, be denied, with costs.

" We must call attention to a defect which appears in the
case as settled, of which the counsel for the respondent has
taken no notice. Section 997 of the Code requires that a case
must be settled and signed by the judge or referee before
whom the action was tried. That very wholesome provision
of the Code does not seem to have been complied with ; at
least it does not appear in the record returned to us that the
case was settled and signed by the judge before whom the
action was tried. But as the Supreme Court received and
acted upon the papers in their apparently imperfect condition,
they constitute the return to us, and we must receive them as
sufficient. If the rule prescribed in section 997 had been complied with, the present dispute and controversy would probably
not have arisen.

" A motion is also made to dismiss the appeal taken in this
case by Raphael J. Moses on behalf of certain policy-holders,

and also an appeal taken by Talcott H. Russell as receiver of the American Life and Trust Company, on the ground that the appellants have not served the undertakings required by section 1326 of the Code.

" We find in the papers no denial of the neglect to serve the undertakings, and those appeals must, therefore, be dismissed unless they are perfected by the service of the proper undertakings within ten days after the service of this órder, with sureties who will justify according to the rules and practice of. the court, and each of such appellants also pay $10 costs of this motion."

_ *Wm. H. Ingersoll* for motion.

Raphael J. Moses, Jr., and *George M. Sanders, Jr.,* opposed.

EARL, J., reads for denial of motion as to defendant Boese, and for dismissal of appeals taken by Raphael J. Moses, Jr., on behalf of certain policy-holders, and by Talcott H. Russell as receiver of the American Trust Company, unless appeals are perfected as stated in opinion.

All concur.

Ordered accordingly.

MARIA DAVIES, Appellant, *v.* DAVID DAVIES et al., Respondents.

(Argued March 16, 1888 ; decided April 17, 1888.)

William Allen Butler for appellant.

Everett P. Wheeler for respondents.

Agree to affirm ; no opinion.
All concur.
Judgment affirmed.

PETER K. KNAPP et al., Appellants, *v.* AUGUSTA S. KNAPP et al., Respondents.

(Argued March 19, 1883; decided April 17, 1888.)

John E. Develin and *Theodore F. Jackson* for appellants.

John E. Parsons and *Edmund Wetmore* for respondents.

Decided on the opinion of the referee.
Per curiam mem. for reversal of judgment of General Term of affirmance of judgment on report of referee.
All concur.
Judgment accordingly.

EDWARD FREEL *v.* THOMAS T. BUCKLEY, Appellant, JAMES S. FEELY et al., Respondents.

(Submitted March 20, 1883; decided April 17, 1888.)

McGuire & Kuhn for appellant.

John U. Shorter for respondents.

Decided on opinion in *Bertles* v. *Nunan* (*ante,* 152) and by the same vote.

Order of General Term reversed. Order of Special Term modified so as to order the county treasurer to pay the whole of the surplus money in his hands to the credit of this action (after deducting $15 for the fees of the referee) to the appellant, Thomas T. Buckley.

ELIZABETH M. CROSBY, as Trustee, etc., Appellant, *v.* MOSES H. MOSES, Respondent.

(Argued March 21, 1883; decided April 17, 1888.)

DEFENDANT was in the occupation of certain premises under a lease which gave to the lessor the option to renew the lease for twenty-one years at an annual rental to be agreed upon by the parties or to be determined by arbitrators, or to take possession at the expiration of the term, paying in such case to the lessee or assigns the value of the buildings on the premises. The complaint asked that such value be determined and that upon payment thereof plaintiff have possession, etc. Defendant claimed a right, and the court below decided he was entitled to a renewal of the lease for twenty-one years. The facts and conclusions of the court are stated in the opinion, as follows :

" The evidence justifies the conclusion that the defendant was entitled to a renewal of the lease, but we think the court below erred in extending the term to twenty-one years. The renewal of December, 1871, was for five years from May 1, 1874, and when the defendant applied for a new lease, the conversation with Lindley, the lessor's agent and attorney, settled down to a declaration that he would be willing to take it for another term of five years, upon, as the defendant thinks, a valuation of $3,500. No objection seems to have been made to the 'terms,' but the lessor's attorney thought the valuation 'too low,' and the defendant told him to inquire, adding, 'this thing must be settled.' I think it obvious, from the testimony both of the defendant and Lindley, the attorney, that the only matter to be adjusted was the amount of rent; that was 'the thing' in question. This further appears, from the reason assigned by the defendant, viz.: that he must know what to do with his tenant, who was bothering him 'the same' as he was the lessor, and Lindley replied, 'go on and let it.' Lindley testifies that the defendant said he did not desire a twenty-one years lease, 'and he (Lindley) said we have no objection to giving a five years lease at a fair valuation.' He agrees with defendant that there was a conflict in regard to valuation, and both agree that these interviews were followed by the selection of arbitrators and an appraisal. One of the arbitrators, Crosby, selected by the plaintiff, valued the property at $5,000. Lovejoy, selected by the defendant, put it at $3,500, while Martin, the umpire, whose decision was, by the terms of the arbitration clause in the lease, to be final, fixed the sum at $3,700.

This was done June 12, 1879, and on the 16th of June Lindley notified the defendant that the lease was drawn and ready for execution. After reaching this point the parties changed their positions. The plaintiff claimed that the arbitration was merely preliminary to her election whether to take the building or give a new lease, and the defendant, that by consenting to arbitrate she became bound, by the terms of the original lease, to a renewal of twenty-one years. Neither claim is admissible. Each is inconsistent with the previous conduct of both parties. There is some evidence that Lovejoy, the defendant's appraiser, and Martin, the umpire, understood a lease for twenty-one years was intended. They were led to this by Crosby, but Crosby was not shown to have authority from the plaintiff. She, so far as appears, referred the matter to Lindley, and the latter acted for her. As to the arbitration, it was no doubt provided for by the lease, but the term was subject to change, and this was effected by parol. We think, therefore, that the judgment as it now stands is erroneous."

Sutherland Tenney for appellant.

George S. Hamlin for respondent.

DANFORTH, J., reads for reversal and a new trial unless the defendant stipulates to accept a lease for five years instead of twenty-one years. If he stipulates to do so, the judgment is so modified, and as modified, affirmed.

All concur.

Judgment accordingly.

FRANK LESLIE, Appellant, *v.* MIRIAM F. LESLIE et al., Respondents.

(Argued March 23, 1883 ; decided April 17, 1883.)

AFFIRMED on opinion of court below.

Scott Lord for appellant.

William Fullerton for respondents.

Per curiam mem. for affirmance.
All concur.
Judgment affirmed.

THE GENESEE RIVER NATIONAL BANK, Appellant *v.* MAR-
GARET M. MEAD, Respondent. *131-*

> The mere fact that an assignment of property by a debtor was voluntary
> and without consideration is not sufficient to require a finding that it was
> fraudulent against creditors.

(Argued March 27, 1888; decided April 17, 1888.)

THIS action was brought by plaintiff, as a judgment creditor of
Jacob A. Mead, deceased, against defendant individually and as
executrix of the will of the deceased, to require her to account as
executrix for the proceeds of a policy of insurance upon the life
of decedent, which the complaint alleged had been assigned by
him to her without consideration and for the purpose of defrauding his creditors. The opinion of the court is given in full.

"The claim of the plaintiff to charge the proceeds of the
$3,000 policy of insurance to the defendant on her accounting
as executrix depended upon the question, whether the assignment of that policy, made to her by the testator, was made
with intent to hinder, delay and defraud his creditors.
The trial court found, as matter of fact, that the assignment
was not made or received with such intent, but that, at the
time and under the circumstances under which it was made, it
was a just and proper settlement upon the defendant.

"There is no finding that the testator was at the time of the
assignment insolvent, but on the contrary, the court expressly
refused such a finding. Unless the insolvency of the testator, at
the time of the assignment, was so clearly and conclusively
proved that it was legal error to refuse the finding requested,
the conclusion of the trial court as to the fact of fraudulent intent cannot be disturbed here. The mere fact that the assign-

ment was voluntary, and without consideration, was not sufficient to require the court to find that it was fraudulent against creditors. (2 R. S. 137, § 4.)

"There was no controlling evidence as to the pecuniary circumstances of the testator at the time the assignment was made. Even assuming that it was made in 1876, as claimed by the plaintiff, it was not shown by any direct proof that the testator then owed any debts, other than that claimed by the plaintiff, nor what was the amount of his property. The only evidence bearing upon these subjects was the account rendered by the executrix in this action, from which it appeared that she had received from the estate, up to the date of rendering her account, $628.79, and had paid out the sum of $1,241.86. This account shows that a considerable part of the payments was for lawyers' fees and expenses of the administration, and the only testimony as to indebtedness included therein is that of the defendant, who says that the amount consisted of the expenses of settling the estate, the funeral expenses, board and doctors' bills, and a few small debts left unpaid at the time of the testator's death. It appears that the defendant expended for a monument $398, of which she paid $50 out of her private purse, the remainder being, presumably, included in the account. What the small debts spoken of amounted to, or when they were incurred, does not appear. It is quite within the range of probability that they were for the expenses of the testator during his last illness, and that his means were exhausted during the same period, and after the assignment of the policy. The evidence was not sufficient to constrain the court to find that the testator was insolvent at the time of that assignment, or that it was made with intent to hinder, delay or defraud his creditors.

"On this ground the judgment should be affirmed, with costs."

W. A. Sutherland for appellant.

John A. Van Derlip for respondent.

RAPALLO, J., reads for affirmance.
All concur.
Judgment affirmed.

HENRY J. WAGGONER, Appellant, *v.* MARY WALRATH, Executrix, etc., Respondent.

(Submitted March 30, 1883 ; decided April 24, 1883.)

REPORTED below (24 Hun, 443).

Wayland F. Ford for appellant.

Porter & Walts for respondent.

Agree to affirm ; no opinion.
All concur.
Judgment affirmed.

ELLA A. DANA, as Administratrix, etc., Appellant, *v.* THE NEW YORK CENTRAL AND HUDSON RIVER RAILROAD COM- /26 PANY, Respondent.

(Argued April 16, 1883 ; decided April 24, 1883.)

THIS action was brought to recover damages for alleged negligence causing the death of C. Frank Dana, plaintiff's intestate, who was killed at the same accident as was Shehan, for whose death defendant was held liable. (See *Sheehan* v. *N. Y. C. & H. R. R. R. Co.*, 91 N. Y. 332.) In this case plaintiff was nonsuited on the trial.

The opinion is given in full.

" This action is to recover damages for the death of C. Frank Dana, caused, as the plaintiff alleges, by the defendant's negligence. Upon the trial the facts in evidence were as follows : On and for sometime before August 22, 1878, Dana was in the service of the defendant as locomotive engineer, and on that day was drawing its regular freight or schedule train, No. ' 50 ' from Rochester, east to Syracuse. There was but a single track with stations at various places between these points, and among others at Cayuga and Auburn. The train was due at Cayuga at 4: 45 P. M., but actually arrived at 4: 30. Regular train ' 61 ' was due at Cayuga from the east at 4: 35, but was delayed. This was known to Kiefer, defendant's telegraph operator at that place, and as train '50' came in, he said to its conductor, ' orders received to hold No. 50 for 61.' The conductor repeated this to Dana. Train ' 61 ' reached Cayuga at 4: 55, and train '50' immediately left for the east. After running a mile and a half, it met and collided with a 'wild cat' train, No. 337. Dana was thereby at once killed, and Shehan, fireman on '337,' was injured. Train '337' had no schedule time or place on the road, and no one upon train ' 50,' nor the telegraph operator at Cayuga, had reason to anticipate its coming. It was made up and set in motion by special telegraphic orders addressed at 2: 50 on that day by defendant's superintendent to its conductor and engineer, then at De Witt (a station just east of Syracuse), to ' wild cat to Auburn and report.' At 4: 46 the defendant's superintendent gave them a further order to ' wild cat to Cayuga regardless of No. 50.' In doing so the collision occurred.

" No doubt the intestate, at the time of entering the defendant's employment, must be deemed to have assumed the ordinary risks incident to the service, but it is equally well settled that the employers cannot avail themselves of this assent of the servant, unless they have taken reasonable precautions to insure his safety while in the performance 'of assigned duties. The principle, therefore, which secures this exemption has no application where the injury is traced to the employers' personal failure to take such precautions, nor where they knew of the existence of a danger of which the servant has no means of knowledge. Within these rules, therefore, a railroad corporation is bound to carry on its business under a proper and reasonable system, or regulations (*Slater* v. *Jewett*, 85 N. Y. 61; 39 Am. Rep. 627), and if, through any defect therein, an injury occurs to the servant, the corporation will be liable. It does not appear from the record that the injury complained of was not immediately due to the defendant's omission of duty in this respect, and the trial court erred in taking the case from the jury. The evidence would justify a finding that they had not taken reasonable precautions to secure the safety of their servants employed upon the train whose time was interfered with.

Upon this question it was in no respect different from that submitted to the jury in *Sheehan's Case*,* and found by their verdict to be enough. We thought it was properly submitted to them, and sustained the judgment. (See opinion of March, 1883.) That decision requires a reversal of the one now before us.

" It is claimed, however, by the learned counsel for the respondent, that Dana knew of the regulations by which trains were run by telegraph orders, and took the risk of their sufficiency. He was furnished with a copy of them. Among other things not material here, they prescribe that ' all telegraph orders must be first copied by the operator on the order-book provided for that purpose, and repeated back immediately to the dispatcher, to be sure it is correct. After receiving ' O. K. ' from the dispatcher, the operator will make a copy on a blank for the persons addressed, who will, after comparing it with the book, and seeing it is correct, sign their names to the book, prefixed by the numeral ' 13.' The operator will transmit the ' 13 ' (accompanied by the signatures addressed) to the dispatcher. The numeral ' 12 ' at the end of order means ' answer how understood,' and ' 13 ' ' we understand to,' etc.

" ' When an agent or operator receives an order to hold any train for any purpose, he must carry out the order strictly. Conductors and engine-men will respect such orders, and comply with the same in all cases.'

" The provisions of the first clause were scrupulously followed in setting ' 337 ' upon the track, and giving it the time of ' 50.' Conductor and engineer were addressed by the superintendent, and their written acknowledgment of receipt of his message obtained. Nothing of the kind was done or attempted with the conductor or engineer of train ' 50.' The starting off of ' 337 ' on the time of ' 50 ' was, in the absence of such communication or some other precaution, a trap from which the second clause furnished no opportunity of escape. Resort was had to the second clause. Kiefer, the operator, was directed by the superintendent at 4: 10, ' hold No. ' 50 ' for orders,'

---

* 91 N. Y. 332.

but there was no information given that ' 337 ' was to be put on the track, nor instruction even to exhibit the order to the conductor or engineer on train ' 50.' The rules do not require it, and the verbal order I have before referred to was given by the operator. For Kiefer's act, in this respect, the defendant is clearly liable. The act he was required to do and did perform was one for which the master was responsible as a duty pertaining to itself, and as to it Kiefer occupied the place of the master. (*Flike* v. *Boston & Albany R. R. Co.*, 53 N. Y. 549; 13 Am. Rep. 545.) The obligation of the master extended to giving notice to the hands on train ' 50 ' that train ' 337 ' was moving on its time, or giving direction to those hands to stay until ' 337 ' arrived. Telling Kiefer to hold the train for orders was a proper step in that direction, but, standing by itself, was not enough. The defendant was to see to it that train ' 50 ' was either held or so notified of the ' wild-cat ' train that it would move, if at all, at its own peril. This was not done. Kiefer told them to go on, and the second clause of the rules above referred to required the conductor and engineer to respect such order and ' comply with it strictly.'

" The jury might well inquire, among other things, why train ' 50,' having schedule right to the road, was not notified before another train was ordered to move toward it in a contrary direction, and why the special order for delay in movement was not addressed by the train dispatcher to its conductor and engineer. The intestate might properly look for both, or equivalent precautions, in such emergency as the defendant created. Knowledge of these rules, therefore, implies no contributory negligence on his part.

" The judgment should be reversed, and a new trial granted, with costs to abide the event."

Thomas Raines for appellant.

Edward Harris for respondent.

DANFORTH, J., reads for reversal and new trial.
All concur.
Judgment reversed.

THE PEOPLE, ex rel. THE OGDENSBURGH AND LAKE CHAMPLAIN RAILROAD COMPANY, Respondent, *v.* GEORGE K. POND et al., Assessors, etc., Appellants.

(Argued April 17, 1883; decided April 24, 1883.)

THIS was an appeal from an order of General Term, which affirmed an order of Special Term made in proceedings by *certiorari* under chapter 269, Laws of 1880, to review and correct an alleged erroneous assessment.

The appeal was dismissed on the ground that there was sufficient evidence to authorize the Supreme Court to exercise its discretionary power.

John P. Badger for appellant.

Louis Hasbrouck for respondent.

Agree to dismiss; no opinion.
All concur.
Appeal dismissed.

JANE VANDERBILT, as Administratrix, etc., Appellant, *v.* JOHN SCHREYER, as Executor, etc., et al., Respondents.

(Submitted April 17, 1883; decided April 24, 1883.)

REPORTED below (28 Hun, 61).

T. M. Tyng for appellant.

J. L. Lindsay for respondents.

Agree to affirm on case *P. M. S. Co. v. Toel* (85 N. Y. 646); no opinion.
All concur.
Order affirmed.

In the Matter of the Application of the EAST. RIVER BRIDGE
AND CONEY ISLAND STEAM TRANSIT COMPANY for the Appointment of Commissioners.

(Argued April 17, 1883; decided April 24, 1883.)

John H. Bergen & Jesse Johnson for appellant.

David Barnett for respondent.

Agree to dismiss appeal; no opinion.
All concur.
Appeal dismissed.

WILLIAM S. MARRIN et al., Appellants, *v.* OWEN A. MARRIN,
Respondent.

(Argued April 17, 1883; decided April 24, 1883.)

MEM. of decision below (27 Hun, 601).

Joseph J. Marrin for appellants.

Benjamin Hitchings for respondent.

Agree to reverse orders of the Special and General Terms and
to deny motion; no opinion.
All concur.
Ordered accordingly.

ALFRED T. BAXTER, Respondent, *v.* FRANKLIN BELL et al.,
Appellants.

(Submitted April 17, 1883; decided April 24, 1883.)

B. F. Tracey & Samuel Hand for appellants.

Frederic A. Ward for respondent.

Agree to dismiss appeal; no opinion.
All concur.
Appeal dismissed

In the Matter of the Petition of CHRISTOPHER PRINCE to Vacate an Assessment.

(Argued April 17, 1883 ; decided April 24, 1883.)

John C. Shaw for appellant.

D. J. Dean for respondent.

Agree to affirm; no opinion.
All concur.
Order affirmed.

In the Matter of the Petition of GERSHOM SEIXAS to Vacate an Assessment.

(Argued April 17, 1883 ; decided April 24, 1883.)

John C. Shaw for appellant.

D. J. Dean for respondent.

Agree to affirm; no opinion.
All concur.
Order affirmed.

ELLA L. WINTON, Respondent, *v.* WALTER W. WINTON, Appellant.

(Argued April 17, 1883 ; decided April 24, 1883.)

B. F. Sawyer for appellant.

Edward P. Wilder for respondent.

Agree to dismiss appeal; no opinion.
All concur.
Appeal dismissed.

STEPHEN TUNSTALL, Respondent, *v.* WALTER W. WINTON, Appellant.

(Argued April 17, 1883; decided April 24, 1883.)

B. F. Sawyer for appellant.

Edward P. Wilder for respondent.

Agree to reverse orders of Special and General Terms and to grant motion; no opinion.

All concur.

Ordered accordingly.

BENJAMIN C. MIFFLIN, Appellant, *v.* JAMES I. BROOKS, Impleaded, etc., Respondent.

(Submitted April 17, 1883 ; decided April 24, 1883.)

Albert Stickney for appellant.

George H. Adams for respondent.

Agree to dismiss appeal; no opinion.

All concur.

Appeal dismissed.

SELINA BARTLETT, Respondent, *v.* JOSEPH MUSLINER et al., Appellants.

A preference on the calendar of this court of an action for dower, authorized by the Code of Civil Procedure (§ 791, subd. 6), can be claimed only when the proof required, *i. e.*, that plaintiff " has no sufficient means of support aside from the estate in controversy," was made and an order allowing the preference obtained as required (§ 793), before the notice of argument was served.

(Submitted April 17, 1883; decided April 24, 1883.)

THIS was a motion to advance the cause on the calendar.

The following mem. was handed down:

"The plaintiff claims to have this cause advanced on the calendar as a preferred cause under subdivision 6 of section 791 of the Code of Civil Procedure, which reads as follows: '§ 6. An action for dower, where the plaintiff makes proof, by affidavit, to the satisfaction of the court, or a judge thereof, that she has no sufficient means of support aside from the estate in controversy.'

"The respondent, in noticing the cause for argument in this court, duly claimed the preference authorized by this section. Section 793 provides, that where the right to a preference depends upon facts, which do not appear in the pleadings or other papers upon which the cause is to be tried or heard, the party desiring a preference must procure an order therefor, from the court, or a judge thereof, upon notice to the adverse party. A copy of the order must be served with or before the notice of trial or argument. 'The order in a case embraced in subdivision 6 may be made *ex parte*, and is conclusive.' It would seem from these provisions that the preference authorized by this subdivision can be claimed only when the proof is made, and the order allowing a preference is obtained before the notice of argument is served. It does not appear that these proceedings were taken in this case, therefore the motion is denied."

RUGER, Ch. J., reads mem. for denial of motion.

All concur.

Motion denied.

THE PEOPLE, ex rel. GUSTAVE AUGERSTEIN, et al., Appellants, *v.* BERNARD KINNEY et al., Respondents.

Where in an action in which the people were parties, and appeared by the attorney-general, the latter did not, at the time of serving notice of argument, give notice of a particular day in the term on which he will move it, as prescribed by the provision of the Code of Civil Procedure (§ 791, subd. 1) to entitle the cause to a preference, but served with the notice of argument notice of motion that the cause be set down for a day named, which motion failed because the court adjourned before the day specified for making it. *Held*, that the action was not entitled to a preference.

(Argued April 17, 1868 ; decided April 24, 1888.)

THIS was a motion to set cause down for a day certain.

The facts are stated in the mem. handed down, of which the following is a copy :

" This action was instituted by the attorney-general of the State of New York in the name of The People, on the relation of the relators, to determine the constitutionality of section 4 of chapter 335 of the Laws of 1873, and the amendments thereto; and to test the title of the defendants to the office of aldermen of the city of New York, and to determine who were entitled to exercise the franchises appertaining to the common council of that city.

" The cause is upon our calendar upon an appeal of the plaintiffs, and a preference is claimed for them under subdivision 1 of section 791 of the Code, which provides for preference in ' an action or special proceeding, in which the people of the State are parties, and appear by the attorney-general ; where the attorney-general has given notice, at the time of service of notice of trial or argument, of a particular day in the term on which he will move it.' But the attorney-general did not give notice at the time of service of notice of argument of the particular day in the term on which he would move it ; and, therefore, there is no right to the preference claimed. It is true that there was served with the notice of argument, a notice of motion for a preference, returnable April 3, 1883, in which notice plaintiffs asked that the cause be set down for argument April 9, 1883, and that that motion failed, because the court adjourned before the 3d day of April. That was a notice of a motion for a preference ; not a notice that the cause would be moved on a certain day, as required by the section of the Code.

"As there is nothing in the papers showing that it is important that this case should have an early hearing, or that any public interests are suffering by the delay, we are disposed to hold them to the strict practice, and, therefore, to deny the motion."

EARL, J., reads mem. for denial of motion.
All concur.
Motion denied.

HENRY C. MILLIGAN, Respondent, *v.* THE LALANCE AND GROSJEAN MANUFACTURING COMPANY, Appellant.

(Submitted April 17, 1888 ; decided May 1, 1888.)

Abram Wakeman for appellant.

Roderick Robertson for respondent.

Agree to dismiss appeal ; no opinion.
All concur.
Appeal dismissed.

THE PEOPLE, ex rel. VINCENT CLARK, Appellant, *v.* STEPHEN B. FRENCH et al., Commissioners, etc., Respondents.

(Argued April 18, 1888 ; decided May 1, 1888.)

John W. Weed for appellant.

D. J. Dean for respondents.

Agree to affirm on authority of *Phillips* v. *Mayor, etc.* (88 N. Y. 245), without opinion.
All concur.
Order affirmed.

WILLIAM L. POMEROY et al., Appellants, *v.* ALFRED D. ISRAEL et al., Respondents.

(Argued April 18, 1883 ; decided May 1, 1883.)

Rufus W. Peckham for appellants.

Samuel Hand for respondents.

Agree to affirm ; no opinion.
All concur.
Judgment affirmed.

———————

FLORA SAMUELS, Respondent, *v.* FREDERICK G. WEAVER, as Sheriff, etc., Appellant.

(Argued April 19, 1883 ; decided May 1, 1883.)

C. D. Adams for appellant.

S. J. Barrows for respondent

Agree to affirm ; no opinion.
All concur.
Judgment affirmed.

———————

THE AMERICAN HOSIERY COMPANY, Appellant, *v.* THOMAS RILEY, as Sheriff, Respondent.

(Argued April 24, 1883 ; decided May 1, 1883.)

Samuel Jones for appellant

Thomas E. Pearsall for respondent

Agree to dismiss appeal ; no opinion.
All concur, except MILLER, J., absent.
Appeal dismissed.

MARCUS T. HUN, as Receiver, etc., Respondent, *v.* JOHN W.
SALTER, Appellant.

Under the Code of Civil Procedure (§ 709), in an action in the Supreme
Court, triable and tried in the first judicial district, an application for an
extra allowance of costs must be made in that district, although the
justice before whom the cause is tried resides in another district.

The rule of the Supreme Court (44), requiring such an application to be
made to the court before which the trial is had or the judgment rendered,
does not authorize it to be made out of the district.

(Argued April 24, 1888; decided May 8, 1888.)

THERE were two appeals in this action, one from a judgment of General Term affirming a judgment of Special
Term, the other from an order of General Term affirming
an order granting an extra allowance of costs to the plaintiff.
The appeal from the judgment was decided on the opinion
below. As to the appeal from the order the court say:

" Order giving extra allowance of costs to the plaintiff, and this
we think should be sustained. The place of trial was the
county of New York, and the action was there tried and decided in February, 1881. It appears affirmatively that no
application was made at the trial for an allowance of costs, nor
was the question then in any way brought to the attention of
the trial judge. His decision upon the issues was filed in
March, 1881. On the 1st of June following, notice of this
motion for an extra allowance of costs was given, to be made
upon an affidavit of plaintiff's counsel, among other papers, verified on that day, and the pleadings and proceedings in the
action, to be brought on before the judge who presided at the
trial, but at his chambers in Canandaigua, Ontario county, and
therefore in the seventh judicial district. The defendant objected to his jurisdiction on the ground that the motion could·
be heard only in the first judicial district, where the action was
triable. The objection was well taken. Section 769 of
the Code declares that where an action of the Supreme
Court is triable within the first judicial district, a motion
upon notice in that action 'must be made in that district.' The respondent relies upon rule 44 of the Supreme

Court, requiring an application for an additional allowance of costs to be made to the court before which the trial is had or the judgment rendered. Such construction of the rule upon the facts of this case is inconsistent with the provision of the statute already cited, and cannot prevail."

George H. Forster for appellant.

Peter B. Olney for respondent.

DANFORTH, J., reads for affirmance of judgment, and for reversal of order without prejudice to any further application to the Supreme Court in reference to the allowance, which plaintiff may be advised to make.

All concur.

Judgment and order accordingly.

FRANK H. CROOKER, by Guardian, etc., Appellant, *v.* THE KNICKERBOCKER ICE COMPANY, Respondent.

It is not negligence *per se* to drive a team at " a lively trot " in the streets of a city. One so driving is not limited to any particular rate of speed, but is bound simply to use proper care and prudence, so as not to cause injury to other persons lawfully upon the streets.

(Argued April 20, 1888; decided May 8, 1888.)

THIS action was brought to recover damages for injuries alleged to have been caused by the negligence of defendant's servant. Plaintiff, while crossing a street in the city of Brooklyn, was run over by one of defendant's ice wagons, which was at the time being driven by a boy, a son of one of the defendant's employes. The court say :

"In the disposition of this case we assume that the lad who was driving the wagon at the time of the accident may be treated as the servant of the defendant, and yet we are of opinion that the plaintiff was properly nonsuited.

"The only proof of negligence was that the driver was driving the team on 'a lively trot.' It cannot be held as matter of law or fact that merely driving at the rate of speed stated, in the streets of a city, is negligence.   Persons driving in the streets of a city are not limited to any particular rate of speed. They may drive slow or fast but they must use proper care and prudence, so as not to cause injury to other persons lawfully upon the streets.   There was no proof in this case or at least not sufficient proof for submission to the jury, that the team was driven carelessly, or that the driver was negligent."

Herman F. Koepe for appellant.

Samuel D. Morris for respondent.

Per curiam opinion for affirmance.   RAPALLO, MILLER, EARL and FINCH, JJ., concur.   RUGER, Ch. J. ANDREWS and DANFORTH, JJ., dissent.

Judgment affirmed.

THE PEOPLE OF THE STATE OF NEW YORK, Appellant. *v.* THEODORE WARE, Respondent.

(Argued April 30, 1883 ; decided May 8, 1883.)

MEM. of decision below (29 Hun, 473).

A. J. Requier for appellant.

William F. Kintzing for respondent.

Agree to affirm ; no opinion.
All concur.
Judgment affirmed.

E. P. GRANT, Respondent, *v.* W. T. BIRDSALL, et al., Appellants

(Submitted May 1, 1883 ; decided May 8, 1883.)

S. W. Valentine for appellants.

D. M. Porter for respondent.

Agree to dismiss appeal; no opinion.
All concur.
Appeal dismissed.

THE AMITY INSURANCE COMPANY, Respondent, *v.* THE PENN-
SYLVANIA RAILROAD COMPANY, Appellant.

(Argued May 1, 1888 ; decided May 8, 1888.)

Osborn E. Bright for appellant.

G. A. Clement for respondent.

Agree to dismiss appeal; no opinion.
All concur.
Appeal dismissed.

In the Matter of the ATTORNEY-GENERAL *v.* THE NORTH
AMERICA LIFE INSURANCE COMPANY.

(Argued May 1, 1888 ; decided May 8, 1888.)

THIS was an appeal from an order of General Term, which
reversed an order of Special Term, directing the superintendent of the insurance department as to the distribution of the
fund held by him, deposited under the insurance laws as security for the policy-holders of the defendant.

Application was made by the superintendent of the insurance department in January, 1880, for the distribution of
that fund. On the 30th day of that month an order was
made at a Special Term of the Supreme Court, directing precisely and fully how the fund should be distributed. Every
person interested in the fund was made a party to that proceeding, in the mode prescribed by the rules and practice
of that court. That order does not appear to have been
appealed from or in any way vacated or modified, and no complaint was made that the superintendent was not proceeding
to distribute the fund as it directs. It did not appear that
these appellants were non-residents of the State, or that they

were not fully cognizant of that proceeding. After a delay of more than two years this motion was made for an order directing the superintendent to dispose of the fund in a manner different from that directed by the prior order. The General Term held that the motion should not have been granted for the reason that the prior order as'long as it remains unvacated and unreversed should be regarded as conclusive. The court here say : " We are of the same opinion. The orderly administration of justice requires that that order should be observed so long as it remains in force. If these appellants desired any relief from that order they should have appealed from it, or upon sufficient grounds should have moved to have it vacated or modified ; but so long·as it remains in force they and all the other policy-holders may be regarded as concluded by it. It is not necessary to hold that it operates as an absolute estoppel so that the same court might not give relief against it. But whether any policy-holder should be relieved or be permitted to have a distribution of the fund different from that prescribed by the order, was, 'at least, in the discretion of the Supreme Court, a discretion which is not reviewable here.

" The claim that the Supreme Court was without jurisdiction to make the order of January 30 is not well founded. We must take notice that a proper proceeding was pending in the Supreme Court for winding up the affairs of the insurance company, and distributing its assets among the persons entitled to share therein. Although this fund was in the custody of the superintendent of the insurance department and could not be taken from him and administered under the direction of the court by the receiver (*Ruggles* v. *Chapman*, 59 N. Y. 165 ; *People, ex rel. Ruggles*, v. *Chapman*, 64 id. 560), yet the fund,. being a portion of the assets of the company, came within the jurisdiction of the court. It could determine who was entitled to share therein, and how the same was to be divided among those interested therein, and its jurisdiction could be invoked for that purpose by the superintendent or other proper parties. As the proceeding was pending in the Supreme Court its jurisdiction in reference to this fund could be invoked by a petition presented in that proceeding ; and we must assume that this was so presented, and that the court acquired jurisdiction to make the order."

Raphael J. Moses, Jr., for appellants.

William Barnes for respondents.

EARL, J., reads for affirmance.
All concur.
Order affirmed.

THE PEOPLE, ex rel. THE EQUITABLE FIRE AND MARINE INSUR-ANCE COMPANY, Appellant, *v.* CHARLES G. FAIRMAN, Superintendent, etc., Respondent.

(Argued May 1, 1888 ; decided May 8, 1888.)

Edward D. McCarthy for appellant.

Austin A. Yates for respondent.

Agree to affirm; no opinion.
All concur.
Order affirmed.

THE PEOPLE OF THE STATE OF NEW YORK, Respondent, *v.* LIZZIE ELLEN WIGGINS, Appellant.

(Argued May 1, 1888 ; decided May 11, 1888.)

MEM. of decision below (28 Hun, 308).

The defendant was indicted and convicted of grand larceny in stealing a pocket-book containing money from one Mrs. Curtis, who was not produced as a witness on the trial. Because of this, it was objected that the prisoner could not be convicted. The court here say:

"It was not necessary to call Mrs. Curtis as a witness. There was sufficient evidence that she was the person in Macy's store; that she owned the pocket-book, and that the defendant took it from her, against her will and without her consent, and for the purpose of stealing it."

Benjamin Steinhardt for appellant.

A. J. Requier for respondent.

EARL, J., reads mem. for affirmance.
All concur.
Judgment affirmed.

THE PEOPLE OF THE STATE OF NEW YORK, Respondent, *v.*
THOMAS McDONNELL, Appellant.

Where, to an indictment for murder, the defendant pleaded "guilty to
manslaughter in the first degree," *held*, that an acceptance of the plea
and a judgment thereon was proper; that it was not necessary to aver in
the indictment the facts which, if proven, would constitute the lesser
crime.

(Submitted May 2, 1888; decided May 11, 1888.)

THE defendant was indicted for murder in the first degree.
He pleaded " guilty to manslaughter in the first degree," and
after sentence by the General Sessions and judgment thereon,
appealed to the Supreme Court, where the judgment was
affirmed.   The court here say :
" In this conclusion we find no error.   The indictment
charges the commission of the offense under circumstances
constituting its highest degree.   Upon trial he might have
been convicted of a lower degree (2 R. S. 702, § 27; *Keefe* v.
People, 40 N. Y. 348), and in that case could not again
be tried or convicted of a different degree thereof. (2 R. S.
702, § 28.)   The same result follows a plea of guilty.   It was
not necessary to aver in the indictment the facts or circumstances which, if proven, would constitute the lesser crime.
These are matters of evidence for the benefit of the accused.   *People* v. *Butler* (3 Park. Cr. 377), cited by the
appellant, is not to the contrary, but recognizes the rule
that an indictment under the common-law form is sufficient
notwithstanding the statute, and permits a conviction for the
offense charged in any degree according to the evidence.   Nor
do the cases referred to by his counsel support his contention."

William F. Kintzing for appellant.

John Vincent for respondent.

DANFORTH, J., reads for affirmance.
All concur.
Judgment affirmed.

ANTHONY BECHT, Administrator, etc., Respondent, *v.* AUSTIN
CORBIN, Receiver, etc., Appellant.

(Argued March 14, 1883 ; decided June 5, 1883.)

THIS action was brought against defendant, who, as receiver
of the Long Island Railroad Company, was operating the railroad of that company, to recover damages for alleged negligence
causing the death of Adam Becht, plaintiff's intestate.

The road runs through Atlantic avenue in the city of Brooklyn, and the deceased, in attempting to cross that avenue, was
struck by an engine passing on said road and was killed. The
opinion, which is given in full, states the other material facts.

"Under the decisions in the cases of *Reynolds* v. *N.
Y. C. & H. R. R. R. Co.* (58 N. Y. 248), and *Cordell* v. *N. Y. C. & H. R. R. R. Co.* (75 id. 330),
the motion for a nonsuit should have been granted. The
plaintiff not only failed to furnish any .affirmative proof of
due care on the part of the deceased in approaching the track,
but the only direct proof in the case is to the contrary. The
only witness who saw the deceased struck testifies that he saw
him when he left the sidewalk, and that he was running at the
time, with his head down ; that he ran obliquely across the
track toward the engine, partially facing the engine as he ran.
The witness noticed deceased from the time he left the sidewalk until he was struck, and that he did not look up toward
the engine at all until he was directly in front of it on the
track. This evidence, though uncontradicted, was not conclusive, the witness being the conductor of the train to which the
engine belonged, and if the burden had been upon the defendant to prove affirmatively the negligence of the deceased, there

might have been a question for the jury as to the truth of the testimony. But the burden of proving due care rested upon the plaintiff, under the cases cited, and the only direct proof, as before said, was to the contrary.

"Independently of this direct proof there is nothing in the circumstances of the case which is not, to say the least, quite as consistent with the negligence of the deceased, as with due care on his part. But the preponderance is greatly on the side of his negligence. Indeed, it is almost if not quite conclusive. The point from which the deceased started to cross the avenue and the point on the track where he collided with the engine are conceded, and these points show that he was crossing the avenue obliquely in a north-easterly direction, partially facing the engine, which was approaching from the east, as stated by the conductor. Although it was dusk, and assuming that the engine had no headlight, yet it appears by the testimony of the plaintiff's witnesses that it could be seen at a much greater distance than was necessary to enable the deceased to avoid it. It must have been within only a few feet of him when he stepped on the track in front of it. If he had looked at all he must have seen it. The only theory upon which it is claimed that the jury could find that the deceased exercised due care is that he may have looked and seen the engine and supposed it was running away from him, instead of toward him. But if he had been attentive he could not have supposed this. From the place where he left the sidewalk to the point on the track where the engine struck him was a distance of more than half the width of the avenue. He was crossing in a north-easterly direction. If the engine had come from the west and was going east it must have passed him while he was crossing. When he stepped upon the track, if he had looked, he would have seen it a few feet to his right, that is, to the east, and that it was in motion. It could not have got in that position without his observing it, had he paid any attention, unless it was coming from the east. If he had seen it under these circumstances, can it be assumed that he exercised due care in attempting to cross the track as he did? The circumstances are all inconsistent with the theory that he exercised such care, and the plaintiff should, under the decisions before cited, have been nonsuited."

Edward E. Sprague for appellant.

Anthony Barrett for respondent.

RAPALLO, J., reads for reversal and new trial.
All concur, except DANFORTH, J., not voting.
Judgment reversed.

THE PEOPLE OF THE STATE OF NEW YORK, Respondent, *v.* THE LA PLATA MINING AND SMELTING COMPANY, Appellant.

THIS case presented a similar question and was argued and decided with *People* v. *N. Y. F. D. D. Co. (ante,* p. 487).

MARCUS T. HUN, as Receiver, etc., Appellant, *v.* HENRY H. VAN DYCK et al., Respondents.

(Argued April 25, 1883 ; decided June 5, 1883.)

REPORTED below (26 Hun, 567).

Peter B. Olney for appellant.

Elliott F. Shepard & Nelson J. Waterbury for respondents.

Agree to affirm ; no opinion.
All concur.
Judgment affirmed.

1

MARY A. HARLINGER, as Administratrix, etc., Respondent, *v.* THE NEW YORK CENTRAL AND HUDSON RIVER RAILROAD COMPANY, Appellant.

(Argued April 27, 1883; decided June 5, 1883.)

George N. Kennedy for appellant.

Louis Marshall for respondent.

Agree to affirm; no opinion.
All concur, except RUGER, Ch. J., not sitting.
Judgment affirmed.

———————

JAMES B. HART, Appellant, *v.* THE MAYOR, ALDERMEN AND COMMONALTY OF THE CITY OF NEW YORK, Respondent.

(Argued May 3, 1883; decided June 5, 1883.)

Thomas Allison for appellant.

D. J. Dean for respondent.

Agree to affirm on opinion of MILLER, J., in *Dickinson* v. *Mayor, etc. (ante,* p. 584).
All concur.
Order affirmed, and judgment absolute against plaintiff on stipulation.

———————

THE PEOPLE OF THE STATE OF NEW YORK, Appellant, *v.* GEORGE W. MATSELL et al. Respondents.

(Submitted May 4, 1883; decided June 5, 1883.)

George P. Andrews for respondents

Affirmed by default; no opinion.

THOMAS DORAN, Respondent, *v.* THE FRANKLIN FIRE INSUR-
ANCE COMPANY, Appellant.

(Argued May 7, 1883; decided June 5, 1883.)

Everett P. Wheeler for appellant.

Amasa J. Parker for respondent.

Agree to affirm ; no opinion.
All concur.
Judgment affirmed.

LEWIS POTTER, Appellant, *v.* THE TOWN OF GREENWICH, Respondent.

(Argued May 7, 1883 ; decided June 5, 1883.)

THERE were two appeals in this action, one from judgment
of the General Term, sustaining a demurrer to the second and
third counts of the complaint.   The other from an order of the
same court, reversing a judgment in favor of plaintiff, and
granting a new trial.   The first appeal was affirmed on the
opinion of RUMSEY, J., at General Term, which is reported in
26 Hun, 326.

The first count of the complaint alleged in substance
that pursuant to chapter 907, Laws of 1869, an application
was duly made by the town of Greenwich, defendant, and it
was duly authorized to issue its bonds to the amount of $40,000,
and invest the same, or the proceeds, in the second mortgage
bonds of the Greenwich and Johnsonville railroad ; that commissioners were duly appointed, who issued the bonds of the
town to the amount specified ; that said bonds were drawn as
said commissioners understood and believed in accordance with
said act, and they intended that they should be so drawn, and
intended and believed they were good and valid obligations of
the town, and so advised plaintiff ; that they supposed the act
authorized the bonds to be issued payable at any time not exceeding thirty years ; that plaintiff, believing and relying on

said statements of the commissioners, purchased one of said bonds, upon which default has been made in the payment of interest. By the terms of the bond the principal was made payable twenty years from its date. Plaintiff asked to have the bond reformed so as to make it conform to the statute; *i. e.*, to be made payable thirty years from date, and asked judgment for the interest due and unpaid. The answer to this count was a general denial.

The material facts as to this issue appear in that portion of the opinion which follows.

" The second appeal presents a more difficult question, whether a court of equity should interfere and reform the bond, which lies at the basis of this action. The case is a peculiar one, and in support of it we have been cited to no precedent. Between the plaintiff and defendant there was no previous contract — there was no contract or agreement at all, except as it is contained in the bond. The plaintiff, after the fullest opportunity for examination, bought the bond on the 25th of March, 1871, and made no objection to it until May 25, 1880, when he commenced this action, on the ground that, although the bond purports to have been issued under the statute known as the Bonding Act (Chap. 907, Laws of 1869), it does not conform therewith as to the time when payable. If the terms of a special authority were always followed, if public officers always performed their duty, a departure from the authority, or an exceptional omission on their part, might be ascribed to mistake, and the mistake rectified as of course. But nothing of that kind is pretended. The finding of the Special Term is that the commissioners intended that the bonds issued by them should conform to the statute, but committed the drafting of them to a scrivener, who ' by mistake made them so read that in effect they are payable at the expiration of twenty years from their date, instead of thirty years from their date,' and the commissioners inadvertently issued and sold the same. It is very properly argued by respondent's counsel that so far as this finding attributes this mistake to a scrivener, or indeed to any draftsman, it is without evidence. It does not even appear by whom, or by whose directions, the bonds were drawn. It does not appear that the person who drew them labored under mistake of any kind, nor but that having — indeed he must be presumed to have had — perfect and present knowledge of the statute, used language and inserted terms in the bonds deliberately. In other words, for aught that appears, or is warranted by the evidence, the bond in question is exactly as the draftsman intended it should be.

"It is said, however, that the commissioners executed the bond under a mistake. The only one of that body who testified, says he read the bond before he signed it. Then he knew its contents. It is not found that he was ignorant of the statute under which he was appointed, and although he testified that he had not read the law, that fact even does not appear in relation to his associates. So the case is, that bonds drawn as the scrivener intended to draw them were executed by the commissioners with knowledge of their contents, and under the influence of no fraud, but by one commissioner under the impression, which proves to have been a mistaken one, that they conformed to the statute. As to the other commissioners there is no evidence. As there is no foundation for the finding that the scrivener was mistaken, no evidence but that two at least of the commissioners had in their mind the statute and the words of the bond, and purposely signed the bond in disregard of the statute, the case presents itself as one where what was done was knowingly and intentionally done, and where, therefore, there could be no mistake. It is contended, however, by the learned counsel for the appellant that the bonds are valid as they now read. That seems also to have been the opinion of the trial judge, who finds as a conclusion of law, 'that the statute providing that such bonds shall become due and payable at the expiration of thirty years from their date fixes thirty years as the time in which said bonds shall become due and payable, and overrules and controls the words of the bonds prescribing an earlier date for their payment.' If that is so, and whether it is so or not is not a question here — for the plaintiff presents the case in no such aspect — no aid from a court of equity is needed, and the plaintiff has vexed the courts without cause. He should be left to his remedy when the bond matures."

Samuel Hand for appellant.

Esek Cowen for respondent.

DANFORTH, J., reads for affirmance of order and judgment absolute against plaintiff, dismissing complaint.

All concur, except ANDREWS and EARL, JJ., dissenting.

Also for affirmance of judgment sustaining demurrer to the second and third counts of the complaint.

All concur.

Judgment accordingly.

THE PEOPLE OF THE STATE OF NEW YORK, Respondent. *v.* MARGARET SMITH, Appellant.

(Submitted May 8, 1888 ; decided June 5, 1888.)

REPORTED below (28 Hun, 626).

Howe & Hummel for appellant.

John Vincent for respondent.

Agree to affirm on opinion of General Term.

All concur.

Judgment affirmed.

FREDERICK A. POTTS, Appellant, *v.* ISAAC MAYER, Impleaded, etc., Respondent.

(Argued May 9, 1888 ; decided June 5, 1888.)

Samuel Hand for appellant.

Payson Merrill for respondent.

Agree to affirm ; no opinion.

All concur.

Judgment affirmed.

WILLIAM R. BREED et al., Executors, etc., Appellants, *v.* JOHN PADGETT et al., Respondents.

R. A. Stanton for appellants.

Samuel S. Stafford for respondents.

Agree to affirm; no opinion.
All concur.
Judgment affirmed.

INDEX.

ACCUMULATION.

1. The provisions of the Revised Statutes (1 R. S. 726, § 37; id. 773, § 3), authorizing an accumulation of the income of real and personal property for the benefit of minors, require that the accumulation shall be for the benefit of a minor solely and during his minority, and that, when the period of accumulation ceases, the accumulated funds shall be released from further restraint and paid over to the person for whose benefit the accumulation is directed. *Pray* v. *Hegeman.* 508

2. A direction for accumulation during a minority, accompanied with a gift of the income of the accumulated fund after the expiration of the minority, to the minor for life, and of the principal, upon his death, to other persons, is void. (1 R. S. 726, § 38.) *Id.*

ACTION.

1. An action may be brought under the Code of Civil Procedure (§ 1937), after the recovery of a judgment against joint debtors, by the judgment creditor "against one or more of the defendants who were not summoned in the original action," although the defendants served have appealed and have given the security, which under said Code (§ 1310) "stays all proceedings to enforce the judgment appealed from." *Morey* v. *Tracey.* 581

2. The second action is not brought to enforce the judgment, but to establish the liability of the defendants not served, which is not determined by such judgment. *Id.*

ADMISSIONS AND DECLARATIONS.

The rule allowing the silence of a person to be taken as an implied admission of the truth of allegations spoken or uttered in his presence does not apply to silence at a judicial proceeding or hearing. *People* v. *Willett.* 29

—— *Where part of a writing or conversation are proved as admissions by a party, he may give in evidence other parts tending to explain or modify the admissions. Grattan* v. *M. L. Ins. Co.* 274

AGREEMENT.

See CONTRACT.

ALBANY (CITY OF).

1. The act of 1881 (Chap. 582, Laws of 1881) purporting to amend the provision of the Code of Civil Procedure (§ 1041), in regard to the selection and drawings of jurors in the city and county of Albany; so far as it relates to grand jurors, is a local act and is within the prohibition of the provision of the State Constitution (Art. 3, § 18), forbidding the passage of a local or pri-

vate bill for "selecting, drawing, summoning or impaneling grand or petit jurors." *People* v. *Petrea.*
128

2. Assuming, therefore, the said act not to have been reported by the commissioners appointed by law to revise the statutes, and so not within the exception (Art. 3, § 25) exempting from the operation of said provision, bills so reported, the said act is as to grand jurors unconstitutional and void.   *Id.*

3. Certain accounts for repairs to the "City Building" and for articles furnished defendant were presented to and audited by its common council, and by resolution ordered to be paid. The common council had power to make the repairs and to purchase the articles. In an action upon the accounts, *held*, that the action of the common council not having been rescinded, it was conclusive recognition of the liability of the city, and precluded it from defending on the ground that it was not originally bound to pay because the indebtedness was incurred without previous authority. *Albany City Nat. B'k* v. *City of Albany.*
363

4. The work was done and articles furnished by direction of individual members of the common council, who were not authorized to bind the city or contract debts on its behalf. The accounts, when presented, were referred to the proper committee, and were reported back with a certificate to each to the effect that the committee had examined the account, that the prices charged were reasonable, and that the expenditure "was duly authorized by the common council," and thereupon that body audited the accounts. *Held*, that assuming the city could only be charged on proof or ratification, the evidence justified a finding of such ratification ; that the common council was chargeable with knowledge of its own records, and this although there had been a change in the individuals composing that body ; and, therefore, it was to be assumed

that, in acting upon the bills, it knew the indebtedness had not been authorized by any resolution, and that it acted independently of the statement in the certificates, and in auditing and directing payment of the bills, intended to adopt the transactions out of which the indebtedness arose.   *Id.*

5. Also *held*, that a clause in the city charter (§ 16, chap. 305, Laws of 1877), prohibiting any member of the common council from incurring any expense in behalf of the city for repairs or supplies unless previously ordered by the common council, did not limit the legislative power of that body, or prevent the city from paying a debt so incurred.   *Id.*

ANTE-NUPTIAL AGREEMENT

1. By an ante-nuptial agreement the woman covenanted that if, after marriage, the man died first, she would accept $1,500 " in full satisfaction of her dower in his estate, and shall bar her from claiming the same, either in his real or personal estate." He covenanted to provide by will for the payment of that sum " in lieu of dower, or her rights as his widow in his estate." The parties married and the husband died, having made provision by will as covenanted. *Held*, that the agreement was valid and remained in full force after marriage (§ 3, chap. 375, Laws of 1849); that the intent was that the woman should take nothing as widow from her husband's estate ; and that, therefore, there being no children living, the issue of such marriage, she was not entitled to the specific articles given by the statute (2 R. S. 83, § 9) to a widow; that, although not to be appraised, they were part of the estate, and she, by her agreement, was estopped from claiming them. *In re Estate of Young* v. *Hicks.*
235

2. As to whether the matter would have been affected by the existence of minor children or others interested, *quære.*   *Id.*

APOTHECARIES.

1. Where, upon the sale by a druggist of a poisonous medicine, he fully and fairly warns the purchaser of its character, and gives accurate information and directions as to the quantity which may be safely taken, and the customer is injured or killed by taking an overdose in disregard of such direction, the druggist is not liable for negligence or tort, simply because of an omission on his part to put a label marked " poison " upon the " parcel in which the sale is made " as required by the statute. (2 R. S. 694, § 23.) The customer may not disregard the warning and direction and charge the consequences of his own negligence or recklessness upon the druggist. *Wohlfahrt* v. *Beckert.* 490

2. In an action against a druggist for alleged negligence in the sale of a poisonous medicine without attaching a label marked poison, thus causing the death of W., plaintiff's intestate, it appeared, that W., having been advised to take a comparatively harmless preparation known as " black draught," and that he could take a small wine glass thereof, which he could procure at any drug store for ten cents, went to defendant's drug store, where, according to the testimony of defendant's clerk, he asked defendant for ten cents worth of " black drops ; " defendant told him that was a poison, and advised him to take another preparation; this W. refused, and defendant thereupon directed the witness to give him black drops, but informed him that he should only take ten or twelve drops for a dose ; witness gave W. two drachms of the medicine asked for in a vial upon which was a label marked " black drops ; " the label did not have the word " poison " thereon. W. took nearly the whole of the contents of the vial and died in consequence. *Held,* that if the testimony of the clerk was to be taken as the truth, a verdict for defendant was properly directed ; but that the jury were at liberty, under the circumstances, to disbelieve such testimony, as the witness was interested, having violated the law by omitting the prescribed label ; and that, therefore, the question as to whether the warning testified to was in fact given was one for the jury, and the direction was error. *Id.*

APPEALS.

1. The provisions of chapter 16 of the Code of Civil Procedure in reference to appeals do not apply to an appeal in a proceeding by *certiorari* commenced prior to September 1, 1880 (Code, § 3347, subd. 11). *People, ex rel. Murphy,* v. *French.* 306

2. *It seems,* the provision of said chapter (§ 2140), declaring that in such a proceeding the court, upon " *the hearing,*" shall have power to determine whether there was such a preponderance of proof against the existence of any fact found, that the verdict of a jury affirming its existence rendered in an action in the Supreme Court, " would be set aside as against the weight of evidence," ' has no application to appeals to this court. It only applies to the " hearing " on return to the writ, and is confined to the court in which such hearing is had. *Id.*

3. *It seems,* also, that the general statutory scheme for the distribution of judicial powers does not contemplate the review by this court of disputed questions of fact, and it will not entertain such questions in the absence of express legislative authority. *Id.*

4. Where an order of Special Term recited that it was made " on reading and filing the decision of the court," referring to an opinion which was the only decision filed, and the minutes of the General Term on affirmance of such order stated that it was affirmed on opinion of the judge at Special Term, *held,* that the opinion was thus made part of the record and could be referred to to ascertain the grounds of the decision ; and, it

appearing therefrom that the decision was based upon the ground of a want of power, *held*, that the order, although a discretionary one, was reviewable here. *Tolman* v. *Syr. & B. R. R. Co.* 853

5. Within the limitations fixed by the provision of the Code of Civil Procedure (§ 3253) in reference to extra allowances for costs, the power of the court below to make allowances is not subject to review here ; but the question whether an allowance exceeds those limitations is one of law, proper to be considered by this court. *Conaughty* v. *Saratoga Co. B'k.* 401

6. In an action brought to restrain a corporation from the exercise of its corporate franchises, *held*, that the subject-matter involved was simply the corporate franchises, not its capital and moneyed assets, that in the absence of any evidence as to the money value of those franchises, an extra allowance was improper, and that an order allowing it was reviewable here. *Id.*

7. The provision of the Code of Civil Procedure (§ 3301, as amended by chap. 399, Laws of 1882), providing that the stipulation of the attorneys for parties to an action may take the place of a clerk's certificate to a copy of a paper whereof a certified copy is required, was not intended to alter the effect of the provision (§ 1315) requiring a return to this court to be certified by the clerk of the court from which the appeal is taken, or of the rule of this court (Rule 1) making the same requirement. *Dow* v. *Darragh.* 537

8. Returns to this court should be made by a responsible officer, under sanction of his official oath, and attorneys for parties cannot, by stipulation, make up a case for the court. *Id.*

9. In the absence of exceptions on a criminal trial this court has no power to review the case upon the facts. *People* v. *Hovey.* 554

10. The provision of the Code of

Criminal Procedure (§ 527), as amended in 1882 (Chap. 360, Laws of 1882), providing that "the appellate court may order a new trial if it be satisfied that the verdict against the prisoner was against the weight of evidence or against law, or that justice required a new trial, whether any exceptions shall have been taken or not," applies only to appeals to the Supreme Court. *Id.*

11. An exception to a charge taken after a criminal trial has terminated does not present any question for the consideration of an appellate court. *Id.*

12. Where, therefore, after a criminal trial, and when the prisoner was before the court for sentence, his counsel moved for a new trial for an alleged error in the charge, and upon denial of the motion took an exception, *held*, that no question was thereby presented here for review. *Id.*

13. The provision of the Code of Criminal Procedure (§ 527) providing that "the appellate court may order a new trial if it be satisfied that the verdict against the prisoner was against the weight of evidence, * * * or that justice requires," is applicable only to the Supreme Court and gives that court a discretionary power. When in the exercise of that discretion it refuses or grants a new trial its determination is not reviewable here. *People* v. *Boas.* 560

14. Under the provision of said Code (§ 519), authorizing an appeal to this court by the people from a judgment of the General Term reversing a judgment of conviction, such an appeal brings up for review only questions of law. *Id.*

15. In determining whether the reversal was solely upon questions of law, the record only can be examined ; the opinion of the General Term forms no part thereof and may not be looked at. *Id.*

16. Unless, therefore, the order of

the General Term shows that the Supreme Court has exercised its discretion and refused a new trial upon the facts and granted it only for errors of law, there is nothing for this court to review on appeal to it. *Id.*

17. An action may be brought under the Code of Civil Procedure (§ 1937), after the recovery of a judgment against joint debtors, by the judgment creditor "against one or more of the defendants who were not summoned in the original action," although the defendants served have appealed and have given the security, which under said Code (§ 1310) "stays all proceedings to enforce the judgment appealed from." *Morey* v. *Tracey.* 581

18. The determination of the trial judge of the fact as to the loss of a paper, secondary evidence of the contents of which is sought to be given, cannot be reviewed here, unless the proof of loss was so clear and conclusive that it was error of law to find against it. *Kearney* v. *Mayor, etc.* 617

19. The complaint herein set forth a demand for $398.71 ; the answer denied liability and set up a counter-claim for $301.29. The trial court found with defendant and gave judgment against plaintiff for the counter-claim. The General Term reversed the judgment. *Held,* that the amount of the two claims constituted "the matter in controversy," within the meaning of the Code of Civil Procedure (§ 191, subd. 3), and that this court had jurisdiction on appeal. *Crawford* v. *West Side B'k.* 631

—— *Objection that evidence of contradictory declarations of witnesses was received without first calling the witness's attention thereto, if not raised on trial cannot be raised on appeal.*
See *Mead* v. *Shea.* 122

—— *When objection as to jurisdiction may be taken on appeal to this court although not taken below.*
See *Foster* v. *Shepard.* 251

—— *Costs upon.*
See *Murtha* v. *Curley.* 859

—— *Where case is prepared and settled by consent of both parties and is properly certified, and no motion is made to amend, no complaint that it is defective can be made here, and argument must be made upon it as returned. The case should be settled and signed by the judge or referee who tried the cause.*
Also when appeal should be dismissed for failure to serve undertaking.
See *Reese* v. *Boese.* (*Mem.*) 632

—— *Order granting preliminary injunction not appealable to this court.*
See *Foster* v. *City of B.* (*Mem.*) 629

APPOINTMENT,

—— *What is proper execution of power of appointment.*
See *Hutton* v. *Benkard.* 295

—— *Construction of, and what is valid execution of power of appointment.*
See *Mott* v. *Ackerman.* 539

ASSESSMENT AND TAXATION.

1. The act (Subd. 9, § 1, chap. 482, Laws of 1875, as amended by chap. 365, Laws of 1880, and by chap. 554, Laws of 1881), giving to the board of supervisors in any county containing an incorporated city of over one hundred thousand inhabitants, where contiguous territory in the county has been mapped out into streets and avenues, power to lay out, open, grade and construct the same, and to provide for the assessment of damages on the property benefited, is not a local law within the meaning of the State Constitution, and so is not violative of the constitutional provision (Art. 3, § 18) prohibiting the passage of a local or private law laying out or opening highways, or of the provision (Art. 3, § 23) requiring the legislature to act by general laws in conferring upon boards of supervisors any power of local legislation. *In re Church.* 1

2. Where a board of supervisors, acting within the authority so conferred, has created the occasion for and has required the appointment of commissioners to estimate and appraise the damages and benefits, the Supreme Court has jurisdiction to make such appointment. *Id.*

3. The board of supervisors may impose the whole cost of the improvement upon the property included in the area which it decides has been benefited to that extent. *Id.*

4. By resolution of the board of supervisors of the county of K. which had directed the opening of a street, under said act, in the town of N. U., the town was authorized to issue bonds to pay for the improvement, to be paid out of the general tax, so far as the assessments proved inadequate. *Held,* that adequate and certain provision was thus made for compensation for property taken, sufficient to meet the constitutional prohibition against the taking of property without compensation. *Id.*

5. The petition upon which proceedings were instituted to vacate an assessment for regulating and grading a street in the city of New York, authorized by the act of 1871 (Chap. 226, Laws of 1871), charged in substance that the commissioner of public works fraudulently combined and colluded with the contractors to let the contract at an extravagant price. The contract in question was not let at a public letting, but was what is known as "a special contract," the commissioner having invited four persons to bid for the work. The persons so invited put in bids for "filling," which was the main item, ranging from $1.43 to $1.60 per cubic yard. The contract was awarded for $1.47. The petitioner upon the hearing offered in evidence the "bid-book" of the department of public works, containing a record of bids received for public lettings prior and subsequent to the contract in question, relating to streets in the same vicinity, by which it appeared that filling was contracted for at prices

not exceeding eighty cents per cubic yard. This evidence was rejected. *Held* error; that the commissioner, in the absence of evidence to the contrary, must be presumed to have known the usual prices paid for the work, and the evidence was competent on the issue of fraud. *In re Righter.* 111

6. Also *held,* that it was competent as bearing upon the alleged combination and collusion to prove the bids by the selected bidders for the other special contract work and the contracts awarded therefor. *Id.*

7. The provision of the act of 1873 entitled "An act to provide for the Eastern boulevard in the city of New York, and in relation to certain alterations of the map or plan of said city, and certain local improvements" (§ 4, chap. 528, Laws of 1873), authorizing the department of public parks to do the work "of regulating, grading or otherwise improving Tenth avenue," authorized the construction of a sewer in said avenue. *In re L. & W. Orphan Home.* 116

8. Under said provision the department was authorized to do the work of constructing such a sewer, or any part thereof, by day's work. *Id.*

9. In proceedings to vacate an assessment for the construction of such a sewer, *held,* that in the absence of evidence that there was no connection or relation between the portion of Tenth avenue specified in the act and the Eastern boulevard, for the purpose of sustaining the constitutionality of the act, the connection was to be assumed; and, therefore, that said act was not violative of the provision of the State Constitution (Art 3,§ 13), declaring that no local or private act shall contain more than one subject, and requiring that to be expressed in the title. *Id.*

10. The greater portion of the work was done by day's work. It appeared that rock excavation cost over $14 per cubic yard, pipe cul-

vert $7.05 per lineal foot, and brick sewer $25 per lineal foot, while the fair value was rock excavation $4 per cubic yard, pipe culvert $1.50 per lineal foot and brick sewer $4.55 per lineal foot. *Held*, that the evidence disclosed not merely a case of improvidence and extravagance, but sufficiently established fraud or irregularity. *Id.*

11. But *held*, that the petitioner was not entitled to have the assessment wholly vacated ; and that an order reducing it, by striking out the amount added by reason of such fraud or irregularity, was proper. *Id.*

12. Also *held*, that an objection that the petition contained no averments of fraud affecting the assessment, not having been taken at Special Term, would not be heard here. *Id,*

13. The act of 1865 (Chap. 694, Laws of 1865), as amended in 1875 (Chap. 60, Laws of 1875), providing that an insurance corporation of another State seeking to do business here shall pay to the superintendent of the insurance department for taxes, fines, etc., an amount equal to that imposed by the " existing or future laws " of the State of its origin, upon companies of this State seeking to do business there, when such amount is greater than that required for such purposes by the then existing laws of this State, is not an unlawful delegation of legislative power. *People* v. *Fire Association.* 311

14. The said act is not repugnant to the provision of the Federal Constitution (Art. 14), declaring that no State shall "deny to any person within its jurisdiction the equal protection of the law." That provision relates wholly to persons rightfully within the jurisdiction, not to the terms and conditions on which alone they can come in. *Ide*

15. Said act is not violative of the provision of the State Constitution (Art. 3, § 20), declaring that "every law which imposes, continues or re-

vives a tax shall distinctly state the tax and the object to which it is to be applied, and it shall not be sufficient to refer to any other law to fix such tax or object," as the condition imposed by the act is in the nature of a license fee. *Id.*

16. The said act is not affected by the provision of the act of 1861 (§ 8, chap. 361, Laws of 1881) in reference to taxing certain corporations, companies and associations, which declares that the organization mentioned by the act shall thereafter " be exempt from assessment and taxation for State purposes," except as therein provided, as the exemption there is only from the general taxes for State purposes. *Id.*

17. By a law of Pennsylvania it is provided that an insurance company of another State doing business in that State shall pay into the State treasury annually three per cent of the premiums received there during the year. *Held*, that said act of 1875 required of an insurance company of that State doing business here a payment to the superintendent of such sum as, with other payments, would make a full payment of three per cent on the premiums received by it; that if it had not paid the two per cent required to be paid by the State law (Chap. 465, Laws of 1875, as amended by chap. 359, Laws of 1876, chap. 188, Laws of 1878, and chap. 153, Laws of 1879), to the treasurers of the fire departments of the cities and villages, on all premiums received on property located therein, because there was no fire department in a particular locality to receive it, such amount must be added to the sum payable to the superintendent. *Id.*

18. The statement in the act (Chap. 542, Laws of 1880, as amended by chap. 361, Laws of 1881) providing for the taxation of certain corporations and associations, that the taxes imposed thereby " shall be applicable to the payment of the ordinary and current expenses of the State," is a sufficient compliance with the requirement of

the State Constitution (Art. 3, § 20) that every law imposing a tax "shall distinctly state * * * the object to which it is to be applied." *People* v. *Home Ins. Co.* 328

19. The taxes upon corporations, imposed by said act, are taxes upon franchises, not upon property and the fact that dividends, a portion of which is derived from securities exempt from taxation, furnish the basis for computing the amount of the tax, does not invalidate it. *Id.*

20. In taxing corporations under the act the State authorities are not required to deduct the amount of stock which the corporation holds in United States bonds from the total amount of its capital stock and to compute the tax only upon dividends derived from the remainder. *Id.*

21. The legislature has, by virtue of its jurisdiction over corporations organized under its laws, authority to impose such a tax. *Id.*

22. In performing the duty of levying taxes the legislature may, in its discretion, impose unequal or double taxes, and in determining the question of legislative power the courts are precluded from considering that question. *Id.*

23. *It seems*, however, that the corporations affected by said act are not thereby subjected to unequal or double taxation. *Id.*

24. The authorities showing the distinction between franchise and property taxes collated. *Id.*

25. Under the act of 1880 (Chap. 542, Laws of 1880), providing for " raising taxes for the use of the State upon certain corporations," etc., the first report required to be made by the officers of the corporation included in the act was to be made in November, 1880, and the first tax paid in January, 1881 ; and this, although at the latter date the corporation had not been

in existence for a year. *People* v. *S. V. Hy. Gold Co.* 388

26. This construction does not give to the act a retroactive effect, as the tax so imposed was to pay the prospective expenditure for the fiscal year commencing October 1, 1880. *Id.*

27. The act of 1865 (Chap. 453, Laws of 1865), providing, where property has been omitted in an assessment-roll, for its assessment and taxation for the omitted year, in the year next succeeding, is to be construed in connection with the general system of taxation of which it forms a part, and so is not subject to the constitutional objection that it does not provide for notice or a hearing. *People, ex rel.* v. *B'd Assrs.* 430

28. The relator, a corporation liable to taxation for State purposes under the act of 1880 (Chap. 542, Laws of 1880), was omitted from the assessment-roll by the assessors of the city of Brooklyn, where it was taxable, and no tax upon its personal property for city and county purposes was imposed for that year. In 1881 it was assessed for that year, and, in addition, for the omitted year, under said act of 1865, the valuation for the year 1879 being taken. Notice was given as prescribed by the statute also calling attention to the laws of both years. *Held*, that the act of 1865 was adjustable to the change made by the act of 1880, and that the assessment was val id, *Id*

29. The acts providing for the taxation of the franchises of certain corporations and associations (Chap. 542, Laws of 1880, as amended by chap. 361, Laws of 1881) are prospective in their character ; the tax thereby imposed is not for the past, but for the future enjoyment of the franchises, and the amount of the dividends made or declared during the year are made simply the measure of the annual value of the franchises. *People* v. *Albany Ins. Co.* 458

30. Defendant, a corporation, taxable

under said act, and having a capital of $200,000, in January, 1881, declared a dividend of six and one-fourth per cent from the earnings and profits of the company for the current year. In February, 1880, having on hand a large surplus fund, all of which had been earned and acquired before January 1, 1880, and in contemplation of the expiration of its charter, which would take place in June, 1880, it was resolved by the company that $100,000 should be taken from such surplus and paid to and divided among its stockholders, and it was at the same time resolved that the charter should be extended. Upon a case submitted under the Code of Civil Procedure (§ 1279), *held*, that this division, even if a dividend within the letter, was not such within the meaning or for the purposes of the act ; that the accumulation of earnings was no measure of the value of the enjoyment of the franchises during the year 1880 or 1881, and was not within the contemplation of the framers of the act ; and that the corporation was not liable to taxation thereon.
Id.

31. *It seems* that should a corporation, for the purpose of evading taxation under the act, divide six per cent or more, but less than its actual earnings in any one year after the passage of said act, and thus create a surplus, the division of such surplus in a subsequent year may be treated as a dividend within the act. *Id.*

32. The defendant was incorporated for the purpose, as expressed in its charter (Chap. 170, Laws of 1843), "of constructing, using and providing one or more dry-docks or wet-docks or other conveniences and structures for building, raising, repairing or coppering vessels and steamers of every description." In an action to recover taxes alleged to be due for the year 1881, under the act of 1880 (Chap. 542, Laws of 1880), *held*, that defendant was not "a manufacturing corporation" within the meaning of the clause in said act (§ 3), which exempts such cor-

porations from its provisions ; and that it was liable to taxation under the act. *People* v. *N. Y. F. Dry-Dock Co.* 487

33. Under the provision of the act (Chap. 296, Laws of 1874) subjecting the property of the N. Y. & O. M. R. R. Co. to taxation, and appropriating the amount of the county taxes thereon, in any town which has issued bonds in aid of the construction of the road of said company, to such town, to be devoted to the payment of its bonds, after any such tax has been collected, the moneys belong to the town, and any diversion thereof from their lawful object is an injury to the rights of the town, which may be protected by an appropriate action in its behalf. *Bridges* v. *Bd of Sup'rs.* 570

34. The town is not confined to the remedy given by the act (§ 4), *i. e.* an action against the collector and the sureties upon his bond. *Id.*

35. The action on behalf of the town might, under the Revised Statutes (2 R. S. 473, § 92), have been properly brought by the supervisor of the town, and may be so brought under the Code of Civil Procedure (§ 1926). *Id.*

36. Where, therefore, the warrant issued to the collector of such a town required him to pay over the moneys so collected to the county treasurer, which command the collector obeyed, instead of paying the amount collected to the railroad commissioners of the town, as prescribed by the act (§ 3), *held*, that an action as for moneys had and received was properly brought by the supervisor of the town against the board of supervisors of the county to recover the amount so paid. *Id.*

37. Also *held*, that it was no defense to the action that the county had received no more money from the town for taxes than it was entitled to receive under the general statutes of the State ; that it was the duty of the board of supervisors, in making an apportionment of the .

49. As to whether an action may be maintained by the city of New York against the State comptroller to recover alleged over-payments on account of taxes for State purposes, *quære* Id.

ASSIGNMENT.

The mere fact that an assignment of property by a debtor was voluntary and without consideration is not sufficient to require a finding that it was fraudulent against creditors. *Genesee River Nat. B'k* v. *Mead.* 637

ATTACHMENT.

1. Pending a contest as to the validity of a will a special administrator was appointed. A judgment had been recovered against the decedent prior to his death. An attachment against the judgment creditor was sought to be executed upon the judgment by service of copy upon the executrix named in the will. The special administrator was then acting, and the contest was then and is still pending. *Held,* that the executrix had no power to represent the estate, and so was not the "individual holding such property" within the meaning of the provision of the Code of Procedure (§ 235), authorizing the execution of an attachment by service of a copy; that, therefore, the judgment was not reached by the attachment; and that an order of the surrogate denying an application of the attachment creditor for the payment of the same to him was proper. *In re Flandrow.* 256

2. Also *held,* the fact that the attorney for the special administrator, upon being inquired of, gave information that the person named in the will was executrix, but concealed the appointment of the special administrator, did not preclude the latter from raising the objection. Id.

ATTORNEY AND CLIENT.

1. In an action by C., an attorney, to recover a compensation agreed to be paid for professional services, it appeared that W., being interested in the success of the plaintiff in an action brought for the purpose of contesting the validity of a will, in which action a verdict had been rendered sustaining the will, entered into a contract with C., by which the latter agreed to appeal and conduct the case to a final determination; for which service W. agreed to pay a sum specified. C. was thereupon substituted as attorney for the plaintiff in said action, and performed services therein. W. having died, his executors, the defendants in this action, settled and discontinued the action. Defendants were permitted to prove, under objection and exception, that after the employment of C., and before the death of W., the former entered into a contract with the attorney for one of the defendants in said action, whereby he agreed, for the consideration of $1,500, to release certain premises from the operation of said action. C., without disclosing the fact that he was to receive compensation, applied to his client and to the nominal plaintiff in said action to consent to such release. Neither consented. Notwithstanding this he executed in his own name, as attorney for plaintiff, a release. *Held,* that the evidence was properly received, and that the facts proved a violation of his professional duty on the part of C., and so constituted a good defense. *Chatfield* v. *Simonson.* 209

2. Defendants' answer contained a general denial, and also, in a separate count, a statement of the facts above stated. The count commenced, "Defendants, for further answer to said complaint," allege, etc. It concluded by alleging that the sum so received by C. in right and equity belonged to W., and that "these defendants will set off the same" against any demand established by plaintiff. *Held,* that the evidence was proper under the general denial, as it showed non-performance of his implied contract by plaintiff; but that if necessary to specifically set forth the facts, this was done, and defendant could

not be precluded from insisting upon the defense, because the special use to be made of the facts was not correctly pointed out. *Id.*

3. Also *held*, that pleading the acts of C. by way of set-off was not a ratification thereof; that it was, at most, but the assertion of a legal conclusion which did not operate as an estoppel. *Id.*

AWARD.

In an action brought under the provision of the act of 1813 (§ 184, chap. 86, Laws of 1813), authorizing a person entitled to an award of the commissioners of estimate and assessment in the city of New York to bring an action against any other person to whom the same has been paid, to recover the same, it is no defense that the award was excessive or inequitable, or that plaintiff was entitled to only nominal damages while the commissioners awarded substantial damages. The award, as to this, is "final and conclusive" (§ 178), and it is sufficient for the plaintiff to show that the award was made for lands owned by him and so that he was entitled to it. *De Peyster* v. *Mali*. 262

—— *When right to interest on award for damages for widening Broadway is waived by accepting award and receipting in full therefor.*
Cutter v. *Mayor*. 166

BAIL.

An indictment for contempt was found by the Court of Sessions of Albany county; an application for a writ of *habeas corpus* was made by the accused who was arrested in New York City, to a justice of the Supreme Court in New York. At the time of the hearing thereon the Court of Oyer and Terminer in and for Albany county was in session. *Held*, that the Oyer and Terminer had authority to try the prisoner (2 R. S. 205, §§ 29, 30), and so that the justice had no authority to let the prisoner to bail. (2 R. S. 728, §§ 56, 57.)
People, ex rel. v. *Mead*. 415

BANKS AND BANKING.

1. By an agreement between plaintiff, a savings institute, and the F. N. Bank, all of the business of the two corporations was to be done in the same office and over the same counter, by the same individuals, the only separation being in the books of account. Plaintiff as such was to receive no money, but all of its funds were to be deposited in the bank, and corresponding credits were to take the place of actual payments by the bank. The business of the institute and the bank was carried on under this arrangement, the former keeping no cash-drawer or safe for the deposit of money. One C. delivered over the counter of the bank to B., who was treasurer of the institute and also cashier of the bank, a sum of money, which she desired deposited with the institute to her credit. B. received the money, entered it in C.'s pass-book, as deposited with the institute, and, as he testified, placed it in the cash-drawer of the bank; it was not entered on the bank cash-book or credited to the institute, and, in some manner unexplained, it disappeared. In an action to recover, among other things, the amount of this deposit, *held*, that while as between C. and the institute B. received the money as its treasurer, as between the bank and the institute at the same instant he received it as cashier, it became the money of the bank, and the bank was liable to the plaintiff therefor; also, that this was so, although the money did not go into the cash-drawer but was embezzled by B. *Fishkill Svgs. Inst.* v. *Bostwick*. 564

2. A check was presented at the bank and received by B. to pay money due plaintiff; it was payable to him as treasurer; was indorsed by him as such, and then by him as cashier of the bank, and remitted for collection. No credit was given plaintiff therefor on the bank-books. *Held*, that under the general arrangement, the check, when received, became at once the property of the bank; the institute was entitled to credit for the

amount and could recover the same of the bank. *Id.*

8. A check drawn upon the bank by a depositor, payable to the order of B. as treasurer, was indorsed by him as such, charged to the drawer in the bank accounts, but not credited to plaintiff. *Held,* that it was entitled to recover the amount. *Id.*

See SAVINGS BANKS.

BANKRUPTCY.

After defendant, as sheriff, had levied upon property and advertised it for sale under executions issued to him, proceedings in bankruptcy were commenced against the judgment debtors; and, with the usual order to show cause, an order was issued by the clerk, as of course, without direction of the court as required by the Bankruptcy Act (U. S. R. S., § 5023), staying defendant from any transfer or disposition of the property. The sale was adjourned by defendant by direction of the attorneys for D., the judgment creditor, who before the adjourned day intervened by petition in the bankruptcy proceedings, setting forth these facts, and the consideration for his judgments, and alleging that they were recovered without collusion with the judgment creditors. The petition asked for a modification of the stay so as to allow defendant to sell under the executions. The application was opposed by affidavits tending to show that the debts and the judgments thereon were in fraud of the bankrupt law. After a hearing the bankrupt court denied the application, but directed the assignee in bankruptcy to sell the property levied upon free from the lien of the executions, which lien the order declared should attach to the proceeds of sale, and gave to D. permission, within a time named, to apply for an order requiring the assignee to apply the proceeds in payment of the judgments. Defendant thereupon returned the executions *nulla bona.* D. failed to make such application and brought

this action for an alleged false return. Thereafter the assignee in bankruptcy filed a bill in equity against D. and the judgment debtors to determine the validity of the judgments, and who was entitled to the proceeds of sale. D. appeared therein and answered, averring, among other things, that "the property was taken from the sheriff by the assignee in obedience to the order of the court and by him in like manner disposed of." After trial had in such action, the court decreed the judgments and executions were obtained in fraud of the Bankrupt Act, that the levy was null and void as against the assignee and that he was entitled to said proceeds. *Held,* that conceding the injunction accompanying the order to show cause was without force, the voluntary appearance of D. made him a party to the bankruptcy proceedings, and gave effect from that moment not only to the subsequent orders but to the one already made, that the United States courts had jurisdiction over the subject-matter and D.; also that D., having appeared in and contested the action brought by the assignee, could not now object that that court had no authority as to him to take the proceedings; and that, therefore, the orders and judgment were a protection to defendant; also that it was immaterial that the decree was made after the commencement of this action; and that it was properly set up by supplemental answer. (Code of Civil Procedure, § 544.) *Dorrance* v. *Henderson.* 406

BENEVOLENT, CHARITABLE, SCIENTIFIC AND MISSIONARY SOCIETIES.

1. A devise or bequest to a corporation organized under the act of 1848 (Chap. 319, Laws of 1848), providing for the incorporation of "benevolent, charitable, scientific and missionary societies," contained in a will made within two months of the testator's death, is, by the terms of the exception in the provision of said act (§ 6) authorizing such cor-

porations to take by devise or bequest, invalid ; and this, although the testator leaves no wife, child or parent. *Stephenson* v. *Short.* 488

2. Where by the charter of a missionary society (§ 3, chap. 41, Laws of 1862) it was authorized to take by bequest or devise " subject to the provisions of law relating to bequests and devises to religious societies," *held*, that said exception in the provision of the act of 1860 applied ; and that a bequest to the society, in the will of one who died within two months after the execution of the will, was invalid. *Id.*

BEQUEST.

See WILLS.

BIGAMY.

1. For the purpose of enforcing the statutory provision (2 R. S. 146, § 49) prohibiting one who has been divorced, on account of his or her adultery, from marrying again " until the death of the complainant," and under the provision of the statute in reference to bigamy (2 R. S. 687, § 8), which declares that " every person having a husband or wife living " who shall marry again shall, except in the cases specified, be adjudged guilty of bigamy, a person against whom a divorce has been obtained because of adultery is regarded as having a husband or wife living, so long as the party obtaining the divorce lives. *People* v. *Faber.* 146

2. A person, therefore, so divorced who marries again, in this State, in violation of said prohibitory provision, is guilty of the crime of bigamy. *Id.*

BOARDS.

See STATE BOARD OF EQUALIZATION.

BOARD OF SUPERVISORS.

See SUPERVISORS.

BOND.

1. The imposition by the board of supervisors of a county upon the county treasurer, during his term of office, of the duty of raising, keeping and disbursing large sums of money, in addition to the usual and ordinary duties of his office, for instance the raising and disbursing money, during a war, for bounty purposes, does not discharge the sureties upon his bond from all liability. *Bd. Sup'rs* v. *Clark.* 391

2. Conceding no liability is imposed upon them on account of such increased duties, their obligations having reference to the usual and ordinary duties of the treasurer remain unaffected. *Id.*

3. In an action upon a county treasurer's bond, the defendants are properly chargeable with interest upon an amount which it appears it was the duty of that officer to pay, but which he failed to pay over at the expiration of his term of office, to his successor. *Id.*

—— *Town bonding, when evidence of mistake in executing town bond insufficient to authorize reformation of the instrument.*
See Potter v. *Town of Greenwich.* (*Mem.*) 662

BROOKLYN (CITY OF).

1. The act of 1865 (Chap. 453, Laws of 1865), providing, where property has been omitted in an assessment-roll, for its assessment and taxation for the omitted year, in the year next succeeding, is to be construed in connection with the general system of taxation of which it forms a part, and so is not subject to the constitutional objection that it does not provide for notice or a hearing. *People, ex rel.* v. *B'd Assrs.* 430

2. The relator, a corporation liable to taxation for State purposes under the act of 1880 (Chap. 542, Laws of 1880), was omitted from the assessment-roll by the assessors of the city of Brooklyn, where it was taxable and no tax upon his par-

sonal property for city and county purposes was imposed for that year. In 1881 it was assessed for that year, and, in addition, for the omitted year, under said act of 1865, the valuation for the year 1879 being taken. Notice was given as prescribed by the statute also calling attention to the laws of both years. *Held*, that the act of 1865 was adjustable to the change made by the act of 1880, and that the assessment was valid. *Id.*

3. The act of 1882 (Chap. 363, Laws of 1882) validating (so far as the same remain unpaid) certain taxes in the city of Brooklyn, which were invalid because of the omission of the assessors to verify the assessment-rolls as prescribed by the city charter (§ 31, title 4, chap. 384, Laws of 1854, as amended by § 21, chap. 63, Laws of 1862) did not validate a sale, made prior to its passage because of non-payment of such a tax; nor did it validate the penalties by way of interest and expenses, imposed by statute for the non-payment of a tax; it simply validated the tax with interest at the rate specified (§ 2) from the date of confirmation, on condition that the property owner might discharge it by paying the amount specified. *In re Clementi* v. *Jackson.* 591

4. The acts chapter 348, Laws of 1882, and chapter 443, Laws of 1881, have no application to such a case. *Id.*

5. A payment by a purchaser at a tax sale, prior to the passage of the act, is not a payment of the tax. Notwithstanding the sale the tax "remains unpaid" within the meaning of the act, and the property owner is entitled to the benefit of said condition, and upon refusal of the registrar of arrears of the city to accept the amount specified, is entitled to a *mandamus* to compel the acceptance thereof and the discharge of the tax. *Id.*

6. The purchaser at the tax sale is not a necessary party to the proceeding by *mandamus.* *Id.*

BURDEN OF PROOF.

Upon settlement of the accounts of executors a claim against the estate, based upon an alleged contract with the deceased, which was presented and sworn to in the ordinary manner, was allowed and paid by the executors. *Held*, that the burden was upon the contestants to show that it was not a just debt, and in the absence of such evidence it was properly allowed. *In re Frazer.* 239

CALENDAR.

1. A preference on the calendar of this court of an action for dower, authorized by the Code of Civil Procedure (§ 791, subd. 6), can be claimed only when the proof required, *i. e.*, that plaintiff " has no sufficient means of support aside from the estate in controversy," was made and an order allowing the preference obtained as required (§ 793), before the notice of argument was served. *Bartlett* v. *Musliner.* 646

2. Where in an action in which the people were parties, and appeared by the attorney-general, the latter did not, at the time of serving notice of argument, give notice of a particular day in the term on which he would move it, as prescribed by the provision of the Code of Civil Procedure (§ 791, subd. 1), to entitle the cause to a preference, but served with the notice of argument notice of motion that the cause be set down for a day named, which motion failed because the court adjourned before the day specified for making it. *Held*, that the action was not entitled to a preference. *People, ex rel.* v. *Kinney.* 647

CASE.

—— *Where a case is prepared and settled by consent of both parties and is properly certified, and no motion is made to amend, no complaint that it is defective can be made here, and argument must be made upon it as returned. The case should be settled and signed by the judge or referee who tried the cause.*

Also when appeal should be dismissed for failure to serve undertaking.

See Reese v. Boese. (Mem.) 682

CASES REVERSED, DISTIN-
GUISHED, ETC.

People v. M. & T. Svgs. Instn. (28 Hun, 375), reversed. *People v. M. & T. Svgs. Instn.* 7

Blake v. Ferris (5 N. Y. 48), distinguished. *Vogel v. Mayor, etc.* 17

Pack v. Mayor, etc. (8 N. Y. 222), distinguished. *Vogel v. Mayor, etc.* 17

Kelly v. Mayor, etc. (11 N. Y. 432), distinguished. *Vogel v. Mayor, etc.* 17

Dillaye v. Greenough (45 N. Y. 438), distinguished. *Wetmore v. Porter.* 84

People v. O. B. S. B. B. Co. (28 Hun, 274), reversed in part. *People v. O. B. S. B. B. Co.* 98

People v. Faber (29 Hun, 320), reversed. *People v. Faber.* 146

People v. Hovey (5 Barb. 117), overruled. *People v. Faber.* 149

Feely v. Buckley (28 Hun, 451), overruled. *Bertles v. Nunan.* 162

Mills v. Hoffman (26 Hun, 594), reversed. *Mills v. Hoffman.* 181

People, ex rel. Mayor, etc., v. Nichols (79 N. Y. 582), distinguished. *People, ex rel. Gere, v. Whitlock.* 198

Houghkirk v. Pres't, etc., D. & H. C. Co. (28 Hun, 407), reversed. *Houghkirk v. Pres't, etc., D. & H. C. Co.* 219

Smith v. Burch (28 Hun, 331), reversed. *Smith v. Burch.* 228

Peck v. Sherwood (56 N. Y. 615), distinguished. *In re Fraser.* 246

De Peyster v. Mali (27 Hun, 439), reversed. *De Peyster v. Mali.* 262

Edington v. Mut. L. Ins. Co. (77 N. Y. 564), distinguished. *Grattan v. Met. L. Ins. Co.* 287

Hounsell v. Smyth (97 E. C. L. 731), distinguished. *Barry v. N. Y. C. & H. R. R. R. Co.* 292

Nicholson v. E. R. Co (41 N. Y. 525), distinguished. *Barry v. N. Y. C. & H. R. R. R. Co.* 293

Sutton v. N. Y. C. & H. R. R. R. Co. (66 N. Y. 243), distinguished. *Barry v. N. Y. C. & H. R. R. R. Co.* 293

Barto v. Himrod (8 N. Y. 483), distinguished. *People v. Fire Assr. of Philadelphia.* 315

Clark v. Port of Mobile (10 Ins. L. J. 361), disapproved. *People v. Fire Assn. of Philadelphia.* 315

Chamberlain v. Taylor (26 Hun, 601), distinguished. *Chamberlain v. Taylor.* 348

Darby v. Condit (1 Duer, 599), overruled. *Tolman v. Syracuse, B. & N. Y. R. R. Co.* 358

Pybus v. Gibbs (6 E. & B. 902), disapproved. *B'd Sup'ers v. Clark.* 396

Conaughty v. Saratoga Co. B'k (28 Hun, 373), reversed. *Conaughty v. Saratoga Co. B'k.* 402

Lawrence v. Elliott (3 Redf. 235), overruled. *Stephenson v. Short.* 433

People v. Canal Appraisers (33 N. Y. 461), distinguished and limited. *Smith v. City of Rochester.* 482

Gould v. H R. R. R. Co. (6 N. Y. 522), distinguished. *Smith v. City of Rochester.* 485

People v. Tibbetts (19 N. Y. 527), distinguished. *Smith v. City of Rochester.* 486

Wohlfahrt v. Beckert (27 Hun, 74), overruled in part. *Wohlfahrt v. Beckert.* 490

CAUSE OF ACTION.

1. One who employs a contractor to do a work, not in its nature a nuisance, but which becomes so by reason of the manner in which the contractor has performed it, if he accepts the work in that condition becomes at once responsible for the nuisance. *Vogel* v. *Mayor, etc.* 10

2. The complaint in an action brought by an executor to recover the value or possession of certain railroad bonds, after alleging the issuing of letters testamentary to plaintiff and his qualification, and that the bonds in question belonged to the estate, alleged in substance that plaintiff, at the request of defendant, who was his partner in business, and who knew that the bonds were trust funds, pledged the same as security for loans made to the firm; that the firm had funds sufficient to pay the debt, and defendant was largely indebted to plaintiff, yet that defendant, without the knowledge or consent of plaintiff, procured the pledge to sell the bonds, and the proceeds were applied to the payment of the firm debt; that the bonds came into the custody and control of defendant, who refused to return them or pay their value. Upon demurrer to the complaint, *held*, that it set forth a good cause of action; and that it was not necessary that plaintiff should have been made individually a party defendant. *Wetmore* v. *Porter*. 76

—— Where *trustees of village enter into a contract as water commissioners for the erection of water-works for village, they act as agents for it, and action is maintainable against it.* See *Fleming* v. *Village of S. B.* 368

CERTIFICATE.

The provision of the Code of Civil Procedure (§ 3301, as amended by chap. 399, Laws of 1882), providing that the stipulation of the attorneys for parties to an action may take the place of a clerk's certificate to a copy of a paper whereof a certified copy is required, was not intended to alter the effect of the provision (§ 1315) requiring a return to this court to be certified by the clerk of the court from which the appeal is taken, or of the rule of this court (Rule 1) making the same requirement. *Dow* v. *Darragh*. 537

CERTIORARI.

The provisions of chapter 16 of the Code of Civil Procedure in reference to appeals do not apply to an appeal in a proceeding by *certiorari* commenced prior to September 1, 1880 (Code, § 3347, subd. 11). *People, ex rel.* v. *French.* 806

CHALLENGE OF JURORS.

Upon the trial of an indictment for murder a juror, challenged by the prisoner for principal cause, testified, in substance, that he had read and talked about the case, and had formed an opinion as to the guilt or innocence of the prisoner, but that such opinion would not, as he believed, influence his verdict, and that he could render an impartial verdict. *Held,* that the challenge was properly overruled. (Code of Criminal Procedure, § 376.) *People* v. *Cornetti.* 85

CHAMPERTY.

The provision of the Revised Statutes (2 R. S. 691, § 5) making it a misdemeanor to accept a conveyance of lands, which, to the knowledge of the grantee, are at the time held adversely, and the title to which is in litigation, does not affect the previous title of the grantor in a deed executed in violation thereof, and the conveyance is no defense to an action of ejectment brought by him. *Chamberlain* v. *Taylor.* 348

CHATTEL MORTGAGE.

1. The provision of the statute in reference to chattel mortgages (§ 3, chap. 279, Laws of 1833), providing that, unless such a mortgage is re-filed, as prescribed, it shall cease to be a lien, as against subsequent purchasers in good faith, after the expiration of a year from the time of filing, does not relieve a purchaser having actual notice of a mortgage when he purchased, which, at the time it was executed, accurately described the mortgaged property, although the appearance of the property had, for the purpose of deception, without the fault of the mortgagee, been changed by the mortgagor. *Mack* v. *Phelan.* 20

2. In November, 1871, C. executed to H. a chattel mortgage on three machines, which were described by numbers and other descriptive particulars, and were stated to be in the possession of the mortgagor in a certain mill. In October, 1872, the mortgagee attempted to renew the mortgage by refiling a copy; this was held not to be effectual, because the paper filed was not an exact copy; it, however, stated accurately the debt and the mortgaged property, and the statement signed by the mortgagee stated correctly the amount unpaid. C. sold the machines to A. H. H. & Co.; immediately prior to the purchase the agent of that firm saw and read the original mortgage, and the copy filed as a renewal, but was informed by the mortgagor that it did not cover the machines in question, and to support this he referred to the fact that the numbers of the machines he was about to sell did not correspond with the numbers as stated in the mortgage; these had in fact been removed, and other numbers appeared upon the machines. The agent, satisfied with this information, concluded the purchase without making further inquiry or going to the mill. In an action for the conversion of the machines, *held,* that the purchasers were chargeable with notice of the mortgage, and of the legal rights of the mortgagee under it; that the paper filed as a copy, although inaccurate, was, with the statement of the mortgagee accompanying it, notice to them that the original mortgage was as between the parties a subsisting security, and the debt secured unpaid; and that it was not essential that they should have had actual knowledge, at the time of the purchase, that the machines were those embraced in the mortgage. *Id.*

3. C. received for the machines a sum

of money, and three other machines; these latter were stored by him with other machinery covered by the mortgage; he procured insurance on all of the machinery, loss, if any, payable to H., as mortgagee. The policies were forwarded to H., who lived in Missouri. A loss having occurred, H. came to this State to collect the insurance. He then learned all the facts of the sale and exchange, of which before he had been ignorant. After acquiring such knowledge H. obtained from C. a power of attorney and assignment of all his interest in the policies. H. then informed A. H. H. & Co. of his claim upon, and demanded the three machines, offering, if they would surrender them, to transfer the claim for insurance; this they refused, and H. thereupon settled with the insurance companies. *Held*, that there was no ratification, either in law or fact, of the acts of C., and no estoppel upon H. from asserting his claim under the mortgage. *Id.*

4. After the adjustment of the loss H. sold the old iron, the remnants of the property. *Held*, that this did not amount to a ratification of the acts of C. *Id.*

5. *It seems* that the most A. H. H. & Co. could claim was that H. should account for the portion of the sum received on sales realized from the remnants of the machines sold by them. *Id.*

CODE OF CIVIL PROCEDURE.

CODE OF CRIMINAL PROCEDURE.

CODE OF PROCEDURE.

COMPLAINT.

See PLEADING.

CONSTITUTIONAL LAW.

1. The act (Subd. 9, § 1, chap. 482, Laws of 1875, as amended by chap. 365, Laws of 1880, and by chap. 554, Laws of 1881), giving to the board of supervisors in any county containing an incorporated city of over one hundred thousand inhabitants, where contiguous territory

in the county has been mapped out into streets and avenues, power to lay out, open, grade and construct the same, and to provide for the assessment of damages on the property benefited, is not a local law within the meaning of the State Constitution, and so is not violative of the constitutional provision (Art. 3, § 18) prohibiting the passage of a local or private law laying out or opening highways, or of the provision (Art. 3, § 23) requiring the legislature to act by general laws in conferring upon boards of supervisors any power of local legislation. *In re Church.* 1

2. By resolution of the board of supervisors of the county of K. which had directed the opening of a street, under said act, in town of N. U., the town was authorized to issue bonds to pay for the improvement, to be paid out of the general tax, so far as the assessments proved inadequate. *Held,* that adequate and certain provision was thus made for compensation for property taken, sufficient to meet the constitutional prohibition against the taking of property without compensation. *Id.*

3. In proceedings to vacate an assessment for the construction of a sewer in Tenth avenue, which improvement was made under the provision of the act of 1873, entitled "An act to provide for the Eastern boulevard in the city of New York, and in relation to certain alterations of the map or plan of said city, and certain local improvements" (§ 4, of chap. 528, Laws of 1873), authorizing the department of public parks to do the work "of regulating, grading or otherwise improving Tenth avenue," *held,* that in the absence of evidence that there was no connection or relation between the portion of Tenth avenue specified in the act and the Eastern boulevard, for the purpose of sustaining the constitutionality of the act, the connection was to be assumed; and, therefore, that said act was not violative of the provision of the State Constitution (Art. 3, §

16), declaring that no local or private act, shall contain more than one subject, and requiring that to be expressed in the title. *In re L. & W. O. Home.* 116

4. The act of 1881 (Chap. 532, Laws of 1881) purporting to amend the provision of the Code of Civil Procedure (§ 1041), in regard to the selection and drawing of jurors in the city and county of Albany, so far as it relates to grand jurors, is a local act and is within the prohibition of the provision of the State Constitution (Art 3, § 18), forbidding the passage of a local or private bill for "selecting, drawing, summoning or impaneling grand or petit jurors." *People* v. *Petrea.* 128

5. Assuming therefore the said act not to have been reported by the commissioners appointed by law to revise the statutes, and so not within the exception (Art. 3, § 25) exempting from the operation of said provision, bills so reported, the said act is as to grand jurors unconstitutional and void. *Id.*

6. In the absence of proof to the contrary it will be presumed in support of the constitutionality of the act that it originated in a bill so reported. *Id.*

7. It is proper, however, to establish by proof *aliunde* that it did not so originate. *Id.*

8. So far as said act relates to the selection of petit jurors, as it is simply an amendment of an existing local law, it is not within the prohibitory provision of the Constitution and is valid. *Id.*

9. The amendment of an existing local act in mere matters of detail is not within the mischief aimed at by said provision, and is not violative thereof. *Id.*

10. Where an indictment was found by a grand jury drawn from the petit jury list as provided for in said act, *held,* upon the trial thereof, that as the grand jurors were drawn by the proper officer,

were regularly summoned and returned, were recognized, impaneled and sworn by the court, were qualified to sit as grand jurors, and as such found the indictment, the arraignment and trial of the accused under it was not a violation of the constitutional guaranty that no person shall be held to answer for a capital or otherwise infamous crime, save as excepted, "unless on presentment or indictment of a grand jury" (Art. 1, § 6); that the indictment was by a grand jury within the meaning of said guaranty.   *Id.*

11. The act entitled "An act to amend an act to provide for the election of police commissioners in the city of Syracuse, and to establish a police force therein, and to repeal certain sections thereof" (Chap. 559, Laws of 1881), is not violative of the provision of the State Constitution (Art. 3, § 16) declaring that no local or private bill shall contain more than one subject and that shall be embraced in the title. *People, ex rel.* v. *Whitlock.*   191

12. The legislature may abridge the term of an office created by it, by express words, or may specify an event upon the happening of which it shall end.   *Id.*

13. It is also within the power of the legislature, where it has given the authority to appoint to an office created by it, to authorize the removal of the incumbent without notice or a hearing.   *Id.*

14. The act of 1865 (Chap. 694, Laws of 1865), as amended in 1875 (Chap. 60, Laws of 1875), providing that an insurance corporation of another State seeking to do business here shall pay to the superintendent of the insurance department for taxes, fines, etc., an amount equal to that imposed by the " existing or future laws " of the State of its origin, upon companies of this State seeking to do business there, when such amount is greater than that required for such purposes by the then existing laws of this State, is not an unlawful delegation of legislative power. *People* v. *Fire Ass'n.*   311

15. The legislature has power to pass an act to take effect upon the happening of some future event, certain or uncertain, which, in its judgment, affects the expediency of the law.   *Id.*

16. The fact that the contingency upon which the operation of the act is made to depend is the action of the legislature of another State does not invalidate the act. It does not follow, therefrom, that the legislative discretion of such other State is substituted for our own.   *Id.*

17. *It seems,* however, that the question of expediency may not be delegated, but must be settled definitely and finally by the legislature itself.   *Id.*

18. The said act is not repugnant to the provision of the Federal Constitution (Art. 14), declaring that no State shall " deny to any person within its jurisdiction the equal protection of the law." That provision relates wholly to persons rightfully within the jurisdiction, not to the terms and conditions on which alone they can come in.   *Id.*

19. The constitutional difference between the rights of non-resident individuals and foreign corporations pointed out.   *Id.*

20. Said act is not violative of the provision of the State Constitution (Art. 3, § 20), declaring that " every law which imposes, continues or revives a tax shall distinctly state the tax and the object to which it is to be applied, and it shall not be sufficient to refer to any other law to fix such tax or object," as the condition imposed by the act is in the nature of a license fee.   *Id.*

21. The statement in the act (Chap. 542, Laws of 1880, as amended by chap. 361, Laws of 1881), providing for the taxation of certain corporations and associations, that the taxes imposed thereby " shall be applicable to the payment of the ordinary and current expenses of the State," is a sufficient compliance with the requirement of the

State Constitution (Art. 3, § 20) that every law imposing a tax "shall distinctly state * * * the object to which it is to be applied." *People* v. *Home Ins. Co.* 328

22. In taxing corporations under the act the State authorities are not required to deduct the amount of stock which the corporation holds in United States bonds from the total amount of its capital stock and to compute the tax only upon dividends derived from the remainder. *Id.*

23. The legislature has, by virtue of its jurisdiction over corporations organized under its laws, authority to impose such a tax. *Id.*

24. In performing the duty of levying taxes the legislature may, in its discretion, impose unequal or double taxes, and in determining the question of legislative power the courts are precluded from considering that question. *Id.*

25. The act of 1865 (Chap. 453, Laws of 1865), providing, where property has been omitted in an assessment-roll, for its assessment and taxation for the omitted year, in the year next succeeding, is to be construed in connection with the general system of taxation of which it forms a part, and so is not subject to the constitutional objection that it does not provide for notice or a hearing. *People, ex rel.* v. *B'd of Assessors.* 430

CONSTRUCTION.

1. Where, upon examination of a will, taken as a whole, the intention of the testator appears clear, but its plain and definite purposes are endangered by inapt or inaccurate modes of expression, the court may, and it is its duty to, subordinate the language to the intention; it may reject words and limitations, supply or transpose them to get at the correct meaning. *Phillips* v. *Davies.* 199

2. Where a will is capable of two interpretations that one should be

adopted which prefers those of the blood of the testator to strangers. *Wood* v. *Mitcham.* 375

CONTEMPT.

1. A warrant issued by a district attorney, as authorized by the statute (Chap. 888, Laws of 1847), for the arrest of the relator, stated that he stood indicted "for contempt." On *habeas corpus*, issued on the petition of the relator, *held*, that this was a sufficient specification of the offense; that as the statement was of a contempt which has already served as a basis of an indictment, it necessarily implied a willful contempt, of a character constituting a misdemeanor. *People, ex rel.* v. *Mead.* 415

2. Also *held*, that as the indictment was found prior to the enactment of the Code of Criminal Procedure the provisions therein (§§ 301, 302) as to the form of bench warrants did not apply (§ 962), nor was it a case of a commitment for contempt specified in the provision of the Revised Statutes (2 R. S. 567, § 40) in relation to *habeas corpus.* *Id.*

3. Also *held*, that it was not essential to the validity of the indictment that the accused should first have been adjudged guilty of contempt by the court whose process he disobeyed. *Id.*

4. The relator was served with a subpœna, requiring him to appear before the Court of Oyer and Terminer in the county of Albany. He was called, and omitted to appear. *Held*, that he was properly indicted for contempt in that county; that the offense was there committed. *Id.*

5. The indictment was found by the Court of Sessions of Albany county: the application for the writ of *habeas corpus* was made to a justice of the Supreme Court in New York. At the time of the hearing thereon the Court of Oyer and Terminer in and for Albany county was in session. *Held*, that the Oyer and Terminer had authority

to try the prisoner (2 R. S. 205, §§ 29, 30), and so that the justice had no authority to let the prisoner to bail. (2 R. S. 728, §§ 56, 57.) *Id.*

CONTRACTS.

1. Where the trustees of an incorporated village organize into a board of water commissioners for the purposes and as prescribed by the act of 1875 (Chap. 181, Laws of 1875), and as such enter into a contract for erecting water-works for the village, they act simply as agents for, and the contract is binding upon it, and an action is maintainable against it thereon. *Fleming* v. *Village of S. B.* 368

2. It is immaterial whether the contract is made in the name of the village, or in the names of the trustees as water commissioners, or as a board. *Id.*

3. Said statute confers upon such water commissioners general power to contract, and the entire control of the work for procuring a water supply; and where a contract has been regularly let as prescribed, if in the substantial performance thereof slight variations or changes are necessary they may be made by their direction without a new letting, and for the extra expense the village is liable. *Id.*

4. The rule excluding evidence of parol negotiations and undertakings, when offered to contradict or substantially vary the legal import of a written agreement, does not prevent a party to the agreement, in an action between the parties thereto, from proving, by way of defense, the existence of an oral agreement made in connection with the written instrument, where the circumstances would make the use of the latter, for any purposes inconsistent with the oral agreement, dishonest or fraudulent. *Juilliard* v. *Chaffee.* 529

5. As also the consideration of an agreement is open to inquiry, a party may show that the design

and object of the written agreement were different from what its language, if alone considered, would indicate. *Id.*

6. He may also show that the written instrument was executed in part performance only of an entire oral agreement, or that the obligation of the instrument has been discharged by the execution of a parol agreement collateral thereto. *Id.*

—— *When party cannot avail himself of objection that contract is against public policy.* See *Juilliard* v. *Chaffee.* 529

See ANTE-NUPTIAL AGREEMENT.

CONTRIBUTORY NEGLIGENCE.

See NEGLIGENCE.

CORPORATIONS.

1. The statement in the act (Chap. 542, Laws of 1880, as amended by chap. 361, Laws of 1881) providing for the taxation of certain corporations and associations, that the taxes imposed thereby "shall be applicable to the payment of the ordinary and current expenses of the State," is a sufficient compliance with the requirement of the State Constitution (Art. 3, § 20) that every law imposing a tax " shall distinctly state * * * the object to which it is to be applied." *People* v. *Home Ins. Co.* 328

2. The taxes upon corporations, imposed by said act, are taxes upon franchises, not upon property, and the fact that dividends, a portion of which is derived from securities exempt from taxation, furnish the basis for computing the amount of the tax, does not invalidate it. *Id.*

3. In taxing corporations under the act the State authorities are not required to deduct the amount of stock which the corporation holds in United States bonds from the total amount of its capital stock and to compute the tax only upon

dividends derived from the remainder. *Id.*

4. *It seems* that the corporations
affected by said act are not thereby
subjected to unequal or double
taxation. *Id.*

5. The authorities showing the distinction between franchise and
property taxes collated. *Id.*

6. Under the act of 1880 (Chap. 542,
Laws of 1880), providing for "raising taxes for the use of the State
upon certain corporations," etc.,
the first report required to be made
by the officers of the corporation
included in the act was to be made
in November, 1880, and the first
tax paid in January, 1881; and this,
although at the latter date the corporation had not been in existence
for a year. *People* v. *S. V. Hy.
Gold Co.* 383

7. The acts providing for the taxation
of the franchises of certain corporations and associations (Chap. 542,
Laws of 1880, as amended by chap.
361, Laws of 1881) are prospective
in their character; the tax thereby
imposed is not for the past, but for
the future enjoyment of the franchises, and the amount of the dividends made or declared during the
year are made simply the measure of the annual value of the
franchises. *People* v. *Albany Ins.
Co.* 458

8. Defendant, a corporation, taxable
under said act, and having a capital of $200,000, in January, 1881,
declared a dividend of six and one-
fourth per cent from the earnings
and profits of the company for the
current year. In February, 1880,
having on hand a large surplus
fund, all of which had been earned
and acquired before January 1,
1880, and in contemplation of the
expiration of its charter, which
would take place in June, 1880, it
was resolved by the company that
$100,000 should be taken from
such surplus and paid to and
divided among its stockholders,
and it was at the same time resolved that the charter should be
extended. Upon a case submitted

under the Code of Civil Procedure
(§ 1279), *held*, that this division,
even if a dividend within the letter, was not such within the meaning or for the purposes of the act;
that the accumulation of earnings
was no measure of the value of
the enjoyment of the franchises
during the year 1880 or 1881, and
was not within the contemplation
of the framers of the act; and that
the corporation was not liable to
taxation thereon. *Id.*

9. *It seems* that should a corporation,
for the purpose of evading taxation
under the act, divide six per cent
or more, but less than its actual
earnings in any one year after the
passage of said act, and thus create
a surplus, the division of such surplus in a subsequent year may be
treated as a dividend within the
act. *Id.*

10. The defendant was incorporated
for the purpose, as expressed in
its charter (Chap. 170, Laws of
1843), "of constructing, using and
providing one or more dry-docks or
wet-docks or other conveniences
and structures for building, raising,
repairing or coppering vessels and
steamers of every description."
In an action to recover taxes alleged to be due for the year 1881,
under the act of 1880 (Chap. 542,
Laws of 1880), *held*, that defendant was not "a manufacturing corporation" within the meaning of
the clause in said act (§ 3) which
exempts such corporations from its
provisions; and that it was liable
to taxation under the act. *People*
v. *N. Y. F. Dry Dock Co.* 487

See BENEVOLENT, ETC., ASSOCIA-
TIONS.
FOREIGN CORPORATIONS
INSURANCE (FIRE).
INSURANCE (LIFE).
MANUFACTURING CORPORA-
TIONS.
MUNICIPAL CORPORATIONS.
RAILROAD CORPORATIONS.
RELIGIOUS CORPORATIONS.

COSTS.

1. During the pendency of an action

against an executor for misappropriation of moneys belonging to the estate, he died and his executor was substituted as party defendant. Judgment was recovered, which the defendant was directed to pay out of the estate; costs were also given, which were directed to be paid in like manner. The real estate of the deceased executor was sold by order of the surrogate. *Held*, that the surrogate properly disallowed the costs, as a claim, payable out of the proceeds of sale. (Code of Civil Procedure, §§ 2756, 2757.) *In re Estate of Fox.* 93

2. Under the provision of the Code of Civil Procedure (§ 3271) giving to the court discretionary power to require the plaintiff in an action brought by or against an executor, administrator, etc., in his representative capacity, to give security for costs, the court has power to require such security of one bringing suit in such capacity, although there is no evidence of mismanagement or bad faith, and aside from the question of his personal liability for costs as prescribed by the Code (§ 3246). *Tolman v. Syr., B. & N. Y. R. R. Co.* 353

3. Where a plaintiff is entitled to costs, under the Code of Civil Procedure (§ 3228), upon entry of judgment in his favor, and such judgment is reversed and new trial granted by the General Term "with costs to appellant to abide the event," but is affirmed on appeal by plaintiff to this court, he is entitled, of course, to the costs of the appeals to the General Term and to this court (Code, § 3238.) *Murtha v. Curley.* 359

4. The provision of the Code of Civil Procedure (§ 3253), in reference to extra allowances of costs, simply authorizes such an allowance in an action wherein rights of property are involved and a pecuniary value may be predicated of the subject-matter; the importance of a litigation in any other than its pecuniary aspect affords no basis for the allowance, and when no money judgment is asked or ren-

dered and the "subject-matter involved" is not capable of a money value, or the value is not shown, the allowance is not authorized. *Conaughty v. Saratoga Co. B'k.* 401

5. The term "subject-matter involved" refers simply to property or other valuable thing, the possession, ownership or title to which is to be determined by the action, it does not include other property although it may be directly or remotely affected by the result. *Id.*

6. Within the limitations fixed by said provision the power of the court below to make allowances is not subject to review here; but the question whether an allowance exceeds those limitations is one of law, proper to be considered by this court. *Id.*

7. In an action, therefore, brought to restrain a corporation from the exercise of its corporate franchises, *held*, that the subject-matter involved was simply the corporate franchises, not its capital and moneyed assets; that in the absence of any evidence as to the money value of those franchises, an extra allowance was improper, and that an order allowing it was reviewable here. *Id.*

8. Under the Code of Civil Procedure (§ 709), in an action in the Supreme Court, triable and tried in the first judicial district, an application for an extra allowance of costs must be made in that district, although the justice before whom the cause is tried resides in another district. *Hun v. Salter.* 651

9. The rule of the Supreme Court (44), requiring such an application to be made to the court before which the trial is had or the judgment rendered does not authorize it to be made out of the district. *Id.*

COUNTER-CLAIM.

—— *In action by executors to foreclose mortgage purchased by them after death of testator, evidence of receipt of money by him from mortgagor, is*

inadmissible; it does not operate as payment, and is not available as a counter-claim.
See *Carter* v. *Holahan.* 498

COUNTY TREASURER.

1. The imposition by the board of supervisors of a county upon the county treasurer, during his term of office, of the duty of raising, keeping and disbursing large sums of money, in addition to the usual and ordinary duties of his office, for instance the raising and disbursing money, during a war, for bounty purposes, does not discharge the sureties upon his bond from all liability. *Bd. Sup'rs* v. *Clark.* 391

2. Conceding no liability is imposed upon them on account of such increased duties, their obligations having reference to the usual and ordinary duties of the treasurer remain unaffected. *Id.*

3. In an action upon a county treasurer's bond, the defendants are properly chargeable with interest upon an amount which it appears it was the duty of that officer to pay, but which he failed to pay over at the expiration of his term of office, to his successor. *Id.*

COURTS.

See COURT OF APPEALS.
SURROGATE'S COURT.

COURT OF APPEALS.

1. The complaint herein set forth a demand for $398.71 ; the answer denied liability and set up a counter-claim for $301.29. The trial court found with defendant and gave judgment against plaintiff for the counter-claim. The General Term reversed the judgment. *Held,* that the amount of the two claims constituted "the matter in controversy," within the meaning of the Code of Civil Procedure (§ 191, subd. 3), and that this court had jurisdiction on appeal. *Crawford* v. *West Side B'k.* 631

2. A preference on the calendar of this court of an action for dower, authorized by the Code of Civil Procedure (§ 791, subd. 6), can be claimed only when the proof required, *i. e.,* that plaintiff "has no sufficient means of support aside from the estate in controversy," was made and an order allowing the preference obtained as required (§ 793), before the notice of argument was served. *Bartlett* v. *Musliner.* 646

3. Where in an action in which the people were parties, and appeared by the attorney-general, the latter did not, at the time of serving notice of argument, give notice of a particular day in the term on which he would move it, as prescribed by the provision of the Code of Civil Procedure (§ 791, subd. 1) to entitle the cause to a preference, but served with the notice of argument notice of motion that the cause be set down for a day named, which motion failed because the court adjourned before the day specified for making it. *Held,* that the action was not entitled to a preference. *People, ex rel.* v. *Kinney.* 647

See APPEALS.

CRIMINAL TRIAL.

1. Upon the trial of an indictment for murder, evidence was received on the part of the prosecution, under objection and exception, to the effect, that upon the coroner's inquest a witness testified that shortly after the murder a stranger called at her house and asked the way to Sandy Hill and also for a drink of water ; that the prisoner and a number of others were placed around a room and the witness pointed out the prisoner as the one who so called ; also, that a number of persons, including the prisoner, passed behind her, each one repeating the question asked her by the stranger, and that she identified the prisoner by his voice, and that the prisoner on that occasion did not deny that he was such stranger. *Held,* that the examina-

tion before the coroner was of a judicial character ; that the experiments so made were part of the proceedings ; that the prisoner was not bound to speak, and his silence could not be regarded as an evidence of guilt ; and therefore that the evidence was improperly received. *People* v. *Willett.* 29

2. Upon the trial of an indictment for murder, a juror, challenged by the prisoner for principal cause, testified, in substance, that he had read and talked about the case, and had formed an opinion as to the guilt or innocence of the prisoner, but that such opinion would not, as he believed, influence his verdict, and that he could render an impartial verdict. *Held*, that the challenge was properly overruled. (Code of Criminal Procedure, § 376.) *People* v. *Cornetti.* 85

3. It appeared that the prisoner and C., the deceased, were at the time of the homicide convicts confined in a State prison On the morning of the homicide another convict, after sharpening a case-knife laid it down and went to another part of the room ; on his return he found the knife had been taken away. The prisoner was near where the knife was left and in a position where he could have seen it. A few moments thereafter the prisoner approached C. and stabbed him with a knife, which was identified as the one so sharpened. C. died in a few minutes. The witnesses for the prosecution testified that no words passed between C. and the prisoner, and there was no assault or provocation by the former. *Held*, that the prisoner was properly convicted of murder in the first degree. *Id.*

4. An indictment for false pretenses averred in substance, that the accused having contracted to sell to B., the complainant, certain premises, fraudulently exhibited to B., who was illiterate and unable to read, a deed which he falsely represented to be a deed of the prem ises, when in fact the description covered other premises, etc. What

purported to be a copy of the deed was set forth in the indictment. The deed offered in evidence on trial showed that in the copy in the indictment the easterly and westerly boundary lines were omitted. The copy, however, showed inferentially the length of these two lines. *Held*, that the variance was not material. *Webster* v. *People*. 422

5. The indictment did not allege that the deed was under seal. It was so stated, however, in the attesting clause, a copy of which was set forth. *Held*, this, with the averment that the instrument was a deed, amounted to a substantial averment that it was under seal. *Id.*

6. Where such an indictment sets forth various pretenses alleged to be false, if one or more are proved to be false, and are sufficient *per se* to constitute the offense, a conviction is proper, notwithstanding the failure of the prosecution to prove the other alleged pretenses to be false. *Id.*

7. In the absence of exceptions on a criminal trial this court has no power to review the case upon the facts. *People* v. *Hovey*. 554

8. The provision of the Code of Criminal Procedure (§ 527), as amended in 1882 (Chap. 360, Laws of 1882), providing that "the appellate court may order a new trial if it be satisfied that the verdict against the prisoner was against the weight of evidence or against law, or that justice required a new trial whether any exceptions shall have been taken or not," applies only to appeals to the Supreme Court. *Id.*

9. An exception to a charge taken after a criminal trial has terminated does not present any question for the consideration of an appellate court. *Id.*

10. Where, therefore, after a criminal trial, and when the prisoner was before the court for sentence, his counsel moved for a new trial for

in such an action and to set it aside if it appears excessive, or the result of sympathy and prejudice. *Id.*

DEBTOR AND CREDITOR.

1. The primary relation of a depositor in a savings bank to the corporation is that of creditor. *People v. M. & T. Svgs. Inst'n.* 7

2. Upon insolvency of the corporation, the depositors stand as other creditors having no greater, but equal rights to be paid ratably out of the insolvent estate. *Id.*

3. Accordingly *held*, where a creditor of a savings bank obtained a judgment against a receiver thereof in an action brought against the bank before the appointment of the receiver, in which action the receiver was substituted as defendant, that the plaintiff was not entitled to a preference over depositors in the payment of his judgment. *Id.*

4. During the pendency of an action against an executor for misappropriation of moneys belonging to the estate, he died and his executor was substituted as party defendant Judgment was recovered, which the defendant was directed to pay out of the estate; costs were also given, which were directed to be paid in like manner. The real estate of the deceased executor was sold by order of the surrogate. *Held*, that in the distribution of the proceeds said judgment creditor was not entitled to a preference for the damages recovered over the other creditors of the decedent, but was entitled to share *pro rata ;* and that the surrogate properly disallowed the costs, as a claim, payable out of such proceeds. (Code of Civil Procedure, §§ 2756, 2757.) *In re Fox.* 93

5. The mere fact that an assignment of property by a debtor was voluntary and without consideration is not sufficient to require a finding that it was fraudulent against creditors. *Genesee River Nat. B'k v. Mead.* 637

—— *Right of insolvent debtor to give preference.*
See *Juilliard* v. *Chaffee.* 529

DEFENSE.

1. It is no defense to an action brought by an executor as such, to recover assets of the estate in the hands of defendant, or for the conversion thereof, that plaintiff in his individual capacity acted in collusion with the defendant in despoiling the estate. *Wetmore* v. *Porter.* 76

2. In an action brought under the provision of the act of 1813 (§ 184, chap. 86, Laws of 1813), authorizing a person entitled to an award of the commissioners of estimate and assessment in the city of New York to bring an action against any other person to whom the same has been paid to recover the same, it is no defense that the award was excessive or inequitable, or that plaintiff was entitled to only nominal damages while the commissioners awarded substantial damages. The award, as to this, is "final and conclusive" (§ 178), and it is sufficient for the plaintiff to show that the award was made for lands owned by him and so that he was entitled to it. *De Peyster* v. *Mali.* 262

3. The provision of the Revised Statutes (2 R. S. 691, § 5) making it a misdemeanor to accept a conveyance of lands, which, to the knowledge of the grantee, are at the time held adversely, and the title to which is in litigation, does not affect the previous title of the grantor in a deed executed in violation thereof, and the conveyance is no defense to an action of ejectment brought by him. *Chamberlain* v. *Taylor.* 848

—— *Irregularity in letters of administration cannot be availed of collaterally in suit brought by administrator.*
See *Martin* v. *D. D. E. B. & B. R. R. Co.* 70

DEFINITIONS.

1. Defendants, as executors and trustees, were required by the will to invest in bonds and mortgages "on unincumbered real estate." At the time of a loan upon bond and mortgage there was an unpaid tax upon the land. *Held*, that this was not a violation of the provision; that the tax was not an incumbrance within the meaning of the provision. *Crabb v. Young.* 56

2. The term "subject-matter involved" in the provision of the Code of Civil Procedure (§ 3253), in reference to extra allowances of costs, refers simply to property or other valuable thing, the possession, ownership or title to which is to be determined by the action, it does not include other property although it may be directly or remotely affected by the result. *Conaughty* v. *Saratoga Co. Bank.* 401

—— *When words "expiration of the term," in lease relate not to the determination of the estate, but to the time specified for the lease to run. See Finkelmeier* v. *Bates.* 172

—— *What is included in the term "ready money" as used in wills. See Smith* v. *Burch.* 228

DEMURRER.

See PLEADING.

DESCENT.

The wife of M., a resident of this State, procured a divorce from him on account of his adultery; the judgment forbade him from marrying again. He thereafter went into the State of New Jersey, and there married during the life of his first wife, returning with his second wife to this State, and continuing to reside here. The statute law of New Jersey declares that "all marriages, where either of the parties shall have a former husband or wife living at the

time of such marriage, shall be invalid, * * * and the issue thereof shall be illegitimate." In an action to test the right of plaintiff, a son born of the second marriage, to inherit, as the lawful heir of M., who died intestate, *held*, that at the time of the second marriage the latter had no former wife living within the meaning of said statute; that the laws of this State and the provision of the judgment prohibiting marriage had no effect in another State whose laws did not prohibit a second marriage by one divorced; and that plaintiff was legitimate and so entitled to inherit. *Moore* v. *Hegeman.* 521

DEVISE.

See WILLS.

DIVORCE.

1. For the purpose of enforcing the statutory provision (2 R. S. 146, § 49) prohibiting one who has been divorced, on account of his or her adultery, from marrying again "until the death of the complainant," and under the provision of the statute in reference to bigamy (2 R. S. 687, § 8), which declares that "every person having a husband or wife living" who shall marry again shall, except in the cases specified, be adjudged guilty of bigamy, a person against whom a divorce has been obtained because of adultery is regarded as having a husband or wife living, so long as the party obtaining the divorce lives. *People* v. *Faber.* 146

2. The wife of M., a resident of this State, procured a divorce from him on account of his adultery; the judgment forbade him from marrying again. He thereafter went into the State of New Jersey, and there married during the life of his first wife, returning with his second wife to this State, and continuing to reside here. The statute law of New Jersey declares that "all marriages, where either of the parties shall have a former hus-

band or wife living at the time of such marriage, shall be invalid, * * * and the issue thereof shall be illegitimate." In ·an action to test the right of plaintiff, a son born of the second marriage, to inherit, as the lawful heir of M., who died intestate, *held*, that at the time of the second marriage the latter had no former wife living within the meaning of said statute; that the laws of this State and the provision of the judgment prohibiting marriage had no effect, and M. had a right to marry in another State whose laws did not prohibit a second marriage by one divorced; and that plaintiff was legitimate and so entitled to inherit. *Moore* v. *Hegeman.* 521

3. After the dissolution of the first marriage M. and his first wife were again married, but in an action brought by her it was adjudged that the second marriage was prohibited by the statutes of this State, and was void ; after the entry of this judgment the marriage in New Jersey took place. It was urged here that such remarriage was valid. *Held*, that the judgment not having been reversed, and having been made by a competent court having jurisdiction of the parties and the subject-matter, was conclusive. *Id.*

4. As to whether after a judgment of divorce on the ground of the adultery of one of the parties, and the consequent prohibition against another marriage by the guilty party, a second marriage of the parties in this State will be valid, *quære.* *Id.*

DOWER.

A preference on the calendar of an action for dower, authorized by the Code of Civil Procedure (§ 791, subd. 6), can be claimed only when the proof required, *i. e.*, that plaintiff "has no sufficient means of support aside from the estate in controversy," was made and an order allowing the preference obtained as required (§ 793), before the notice of argument was served. *Bartlett* v. *Musliner.* 646

—— *When acceptance by widow of provisions in will for benefit, does not deprive her of the right to claim dower.* See *In re Frazer.* 239

DRUGS.

See APOTHECARIES.

EASEMENT.

—— *Nature of public easement in fresh-water navigable' streams and small lakes* See *Smith* v. *City of R.* . 463

EJECTMENT.

1. The provision of the Revised Statutes (2 R. S. 691, § 5) making it a misdemeanor to accept a conveyance of lands, which, to the knowledge of the grantee, are at the time held adversely, and the title to which is in litigation, does not affect the previous title of the grantor in a deed executed in violation thereof, and the conveyance is no defense to an action of ejectment brought by him. *Chamberlain* v. *Taylor.* 348

2. If the deed be utterly void, the grantor may recover as owner of the legal title; if void only as to the defendants, the action is authorized by the Code of Civil Procedure (§ 1501) in the name of the grantor for the benefit of the grantee. *Id.*

ELECTION (OF RIGHTS AND REMEDIES).

1. A principal upon being informed of an unauthorized act of an agent has a right to elect whether he will adopt it or not, and so long as the condition of the parties is unchanged, cannot be prevented from such adoption by the fact that the other party prefers to treat the contract as invalid. *Andrews* v. *Ætna Life Ins. Co.* 596

2. An election once made, however, is irrevocable. *Id.*

EMINENT DOMAIN.

—— *What is sufficient provision for compensation for property taken for public use to meet requirements of Constitution.*
See *In re Church.* 1

—— *Waters of fresh-water navigable streams and small lakes, in which the public has an easement as on a highway, may not be diverted for other public uses, except under right of eminent domain, on making compensation to riparian owners.*
See *Smith* v. *City of R.* 463

ERROR (WRIT OF).

Upon a writ of error no exception lies to a refusal to postpone a criminal trial because of the absence of witnesses. *Webster* v. *People.* 422

See APPEAL.

ESTOPPEL.

1. In an action to recover back premiums paid upon certain policies of life insurance issued by defendant, each of which when delivered contained a provision that the policy would " be good at any time, after three payments, for its equitable value," the complaint, after alleging the issuing of the policies and the payment of more than three years premiums, averred, in substance, that plaintiff, having concluded not to continue to pay premiums, demanded of defendant the equitable value of the policies, and on its refusal to allow the same, commenced an action to recover such equitable value ; that thereafter defendant notified plaintiff that said provision was inserted in the policies without its authority or consent, and set up such claim in the answer. Whereupon the plaintiff discontinued the said action, and paid the taxable costs thereof. *Held,* that assuming the first action was discontinued in consequence of said averments in the answer, defendant was not estopped, as it did not damage plaintiff, because whether the clause

was part of the contract or not the former action could not have been sustained ; that the clause if binding upon defendant imposed no obligation upon the company to pay any thing until plaintiff's death ; it simply continued the policies in force for their equitable value in case no further payments were made. *Andrews* v. *Ætna L. Ins. Co.* 596

2. It appeared upon the trial of this action that the notice referred to was a letter written to defendant's secretary, which, while it asserted that the clause was written in the policies without authority, stated that defendant was willing to perform it, and the answer in the former action which asserted that the clause was inserted without authority denied that defendant had refused to pay the equitable value. *Held,* that this was an unequivocal election on the part of defendant to affirm or ratify the alleged unauthorized act, and so the proceedings in the former action furnished no basis for an equitable estoppel. *Id.*

—— *When mortgages not estopped from asserting claim under chattel mortgage.*
See *Mack* v. *Phelan* 20

—— *When minor, on coming of age, estopped from questioning acts of general guardian.*
See *Mills* v. *Hoffman.* 181

—— *When pleading the unlawful acts of attorney, by way of set-off, in action by him for services is not a ratification thereof, and does not estop defendant from using them as an absolute defense under a general denial in the answer.*
See *Chatfield* v. *Simonson* 203

EVIDENCE.

1. Upon the trial of an indictment for murder, evidence was received on the part of the prosecution, under objection and exception, to the effect, that upon the coroner's inquest a witness testified that shortly after the murder a stranger

testified to could only be proved to contradict him or refresh his memory ; second, the plaintiff's inquiry on the former trial did not preclude his objecting to the evidence. *Id.*

13. The rule excluding evidence of parol negotiations and undertakings, when offered to contradict or substantially vary the legal import of a written agreement, does not prevent a party to the agreement, in an action between the parties thereto, from proving, by way of defense, the existence of an oral agreement made in connection with the written instrument, where the circumstances would make the.use of the latter, for any purposes inconsistent with the oral agreement, dishonest or fraudulent. *Juilliard* v. *Chaffee.*   529

14. As also the consideration of an agreement is open to inquiry, a party may show that the design and object of the written agreement were different from what its language, if alone considered, would indicate.   *Id.*

15. He may also show that the written instrument was executed in part performance only of an entire oral agreement, or that the obligation of the instrument has been discharged by the execution of a parol agreement collateral thereto.   *Id.*

16. In an action to recover a sum of money, alleged to have been loaned by H. S. & Co. to defendant, plaintiff put in evidence a written instrument executed by defendant, which stated that he had " borrowed and received " of S. M. & Co. the sum claimed, and that the same was " payable to them or order on demand, with interest." Defendant offered and was permitted to prove, as a defense, that the instrument was executed as part of a prior oral agreement by the terms of which the payees were to advance the money in anticipation, upon debts owing by them and on the defendant's promise that it should be applied in discharge of those debts, and that the writing should be executed, but when the

money was so applied that it should be returned to the defendant ; also, that the latter had applied the money as agreed. *Held* no error ; that the paper was but evidence of part of the agreement, and it was proper to show in defense the whole transaction. *Id.*

17. A party alleging the loss of a material paper, to make out a case authorizing secondary evidence of its contents, must show that he has in good faith exhausted, to a reasonable degree, all the sources of information and means of discovery which the nature of the case would naturally suggest and which were accessible to him. *Kearney* v. *Mayor, etc.*   617

18. The person last known to have been in possession of the paper must be examined as a witness to prove the loss ; if out of the State his deposition must be procured or some good excuse given for not doing so.   *Id.*

—— *When competent to establish by proof aliunde that statute was not constitutionally passed. See People* v. *Petrea.*   128

—— *In action to foreclose mortgage purchased by executors after death of testator, evidence of receipt of money by him from mortgagor, it does not operate as payment and is not available as a counter-claim. See Carter* v. *Holahan.*   498

EXCEPTIONS.

1. Upon a writ of error no exception lies to a refusal to postpone a criminal trial by reason of the absence of witnesses. *Webster* v. *People.*   422

2. In the absence of exceptions on a criminal trial this court has no power to review the case upon the facts. *People* v. *Hovey.*   554

3. An exception to a charge taken after a criminal trial has terminated does not present any question for the consideration of an appellate court.   *Id.*

4. Where therefore, after a criminal trial, and when the prisoner was before the court for sentence, his counsel moved for a new trial for an alleged error in the charge, and upon denial of the motion took an exception, *held*, that no question was thereby presented here for review.   *Id.*

EXECUTION.

—— *When order in bankruptcy proceedings, staying proceedings of sheriff on execution, and directing assignee to sell property levied on, and judgment in favor of assignee adjudging judgment on which execution was issued invalid, is a defense to an action against sheriff for a false return, in returning execution nulla bona.*
See Dorrance v. Henderson. 406

EXECUTORS AND ADMINISTRATORS.

1. An executor, having notice that there is a debt due the estate, is bound to active diligence for its collection ; he may not wait for a request from the distributees. *Harrington* v. *Keltelas.*   40

2. In case the debt is lost through his negligence he becomes liable as for a *devastavit*.   *Id.*

3. *It seems*, that if the case is one of such doubt, that an indemnity is proper, he must at least ask for it ; and at any rate he takes the risk of showing that the debt was not lost through his negligence.   *Id.*

4. The statute of limitations does not begin to run in favor of an executor, as against a claim for damages occasioned by his negligence in collecting a debt due the estate from the time of the probate of the will, but at best only from the time of the loss.   *Id.*

5. Where, therefore, it was claimed that a debt was lost by reason of the running of the said statute, and it appeared that the will was admitted to probate, in 1870, that the defense of the statute became available to the debtor in 1874, and his pecuniary ability up to that time was unquestioned, that the executor died in 1876, and that an action against his executors was commenced in 1878. *Held*, that the action was not barred by the said statute.   *Id.*

6. As to whether an executor will be permitted to allege his own wrong so as to have time run in his favor, or whether each day before his accounting will not be deemed a commencement of the cause of action, or he be chargeable for the amount he could have collected as for assets in his hands, *quære.*   *Id.*

7. In an action brought by one of the beneficiaries under a will against the executors, who by the will were authorized to sell the real estate, and to invest and hold the proceeds with that of the personalty, as trustees for certain specified trusts, to recover damages for alleged willful delay and neglect in selling the real estate, and for improvident investments of the trust funds and to remove the trustees, it appeared that a former action was brought by plaintiff against defendants and others, wherein the complaint charged willful and fraudulent misconduct in the management of the estate and delay in selling the real estate, and demanded judgment that the executors be directed to sell immediately, also, to pay plaintiff the sums lost by such negligence, and that some other person be appointed to take charge of the portion of the funds in which plaintiff was interested. By the judgment in that action the trustees were directed to sell the real estate at auction within five months, and one of the trustees was suspended until the further order of the court on the ground of his insolvency. It also appeared and the court found that plaintiff upon being paid a consideration by the other *cestuis que trust*, who were satisfied with defendants' management, consented to a delay in the sale ; that certain securities were set aside as and for her portion of the trust fund, and that the lands were sold within the time agreed. *Held*, that

the former judgment in effect determined that upon the facts existing at the time it was rendered plaintiff was neither entitled to recover damages for delay, nor for a judgment removing defendants from their trusteeship; and that said judgment was conclusive and estopped plaintiff from any claim for relief based on facts occurring prior to said judgment; also, that no claim could be based upon the subsequent delay in selling the real estate. *Crabb* v. *Young.*   56

8. The will provided that the executors should not be liable for any loss or damage except such as occurred "from their willful default, misconduct or neglect." The complaint alleged and the court found that defendants imprudently and carelessly invested a portion of the fund set apart for plaintiff in insufficient securities, but such imprudence was not alleged or found to have been "willful." *Held,* that a judgment requiring defendants to restore to the trust fund the amount so invested was not authorized. *Id.*

9. It did not appear that any loss had actually occurred to the income because of such investments, and it seemed probable that no loss would even eventually occur to the fund itself, and the evidence disclosed no ground for imputing bad faith or want of prudence in making said investments. *Held,* that a judgment removing defendants was not justified; that if they acted in good faith subsequent events which they could not foresee, over which they had no control, could not render them liable. *Id.*

10. Defendants were required by the will to invest in bonds and mortgages "on unincumbered real estate." At the time of a loan upon bond and mortgage there was an unpaid tax upon the land. *Held,* that this was not a violation of the provision; that the tax was not an incumbrance within the meaning of the provision. *Id.*

11. A surrogate, in issuing letters of administration, has authority, and

it is within his discretion, to limit the powers conferred upon the administrator. *Martin* v. *D. D. E. B. & B. R. R. Co.*   70

12. Where, therefore, such letters contain this clause, these letters are issued with limited authority to prosecute only, and not with power to collect or compromise," *held,* that the surrogate had power to insert the limitation.   *Id.*

13. *It seems,* that if such a limitation was in excess of the powers of the surrogate, it did not invalidate the letters, but was at most only an irregularity.   *Id.*

14. *It seems* also (MILLER, J., DANFORTH and FINCH, JJ., concurring), that the objection is one that may not be raised collaterally, in a suit brought by the administrator. *Id.*

15. It is no defense to an action brought by an executor as such, to recover assets of the estate in the hands of defendant, or for the conversion thereof, that plaintiff in his individual capacity acted in collusion with the defendant in despoiling the estate. *Wetmore* v. *Porter.*   76

16. The complaint in an action brought by an executor to recover the value or possession of certain railroad bonds, after alleging the issuing of letters testamentary to plaintiff and his qualification, and that the bonds in question belonged to the estate, alleged in substance that plaintiff, at the request of defendant, who was his partner in business, and who knew that the bonds were trust funds, pledged the same as security for loans made to the firm; that the firm had funds sufficient to pay the debt, and defendant was largely indebted to plaintiff, yet that defendant, without the knowledge or consent of plaintiff, procured the pledgee to sell the bonds, and the proceeds were applied to the payment of the firm debt; that the bonds came into the custody and control of defendant, who refused to return them or pay their value. Upon demurrer to the complaint, *held,*

that it set forth a good cause of action; and that it was not necessary that plaintiff should have been made individually a party defendant. *Id.*

17. During the pendency of an action against an executor for misappropriation of moneys belonging to the estate, he died and his executor was substituted as party defendant. Judgment was recovered, which the defendant was directed to pay out of the estate; costs were also given, which were directed to be paid in like manner. The real estate of the deceased executor was sold by order of the surrogate. *Held*, that in the distribution of the proceeds said judgment creditor was not entitled to a preference for the damages recovered over the other creditors of the decedent, but was entitled to share *pro rata;* and that the surrogate properly disallowed the costs, as a claim, payable out of such proceeds. (Code of Civil Procedure, §§ 2756, 2757.) *In re Fox.* 93

18. In proceedings to compel a purchaser of real estate, at a receiver's sale, to complete the purchase, the receiver claimed title under two deeds; one dated March 21, 1863, from an executor, having power under the will to sell the real estate, to a third person, having the same family name as the executor; the other dated March 25, 1863, by said grantee, conveying the premises back to the executor, individually. The deeds were both recorded April 1, 1863, with an interval of but five minutes between. The receiver's sale was made January 11, 1882. No accounting or settlement of the estate by the executor had been had; no explanation was made by the receiver, and no ratification of the transfer by those interested, under the will, was proved. *Held*, that the title was defective, as it appeared that the conveyances were but one transaction, the executor acting in the double capacity of seller and purchaser; and, therefore, the title was voidable at the election of the beneficiaries named in the will; also that the lapse of

time, it being less than twenty years, was not conclusive upon them. *People* v. *O. B. of S. B. B. Co.* 98

19. The court below directed the purchaser to take the premises if the seller should produce sufficient evidence showing a confirmation of the executor's purchase by the proper parties. Such evidence to be taken in a proceeding instituted within sixty days. *Held* error; that the purchaser should have been relieved wholly from his contract. *Id.*

20. In proceedings before a surrogate to compel an accounting, by an executor, instituted prior to September 1, 1880, a hearing was had and a decree rendered, after that time, which was appealed from. The appellant, at the close of the evidence, requested the surrogate to find upon certain questions of fact, as provided by the Code of Civil Procedure (§ 2545), which he refused. *Held*, that an exception to the refusal was not well taken; as, by the said Code (§ 3347, subd. 11), all proceedings pending in Surrogate's Court on that date are exempted from the operation of any of the provisions of the chapter (18) containing said provision. *Mills* v. *Hoffman.* 181

21. In an action brought by a legatee against the other beneficiaries, and the heirs at law and next of kin of the testator, and against an administrator, with the will annexed, for the purpose of determining, among other things, the rights of the parties in the estate, and for an accounting by the administrator, and payment by him, to the parties entitled, of the amount found in his hands; judgment was rendered determining those questions and adjudging that upon compliance with the provisions of the judgment by the administrator he should be discharged from all claims and demands. A guardian *ad litem* was appointed in said action for an infant who, with her general guardian, was made a party defendant, and by the judgment

she was adjudged to be entitled to a certain sum out of the funds in the hands of the administrator. The latter fully performed all the requirements of said judgment, paying over the share of said infant to her general guardian, and was thereupon discharged from such administration. After said infant became of age, with full knowledge of the terms of the judgment, she received from her general guardian the moneys so paid to him, and also other moneys which the judgment required other defendants to pay to her, and which they had previously paid in compliance therewith to said guardian. She also commenced proceedings to vacate said judgment upon the ground that the appointment of the guardian *ad litem* was irregular, and an order was granted vacating the same, so far as she was concerned. Four years after the payment so made to her she commenced proceedings before the surrogate to compel said administrator to account. *Held,* that the proceedings were not maintainable ; that assuming the judgment has, so far as the petitioner is concerned, been deprived of any force as an adjudication of the question involved, she could and did, by acceptance of the moneys paid, ratify the acts of the general guardian and estopped herself from controverting either the judgment or the settlement made thereunder. *Id.*

22. The will of W. gave to his widow "all of the household property in the dwelling house, and the use of the dwelling-house during her life." In the dwelling-house, at the time of the testator's death, was a quantity of coal and wood, provided for family use, and a shot-gun. Upon settlement of the accounts of the executors, *held,* that these articles were properly allowed to the widow ; that the shot-gun might have been provided for the defense of the house, and in the absence of proof the court was not required to presume the contrary. *In re Frazer.* 239

23. The appraisers set apart as ex-

empt and for the use of the widow, a horse, phaeton and harness, of the value of $150. *Held,* that the gift of the household property did not preclude this allowance ; that "other personal property" was available for the exemption and might be necessary. *Id.*

24. A claim against the estate, based upon an alleged contract with the deceased, which was presented and sworn to in the ordinary manner, was allowed and paid by the executors. *Held,* that the burden was upon the contestants to show that it was not a just debt, and in the absence of such evidence it was properly allowed. *Id.*

25. M., the claimant, was allowed to testify as a witness to the contract. *Held* no error ; as he was not a party, nor did the executors derive any title through or from him. (Code of Civil Procedure, §§ 828, 829.) *Id.*

26. Also *held,* that it was no objection to the allowance that the executors could, had they resisted the claim, have excluded M. as a witness to personal transactions with the deceased. *Id.*

27. The executors allowed to a widow a claim for the wages of her son P. This was objected to on the ground that she was not authorized to receive them, and that the claim was outlawed when paid. The services ended in March, 1871. P. was then eighteen years of age. His father died in 1877 ; the payment was made in 1879, previous to which P. had died. No administrator was appointed. *Held,* that as the payment was of a just debt and had gone to the benefit of those entitled, and as the estate could not be required to pay a second time, and so had suffered no wrong, the executors were properly credited with the payment. *Id.*

28. The testator, having in his hands a sum of money belonging to his wife, loaned it in 1869, taking notes in the name of his wife. Afterward he included the amount in a

mortgage executed to himself by the borrower. The amount, with interest, was allowed to the widow by the executors. It was claimed by the contestant that it was to be presumed that the wife did not consent; that the husband was guilty of a conversion of her money, and so the statute of limitations was set running and the claim outlawed prior to the testator's death. *Held* untenable; that it was to be presumed, in the absence of evidence to the contrary, that the security was taken by the husband, with the consent of the wife; and therefore to the extent of her interest, he held the mortgage as agent or trustee for her.   *Id.*

29. Also *held*, that interest was properly allowed, as it was earned by the investment and received by the testator.   *Id.*

30. The will directed the executors to expend a sum not exceeding $2,000 "in repair" of a cemetery lot. A sarcophagus was erected on the lot at the expense of $500, and the testator's remains placed therein. A monument on the lot was exchanged for a better one and headstones to graves erected, and coping replaced at a cost of $935.05. *Held*, that what was done was within the authority and discretion given to the executors. *Id.*

31. The testator's residuary estate, including the homestead in which his wife was given a life estate, he gave to his wife, to H., the contestant, and to W. in equal proportions. The executors, at the request of the widow and H., expended $320 in repair to the premises, one-half of which they charged to each. It was objected that but one-third should be so charged. *Held* untenable.   *Id.*

32. Also *held*, that as the will contained no provisions excluding the widow from dower or repugnant to a claim therefor, the acceptance by her of the provisions in the will for her benefit did not deprive her of the right to make the claim.   *Id.*

33. Pending a contest as to the validity of a will a special administrator was appointed. A judgment had been recovered against the decedent prior to his death. An attachment against the judgment creditor was sought to be executed upon the judgment by service of copy upon the executrix named in the will. The special administrator was then acting, and the contest was then and is still pending. *Held*, that the executrix had no power to represent the estate, and so was not the "individual holding such property" within the meaning of the provision of the Code of Procedure (§ 235), authorizing the execution of an attachment by service of a copy; that, therefore, the judgment was not reached by the attachment; and that an order of the surrogate denying an application of the attachment creditor for the payment of the same to him was proper. *In re Flandrow.*   256

34. Also *held*, the fact that the attorney for the special administrator, upon being inquired of, gave information that the person named in the will was executrix, but concealed the appointment of the special administrator, did not preclude the latter from raising the objection. *Id.*

35. Under the provision of the Code of Civil Procedure (§ 3271) giving to the court discretionary power to require the plaintiff in an action brought by or against an executor, administrator, etc., in his representative capacity, to give security for costs, the court has power to require such security of one bringing suit in such capacity, although there is no evidence of mismanagement or bad faith, and aside from the question of his personal liability for costs as prescribed by the Code (§ 3246). *Tolman v. Syr., etc., R. R. Co.*   353

36. Where a power of sale is given to executors for the purpose of paying debts or legacies, and especially where there is an equitable conversion of land into money for the purpose of such payment and for

distribution, and the power is imperative and does not grow out of a personal discretion confided to the individual, such power belongs to the office of the executor and under the statute passes to and may be exercised by an administrator with the will annexed. *Mott v. Ackerman.* 539

FALSE PRETENSES.

1. An indictment for false pretenses averred in substance, that the accused having contracted to sell to B., the complainant, certain premises, fraudulently exhibited to B., who was illiterate and unable to read, a deed which he falsely represented to be a deed of the premises, when in fact the description covered other premises, etc. What purported to be a copy of the deed was set forth in the indictment. The deed offered in evidence on trial showed that in the copy in the indictment the easterly and westerly boundary lines were omitted. The copy, however, showed inferentially the length of these two lines. *Held*, that the variance was not material. *Webster v. People.* 422

2. The indictment did not allege that the deed was under seal. It was so stated, however in the attesting clause, a copy of which was set forth. *Held*, this, with the averment that the instrument was a deed, amounted to a substantial averment that it was under seal. *Id.*

3. Where such an indictment sets forth various pretenses alleged to be false, if one or more are proved to be false, and are sufficient *per se* to constitute the offense, a conviction is proper, notwithstanding the failure of the prosecution to prove the other alleged pretenses to be false. *Id.*

FISH AND FISHERIES.

1. The town of B., which claimed title under certain letters patent executed in 1666 and 1686 by the Colonial governors of the Province of New York, executed to plaintiff a lease of certain lands under water in a bay included in the boundaries of the said grants. In an action for alleged trespass in entering upon said lands and removing oysters therefrom, it appeared that the town, by various acts continuing from the time of said grants, assumed the rights of rental and exercised control of the lands under water in the bay. *Held*, that the title was in the town and the lease conferred upon plaintiff the exclusive right to take oysters from the lands covered by the lease; and that it was immaterial whether or not there was a natural oyster-bed on the land. *Hand v. Newton.* 88

2. The board of trustees of the town in 1871 passed a resolution declaring it not to be the intention of the trustees "to lease oyster lots on ground where oysters are naturally growing." In 1880 and before the granting of the lease in question, said resolution was, by another resolution passed by said board, repealed or modified so as to allow such leasing. *Held*, that the first resolution did not affect the validity of the lease; but that in any event the trustees had the right to repeal or modify it, and having so done, their right to lease without regard to the fact of the existence of a natural oyster-bed was restored. *Id.*

FIXTURES.

—— *What to be considered as such as between landlord and tenant.* See *Finkelmeier v. Bates.* 172

FORECLOSURE.

1. D. purchased certain premises, upon which was a mortgage, the payment whereof was guaranteed by K., plaintiff's testator. The conveyance was by the deed made subject to the mortgage. D., in making the purchase, acted as agent for K., who advanced the money therefor. D. subsequently conveyed the premises to K., the deed containing the same provision as to the mortgage. After K.'s death plaintiffs, as his executors, purchased the

mortgage with accompanying bond, and took an assignment thereof. In an action to foreclose the mortgage, in which the mortgagor was sought to be charged with any deficiency, *held*, that K., by the acceptance of the deed, did not become primarily liable to pay the mortgage, and that the relief sought was properly granted. *Carter* v. *Holahan*. 498

2. It was claimed that K. acted as agent for the mortgagor in making the purchase of the premises. *Held*, that conceding this to be so, as neither D. nor K. received any consideration which would support a contract to pay the mortgage, the mortgagor was not discharged from liability. *Id.*

8. By the will of K. no disposition was made of the premises. *Held*, that as the legal title on his death went to his heirs, and, therefore, there was no union of the equitable and legal estates in the same person, the mortgage was not merged upon its transfer to plaintiffs. *Id.*

4. Defendants offered in evidence on the trial a number of receipts for moneys paid by the mortgagor to K., during his life-time ; which were alleged to have been payments upon the mortgage ; these were excluded. *Held* no error ; that as, at the time the payments were made, K. was neither the holder nor owner of the bond and mortgage, they would not operate as payments thereon ; that they were not available as a counter-claim to a demand acquired by plaintiffs after the death of their testator. *Id.*

FOREIGN CORPORATIONS.

1. The act of 1865 (Chap. 694, Laws of 1865), as amended in 1875 (Chap. 60, Laws of 1875), providing that an insurance corporation of another State seeking to do business here shall pay to the superintendent of the insurance department for taxes, fines, etc., an amount equal to that imposed by the " existing or future laws " of the State of its origin, upon companies of

this State seeking to do business there, when such amount is greater than that required for such purposes by the then existing laws of this State, is not an unlawful delegation of legislative power. *People* v. *Fire Ass'n.* 311

2. The said act is not repugnant to the provision of the Federal Constitution (Art. 14), declaring that no State shall " deny to any person within its jurisdiction the equal protection of the law." That provision relates wholly to persons rightfully within the jurisdiction, not to the terms and conditions on which alone they can come in. *Id.*

3. A foreign corporation may not come or transact business within the jurisdiction except by permission, express or implied ; the State may prohibit it entirely, or may impose conditions, on compliance with which only it may come. *Id.*

4. Said provision, therefore, applies only to foreign insurance companies after they have performed the conditions upon which they are entitled to admission. *Id.*

5. *It seems* that, even if the conditions were unconstitutional, the foreign corporation waives the objection when it accepts the conditions by coming in under them, and is estopped from raising it. *Id.*

6. The constitutional difference between the rights of non-resident individuals and foreign corporations pointed out. *Id.*

7. Said act is not violative of the provision of the State Constitution (Art. 3, § 20), declaring that "every law which imposes, continues or revives a tax shall distinctly state the tax and the object to which it is to be applied, and it shall not be sufficient to refer to any other law to fix such tax or object," as the condition imposed by the act is in the nature of a license fee. *Id.*

8. The said act is not affected by the provision of the act of 1881 (§ 8, chap. 361, Laws of 1881) in refer-

ence to taxing certain corporations, companies and associations, which declares that the organization mentioned by the act shall thereafter "be exempt from assessment and taxation for State purposes," except as therein provided, as the exemption there is only from the general taxes for State purposes. *Id.*

9. By a law of Pennsylvania it is provided that an insurance company of another State doing business in that State shall pay into the State treasury annually three per cent of the premiums received there during the year. *Held*, that said act of 1875 required of an insurance company of that State doing business here a payment to the superintendent of such sum as, with other payments, would make a full payment of three per cent on the premiums received by it ; that if it had not paid the two per cent required to be paid by the State law (Chap. 465, Laws of 1875, as amended by chap. 359, Laws of 1876, chap. 138, Laws of 1878, and chap. 153, Laws of 1879), to the treasurers of the fire departments of the cities and villages, on all premiums received on property located therein, because there was no fire department in a particular locality to receive it, such amount must be added to the sum payable to the superintendent. *Id.*

FORMER ADJUDICATION.

1. In an action brought by one of the beneficiaries under a will against the executors, who by the will were authorized to sell the real estate, and to invest and hold the proceeds with that of the personalty, as trustees for certain specified trusts, to recover damages for alleged willful delay and neglect in selling the real estate, and for improvident investments of the trust funds and to remove the trustees, it appeared that a former action was brought by plaintiff against defendants and others, wherein the complaint charged willful and fraudulent misconduct in the management of the estate and delay in selling the real estate, and demanded judgment that the executors be directed to sell immediately, also, to pay plaintiff the sums lost by such negligence, and that some other person be appointed to take charge of the portion of the funds in which plaintiff was interested. By the judgment in that action the trustees were directed to sell the real estate at auction within five months, and one of the trustees was suspended until the further order of the court on the ground of his insolvency. It also appeared and the court found that plaintiff, upon being paid a consideration by the other *cestuis que trust*, who were satisfied with defendants' management, consented to a delay in the sale; that certain securities were set aside as and for her portion of the trust fund, and that the lands were sold within the time agreed. *Held*, that the former judgment in effect determined that upon the facts existing at the time it was rendered plaintiff was neither entitled to recover damages for delay, nor for a judgment removing defendants from their trusteeship; and that said judgment was conclusive and estopped plaintiff from any claim for relief based on facts occurring prior to said judgment; also, that no claim could be based upon the subsequent delay in selling the real estate. *Crabb* v. *Young.* 56

2. A party may not enjoy the rights awarded to him by a judgment and deny its force as an adjudication. *Mills* v. *Hoffman.* 181

—— *When prior order as to distribution of funds in hands of superintendent of insurance department conclusive upon application for order directing a different distribution. See In re Att'y-Gen'l* v. *N. A. L. Ins. Co. (Mem.)* 654

FRAUD.

1. In an action to recover a sum of money, alleged to have been loaned by H. S. & Co. to defendant, plaintiff put in evidence a written instrument executed by defendant,

which stated that he had "borrowed and received" of S. M. & Co. the sum claimed, and that the same was "payable to them or order on demand with interest." Defendant offered and was permitted to prove, as a defense, that the instrument was executed as part of a prior oral agreement by the terms of which the payees were to advance the money in anticipation, upon debts owing by them and on the defendant's promise that it should be applied in discharge of those debts, and that the writing should be executed, but when the money was so applied that it should be returned to the defendant ; also, that the latter had applied the money as agreed. Plaintiff sued, as receiver of said firm of S. M. & Co. It appeared that the form of the writing was adopted at the request of the payees, so that if creditors, other than those benefited by the advance, should make inquiry, they might suppose the transaction was as the paper indicated. Plaintiff claimed that this was fraudulent as to other creditors represented by the receiver. *Held* untenable ; that in providing beforehand for the payment of one rather than another obligation, the firm violated no duty, although insolvent ; also, that it could not be said as matter of law that any fraud was intended by either, it was a question of fact for the jury. *Juilliard* v. *Chaffee*.   529

2. *It seems* that if a creditor was here, who, on the faith of the security apparently afforded by the instrument, had either sold goods or given credit, or in any way changed his position to his detriment, a different question would arise.   *Id.*

3. *It seems*, also, that if the agreement was against the spirit of the bankrupt or insolvent laws, or otherwise contrary to public policy, plaintiff's position was no better than that of defendant and he could not avail himself of the objection.   *Id.*

—— *In assessment for a local im-*

provement in New York city, what proper evidence of.
See *In re L. & W. Orphan Home.*   16

FRAUDULENT CONVEYANCES.

The mere fact that an assignment of property by a debtor was voluntary and without consideration is not sufficient to require a finding that it was fraudulent against creditors. *Genesee Riv. Nat. B'k* v. *Mead*.   637

GENERAL TERM.

The General Term has power and it is its duty to review the verdict in an action to recover damages for death caused by negligence, and to set it aside if it appears excessive or the result of sympathy and prejudice. *Houghkirk* v. *Pres't., etc., D. & H. C. Co.*   219

GRAND JURY.

1. The act of 1881 (Chap. 532, Laws of 1881) purporting to amend the provision of the Code of Civil Procedure (§ 1041), in regard to the selection and drawing of jurors in the city and county of Albany, so far as it relates to grand jurors, is a local act and is within the prohibition of the provision of the State Constitution (Art. 3, § 18), forbidding the passage of a local or private bill for "selecting, drawing, summoning or impaneling grand or petit jurors." *People* v. *Petrea.*   128

2. Assuming, therefore, the said act not to have been reported by the commissioners appointed by law to revise the statutes, and so not within the exception (Art. 3, § 25) exempting from the operation of said provision, bills so reported, the said act is as to grand jurors unconstitutional and void.   *Id.*

3. In the absence of proof to the contrary it will be presumed in support of the constitutionality of the act that it originated in a bill so reported.   *Id.*

4. It is proper, however, to establish by proof *aliunde* that it did not so originate. *Id.*

5. So far as said act relates to the selection of petit jurors, as it is simply an amendment of an existing local law, it is not within the prohibitory provision of the Constitution and is valid. *Id.*

6. The amendment of an existing local act in mere matters of detail is not within the mischief aimed at by said provision, and is not violative thereof. *Id.*

7. Where an indictment was found by a grand jury drawn from the petit jury list as provided for in said act, *held*, upon the trial thereof, that as the grand jurors were drawn by the proper officer, were regularly summoned and returned, were recognized, impaneled and sworn by the court, were qualified to sit as grand jurors, and as such found the indictment, the arraignment and trial of the accused under it was not a violation of the constitutional guaranty that no person shall be held to answer for a capital or otherwise infamous crime, save as excepted, "unless on presentment or indictment of a grand jury" (Art. 1, § 6); that the indictment was by a grand jury within the meaning of said guaranty. *Id.*

8. Also *held*, that under the Code of Criminal Procedure (§§ 312, 313, 321, 328, 329), the accused was not entitled to avail himself, by plea or objection in other form, of the defect in the proceedings in drawing the grand jury *Id.*

HABEAS CORPUS.

1. A warrant so issued by a district attorney as authorized by the statute (Chap. 338, Laws of 1847) for the arrest of the relator, stated that he stood indicted "for contempt." On *habeas corpus*, issued on the petition of the relator, *held*, that this was a sufficient specification of the offense; that as the statement was of a contempt which has already served as a basis of an indictment, it necessarily implied a willful contempt, of a character constituting a misdemeanor. *People, ex rel. v. Mead.* 415

2. Also *held*, that as the indictment was found prior to the enactment of the Code of Criminal Procedure the provisions therein (§§ 301, 302) as to the form of bench warrants did not apply (§ 962), nor was it a case of a commitment for contempt specified in the provision of the Revised Statutes (2 R. S. 567, § 40) in relation to *habeas corpus*. *Id.*

3. The indictment was found by the Court of Sessions of Albany county; the application for the writ of *habeas corpus* was made to a justice of the Supreme Court in New York. At the time of the hearing thereon the Court of Oyer and Terminer in and for Albany county was in session. *Held*, that the Oyer and Terminer had authority to try the prisoner (2 R. S. 205, §§ 29, 30), and so that the justice had no authority to let the prisoner to bail. (2 R. S. 728, §§ 56, 57.) *Id.*

HIGHWAYS.

It is not negligence *per se* to drive a team at "a lively trot" in the streets of a city. One so driving is not limited to any particular rate of speed, but is bound simply to use proper care and prudence, so as not to cause injury to other persons lawfully upon the streets. *Crocker* v. *Knick. Ice Co.* 652

—— *Jurisdiction of Supreme Court to appoint commissioners under act chap.* 482, *Laws of* 1875, *as amended, to appraise damages and benefits for opening streets in territory contiguous to city.*
See *In re Church.* 1

HUSBAND AND WIFE.

1. Under a conveyance to a husband and wife jointly, they take, not as tenants in common or as joint tenants, but as tenants by the entirety, and upon the death of either, the survivor takes the whole estate. *Bertles* v. *Nunan.* 152

2. This common-law doctrine has not been abrogated by the statutory provisions (§ 3, chap. 200, Laws of 1848, amended by chap. 375, Laws of 1849; §§ 1, 2, chap. 90, Laws of 1860, amended by chap. 172, Laws of 1862), enabling a wife to acquire and hold a separate estate and to sell and convey the same. (DANFORTH and FINCH, JJ., dissenting.) *Id.*

8. As to whether those provisions apply to lands so conveyed, *quære Id.*

4. So also as to whether the husband still retains the common-law right of control and use of lands so conveyed, during the joint lives. *Id.*

5. On settlement of the accounts of executors, it appeared that the testator, having in his hands a sum of money belonging to his wife, loaned it in 1869, taking notes in the name of his wife. Afterward he included the amount in a mortgage executed to himself by the borrower. The amount, with interest, was allowed to the widow by the executors. It was claimed by the contestant that it was to be presumed that the wife did not consent; that the husband was guilty of a conversion of her money, and so the statute of limitations was set running and the claim outlawed prior to the testator's death. *Held* untenable; that it was to be presumed, in the absence of evidence to the contrary, that the security was taken by the husband, with the consent of the wife; and therefore to the extent of her interest, he held the mortgage as agent or trustee for her *In re Frazer.* 239

6. Also *held*, that interest was properly allowed, as it was earned by the investment and received by the testator. *Id.*

See ANTE-NUPTIAL AGREEMENT. MARRIED WOMEN.

INDICTMENT.

1. It is not essential to the validity of an indictment for contempt that the accused should first have been adjudged guilty of contempt by the court whose process he disobeyed. *People, ex rel.* v. *Mead.* 415

2. The relator was served with a subpœna, requiring him to appear before the Court of Oyer and Terminer in the county of Albany. He was called, and omitted to appear. *Held*, that he was properly indicted for contempt in that county; that the offense was there committed. *Id.*

3. An indictment for false pretenses averred in substance, that the accused having contracted to sell to B., the complainant, certain premises, fraudulently exhibited to B., who was illiterate and unable to read, a deed which he falsely represented to be a deed of the premises, when in fact the description covered other premises, etc. What purported to be a copy of the deed was set forth in the indictment. The deed offered in evidence on trial showed that in the copy in the indictment the easterly and westerly boundary lines were omitted. The copy, however, showed inferentially the length of these two lines. *Held*, that the variance was not material. *Webster* v. *People.* 422

4. The indictment did not allege that the deed was under seal. It was so stated, however, in the attesting clause, a copy of which was set forth. *Held*, this, with the averment that the instrument was a deed, amounted to a substantial averment that it was under seal. *Id.*

5. Where such an indictment sets forth various pretenses alleged to be false, if one or more are proved to be false, and are sufficient *per se* to constitute the offense, a conviction is proper, notwithstanding the failure of the prosecution to prove the other alleged pretenses to be false. *Id.*

6. Where, to an indictment for murder, the defendant pleaded "guilty to manslaughter in the first degree," *held*, that an acceptance of

the plea and a judgment thereon was proper ; that it was not necessary to aver in the indictment the facts which, if proven, would constitute the lesser crime. *People* v. *McDonnell.* 657

INFANTS.

1. In the case of a child of tender years, injured by alleged negligence, where the circumstances would justify an inference that he was misled or confused in respect to the actual situation, and that his conduct was not unreasonable in view of those circumstances, and his age, the question of contributory negligence is for the jury, although he may have omitted some precaution which in the case of an adult would be deemed conclusive evidence of negligence. *Barry* v. *N. Y. C.*, etc. 289

2. The provisions of the Revised Statutes (1 R. S. 726, § 87 ; id. 773, § 3, authorizing an accumulation of the income of real and personal property for the benefit of minors, require that the accumulation shall be for the benefit of a minor solely and during his minority, and that, when the period of accumulation ceases, the accumulated funds shall be released from further restraint and paid over to the person for whose benefit the accumulation is directed. *Pray* v. *Hegeman.* 508

3. A direction for accumulation during a minority, accompanied with a gift of the income of the accumulated fund after the expiration of the minority, to the minor for life, and of the principal, upon his death, to other persons, is void. (1 R. S. 726, § 38.) *Id.*

—— *When minor on coming of age, estopped from questioning acts of general guardian.* See *Mills* v. *Hoffman.* 181

INJUNCTION.

Where in a controversy sought to be submitted under the Code of

Civil Procedure (§ 1279) between the State and a corporation, the only relief to which the former is entitled, if any, is to restrain the corporation from exercising franchises unlawfully, the proceeding should be dismissed, as that relief may not be given therein. (Code, § 1281.) *People* v. *Mut. En. & Ac. Assn.* 622

—— *Order granting preliminary injunction not appealable to this court.* See *Foster* v. *City of B.* (*Mem.*) 629

INSURANCE.

—— *Validity of act* (*Chap.* 694, *Laws of* 1865), *providing for taxation of foreign insurance companies.* See *People* v. *Fire Assn.* 311

INSURANCE (FIRE).

1. A policy of insurance, issued by defendant upon a dwelling-house, contained a condition, avoiding it, " if the building *become* unoccupied without the consent of the company indorsed " thereon ; this was in connection with other conditions relating to the future. It was provided in the policy that nothing but a specific agreement, indorsed thereon, should be construed as a waiver of any of its conditions, and that an agent " has no authority to waive, modify or strike from this policy any of its printed conditions." The insurance was effected, and the policy delivered by an agent of the defendant. The building was then unoccupied, which fact was known to the agent. He had authority to insure unoccupied buildings, and the premium charged was at the rate for such buildings, which was more than double that for those occupied. No indorsement, however, of defendant's consent was made upon the policy. In an action upon the policy, *held*, that the condition as to an indorsement might have been fairly interpreted by the insured as relating only to the future ; but, assuming it to be otherwise, it was to be assumed that the agent accounted for and paid over to defend-

ant the premium received, and as it had not only not repudiated the contract, but recognized its original validity, it must be deemed to have waived the condition essential to such validity ; that it would not be permitted to receive and keep the fruits of the contract and yet repudiate its existence. *Haight* v. *Cont'l Ins. Co.* 51

2. The premises had been sold on foreclosure, but no deed had been executed or report of sale made. *Held*, that as the sale yet remained inchoate and conditional, there was no breach of a condition of the policy avoiding it in case of a transfer of interest without consent indorsed. *Id.*

INSURANCE (LIFE).

1. One holding a policy of life insurance does not forfeit his policy by omitting to pay annual premiums thereon after the company issuing the policy has ceased to do business, transferred all of its assets and become insolvent. *People* v. *Em. Mut. L. Ins. Co.* 105

2. The fact that a life insurance company is authorized to reinsure its risks, or that it is by statute permitted to discontinue its business and wind up its affairs, does not release it from any of its existing obligations ; such a company has no power to turn its policy-holders against their consent over to another company, and the policy-holders are under no obligations, in order to protect their legal rights, to protest against an effort so to do. *Id.*

3. The implied contract of the company with its policy-holders is, that it will continue its business, keep on hand the fund required by law for their security, and remain in a condition, so long as its contracts continue, to perform its obligations. *Id.*

4. The E. M. L. Ins. Co. entered into a contract with the C. L. Ins. Co., by which the latter agreed to insure the outstanding risks of the former

for a sum specified, it agreeing to cease business and to wind up its affairs ; it transferred all of its assets to the C. L. Ins. Co., and still owed that company a balance which it had no means of paying and has not paid. The E. M. L. Ins. Co. thereupon surrendered its offices, notified the comptroller of that fact, and seven years thereafter, at the suit of the attorney-general, it was dissolved and a receiver appointed. Certain of its policy-holders refused or neglected to accept new policies from the C L Ins. Co., and omitted to pay premiums after such transfer. *Held*, that the E. M. L. Ins. Co., having voluntarily disabled itself from the performance of its contract, said policy-holders were excused from further performance or offer to perform on their part, and were entitled to recover as damages for the breach on the part of the company, the value of their policies at the time of such breach ; that by virtue of their position they were beneficiaries of the fund held by the State as security for policy-holders, and their claims followed that fund into the hands of the receiver and were first entitled to be paid therefrom. *Id.*

5. A warranty in an application for a policy of life insurance that a third person is in good health does not mean an actual freedom from illness or disease, but simply that the person has indicated in his actions and appearance no symptoms or traces of disease, and to the ordinary observation of a friend or relative is in truth well. *Grattan* v. *Met. L. Ins. Co.* 274

6. Where, therefore, in an action upon a policy, upon the question as to a breach of such a warranty, the court charged that if from the appearance of the person he was in good health so that anybody would so pronounce him, and there was nothing to indicate he was not in good health, the warranty was not broken although in fact the germs of a hidden and lurking disease then existed. *Held* no error. *Id.*

7. An application contained a war-

ranty that the answers to the questions in the report of the medical examiner were " fair and true," and the applicant signed a certificate at the foot of said report to the effect that he had given true answers to the questions, and " that they agree exactly with the foregoing." He gave a truthful answer to a question by the medical examiner, but the latter wrote a different and untruthful answer in his report. The evidence authorized a finding that the applicant did not see the answer as written in the report, and was ignorant of the fact that it differed from that given by him. *Held*, that this having been found, the company, not the insured, was responsible for the falsehood. *Id.*

8. Such a certificate can only be met and answered by proof establishing either that the answer was not written or was not known to the applicant when the certificate was signed by him; the burden of the untruth must be shown to rest solely on the agent of the company. *Id.*

9. To prove the falsity of the answer as given in the report, defendant put in evidence a portion of a letter written by the insured. Plaintiff was permitted, under objection and exception, to read in evidence the remainder of the letter, which gave a history of the transaction, showing that the writer gave a correct answer, and was ignorant of the fact that an untruthful answer was written in the report. *Held*, that the ruling was proper. *Id.*

10. A physician who was called upon professionally to make an examination of T., brother of the insured, was asked " what opinion did you form, based on the general sight of the man before you made an examination, or before you had any conversation with him." *Held*, that the question was properly excluded as privileged within the statute. (Code of Civil Procedure, § 834) *Id.*

11. After a physician called by de-

fendant had been asked if T., upon whom he attended, died of consumption, and the question had been excluded, he was asked whether, in response to questions put by plaintiff's counsel on a former trial, he had not answered that T. died of consumption. This was objected to and excluded. *Held* no error; first, what the witness had testified to could only be proved to contradict him or refresh his memory ; second, the plaintiff's inquiry on the former trial did not preclude his objecting to the evidence. *Id.*

12. In an action to recover back premiums paid upon certain policies 'of life insurance issued by defendant, each of which when delivered contained a provision that the policy would " be good at any time, after three payments, for its equitable value," the complaint, after alleging the issuing of the policies and the payment of more than three years premiums, averred, in substance, that plaintiff, having concluded not to continue to pay premiums, demanded of defendant the equitable value of the policies, and on its refusal to allow the same, commenced an action to recover such equitable value; that thereafter defendant notified plaintiff that said provision was inserted in the policies without its authority or consent, and set up such claim in the answer. Whereupon the plaintiff discontinued the said action, and paid the taxable costs thereof. *Held*, that assuming the first action was discontinued in consequence of said averments in the answer, defendant was not estopped, as it did not damage plaintiff, because whether the clause was part of the contract or not the former action could not have been sustained; that the clause if binding upon defendant imposed no obligation upon the company to pay any thing until plaintiff's death ; it simply continued the policies in force for their equitable value in case no further payments were made. *Andrews* v. *Ætna L. Ins. Co.* 596

13. It appeared upon the trial of this

action that the notice referred to was a letter written to defendant's secretary, which, while it asserted that the clause was written in the policies without authority, stated that defendant was willing to perform it, and the answer in the former action which asserted that the clause was inserted without authority denied that defendant had refused to pay the equitable value. *Held*, that this was an unequivocal election on the part of defendant to affirm or ratify the alleged unauthorized act, and so the proceedings in the former action furnished no basis for an equitable estoppel. *Id.*

14. The court refused to submit to the jury the questions as to the original validity of the policies, and whether they had been affirmed by defendant. *Held* no error; because, *first*, no such issue was tendered by the complaint; *second*, the evidence of ratification was so conclusive there was no question for the jury. *Id.*

—— *When prior order as to distribution of funds in hands of superintendent of insurance department conclusive upon application for order directing a different distribution.*
See *In re Att'y-Gen.* v. *N. A. L. Ins. Co.* (Mem.)   654

INTEREST.

1. Where one, entitled to an award for damages by reason of the widening of Broadway in the city of New York, made in proceedings under the act of 1869 (Chap. 890, Laws of 1869), accepted the sum awarded, and gave a receipt acknowledging payment in full of its amount, *held*, that the right to interest was thereby waived, and an action to recover the same could not thereafter be maintained against the city; and this, although the claimant demanded payment of interest at the time and protested against the refusal of the comptroller to pay the same. *Cutter* v. *Mayor, etc.*   166

2. Interest in such case is given as damages for non-payment or deten-

tion of the money awarded (§ 183, chap. 86, Laws of 1813), and is only to be recovered with the principal by action; it does not constitute a debt capable of a distinct claim. Acceptance, therefore, without action, of the sum awarded, in full payment of the principal, bars an action for such damages.   *Id.*

—— *When allowable on moneys in hands of agent or trustee.*
See *In re Frazer.*   239

JOINT DEBTORS.

1. An action may be brought under the Code of Civil Procedure (§ 1937), after the recovery of a judgment against joint debtors, by the judgment creditor " against one or more of the defendants who were not summoned in the original action," although the defendants served have appealed and have given the security, which under said Code (§ 1310) "stays all proceedings to enforce the judgment appealed from." *Morey* v. *Tracey.*   581

2. The second action is not brought to enforce the judgment but to establish the liability of the defendants not served, which is not determined by such judgment. *Id.*

JOINT TENANTS.

See TENANTS IN COMMON AND JOINT TENANTS.

JUDICIAL SALES.

1. In proceedings to compel a purchaser of real estate, at a receiver's sale, to complete the purchase, the receiver claimed title under two deeds; one dated March 21, 1863, from an executor, having power under the will to sell the real estate, to a third person, having the same family name as the executor; the other dated March 25, 1863, by said grantee, conveying the premises back to the executor, individually. The deeds were both recorded April 1, 1863, with an interval of but five minutes between.

The receiver's sale was made January 11, 1882. No accounting or settlement of the estate by the executor had been had; no explanation was made by the receiver, and no ratification of the transfer by those interested, under the will, was proved. *Held,* that the title was defective as it appeared that the conveyances were but one transaction, the executor acting in the double capacity of seller and purchaser; and, therefore, the title was voidable at the election of the beneficiaries named in the will; also that the lapse of time, it being less than twenty years, was not conclusive upon them. *People* v. *O. B. of S. B. B. Co.* 98

2. The court below directed the purchaser to take the premises if the seller should produce sufficient evidence showing a confirmation of the executor's purchase by the proper parties. Such evidence to be taken in a proceeding instituted within sixty days. *Held* error; that the purchaser should have been relieved wholly from his contract. *Id.*

JURISDICTION.

1. A surrogate, in issuing letters of administration, has authority, and it is within his discretion, to limit the powers conferred upon the administrator. *Martin* v. *D. D. E. B. & B. R. R. Co.* 70

2. Under the Code of Civil Procedure (§§ 2717, 2718) a surrogate has no jurisdiction to entertain proceedings instituted by one claiming a legacy, to compel an executor to pay the same, when the executor "files a written answer duly verified, setting forth facts which show that it is doubtful whether the petitioner's claim is valid and legal, and denying its validity." In such a case, the surrogate must dismiss the petition. *Fiester* v. *Shepard.* 251

3. The complaint herein set forth a demand for $398.71; the answer denied liability and set up a counter-claim for $301.29. The

trial court found with defendant and gave judgment against plaintiff for the counter-claim. The General Term reversed the judgment. *Held,* that the amount of the two claims constituted "the matter in controversy," within the meaning of the Code of Civil Procedure (§ 191, subd. 3), and that this court had jurisdiction on appeal. *Crawford* v. *West Side B'k.* 631

—— *Jurisdiction of Supreme Court to appoint commissioners under act chap.* 482, *Laws of* 1875, *as amended, to appraise damages and benefits for opening streets in territory contiguous to city.*
See *In re Church.* 1

—— *Jurisdiction of surrogate to determine question as to widow's right to the articles of household furniture specified in the statute, when in accordance with an ante-nuptial contract she has accepted a sum "in lieu of her rights" as widow.*
See *In re Young* v. *Hicks.* 235

JURY.

The act of 1881 (Chap. 532, Laws of 1881) purporting to amend the provision of the Code of Civil Procedure (§ 1041), in regard to the selection and drawings of jurors in the city and county of Albany, so far as it relates to the selection of petit jurors, as it is simply an amendment of an existing local law, is valid. *People* v. *Petrea.* 128

See CHALLENGE (OF JURORS).

LAKES.

See WATER-COURSES.

LANDLORD AND TENANT.

See LEASE.

LARCENY.

—— *It is not necessary, on trial of indictment for grand larceny in stealing a pocket-book, to call as witness the person from whom it was stolen ; that defendant took it against the will and consent of said person may be shown by other evidence.*

See People v. Wiggins (Mem.) 657

LEASE.

1. By a lease for a term of twenty-one years the lessee covenanted to pay an annual rental, and all taxes and assessments, also to build a "first-class commercial building," of a size and material specified, to cost not less than $30,000. A right of re-entry in case of non-payment of the rent was reserved, and it was covenanted, that "at the expiration of the aforesaid term" the value of the building should be appraised, and upon payment of one-half of the appraised value the building should belong to the lessor, and "on the last day of said term or other sooner determination of the estate" granted, the lessee would peaceably surrender possession The lessor was given the option of giving a renewal lease for a further term of twenty-one years instead of paying half the value of the building, and at the expiration of that term it was declared that the building should belong to him. The lessee erected the building, and at the expiration of about five years his assignees were dispossessed for non-payment of rent. In an action to recover the rent due defendants set up as a counter-claim the half value of the building, claiming that the words "expiration of the term" when the lessor was to pay the half value in case he determined not to re-lease related not to time, but to the estate of the lessee, and that upon termination of the estate the liability of the lessor arose. *Held* untenable ; that assuming the covenant to pay such half value to be an independent one, not conditioned upon the prior payment of rent, the word "term" was used in the sense of time, and such liability did not arise until the end of the twenty-one years. *Finkelmeier v. Bates.* 172

2. The lessor, as part of the original construction, put into the building

an elevator, an engine to run the same; a boiler was also placed in a vault under the sidewalk to furnish steam for the engine, and for heating the building. The boiler was set in brick work, and could only be removed by taking up the sidewalk. Defendants sought to counter-claim the value of the elevator and boiler ; *held* untenable; that in the absence of evidence to the contrary, it was to be assumed the price of these articles went to make up the stipulated expenditure of $30,000, and under the lease, as between the parties, they were to be considered as part of the building. *Id.*

—— *Right of town to lease lands under water for cultivating oysters.*
See Hand v. Newton. 88

—— *Provision in lease as to renewal thereof may be modified by parol, and as to what is to be considered as a modification.*
See Crosby v. Moses. (Mem.) 634

LEGACIES.

The will of C. gave to two grandchildren "the sum of $1,000 each, to be paid to them respectively as they arrive at the age of twenty-five years." To five children he gave $1,000 each, payable one legacy each year for five years after his decease. After certain devises and bequests, he gave his residuary estate to defendant, his son, subject to the payment of his debts and the legacies. In an action by the administrator of the estate of one of said grandchildren, who died before reaching the age of twenty-five, brought after she would have reached that age, had she lived, to recover the legacy, *held*, that the postponement of the time of payment did not make the gift contingent; that the testator's intent, as disclosed by the will, was simply to postpone payment for the benefit of the estate ; that the legacy vested upon the death of the testator, and that plaintiff was entitled to recover. *Bushnell v. Carpenter.* 270

See WILLS.

LEGITIMACY.

The wife of M., a resident of this State, procured a divorce from him on account of his adultery; the judgment forbade him from marrying again. He thereafter went into the State of New Jersey, and there married during the life of his first wife, returning with his second wife to this State, and continuing to reside here. The statute law of New Jersey declares that "all marriages, where either of the parties shall have a former husband or wife living at the time of such marriage, shall be invalid, * * * and the issue thereof shall be illegitimate." In an action to test the right of plaintiff, a son born of the second marriage, to inherit, as the lawful heir of M., *held*, that at the time of the second marriage the latter had no former wife living within the meaning of said statute; that the laws of this State and the provision of the judgment prohibiting marriage had no effect, and M. had a right to marry in another State whose laws did not prohibit a second marriage by one divorced; and that plaintiff was legitimate and so entitled to inherit. *Moore* v. *Hegeman.* 521

LIMITATIONS OF ACTIONS.

1. The statute of limitations does not begin to run in favor of an executor, as against a claim for damages occasioned by his negligence in collecting a debt due the estate from the time of the probate of the will, but at best only from the time of the loss. *Harrington* v. *Ketellas.* 40

2. Where, therefore, it was claimed that a debt was lost by reason of the running of the said statute, and it appeared that the will was admitted to probate in 1870, that the defense of the statute became available to the debtor in 1874, and his pecuniary ability up to that time was unquestioned, that the executor died in 1876, and that an action against his executors was commenced in 1878. *Held*, that the action was not barred by the said statute. *Id.*

3. As to whether an executor will be permitted to allege his own wrong so as to have time run in his favor, or whether each day before his accounting will not be deemed a commencement of the cause of action, or he be chargeable for the amount he could have collected as for assets in his hands, *quære.* *Id.*

4. Upon settlement of the accounts of executors it appeared that the testator, having in his hands a sum of money belonging to his wife, loaned it in 1869, taking notes in the name of his wife. Afterward he included the amount in a mortgage executed to himself by the borrower. The amount, with interest, was allowed to the widow by the executors. It was claimed by the contestant that it was to be presumed that the wife did not consent; that the husband was guilty of a conversion of her money, and so the statute of limitations was set running and the claim outlawed prior to the testator's death. *Held* untenable; that it was to be presumed, in the absence of evidence to the contrary, that the security was taken by the husband, with the consent of the wife; and therefore to the extent of her interest, he held the mortgage as agent or trustee for her. *In re Frazer.* 239

5. Plaintiff's complaint alleged that defendant "improperly, carelessly, negligently and unlawfully suffered ice and snow to be and remain upon the crosswalk," at the intersection of two streets in the city of New York; that in consequence thereof, plaintiff, while passing over said crosswalk, was thrown to the ground and injured, and plaintiff asked to recover the damages sustained. *Held*, that the action was "to recover damages for a personal injury resulting from negligence" within the meaning of the provision of the Code of Civil Procedure (§ 383), limiting the time for the commencement of such action to three years. *Dickinson* v. *Mayor, etc.* 584

6. The provision of said Code (§ 410) providing that where "a demand

is necessary to entitle a person to maintain an action, the time within which the action must be computed from the time when the right to make the demand is complete," is applicable to actions against the city of New York. . *Id.*

7. Such an action is not saved from the operation of said provision by the provision (§ 3341) declaring that " any special provision of the statutes remaining unrepealed * * * which is applicable exclusively to an action " against said city shall not be affected by the Code. *Id.*

8. The provision of the charter of said city of 1873 (§ 105, chap. 335, Laws of 1873) providing that no action shall be maintained against the city "unless the claim upon which the action is brought has been presented to the comptroller and he has neglected for thirty days after such presentment to pay the same," was intended for the benefit of the city, not of claimants, and does not deprive the city of the benefit of the said provision as to the time when the statute of limitations begins to run. *Id.*

9. Accordingly, *held*, that, as it was set forth in the complaint that the accident happened in January, 1877, and that the claim was presented to the comptroller in April, 1881, the action was barred. *Id.*

LOST INSTRUMENTS.

1. A party alleging the loss of a material paper, to make out a case authorizing secondary evidence of its contents, must show that he has in good faith exhausted, to a reasonable degree, all the sources of information and means of discovery which the nature of the case would naturally suggest and which were accessible to him. *Kearney* v. *Mayor, etc.* 617

2. The person last known to have been in possession of the paper must be examined as a witness to prove the loss; if out of the State his deposition must be procured or

some good excuse given for not doing so. *Id.*

3. The determination of the trial judge of the fact as to the loss cannot be reviewed here, unless the proof of loss was so clear and conclusive that it was error of law to find against it. *Id.*

4. Where the only witness called to prove the loss is the party claiming it, the trial court is not bound as matter of law to credit his statements, although they are not contradicted by any other witness. *Id.*

MANDAMUS.

1. The act of 1882 (Chap. 363, Laws of 1882) validating (so far as the same remain unpaid) certain taxes in the city of Brooklyn, which were invalid because of the omission of the assessors to verify the assessment-rolls as prescribed by the city charter (§ 31, title 4, chap. 384, Laws of 1854, as amended by § 21, chap. 63, Laws of 1862) did not validate a sale, made prior to its passage because of non-payment of a tax ; and a payment by a purchaser at such a tax sale is not a payment of the tax. Notwithstanding the sale the tax " remains unpaid" within the meaning of the act, and the property owner is entitled to the benefit of said condition, and upon refusal of the registrar of arrears of the city to accept the amount specified, is entitled to a *mandamus* to compel the acceptance thereof and the discharge of the tax. *In re Clementi* v. *Jackson.* 591

2. The purchaser at the tax sale is not a necessary party to the proceeding by *mandamus.* *Id.*

MANUFACTURING CORPORATION.

—— *What is not, within meaning of Tax Act of* 1880. (*Chap.* 542, *Laws of* 1880.)
See *People* v. *N. Y. F. D. D. Co.* 487

MARRIAGE.

1. The wife of M., a resident of this State, procured a divorce from him on account of his adultery ; the judgment forbade him from marrying again. He thereafter went into the State of New Jersey, and there married during the life of his first wife, returning with his second wife to this State, and continuing to reside here. The statute law of New Jersey declares that "all marriages, where either of the parties shall have a former husband or wife living at the time of such marriage, shall be invalid, * * * and the issue thereof shall be illegitimate." In an action to test the right of plaintiff, a son born of the second marriage, to inherit, as the lawful heir of M, *held*, that at the time of the second marriage the latter had no former wife living within the meaning of said statute ; that the laws of this State and the provision of the judgment prohibiting marriage had no effect, and M. had a right to marry, in another State whose laws did not prohibit a second marriage by one divorced ; and that plaintiff was legitimate and so entitled to inherit. *Moore* v. *Hegeman.* 521

2. Also *held*, that as there were statutory provisions on the subject, there was no presumption that the rule of the common law still existed in New Jersey; that the statute superseded and took the place of such rule. *Id.*

3. The distinction between the New Jersey statutes upon this subject and those of this State pointed out. *Id.*

4. After the dissolution of the first marriage M. and his first wife were again married, but in an action brought by her it was adjudged that the second marriage was prohibited by the statutes of this State, and was void ; after the entry of this judgment the marriage in New Jersey took place. It was urged here that such re-marriage was valid. *Held*, that the judgment not having been reversed, and having been made by a com-

petent court having jurisdiction of the parties and the subject-matter, was conclusive. *Id.*

5. As to whether after a judgment of divorce on the ground of the adultery of one of the parties, and the consequent prohibition against another marriage by the guilty party, a second marriage of the parties in this State will be valid, *quære.* *Id.*

See ANTE-NUPTIAL AGREEMENT.

MARRIED WOMEN.

See HUSBAND AND WIFE.

MASTER AND SERVANT.

—— *As to what is sufficient evidence of negligence on the part of a railroad corporation, to subject it to liability to an employe, and as to what is not contributory negligence on his part.* See *Dana* v. *N. Y. C. & H. R. R. Co.* (*Mem.*) 639

MERGER.

—— *When mortgage not merged upon transfer to executors of owner of equity of redemption.* See *Carter* v. *Holahan.* 498

MISDEMEANOR.

The provision of the Revised Statutes (2 R. S. 691, § 5) making it a misdemeanor to accept a conveyance of lands, which, to the knowledge of the grantee, are at the time held adversely, and the title to which is in litigation, does not affect the previous title of the grantor in a deed executed in violation thereof, and the conveyance is no defense to an action of ejectment brought by him. *Chamberlain* v. *Taylor.* 848

MISTAKE.

—— *Where evidence of mistake in executing town bond insufficient to authorize reformation of the instrument.* See *Potter* v. *Town of G.* (*Mem.*) 662

minutes. The witnesses for the prosecution testified that no words passed between C. and the prisoner, and there was no assault or provocation by the former. *Held*, that the prisoner was properly convicted of murder in the first degree. *People* v. *Cornetti.* 85

2. Where, to an indictment for murder, the defendant pleaded "guilty to manslaughter in the first degree," *held*, that an acceptance of the plea and a judgment thereon was proper ; that it was not necessary to aver in the indictment the facts which, if proven, would constitute the lesser crime. *People* v. *McDonnell.* 657

NEGLIGENCE.

1. An executor, having notice that there is a debt due the estate, is bound to active diligence for its collection ; he may not wait for a request from the distributees. *Harrington* v. *Keteltas.* 40

2. In case the debt is lost through his negligence he becomes liable as for a *devastavit.* *Id.*

3. Under the statute (Chap. 450, Laws of 1847, as amended by chap. 256, Laws of 1849) authorizing an action to recover damages for death caused by negligence, the pecuniary loss which a party named in the statute is entitled to recover may consist of special damages, *i. e.*, of actual definite loss, and also of prospective general damages. *Houghkirk* v. *Pres't, etc., D. & H. C. Co.* 219

4. Plaintiff's intestate was run over and killed in attempting to cross the tracks of defendant's road at a place where plaintiff claimed a right of crossing ; there was no flagman present at the scene of the accident. The court submitted it to the jury to determine whether, under the circumstances, due care required the presence of a flagman, and whether for the omission of that precaution defendant was chargeable with negligence. *Held* error. *Id.*

5. In an action against a railroad company for alleged negligence, causing the death of plaintiff's intestate, it appeared that the decedent was run over and killed in attempting to cross defendant's tracks at a point where the owners of adjoining lands had a right of way, and where the public for thirty years had been in the habit of crossing. *Held*, that the acquiescence of defendant for so long a time in this public use amounted to a license or permission to all persons to cross at this point, and imposed a duty upon it as to persons so crossing to exercise reasonable care in the movement of its trains, so as to protect them from injury. *Barry* v. *N. Y. C., etc.* 289

6. The train which caused the death was backing up without a bell being rung or other signal given, in charge of a brakeman, who was on a platform between two cars, where he could not see persons on the track or have notice to apply the brakes in case of danger. Persons were at all times crossing the tracks, several hundreds crossing daily. *Held*, that the evidence justified the submission of the question of defendant's negligence to the jury. *Id.*

7. The intestate was a boy ten years old. The train which ran over him went past the crossing followed by a freight train. The bell on the freight train was ringing and the flagman on the crossing was flagging it, paying no attention to the other. The first train was switched on to another track and backed up on the track the boy attempted to cross. There was no direct proof as to what precautions he took before crossing the track. *Held*, that the question of contributory negligence was properly submitted to the jury ; that it was competent for them to infer that the boy seeing the first train pass supposed it was going on, and his attention being attracted by the freight train, he did not observe that the first train had changed its direction and was backing up. *Id.*

8. In the case of a child of tender years, where the circumstances would justify an inference that he was misled or confused in respect to the actual situation, and that his conduct was not unreasonable in view of those circumstances, and his age, the question of contributory negligence is for the jury, although he may have omitted some precaution which in the case of an adult would be deemed conclusive evidence of negligence. *Id.*

9. *It seems* it cannot be held as matter of law, that, under the circumstances of this case, the ringing of the bell would fulfill the whole duty resting on defendant. *Id.*

10. Where, upon the sale by a druggist of a poisonous medicine, he fully and fairly warns the purchaser of its character, and gives accurate information and directions as to the quantity which may be safely taken, and the customer is injured or killed by taking an overdose in disregard of such direction, the druggist is not liable for negligence or tort simply because of an omission on his part to put a label marked " poison " upon the " parcel in which the sale is made " as required by the statute. (2 R. S. 694, § 23.) The customer may not disregard the warning and direction and charge the consequences of his own negligence or recklessness upon the druggist. *Wohlfahrt* v. *Beckert.* 490

11 It is not negligence *per se* to drive a team at "a lively trot" in the streets of a city. One so driving is not limited to any particular rate of speed, but is bound simply to use proper care and prudence, so as not to cause injury to other persons lawfully upon the streets. *Crocker* v. *Knick. Ice Co.* 652

—— *When executors and trustees not liable for.*
See *Crabb* v. *Young.* 56

—— *As to what is sufficient evidence of negligence, on the part of a railroad corporation, to subject it to liability to* an *employe, and as to what is not contributory negligence on his part.*
See *Dana* v. *N. Y. C. & H. R. R. Co.* (*Mem.*) 68*

—— *When evidence as to due care insufficient to authorize submission of question to jury.*
See *Becht* v. *Corbin.* (*Mem.*) 658

NEW TRIAL.

The provision of the Code of Criminal Procedure (§ 527) providing that "the appellate court may order a new trial if it be satisfied that the verdict against the prisoner was against the weight of evidence, * * * or that justice requires," is applicable only to the Supreme Court and gives that court a discretionary power When in the exercise of that discretion it refuses or grants a new trial its determination is not reviewable here. *People* v. *Boas.* 560

NEW YORK (CITY OF).

1. In May, 1857, one K. entered into a contract with defendant to regulate, grade, etc., a portion of one of its streets, the work to be completed on or before August 19, 1858. The contract required the work to be done under the supervision of a person appointed by the street commissioner, and to be approved of by that officer or the person so appointed, and if at any time the work should not progress according to the terms of the contract, said officer was authorized to complete the work at the expense of the contractor. K. commenced the work and dug a deep hole or trench in the street near plaintiff's lots, adjoining the street: in 1859 he dug another hole, but did little else toward the performance of the contract, and in 1859 abandoned it. In 1873 the city employed another person who completed the work. In consequence of said excavations, surface water, which before that had been accustomed to flow in a natural channel, was diverted and thrown upon plaintiff's premises,

causing damage. This damage was done after the time for the performance of the contract had expired, and ceased when the work was completed. In an action to recover said damage, *held* (MILLER, DANFORTH and FINCH, JJ., dissenting), that defendant was liable, as it permitted these excavations to remain when it had the power and right to take charge of and complete the work, and thus protect plaintiff's property from injury. *Vogel* v. *Mayor, etc.* 10

2. The petition upon which proceedings were instituted to vacate an assessment for regulating and grading a street in the city of New York, authorized by the act of 1871 (Chap. 226, Laws of 1871), charged in substance that the commissioner of public works fraudulently combined and colluded with the contractors to let the contract at an extravagant price. The contract in question was not let at a public letting, but was what is known as "a special contract," the commissioner having invited four persons to bid for the work. The persons so invited put in bids for "filling," which was the main item, ranging from $1.43 to $1.60 per cubic yard. The contract was awarded for $1.47. The petitioner upon the hearing offered in evidence the "bid-book" of the department of public works, containing a record of bids received for public lettings prior and subsequent to the contract in question, relating to streets in the same vicinity, by which it appeared that filling was contracted for at prices not exceeding eighty cents per cubic yard. This evidence was rejected. *Held* error ; that the commissioner, in the absence of evidence to the contrary, must be presumed to have known the usual prices paid for the work, and the evidence was competent on the issue of fraud. *In re Righter.* 111

3. Also *held*, that it was competent as bearing upon the alleged combination and collusion to prove the bids by the selected bidders for the other special contract work and the contracts awarded therefor. *Id.*

4. The provision of the act of 1878, entitled "An act to provide for the Eastern boulevard in the city of New York, and in relation to certain alterations of the map or plan of said city, and certain local improvements" (§ 4, chap. 528, Laws of 1873), authorizing the department of public parks to do the work "of regulating, grading or otherwise improving Tenth avenue," authorized the construction of a sewer in said avenue. *In re L. & W. O. H.* 116

5. Under said provision the department was authorized to do the work of constructing such a sewer, or any part thereof, by day's work. *Id.*

6. In proceedings to vacate an assessment for the construction of such a sewer, *held*, that in the absence of evidence that there was no connection or relation between the portion of Tenth avenue specified in the act and the Eastern boulevard, for the purpose of sustaining the constitutionality of the act, the connection was to be assumed ; and, therefore, that said act was not violative of the provision of the State Constitution (Art. 3, § 16), declaring that no local or private act shall contain more than one subject, and requiring that to be expressed in the title. *Id.*

7. The greater portion of the work was done by day's work. It appeared that rock excavation cost over $14 per cubic yard, pipe culvert $7.05 per lineal foot, and brick sewer $25 per lineal foot, while the fair value was rock excavation $4 per cubic yard, pipe culvert $1.50 per lineal foot, and brick sewer $4.55 per lineal foot. *Held*, that the evidence disclosed not merely a case of improvidence and extravagance, but sufficiently established fraud or irregularity. *Id.*

8. But *held*, that the petitioner was not entitled to have the assessment wholly vacated ; and that an order reducing it, by striking out the amount added by reason of such fraud or irregularity, was proper. *Id.*

9. Also *held*, that an objection that the petition contained no averments of fraud affecting the assessment, not having been taken at Special Term, would not be heard here. *Id.*

10. Where, one entitled to an award for damages by reason of the widening of Broadway in the city of New York, made in proceedings under the act of 1869 (Chap. 890, Laws of 1869), accepted the sum awarded, and gave a receipt acknowledging payment in full of its amount, *held*, that the right to interest was thereby waived, and an action to recover the same could not thereafter be maintained against the city; and this, although the claimant demanded payment of interest at the time, and protested against the refusal of the comptroller to pay the same. *Cutter* v. *Mayor, etc.* 166

11. Interest in such case is given as damages for non-payment or detention of the money awarded (§ 183, chap. 86, Laws of 1813), and is only to be recovered with the principal by action; it does not constitute a debt capable of a distinct claim. Acceptance, therefore, without action, of the sum awarded, in full payment of the principal, bars an action for such damages. *Id.*

12. In an action brought under the provision of the act of 1813 (§ 184, chap. 86, Laws of 1813), authorizing a person entitled to an award of the commissioners of estimate and assessment in the city of New York to bring an action against any other person to whom the same has been paid to recover the same, it is no defense, that the award was excessive or inequitable, or that plaintiff was entitled to only nominal damages while the commissioners awarded substantial damages. The award, as to this, is "final and conclusive" (§ 178), and it is sufficient for the plaintiff to show that the award was made for lands owned by him, and so that he was entitled to it. *De Peyster* v. *Mali.* 262

13. A regular clerk in a department of the government of the city of New York, whose services are no longer needed, may under the charter of that city of 1873 (Chap. 835, Laws of 1873) be removed by the head of the department without any previous trial, hearing or notice; the provision of said charter (§ 28) declaring that "no regular clerk * * * shall be removed until he has been informed of the cause of the proposed removal, and has been allowed an opportunity of making an explanation," does not apply to such a case. *Langdon* v. *Mayor, etc.* 427

14. Plaintiff's complaint alleged that defendant " improperly, carelessly, negligently and unlawfully suffered ice and snow to be and remain upon the crosswalk," at the intersection of two streets in the city of New York; that in consequence thereof, plaintiff, while passing over said crosswalk, was thrown to the ground and injured, and plaintiff asked to recover the damages sustained. *Held*, that the action was "to recover damages for a personal injury resulting from negligence" within the meaning of the provision of the Code of Civil Procedure (§ 383), limiting the time for the commencement of such action to three years. *Dickinson* v. *Mayor, etc.* 584

15. The provision of said Code (§ 410) providing that where "a demand is necessary to entitle a person to maintain an action, the time within which the action must be commenced must be computed from the time when the right to make the demand is complete," is applicable to actions against the city of New York. *Id.*

16. Such an action is not saved from the operation of said provision by the provision (§ 8341) declaring that " any special provision of the statutes remaining unrepealed * * * which is applicable exclusively to an action " against said city shall not be affected by the Code. *Id.*

17. The provision of the charter of said city of 1873 (§ 105, chap. 385,

Laws of 1878), providing that no action shall be maintained against the city "unless the claim upon which the action is brought has been presented to the comptroller and he has neglected for thirty days after such presentment to pay the same" was intended for the benefit of the city, not of claimants, and does not deprive the city of the benefit of the said provision as to the time when the statute of limitations begins to run. *Id.*

18. Accordingly, *held*, that, as it was set forth in the complaint that the accident happened in January, 1877, and that the claim was presented to the comptroller in April, 1881, the action was barred. *Id.*

19. Losses from taxes for State purposes assessed in the city of New York, but not collected, are to be borne by the city, not the State, which is entitled to the whole amount. *Mayor, etc.,* v. *Davenport.* 604

20. As to whether an action may be maintained by the city of New York against the State comptroller to recover alleged over-payments on account of taxes for State purposes, *quære.* *Id.*

NOTICE.

—— *What sufficient to charge purchaser of chattel with notice of mortgage thereon.*
See Mack v. *Phelan.* 20

NUISANCE.

One who employs a contractor to do a work, not in its nature a nuisance, but which becomes so by reason of the manner in which the contractor has performed it, if he accepts the work in that condition, becomes at once responsible for the nuisance. *Vogel* v. *Mayor, etc.* 10

OFFICE AND OFFICER.

1. The legislature may abridge the term of an office created by it, by

express words, or may specify an event upon the happening of which it shall end. *People, ex rel.* v. *Whitlock.* 191

2. It is also within the power of the legislature, where it has given the authority to appoint · to an office created by it, to authorize the removal of the incumbent without notice or a hearing. *Id.*

3. A regular clerk in a department of the government of the city of New York, whose services are no longer needed, may under the charter of that city of 1873 (Chap. 335, Laws of 1873) be removed by the head of the department without any previous trial, hearing or notice; the provision of said charter (§ 28) declaring that "no regular clerk * * * shall be removed until he has been informed of the cause of the proposed removal, and has been allowed an opportunity of making an explanation," does not apply to such a case. *Langdon* v. *Mayor, etc* . 427

—— *Liability of bank for acts of its cashier.*
See F. S. Institute v. *Bostwick.* 564

See COUNTY TREASURER.
  SHERIFFS.
  STATE BOARD OF EQUALIZATION.
  SUPERVISORS.

OYSTERS.

——*Right of town to lease lands under water for cultivating oysters.*
See Hand v. *Newton.* 88

PARTIES.

—— *Where trustees of village enter into a contract as water commissioners for the erection of water-works for village they act as agents for it and action is maintainable against it.*
See Fleming v. *Village of S. B.* 368

—— *When purchaser at a tax sale in Brooklyn not a necessary party to a proceeding by mandamus by the owner of land sold to compel the reg-*

*istrar of arrears to accept the amount
authorized to be paid in satisfaction of
tax by act chap. 363. Laws of 1882.*
See *In re Clementi* v. *Jackson.* 591

PATENTS (FOR LANDS).

1. The town of B., which claimed
title under certain letters-patent
executed in 1666 and 1686 by the
Colonial governors of the Province
of New York, executed to plaintiff
a lease of certain lands under water
in a bay included in the boundaries
of the said grants. In an action
for alleged trespass in entering
upon said lands and removing
oysters therefrom, it appeared that
the town, by various acts continuing from the time of said grants,
assumed the rights of rental and
exercised control of the lands under
water in the bay. *Held*, that the
title was in the town and the
lease conferred upon plaintiff the
exclusive right to take oysters
from the lands covered by the
lease; and that it was immaterial
whether or not there was a natural
oyster-bed on the land. *Hand* v.
Newton. 88

2. The board of trustees of the town
in 1871 passed a resolution declaring it not to be the intention of
the trustees "to lease oyster lots
on ground where oysters are naturally growing." In 1880 and before the granting of the lease in
question, said resolution was, by
another resolution passed by said
board, repealed or modified so as
to allow such leasing. *Held*, that
the first resolution did not affect
the validity of the lease; but that
in any event the trustees had the
right to repeal or modify it, and
having so done, their right to
lease without regard to the fact
of the existence of a natural oyster-
bed was restored. *Id.*

PAYMENT.

—— *Sum in excess of lawful interest
accepted on making a loan by agent,
without authority or knowledge of
principal, but received by latter, should
be allowed as payment.*
See *Philips* v. *Mackellar.* 34

PLACE OF TRIAL.

Plaintiff's complaint alleged, in substance, that defendants, as trustees,
held the legal title to certain hotel
property situate in the county of
Saratoga, and as such issued to
plaintiff a certificate showing him
to be entitled to an interest therein
and in the rents and profits; that
as such trustees defendants had
declared a dividend on said certificate, which he claimed to recover.
The answer averred payment of
the dividend. The venue was laid
in the county of New York. On
motion to change the place of trial
to Saratoga county, *held*, that the
action was not to determine or
affect any interest in land within
the meaning of the provision of
the Code of Civil Procedure (§
982), requiring such action to be
tried in the county where the subject of the action or some part
thereof is situated; but that the action was in the nature of one for
moneys had and received, and so
was triable in New York. *Roche*
v. *Marvin.* 396

PLEADING.

1. A complaint which states facts
constituting a good cause of action
is not demurrable, simply because
the facts are inartificially stated or
because several different causes of
action are joined in one count.
Wetmore v. *Porter.* 76

2. Nor is a complaint demurrable
where the facts stated show that
plaintiff is entitled to some relief
because the relief demanded is not
precisely that to which plaintiff is
entitled. *Id.*

3. In this action by C., an attorney,
to recover a compensation agreed
to be paid for professional services,
it appeared that W., being interested in the success of the plaintiff in an action brought for the
purpose of contesting the validity
of a will, in which action a verdict had been rendered sustaining
the will, entered into a contract
with C., by which the latter agreed
to appeal and conduct the case to

a final determination, W. to pay a sum specified therefor. C. was thereupon substituted as attorney for the plaintiff in said action, and performed services therein. W. having died, his executors, the defendants in this action, settled and discontinued the action. Defendants were permitted to prove, under objection and exception, that after the employment of C., and before the death of W., the former entered into a contract with the attorney for one of the defendants in said action, whereby he agreed, for the consideration of $1,500, to release certain premises from the operation of said action. C., without disclosing the fact that he was to receive compensation, applied to his client and to the nominal plaintiff in said action to consent to such release. Neither consented. Notwithstanding this he executed in his own name, as attorney for plaintiff, a release. Defendant's answer contained a general denial, and also, in a separate count, a statement of the facts above stated. The count commenced, "Defendants, for further answer to said complaint," allege, etc. It concluded by alleging that the sum so received by C. in right and equity belonged to W., and that "these defendants will set off the same" against any demand established by plaintiff. *Held*, that the evidence was proper under the general denial, as it showed non-performance of his implied contract by plaintiff; but that if necessary to specifically set forth the facts, this was done, and defendant could not be precluded from insisting upon the defense, because the special use to be made of the facts was not correctly pointed out. *Chatfield* v. *Simonson.* 209

4. Also *held*, that pleading the acts of C. by way of set-off was not a ratification thereof; that it was, at most, but the assertion of a legal conclusion which did not operate as an estoppel. *Id.*

5. Plaintiff's complaint alleged that defendant "improperly, carelessly, negligently and unlawfully suffered ice and snow to be and remain upon the crosswalk," at the intersection of two streets in the city of New York; that in consequence thereof, plaintiff, while passing over said crosswalk, was thrown to the ground and injured, and plaintiff asked to recover the damages sustained. *Held*, that the action was "to recover damages for a personal injury resulting from negligence" within the meaning of the provision of the Code of Civil Procedure (§ 383), limiting the time for the commencement of such action to three years. *Dickinson* v. *Mayor, etc.* 584

POISON.

In an action against a druggist for alleged negligence in the sale of a poisonous medicine without attaching a label marked poison, thus causing the death of W., plaintiff's intestate, it appeared, that W., having been advised to take a comparatively harmless preparation known as "black draught," and that he could take a small wine glass thereof, which he could procure at any drug store for ten cents, went to defendant's drug store, where, according to the testimony of defendant's clerk, he asked defendant for ten cents worth of "black drops;" defendant told him that was a poison, and advised him to take another preparation; this W. refused, and defendant thereupon directed the witness to give him black drops, but informed him that he should only take ten or twelve drops for a dose; witness gave W. two drachms of the medicine asked for in a vial upon which was a label marked "black drops;" the label did not have the word "poison" thereon. W. took nearly the whole of the contents of the vial and died in consequence. *Held*, that if the testimony of the clerk was to be taken as the truth, a verdict for defendant was properly directed; but that the jury were at liberty, under the circumstances, to disbelieve such testimony, as the witness was interested, having violated the law by omitting the prescribed label; and that, therefore, the question as to whether the warning testified to was in fact given was one for the jury, and the direction was error. *Wohlfahrt* v. *Beckert*.   490

POWERS.

1. M., at the time of making her will, and of her death, owned a large amount of real estate but only a small amount of personal property. By her will, after providing for the payment of debts, she first gave her estate, real and personal. to her executors in trust, to rent, etc., and apply the rents, income, etc., to the use of her husband during his life. Then followed ten clauses purporting to create separate and independent trusts ; also numerous legacies, all of which would substantially fail in the absence of a trust estate, or power in trust vested in the executors, by force of which the real estate could be sold and converted into money. Certain real estate was also specifically devised, and the executors were directed to pay off incumbrances thereon, which, in the absence of such power, could not be done. The clause appointing executors contained the following : " and during the life-time of my said husband my said executors, and such and whichever of them as shall act, are authorized and empowered, by and with the consent of my said husband, to sell and dispose of any part of my estate, real and personal, not specifically bequeathed." In an action for a construction of the will, *held*, that said clause was to be construed as conferring upon her executors a power of sale, which, during the life of her husband, was to be exercised only with his consent, but thereafter continuing to exist ; and that, therefore, the executors had power to sell after the death of the husband, and convert into money so much of the real estate as was not specifically devised. *Phillips* v. *Davies*.   99

2. In 1869 S. conveyed all of her estate to trustees, in trust, to convert into money, and keep the proceeds invested, applying the income and such portion of the principal as they should deem proper to her use during her life, and paying over the residue as she should by will appoint. In 1877 S. made a will, which made no reference to the trust, but by which she devised certain real estate, part of the trust estate, gave legacies amounting to $275,500, and gave her residuary estate, including that she might thereafter acquire or become possessed of, to seventeen beneficiaries named. At the time of the execution of the will and of her death, S., aside from the trust estate, only owned property of the value of about $25,000, which consisted principally of an undivided interest in the estate of a deceased sister. She was in the habit of spending all the income paid her by the trustees, and was well acquainted with the condition and amount of her estate. At the time of executing the will, S. was in delicate health, and was apprehensive that she might die at any moment. In an action by the trustees for an accounting and for directions as to the disposition of the trust estate, *held*, that the power of appointment reserved in the trust deed was properly and effectually executed both as to real and personal estate   *Hutton* v. *Benkard.*   295

3. Where it appears, from the terms of a will, taken as a whole, and construed in the light of surrounding circumstances, that it was the intention of the testator in the dispositions made by him to execute a power of appointment, such intention will have effect although the power is not referred to in express words.   *Id.*

4. The provisions of the Revised Statutes in reference to powers (1 R. S., part 2, chap. 1, title 2, art. 3, p. 732 *et seq.*) apply so far as they can be made applicable to personal as well as to real estate, and the rules governing the construction of testamentary appointments in regard to real estate apply when they affect personal property.   *Id.*

5. The provision, therefore, of such statutes (1 R. S. 787, § 126), declaring that lands embraced in a power to devise shall pass by a will purporting to convey all the testator's real estate "unless the intent that the will shall not operate as an execution of the power shall appear, expressly or by necessary implication," applies to personalty. *Id.*

6. The will of M. devised his real estate to his executors in trust, to hold one-third part thereof for the benefit of each of his three daughters during life. Upon the death of a daughter, leaving a husband and lawful issue living, it was declared that the executors should stand seized of her third "from and immediately after her death, upon trust for the sole use and benefit of such issue;" in case of the death of a daughter single and unmarried, "upon such trust, and for such purpose as she shall or may appoint by her last will;" in default of such appointment "for the sole use and benefit of her next of kin." *Held*, that the power of appointment related to the remainder in fee; that in each event provided for, the trust in the executors upon the death of the daughter would be purely passive, the remainder vesting in the beneficiaries; that the phrase in the clause giving such power of appointment "upon such trust" meant, not a trust to be created by the daughter and so limiting the power of disposition, but related to the trust in the executors. *Mott* v. *Ackerman*. 539

7. As to one of the daughters who was married at the time of the execution of the will, it provided that in case she should give to her husband any part of her income from the estate or pay any of his debts she should thereupon forfeit all right and interest in and to such income. *Held*, that this did not affect the conclusion above stated; it did not show any intent to limit the power of appointment. *Id.*

8. One of the daughters died unmarried, leaving a will by which she gave all of her estate, real and personal, after payment of debts, to her two sisters who survived her, "and to the survivor of them," and to the heirs, executors and administrators of such survivor. *Held*, that this was a valid execution of the power of appointment and the title to one-third of the real estate passed under it; that the limitation in the devise to the survivor did not work an unlawful suspension of the power of alienation (1 R. S. 724, § 24); that the estate upon the death of the testatrix passed to her two sisters as tenants in common, each taking a fee, that of the one dying first being defeasible by such death, and thereupon the entire absolute estate vested, which, therefore, could be aliened after two lives at most. *Id.*

9. The two surviving sisters purchased and owned as tenants in common certain other real estate; one of them subsequently died, leaving a will by which she gave to her executors a power of sale, to be exercised during the life of the surviving sister with her concurrence, and (the will then proceeds) "on the death of my said sister Maria, or as soon afterward as they may think advisable * * * and within three years from the proof of this will," the executors were empowered and directed to convert into money the real estate, etc. Maria lived more than three years after probate of the will. After her death and about twelve years after such probate the surviving executors contracted to sell the real estate to defendant, who refused to complete the purchase, claiming, among other things, that the power of sale could only be exercised within the three years. *Held* untenable; that as the purposes of the will required a sale the power was imperative (1 R. S. 734, § 96), and was so intended by the testatrix, and the neglect to sell within the time specified did not destroy the authority conferred. *Id.*

10. The executor before bringing this action tendered a deed which was refused. Pending the appeal to this court said executor died and

the present plaintiff was appointed administrator, with the will annexed, and the action was revived in his name. *Held*, that the deed so tendered could not now be delivered or treated as delivered with the effect of passing the title; but that plaintiff could make the conveyance. (2 R. S. 72, § 22.) *Id.*

11. Where a power of sale is given to executors for the purpose of paying debts or legacies, and especially where there is an equitable conversion of land into money for the purpose of such payment and for distribution, and the power is imperative and does not grow out of a personal discretion confided to the individual, such power belongs to the office of the executor and under the statute passes to and may be exercised by an administrator with the will annexed. *Id.*

PRACTICE.

1. Returns to this court should be made by a responsible officer, under sanction of his official oath, and attorneys for parties cannot, by stipulation, make up a case for the court. *Dow* v. *Darragh.* 537

2. A preference on the calendar of an action for dower, authorized by the Code of Civil Procedure (§ 791, subd. 6), can be claimed only when the proof required, *i. e.*, that plaintiff " has no sufficient means of support aside from the estate in controversy," was made and an order allowing the preference obtained as required (§ 793), before the notice of argument was served. *Bartlett* v. *Musliner.* 646

3. Where in an action in which the people were parties, and appeared by the attorney-general, the latter did not, at the time of serving notice of argument, give notice of a particular day in the term on which he would move it, as prescribed by the provision of the Code of Civil Procedure (§ 791, subd. 1) to entitle the cause to a preference, but served with the notice of argument notice of motion that the

cause be set down for a day named, which motion failed because the court adjourned before the day specified for making it. *Held*, that the action was not entitled to a preference. *People, ex rel.* v. *Kinney.* 647

4. Under the Code of Civil Procedure (§ 709), in an action in the Supreme Court, triable and tried in the first judicial district, an application for an extra allowance of costs must be made in that district, although the justice before whom the cause is tried resides in another district. *Hun* v. *Salter.* 651

—— *Where case is prepared and settled by consent of both parties and is properly certified, and no motion is made to amend, no complaint that it is defective can be made here, and argument must be made upon it as returned. The case should be settled and signed by the judge or referee who tried cause.*
Also where appeal should be dismissed for failure to serve undertaking.
See Reese v. *Boese.* (*Mem.*) 632

See PLEADING.
TRIAL.

PRESUMPTIONS.

1. The will of W. gave his widow "all of the household property in the dwelling-house and the use of the dwelling-house during her life." In the dwelling-house, at the time of the testator's death, was a quantity of coal and wood, provided for family use, and a shot-gun. Upon settlement of the accounts of the executors, *held*, that these articles were properly allowed to the widow; that the shot-gun might have been provided for the defense of the house, and in the absence of proof the court was not required to presume the contrary. *In re Frazer.* 389

2. The testator, having in his hands a sum of money belonging to his wife, loaned it in 1869, taking notes in the name of his wife. After-

ward he included the amount in a mortgage executed to himself by the borrower. The amount, with interest, was allowed to the widow by the executors. It was claimed by the contestant that it was to be presumed that the wife did not consent; that the husband was guilty of a conversion of her money, and so the statute of limitations was set running and the claim outlawed prior to the testator's death. *Held* untenable; that it was to be presumed, in the absence of evidence to the contrary, that the security was taken by the husband, with the consent of the wife; and therefore to the extent of her interest, he held the mortgage as agent or trustee for her. *Id.*

—— *That act is constitutionally passed.*
See *People* v. *Petrea.* 128

—— *When trustees of village are presumed to have knowledge of and to have assented to the doing of extra work.*
See *Fleming* v. *Village of S. B.* 368

—— *Where there are statutory provisions of a State on a particular subject there is no presumption that the rule of the common law in reference thereto is in force.*
See *Moore* v. *Hegeman* 521

PRINCIPAL AND AGENT.

1. The fact that an agent, without the authority, consent or knowledge of his principal, upon loaning the money of the latter, exacted a sum in excess of lawful interest, does not make the loan usurious; nor does the fact of the receipt by the principal of the sum so paid, in the absence of evidence of knowledge on his part that it was paid as a usurious consideration for the loan, establish a ratification of the act of the agent. *Philips* v. *Mackellar.* 84

2. *It seems,* however, in such case, the sum so paid should be allowed and applied as a payment. *Id.*

3. A principal upon being informed of an unauthorized act of an agent has a right to elect whether he will adopt it or not, and so long as the condition of the parties is unchanged, cannot be prevented from such adoption by the fact that the other party prefers to treat the contract as invalid. *Andrews* v. *Ætna Life Ins. Co.* 596

4. An election once made, however, is irrevocable. *Id.*

—— *Where trustees of village enter into a contract as water commissioners for the erecting of water-works for village they act as agents for it, and action is maintainable against it.*
See *Fleming* v. *Village of S. B.* 368

—— *Liability of bank for acts of its cashier.*
See *F. S. Institute* v. *Bostwick.* 564

PRIVILEGED COMMUNICATIONS.

1. A physician who was called upon professionally to make an examination of T., brother of the insured, was asked " what opinion did you form, based on the general sight of the man before you made an examination, or before you had any conversation with him " *Held,* that the question was properly excluded as privileged within the statute. (Code of Civil Procedure, § 834.) *Grattan* v. *Met. L. Ins. Co.* 274

2. After a physician called by defendant had been asked if T., upon whom he attended, died of consumption, and the question had been excluded, he was asked whether, in response to questions put by plaintiff's counsel on a former trial, he had not answered that T. died of consumption. This was objected to and excluded. *Held* no error; first, what the witness had testified to could only be proved to contradict him or refresh his memory; second, the plaintiff's inquiry on the former trial did not preclude his objecting to the evidence. *Id.*

PROMISE OF MARRIAGE.

See ANTE-NUPTIAL CONTRACT.

PUBLIC POLICY.

—— *When party cannot avail himself of objection that contract is against public policy.*

QUESTIONS OF LAW AND FACT.

—— *When question of negligence one of fact.*

—— *When question as to original validity of policy of insurance, and as to ratification by company of provision therein inserted by agent without authority is one of law and a refusal to submit the same to a jury proper.*

—— *When evidence as to due care insufficient to authorize submission of question to jury.*

RAILROAD CORPORATIONS.

1. In an action against a railroad company for alleged negligence, causing the death of plaintiff's intestate, it appeared that the decedent was run over and killed in attempting to cross defendant's tracks at a point where the owners of adjoining lands had a right of way, and where the public for thirty years had 'been in the habit of crossing. *Held,* that the acquiescence of defendant for so long a time in this public use amounted to a license or permission to all persons to cross at this point, and imposed a duty upon it as to persons so crossing to exercise reasonable care in the movement of its trains, so as to protect them from injury. *Barry* v. *N. Y. C., etc.* 289

2. The train which caused the death was backing up without a bell being rung or other signal given, in charge of a brakeman, who was on a platform between two cars, where he could not see persons on the track or have notice to apply the brakes in case of danger. Persons were at all times crossing the tracks, several hundreds crossing daily. *Held,* that the evidence justified the submission of the question of defendant's negligence to the jury. *Id.*

3. The intestate was a boy ten years old. The train which ran over him went past the crossing followed by a freight train. The bell on the freight train was ringing and the flagman on the crossing was flagging it, paying no attention to the other. The first train was switched on to another track and backed up on the track the boy attempted to cross. There was no direct proof as to what precaution he took before crossing the track. *Held,* that the question of contributory negligence was properly submitted to the jury; that it was competent for them to infer that the boy seeing the first train pass supposed it was going on, and his attention being attracted by the freight train, he did not observe that the first train had changed its direction and was backing up. *Id.*

4. *It seems* it cannot be held as a matter of law, that, under the circumstances of this case, the ringing of the bell would fulfill the whole duty resting on defendant. *Id.*

5. Under the provision of the act (Chap. 296, Laws of 1874) subjecting the property of the N. Y. & O. M. R. R. Co. to taxation, and appropriating the amount of the county taxes thereon, in any town which has issued bonds in aid of the construction of the road of said company, to such town, to be devoted to the payment of its bonds, after any such tax has been collected, the moneys belong to the town, and any diversion thereof from their lawful object is an injury to the rights of the town, which may be protected

by an appropriate action in its behalf. *Bridges* v. *Bd. Suprs.* 570

—— *As to what is sufficient evidence of negligence on the part of a railroad corporation, to subject it to liability to an employe, and as to what is not contributory negligence on his part.*
See *Dana* v. *N. Y. C. & H. R. R. R. Co.* (*Mem.*) 639

—— *When evidence as to due care insufficient to authorize submission of question to jury.*
See *Becht* v. *Corbin.* (*Mem.*) 658

RATIFICATION.

1. In an action brought by a legatee against the other beneficiaries, and the heirs at law and next of kin of the testator, and against an administrator, with the will annexed, for the purpose of determining, among other things, the rights of the parties in the estate, and for an accounting by the administrator, and payment by him, to the parties entitled, of the amount found in his hands; judgment was rendered determining those questions and adjudging that upon compliance with the provisions of the judgment by the administrator he should be discharged from all claims and demands. A guardian *ad litem* was appointed in said action for an infant who, with her general guardian, was made a party defendant, and by the judgment she was adjudged to be entitled to a certain sum out of the funds in the hands of the administrator. The latter fully performed all the requirements of said judgment, paying over the share of said infant to her general guardian, and was thereupon discharged from such administration. After said infant became of age, with full knowledge of the terms of the judgment, she received from her general guardian the moneys so paid to him, and also other moneys which the judgment required other defendants to pay to her, and which they had previously paid in compliance therewith to said guardian.

She also commenced proceedings to vacate said judgment upon the ground that the appointment of the guardian *ad litem* was irregular, and an order was granted vacating the same, so far as she was concerned. Four years after the payment so made to her she commenced proceedings before the surrogate to compel said administrator to account. *Held*, that the proceedings were not maintainable; that assuming the judgment has, so far as the petitioner is concerned, been deprived of any force as an adjudication of the question involved, she could and did, by acceptance of the moneys paid, ratify the acts of the general guardian and estopped herself from controverting either the judgment or the settlement made thereunder. *Mills* v. *Hoffman.* 181

2. In an action to recover back premiums paid upon certain policies of life insurance issued by defendant, each of which when delivered contained a provision that the policy would "be good at any time, after three payments, for its equitable value," the complaint, after alleging the issuing of the policies and the payment of more than three years premiums, averred, in substance, that plaintiff, having concluded not to continue to pay premiums, demanded of defendant the equitable value of the policies, and on its refusal to allow the same, commenced an action to recover such equitable value; that thereafter defendant notified plaintiff that said provision was inserted in the policies without its authority or consent, and set up such claim in the answer. Whereupon the plaintiff discontinued the said action, and paid the taxable costs thereof. It appeared upon the trial of this action that the notice referred to was a letter written to defendant's secretary, which, while it asserted that the clause was written in the policies without authority, stated that defendant was willing to perform it, and the answer in the former action which asserted that the clause was inserted without authority denied that defendant had refused to pay

4. Where the precedent or particular estate is given to several persons as tenants in common, the remainders limited upon the estates of part of the tenants in common may fail without affecting the remainders limited upon the estates of the others. *Id.*

RETURNS.

1. The provision of the Code of Civil Procedure (§ 3301, as amended by chap. 399, Laws of 1882), providing that the stipulation of the attorneys for parties to an action may take the place of a clerk's certificate to a copy of a paper whereof a certified copy is required, was not intended to alter the effect of the provision (§ 1315) requiring a return to this court to be certified by the clerk of the court from which the appeal is taken, or of the rule of this court (Rule 1) making the same requirement. *Dow* v. *Darragh.* 587

2. Returns to this court should be made by a responsible officer, under sanction of his official oath, and attorneys for parties cannot, by stipulation, make up a case for the court. *Id.*

RIPARIAN OWNERS.

1. The riparian owners of lands adjoining fresh-water non-navigable streams take title to the thread of the stream, and as incident to the title acquire the right to the usufructuary enjoyment of the undiminished and undisturbed flow of said stream. *Smith* v. *City of Rochester.* 463

2. This is so also as to the fresh-water navigable streams and small lakes within this State where the tide does not ebb and flow; save that the public has an easement in such waters for the purpose of travel, as on a public highway, which easement, as it pertains to the sovereignty of the State, is inalienable and gives to the State the right to use, regulate and control the waters for the purposes of navigation. *Id.*

3. This public easement gives the State no right to convert the waters or to authorize their conversion to any other uses than those for which the easement was created, *i. e.*, for the purposes of navigation. *Id.*

4. The right to divert the waters for other uses, although public in their nature, can only be acquired under and by virtue of the sovereign right of eminent domain, and upon making " just compensation." *Id*

5. Plaintiffs are the owners of certain premises, on the banks of Honeoye creek, used and occupied by them for milling purposes, and their mills are operated by the waters of the stream; said creek is a fresh-water non-navigable stream, formed by the junction of the surplus waters of three small inland lakes; one of these, Hemlock lake, is about seven miles in length, and one-half mile in width; it is to a certain extent navigable and has for many years been navigated for local purposes by those living upon its shores. Said lake and the lands adjoining and the plaintiffs' premises are included in the territory of which the proprietorship was ceded by this State to Massachusetts by the treaty of 1786. Under the authority of the act chapter 754, Laws of 1873, defendant constructed a conduit from the said lake to the city, for the purpose of furnishing water for the inhabitants of the city, which conduit draws from the lake 4,000,000 gallons of water daily. In an action to restrain the continued diversion of the surplus waters of the lake from said creek, *held*, that, conceding the lake was part of the navigable waters of the State and subject to all the rules pertaining to such waters, and that the State by the act aforesaid conferred upon the defendant all of the rights in the lake which remained in the State subsequent to the treaty, it imposed the same liability to those who might be injured by defendant's use of such waters as the State itself would have incurred for a similar use ; that the diversion of the waters for the purpose speci-

fied was for an object totally inconsistent with their use as a public highway or the common right of all the people to their benefits; that the State had no right, and by the said act did not attempt to grant a right to such use to the detriment of the riparian owners upon said creek and without making compensation; and that, as the evidence tended to show plaintiffs were injured by the diversion complained of, a dismissal of their complaint was error.   *Id.*

6. The rights of the riparian owners upon the Hudson (aside from its tidal character) and the Mohawk `rivers are affected by the doctrines of the civil law, prevailing in the Netherlands from whose government they were derived, and are distinguishable from the rights of riparian owners upon other navigable waters of the State.   *Id.*

7. *It seems* that the doctrine above stated, as to the·rights of riparian owners, does not apply to the vast fresh-water lakes or inland seas of this country, or to the streams forming the boundary lines of States.   *Id.*

RULES.

1. The provision of the Code of Civil Procedure (§ 3301, as amended by chap. 399, Laws of 1882), providing that the stipulation of the attorneys for parties to an action may take the place of a clerk's certificate to a copy of a paper whereof a certified copy is required, was not intended to alter the effect of the rule of this court (Rule 1) requiring a return to this court to be certified by the clerk of the court below. ·*Dow* v. *Darragh*.   537

2. Under the Code of Civil Procedure (§ 709), in an action in the Supreme Court, triable and tried in the first judicial district, an application for an extra allowance of costs must be made in that district, although the justice before whom the cause is tried resides in another district. *Hun* v. *Salter*. 651

3. The rule of the Supreme Court (44), requiring such an application to be made to the court before which the trial is had or the judgment rendered does not authorize it to be made out of the district. *Id.*

SALES.

See JUDICIAL SALES.

SAVINGS BANKS.

1. The primary relation of a depositor in a savings bank to the corporation is that of creditor. *People* v. *M. & T. S'v'gs Inst.*   7

2. Upon insolvency of the corporation, the depositors stand as other creditors, having no greater, but equal rights, to be paid ratably out of the insolvent estate.   *Id.*

3. Accordingly *held*, where a creditor of a savings bank obtained a judgment against a receiver thereof in an action brought against the bank before the appointment of the receiver, in which action the receiver was substituted as defendant, that the plaintiff was not entitled to a preference over depositors in the payment of his judgment.   *Id.*

See BANKS AND BANKING.

SHERIFF.

After defendant, as sheriff, had levied upon property and advertised it for sale under executions issued to him, proceedings in bankruptcy were commenced against the judgment debtors; and, with the usual order to show cause, an order was issued by the clerk, as of course, without direction of the court as required by the Bankruptcy Act (U. S. R. S., § 5023), staying defendant from any transfer or disposition of the property. The sale was adjourned by defendant by direction of the attorneys for D., the judgment creditor, who before the adjourned day intervened by petition in the bankruptcy proceedings, setting forth these facts, and the consideration for his judgments, and alleging that they were recovered without collusion with the judgment creditors. The petition asked for a modification of the stay so as to allow defendant to sell under the executions. The application was opposed by affidavits tending to show that the debts and the judgments thereon were in fraud of the bankrupt law. After a hearing the bankrupt court denied the application, but directed the assignee in bankruptcy to sell the property levied upon free from the lien of the executions, which lien the order declared should attach to the proceeds of the sale, and gave to D. permission, within a time named, to apply for an order requiring the assignee to apply the proceeds in payment of the judgments. Defendant thereupon returned the execution *nulla bona*. D. failed to make such application and brought this action for an alleged false return. Thereafter the assignee in bankruptcy filed a bill in equity against D. and the judgment debtors to determine the validity of the judgments, and who was entitled to the proceeds of sale. D. appeared therein and answered averring, among other things, that "the property was taken from the sheriff by the assignee in obedience to the order of the court and by him in like manner disposed of." After trial had in such action, the court decreed the judgments and executions were obtained in fraud of the Bankrupt Act, that the levy was null and void as against the assignee and that he was entitled to said proceeds. *Held*, that conceding the injunction accompanying the order to show cause was without force, the voluntary appearance of D. made him a party to the bankruptcy proceedings, and gave effect from that moment not only to the subsequent orders but to the one already made, that the United States courts had jurisdiction over the subject-matter and D.; also that D., having appeared in and contested the action brought by the assignee, could not now object that that court had no authority as to him to take the proceedings; and that, therefore,

the orders and judgment were a protection to defendant; also that it was immaterial that the decree was made after the commencement of this action; and that it was properly set up by supplemental answer. (Code of Civil Procedure, § 544.) *Dorrance* v. *Henderson.*
406

STATE BOARD OF EQUALIZATION.

1. The action of the State board of equalization in the discharge of the duty imposed upon it of equalizing "the State tax among the several counties of this State" (Chap. 312, Laws of 1859), is judicial in its character, and when it has acquired jurisdiction any error in its judgment or mistake in its conclusions can be asserted only in some direct proceeding for review. *Mayor, etc.*, v. *Davenport.*
604

2. The fact that said board did not have before it at its meeting a written digest of facts required by the statute (§ 7) to be prepared by the State assessors is not a jurisdictional defect, and is immaterial. *Id.*

3. The fact that the board increased the valuation of a county without swearing and examining witnesses is immaterial ; that is the duty of the State assessors, and upon the information given by them to the board, it is authorized to act. *Id.*

4. Nor does the fact that the board after a short secret session adopted a schedule of equalization prepared by one of the assessors affect the validity of its decision. *Id.*

STATUTES.

STATUTE OF LIMITATIONS.

See LIMITATION OF ACTIONS.

STIPULATION.

1. The provision of the Code of Civil

Procedure (§ 3301, as amended by chap. 399, Laws of 1882), providing that the stipulation of the attorneys for parties to an action may take the place of a clerk's certificate to a copy of a paper whereof a certified copy is required, was not 'intended to alter the effect of the provision (§ 1315) requiring a return to this court to be certified by the clerk of the court from which the appeal is taken, or of the rule of this court (Rule 1) making the same requirement. *Dow* v. *Darragh.* 537

2. Returns to this court should be made by a responsible officer, under sanction of his official oath, and attorneys for parties cannot, by stipulation, make up a case for the court. *Id.*

STREETS.

See HIGHWAYS.

SUBMISSION OF CONTROVERSY.

1. To give the court cognizance of a case submitted under the provision of the Code of Civil Procedure (§ 1279), providing for the submission of controversies upon facts admitted, the facts stated must show that there was, at the time the submission was made, a controversy or question of difference between the parties on the point presented for decision, and that a judgment can be rendered thereon: the court may not pass upon a mere abstract question. *People* v. *Mut. En. & Ac. Assn.* 622

2. Where in a controversy sought to be submitted between the State and a corporation the only relief to which the former is entitled, if any, is to restrain the corporation from exercising franchises unlawfully, the proceeding should be dismissed, as that relief may not be given therein. (Code, § 1281.) *Id.*

SUPERVISORS.

1. The act (Subd. 9, § 1, chap. 482, Laws of 1875, as amended by chap. 365, Laws of 1880, and by chap. 554, Laws of 1881), giving to the board of supervisors in any county containing an incorporated city of over one hundred thousand inhabitants, where contiguous territory in the county has been mapped out into streets and avenues, power to lay out, open, grade and construct the same, and to provide for the assessment of damages on the property benefited, is not a local law within the meaning of the State Constitution, and so is not violative of the constitutional provision (Art. 3, § 18) prohibiting the passage of a local or private law laying out or opening highways, or of the provision (Art. 3, § 23) requiring the legislature to act by general laws in conferring upon boards of supervisors any power of local legislation. *In re Church.* 1

2. Where a board of supervisors acting within the authority so conferred has created the occasion for and has required the appointment of commissioners to estimate and appraise the damages and benefits, the Supreme Court has jurisdiction to make such appointment. *Id.*

3. The board of supervisors may impose the whole cost of the improvement upon the property included in the area which it decides has been benefited to that extent. *Id.*

4. By resolution of the board of supervisors of the county of K. which had directed the opening of a street, under said act, in the town of N. U., the town was authorized to issue bonds to pay for the improvement, to be paid out of the general tax, so far as the assessments proved inadequate. *Held,* that adequate and certain provision was thus made for compensation for property taken, sufficient to meet the constitutional prohibition against the taking of property without compensation. *Id.*

—— *When action as for money had and received may be brought by supervisor on behalf of town, against board of supervisors of county, to recover moneys belonging to town paid improperly into the county treasury. See Bridges* v. *Board of Supervisors.* 570

SUPREME COURT.

—— *Jurisdiction of Supreme Court to appoint commissioners under act chap.* 482, *Laws of* 1875, *as amended, to appraise damages and benefits for opening streets in territory contiguous to city.*
See *In re Church.* 1

SURROGATE'S COURT.

1. A surrogate, in issuing letters of administration, has authority, and it is within his discretion, to limit the powers conferred upon the administrator. *Martin* v. *D. D. E. B. & B. R. R. Co.* 70

2. Where, therefore, such letters contain this clause, " these letters are issued with limited authority to prosecute only, and not with power to collect or compromise," *held*, that the surrogate had power to insert the limitation. *Id.*

3. *It seems*, that if such a limitation was in excess of the powers of the surrogate, it did not invalidate the letters, but was at most only an irregularity. *Id.*

4. In proceedings before a surrogate to compel an accounting, by an executor, instituted prior to September 1, 1880, a hearing was had and a decree rendered, after that time, which was appealed from. The appellant, at the close of the evidence, requested the surrogate to find upon certain questions of fact, as provided by the Code of Civil Procedure (§ 2545), which he refused. *Held*, that an exception to the refusal was not well taken; as, by the said Code (§ 3347, subd. 11), all proceedings pending in Surrogate's Court on that date are exempted from the operation of any of the provisions of the chapter (18) containing said provision. *Mills* v. *Hoffman.* 181

5. Under the Code of Civil Procedure (§§ 2717, 2718) a surrogate has no jurisdiction to entertain proceedings instituted by one claiming a legacy, to compel an executor to pay the same, when the executor " files a written answer duly verified, setting forth facts which show that it is doubtful whether the petitioner's claim is valid and legal, and denying its validity." In such a case, the surrogate must dismiss the petition. *Fiester* v. *Shepard.* 251

6. The objection, although not raised in the Surrogate's Court or at General Term, may be taken on appeal to this court. *Id.*

—— *Jurisdiction of surrogate to determine question as to widow's right to the articles of household furniture specified in the statute, where in accordance with an ante-nuptial contract she has accepted a sum " in lieu of her rights " as widow.*
See *In re Young* v. *Hicks.* 235

SUSPENSION OF POWER OF ALIENATION.

1. The provision of the Revised Statutes (1 R. S. 723, § 17) declaring that " where a remainder shall be limited on more than two successive estates for life, all the life estates subsequent to those of the two persons first entitled thereto shall be void, and upon the death of those persons the remainder shall take effect," refers only to vested, not to contingent remainders, and executes the remainders in possession only in favor of such ascertained persons, as except for the void life estate, would under the will or deed be entitled to the immediate possession. *Purdy* v. *Hayt.* 446

2. Where, therefore, the gift in remainder is upon a contingency which has not happened at the time of the death of the second life tenant, the provision does not 'apply, and the gift is invalid. *Id.*

3. It is no objection to the validity of a remainder in fee that it is limited in favor of persons not in being when the limitation is created, or who are not ascertainable until the termination of the precedent es-

tate, provided the contingency upon which it depends must happen within or not beyond the prescribed period for the vesting of estates. *Id.*

4. The will of M. gave his residuary estate to his executors, to be divided into shares as specified, a share to be held in trust during the life of each child of the testator who should survive him. After authorizing an expenditure of an amount, not exceeding a sum specified, out of the rents and profits of the share of each child for its support and education, the will directed that "the balance of such income shall from time to time be added to the share or sub-share from which the same proceeded, and accumulated as principal until he or she arrives at the age of twenty-one years, after which period the whole of such income shall be paid over, quarter-yearly, to such child. *Held,* it was the intention of the testator that during the minority of each child the surplus income of his or her share should be capitalized and thereafter the beneficiary should be entitled only to the income during life on the original share as augmented by the accumulations, and upon the death of the child the share, together with the accumulations should go to the remaindermen as provided; that the direction for accumulation was void, and so was to be regarded as stricken out of the will, thus leaving to each child a gift of a life estate in the share held for him or her, which would carry all the accruing income; and it appearing that the surplus income of the share of A., a son of the testator, had accumulated during his minority, *held,* that the accumulation belonged to him and could be reached by a judgment creditor of his in an action brought for that purpose. *Pray* v. *Hegeman.* 508

5. Also *held,* that the same result would be reached if the right to the accumulated fund was to be governed by the provision of the statute (1 R. S. 726, § 40), providing that where, in consequence of a

valid limitation of an expectant estate, there is a suspense of the power of alienation or ownership, during which the rents and profits are undisposed of, they "shall belong to the persons presumptively entitled to the next eventual estate;" that the provision of the will might be treated as creating an equitable expectant life interest or estate in the son after his arrival at majority, and so constituting the "next eventual estate" within the meaning of the statute. *Id.*

6. The will of M. devised his real estate to his executors in trust, to hold one-third part thereof for the benefit of each of his three daughters during life. Upon the death of a daughter, leaving a husband and lawful issue living, it was declared that the executors should stand seized of her third "from and immediately after her death, upon trust for the sole use and benefit of such issue," in case of the death of a daughter single and unmarried, "upon such trust, and for such purpose as she shall or may appoint by her last will;" in default of such appointment "for the sole use and benefit of her next of kin." One of the daughters died unmarried, leaving a will by which she gave all of her estate, real and personal, after payment of debts, to her two sisters who survived her, "and to the survivor of them," and to the heirs, executors and administrators of such survivor. *Held,* that this was a valid execution of the power of appointment and the title to one-third of the real estate passed under it; that the limitation in the devise to the survivor did not work an unlawful suspension of the power of alienation (1 R. S. 724, § 24); that the estate, upon the death of the testatrix, passed to her two sisters as tenants in common, each taking a fee, that of the one dying first being defeasible by such death, and thereupon the entire absolute estate vested, which, therefore, could be aliened after two lives at most. *Mott* v. *Ackerman.* 589

7. *It seems* that the two sisters took

received no more money from the town for taxes than it was entitled to receive under the general statutes of the State; that it was the duty of the board of supervisors, in making an apportionment of the taxes for county purposes, after the passage of said act, to lay out of view the amount so withdrawn by the act and to assess generally, upon the county at large, a sufficient sum to cover the county charges, in addition to the tax for county purposes levied upon the property of the railroad, in the towns specified. *Id.*

6. But *held*, that the act only appropriated to the towns that portion of the taxes in question known and described as county taxes; that they were not entitled to receive the portion collected for State purposes. *Id.*

—— - *Right of town to lease lands under water for cultivating oysters.* See *Hund* v. *Newton.* 88

TOWN BONDING.

—— *When evidence of mistake in executing town bond insufficient to authorize reformation of the instrument.* See *Potter* v. *Town of G.* (Mem.) 662

TRIAL.

1. A request to the court on trial to rule as to the order in which counsel shall address the jury can only properly be made after the whole evidence has been presented. *Mead* v. *Shea.* 122

2. Plaintiff's complaint stated two causes of action, one upon two promissory notes indorsed by S., defendant's testator, the other for goods sold. To the first defendant pleaded payment; to the second, a general denial. Plaintiff opened the case and gave evidence as to both causes of action. After the evidence had been substantially closed defendant's counsel moved for judgment on the last cause of action To this

the court replied, "my impression is there is not evidence to warrant a recovery. I think I shall so direct the jury." No further request as to that cause of action was made, and no exception was taken to the omission of the court to rule on the request. Said counsel then stated to the court " we have established the affirmative of the issue." The court replied, "I think not, I think the pleadings control that." To which said counsel excepted. Some further evidence was given by defendant, and the court, in submitting the case to the jury, withdrew from their consideration the claim for goods sold. *Held*, that the colloquy between court and counsel did not amount to a claim or denial of the right of the latter to the closing address to the jury; but conceding this, the court properly declined to allow the right, as at the time nothing had occurred which prevented the final submission to the jury of the issue as to the second cause of action, and there was, therefore, at the time the request was made an issue undisposed of as to which plaintiff had the affirmative and the right to close. *Id.*

3. It appeared that H., in the spring of 1876, doing business in the name of his wife, purchased stone of plaintiff to the amount of $800, giving in payment her notes indorsed by S., which were renewed from time to time until April 7, 1877, when the notes in suit were given. In October, 1876, the H.s purchased another lot of stone of plaintiff, and on the 27th of the month Mrs. H. delivered to him an order on R. for $800, which was accepted and paid in the spring and summer of 1877. The H.s both testified that this order was given in payment of the notes indorsed by S. Plaintiff testified in his own behalf that the order was given to apply on the October purchase. Plaintiff was permitted to prove, as bearing upon the credibility of the H.s, their letters and declarations as to the purchases and the manner of payment, written and made both before and after the giving of the order.

Held, that the evidence was properly received. Also that the objection that as the evidence tended to contradict the testimony of the H.s their attention should have first been called to, and they interrogated in regard thereto, could not be presented here, it not having been raised on the trial. *Id.*

——— *When question as to original validity of policy of insurance, and as to ratification by company of provision therein inserted by agent without authority, is one of law, and a refusal to submit the same to a jury proper.*
See *Andrews* v. *Æ. L. Ins. Co.* 596

See CRIMINAL TRIAL

TRUSTS AND TRUSTEES.

1. A testator has the right to impose the terms and conditions under which his bounty shall be distributed, and the court has no authority to increase the responsibility of, or impose obligations upon, the trustees selected by him from the burden of which he has in his will protected them. *Crabb* v. *Young.* 56

2. While trustees will be held to great strictness in their dealings with trust property, the courts will regard them with leniency when it appears they have acted in good faith. *Id.*

3. Whoever receives property knowing that it is the subject of a trust, and has been transferred by the trustee in violation of his duty or power, takes it subject to the right, not only of the *cestui que trust*, but also of the trustee, to reclaim possession or to recover for its conversion. *Wetmore* v. *Porter.* 76

——— *When transfer by executor having power to sell, of real estate, to a third person and by the latter back to the executor individually, voidable at the election of the beneficiaries named in the will.*
See *People* v. *O. B. of S. B. B. Co.* 98

USURY.)

1. The fact that an agent, without the authority, consent or knowledge of his principal, upon loaning the money of the latter, exacted a sum in excess of lawful interest, does not make the loan usurious; nor does the fact of the receipt by the principal of the sum so paid, in the absence of evidence of knowledge on his part that it was paid as a usurious consideration for the loan, establish a ratification of the act of the agent. *Philips* v. *Mackellar.* 84

2. To make out the defense of usury, it must be made to appear that the lender had knowledge of the usurious agreement and assented to the same. *Id.*

3. *It seems*, however, in such case, the sum so paid should be allowed and applied as a payment. *Id.*

VILLAGES.

1. Where the trustees of an incorporated village organized into a board of water commissioners for the purposes and as prescribed by the act of 1875 (Chap. 181, Laws of 1875), and as such enter into a contract for erecting water-works for the village, they act simply as agents for and the contract is binding upon it, and an action is maintainable against it thereon. *Fleming* v. *Vill. of S. B.* 368

2. It is immaterial whether the contract is made in the name of the village, or in the names of the trustees as water commissioners, or as a board. *Id.*

3. Said statute confers upon such water commissioners general power to contract, and the entire control of the work for procuring a water supply; and where a contract has been regularly let as prescribed, if in the substantial performance thereof slight variations or changes are necessary they may be made by their direction without a new letting, and for the extra expense the village is liable. *Id.*

4. In an action to recover for such extra work it did not appear that it was formally ordered by the board at any regular meeting thereof, or that any formal action was taken in reference to it. It appeared, however, that some one or more of the commissioners were upon the work nearly every day, and sometimes all of them, supervising and inspecting the same. It was provided in the contract that the work should be at all times under their control. *Held*, it was to be presumed they all had knowledge of what was being done and assented to the extra work; and so, a finding that such work was ordered by the board was justified. *Id.*

WAIVER.

—— *Of condition in policy of insurance, what amounts to.*
See *Haight* v. *C. I. Ins. Co.* 51

—— *When right to interest on award for damages for widening Broadway, by accepting award and receipting in full therefor.*
See *Cutter* v. *Mayor.* 166

WARRANTS.

1. A warrant issued after indictment found may briefly state the offense, and need not be more precise and accurate than is sufficient to apprise the prisoner of the charge against him. *People, ex rel.* v. *Mead.* 415

2. A warrant so issued by a district attorney as authorized by the statute (Chap. 338, Laws of 1847) for the arrest of the relator, stated that he stood indicted "for contempt." On *habeas corpus*, issued on the petition of the relator, *held*, that this was a sufficient specification of the offense; that as the statement was of a contempt which has already served as a basis of an indictment, it necessarily implied a willful contempt, of a character constituting a misdemeanor. *Id.*

3. Also *held*, that as the indictment was found prior to the enactment of the Code of Criminal Procedure the provisions therein (§§ 301, 302) as to the form of bench warrants did not apply (§ 962), nor was it a case of a commitment for contempt specified in the provision of the Revised Statutes (2 R. S. 567, § 40) in relation to *habeas corpus*. *Id.*

WARRANTY.

A warranty in an application for a policy of life insurance that a third person is in good health does not mean an actual freedom from illness or disease, but simply that the person has indicated in his actions and appearance no symptoms or traces of disease, and to the ordinary observation of a friend or relative is in truth well. *Grattan* v. *Met. L. Ins. Co.* 274

WATER-COURSES.

1. The riparian owners of lands adjoining fresh-water non-navigable streams take title to the thread of the stream, and as incident to the title acquire the right to the usufructuary enjoyment of the undiminished and undisturbed flow of said stream. *Smith* v. *City of Rochester.* 463

2. This is so also as to the fresh-water navigable streams and small lakes within this State where the tide does not ebb and flow; save that the public has an easement in such waters for the purpose of travel, as on a public highway, which easement, as it pertains to the sovereignty of the State, is inalienable and gives to the State the right to use, regulate and control the waters for the purposes of navigation. *Id.*

3. This public easement gives the State no right to convert the waters or to authorize their conversion to any other uses than those for which the easement was created, i. e., for the purposes of navigation. *Id.*

4. The right to divert the waters for other uses, although public in their

the executor to set apart said articles for her, had jurisdiction to determine the question. *Id.*

3. The will of W. gave to his widow "all of the household property in the dwelling-house and the use of the dwelling-house during her life." In the dwelling-house, at the time of the testator's death, was a quantity of coal and wood, provided for family use, and a shot-gun. Upon settlement of the accounts of the executors, *held*, that these articles were properly allowed to the widow; that the shotgun might have been provided for the defense of the house, and in the absence of proof the court was not required to presume the contrary. *In re Frazer.* 239

4. The appraisers set apart as exempt and for the use of the widow, a horse, phaeton and harness, of the value of $150. *Held*, that the gift of the household property did not preclude this allowance; that "other personal property" was available for the exemption and might be necessary. *Id.*

5. The executors allowed to a widow a claim for the wages of her son P. This was objected to on the ground that she was not authorized to receive them, and that the claim was outlawed when paid. The services ended in March, 1871. P. was then eighteen years of age. His father died in 1877, the payment was made in 1879, previous to which P. had died. No administrator was appointed. *Held*, that as the payment was of a just debt and had gone to the benefit of those entitled, and as the estate could not be required to pay a second time, and so had suffered no wrong, the executors were properly credited with the payment. *Id.*

6. The testator, having in his hands a sum of money belonging to his wife, loaned it in 1869, taking notes in the name of his wife. Afterward he included the amount in a mortgage executed to himself by the borrower. The amount, with interest, was allowed to the widow

by the executors. It was claimed by the contestant that it was to be presumed that the wife did not consent; that the husband was guilty of a conversion of her money, and so the statute of limitations was set running and the claim outlawed prior to the testator's death. *Held* untenable; that it was to be presumed, in the absence of evidence to the contrary, that the security was taken by the husband, with the consent of the wife; and therefore to the extent of her interest, he held the mortgage as agent or trustee for her. *Id.*

7. Also *held*, that interest was properly allowed, as it was earned by the investment and received by the testator. *Id.*

8. Also *held*, that as the will contained no provisions excluding the widow from dower or repugnant to a claim therefor, the acceptance by her of the provisions in the will for her benefit did not deprive her of the right to make the claim. . *Id.*

WILLS.

1. A testator has the right to impose the terms and conditions under which his bounty shall be distributed, and the court has no authority to increase the responsibility of, or impose obligations upon, the trustees selected by him from the burden of which he has in his will protected them. *Crabb v. Young.* 56

2. Where, upon examination of a will, taken as a whole, the intention of the testator appears clear, but its plain and definite purposes are endangered by inapt or inaccurate modes of expression, the court may, and it is its duty to, subordinate the language to the intention; it may reject words and limitations, supply or transpose them to get at the correct meaning. *Phillips v. Davies.* 199

3. M., at the time of making her will, and of her death, owned a large amount of real estate but

only a small amount of personal property. By her will, after providing for the payment of debts, she first gave her estate, real and personal, to her executors in trust, to rent, etc., and apply the rents, income, etc.. to the use of her husband during his life. Then followed ten clauses purporting to create separate and independent trusts ; also numerous legacies, all of which would substantially fail in the absence of a trust estate, or power in trust vested in the executors, by force of which the real estate could be sold and converted into money. Certain real estate was also specifically devised, and the executors were directed to pay off incumbrances thereon, which, in the absence of such power, could not be done. The clause appointing executors contained the following: " and during the life-time of my said husband my said executors, and such and whichever of them as shall act, are authorized and empowered, by and with the consent of my said husband, to sell and dispose of any part of my estate, real and personal, not specifically bequeathed." In an action for a construction of the will, *held*, that said clause was to be construed as conferring upon her executors a power of sale, which during the life of her husband was to be exercised only with his consent, but thereafter continuing to exist ; and that, therefore, the executors had power to sell after the death of the husband, and convert into money so much of the real estate as was not specifically devised. *Id.*

4. In 1877, M., plaintiff's testatrix, made her will, which contained this clause: " I further give and bequeath to my beloved husband all the ready money I may have, either in bank or elsewhere, at my decease." In 1879 she gave to defendant, her husband, authority to collect a legacy due to her, which he collected during the year 1880. From January 1st of that year up to her death, which occurred in September, 1881, the testatrix was of unsound mind and

incompetent to transact business. The money so collected was used by defendant with his own money in defraying household expenses and in procuring nurses and medical attendance for his wife, and none of it remained at her death. Defendant was able to provide suitably for his family out of his own property. In an action to recover the amount so collected, *held*, that under said clause of the will, defendant was entitled to retain the same ; that when collected it could properly be treated as " ready money ;" it remained in his hands as such, liable to be paid on demand, he holding it simply as a depositary, and he used it subject to this liability. *Smith* v. *Burch.* 228

5. The authorities as to what is included in the word " money," as used in wills, collated. *Id.*

6. The will of W. gave to his widow " all of the household property in the dwelling-house and the use of the dwelling-house during her life." In the dwelling-house, at the time of the testator's death, was a quantity of coal and wood, provided for family use, and a shotgun. Upon settlement of the accounts of the executors, *held*, that these articles were properly allowed to the widow ; that the shotgun might have been provided for the defense of the house, and in the absence of proof the court was not required to presume the contrary. *In re Fraser*. 239

7. The will of C. gave to two grandchildren " the sum of $1,000 each, to be paid to them respectively as they arrive at the age of twenty-five years." To five children he gave $1,000 each, payable one legacy each year for five years after his decease. After certain devises and bequests, he gave his residuary estate to defendant, his son, subject to the payment of his debts and the legacies. In an action by the administrator of the estate of one of said grandchildren, who died before reaching the age of twenty-five, brought after she would have reached that age, had

she lived, to recover the legacy, *held*, that the postponement of the time of payment did not make the gift contingent ; that the testator's intent, as disclosed by the will, was simply to postpone payment for the benefit of the estate ; that the legacy vested upon the death of the testator, and that plaintiff was entitled to recover. *Bushnell* v. *Carpenter.* 270

8. In 1809 S. conveyed all of her estate to trustees, to convert into money, and keep in trust the proceeds invested, applying the income and such portion of the principal as they should deem proper to her use during her life, and paying over the residue as she should by will appoint. In 1877 S. made a will, which made no reference to the trust, but by which she devised certain real estate, part of the trust estate, gave legacies amounting to $275,500, and gave her residuary estate, including that she might thereafter acquire or become possessed of, to seventeen beneficiaries named. At the time of the execution of the will and of her death, S., aside from the trust estate, only owned property of the value of about $25,000, which consisted principally of an undivided interest in the estate of a deceased sister. She was in the habit of spending all the income paid her by the trustees, and was well acquainted with the condition and amount of her estate. At the time of executing the will, S. was in delicate health, and was apprehensive that she might die at any moment. In an action by the trustees for an accounting and for directions as to the disposition of the trust estate, *held*, that the power of appointment reserved in the trust deed was properly and effectually executed both as to real and personal estate. *Hutton* v. *Benkard.* 295

9. Where it appears, from the terms of a will, taken as a whole, and construed in the light of surrounding circumstances, that it was the intention of the testator in the dispositions made by him to execute a power of appointment, such intention will have effect although

the power is not referred to in express words. *Id.*

10. R. died, leaving a will, prior to the execution of which, C., a married daughter, had died, leaving four children, a son and three daughters. Her husband had remarried and had by the second marriage two children, daughters, who were of no kin to R. All of said children survived him. By his will he directed a seventh part of his residuary estate to be subdivided into four equal shares, to be held in trust, one for each of the four children of C. during their respective minorities, and then to be paid over. Substantially similar provisions were made for the disposition of each of said shares in case the beneficiary died before coming of age. The direction as to the share of E., one of the testator's said grandchildren, was that in case of such death and in default of issue " living at her death, then to pay over the same with its accumulations to her then living brother and sisters and the issue of any deceased brother or sister who shall have died having lawful issue then living, each then living brother and sister taking one equal share thereof, and the issue of any deceased brother or sister taking by representation the share the parent of such issue would have taken if then living." E. died before coming of age leaving no issue, but leaving her brother and two sisters and her two half sisters surviving. In an action for a construction of the will, *held*, that her share went to her brother and sisters of the full-blood, and that her sisters of the half-blood were not entitled to any portion thereof ; that as the contrary construction would result in diverting a portion of the testator's estate from his lineal descendants to strangers to his blood, the burden was upon them to establish that the testator in using the word " sisters " intended to include them ; that the presumption to the contrary could only be overcome by clear and unequivocal language ; and, therefore, the fact that in the direction as to the disposition of the shares of two of the other of his

and accumulated as principal until he or she arrives at the age of twenty-one years, after which period the whole of such income shall be paid over, quarter-yearly, to such child. *Held*, it was the intention of the testator that during the minority of each child the surplus income of his or her share should be capitalized and thereafter the beneficiary should be entitled only to the income during life on the original share as augmented by the accumulations, and upon the death of the child the share, together with the accumulations, should go to the remaindermen as provided ; that the direction for accumulation was void, and so was to be regarded as stricken out of the will, thus leaving to each child a *gift of a life estate* in the share held for him or her, which would carry all the accruing income; and it appearing that the surplus income of the share of A., a son of the testator, had accumulated during his minority, *held*, that the accumulation belonged to him and could be reached by a judgment creditor of his in an action brought for that purpose. *Pray* v. *Hegeman.*   508

17. Also *held*, that the same result would be reached if the right to the accumulated fund was to be governed by the provision of the statute (1 R. S. 726, § 40), providing that where, in consequence of a valid limitation of an expectant estate, there is a suspense of the power of alienation or ownership, during which the rents and profits are undisposed of, they "shall belong to the persons presumptively entitled to the next eventual estate;" that the provision of the will might be treated as creating an equitable expectant life interest or estate in the son after his arrival at majority, and so constituting the "next eventual estate" within the meaning of the statute.   *Id.*

18. The will of M. devised his real estate to his executors in trust, to hold one-third part thereof for the benefit of each of his three daughters during life. Upon the death of a daughter, leaving a husband

and lawful issue living, it was declared that the executors should stand seized of her third "from and immediately after her death, upon trust for the sole use and benefit of such issue;" in case of the death of a daughter single and unmarried, "upon such trust, and for such purpose as she shall or may appoint by her last will;" in default of such appointment "for the sole use and benefit of her next of kin." *Held*, that the power of appointment related to the remainder in fee ; that in each event provided for the trust in the executors upon the death of the daughter would be purely passive, the remainder vesting in the beneficiaries ; that the phrase in the clause giving such power of appointment "upon such trust" meant, not a trust to be created by the daughter and so limiting the power of disposition, but related to the trust in the executors. *Mott* v. *Ackerman.*   589

19. As to one of the daughters who was married at the time of the execution of the will, it provided that in case she should give to her husband any part of her income from the estate or pay any of his debts she should thereupon forfeit all right and interest in and to such income. *Held*, that this did not affect the conclusion above stated ; it did not show any intent to limit the power of appointment.   *Id.*

20. One of the daughters died unmarried, leaving a will by which she gave all of her estate, real and personal, after payment of debts, to her two sisters who survived her, " and to the survivor of them," and to the heirs, executors and administrators of such survivor. *Held*, that this was a valid execution of the power of appointment and the title to one-third of the real estate passed under it; that the limitation in the devise to the survivor did not work an unlawful suspension of the power of alienation (1 R. S. 724, § 24) ; that the estate upon the death of the testatrix passed to her two sisters

as tenants in common, each taking a fee, that of the one dying first being defeasible by such death, and thereupon the entire absolute estate vested, which, therefore, could be aliened after two lives at most.　　*Id.*

21. The two surviving sisters purchased and owned as tenants in common certain other real estate; one of them subsequently died, leaving a will by which she gave to her executors a power of sale, to be exercised during the life of the surviving sister with her concurrence, and (the will then proceeds) "on the death of my said sister Maria, or as soon afterward as they may think advisable * * * and within three years from the proof of this will," the executors were empowered and directed to convert into money the real estate, etc. Maria lived more than three years after probate of the will. After her death and about twelve years after such probate the surviving executors contracted to sell the real estate to defendant, who refused to complete the purchase, claiming, among other things, that the power of sale could only be exercised within the three years. *Held* untenable; that as the purposes of the will required a sale the power was imperative (1 R. S. 734, § 96), and was so intended by the testatrix, and the neglect to sell within the time specified did not destroy the authority conferred.　　*Id.*

ERRATA.

In *Hynes* v. *McDermott* (82 N. Y. 52), "51 N. Y." in seventeenth line from top of page, should read "54 N. Y."

In *Young* v. *Guy* (87 N. Y. 458), in first line of second paragraph of head-note 'assigned by G." should read " assigned by S."

In *Bradley* v. *Mirick* (91 N. Y. 293), erase, at end of head-note, the words "*Bradley* v. *Mirick* (25 Hun, 272), reversed," as the case was in fact affirmed; also on page 688 (91 N. Y.), erase same words

ERRATA

Lightning Source UK Ltd.
Milton Keynes UK
UKHW021213041218
333417UK00019B/174/P